Bolivia
a Lonely Planet travel survival kit

Deanna Swaney

Bolivia

3rd edition

Published by
   Lonely Planet Publications
   Head Office: PO Box 617, Hawthorn, Vic 3122, Australia
   Branches: 155 Filbert St, Suite 251, Oakland, CA 94607, USA
                  10 Barley Mow Passage, Chiswick, London W4 4PH, UK
                  71 bis rue du Cardinal Lemoine, 75005 Paris, France

Printed by
   SNP Printing Pte Ltd, Singapore

Photographs by
   Ward Hulbert (WH), Todd Miner (TM), Robert Strauss (RS), Deanna Swaney (DS), Mary Trigger (MT)

   Front cover: Woven Cloths (photograph by Richard I'Anson)

First Published
   December 1988

This Edition
   November 1996

National Library of Australia Cataloguing in Publication Data

Swaney, Deanna
   Bolivia.

   3rd ed.
   Includes index.
   ISBN 0 86442 396 9.

   1. Bolivia – Guidebooks. I. Title. (Series: Lonely Planet travel survival kit)

918.0452

918.40452 S972b 1996   Swaney, Deanna.   Bolivia

text & maps © Lonely Planet 1996
photos © photographers as indicated 1996
climate charts for Cochabamba and Santa Cruz compiled from information supplied by Patrick J Tyson,
© Patrick J Tyson, 1996

Deanna Swaney

After completing university studies, Deanna made a shoestring circuit of Europe and has been addicted to travel ever since. Despite an erstwhile career in computer programming, she managed intermittent forays away from the corporate bustle of midtown Anchorage, Alaska, and at first opportunity, made a break for South America where she wrote the 1st edition of this book. Subsequent travels steered her through a course of island paradises – Arctic and tropical – and resulted in three more Lonely Planet travel survival kits: *Tonga, Samoa* and *Iceland, Greenland & the Faroe Islands.*

She returned to dry land for *Zimbabwe, Botswana & Namibia,* and has since coauthored the 2nd editions of the *Brazil* and *Mauritius, Réunion & Seychelles* travel survival kits, updated the 2nd edition of *Madagascar & Comoros* and contributed to shoestring guides to Africa, South America and Scandinavia.

Deanna now divides her time between travelling and her froggy lakeside base in the English West Country.

From the Author

Thanks to Yossi Brain, for his considerable help with the hiking, trekking and mountaineering information and major contributions to the La Paz and Cordilleras & Yungas chapters; Matthew Parris, for a head-swelling vote of confidence and excellent info on the Mapiri Trail; Dr Hugo Berrios, for mountaineering info and a nice little hike on Huayna Potosí; and the whole Reseguín gang – Peter Hutchison, Andy St Pierre, Ulli Schatz, Sylvie, Alix Shand, Alex downstairs, and the enormous slug. Also, thanks for various reasons to Trex, Jonathon Derksen, Carmen Julia, Álvaro, Planet José, Pig & Whistle Martin and lots of other clued-in *paceños.*

I'm also grateful to Guy Cox – the Birdman of Buena Vista – as well as Robin Clarke and Miriam Melgar for help relating to Parque Nacional Amboró; John Carey, for enlightened perspectives on Uyuni (I wanted to get back to you, but your letter didn't include a postal address!); Margarita van 't Hoff & Pieter de Raad, for good company in Samaipata and useful information on Samaipata and Vallegrande; Tito Ponce Lopez, who knows Uyuni and surrounds better than the back of his hand; and Anne Meadows & Daniel Buck for the lowdown on Butch & Sundance in Tupiza and San Vicente, and for providing the related aside in the Southern Altiplano chapter; Tim Killeen, associate curator of the Museo de Historia Natural Noel Kempff Mercado in Santa Cruz, for his invaluable information and advice on Noel Kempff Mercado National Park (Tim would also like to acknowledge the research and contributions of the Missouri Botanical Garden, the Field Museum, and Conservation International); Tim Bowyer in London, for his welcome input on Vallegrande, Pucara and La Higuera; Robert Eichwald, USA, for expert recommendations and good company in Cochabamba; Fabiola, Beatriz and Nicolás for a couple of wonderful days exploring around Tupiza; Marc Steininger, for conservation information and excursions around Amboró; Wayne Bernhardson for assistance with the Chilean connection and permission to use his spiffy cameloid material; Louis Demers of Sorata for his expert information and direction on the Mapiri Trail and other hiking routes in the Sorata area; and Norbert Schürer, who researched and wrote the discussion of Bolivian literature in the Facts about the Country chapter.

And there were many more: Loreen Olufsen, USA, for a happy couple of weeks and a memorable hike to Yampupata and Isla del Sol; Uta Lütke-Wöstmann, Germany, for lots of pleasant chat and help in Cochabamba and Villa Tunari; Eduardo Garnica, for many helpful details on Potosí; Ernst and Norbert Schürer for their long-suffering natures, which accommodated road-building in the Chaco, blizzards in Boyuibe and revolving tropical ailments, and for their endless dedication to hotel-checking – especially when I was struck down by laryngitis in Santa Cruz; Evangelos Kotsopoulos (Germany), for his helpful remarks on cycling in Bolivia; Anne Bois d'Enghien for great company on the first ascent of Rum Doodle (aka Muyuloma) with Tarija's New Age fringe, a merciful late-night run to the tranca in Tarija and dedication beyond the call of duty in both Tarija and La Paz; François Laviolette, for keen eyes and ears in and around Tarija; and Greg & Katie Cumberford, for their information on Mizque and Aiquile. Most of the mountaineering and climbing information in this book was originally prepared by Todd Miner, the director and coordinator of Alaska Wilderness Studies at the University of Alaska, Anchorage. The updated climbing information is courtesy of Yossi Brain, a British-born, La Paz-based mountaineering and trekking guide. He's now the Climbing Secretary of the Club Andino Boliviano, and runs Ozono, a top notch climbing and trekking agency in La Paz.

Special thanks to readers Bruce & Cheryl McLaren, New Zealand, for their long and very helpful letters and maps, and to J Azevedo, USA, for his brilliant info on Tarija and the Jesuit missions – if I could only write so well! (If you see this, please get in touch with me – your address was removed from the letter.) Other particularly useful letters, some of which were extracted for use in the text, came from Martin Bottenberg, Netherlands; Lisa Durham, MRCVS, UK; Malcolm James, UK; Ed Maurer, Peru; Tim Eryre, UK (who introduced me to the joys of 1-point type – you'll get a bill from my optometrist!); James Lind, UK; Mary Ann Springer, USA; Louise Cyr, Canada; Quentin Given & Lorna Reith, UK; Geoffrey Groesbeckj, USA; Anne Burrill, Italy.

Finally, love, thanks and lots of other positive sentiments to Earl, Dean & Jennifer Swaney in Fresno, Robert Strauss in Kyre Park, Rodney Leacock in Colorado Springs, and Keith & Holly Hawkings and Dave Dault, back home in Anchorage.

From the Publisher

This edition was coordinated by Karin Riederer, with assistance from Janet Austin, Katie Cody, Adrienne Costanzo, Jane Fitzpatrick, Kirsten John, Anne Mulvaney, Nick Tapp and Steve Womersley. The maps were drawn or updated by Jenny Jones with help from Paul Clifton, Jane Hart, Dorothy Natsikas and Michael Signal. Jenny was also responsible for design, layout and some illustrations. Michael Signal, Tamsin Wilson, Matt King, Trudi Carnavan and Ann Jeffree also helped draw the illustrations. The cover was designed by David Kemp and Michael Signal. Karin Riederer and Kerrie Williams compiled the index, and Leonie Mugavin provided library assistance. Thanks to the readers' letters team of Julie Young and Shelley Preston in Australia, Simon Goldsmith in the UK, Sacha Pearson in the USA and Arnaud Lebonnois in France, and to Dan Levin for technical assistance.

This Book

Deanna Swaney and Robert Strauss researched and wrote the previous edition of this book. This edition was thoroughly updated by Deanna Swaney. Many readers wrote with helpful information and suggestions; a complete list of all their names appears near the back of this book.

Warning & Request

Things change – prices go up, schedules change, good places go bad and bad places go bankrupt – nothing stays the same. So if you find things better or worse, recently opened or long since closed, please write and tell us and help make the next edition better.

Your letters will be used to help update future editions and, where possible, important changes will also be included in an Update section in reprints.

We greatly appreciate all information that is sent to us by travellers. Back at Lonely Planet we employ a hard-working readers' letters team to sort through the many letters we receive. The best ones will be rewarded with a free copy of the next edition or another Lonely Planet guide if you prefer. We give away lots of books, but, unfortunately, not every letter/postcard receives one.

Contents

Map Legend

BOUNDARIES

————————— International Boundary

————·——— Regional Boundary

ROUTES

———————— Freeway

———————— Highway

— — — — — Unsealed Highway

———————— Major Road

— — — — — Unsealed Road or Track

———————— City Road

———————— City Street

— — — — — Jeep, 4WD Track

+++++++++ Railway

▬▬▬▬▬▬ Underground Railway

- - - - - - - Walking Track

———————— Ferry Route

-+-+-+-+-+- Cable Car or Chairlift

AREA FEATURES

.... Parks, Plaza

.... Built-Up Area

.... Pedestrian Mall

.... Market

+ + + + + + Cemetery

.... Reef

.... Beach or Desert

.... Rocks

HYDROGRAPHIC FEATURES

.... Coastline

.... River, Creek

— — — — — Intermittent River or Creek

>>> ——— Rapids, Waterfalls

.... Lake, Intermittent Lake

.... Canal, Aqueduct

.... Swamp

SYMBOLS

✪ CAPITAL	National Capital	◗	☗	Embassy, Petrol Station
◉ Capital	Regional Capital	✈	✝	Airport, Airfield
◍ CITY	Major City	▭	✿	Swimming Pool, Gardens
● City	City	❖	🐘	Shopping Centre, Zoo
● Town	Town	⚲	⋔	Winery or Vineyard, Picnic Site
● Village	Village	◄—	A25	One Way Street, Route Number
■ ▼	Place to Stay, Place to Eat	🏛	⚶	Stately Home, Monument
☕ ☗	Cafe, Pub or Bar	☗	◙	Castle, Tomb
✉ ☎	Post Office, Telephone	⌒	⌂	Cave, Hut or Chalet
❶ ❸	Tourist Information, Bank	▲	☀	Mountain or Hill, Lookout
◓ 🅿	Transport, Parking	⚱	⌇	Lighthouse, Shipwreck
🏛 ⛨	Museum, Youth Hostel	)(	◎	Pass, Spring
⌂ ⚐	Caravan Park, Camping Ground	⚑	↑	Beach, Golf Course
✚ ✛	Church, Cathedral	∴	✗	Ruins, Mine
☪ ✡	Mosque, Synagogue	▬▬		Ancient or City Wall
卍 ✵	Buddhist Temple, Hindu Temple	⌢⟹ ⟸		Cliff or Escarpment, Tunnel
✚ ★	Hospital, Police Station	+++▬+++		Railway Station

Note: not all symbols displayed above appear in this book

Introduction

Bolivia is the Tibet of the Americas – the highest and most isolated of the Latin American republics. A landlocked country lying astride the widest stretch of the Andean Cordillera, Bolivia spills through a maze of tortured hills and valleys into the vast forests and savannas of the Amazon and Paraná basins, its geographical and climatic zones ranging from snowcapped Andean peaks to vast, low-lying savannas and jungles. With two major indigenous groups and several smaller ones, Bolivia is also the most Indian country on the South American continent. Over 50% of the population are of pure Amerindian blood and many people maintain traditional cultural values and belief systems.

Bolivia has certainly had a turbulent and explosive history, but nowadays, its image as a haunt of revolutionaries and drug barons is greatly overstated and although it still faces some difficult problems, it remains one of South America's most peaceful, secure and inviting countries. In fact, the word most often used by locals is *tranquilo*, 'tranquil'.

The country combines awe-inspiring landscapes, colonial treasures, colourful indigenous cultures and remnants of mysterious ancient civilisations. Its natural attractions range from the peaks of the Andean Cordillera to the stark beauty and startling colours of the lakes and windswept deserts of the Altiplano; from the jungle-choked waterways of the Amazon and Paraná basins to the thorny scrublands of the Chaco.

There are plenty of opportunities for hiking, trekking and wildlife viewing. The Bolivian Amazon is ideal for rainforest excursions, and several national parks now offer visitor facilities. Dinosaur trackers and fossil fiends will enjoy the dinosaur footprints at Torotoro south of Cochabamba or the many fossil sites around Tarija.

History abounds in such wonders as the ancient ceremonial site of Tiahuanaco; the

legendary mines of Potosí – dating from the 16th century and still worked under tortuous conditions; the ornate Jesuit churches of the eastern lowlands; and the vestiges of Inca culture set against the dramatic backdrop of the Andean cordilleras and Lake Titicaca. Bolivia's world-renowned music is in itself a compelling reason to visit, especially when it's played on native instruments in the context of a *peña* (folk music programme) or one of the country's many festivals. There are plenty of examples of colonial architecture to explore, the best of which is preserved in the churches, narrow streets and museums of Sucre and Potosí.

Foreign visitors have only recently begun to discover this intriguing and underrated country, so it's still surprisingly easy to stray

9

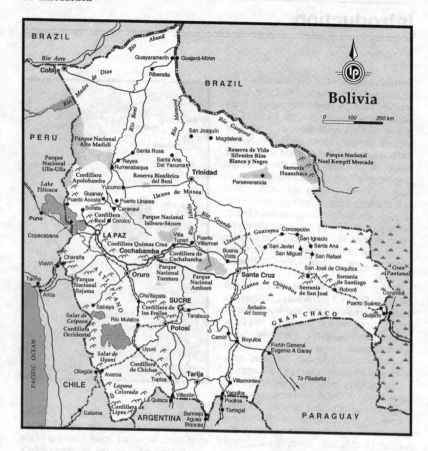

from the worn routes. Every corner of Bolivia will overwhelm curious and motivated travellers with cultural and natural beauty, as well as unforgettable experiences and characters to match the classic expectations of those who dream of South America.

Facts about the Country

HISTORY

The Central Andes

The great Altiplano (High Plateau), the largest expanse of arable land in the Andes, extends from present-day Bolivia into southern Peru, north-western Argentina and northern Chile. It has been inhabited for thousands of years, but the early cultures of the Altiplano were shaped by the imperial designs of two major forces: the Tiahuanaco culture of Bolivia and the Inca of Peru.

Most archaeologists define the prehistory of the Central Andes in terms of 'horizons' – Early, Middle and Late – each of which was characterised by distinct architectural and artistic trends. Cultural interchanges between early Andean peoples occurred mainly through peaceful trade and exchange, often between nomadic tribes or as a result of the diplomatic expansionist activities of powerful and well-organised societies. These interchanges resulted in the Andes' emergence as the cradle of South America's highest cultural achievements.

Early Horizon – The Chavíns

The original Andean arrivals are presumed to have descended from nomadic hunters who wandered across the Bering Strait from Siberia and eventually settled down to a sedentary agricultural existence in permanent communities. During the initial settlement of the Andes, which lasted until about 1400 BC, villages and ceremonial centres were established, and trade then emerged between coastal fishing communities and the farming villages of the highlands.

The so-called Early Horizon, which lasted from about 1400 to 400 BC, was an era of architectural innovation and activity. Its culmination is most evident in the ruins of Chavín de Huantar, on the eastern slopes of the Andes in Peru. It's postulated that during this period, a wave of Aymara-speaking Indians, possibly from the mountains of central Peru, swept across the Andes into

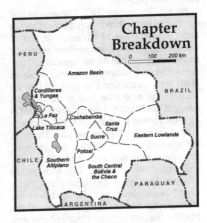

Chapter Breakdown

0   100   200 km

PERU

Amazon Basin

BRAZIL

Cordilleras & Yungas

La Paz   Cochabamba

Lake Titicaca   Santa Cruz

Sucre   Eastern Lowlands

CHILE   Potosí

Southern Altiplano   South Central Bolivia & the Chaco

PARAGUAY

ARGENTINA

Alto Perú (Bolivia) and occupied the Altiplano, driving out most of the region's original settlers.

Chavín influences resounded far and wide, even after the decline of Chavín society, and spilled over into the Early Middle Horizon (400 BC to 500 AD) that followed.

Middle Horizon – Tiahuanaco

The core centuries of the Middle Horizon, from about 500 to 900 AD, were marked by the imperial expansion of the new Tiahuanaco-Huari culture.

The ceremonial centre of Tiahuanaco, on the shores of Lake Titicaca, grew and prospered through the Middle Horizon and developed into the religious and political capital of the Alto Peruvian Altiplano. The Tiahuanaco people produced technically impressive work, the most notable example of which was the city itself. They created impressive ceramics and gilded ornamentation, and engraved pillars and slabs with calendar markings and designs representing their bearded white leader/deity Viracocha, as well as other designs and hieroglyphs that

11

remain undeciphered. It's believed that Tiahuanaco culture introduced and encouraged the extensive planting of maize for ceremonial purposes.

By the 7th century BC, Tiahuanaco had developed into a thriving civilisation, and in many respects was as advanced as that of ancient Egypt. It had an extensive system of roads, irrigation canals and agricultural terraces. Over the following centuries, wooden boats were constructed to ferry 55,000 kg slabs 48 km across the lake to the building site, and sandstone blocks weighing 145,000 kg were moved from a quarry 10 km away.

Tiahuanaco and its counterpart, Huari, in the Ayacucho valley (which is now in Peru), developed into well-organised, prosperous and ambitious societies. The relationship between these two widely separated communities isn't clear, but the architecture, iconography and changing art forms of the Middle Horizon suggest close cultural ties. Though they may have been dual capitals of the same state, many theories favour the idea that Tiahuanaco was the real power centre. Its art and architecture were more refined than that of Huari, which might have functioned as a strategic military outpost. Whatever the relationship, through trade and political expansion, the Tiahuanaco-Huari influence – particularly artistic values and construction methods – eventually extended as far north as Ecuador.

The Tiahuanaco site had been inhabited since about 1500 BC and remained occupied until 1200 AD, but its period of power lasted only from the 6th century BC to the 9th century AD (Huari had been abandoned before 800 AD). During the Late Middle Horizon, Tiahuanaco's power waned, and its civilisation declined. One theory speculates that Tiahuanaco was uprooted by a drop in the Lake Titicaca water level, which left the lakeside settlement far from shore. Another postulates that it was attacked and its population massacred by the warlike Kollas (sometimes spelt Collas; also known as Aymara) from the west. When the Spanish arrived, they learnt of an Inca legend about a battle between the Kollas and 'bearded white men' on an island in Lake Titicaca. These men were presumably Tiahuanacans, of whom only a few were able to escape. Some researchers believe the displaced survivors migrated southward, and developed into the Chipaya people of western Oruro department.

Today, the remains of the city lie on the plain between La Paz and the southern shore of Lake Titicaca, and collections of Tiahuanaco relics can be seen in several Bolivian museums. For further information, refer to Tiahuanaco in the La Paz chapter.

Late Horizon – the Inca

The Inca, the last of South America's indigenous conquerors, arrived shortly after the fall of Tiahuanaco. The Late Horizon, from 1476 to 1534 AD, marked the zenith of Inca civilisation. They pushed their empire from its seat of power in Cuzco (Peru) eastward into present-day Bolivia, southward to the northern reaches of modern Argentina and Chile, and northward through present-day Ecuador and southern Colombia. For all its widespread power and influence, however, the Inca political state thrived for less than a century before falling to the might of the invading Spanish.

Although the Inca had inhabited the Cuzco region from the 12th century, they were little more than a minor chiefdom. Inca legend recounts tales of bearded white men coming to them from the shores of Lake Titicaca and bringing civilisation before pushing off to sea. It wasn't until about 1440 that the Inca became serious about extending their political boundaries beyond the immediate neighbourhood. In the space of just over 50 years, they managed to establish a highly unified state that took in most of the central Andes.

The origins of the Inca are the stuff of myths and legends (see under History in the Lake Titicaca chapter), but their achievements certainly are not. Renowned for their great stone cities and their skill in working with gold and silver, the Inca also set up a hierarchy of governmental and agricultural overseers, a viable social welfare scheme, and a complex road network and communication system that defied the difficult terrain of their far-flung empire.

The Inca Manco Capac, first in the line of Inca emperors, and his sister/wife Mama Ocllo (also known as Mama Huaca), convinced their people they were children of the Sun God. Their progeny were the first of the Inca nobles, and to keep the lineage pure and to extend it, they adopted a structured system of marriage. Consequently, each subsequent Inca ruler, the Sapa Inca, was considered a direct descendant of the Sun God. Nobles were permitted an unlimited number of wives and their children were considered legitimate Inca nobles.

The traditional history of the Inca is intriguing, but naturally there are other more down-to-earth theories regarding their origins. These include that of the 17th-century Spanish chronicler Fernando Montesinos, who believed the Inca had descended from a lineage of Tiahuanaco wise men. There were indeed many similarities between Tiahuanaco and Inca architecture, and when the Inca arrived to conquer the shores of Lake Titicaca, the Kollas who inhabited the region around Tiahuanaco regarded the site as taboo.

In a sense, the Inca government could be described as an imperialist socialist dictatorship, with the Sapa Inca as reigning monarch, head of the noble family and the extended Inca clan, and unquestionable ruler of the entire state. The state technically owned all property within its vast and expanding realm and taxes were collected in the form of labour. The government organised a system of mutual aid in which relief supplies were collected from prosperous areas and distributed in areas suffering from natural disasters or local misfortune.

This system of benevolent rule was largely attributable to the influence of the eighth Inca, Viracocha (not to be confused with the Tiahuanaco leader/deity, Viracocha), who believed that the mandate from the Sun God was not just to conquer, plunder and enslave, but to organise defeated tribes and absorb them into the realm of the benev-olent Sun God. When the Inca arrived in Kollasuyo (present-day Bolivia), they assimilated local tribes – as they had done elsewhere – by imposing taxation, religion and their own Quechua language (the *lingua franca* of the empire) upon the region's inhabitants.

The Kollas living around the Tiahuanaco site were among the most recalcitrant additions to the empire. Although they were absorbed by the Inca and their religion was supplanted, they were permitted to keep their language and social traditions.

By the late 1520s, internal rivalries had begun to take their toll on the empire; in a brief civil war over the division of lands, Atahuallpa, the true Inca emperor's half-brother, had imprisoned the emperor and assumed the throne himself.

The Spanish Conquest

The arrival of the Spanish in 1531 dealt the ultimate blow. Within a year, Francisco Pizarro, Diego de Almagro and their bands of merry conquistadores had pushed inland toward Cuzco in search of land, wealth and adventure. When they arrived in the capital, Atahuallpa was still the incumbent emperor, but he was not considered the true heir of the Sun God. The Spanish were aided by the Inca belief that the bearded white men had been sent by the great Viracocha Inca as revenge for Atahuallpa's breach of established protocol. In fear, Atahuallpa ordered the murder of the real king, which not only ended the bloodline of the Inca dynasty, but brought shame on the family and dissolved the psychological power grip held by the Inca hierarchy.

The Spanish were unconcerned about the death of the true emperor, but they did turn the resulting guilt to their own advantage. Atahuallpa's shame at having killed the divine descendant of the Sun God, combined with the Inca nobility's initial trust in the Spanish 'gods', made the conquistadores' task easy. Within two years, the government had been conquered, the empire had been dissolved, and the invaders had divided Inca lands and booty between the two leaders of the Spanish forces.

Alto Perú, which would later become Bolivia, fell for a brief period into the possession of Diego de Almagro, who was assassinated in 1538 and didn't have the chance to make the most of his prize. Three years later, Pizarro himself suffered the same fate at the hands of mutinous subordinates. It was during this period that the Spanish got down to exploring and settling their newly conquered land. In 1538, the town of La Plata was founded as the Spanish capital of the Charcas region.

The Legacy of Potosí

By the time the wandering Indian Diego Huallpa revealed his earth-shattering discovery of silver at Potosí in 1544, Spanish conquerors had already firmly implanted their language, religion and customs upon the remnants of Atahuallpa's empire. Spanish Potosí, or the 'Villa Imperial de Carlos V', was founded in 1545 when the riches of Cerro Rico (Rich Hill) were already on their way to the Spanish treasuries. Potosí, with 160,000 residents, became the largest city in the western hemisphere.

The Potosí mine became the world's most prolific. The silver extracted from it underwrote the Spanish economy, particularly the extravagance of its monarchy, for at least two centuries, and spawned a legendary maritime crime wave on the Caribbean Sea.

Atrocious conditions in the gold and silver mines of Potosí guaranteed a short life span for the local Indian conscripts who were herded into work gangs, as well as for the millions of African slaves brought to the mines. Those not actually worked to death or killed in accidents succumbed to pulmonary silicosis within just a few years. Africans who survived migrated to the more amenable climes of the Yungas north-east of La Paz, and developed into an Aymara-speaking minority.

The Spanish soldiers, administrators, settlers, adventurers and miners who poured into the region developed into a powerful land-owning aristocracy. The indigenous peoples became tenant farmers, subservient to the Spanish lords, and were required to supply their conquerors with food and labour, in exchange for subsistence-sized plots of land. Coca, once the exclusive privilege of Inca nobles, was introduced among the general populace to keep people working without complaint.

Independence

In May of 1809, the first independence movement in Spanish America had gained momentum and was under way in Chuquisaca (Sucre). Other cities soon followed the example, and the powder keg exploded. During the first quarter of the 19th century, the soldier and liberator General Simón Bolívar succeeded in liberating Venezuela and Colombia from Spanish domination. In 1822 he dispatched Mariscal (Major-General) Antonio José de Sucre to Ecuador to defeat the Royalists at the battle of Pichincha. In 1824, after years of guerrilla action against the Spanish and the victories of Bolívar and Sucre in the battles of Junín (6 August) and Ayacucho (9 December), Peru won its independence.

At this point, Sucre incited a declaration of independence for Alto Perú, and exactly one year later, the new Republic of Bolivia was born (for further information, see under History in the Sucre chapter). Bolívar and Sucre became Bolivia's first and second presidents. After a brief attempt by Andrés Santa Cruz, the third president, to form a confederation with Peru, things began to go awry. One military junta after another usurped power from its predecessor, setting a pattern of political strife that would haunt the nation for the next 162 years.

Few of Bolivia's 191 governments to date have remained in power long enough to have much intentional effect, and some were more than a little eccentric. The bizarre, cruel General Mariano Melgarejo, who ruled from 1865 to 1871, once drunkenly set off with his army on an overland march to the aid of France at the outset of the Franco-Prussian War. History has it that he was sobered up by a sudden downpour and the project was abandoned (to the immense relief of the Prussians, of course).

Melgarejo is also credited with a host of other gaffs, including murdering a penitent conspirator; appropriating Indian lands; squandering the nation's reserves on his mistresses and alcohol habit (among other personal projects); ceding territory to Brazil in exchange for a horse; and tying the British ambassador naked to the back of a mule and banishing him for failing to drink enough beer. This last infringement, which was the final straw for Queen Victoria, led her to declare that Bolivia did not exist and that it would thenceforth not appear on British maps.

Shrinking Territory

Bolivia's misfortunes during its earlier years were not limited to internal strife. At the time of independence, its boundaries encompassed well over two million sq km, but by the time its neighbours had finished paring away at its territory, only half the original land area remained.

The first and most significant loss occurred in the War of the Pacific, which was fought with Chile between 1879 and 1884. In the end, Chile wound up with 850 km of coastline from Peru and Bolivia. The loss was most severe for Bolivia, which had been robbed of its port of Antofagasta, the copper and nitrate-rich sands of the Atacama Desert and, most significantly, the country's only outlet to the sea. Although Chile did attempt to recompense the loss by building a railroad from La Paz to the coast and allowing Bolivia free port privileges in Antofagasta, Bolivians have never forgotten the devastating *enclaustromiento* which left them without a seacoast. Even today, the government uses the issue as a rallying cry whenever it wants to unite the people behind a common cause.

During the years that followed, Peru, Brazil and Argentina each had their turn hacking away at Bolivia's borders. The next major loss was in 1903 during the rubber boom. Both Brazil and Bolivia had been ransacking the forests of the remote Acre territory, which stretched from Bolivia's present Amazonian borders to about halfway up Peru's eastern border. The area was so rich in rubber trees that Brazil engineered a dispute over sovereignty and sent in its army. Brazil convinced Acre to secede from the Bolivian republic, and then promptly annexed it.

Brazil attempted to compensate Bolivia's loss with a new railway, this one intended to open up the remote northern reaches of the country and provide an outlet to the Amazon Basin by circumventing the rapids that rendered the Río Mamoré unnavigable below Guayaramerín. The Madeira to Mamoré line (nicknamed Mad María), however, never reached Bolivian soil. Construction ended at Guajará-Mirim on the Brazilian bank of the Mamoré, and is now used only infrequently as a tourist novelty.

The boundaries between Bolivia and Paraguay had never been formally defined, and in 1932, a border dispute with Paraguay for control of the Chaco erupted into full-scale warfare. This time the conflict was caused partly by rival foreign oil companies that had their eye on concessions, should their prospecting activities reveal huge

deposits of oil in the Chaco. In a bid to secure favourable franchises, a quarrel was engineered, with Standard Oil supporting Bolivia, and Shell siding with Paraguay.

Paraguay, badly beaten after taking on Argentina, Uruguay and Brazil in the War of the Triple Alliance, needed an outlet to avenge its loss. Victory in this respect would also guarantee a prosperous economic future – if the oil companies' theories regarding the prevalence of oil proved correct. Bolivia fell victim to Paraguayan pride and, within three years, lost another 225,000 sq km, 65,000 young men and a dubious outlet to the sea via the Río Paraguaí before the dispute was finally settled in 1935 in Paraguay's favour. (although it was not until 1938 that Bolivia formally ceded to Paraguay all land taken over and occupied by Paraguay during the 1932-35 war.) The anticipated reserves of oil were never discovered, but several fields in the area that remained Bolivian territory now keep the country self-sufficient in oil production.

Modern Problems

During the 20th century, Bolivian farming and mining interests were controlled by tin barons and wealthy landowners, while the peasantry was relegated to a non-feudal system of peonage known as *pongaje*. The beating Bolivia took in the Chaco War paved the way for the creation of reformist associations, civil unrest among the *cholas* (see the Population & People section in this chapter for details about these people), and a series of coups by ostensibly reform-minded military leaders.

The most significant development was the emergence of the Movimiento Nacionalista Revolucionario (MNR), which united the masses behind the common cause of popular reform. It sparked labour unrest and friction between peasant miners and absentee tin bosses. The miners' complaints against outrageous working conditions, pitifully low pay and the export of profits to Europe raised the political consciousness of all Bolivian workers. Under the leadership of Victor Paz Estenssoro, the MNR prevailed in the 1951

elections, but a last-minute military coup prevented it actually taking power. The coup provoked a popular armed revolt by the miners, which became known as the April Revolution of 1952, and after heavy fighting, the military was defeated and Victor Paz's MNR took the helm for the first time. He nationalised mines, evicted the tin barons, put an end to pongaje and set up COMIBOL (Corporación Minera de Bolivia), the state entity in charge of mining interests.

The revolutionaries were also concerned with agrarian and educational reform and universal suffrage, and pressed ahead with a diverse reform programme, which included redistribution of land among share-cropping peasants and restructuring of the educational system to include primary education in villages. To open up the long-isolated and under-represented Oriente lowlands, a road was constructed from Cochabamba to Santa Cruz.

All these social and economic reforms were aimed at ensuring political participation of all sectors of the population. In the end, the miners and peasants felt they were

Victor Paz Estenssoro served
as Bolivia's president for three terms

being represented, and the relatively popular MNR government lasted an incredible 12 years under various presidents. Victor Paz himself served three nonconsecutive terms of varying lengths.

Even with US support, however, MNR was unable to raise the standard of living or increase food production substantially, and its effectiveness and popularity ground to a standstill. As dissent increased within his ranks, Victor Paz was forced to become more and more autocratic. In 1964 his government, weakened by internal quarrels, was overthrown by a military junta headed by General René Barrientos Ortuño.

This fresh round of military rule was strongly opposed, and General Barrientos lashed back at his detractors. In 1967 the Argentine-born Marxist folk hero Ché Guevara, who had been advocating a peasant revolt in south-eastern Bolivia, was executed by a US-backed military squad working with the Bolivian Armed Forces. In the same year, military forces massacred miners who had gathered at Catavi to form an antigovernment front.

Following the death of General Barrientos in a 1969 helicopter accident, one coup followed another and military dictators and juntas came and went with some regularity. Right-wing coalition leader General Hugo Bánzer Suárez took over in 1971 and served a turbulent term, punctuated by right-wing extremism and human rights abuses, until 1978 when he scheduled general elections amid demand for a return to democratic process. Although Bánzer lost the elections, he ignored the results and accused the opposition of serious tampering.

Shortly thereafter Bánzer was forced to step down in a coup by General Juan Pereda Asbún. Pereda tenuously held power very briefly until the job was snatched from him by General David Perdilla, who at least had the support of the democratic opposition. Perdilla announced elections in 1979, but they failed, and the National Congress appointed Walter Guevara Arze as interim president. His government was overthrown, however, in the bloody 1979 coup by Colonel Alberto Natusch Busch, who stepped down after only two weeks in office due to widespread lack of support.

That same year, Congress appointed Lidia Gueilar, a woman, as interim president, and the country enjoyed a brief respite from military mania. When elections were held the following year, no candidate achieved a majority and it became apparent that Congress would select Hernán Siles Zuazo and his Unión Democrática y Popular (UDP) party, but the process was interrupted by a military coup led by General Luis García Meza Tejada under the direction of cocaine traffickers and resident Nazi activist, Klaus Barbie, the Butcher of Lyons. During this hideous regime came a rash of tortures, arrests and disappearances, as well as an incredible increase in cocaine production and trafficking.

By 1981, however, García Meza had lost control of the military and was forced to step down, to be replaced by General Celso Torrelio Villa. By this time, the populace had had enough of military scuffling and called for democratic rule, but the Torrelio government resisted. In 1982, an attempted coup by García Meza led to the appointment of General Guido Vildoso Calderón to oversee a peaceful return to democratic rule. (García Meza fled the country but in April 1993, was convicted *in absentia* of genocide, treason, human rights abuses and armed insurrection and sentenced to 30 years imprisonment; in March 1995, the unrepentant 64-year-old former dictator was extradited from Brazil and brought back to Bolivia to serve his sentence.)

In 1982, Congress elected Dr Hernán Siles Zuazo, the civilian left-wing leader of the Communist-supported Movimiento de la Izquierda Revolucionaria (MIR). His term was beleaguered with labour disputes, ruthless government spending and monetary devaluation, resulting in a staggering inflation rate that at one point reached 35,000% annually!

When Siles Zuazo gave up after three years and called general elections, Victor Paz Estenssoro returned to politics to become

The Drug War

In 1989, one-third of the Bolivian work force was dependent on the illicit production and trafficking of cocaine. Far and away the most lucrative of Bolivia's economic mainstays, it was generating an annual income of US$1.5 billion, of which just under half remained in the country. Most of the miners laid off during Victor Paz's austerity measures turned to cocaine as a source of income. Ensuing corruption, acts of terrorism and social problems threatened government control over the country, which in the international perspective had by now become synonymous with cocaine production.

US threats to cease foreign aid unless efforts were made to stop cocaine production forced Victor Paz to comply with their proposed coca eradication programme. Instead of eliminating the trade, however, the US eradication directive brought about the organisation of increasingly powerful and vociferous peasant unions and interest groups. This, combined with lax enforcement, corruption and skyrocketing potential profits, actually resulted in an increase in cocaine production. The Bolivian government refused to chemically destroy coca fields, and instead urged coca farmers to replace their crops with other cash-producing commodities such as coffee, bananas, spices and cacao.

Peasants were offered US$2000 each by the government to destroy their coca plantations and plant alternative crops. In early 1990, a drop in the price of coca paste brought about a temporary lull in production, and some farmers sold out to the government's proposed crop substitution programme. Many, however, simply collected the money and moved farther north to replant.

All Bolivian drug enforcement police and military units were paid by the US government, and as early as 1987, the USA had been sending Drug Enforcement Agency (DEA) squadrons into the Beni and Chapare regions to assist the programme. In May 1990, Paz Zamora appealed for a major increase in US aid to augment the weakened Bolivian economy. In response, US President George Bush sent US$78 million in aid and stepped up US 'Operation Support Justice' activities in northern Bolivia. In June 1991, Bolivian police and DEA agents staged a daylight helicopter raid on Santa Ana del Yacuma, north of Trinidad, and seized 15 cocaine labs, nine estates, numerous private aircraft and 110 kg of cocaine base; however, no traffickers were captured, having been given sufficient warning to escape. Several surrendered later under Bolivia's lenient 'repentance law'.

The US forces' greatest fear was that peasant resistance would fuel leftist insurgences and guerrilla groups, while the millions pumped into Bolivia for drug enforcement operations would serve to fatten corrupt military and government officials. At the same time, some US military personnel in Bolivia claimed that the ultimate winners would be the drug cartels; at least 85% of Bolivian antinarcotic trainees, many of whom had family members involved in cocaine production and trafficking, were on one-year stints. It's presumed that once they're free of active duty, they'll simply use their expertise in US military operations to secure work as highly paid informants and security

president for the third time. He immediately enacted harsh measures to revive and stabilise the shattered economy; he ousted labour unions; removed government restrictions on internal trade; slashed the government deficit; imposed a wage freeze; eliminated price subsidies; laid off workers at inefficient government-owned companies; allowed the peso to float against the US dollar; and deployed armed forces to keep the peace.

Inflation was curtailed within weeks, but spiralling unemployment, especially in the poor mining areas of the Altiplano, caused enormous suffering and threatened government stability. Throughout his term, however, Victor Paz remained committed to programmes that would return the government mines to private cooperatives and

develop the largely uninhabited lowland regions of the north and east of the country. To encourage the settlement of the Amazon region, he promoted road building (with Japanese aid) in the wilderness and opened up vast Indian lands and pristine rainforest to logging interests.

The 1989 presidential elections, free from threat of military intervention, were characterised mostly by apathy. Hugo Bánzer Suárez of the Acción Democrática Nacionalista (ADN) resurfaced, the MIR nominated Jaime Paz Zamora and MNR put forth mining company president and economic reformist Gonzalo Sánchez de Lozada ('Goni'). Although Banzer and Sánchez placed ahead of Paz Zamora, no candidate received a majority, so it was left to National guards for cocaine producers and traffickers. Even so, the US 1992 budget for South American anti-narcotic operations was US$1.2 billion.

In mid-1992, Bolivia's Senate voted to expel US troops participating in antinarcotic activities, but the USA was unwilling to resume aid unless they had a part in the programme. However, they also remained unwilling – at least outwardly – to admit that drug addiction was a domestic problem and the result of shortcomings in their own social structure. It was far easier and more acceptable to most American voters to lay the blame on drug-producing countries.

By early 1995, the US government had grown impatient with what it considered Bolivia's failure to destroy its coca crop in a timely manner, and set a deadline of 30 June 1995 for the eradication of nearly 2000 hectares of coca in the Chapare and an additional 3500 hectares by the end of the year. It also demanded Bolivia's signature on an extradition treaty that would send drug traffickers to trial in the US. If Bolivia refused or failed, US loans, aid and funding would be cut off.

In April, a rather geographically-challenged US Congressman, Dan Burton, suggested the US take its own initiative and spray the Bolivian coca crop with herbicides to be dropped by planes based on an aircraft carrier 'off the Bolivian coast'. When the laughter had subsided, protests were launched against the US and Bolivian governments for even suggesting that sort of force and the Coca Leaf Growers Association again pointed out that the problem lay not with Bolivian coca growers, but with a burgeoning US market for cocaine and related drugs.

In any case, Bolivia met the 30 June deadline by paying farmers US$2500 for each hectare destroyed, which placed a heavy strain on government resources, and predictably, most farmers simply collected the money and moved elsewhere to replant.

A bone of contention arose in Isiboro-Sécure National Park, where UMOPAR (Anti-drug Mobile Rural Patrol Unit) was eradicating coca fields without paying farmers because the coca was being grown on public land. With the expiration of a 90-day state of siege imposed on 18 April, the violence resumed, resulting in 187 arrests, the deaths of five campesino growers and eventually, renewal of the state of siege. At this point, the US began moaning about human rights abuses surrounding the coca eradication programme – apparently oblivious to their own culpability – and DEA officers openly admitted they'd done nothing to prevent the violence.

A relative calm returned over the following weeks, but the agreement between the USA and Bolivia required a total reduction of 5400 hectares of coca by 31 December 1995. Bolivia managed to meet the quota, but US cuts in foreign aid payments meant that some of the burden had to be borne by Bolivian taxpayers. As things stand now, the coca eradication programme is running out of steam and the Bolivian government is again levelling criticisms at the USA for ignoring – or failing to tackle – the home issues that make drug production and trafficking profitable. ∎

Congress to select one. Longtime rivals Bánzer and Paz Zamora formed a coalition to prevail over Sánchez, and Congress selected Paz Zamora as the new president.

In the following election, on 6 June 1993, Sánchez returned to defeat Bánzer. Sánchez and his Aymara running mate, Victor Hugo Cárdenas, appealed to Indian peoples, whereas urbanites generally embraced his free-market economic policies.

Thus far, his emphases have been to stamp out the millstone of corruption and to implement *capitalización*, opening up state-owned companies and mining interests to overseas investment in the hope that private enterprise can run things more efficiently and cost-effectively than government. The idea isn't privatisation, per se, but stabilisa-tion and streamlining so the companies can be made to pay. Overseas interests willing to invest in and operate formerly state-owned companies receive 49% equity, total voting control, licence to operate the company and up to 49% of the profits. The remaining 51% shares are to be distributed to the Bolivian people in the form of pensions and through another scheme dubbed *Participación Popular*, which was announced in early 1994. This operates on a per capita basis, and channels spending away from cities, where it has traditionally rested, and into rural municipalities, to be used for schools, clinics and other local infrastructure.

It was a brilliant but little-understood plan, and most people disapproved of it. City dwellers didn't want to lose their advantage and rural people feared a hidden agenda or simply didn't understand it. The 'working classes' in general, assumed it was privatisation by another name, and concluded that it would lead to the closure of nonprofitable operations and greater unemployment. They had a point – lots of potential investors had their eye on the oil company YPFB and the huge agribusinesses of Santa Cruz department, but no one wanted to touch ENFE (the railroad), for example, or many of the antiquated mining operations.

On 19 April 1995, violent labour protests and strikes over the new economic policies resulted in the declaration of a 90-day state of siege and the arrest of 374 labour leaders, who were taken to remote parts of the country and detained until things calmed down. Initially, travel was restricted and curfews were imposed, but enforcement became impossible and gradually the measures were relaxed. In mid-1995 labour grievances still hadn't been resolved, but apart from protests by university students against funding cuts, objections to reform took a back seat to violence and unrest surrounding US-directed coca eradication in the Chapare. On 19 July 1995, the government cited that, as well as labour unrest in Oruro and Potosí, as sufficient cause to renew the state of siege.

GEOGRAPHY

Bolivia currently encompasses 1,098,581 sq km, which makes it 3½ times the size of the British Isles, slightly smaller than Alaska, and just less than half the size of Western Australia. It's bordered on the west by Chile and Peru, on the north and east by Brazil, and on the south by Argentina and Paraguay. The country is shaped roughly like an equilateral triangle. At its greatest extents, it measures 1300 km from east to west and 1500 km from north to south.

Much of Bolivia's appeal for the visitor lies in its awesome geography. Physically, the land is divided into five basic and diverse regions: the high Altiplano, the highland valleys, the Yungas, the Chaco and the forested lowlands of the Amazon and Paraná basins.

Altiplano

The Altiplano ('high plain') is the most densely populated region of the country, although it is by no means crowded. This

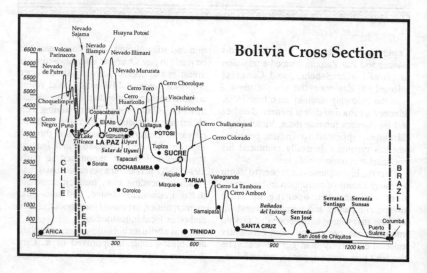

Bolivia Cross Section

great plateau, which is characterised by *puna* vegetation (high open grasslands), runs from the Peruvian border north of Lake Titicaca southward to the Argentine border, and spills over into neighbouring Peru, Chile and Argentina.

Despite its name, the Altiplano is anything but flat. Basin altitudes range from 3500 to 4000m, but the snow-capped peaks of the Cordillera Real and the many isolated volcanic summits of the Cordillera Occidental reach much higher. Nevado Sajama, a volcano near the Chilean border and disputably Bolivia's highest peak, rises to an elevation of 6542m. The average elevation of peaks in the Cordillera Real near La Paz is 5500m.

Bolivia's 'great lakes' are also found on the Altiplano. Lake Titicaca, the most important and beautiful, is the second largest in South America. Lakes Uru Uru and Poopó, south of Oruro, are little more than immense puddles just a few metres deep.

South of the lakes, where the land becomes drier and less populated, are the remnants of two other lakes, the Salar de Uyuni and the Salar de Coipasa. These two salt deserts and the surrounding plains form eerie white expanses of salt deposited by leeching from the surrounding peaks.

The Highland Valleys

The highland valleys south and east of the Altiplano boast the most hospitable living conditions in the country, with near optimum climatic conditions and fertile soils. This is the Cordillera Central, an area of scrambled hills and valleys, fertile basins and intense agriculture. With a reversed Mediterranean climate – rain falls in summer instead of winter – the land supports olives, nuts, wheat, maize and grapes, and wine is produced in the city of Tarija. The cities of Cochabamba, Sucre, Potosí and Tarija support most of the population. Only Potosí, with its exposed and lofty location, suffers from an unfavourable climate.

The Yungas

North and east of Cochabamba and La Paz, where the Andes fall away into the Amazon Basin, are the Yungas – the transition zone between dry highlands and humid lowlands. Above the steaming, forested depths rise the near-vertical slopes of the Cordillera Real and the Cordillera Quimsa Cruz, which halt Altiplano-bound clouds, causing them to deposit bounteous rainfall on the Yungas. Vegetation is abundant and tropical fruits, coffee, sugar, coca, cacao, vegetables and tobacco grow with minimal tending.

The Chaco

In the south-eastern corner of Bolivia, along the Paraguayan and Argentine borders, lies the flat, nearly impenetrable, scrubland of the Chaco. Because the region is almost entirely uninhabited, native flora and fauna thrive, and the Chaco provides a refuge for such rare animal species as the jaguar and peccary, which have been largely displaced in other parts of the country. The only settlement of any size is Villamontes, on the rail line, which prides itself on being the hottest spot in Bolivia. Temperatures frequently reach the mid-forties and thick red dust (or if it's raining, sticky mud) covers everything.

The Lowlands

Encompassing about 60% of Bolivia's total land area, the lowlands of the north and east are hot, flat and sparsely populated. Recently, efforts have been made to develop the forestry, agricultural and mineral potential of the region.

Two great river systems drain this vast area. The Acre, Madre de Dios, Abunã, Beni, Mamoré, Ichilo, Ibare, Grande, Paraguá and a score of other rivers flow northward toward Brazil into Amazon tributaries. The Río Paraguaí flows southward into the Paraná Basin and eventually to the Atlantic via the Río de la Plata.

The only breaks in the flat, green monotony of the south-western Beni and northern Santa Cruz departments are the natural monoliths and ranges of low hills that rise from the Llanos de Moxos, Guarayos and Chiquitos.

CLIMATE

Bolivia has as wide a range of climatic patterns as it has of elevation and topography, but the overall temperatures are probably cooler than most people expect. Even in the humid forest regions of the north, frosts and subzero temperatures are not unheard of during a *surazo*, a cold wind blowing from Patagonia and the Argentine pampa.

Although most of Bolivia lies as near the equator as Tahiti or Hawaii, its elevation and unprotected expanses contribute to variable weather conditions. The two poles of climatic misery in Bolivia are Puerto Suárez for its stifling, humid heat, and Uyuni for its near-Arctic cold and icy winds. But there are no absolutes in the Bolivian climate; there

are times when you can sunbathe in Uyuni and freeze stiff in Puerto Suárez!

The summer rainy period lasts from November to March. In La Paz, mists swirl through the streets and the city is literally wrapped in the clouds; rain falls daily and cold air currents sweep down the canyon from the Altiplano. On the Altiplano above La Paz, the lakes swell to devour the landscape, and livestock stand in knee-deep puddles. Of the major cities, only Potosí normally has snow, but it isn't uncommon in Oruro and La Paz.

During the winter, the climate is drier and more pleasant. Throughout the country, night-time temperatures drop dramatically, and on the high Altiplano, the sun has only to pass behind a cloud for a significant temperature difference to be noticed. Subzero temperatures are frequent, especially at night, and precipitation is not uncommon, but is of shorter duration than in the rainy season.

In Cochabamba, Sucre and Tarija, winter is the time of clear, beautiful skies and optimum temperatures, and there is hardly a healthier or more ideal climate on earth. The lowlands experience hot sunny days and an occasional 10-minute shower to cool things off and settle the dust. Because of its steep elevation, the Yungas may experience rain on any day of the year.

La Paz

Cochabamba

Santa Cruz

ECOLOGY & ENVIRONMENT

The early 1990s have seen a dramatic surge in international and domestic interest in ecological issues and environmental attitudes in the Amazon region. This was clearly demonstrated by the choice of Brazil as the venue for ECO-92, an enormous environmental bash organised by the United Nations to thrash out priorities for the environment and economic development.

Little explored and for years relatively ignored, Bolivia's lowlands have only in the past decade begun to figure in the consciousness of the Bolivian government. With the current push towards the securing of undeniable sovereignty of the lowland regions, and the potential fortunes to be made in minerals, agricultural opportunities and forest products, conservation isn't as convenient as it once was. With so many economic advantages, there's unfortunately little incentive to consider long-term effects.

Environmental problems have not yet reached apocalyptic proportions, but change is coming rapidly, and it is not being accompanied by the sort of careful thought required to maintain a sound ecological balance. Bolivia fortunately lacks the population pressures of Brazil, but it is nevertheless promoting indiscriminate development of its lowlands. With government encouragement, settlers are leaving the highlands to clear lowland forest and build homesteads. Despite increasing criticism at home and abroad, this movement continues, and unless some intelligent controls are instituted soon, Bolivia will head down the path to exhaustion of its forest and wildlife resources.

The Fate of the Amazon

Although books, magazines, TV shows and myriad international causes seem to be debating ecological issues, and the words 'fate of the Amazon' have begun to seem trite, it is appropriate to consider the issue a planetary concern. The Amazon, a very large, complex and fragile ecosystem – which contains one-tenth of the earth's total number of plant and animal species and draining one-fifth of the world's fresh water – is endangered.

Without change, the rainforests will be cleared for more ranches and industries, the land will be stripped for mines and the rivers will be dammed for electricity. Already jaguars, caymans, anteaters, armadillos, dolphins, monkeys and a host of other species are threatened with extinction. As in the past, Indians will inevitably be displaced and the irreplaceable Amazon forests may dwindle irreversibly.

The construction of roads is a prerequisite for exploiting the Amazon. The new roads have created a swathe of development across the former Beni wilderness from La Paz to Guayaramerín and Yucumo to Trinidad. The Riberalta-Cobija road is currently spreading the frenzy into the Pando Department.

These roads are the direct result of 'humanitarian aid' and earth-moving equipment donated by outside logging interests (Japan and the USA have seemingly insatiable appetites for forest products!), but similar projects throughout the Amazon have been encouraged and financed with collaboration from the World Bank, the International Monetary Fund (IMF), US and other international banks, and a variety of private corporations, politicians and military interests.

The inevitable conclusion is that new highway projects such as these will follow established patterns of development and open up the region for further decimation. According to calculations based on Landsat photos, the damming of rivers, and the burning and clearing of the forests between 1970 and 1989, destroyed about 400,000 sq km, or about 10%, of the Amazon forest.

In late 1988, Chico Mendes, a rubber tapper and opponent of rainforest destruction, was assassinated in the town of Xapurí, Acre, Brazil, by a local landowner. This sparked an international outcry that eventually pressured the World Bank and the IMF to place a moratorium on funding of rainforest development projects.

Economic Development of the Amazon

Most biologists doubt that the Amazon can support large-scale agriculture. The rainforest lushness is deceptive: the volcanic lands and flood plains can support continuous growth, but the forest topsoil is thin and infertile, and much of it is acidic and contains insufficient calcium, phosphorus and potassium for effective crop production.

Small-scale slash-and-burn, a traditional agricultural technique adopted by nomadic Indians, supported small populations on such fragile lands as those of the Amazon Basin, without ecological compromises. Indians would fell an approximately 12 or 24-hectare plot of land and burn off the remaining material. The resulting ash would support a few years of crops: squash, maize, manioc, plantains and beans. Clearings were small and few, and once the land was no longer productive, it was left fallow long enough for the forest to recover.

In contrast, modern agricultural interests in the region have emphasised cattle ranching, which does not give the land a rest. Ranchers clear enormous tracts of land – some larger than European nations – which are never left fallow, so once any nutrients or topsoil are gone, the land is permanently wasted.

Effects of Development The Amazon's indigenous population has borne the brunt of the destruction that has systematically wiped out their lands and their forest habitat. New roads have attracted settlers and opportunists into the last refuges of tribes which, as a consequence, have been virtually wiped out by new diseases, pollution, over-hunting and violent confrontations.

Due to the presence of valuable minerals in the northern rivers, parts of northern La Paz department are facing environmental catastrophe. Both commercial mining companies and maverick prospectors stream into the Alto Beni region to work the streams and rivers. Tragically, their principal technique involves the use of highly poisonous mercury to extract gold from ore. Large quantities of mercury are washed into the water and become a major health hazard for local inhabitants and remaining wildlife.

Since the failure of its early 1950's attempt at agrarian reform on the Altiplano, the Bolivian government has officially encouraged immigration and development in the lowland regions of the country. The 1950's programme entailed allotting each farmer with a plot of land known as a *minifundio*. These private plots made obsolete the communal *ayllu* system of shared responsibility and production practised since Inca days. However, the minifundio parcels were too small to sustain life on the harsh Altiplano and, in the end, farmers were forced to somehow wrest a living from the land or relocate. For the past decade, the govern-

ment has been actively promoting development in the lowland regions with promises of land and loans. Although it has meant a complete change in lifestyle, the advantages of migrating to the verdant and productive lowlands have been too inviting for many to pass up.

The theory that the Amazon forests are the prime source of the world's oxygen is no longer given much credence by the scientific community, but there is increasing concern over the regional and global climatic changes brought on by the forest clearing. One of the most dramatic and disturbing developments is *el chaqueo*, the burning of immense tracts to clear forest for agriculture or cattle ranching, which in Bolivia amounts to up to 200,000 sq km annually. A prevailing notion is that the rising smoke forms rain clouds and ensures good rains. In reality, it has just the opposite effect. The hydrological cycle, which depends on transpiration from the forest canopy, is interrupted by the deforestation, resulting in diminished rainfall. In extreme cases, deforested zones may be baked by the sun into desert-like wastelands.

According to meteorologists, the smoke cloud, primarily from the burning of the Brazilian forests, has already reached Africa and Antarctica. In September, the Altiplano skies are obscured by a dirty grey haze that blots out the mountains and turns the sun into an egg yolk. In the northern lowlands, visibility can diminish to as little as 200m. Scientists generally agree that the torching of the forest on such a massive scale contributes to the greenhouse effect, but opinions differ regarding the scale of damage involved.

Perhaps the most devastating long-term effect is the extinction each year of thousands of forest species. This loss reduces the genetic pool that is vital (as a source of foods, medicines and chemicals) for sustaining life.

Remedies & Compromise Although Brazil's policy toward development of the Amazon has been singled out for criticism, the Amazon Basin also includes vast tracts of six other countries – Bolivia, Colombia,

Venezuela, Guyana, Ecuador and Peru. It's only fair to point out that many countries outside the region were once supporters of such development, and have been reminded only recently that their own treatment of the environment was hardly exemplary. The general consensus for the 1990s, however, is that a series of different approaches must be developed to halt and remedy the destruction. The following are a few of the ways now being tried:

Debt-for-nature swaps are international agreements whereby a portion of a country's external debt is cancelled in exchange for funding of conservation initiatives. Negotiation of such swaps requires that the sovereignty of recipient countries remains intact, and economic damage avoided.

In August 1987, the US-based organisation Conservation International kicked off the idea by making Bolivia an offer: it agreed to pay US$650,000 of Bolivia's foreign debt (which totals US$4 billion!) in exchange for permanent official protection of the 334,200-hectare Reserva Biosférica del Beni near San Borja. Bolivia retains management of the land but, theoretically, wildlife is protected and haphazard development is curtailed.

Conservation International has also succeeded in setting aside the 351,000-hectare Parque Regional Yacuma in the central Beni, and creating the 1.15 million-hectare Reserva Forestal Chimane, which adjoins the Reserva Biosférica del Beni, for sustained development by local indigenous populations.

Another concept, which has been tried in Brazil, involves creation of extractive reserves for the sustainable harvesting of brazil nuts, rubber, and other non-timber products. The idea is to use the forest as a renewable resource, without destroying it. These reserves gained worldwide attention when Chico Mendes, an enthusiastic advocate of the idea, was assassinated in Brazil's Acre state.

Alternatives are also being suggested to stop wasteful clear-felling of timber. Proposed management schemes include control over the size of parcels being logged and the manner in which they're logged so that forest land will continue to be a sustainable resource. In many cases, huge tracts of forest are flattened and laid waste in order to extract a few commercially valuable tree species. When land is cleared exclusively for cattle ranching, however, timber is often burnt and squandered. I've encountered teams from US universities in Bolivia examining different methods of controlling the types of timber cut, of utilising 'waste' species and of thwarting exploitation of local workers who don't recognise the true value of forest products (or the scope of commercial profits) on the international market.

Ecotourism & Conservation Environmental conservation and carefully managed development must be achieved through the combined efforts of concerned individuals and groups both within Bolivia and abroad. Bolivia requires capable people and organisations to educate the public and enlist its support in reducing consumption of tropical forest products; to pressure US and other international banks to stop financing wasteful or destructive development projects; and to persuade Amazon-region governments to adopt rational and sustainable rainforest plans.

Ecotourism provides a financial incentive for countries such as Bolivia to preserve rather than exploit their environment, and the boom in ecotourism worldwide has prompted the creation of groups and organisations to monitor the effects of tourism and provide assessments and recommendations for those involved. It's important that organisations proclaiming an interest in environmental issues prove they are actively making progress towards environmental protection and preservation. One positive force in this direction is the growing consumer pressure, which has the power to change economic trends on a global scale simply by changing purchasing patterns.

For information on groups in Bolivia working towards general cultural preservation and/or environmental conservation, contact any of the organisations listed here.

Asociación Boliviana para la Protección de las Aves, Calle Jordán O-151, Casilla 3257, Cochabamba (☎ 26322, fax 24837)

Asociación para la Protección del Medio Ambiente de Tarija, Calle O'Connor 449, Casilla 59, Tarija (☎ 33873, fax 45865)

Asociación Sucrense Ecológica, Calle Avaroa 326, Sucre (☎ 32079, fax 22091)

Armonía, Casilla 3045, La Paz (☎ 792337) or Casilla 3081, Santa Cruz (☎ 522919, fax 324971)

Conservación Internacional, Casilla 5633, Avenida Villazón 1958-10A, La Paz (☎ 341230)

Instituto de Ecología, Casilla 10077, Calle 27, Cotacota, La Paz (☎ 792582, fax 391176)

FLORA & FAUNA

Field guides are listed under Books in the Facts for the Visitor chapter.

Flora

Because of its enormous range of altitudes, Bolivia enjoys a wealth and diversity of flora rivalled only by its Andean neighbours.

In the overgrazed highlands, the only remaining vegetable species are those with some sort of defence against ravenous livestock or those that are unsuitable for use as firewood. Even this near to the equator, there's little forest above 3000m elevation, although hardy dwarf trees such as the *queñua* survive at altitudes of up to 5300m. Another oddity of the high puna (Altiplano) is the giant pineapple-like *Puya raimondii*, which is found only in Bolivia and southern Peru. (For more on this plant, see Comanche in the Southern Altiplano chapter.)

Moving down in elevation, the moist upper slopes of the Yungas are characterised by dwarf forest. This is composed mostly of small trees and shrubs, thick with moss and ferns, which are permanently soaked with moisture from clouds. As you descend further, you enter the cloud forest, where the trees grow larger and the vegetation even thicker.

At lower elevations, the temperate hills and valleys of the highlands support vegetation similar to that found in Spain or California, including date palms and cactus; there are few forests, and most of the trees are eucalyptus which were transplanted there to counter soil erosion.

The lowland flats of northern Bolivia are characterised by true rainforest specked with vast soaking wetlands and open savanna grasslands. The Amazon Basin contains the richest botanical diversity on earth and botanists have spent their lives cataloguing the thousands of species endemic there. In the more humid regions, the land is comprised largely of swampland, low jungle scrub and rainforest. Although the northern grasslands are maintained by annual burning, there's evidence that this is the natural vegetation in these areas.

Several species of cactus and other succulents have adapted to the typically dry conditions of Bolivia's south-western deserts and grow at altitudes between about 2000 and 3000m. As you descend towards the better-watered Chaco plains farther east, the vegetation increases in size and becomes more dense. Most of south-eastern Bolivia is covered by an almost impenetrable thicket of cactus and thorn scrub, which erupts into colourful bloom in the spring. Instantly recognisable are the hideously spiky *toboroche* (also known as *palo borracho)* and the red-flowering *quebracho* or 'break-axe' tree.

Fauna

Thanks to its varied geography, sparse human population and lack of extensive development, Bolivia is one of the best places on the continent for viewing South American wildlife. You'll need to venture beyond the cities, but that doesn't necessarily mean you'll have to slog through snow, swamp and rainforest to see something. A boat journey along a northern river or a rail trip through the far south-west or the Oriente will probably present at least a glimpse of it.

The Altiplano Although llamas and alpacas are hardly wild, having been domesticated for centuries in the Andean highlands, you're bound to see plenty of them on the Altiplano. Despite their cute and cuddly appearance, they have a nasty reputation for biting and spitting, so beware when observing at close range. These ill-tempered cameloid domesticates, cousins of the equally ill-tempered Arabian and Bactrian camels of Africa and Asia, also have other cousins in the New World. Guanacos are quite rare in Bolivia, but the delicate little *vicuñas* are occasionally seen along the railway line between Uyuni and the Chilean border, as well as throughout the remote south-western part of the country.

As for vicuñas, the problem is their soft and fuzzy hides, which fetch a bundle on the illicit market. As a result, vicuñas are on the decline in the wild, but in several Bolivian reserves – the Reserva de Fauna Andina Eduardo Avaroa and Parque Nacional Ulla Ulla – their numbers have been increasing. The best place to observe them is just across the Chilean border in Parque Nacional Lauca, which harbours thousands of zealously protected vicuñas. Other wild inhabitants of the Altiplano include Andean wolves, foxes, and deer (known as *huemules*), but again, your best chance of seeing them is in Parque Nacional Lauca.

The Southern Altiplano is the exclusive habitat of the James flamingo; just look for any shallow lake and it will probably be full of them. Also relatively common is the versatile *ñandu* or rhea (the South American ostrich) which is found from the Altiplano to the Beni, the Chaco and the Santa Cruz lowlands. Then there's the *viscacha*, a long-tailed rabbit-like creature that spends most of its time huddled under rocks. Viscachas are very docile but, like rabbits, they are easily alarmed and disappear at the approach of humans.

If you're lucky, you may see a condor or two in the highland regions. Highly revered by the Inca, these rare vultures are the world's heaviest birds of prey. They have a wingspan of over three metres and have been known to effortlessly drag a carcass weighing 20 kg.

The Highland Valleys Unfortunately, this well-populated region is nearly devoid of wildlife. The puma, native throughout the Americas, was considered sacred by many of the tribes conquered by the Inca, and the Inca

Blue-and-yellow macaw

capital at Cuzco was laid out in the shape of this feline deity. Even today, many Bolivians believe that eclipses are caused by hungry pumas nibbling at the sun or the moon, both of which are considered deities. On such occasions, the people stage noisy celebrations in the hope of frightening it away. After centuries of human interference, however, the puma is now wisely reclusive. Tracks are occasionally seen in the Cordillera de los

Sombreros and other remote ranges, but there's little chance of spotting one without mounting a special expedition.

The Chaco The jaguar, tapir and *javeli* (peccary), which occupy the nearly inaccessible expanses of the Chaco in relatively healthy numbers, are quite elusive. Slightly more common, but still threatened with extinction, is the giant anteater, which exists in far eastern Bolivia near the Pantanal.

The Amazon Basin There is an incredible variety of lizards, parrots, monkeys, snakes, butterflies, fish and bugs (by the zillions!) in this region. River travellers in the Amazon Basin are almost certain to spot capybaras (large amphibious rodents), turtles, alligators, pink dolphins and, occasionally, giant river otters. It's not unusual to see anacondas in the rivers of the Beni, and overland travellers frequently see armadillos, rheas, sloths and the agile, long-legged *jochis* or agoutis.

Many of the more common animals wind up in the stew pot. Locals roast turtles in the shell and eat their eggs. Jochi and armadillo are considered staples in some areas, and a great many of the latter are also turned into *charangos*, traditional Andean ukulele-type instruments.

Rarer still, but present in national parks and remote regions of the Beni, Pando and northern Santa Cruz and Cochabamba departments, are jaguars, peccaries, tapirs, giant anteaters and spectacled bears. However, your chances of seeing any of these are rather slim – and getting slimmer every day.

National Parks & Reserves

Bolivia boasts a number of national parks and reserves that are the habitat of a myriad of plant, bird and animal species. Some of these parks have only recently become accessible to visitors. There are other areas that may become national parks but the boundaries are loosely defined and, in many, conservation enforcement is either a low priority or nonexistent. Following is a brief outline of the parks and reserves included in this book. For more information, see the relevant chapters.

Parque Nacional & Área de Uso Múltiple Amboró
Amboró, near Santa Cruz, was created with 180,000 hectares in 1973, became a national park in 1984, was expanded to 630,000 hectares in 1990 and decreased to 430,000 hectares in 1995. It is home to the rare spectacled bear, jaguars, capybaras, peccaries and an astonishing variety of bird life. Further information is available from the Fundación Amigos de la Naturaleza (☎ 524921, fax 533389) Casilla 2241, Santa Cruz. The FAN office is in the village of La Nueve, eight km west of Santa Cruz on the Samaipata road. The small Carrasco portion of the park attempts to protect some remaining stands of rainforest in the volatile Chapare region. The most accessible site is the Cuevas de los Pájaros Nocturnos.

Reserva Biosférica del Beni
The 334,200-hectare Beni Biosphere Reserve, near San Borja in the Amazon Basin, exists in conjunction with the adjacent Reserva Forestal Chimane. It is home to at least 500 species of tropical birds and more than 100 species of mammals.

Parque Nacional Isiboro-Sécure
Unfortunately, due to a 1905 policy to colonise this area of the Chapare (northern Cochabamba Department), the Indian population has been either displaced or exterminated, and most of the wildlife has vanished, except in remote areas. Access is difficult, and because this park lies along a major coca and cocaine-trafficking route you should exercise caution.

Parque Nacional Alto Madidi
This enormous new national park in northern La Paz department protects some of Bolivia's wildest remaining rainforest and harbours its richest concentrations of rainforest species. Areas have also been set aside for traditional use by indigenous people. Access is on foot from Apolo or by boat from Rurrenabaque.

Parque Nacional Noel Kempff Mercado
This remote park near the Brazilian border is named in honour of the distinguished Bolivian biologist who was murdered by renegades in 1986. It contains a variety of Amazonian wildlife and some of the most inspiring natural scenery in Bolivia.

Reserva de Vida Silvestre Ríos Blanco y Negro
This remote 1.4 million-hectare wildlife reserve consists of vast tracts of undisturbed rainforest. Wildlife includes giant anteaters, peccaries and tapirs, and there are over 300 bird species.

Parque Nacional Sajama
This national park, which adjoins Chile's mag-

nificent Parque Nacional Lauca, contains Volcán Sajama (6542m), Bolivia's highest peak. Apart from a couple of private alojamientos, no tourist facilities are available on the Bolivian side.

Parque Nacional Torotoro

Palaeontologists will be interested in the biped and quadruped dinosaur tracks from the Cretaceous period, which can be found in the enormous rock formations near the village of Torotoro. The park also boasts caves, ancient ruins and lovely landscapes.

Parque Nacional Tunari

This park, right in Cochabamba's backyard, features Lagunas de Huarahuara, small lakes containing trout, and pleasant mountain scenery.

Parque Nacional Ulla Ulla

Excellent hiking is possible in this remote park abutting the Peruvian border beneath the Cordillera Apolobamba. It was established in 1972 as a vicuña reserve and presently contains 2500 vicuñas and a large population of condors.

GOVERNMENT & POLITICS

In theory, Bolivia is a republic, much like the USA, with legislative, executive and judicial branches of government. The first two convene in La Paz, the de facto capital, and the Supreme Court sits in Sucre, the constitutional capital. Politically, Bolivia is

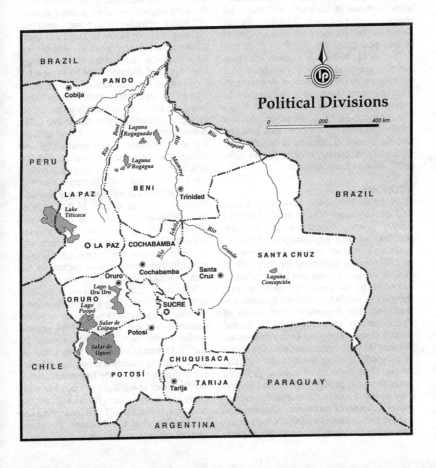

divided into nine departments, which are subdivided into 112 provinces. These are divided into 294 sections and the sections are subdivided into 1408 cantons.

The president is elected to a four-year term by popular vote and cannot hold more than one consecutive term. Once elected, the president appoints a cabinet of 15 members and also selects departmental and local government officers.

The Legislature consists of a Senate and a Chamber of Deputies that convenes in legislative session for 90 days per year. Each of the nine departments send three elected senators for terms of six years, with one-third elected every two years. The Chamber of Deputies has 102 members who are elected to four-year terms.

Bolivia has had nearly as many leaders as years of independence and it has been ruled by military juntas for much of its existence. This may seem to make a mockery of the democratic processes outlined in Bolivia's constitution. In truth, however, the late 1980s and early 1990s have seen peaceful and democratic transitions of government. Politically, the country is currently one of the most stable in Latin America.

ECONOMY

With the decline of the world tin markets, and the ensuing labour strife between miners' unions, cooperatives and the state, the days of tin's supremacy as Bolivia's mainstay export are over for the time being. In 1987, mining accounted for only 36% of Bolivia's export income and 2% of its labour force. In the far south-west there are rich deposits of sulphur, antimony, bismuth and lead/zinc. The legendary silver mines of Potosí are now being reworked for tin and other lesser minerals, and Oruro's mines are winding down to a near standstill. The nation is currently looking towards the Oriente, where large deposits of natural gas, iron manganese and petroleum have been discovered and have supplanted ores as the primary mineral exports of the country. Currently, oil exploration is underway in the Chapare and the eastern lowlands, and a natural gas pipeline is planned between Santa Cruz and Brazil.

Bolivia currently has the second-lowest per capita GNP (US$900 annually) in South America (after Guyana) and the third in the western hemisphere (Haiti is the poorest). Fortunately, this is not as severe as it sounds because a good many rural Bolivians operate outside the currency system and enjoy relatively comfortable subsistence lifestyles.

Agriculturally, Bolivia remains a subsistence country, but does manage to satisfy most of its own requirements. Agricultural exports are dominated by cotton and soya from the eastern lowlands. A small amount of Yungas coffee is exported and a moderate quantity of sugar, grown in Tarija and Santa Cruz departments, goes to Argentina. Natural gas is the largest source of legal export income, contributing 43% of the total.

However, illicit exports of coca products exceed all legal agricultural exports combined. In 1986 alone, Bolivia's star export brought between US$600 million and US$1 billion into the country – more than all legal exports combined. Coca production and refining currently account for about 350,000 jobs and it's clear that as long as there's a strong market and profit potential, one way or another, Bolivia will continue to produce. Currently there are at least 54,000 hectares of coca under cultivation in the Chapare region alone, and in 1986, they yielded 100,000 kg of cocaine, all of which was exported. Most of the Yungas coca is used primarily for domestic consumption in the form of tea and leaves for chewing.

Bolivia currently hopes to boost its weak economy by promoting tourism. However, the country's image as a politically unstable, cocaine-producing country – and general confusion with more crime-ridden countries, such as Peru and Colombia – tends to put off the sort of big-money tourism the industry hopes to attract. Currently, tourist arrivals are mainly either low-budget independent travellers or holiday-makers from neighbouring countries, particularly Brazil, Argentina and Chile. See also the Modern Problems section, earlier in this chapter.

POPULATION & PEOPLE

With just 7.4 million people, Bolivia is relatively thinly populated. Despite its cold, arid climate, the Altiplano supports 70% of the people and for centuries has been the country's most densely populated region. Most of these people are concentrated in the northern end of this region in the environs of La Paz, Lake Titicaca and Oruro.

Between 50% and 60% of the total population is of pure Indian stock; most of these largely traditional people speak either Quechua or Aymara as a first language and strongly resist cultural change. They're known locally as *campesinas* (female) or *campesinos* (male) or *cholas/os* (female/male), although this latter term also refers to anyone who has migrated to the city but continues to wear ethnic dress. About 35% are *mestizo*, people of Spanish American and American Indian parentage or descent. Nearly 1% of the population is of African heritage, mostly descended from the slaves conscripted to work in the Potosí mines.

Most of the remainder of Bolivia's people are of European extraction. Some are descendants of the early Spanish conquerors, but there are also colonies of Platt-Deutsch-speaking Mennonites, some Nazi war criminals, and hordes of researchers, aid workers and missionaries. Small Middle Eastern and Asian minorities, consisting mainly of Palestinians, Punjabis, Japanese and Chinese, have immigrated. Most of these have settled in the rapidly developing lowlands of Santa Cruz department.

Things Go Better With Coca

Cocaine, marijuana, hashish and other drugs are illegal, but the coca leaf, which is the source of cocaine and related drugs, is chewed daily by many Bolivians and is even venerated by indigenous peoples. Mama Coca is the daughter of Pachamama, the earth mother, and coca is considered a gift to the people to be used to drive evil forces from their homes and fields. Both the Quechua and Aymara people make sacrifices of coca leaves when planting or mining to ensure a good harvest or lucky strike. The *yatiri* use them in their healing and exorcising rituals, and in remote rural areas leaves are often used in place of money. People embarking on a journey also use them as offerings to Pachamama in the hope that she'll keep their way safe; this is done by first placing several leaves beneath a rock at the start. If you're walking in the mountains or countryside, you may want to hedge your bets and do the same, or at least carry some leaves along as a gift for helpful locals. They'll always be gratefully received.

The leaf itself grows on bushes that are cultivated in the Yungas and Upper Chapare regions at altitudes of between 1000 and 2000m. They are sold by the kg in nearly every market in Bolivia along with *legía*, an alkaloid usually made of mineral lime, potato and *quinoa* ash, which is used to draw the drug from the leaves when chewed. There are two kinds of legía: *achura*, which is sweet, and *cuta*, which is salty.

The conquering Spanish found that labourers who chewed the leaf became more dedicated to their tasks, so they promoted its use among the peasants. Today, nearly all campesinos and *cholas*, men and women alike, take advantage of its benefits. It's also becoming popular among younger middle-class people, particularly those who sympathise with the causes of Indian peasants. Most Bolivians of European origin, however, still regard chewing coca as a disgusting 'Indian' habit and generally avoid its use.

Used therapeutically, coca serves as an appetite suppressant and a central nervous system stimulant. Indian people use it while working to lessen the effects of altitude and eliminate the need for a lunch break. They also chew it recreationally and socially in much the same way people smoke cigarettes or drink coffee. Among Bolivian miners, the 'coca break' is an institution.

The effects of coca-chewing are not startling. It will leave you feeling a little detached, reflective, melancholy or pleasantly contented. The Indians normally chew about 30 to 35 leaves at a time. If you want to try it, place a few leaves, say, five to 10, between your gums and cheek until they soften. Then repeat the process, placing a little legía between the leaves. Don't start chewing until you've stuffed in the desired amount. Once you've chewed it into a pulpy mess, you're meant to swallow the bitter-tasting juice, which will numb your mouth and throat. (In fact, novocaine and related anaesthetics are coca derivatives.) ∎

Generally speaking, modern Bolivians are a rugged and strong-spirited people. Many of the dispersed Altiplano communities of Aymara-speaking Indians fought historic battles against the cultural dominance and oppression of the expanding Inca Empire. In pre-Hispanic Bolivia, they flourished as one of the most influential cultures in the Andes.

Furthermore, Bolivia organised the first resistance to Spanish rule in South America, which included mestizo revolts in 1661 and 1780, and Indian insurrections that lasted from 1776-80.

The standard of living of most Bolivians is low and in places such as the El Alto suburb of La Paz (which is becoming a city in its own right), housing, nutrition, education, sanitation and hygiene standards are appalling.

The state of health care, particularly in rural areas, is also quite poor. It's estimated that 8% of infants born in Bolivia can be expected to die before their first birthday. Similarly, the average life expectancy in the country is only about 60 years for men and 65 years for women, compared with 70 to 75 years in most developed nations.

EDUCATION

Although school attendance is theoretically compulsory for children aged six to 14, schools in many rural areas are either poor or nonexistent. Overall, only 87% of primary school-aged children are enrolled in classes and for those who are enrolled, attendance isn't necessarily a high priority. As a result, Bolivia's official literacy rate of 75% is one of the lowest in Latin America. There are several universities in the country, the major ones being the Universidad de San Simón in Cochabamba and the Universidad Mayor de San Andrés (UMSA) in La Paz. Sucre and Santa Cruz also have large universities.

ARTS
Literature

Like all other South American nations, Bolivia has developed a literature of its own. Unfortunately, only three Bolivian novels have ever been translated into English, and

two of these aren't very recent translations. Nevertheless, as they were published by large publishers in the US and the UK, they're fairly easy to track down in libraries. To become familiar with Bolivia's literature, however, will require a knowledge of Spanish.

The main sources for information on Bolivian literature are Fernando Diez de Medina's literary history *Literatura Boliviana* (4th edn, 1980); Adolfo Cáceres Romero's monumental *Nueva Historia de la Literatura Boliviana* (1987); and the annual *Bio-Bibliografía Boliviana*, which lists all books published in Bolivia, published by Werner Guttentag Tichauer & M Rita Arze Ramirez. In addition, a fine article by Oscar Rivera-Rodas on the history of Bolivian literature is published in the *Handbook of Latin American Literature* (Garland, 1992).

Bolivia's indigenous people had no written language, but the first volume of Cáceres Romero's study is devoted to the oral literature of the four indigenous cultures – Aymara, Quechua, Kallahuaya and Guaraní. There is a slim collection of *Quechua People's Poetry* by Jesús Lara (Curbstone Press, 1986), which includes some melodies.

Bolivia's most prominent Colonial-era writer is Bartolomé Arzáns Orsúa y Vela (1676-1736), whose immense *Historia de la Villa Imperial de Potosí* relates the history of that city year by year from its founding in 1545 until the author's death in 1736. The emphasis was on what we would now call 'human interest stories' and grand narrative sweep. Some of these wonderful stories and anecdotes have been translated into English in *Tales of Potosí* (Brown University Press, 1975).

After Bolivian independence, the first literary movement was Romanticism, which spawned two prominent writers. Julio Lucas Jaimes (1840-1914), in contrast to conventional European Romanticism, reread history and oral narratives in short tales. He also founded the 'traditionalist' genre, which attempted to recover a local style and thereby create a national literature. In the works of

A	B
C	D
E	F

A: (DS)   D: (DS)
B: (RS)   E: (RS)
C: (RS)   F: (RS)

A	B
C	D
E	

A: Butterflies on the riverbank, Amazon Basin (DS)
B: Armadillo (DS)
C: Alpacas, near Tupiza (RS)
D: Tapir (RS)
E: Capybaras (RS)

Nathaniel Aguirre (1843-1888), also a traditionalist, the narrator plays an important role, and foreshadows a predominant construct in contemporary Latin American fiction.

Bridging the transition from Romanticism to modernism was the poet Adela Zamudio (1854-1928). The modernist Ricardo Jaimes Freyre (1866-1933) was the first Bolivian author to gain international recognition. His story *Indian Justice*, which dealt with the exploitation of the indigenous population, is translated in *The Spanish American Short Story – A Critical Anthology* (University of California Press, 1980). Other notable modernist writers include the poet Franz Tamayo (1879-1956) and Gregorio Reynolds (1882-1948).

The first and most influential of the new generation of realist Bolivian authors was the historian and novelist Alcides Arguedas. His sociological treatise *Pueblo Enfermo*, 'sick nation', published in 1909, and his novel *Raza de Bronce* (1919), emphasise the diversity of Bolivian culture and strongly criticise the predominant feudal system for its enslavement of the indigenous population.

Another writer of this generation was novelist, dramatist, poet and diplomat Adolfo Costa du Rels (1891-1980), who spent much of his career in Europe – as the president of the League of Nations Council, among other things – and some of his works were written in French. His drama *Les Étendards du Roi* has been translated as *The King's Standards* (1958) and his novel, *Terres Embrasées* (1932), was re-written in Spanish as *Tierras Hechizadas* and translated into English as *Bewitched Lands* (Knopf, 1945). This realistic novel describes the rivalry between an authoritarian mestizo Chaco landholder and his European-educated, democratically-minded son, as seen by two Englishmen looking for oil. It's all interlaced with evocative descriptions of the Bolivian rainforests and Chaco.

The Chaco War provided material for a range of novels. Augusto Céspedes published his collection of short stories *Sangre de Mestizos* in 1936; Jesús Lara published his diary-novel *Repete* in 1937; and Costa du Rels wrote *Laguna H-3* in 1967. Céspedes *Metal del Diablo* ('the devil's metal'), which appeared in 1946, depicts the wretched conditions of the workers in Bolivian tin mines and sharply attacks the wealthy owners and exploiters.

The Revolution of 1952 and the military dictatorship of General René Barrientos and subsequent guerrilla uprising ushered in the contemporary period and coincided with innovations in narrative technique.

In 1957, two influential books were published. Marcelo Quiroga Santa Cruz's (1931-1980) existentialist novel *Los Deshabitados* ('the vacant ones') was concerned with the meaninglessness of reality and experiences. Similarly, Oscar Cerruto's (1912-1981) collection of short stories, *Cerco de Penumbras* ('fence of shadows'), grapples with failure and the absurdity of existence.

One novel inspired by Ché Guevara's struggle was Renato Prada Oropeza's *Los Fundadores del Alba* (1969), 'founders of the dawn', translated into English as *The Breach* (Doubleday, 1971). This novel, which won the 1969 *Casa de las América's* prize in Cuba, revolves around the experiences of two young men, one a saint-like guerrilla modelled on Ché Guevara and the other a soldier who lacks ideals and is only fighting because he has been drafted.

Three notable contemporary Bolivian poets are Jaime Sáenz (1921-1986), Pedro Shimose (born 1940) and Eduardo Mitre (born 1943). Sáenz's *Muerte por el Tacto* (1957), 'death by touch', and *Obra Poética* (1975), 'poetic work', are written in free verse and deal with love on an abstract level. Shimose's eight volumes of poetry, published in *Poemas* (1988), are presented in colloquial idiom and controversially attack tyranny and social inequality. Five short poems by Mitre are translated into English in the *Anthology of Contemporary Latin American Literature, 1960-1984* (Fairleigh Dickenson University Press, 1986).

The Bolivian novel most recently published in English (and still in print) is Arturo von Vacano's *Morder el Silencio* (1980), which was translated as *The Biting Silence* (Avon, 1987). This autobiographical novel runs through the life, career and ultimate arrest of the journalist-narrator, who has written an article critical of the military government and is accused of being a communist. The solution offered in the end is distinctively Maoist: to let the country die along with its government and start all over again from scratch.

A new and worthwhile Bolivian novel is the hard-to-find *Barriomundo* by Jaime Nisttahuz, whose characters are borrowed from classical Greek figures but the story is told through the eyes of boys growing up in a La Paz neighbourhood. It presents a refreshingly honest view of the world and presents the eternal conflict between childhood and eternal political agendas. And why is it so hard to find? Because it's priced for the common reader – only US$2.20 – and no mainstream bookshop will accept such a low profit margin. (Try the La Paz Casa de la Cultura, at the corner of Potosí and Mariscal Santa Cruz.)

Painting

In the early colonial days, a number of artists worked on religious themes in Bolivia, among them Italian-born Bernardo Bitti, Gregoria Gamarra, Matías Sanjinés, Zurbarán and Leonardo Flores. Look for all of these early artists in Bolivian museums and churches.

Bolivia's major contribution to religious painting, however, is represented by the Escuela Potosina Indígena, which was inspired by the Potosí master Melchor Pérez de Holguín. Hallmarks of this tradition include gilded highlights and triangular representations of the Virgin Mary.

Holguín, who was born in Cochabamba, arrived in Potosí in 1670 and entered the workshop of Francisco Herrar y Velarde, a Spanish painter who had settled there. His earliest works were paintings of the saints, portrayed as gaunt and wrinkled, presumably from pious asceticism. Once his talents were known, commissions poured in and his

reputation spread. His last signed canvas was completed in 1732, but his tradition was carried on by *potosino* students, including Gaspar Miguel de Berrio, Nicolás de los Ecoz, Joaquín Caraballo and Manuel Córdoba.

In the mid-1800s, Bolivian life was depicted in naïve watercolours by Melchor María Mercado, the USA-born son of Spanish parents living in Sucre. His work was clearly influenced by the French artist-explorer Alcides d'Orbigny, who spent three months in Sucre during Mercado's early years.

A distinctive modern artist was Alejandro Mario Yllanes, an Aymara tin miner from Oruro who turned to art in the 1930s as an engraver and muralist. He drew on themes from Andean mythology and pre-Hispanic history, which raised consciousness and a sense of identity among Aymara campesinos. The government of General Toro recognised the threat this represented and exiled him to the lowlands, where he absorbed the brilliant tropical colours that suffuse his later work. He somehow wound up in New York City, where he stayed until his death in 1960. His paintings, which depict the fiery side of the Aymara tradition, were first exhibited in New York in 1992, and received favourable reviews. There's now a drive in La Paz to bring his work home to Bolivia.

Also of note was Miguel Alandia Pantoja who, in the late 1940s, painted scenes of popular revolution – superimposed on industrial revolution – in the time leading up to the reforms instituted by Victor Paz Estenssoro in 1952. His scenes of good (the workers) versus evil (the establishment) are vibrant, angular and colour-rich.

The modern Aymara artist Mamani Mamani, from Tiahuanaco village, strives to portray the true 'colour' of the Altiplano – not the landscape but the images that inspire the people – and it is brilliant. The *paceño* artist, Gil Imana, brings out the stark, cold and isolated nature of life in the Andes, using only tiny splashes of colour on drab backgrounds to hint at the underlying vibrancy of the culture.

Other names to watch for are Andrés Chambi, of La Paz, who's concerned with the hopes of Bolivia's working classes; Elsa Quintanilla, also from La Paz, who uses watercolours to interpret the female character in brilliant colours; Gilka Wara Libermann, who turns religious art into a modern riot of colour; Alfredo La Placa, former Bolivian ambassador to the UN, with his surreal interpretations of his country, its mining heritage and its desire for order and progress; and Ricardo Pérez Alcalá, from Potosí, who eschews political and moral messages in favour of realistic whimsy, such as his preoccupation with Simón Bolívar or his painting of Leonardo da Vinci riding the bicycle he was never able to invent. Another realist is David Dario Antezana, whose watercolours of Bolivian rural life reflect obsession with detail and the rich red light of late afternoon; it's a stunning and evocative effect.

For more on Bolivian visual arts, see the book *La Pintura en los Museos de Bolivia* by José de Mesa & Teresa Gisbert.

Music

Although the musical traditions of the Andes have evolved from a series of pre-Inca, Inca, Spanish, Amazonian and even African influences, each region of Bolivia has developed distinctive musical traditions, dances and instruments. The strains of the Andean music from the cold and bleak Altiplano are suitably haunting and mournful, while those of warmer Tarija, with its complement of bizarre musical instruments, take on more vibrant and colourful tones.

Although the original Andean music was exclusively instrumental, recent trends towards popularisation of the magnificent melodies has inspired the addition of appropriately tragic, bittersweet or morose lyrics.

In the far eastern and northern lowland regions of Bolivia, Jesuit influences upon Chiquitano, Moxos and Guaraní musical talent left a unique legacy that is still in evidence and remains particularly strong in the musical traditions of neighbouring Paraguay. In addition to economic ventures,

the Jesuits promoted education and culture among the tribes. Extremely able artists and musicians, the Indians handcrafted musical instruments – the renowned violins and harps featured in Chaco music today – and learned and performed Italian baroque music, including opera! In the remotest of settings, they gave concerts, dances, and theatre performances that could have competed on a European scale.

Musical Instruments Although the martial honking of tinny and poorly practised brass bands seems an integral part of most South American celebrations, the Andean musical traditions employ a variety of instruments dating back to pre-colonial days.

Only the popular ukelele-like *charango*, based on the Spanish *vihuela* and *bandurria*, early forms of the guitar and mandolin, has European roots. By the early 17th century, Andean Indians had blended and adapted the Spanish designs into one that would better reproduce their pentatonic scale: a 10-stringed instrument with llama-gut strings arranged in five pairs and a *quirquincho* (armadillo carapace) soundbox. Modern charangos are scarcely different from the earliest models, but because of the paucity and fragile nature of quirquinchos, as well as efforts to improve sound quality, wood is nowadays the material of choice for charango soundboxes. Another stringed instrument, the *violín chapaco*, originated in Tarija and is a variation on the European violin. Between Easter and the Fiesta de San Roque (held in early September) it is the favoured instrument.

Prior to the advent of the charango, melody lines were carried exclusively by woodwind instruments. Best recognised are the *quena* and the *zampoña* (pan flute), which feature in the majority of traditional musical performances. Quenas are simple reed flutes played by blowing into a notch at one end. The more complex zampoñas are played by forcing air across the open ends of reeds lashed together in order of their size, often in double rows. Both quenas and zampoñas come in a variety of sizes and

The zampoña dates back to pre-Conquest times and is often played at fiestas

tonal ranges. Although the quena was originally intended for solo interpretation of musical pieces known as *yaravíes*, the two flutes are now played as part of a musical ensemble. The *bajón*, an enormous pan flute with separate mouthpieces in each reed, accompanies festivities in the Moxos communities of the Beni lowlands. While being played, it must be rested on the ground or carried by two people.

Other prominent wind instruments include the *tarka* and the *sikuri*, the lead instrument in the breathy *tarkeadas* and *sikureadas* of the rural Altiplano, and the *pinquillo*, a *Carnaval* (carnival) flute available in various pitches.

Woodwinds unique to the Tarija area are the *erke*, the *caña* and the *camacheña*. The erke, also known as the *phututu*, is made from a cow's horn and is played exclusively

between New Year's and Carnival. From San Roque in early September to the end of the year, the camacheña, a type of flute, is used. The caña, a three-metre-long cane pole with a cow's horn on the end, is similar in appearance and tone to an alphorn. It's played throughout the year in Tarija.

Percussion also figures in most festivals and other folk musical performances as a backdrop for the typically lilting strains of the woodwind melodies. In highland areas, the most popular drum is the largish *huankara*. The *caja*, a tambourine-like drum played with one hand, is used exclusively in Tarija.

Artists & Recordings Although there is a wealth of yet-to-be-discovered musical talent in Bolivia, key players are influencing musical trends and tastes worldwide with their recordings and occasional performances abroad.

Many visitors to Bolivia, especially those who have attended *peñas* (folk music shows for locals and tourists) or fiestas, are taken with the music and set out in search of recordings to take home. Compact disks haven't yet made their debut in Bolivia, so unless you have space to carry bulky and fragile record albums in your luggage, you'll have to resort to cassette tapes. Unfortunately, original recordings are hard to come by and those sold in music shops and markets are typically low quality bootlegged copies which are prone to rapid self-destruction. They are cheap however – about US$2.20 each – but copy them onto a better tape before giving them much play time.

Major artists you may want to look for include charango masters Ernesto Cavour, Celestino Campos and Mauro Núñez. Look especially for the recording *Charangos Famosos*, a selection of well-known charango pieces.

The Bolivian group that's been the most successful abroad is Los Kjarkas. They've recorded at least a dozen albums and their superb *Canto a la Mujer de Mi Pueblo* is unsurpassed. The track entitled *Llorando se Fue* by the late Bolivian composer Ulisses

Hermosa and his brother Gonzalo, was recorded by the French group Kaoma in 1989 and became a worldwide hit as *The Lambada*. In June 1990, the Hermosa brothers finally received official recognition for their authorship of the song.

Other groups worth noting are Savia Andina, known for their protest songs, Chullpa Ñan, Rumillajta, Los Quipus, Grupo Cultural Wara, Los Masis and Yanapakuna.

In the USA, tapes of Bolivian music are available through the SAEC (see Useful Organisations in the Facts for the Visitor chapter).

Dance

The pre-Hispanic dances of the Altiplano were celebrations of war, fertility, hunting prowess, marriage or work. After the Spanish arrived, traditional European dances and those of the African slaves brought to work in the mines were introduced and massaged into the hybrid dances that characterise Bolivian festivities today.

If Bolivia has a national dance, it's the *cueca*. This heartfelt dance is derived from the Chilean cueca, which in turn is a Creole adaptation of the Spanish fandango. Its liberally interpreted choreography is rendered by whirling handkerchief-waving couples, called *pandillas*, to three-four time. Cuecas are intended to convey a story of courtship, love, loss of love and reconciliation. A favourite part of the dance comes with the shouting of *Aro, aro, aro*, which indicates that it's time for the couple to stop dancing for a moment and celebrate with a glass of spirits each.

The *auqui-auqui*, or 'old man' dance, parodies high-born colonial gentlemen by portraying them ludicrously with a top hat, gnarled cane and an exaggerated elderly posture. Another popular dance is the *huayño*, which originated on the Altiplano.

In the south around Tarija, where musical traditions depart dramatically from those of the rest of Bolivia, the festival dance is known as the *chapaqueada*. It is usually associated with religious celebrations, especially San Roque, and is performed to the

strains of Tarija's host of unusual musical instruments. Also popular in Tarija is *la rueda* (the wheel) which is danced at all fiestas throughout the year.

In San Ignacio de Moxos and around the Beni lowlands, festivities are highlighted by the dancing of the *machetero*, a commemorative folkloric dance accompanied by drums, violins and *bajones*. Dancers carry wooden machetes and wear elaborate crowns of brilliant macaw feathers, wooden masks, and costumes made of cotton, bark and feathers.

Other popular dances in the northern lowlands include the *carnaval* and the *taquirari Beniano*, both adapted from the Altiplano, and the *chovena*, indigenous to north-eastern Bolivia.

Some of the most unusual and colourful dances are those performed at festivals on the high Altiplano, particularly during Carnival. *La Diablada* (The Dance of the Devils) fiesta at Oruro draws a large number of both foreign and Bolivian visitors.

The most famous and recognisable of the Diablada dances is *la morenada*, which is a re-enactment of the dance of the African slaves brought to the courts of Viceroy Felipe III. The costumes consist of hooped skirts, shoulder mantles, and dark-faced masks adorned with plumes. Another dance with African origins is *los negritos*. Performers beat on drums and the rhythm is reminiscent of the music of the Caribbean. In the *suri sikuri*, dancers gyrate wearing enormous hats decked with rhea feathers.

The *los llameros* dancers represent Andean llama herders, the *waca takoris* satirise Spanish bullfighters and the *waca tintis* represent the *picadores*, also of bullfighting fame. The *los Incas* commemorates the original contact between the Incan and Southern European cultures; and the *las tobas* is performed in honour of those Indian groups of the tropical lowlands (inaccurately called 'los apaches') that were conquered by the Inca and forcefully absorbed into the empire.

Potosí and La Paz both claim to be the birthplace of the *caporral de Potosí*, but it was almost certainly inspired by the harsh treatment of slaves in the Potosí mines. Caporrales were slave drivers and the dance commemorates the slaves who were whipped with *latigos* (whips) and forced to wear leggings made of *cascaveles* (rattles), which prevented them from moving silently. Modern dancers wear strings of bottle caps to simulate the effect.

Another Potosí tradition is the *tinku*; although it resembles a kind of disorganised dance, it is actually a ritual fight that takes place primarily in the northern part of the department during festivals. Tinkus usually begin innocently enough, but near the end of the celebrations, they tend to erupt into drunken – and often rather violent – mayhem.

Cinema

Bolivian film-making is only now getting off the ground. Perhaps the best-known Bolivian movie-maker is Jorge Sanjinés, who has made a dozen films and garnered 18 international awards with his popular, politically oriented works. Films such as *Ukamau* and *La Nación Clandestina* extol indigenous society in conflict with the prevailing imperialist values.

An early Bolivian film-making venture was the brilliant *Chuquiago*, by directors Oscar Soria and Antonio Equino, which appeared in the 1970s. Much of the dialogue is in Aymara and the theme concerns the enormous cultural and economic divides in modern La Paz – from El Alto to Calacoto – and is developed in four vignettes: the lives of Isico, a poor Aymara boy who has migrated to the city to find work, however meagre; the *cholo* Johnny, who works as a bricklayer and dreams of migrating to the USA; Carlos, the tax inspector, whose main concerns seem to be crossword puzzles and soliciting bribes from the public; and Patricia, a student and the daughter of a wealthy entrepreneur, who idolises Ché Guevara and joins an ill-fated revolutionary movement.

In 1988 Jac Ávila, who studied his trade in New York, came up with a semi-documentary shot in Haiti before the fall of Baby Doc Duvalier. In 1995, he master-minded a distinctly Bolivian murder mystery entitled *El Hombre de la Luna* ('The Man in the Moon'), a five-part mini-series that aired on Bolivian television. It was made on an extremely low budget but has attracted international attention. He now wants to draw on Bolivia's unique traditions in a planned feature film entitled *Pachamama*.

Another name to watch for is Juan Carlos Valdivia who, in 1992, produced an award-winning documentary for CNN about the unauthorised US military activities in Santa Ana del Yacuma. He also won an award from the Foundation for New Latin American Cinema for his screenplay of the Bolivian novel, *Jonah and the Pink Whale*, a critique of the Santa Cruz 'new rich' in the chaotic and drug-ridden mid-1980s. Hopefully it will attract sufficient funds to bring it to the screen.

With the 1995 release of the Latin 'road movie', Marcos Loayza's *Cuestión de Fe*, Bolivian film was given a further boost internationally. This sensitive and original comedy tells the story of three bumbling friends charged with a religious quest that takes them from La Paz to Coroico and around the Yungas in a classic pick-up truck called *Ramona*. The scenery is predictably inspiring and the story provides a revelation of Bolivian values.

For more, see the 1985 book *Adventures of Bolivian Film* by Carlos Mesa.

Weaving

Spinning and weaving methods have changed little in Bolivia for 3000 years. In rural areas, girls learn to weave before they reach puberty, and women spend nearly all their spare time spinning with a drop spindle or weaving on heddle looms. Prior to Spanish colonisation, llama and alpaca wool were the materials of choice, but sheep's wool is now the most readily available and least expensive medium.

Regional differences are manifest in weaving style, motif and use. Bolivian textiles have diverse patterns and the majority display a degree of skill that results from millennia of experience. The beautiful and practical creations are true works of art, and away from major tourist haunts, you can find real quality for good prices.

Weavings from Tarabuco, near Sucre, are made into the colourful costumes (men wear a *chuspa* – or coca pouch – and a trademark red poncho) and zoomorphic patterns seen around the popular and touristy Sunday market in Tarabuco. Designs are typically arranged in orderly bands of proportionally-sized figures – humans, animals and ordinary objects – and rendered in a rainbow of colours. Articles woven when in mourning are executed in a spectrum of blue hues. The most commonly decorated article is a rectangular women's overskirt that is known in Quechua as an *axsu*. This style is sometimes known as *Candelaria*, after a nearby village.

The most famous and celebrated of Bolivian weavings are the red or magenta and black zoomorphic designs from the Jalq'a region, which is centred on the village of Potolo, north-west of Sucre. Patterns range from faithful representations of *khurus*, wild animals that cannot be domesticated such as frogs, pumas, squirrels and owls, to creative and mythical combinations of animal forms: llamas, horses, dragons and a menagerie of avian aberrations. The patterns are typically asymmetrical, and the relative sizes of figures represented often don't conform to reality – it is not unusual for a gigantic horse to be depicted alongside a tiny building. Jalq'a pieces are prized by weavings buffs and command relatively high prices.

Zoomorphic patterns are also prominent in the wild Charazani country north of Lake Titicaca and in several areas in the vicinity of La Paz, including Lique and Calamarka. Some extremely fine weavings originate in Sica Sica, one of the many dusty and nondescript villages between La Paz and Oruro, and in Calcha, south-east of Potosí near the boundary of Chuquisaca. Some of Bolivia's best clothing textiles are produced here, with expert spinning and an extremely tight weave – over 60 threads per centimetre.

Anyone interested in Bolivian textiles should look for the books *A Travellers' Guide to Eldorado and the Inca Empire* by weavings expert Lynn Meisch, or the hard-to-find *Weaving Traditions of Highland Bolivia* by Laurie Adelson & Bruce Takami, published by the Los Angeles Craft & Folk Art Museum. If you read Spanish, a good

---

Chola Dress

The characteristic dress worn by many Bolivian Indian women was imposed on them in the 18th century by the Spanish king, and the customary centre-parting of the hair was the result of a decree by the Viceroy Toledo.

This distinctive ensemble, both colourful and utilitarian, has almost become Bolivia's defining image. The most noticeable characteristic of the traditional Aymara dress is the ubiquitous dark green, black or brown bowler hat that would seem more at home on a London street than in the former Spanish empire. You'd be hard pressed to find a chola or campesina without one.

The women normally braid their hair into two long plaits that are joined by a tuft of black wool known as a *pocacha*. The short *pollera* skirts they wear are constructed of several horizontal bands tucked under each other. This garment tends to make most of the women appear overweight, especially when several of them are combined with multiple layers of petticoats.

On top, the outfit consists of a factory-made blouse, a woollen *chompa* (pullover/jumper), a short vest-like jacket, and a cotton apron, or some combination of these. Usually, women add a woollen shawl known as a *llijlla* or *phullu*.

Slung across the back and tied around the neck is the *ahuayo*, a rectangle of manufactured or handwoven cloth decorated with colourful horizontal bands. It's used as a carryall and is filled with everything from coca or groceries to babies.

The Quechua of the highland valleys wear equally colourful but not so universally recognised attire. The hat, called a *montera*, is a flat-topped affair made of straw or finely woven white wool. It's often taller and broader than the bowlers worn by the Aymara. The felt montera of Tarabuco, patterned after the Spanish conquistadores' helmets, is the most striking. ■

information source on the Chuquisaca traditions is *Los Diseños de los Textiles Tarabuco y Jalq'a* by Veronica Cevececa, Johnny Dávalos & Jaime Mejía. It's sold at ASUR (Antropólogos del Surandino) at the Caserón de la Capellanía in Sucre. Another excellent booklet on Bolivian textile arts is *Bolivian Indian Textiles* by Tamara E Wasserman & Jonathon S Hill, available through the SAEC (see Useful Organisations in the Facts for the Visitor chapter.)

Architecture

The pre-Columbian architecture of Bolivia is represented primarily by the largely ruined walls and structures of Tiahuanaco and the numerous Inca remains scattered about the country. Restoration of these sites has not revealed much about the artistic values of the Inca or other groups. The only examples of the classic polygonal cut stones that dominate many Peruvian Inca sites are on Isla del Sol and Isla de la Luna in Lake Titicaca.

Surviving colonial architectural trends correspond with four major overlapping periods: renaissance (1550-1650), baroque (1630-1770), mestizo (1690-1790), which was actually a variation on baroque, and the modern period (post-1790). The beginnings of the modern period were marked by a brief experimentation with the neoclassical style, which was then followed by a return to the neo-Gothic.

Some Andean renaissance churches indicate *mudéjar* (Moorish) influences. Renaissance churches are simple in design. They were constructed primarily of adobe with courtyards, aisle-less naves and massive buttresses. One of the best examples is in the village of Tiahuanaco. The three classic examples of mudéjar renaissance design are found at San Miguel and San Francisco in Sucre, and at Copacabana on the shores of Lake Titicaca.

Baroque churches were constructed in the form of a cross with an elaborate dome and walls made of either stone or reinforced adobe. Late in the baroque period, mestizo elements in the form of whimsical decorative carvings were introduced and applied with what appears to be wild abandon. Prominent elements included densely-packed Inca deities and designs, masks, Christian cherubs, sirens, gargoyles and a riot of tropical flora and fauna – vine leaves, frogs, pineapples, chirimoyas etc.

Neoclassical design, which dominated between 1790 and the early 20th century, can be seen in the church of San Felipe Neri in Sucre, and the cathedrals in Potosí and La Paz.

Paralleling the mainstream church construction in the mid-18th century, the Jesuits in the Beni and Santa Cruz lowlands were designing churches reflecting Bavarian Rococco and Gothic influences. Their most unusual effort was the bizarre mission church at San José de Chiquitos, whose design is unique in Latin America.

SOCIETY & CONDUCT
Meeting Bolivians

Making contact with Bolivians, particularly in the cities, will be no problem at all. Few people are shy about striking up a conversation – in a shop or on a bus or micro, for example – and your attempts at friendly conversation are almost certain to be reciprocated. Even if your Spanish is limited, people will be happy to tax your abilities as far as they'll go, and will probably welcome the opportunity to dredge up their own English vocabulary, however meagre it may be.

What may seem off-putting at first is that nearly everyone you meet – even total strangers – will be interested in subjects that are considered taboo in much of the West. You'll frequently be asked about your marital and reproductive status; if you appear to be of marriageable age and profess to be unmarried or childless, you're likely to be met with sympathy, further probing questions and advice about how to remedy your 'problems'. To avoid this sort of innocent but perhaps off-putting reaction, you may want to conveniently invent a spouse and children waiting for you in another city or back home.

People will also want to know your profession, how much you earn and what your trip is costing. Many people believe all foreigners are wealthy beyond imagining, and because most foreigners they meet are on holiday – most Bolivians travel only to visit family or for some sort of economic gain – they also assume that little of this wealth is derived from work. If you're uncomfortable with this, perhaps explain your interest in their country and that you had to work, save and sacrifice to pay for your holiday in Bolivia. Talk about your profession and explain the prices of housing and staples back home. If you are involved in a project in Bolivia – even if it's a possible newspaper article to write when you get home – it's worth mentioning; this is a concept that will hit home and partially explain your mysterious globe-trotting behaviour.

Noise

Noise is a constant companion in Bolivian cities and locals seem undisturbed by noise levels 50 decibels above anything a European could tolerate. Music blares in restaurants and buses; horns honk constantly; TVs are turned up to full volume; rusted-off vehicle silencers (mufflers) are rarely replaced; urchins holler destinations from every passing *micro* or *trufi*; vendors screech at potential customers or at each other; brass bands honk away at any opportunity; and people converse at a volume that would suggest a heated argument. To say it can be annoying doesn't mean it isn't colourful, but in any case, there isn't much you can do about it.

Time

Since the invention of the clock, the world has become a more organised place, but in Bolivia, the concept of time has taken hold only superficially. Time-related terminology does exist but its interpretation isn't necessarily what visitors might expect. For example, *mañana*, 'tomorrow', could mean almost anytime in the indefinite future. In many places – particularly government offices – 'come back tomorrow' is the equivalent of 'go away and don't bother me with your problems'.

Bolivians invited to lunch on a Tuesday might arrive on a Wednesday and, by their understanding of time, may regard themselves as only a little late. You should not adopt local habits to this extent, but arriving a bit late is normal. If you're invited to a party at, say, 8 pm and you turn up at 9 pm, you're likely to be the first guest to arrive.

The same applies to meeting in the street. Arriving half an hour later than arranged will still give you time to read a newspaper before your friend arrives (if they arrive at all). If you become versed in this local custom, it can be a good idea to fix two or three meetings with different people at the same time and place – somebody will probably turn up!

Offices and institutions have a similarly flexible grasp of their advertised working hours. The rule seems to be that if money is directly involved, the hours are more likely to be adhered to. Banks, for instance, run like clockwork (Swiss, not Bolivian!) and shops and other commercial establishments are normally open the hours stated.

Another problem word is *ahora*, 'now', or its more common variation, *ahorita*, 'in a moment'. If, for example, you're waiting for a bus and ask a bystander when the bus should arrive, the answer will almost invariably be *ahorita* or more exasperatingly *ya viene*, 'it's already coming.' This probably means that the bystander has no idea when the bus is coming, but is hopeful that it will come and has taken an optimistic approach. The pessimist, on the other hand, might say that the bus you're waiting for *no existe*, *ya pasó* or *está plantado* – it 'doesn't exist', 'already passed' or 'is broken down'. Don't give up and go away – get a second or third opinion.

The moral is, have a relaxed and flexible travel schedule and take it easy if things don't always go according to plan.

Litter

As with noise, litter is an integral part of Bolivian life, so prepare for it. Bolivian people are accustomed to throwing things away wherever they happen to be – in the streets, on the floor, in buses, along the highway and in the countryside. In extreme cases, such as in Puerto Pailas near Santa Cruz, you'll wade through the streets ankle-deep in pastel plastic bags.

In time, you'll get used to the local standards and the general absence of litter bins. In La Paz, litter bins have been set up around the city bearing proud slogans about keeping the city clean, but the campaign is enjoying only limited success; people are just too accustomed to throwing things on the street. About all you can do is set an example, although you may be the only one walking around all day carrying plastic cups, tissues and greasy *salteña* napkins.

In budget hotels and restaurants you'll only rarely find an ashtray and asking for one may embarrass the management, because they probably won't have one. Nobody will pay any attention at all if you throw your cigarette ash and butts on the floor, and you're keeping someone employed sweeping them up.

Dos and Don'ts

One thing to remember about Bolivia is that every part of the country is different, but generally, the higher the altitude or smaller the town, the more conservative and traditional the society.

The fiercely proud rural Aymara, for example, may sometimes appear as harsh and cold as the land they inhabit, and may understandably question the motives of visitors who venture in with what appears to be a lot of money and no visible means of support. These people who work hard at meagre survival can't fathom someone trotting around the globe rather than attending to work, religious and family responsibilities at home (some of your relatives may feel the same way!). With patience and diplomacy, however, you can break the icy barrier and catch a glimpse of their unimaginably harsh lifestyle. Generally, Quechua speakers in the central highlands are more open to outsiders, but they may still harbour suspicions.

In rural areas, very few people speak any

Spanish and, in places, uninvited outsiders, particularly those who don't speak the local language or aren't familiar with the society's customs, are likely to be misconstrued. Off the trodden track, you'll probably be much happier with a local guide, who can smooth the way and reassure people that you mean no threat.

Religion plays a major role in the lives of most Bolivians, whether they follow Catholicism or animistic beliefs. Most people will be more comfortable if you profess some sort of religion – whether or not you actually practice or believe in it. Superstition is also deeply rooted and has a great deal of influence, and there's no point in attempting to explain it away with logic.

Perhaps the most important advice is to remember that to traditional Bolivians, their own culture is a natural state of being. The best approach is to accept that things are done differently here and to resist the temptation to introduce your own notions or values. Respect peoples' beliefs and values, whether or not they coincide with your own, and avoid making light of anything, however unusual, that appears to be taken seriously by the local community. Don't assume that outsiders are welcome to join in local fiestas or dance in processions; wait until you're invited to do so.

Similarly, if you find something disturbing, bow out rather than criticise. Tinku fights, for example, can become extremely violent and, on occasion, may even result in deaths, but any bloodshed is considered an offering to the earth mother Pachamama. To outsiders, llama sacrifices may represent animal cruelty, but to many Bolivians, it's an essential ritual to preserve a harmonious relationship with the elements. If you find it impossible to tune out your cultural tendencies, it's probably best to avoid these scenarios.

RELIGION

Roughly 95% of Bolivia's population professes Roman Catholicism and follows it to varying degrees. The absence of Roman

Catholic clergy in rural areas has led to the emergence of a hybrid Christian/folk religion in which the Inca and Aymara belief systems blend with Christianity into an interesting amalgamation of doctrines, rites and superstitions.

The most obvious aspect of native religion is the belief in natural gods and spirits, which dates back to Inca times and earlier. People are aware that the sun and the earth make human life possible, that lunar cycles are linked to human reproduction and that the mountains govern the weather and the availability of water. From these basic precepts emerge an array of beneficent and malevolent figures who regularly expect veneration by their devotees to keep the world on an even keel. Many Christians see no conflict between Christianity and homage to the gods of nature; they believe that God in His far-off Heaven uses the mountains and the elements as His intermediaries.

Perhaps the most ubiquitous of these deities is the earth mother. Pachamama shares herself with human beings, helps bring forth crops and distributes riches to those she favours. She seems to have quite an appetite for coca, alcohol and the blood of animals, particularly llamas. If the earth must be disturbed – for ploughing, construction or mining – an apology is offered in the form of a sacrifice. The bigger the wound, the greater the sacrifice expected; in the case of a mine or a building foundation, Pachamama expects a llama dressed in a silk jacket and adorned with gold, silver and valuable trinkets. Alcohol is considered an integral part of the procedure, and even the llama gets to imbibe heavily before it's given the chop.

Fortunately, Pachamama does have mercy on poorer campesinos, who can't spare a llama whenever they need a new adobe dwelling. The next best thing is a *mesa con sullo*, an aborted llama foetus that is smeared with fat, dressed in a jacket (preferably silk) and laid on white wool with a variety of tokens, including *confites* (ritual sweets), nuts, herbs, coca and bits of jewellery. When the sacrifice is ready, it's wrapped up and buried beneath the foundations of the building.

Talismans are also used in daily life to bring out the better elements of life, or to protect a person from evil. A turtle is thought to bring health, a frog carries good fortune, an owl signifies wisdom and success in school and a condor talisman will ensure a good journey. For general good luck, the answer is an image of Pachamama.

Another fundamental belief among the Aymara is in mountain gods, the *apus* and *achachilas*. The apus, mountain spirits who provide protection for travellers, are often associated with a particular *nevado* (snow-capped peak). Achachilas are the spirits of the high mountains, who are believed to be ancestors of the people and look after their *ayllu* (native group of people, loosely translates as 'tribe') and provide bounty from the earth. In La Paz, they're thought to be incarnated in the dogs that await handouts along the Yungas road! It is these spirits that are propitiated in order to ensure sufficient water for a bountiful harvest, or to permit a safe journey through their ranks.

There are also other characters worth mentioning. Ekeko, which means 'dwarf' in Aymara, is the usually pleasant little household god of abundance, and because he's responsible for matchmaking, finding homes for the homeless and ensuring success for business people, he's a good friend to have. He's also a symbol of the abundance a family has to share with its community. The Alasitas festival in La Paz is dedicated to Ekeko.

There are also negative forces. The evil and dreaded *Happiñuñoz*, for example, are personifications of beautiful women who seduce men, cause them to lose their powers of reason and eventually abscond with their souls. The inevitable result is death for their poor victims. Another unsavoury lot are the *liquichiri*, harmful spirits who suck out a person's vitality, causing death for no visible reason.

If a person has a problem with a particular god, a *yatiri* (witch doctor) will often be able to help. To find out what dangers lie ahead in life, a visit to a *thaliri* (fortune-teller) is in order. This will tell the yatiri what should be prevented from happening and which god can be encouraged (or bribed) to prevent it. There is, however, a particularly insidious night phantom called Kharisiri who preys on sleeping humans, and once a person is on his bad side, not even the best yatiri will be able to help.

In the mines of Oruro and Potosí, a number of beliefs and superstitions have developed and persisted over the years. Luck, the miners assume, is procured by avoidance of certain 'unlucky' practices, and by propitiation of El Tío, the sovereign ruler of hell and owner of the minerals, and he must be constantly appeased with gifts of alcohol, cigarettes, coca, incense and sweets. Miners' wives may not enter certain mines lest El Tío become jealous, and while underground, miners may not whistle, eat toasted *haba* beans, or season llama meat with salt. Breaking any of these taboos will bring down the wrath of El Tío and thereby invite bad luck and low mineral yield.

LANGUAGE

The official language of Bolivia is Latin American Spanish, but only 60 to 70% of the people speak it, and then often only as a second language. The remainder speak Quechua, the language of the Inca, or Aymara, the pre-Inca language of the Altiplano. A host of other minor indigenous tongues are used in limited areas throughout the country.

Most travellers in South America either arrive with at least a basic knowledge of Spanish or very quickly acquire a workable vocabulary of 300 to 500 words. English in Bolivia won't get you very far, but fortunately it's not difficult to learn the basics of Spanish. With a short course or self-teaching programme, you may not be able to carry on a philosophical or political discussion, but you will be able to communicate, and will gain a basis on which to improve your Spanish language skills.

For those who haven't studied Spanish, the following is a brief rundown of basic grammar and pronunciation, and common words and phrases. For a more comprehensive reference, track down Lonely Planet's *Latin American Spanish phrasebook*.

Pronunciation

Vowel pronunciation in Bolivian Spanish is easy and consistent:

a	similar to 'f**a**ther'
e	similar 'gr**e**y'
i	similar to 'mar**i**ne'
o	similar to '**o**ld'
u	similar to 'p**oo**l'
y	same as **i** above

Spanish consonants are more or less the same as their English counterparts, but with a few variations:

c	soft (as 's') before *i* or *e* ; hard (as 'k') before *a, u* or *o*
d	a cross between English 'd' and 'th'
g	soft before *i* or *e* (ie like German 'ch', something like an English 'h' but with more friction)
gu	is used when a hard 'g' or 'c' sound (that is, like the 'g' and 'c' in 'get' and 'cake', respectively) is followed by *e* or *i* (which, without the following **u**, would normally render a soft 'g' or 'c' sound). The **u** is silent unless a **gu** appears in front of an *a* or *o*, or the **u** is altered with an umlaut; in such cases, **gu** is pronounced more or less like an English 'w'.
h	never pronounced
j	pronounced as English 'h', only with more friction
ll	often pronounced as 'll y' in 'wi**ll y**ou'; in Bolivia, it often sounds more like the simple English 'y'
ñ	the equivalent of the 'ny' in 'ca**ny**on'
qu	is the same as **gu**
rr	a rolled or trilled 'r'
r	a slap of the tongue against the palate; sounds like a very quickly spoken 'd' in 'ladder'. At the beginning of a word, some Bolivians pronounce it as 'zh'
v	a cross between English 'v' and 'b'
x	as in 'ta**x**i'
z	pronounced as 's'

Stress

For words ending in a vowel or the letters 'n' or 's', stress is placed on the next to last syllable. For words ending in a consonant other than 'n' or 's', the stress is placed on the final syllable. Any deviation from these rules is indicated by an acute accent placed over the stressed vowel. For example: *camión* (truck), *sótano* (basement), or *almacén* (shop). Accents are often omitted from single-syllable words which would technically require one, such as *más* (more), *trés* (three) or *grán* (great). The word *él* only takes an accent when it's used as 'he' or 'him', and *qué* takes one when it's used as 'what?'. Accents may also be used to break up the vowel sounds in a diphthong (vowel combination), as in *increíble* (incredible) or *artesanía* (arts and crafts).

Note

Nouns ending in *a* are generally feminine and the corresponding definite articles are *la* (singular) and *las* (plural). Those ending in *o* are usually masculine and require the definite articles *el* (singular) and *los* (plural).

There are, however, hundreds of exceptions that can only be memorised or deduced by the referent of the word. Plurals are formed by adding *s* to words ending in a vowel and *es* to those ending in a consonant.

Articles, adjectives and demonstrative pronouns must agree with the noun in both gender and number.

Basics

Yes.	*Sí.*
No.	*No.*
Please.	*Por favor.*
Thank you.	*Gracias.*
It's a pleasure.	*Con mucho gusto.*
Sorry.	*Disculpa* (familiar)
	Disculpe (formal)
What time is it?	*¿Que hora tiene?*
When?	*¿Cuando?*
How?	*¿Como?*
What/Pardon?	*¿Como/Perdón?*
Where?	*¿Donde?*

Greetings

Good morning.
Buén día/Buenos días.
Good afternoon/Good evening.
Buenas tardes.
Hello.
Hola.
See you later.
Hasta luego.

Small Talk

What is your name?
¿Cómo se llama usted?
My name is ...
Me llamo ...
How are you?
¿Que tal/Como estás? (familiar)
¿Como está? (formal)
Where do you come from?
¿De donde es usted?
I'm from ...
Soy de ...
Where are you staying?
¿Donde estás alojado? (familiar)
What is your profession/work?
¿Cuál es su profesión/trabajo?

son/daughter	*hijo/a*
husband/wife	*marido/esposa*
Indian/subsistence farmer	*campesina/o*
(if in the city)	*hola/o* (never *indio*)
mother/father	*madre/padre*

Language Difficulties

Do you speak Spanish?
¿Habla usted castellano?
Do you speak English?
¿Habla inglés?
Do you understand?
¿Me entiende?
I (don't) understand.
(No) entiendo.
Please write that down.
Por favor escríbalo.

Getting Around

I want to go to ...
Quiero ir a ...

Where is ...?
¿Dónde está ...?
What time does the next plane/
bus/train leave for ...?
*¿A que hora sale el próximo
avión/bús/trén para ...?*
Where from?
¿De donde?
Where can I buy a ticket?
¿Dónde puedo comprar un boleto?
I'd like a (one-way/return) ticket.
*Quisiera un boleto (sencillo/di ida
y vuelta).*

bus	*bus*
bus terminal	*terminal terrestre*
train	*tren*
railway station	*estación de ferrocarril*
plane	*vuelo*
truck	*camión*
backpack/rucksack	*mochila*
tent	*carpa*
mountain	*montaña/cerro/ nevado*
mountain pass	*paso/pasaje/abra/ portachuelo*

Directions

To the right.	*A la derecha.*
To the left.	*A la izquierda.*
Go straight ahead.	*Siga derecho.*
Around there.	*Por allá.*
Around here.	*Por aquí.*
downhill	*para abajo*
uphill	*para arriba*
here	*aquí*
there	*allí/allá*
north	*norte*
south	*sur*
east	*este/oriente*
west	*oeste/occidente*

Accommodation

Do you have any rooms available?
¿Tiene habitaciones libres?
I'd like a single/double room.
Quieiera un carto sencillo/doble.
How much is it per night/per person?
¿Cuánto cuesta por noche/por persona?

Does it include breakfast?
¿Incluye el desayuno?
Can I see it?
¿Puedo verlo?

hotel	*hotel*
boarding house	*pensión/residencia*
guesthouse	*casa de huépedes*
youth hostel	*albergue juvenil*

Around Town

Where can I change money/
travellers cheques?
*¿Donde se cambia moneda/
cheques de viajeros?*
Where is the toilet?
¿Donde están los servicios?
¿Donde está el baño?
(*servicios* may be identified by the
initials *SS.HH*)
Where is the ...?
¿Donde está el/la ...?
¿Donde se queda el/la ...?
What time does it open/close?
¿A qué hora abren/cierran?

bank	*banco*
block	*cuadra*
church	*templo/catedral/ iglesia*
city	*ciudad*
embassy	*embajada*
exchange house	*casa de cambio*
market	*mercado*
police	*policía*
post office	*correo*
town square	*plaza*
tourist office	*oficina de turismo*

Shopping

I would like (a) ...
Quisiera (un/a) ...
How much is this?
*¿A como/Por cuanto sale esto/Cuanto
cuesta esto/Cuanto vale esto?*
It's too expensive.
Es muy caro.
Do you have anything cheaper?
¿Hay algo más barato?

I'll take it.
Lo llevo.
Buy from me!
¡Comprame!
Don't you have smaller change?
¿No tiene sencillo?

shop	tienda/almacén
more	*más*
less	*menos*
bigger	*más grande*
smaller	*menos grande*

Weather
What's the weather like?
¿Que tiempo hace?
It's hot/cold.
Hace calor/frío.

rain	*lluvia*
snow	*nieve*
wind	*viento*
Spring	*primavera*
Summer	*verano*
Autumn	*otoño*
Winter	*invierno*

Health/Emergencies
Help!
¡Socorro/Auxilio!
Call the police!
¡Llame a al policía!
I've been robbed!
¡Me han robado!
I'm lost.
Estoy perdido/a.
I need a doctor.
Necesito un doctor.
Where's the nearest hospital/chemist?
¿Dónde está el hospital/la farmacia más cercano?
I'm pregnant.
Estoy encinta.

I'm ...	*Soy ...*
diabetic	*diabético/a*
epileptic	*epiléptico/a*
asthmatic	*asmático/a*

Time
What time is it?
¿Que hora es/Que horas son?

It's one o'clock.	*Es la una.*
It's two o'clock.	*Son las dos.*
half past two	*dos y media*
quarter past two	*dos y cuarto*
two twenty-five	*dos con veinticinco minutos*
twenty to two	*veinte para las dos*
in the afternoon	*de la tarde*
in the morning	*de la mañana*
midnight	*medianoche*
noon	*mediodía*
at night	*de la noche*
today	*hoy*
tomorrow	*mañana*
yesterday	*ayer*
day before yesterday	*anteayer*
day after tomorrow	*pasado mañana*

Days of the Week
Sunday	*domingo*
Monday	*lunes*
Tuesday	*martes*
Wednesday	*miércoles*
Thursday	*jueves*
Friday	*viernes*
Saturday	*sábado*

Numbers
1	*uno*
2	*dos*
3	*tres*
4	*cuatro*
5	*cinco*
6	*seis*
7	*siete*
8	*ocho*
9	*nueve*
10	*diéz*
11	*once*
12	*doce*
13	*trece*
14	*catorce*
15	*quince*
16	*dieciseis*
17	*diecisiete*
18	*dieciocho*

19	*diecinueve*
20	*veinte*
21	*veintiuno*
30	*treinta*
40	*cuarenta*
50	*cincuenta*
60	*sesenta*
70	*setenta*
80	*ochenta*
90	*noventa*
100	*cién (to)*
101	*ciento uno*
200	*doscientos*
201	*doscientos uno*
300	*trescientos*
400	*quatrocientos*
500	*quinientos*
600	*seiscientos*
700	*setecientos*
800	*ochocientos*
900	*novecientos*
1000	*mil*
100,000	*cien mil*
one million	*un millón*

Aymara & Quechua

For your interest, here's a brief list of Quechua and Aymara words and phrases. The grammar and pronunciation of these languages are quite difficult for native English speakers. If you're serious about learning them, or will be spending lots of time in remote areas, you should look around in La Paz or Cochabamba for a good language course.

Dictionaries and phrasebooks are available through Los Amigos del Libro and larger bookstores in La Paz, but a fairly sound knowledge of Spanish will be needed to use them. Lonely Planet's *Quechua phrasebook* is primarily for travellers to Peru but it will also be of use in the Bolivian highlands. It provides useful phrases and vocabulary in the Cuzco dialect.

Pronunciation of the following words and phrases is similar to the way they would be pronounced in Spanish. An apostrophe is a glottal stop (the 'sound' in the middle of 'Oh-oh!').

Aymara & Quechua: Some Useful Words & Phrases

English	Aymara	Quechua
cheap	*pisitaqui*	*pisillapa'g*
distant	*haya*	*caru*
downhill	*aynacha*	*uray*
father	*auqui*	*tata*
food	*manka*	*mikíuy*
friend	*kgochu*	*kgochu*
grandfather	*achachila*	*awicho-machu*
grandmother	*hacha-mama*	*paya*
Hello.	*laphi!*	*Raphi!*
I	*Haya*	*Ñoka*
lodging	*korpa*	*pascana*
mother	*taica*	*mama*
near	*maka*	*kailla*
no	*janiwa*	*mana*
river	*jawira*	*mayu*
ruins	*champir*	*champir*
thirst	*phara*	*chchaqui*
to work	*irnakaña*	*lank'ana*

trail	*tapu*	*chakiñan*
very near	*hakítaqui*	*kaillitalla*
water	*uma*	*yacu*
When?	*Cunapacha?*	*Haiká'g?*
Yes.	*Jisa.*	*Ari.*
you	*huma*	*khan*
Where is ...?	*Kaukasa ...?*	*Maypi ...?*
to the left	*chchekaru*	*lokeman*
to the right	*cupiru*	*pañaman*
How do you say ...?	*Cun sañasa uca'ha ...?*	*Imainata nincha chaita ...?*
It is called ...	*Ucan sutipa'h ...*	*Chaipa'g sutin'ha ...*
Please repeat.	*Uastata sita.*	*Ua'manta niway.*
It's a pleasure.	*Take chuima'hampi.*	*Tucuy sokoywan.*
What does that mean?	*Cuna sañasa muniucha'ha?*	*Imata'nita munanchai'ja?*
I don't know.	*Janiwa yatkti.*	*Mana yachanichu.*
I'm hungry.	*Mankatawa hiu'ta.*	*Yarkaimanta wañusianiña.*
How much?	*K'gauka?*	*Maik'ata'g?*

Numbers	Aymara	Quechua
1	*maya*	*u'*
2	*paya*	*iskai*
3	*quimsa*	*quinsa*
4	*pusi*	*tahua*
5	*pesca*	*phiska*
6	*zo'hta*	*so'gta*
7	*pakalko*	*khanchis*
8	*quimsakalko*	*pusa'g*
9	*yatunca*	*iskon*
10	*tunca*	*chunca*
100	*pataca*	*pacha'g*
1000	*waranka*	*huaranca*
one million	*mapacha'*	*hunu*

Facts for the Visitor

PLANNING

When to Go

Bolivia lies within the southern hemisphere, so winter lasts from May to October and summer from November to April. The most important climatic factor to remember is that the weather is generally wet in the summer and dry in the winter.

On the Altiplano, winters can be icy but days are normally crystal clear and dry. Summers are warmer, but there's usually at least some rainfall every day, most often in the afternoon.

In the highland valleys you can expect a comfortable climate in either summer or winter.

For travel in the humid lowlands winter is generally the best season. The summer wet season can be utterly miserable with mud, steamy heat, bugs and relentless tropical downpours. Travel is particularly difficult at this time of year, since transport services are often delayed or shut down altogether by mud or flooding. On the other hand, these conditions will necessitate an increase in river transport, so it can be the best time of year to look for cargo boats in northern Bolivia.

It's also worth considering that the high tourist season in Bolivia falls in the winter, mainly from late June to early September. This is only partially due to climatic factors: not only is this the time of European and North American summer holidays, but it is also the season with most of Bolivia's major fiestas. This means that lots of Bolivians and other South Americans – as well as overseas travellers – will be visiting during this period. This can be an advantage if you're looking for people to form a tour group to the Far South-west or the Cordillera Apolobamba, but bear in mind that average prices for food, accommodation, transport and *artesanìa* (handicrafts) will be somewhat higher at this time than during the rest of the year.

Maps

Internationally Distributed Maps
For general mapping of South America with excellent topographical detail, it's hard to beat the sectional maps published by International Travel Map Productions, PO Box 2290, Vancouver, BC V6B 3W5, Canada. Coverage of Bolivia is provided in *South America – South* (1987); *South America – North East* (1989); *South America – North West* (1987); and *Amazon Basin* (1991). Climbing maps of Illimani and Illampu at a scale of 1:50,000 are published in Germany by the Deutscher Alpenverein and are distributed internationally.

A recent addition to Bolivian mapping is the superb new *Cordillera Real* map, published by the Defense Mapping Agency in La Paz. This is a good resource for climbers and trekkers, and anyone wanting to get their bearings in the Cordillera Real, from Ancohuma to Illimani. It's distributed in the USA, UK and Bolivia. You can also order direct from Liam O'Brien, 28 Turner Terrace, Newtonville, MA 02160, USA. It costs US$10 plus postage and packing.

In the USA, *Maplink* (☎ (1 805) 965 4402), 25 E Mason St, Dept G, Santa Barbara, CA 93101, is an excellent and exhaustive source for maps of Bolivia and just about anywhere else in the world. A similarly extensive selection of maps is available in the UK from *Stanfords* (☎ (0171) 836 1321), 12-14 Long Acre, London WC2E 9LP.

In Bolivia Maps are available in La Paz, Cochabamba and Santa Cruz through Los Amigos del Libro. Government mapping topo sheets and speciality maps are available from the Instituto Geográfico Militar (IGM), whose head office is on Avenida Bautista Saavedra in Miraflores, La Paz. It's open weekdays from 9 to 11 am and 2.30 to 4.30 pm. The office is in a military compound, so you have to leave your passport at the entrance. At the small central La Paz outlet at Oficina 5, Calle Juan XXIII 100, which is a dead end off Calle Rodríguez between Calles Linares and Murillo, you select and pay for maps, and they're ready for collection the following day.

Both offices sell good topographic sheets at a scale of 1:50,000 and 1:250,000, covering some 70% of the country for US$7.50 each. Unfortunately, they frequently run out of the more popular sheets, such as Cordillera Real treks and peaks, Lake Titicaca etc. If the sheet you want is sold out, they'll provide photocopies for US$5.20, but these are typically poor quality and aren't recommended unless you're desperate. Notable areas that are unavailable (for security reasons) include the Tipuani Valley, the Cordillera Apolobamba and Parque Nacional Noel Kempff Mercado.

IGM also publishes a very good 1994 map of the entire country at a scale of 1:1 million. It comes in four sheets and shows communities, political divisions, transport routes and named physical features. This is the best national map, but it still has serious problems, roads that appear to run in circles and the omission of some major roads. From IGM, it costs US$18.60, but it's sometimes available from bookshops or street sellers for considerably less.

Earlier versions of the same maps are also sometimes sold in bookshops. They're easily recognisable because they're attributed to the president who was in power when the map was commissioned. Check the publication date as there are still a lot of 1937 and 1952 maps floating around!

Bolivian geological maps are sold at Geobol, at the corner of Ortiz and Federico Suazo in La Paz; take your passport. For US$5, you can buy a four-sheet geologic map of the entire country.

For detailed trekking maps around the Cordillera Real and Sajama, look for the colourful contour maps produced by Walter Guzmán Cordova, which are sold for US$5 to US$8.25 at the Librería Don Bosco and the Librería del Turista, both in La Paz. Titles include the *Choro/Taquesi/Yunga Cruz*,

Mururata/Illimani, Huayna Potosí/Conoriri and *Sajama*. However, they are based on the IGM maps and contain many of the same errors. Climbing maps of major Bolivian peaks are available from Club Andino Boliviano (☎ 324682) at Calle México 1638, Casilla 1346, La Paz.

A widely available road map entitled *Red de Caminos* (Highway Network) seems to be the result of an optimistic highway commissioner's game of connect the dots. It's still the best road map around, but make sure you get the most recent edition, which was issued in the early 1990s.

For more information about hiking and trekking maps, see Maps in the Activities section later in this chapter.

What to Bring

When preparing for a trip, your packing list will depend on your intended budget, itinerary, mode of travel, time of visit and length of stay. While travelling as light as possible is always a good idea if you want to enjoy the trip, if you can't splash out, you'll have to bring certain items from home.

Bags The type of luggage you should carry will depend largely upon your style of travel. If you prefer prearranged tours and finer hotels, and consistently use taxis around town, then traditional but strong suitcases or shoulder bags will work fine.

For independent travellers, a backpack – or a pack that zips into a suitcase – is probably the most practical and useful carry-all. The most important factors to consider are comfort, strength, weight and manageability.

Essentials As always, the most important advice is to travel light: only take along that which is indispensable. Unfortunately, everyone has a different idea about what indispensable means and when it comes to travelling light, I'm not the best authority. On my most recent trip, with what I considered only the bare essentials, my pack weighed in at 25 kg! I wasn't sure how it got that way, but at times, I wouldn't have complained had it been stolen. To help you avoid disdain for your belongings, the following checklist outlines items that either are difficult to obtain in Bolivia or will probably be used often enough to justify their weight.

- First-aid kit (refer to the Health section for specifics)
- Antimalarial tablets (for the lowlands)
- Travel alarm clock
- Small torch and extra batteries
- Water bottle – aluminium or plastic
- Water purification tablets – iodine-based to kill amoebas
- Swiss Army-type pocketknife with bottle opener, corkscrew, scissors etc
- Spare glasses or contact lenses and a copy of your optical prescription
- Towel
- Flip-flops (thongs) – for relaxing or dealing with dodgy Bolivian plumbing
- Clothesline – two or three metres of cord is useful for all sorts of things
- Sewing kit
- Writing implements – few South American biros function well on airmail paper
- Spanish/English dictionary and possibly Lonely Planet's Quechua and Latin American Spanish phrasebooks
- Contraceptives
- Tampons – sanitary napkins are inexpensive, but tampons are still considered quite a luxury item
- Any prescription medications you normally take

Amazon Basin Essentials For jungle trips in the northern lowlands, the following items should be included in your checklist: two sets of clothing, one for slogging through the forests, rivers and mud and an extra set to keep dry and wear in camp; extra shoes, also to keep dry; plastic bags for wet gear, shoes and other items that should never get wet; binoculars; camera and zoom or telephoto lens; gaiters; strong torch for night walks and animal spotting; *effective* insect repellent; sleeping bag; swimming costume (bathing suit); long-sleeved shirt for cool and/or bug-infested evenings; sunscreen; hat; and a large plastic bag for rubbish.

Clothing Without going overboard and carrying your entire wardrobe along, you will need to be reasonably prepared for the extremes of Bolivia's climate. The minimum recommended for the cold is a warm jacket

suitable for freezing temperatures, several pairs of warm wool or polypropylene socks, a pullover, a pair of woollen gloves and a hat with ear coverings (the last three items are inexpensive and readily available in Bolivia). If you have the slightest tendency toward chills, thermal underwear won't go amiss on winter nights and a set of Gore-Tex rain gear will come in handy if you're visiting during the wet season or hiking in the mountains.

For travel in the lowlands, two sleeveless shirts, a pair of flip-flops or sandals and shorts will be about all you'll need. On the Altiplano and in the Andes, there is still a prejudice against women wearing shorts, so bring a light skirt or dress (see the Women Travellers section later in this chapter). Men will encounter no cultural restrictions regarding dress.

You'll also need two pairs of trousers – one to wash and one to wear; a long-sleeved, lightweight shirt to wear under itchy woollen or alpaca sweaters; underwear and socks; swimming gear – there are lots of waterfalls and hot springs; one pair of sneakers or comfortable walking shoes; and perhaps even a nicer set of clothing for evenings out or other occasions.

If you don't want to carry a pack full of clothing in preparation for all the variables in climate, it's not difficult to find fairly inexpensive clothing in major Bolivian cities. The average Bolivian is smaller than the average foreigner, however, and anyone needing extreme sizes may have difficulties. Even in tourist shops, larger shoe and clothing sizes, as well as children's pullovers and gloves, are hard to come by.

Outdoor Gear For information on gear for hiking, trekking and mountaineering, see the Activities section later in this chapter.

SUGGESTED ITINERARIES

Naturally, I recommend that you allow as much time as possible for a trip to Bolivia. Even after a couple of years travelling around the country, I've only scratched the surface of what there is to see and do. If you're travelling independently and your time is limited, the following suggestions might help you spend your time rewardingly.

One week
> Spend three or four days exploring La Paz and perhaps take a day trip to Tiahuanaco and an overnight excursion to Copacabana.

Two weeks
> Add two days trekking on Isla del Sol and an excursion to Coroico in the Yungas; or a hike on the Taquesi, La Cumbre to Coroico (Choro) or Yunga Cruz routes.

Three weeks
> To the above, add any of the following: three days hiking around Sorata plus a couple of days hiking in the Zona Sur; a jungle or pampas excursion around Rurrenabaque; or visits to Potosí and Sucre.

One month
> All of the above, plus an excursion from Uyuni through the Far South-west. Alternatively, you can add Santa Cruz, Samaipata and the Jesuit Missions Circuit; Tupiza and Tarija; or a trek in the Cordillera Apolobamba.

Two months
> All options listed under one month plus one of the following: Parque Nacional Noel Kempff Mercado; Parque Nacional Amboró; a river trip on the Mamoré from Trinidad to Guayaramerín; or a trek in the Cordillera de los Frailes, near Sucre.

HIGHLIGHTS
If you have only limited time in Bolivia and can't do the sort of exploration the country so amply rewards, you'll need to simply seek out highlights. Although taste is subjective, there are some sites and experiences that will appeal to most visitors.

Arts
Few visitors to Bolivia would argue that artesanía and music are exceptional. Bolivia has no bad music except, perhaps, that of unpractised brass bands and traditional music that has been adapted for lifts and dentists' offices! You'll be able to catch *peñas* (folk music shows) all over the country; an exceptionally good one is at Don Lucho in Potosí.

You'll find a range of musical instruments, lovely woollen clothing and colourfully decorated bags at tourist shops

around the country, but the best and least expensive are bought either directly from the artesan or around Calle Sagárnaga in La Paz. To see the origins of Bolivia's world-famous weavings, visit the smaller villages around Sucre or north of Lake Titicaca.

Landscape
The Bolivian landscape is awesome, offering everything from snow-capped peaks to colourful canyons and steaming rainforest. Particularly inspiring – and accessible – areas include the *salares* (salt pans), volcanos and colourful lakes of the south-west, and the jungle and savanna lowlands around Rurrenabaque. If you're looking for a magical Amazon Basin experience, you can also look for a cargo boat along one of the northern rivers.

For some excellent hiking, set off into the Cordillera Real, where you can follow ancient Inca roads into the dramatic Yungas region. The more remote Cordillera Quimsa Cruz and Cordillera de los Frailes offer equally attractive alternatives. The area around Tupiza strongly resembles the North American Southwest, and not surprisingly, it was here that Butch Cassidy and the Sundance Kid concentrated their Bolivian activities – and met their untimely demise. The area presents a number of great day hikes and longer expeditions.

When you feel like holing up in a small, picturesque village and relaxing for a few days – as many Bolivians like to do – some prime choices include Coroico or Sorata in the Yungas, Copacabana on the shores of Lake Titicaca, Samaipata west of Santa Cruz, and Rurrenabaque or San Ignacio de Moxos in the northern lowlands.

Food
Bolivian cuisine isn't world renowned, but some dishes and drinks are worth trying. Some, such as trout from Lake Titicaca; *jugos* and *licuados* (fresh fruit juices and fruit shakes from market stalls; *salteñas* (Bolivia's favourite mid-morning snack); *sopa de quinoa* (quinoa soup); and *surubí* (an Amazonian catfish), are delicious. Sampling

others – *charque kan* llama meat jerky with hominy); *yuca* (cassava); *masaco* (beef jerky with plantain) and the various types of *chicha* – will at least satisfy curiosity, and you might even like them! For more information, see the Food section later in this chapter.

Buildings & Sites

For church fans, the Jesuit Mission Circuit in the Eastern Lowlands will provide plenty of inspiration. Of particular interest are San Miguel, San Rafael, and San José de Chiquitos. The Moorish-style cathedral in Copacabana and the Mestizo-influenced churches of San Francisco in La Paz and San Lorenzo in Potosí are all beautiful and inspiring. Other forms of colonial architecture are most in evidence around Sucre and Potosí, although La Paz does have a few colonial-era buildings.

There are also highly worthwhile historical and archaeological sites; among them are the ancient ruins of Tiahuanaco near La Paz; the ruins on Isla del Sol in Lake Titicaca; the pre-Inca hill-top ritual site of El Fuerte near Samaipata; and remote Iskanwaya northwest of La Paz. A visit to the Potosí mines will provide you with an eye-opening perspective on the hardships miners faced nearly a millennium ago in Europe – and still endure in highland Bolivia.

Fiestas

Some of the best and most interesting annual fiestas include La Diablada, which takes place in Oruro during Holy Week; Phujllay, a commemoration of *campesino* resistance in Tarabuco; La Festividad de Nuestro Señor Jesús del Gran Poder, which takes place in La Paz in late May or early June; Alasitas, which is dedicated to Ekeko, the household god of abundance, in La Paz in late January; the Fiesta de San Roque, which is a week-long celebration in mid-August; the Fiesta del Santo Patrono de Moxos, a colourful Moxos Indian celebration in San Ignacio de Moxos, in the Beni; the Virgen de Candelaria, both a solemn and riotous bash in Copacabana in early February; Chu'tillos, an international dance and music festival held in Potosí in late August; and the Virgen de Urcupiña, the biggest festival in Cochabamba department, which occurs in Quillacollo around mid-August.

TOURIST OFFICES

Although Bolivia's appeal should not be underestimated, much of its attraction lies in the fact that it has been largely ignored by large-scale tourism. While this does seem to be changing, the Bolivian tourist industry is still in its formative stages, and the government hasn't committed lots of resources to developing and touting the country's attractions.

The cities of La Paz, Oruro, Cochabamba, Sucre, Tarija, Potosí and Santa Cruz all have offices of SENATUR, the Secretaria Nacional de Turismo (but it's predecessors' names still appear on some publications). These offices range in quality from helpful to worthless, but most will at least provide street plans of their respective city and can answer simple questions about local transport and attractions. The SENATUR offices in La Paz, Uyuni and Tarija are especially worth visiting.

In this book, tourist office locations are marked on city maps where applicable. Opening hours are officially 9 am to noon and 2 to 6 pm, but as with many Bolivian government operations, the actual hours of operation is left largely to the whims of employees.

VISAS & DOCUMENTS
Passport

A passport is essential and if yours is within a few months of expiration, get a new one before you leave on a South American circuit. Many countries won't issue a visa or admit you at the border if your passport has less than six months validity remaining. For Bolivia, passports must be valid for one year beyond the date of entering the country. Even if it isn't about to expire, make sure it has a few blank pages for visas and entry and exit stamps. It could be very inconvenient to run out of space when you're too far from an embassy to have extra pages added.

In Bolivia, foreigners must always have proof of identification. Some travellers carry photocopies of their passport (preferably certified) while they amble about town, and leave the passport locked up somewhere safe. Although Bolivia doesn't really have a market for passports, in some countries, a passport is worth several thousand dollars, so keep a close eye on it. Losing your passport is very inconvenient, and getting a replacement takes time and money.

If you'll be staying in Bolivia (or any foreign country) for a longer period of time, it helps to register your passport with your embassy. This will eliminate the need to send faxes to your home country to verify that you really exist. It's also wise to have a copy of your birth certificate or a driving licence, student card, or some such thing with your photo on it – some embassies require photo ID before they'll issue a replacement passport. US citizens should note that replacement passports may be purchased only with US dollars cash.

Personal documents – passports, visas, cédulas (identification cards) etc, or photocopies of these items – must be carried at all times to avoid fines during police checks and lost time at the police station while paperwork is shuffled. This is most strictly enforced in lowland regions. Carrying an expired passport can also be useful as backup ID to give to hotels if they demand your documents as 'security'.

Visas

Currently, citizens of Argentina, Austria, Chile, Colombia, Ecuador, Israel, Paraguay, Switzerland, Uruguay, Scandinavian countries (including Finland and Iceland), the UK, Germany, Ireland, Italy and Spain – do not require visas for stays of up to 90 days. Citizens of Australia, New Zealand, Belgium, France, Luxembourg, the Netherlands, Portugal, the USA and most other non-Communist countries outside the Middle East, South or South-east Asia, North Africa or republics of the former Soviet Union are granted stays of 30 days witho a visa.

Bolivian visa requirements change with astonishing frequency and may at times seem arbitrary. Currently, citizens of South Africa and Brazil require visas, which are issued by Bolivian consular representatives in their home countries or in neighbouring South American countries. Visa rates vary according to the consulate and nationality of the applicant, and cost up to US$50 for a one-year multiple entry visa. To confuse matters further, each consulate – particularly those in border towns – has its own tariff schedule for different nationalities.

In addition to a visa, citizens of many Middle Eastern, Asian and Communist countries (including South Korea, Malaysia, Singapore, Thailand, Jordan and Pakistan) require 'official permission' by cable from the Bolivian Ministry of Foreign Affairs before a visa will be issued. Information is available from Bolivian consulates and embassies.

Officially, everyone requires proof of onward transport and sufficient funds for their intended stay; in practice officials rarely scrutinise these items. Entry or exit stamps are free of charge and attempts at charging should be met with polite refusal.

Minors under 18 must be accompanied by their parents. Those travelling with only one parent may be required to produce a notarised letter from the parent not accompanying them to Bolivia, which grants permission to travel and guarantees financial responsibility. An official-looking statement that the missing parent is deceased should obviate this requirement.

All business travellers must obtain a business visa. To apply, you'll need a passport, letter of intent and a financial guarantee from your employer. Business visas cost US$50 and are valid for visits of up to 90 days.

Visa & Length of Stay Extensions Visas and lengths of stay may be extended with little ado at immigration offices in major cities. If you're from a country for which a visa is not a requirement, ask for a length of stay extension, not a visa extension, otherwise you could have problems when leaving the country. Length of stay extensions are free to most nationalities, but US passport holders must pay US$20 for each month over their original 30 days and EU citizens pay the same for stays of over 90 days. Overstayers are fined US$1.10 per day at immigration in La Paz and US$5 per day at the airport, and even those who do pay up

may face a measure of red tape at the border or airport when leaving the country.

Long-Term Visas Diplomatic, official, student and missionary visas are officially issued free of charge. Permanent residence and work visas are extremely difficult to obtain, so be prepared for a complex stream of paperwork and expenditure. In any case, they're practically impossible to get unless you already have a job lined up.

Getting a Work Visa

If you're offered paid employment, you'll need to obtain a Bolivian work visa, which must be done in La Paz. Here's the rather long and murky procedure:

- You'll need a copy of a three-month employment contract from your prospective employer.

- See a solicitor to obtain a *memorial* requesting a *domiciliario* (proof that you have an address) and *antecedentes* (a copy of your criminal record – or preferably lack of one) from Señor Comandante de la Policía Técnica Judicial. Memoriales signed by a lawyer cost US$5, plus US$0.40 for *papel sellado* (legal paper). You may collect it the following day.

- Take your memoriales to PTJ (pronounced 'peh-teh-hota') in Calle Landaeta, near Plaza del Estudiante, and buy a domiciliario (US$1.40), and antecedentes forms (US$3.20). These are sold at the desk on the ground floor (look for the employee with the suitcase).

- Go to the 4th floor of the PTJ, present the forms and have your fingerprints taken. Fill in the forms and leave your passport. You'll then have to arrange for someone to visit your home and confirm that your domiciliario is legitimate. For this, you'll usually be asked for an unofficial gift – the farther you live from the PTJ, the higher the price. When you exit the PTJ, note the arrow indicating the 'División Contra la Corrupción Pública' (Division Against Public Corruption).

- After one or two days, return to collect your forms and passport.

- Go to the foreigners division on the mezzanine at Immigration ('migración') on Calle Camacho, where you must leave your domiciliario and antecedentes forms, your passport and a copy of your work contract.

- Return the following day to (hopefully) pick up your passport. If it isn't ready, persist until it is.

- Take your passport to the small, nameless and hard-to-find office in Calle Indaburo, above Plaza Murillo (the immigration office will direct you) and pay US$25 for two adhesive stamps to be placed in your passport.

- Return to immigration and pay US$103 for a form and again leave your passport.

- Return the following day to (hopefully) retrieve your passport, which should now contain a large rubber stamp over the two adhesive stamps. It can take up to a week to get this essential stamp and you may be asked to pay unofficial 'fees' of up to U$50.

- Congratulations! You are now the proud owner of a three-month work visa and can happily live and work in Bolivia until it runs out. To remain longer, you must repeat the entire process, which this time also involves securing a one-year employment contract that must be approved by the Ministerio de Trabajo (Ministry of Labour). For this one-year visa, the official charge is US$165. The only alternatives are to marry a Bolivian citizen (which involves an entirely different stream of red tape) or work illegally and risk being deported (or being given free accommodation in San Pedro prison). ■

Photocopies

When it comes to passports, identification and other valuable documents, prepare for the worst. Even if your passport is registered with your embassy, it's wise to keep separate records of your passport number and issue date, and photocopies of the pages with the passport number, name, photograph, place issued and expiration date. Also make copies of visas and your birth certificate.

Photocopy your travellers cheque receipt slips, health and travel insurance policies and addresses, personal contact addresses, credit card numbers and airline tickets and keep all that material separate from your passport and money (better hotels have a safe for valuables). Keep one copy with you, one copy inside your luggage and if applicable, deposit another with a travelling companion. Slip US$100 or so into an unlikely place to use as an emergency stash.

Travel Insurance

In general, all travellers should buy a travel insurance policy, which will provide some sense of security in the case of a medical emergency or the loss or theft of money or belongings. It may seem an expensive luxury, but if you can't afford a travel health insurance policy, you probably can't afford a medical emergency abroad, either. Travel health insurance policies (see the Health section in the Facts for the Visitor chapter) can usually be extended to include baggage, flight departure insurance and a range of other options. It's sensible to buy your policy as early as possible. If you wait until the week of departure, you may find, for example, that you're not covered for delays caused by industrial action.

Some policies are very good value, but to find them, you'll have to do a great deal of shopping around. Long-term or frequent travellers can generally find something for under US$200 per year, but these will normally be from a general business insurance company rather than one specialising in travel. Note, however, that such inexpensive policies may exclude travel to the USA (where health care costs are extremely high)

and may offer very limited baggage protection. Always read the fine print!

If you do need to make a claim on your travel insurance, you must produce proof of the value of any items lost or stolen (purchase receipts are the best, so if you buy a new camera for your trip, for example, hang onto the receipt). In the case of medical claims, you'll need detailed medical reports and receipts for amounts paid. If you're claiming on a trip cancelled by circumstances beyond your control (illness, airline bankruptcy, industrial action etc), you'll have to produce all flight tickets purchased, tour agency receipts and itinerary and proof of whatever glitch caused your trip to be cancelled.

If you book an organised tour, the company will probably encourage you to purchase their own travel insurance policy, which may or may not be a good deal. Bear in mind that some unscrupulous companies – particularly in Europe – manage to keep their tour prices low and appealing by requiring overpriced travel insurance as part of the package.

Driving Licence

Most car hire agencies in Bolivia will accept your home driving licence, but if you intend to do a lot of driving, it's a good idea to get an International Driver's Licence from your local automobile association. Bolivia doesn't require special motorcycle licences, but some other countries do, so if you intend to ride a motorcycle, make sure your international driving licence states that it's valid for motorcycles.

International Health Card

An international health card lists all current vaccines the bearer has taken and will be provided by your doctor at the time of vaccination. It's not required for entry into Bolivia unless you're arriving from an area where yellow fever is endemic – which usually means Sub-Saharan Africa, some parts of Central America, the Caribbean and the Guianas – but it's still a good idea to have one. You'll also need proof of yellow-fever vaccination to enter Brazil overland from Bolivia; this requirement is generally strictly enforced. Technically, you'll also need a yellow-fever vaccination for travel in Santa Cruz department, although visitors are rarely, if ever, asked to produce proof.

EMBASSIES & CONSULATES
Bolivian Embassies Abroad

Here's a partial listing of Bolivian diplomatic representation abroad:

Australia/New Zealand
  Bolivian Consulate, Suite 512, Pennys Building, 210 Queen St, Brisbane, Qld (GPO Box 53, Brisbane, Qld 4001) (☎ (07) 3221 1606; fax (07) 3229 7175)
Canada
  Bolivian Embassy, 17 Metcalfe St, Suite 608, Ottawa, Ontario K1P 426 (☎ (613) 236 5730)
France
  Consulate General of Bolivia, 12 Avenue du Presidente Kennedy, 75016 Paris 16 (☎ 01 42 88 34 32)
Germany
  Embassy of Bolivia, Konstantinstrasse 16, D-5300 Bonn 2 (☎ (0228) 362038)
UK
  Embassy of Bolivia, 106 Eaton Square, SW12W London (☎ (0171) 235 4248)
USA
  Consulate General of Bolivia, 211 E 43rd St, Room 802, New York, NY 10017 (☎ (212) 687 0530)
  Bolivian Embassy, 3014 Massachusetts Ave, NW, Washington, DC 20008 (☎ (202) 483 4410)
  Consulate of Bolivia, 870 Market St, San Francisco, CA

Foreign Embassies in Bolivia

The following countries are among those with diplomatic representation in Bolivia. Opening hours listed are Monday to Friday only; note that holidays and opening hours of foreign embassies vary depending on the country and the sort of services required; it's wise to phone in advance so you don't waste a trip.

Visas for neighbouring countries – Chile, Peru, Brazil, Paraguay, Argentina and other Latin American countries – may be obtained at consulates in most large Bolivian cities and in smaller towns near frontiers. For details, see under individual cities and towns throughout the book.

Argentina
  Avenida 16 de Julio, Edificio Banco de la Nación Argentina, 2nd floor, La Paz (☎ 353089); 8.30 am to 1.30 pm
Brazil
  Avenida 20 de Octubre 2038, Edificio Foncomín, 9th to 11th floors, La Paz (☎ 350769); 9 am to 1 pm
Canada
  Plaza Avaroa, Avenida 20 de Octubre 2475, La Paz (☎ 375224); 9 am to noon
Chile
  Avenida Hernando Siles 5843, Calle 13, Obrajes, La Paz (☎ 785046); 8.30 am to 1 pm and 3 to 6 pm
Colombia
  Plaza Avaroa, Avenida 20 de Octubre 2427, 2nd floor, La Paz (☎ 359658); 9 am to 2 pm
France
  Avenida Hernando Siles 5390, Calle 8, Obrajes, La Paz (☎ 786189); 9 am to noon
Germany
  Avenida Arce 2395, La Paz (☎ 390850); 9 am to noon
Israel
  Avenida Mariscal Santa Cruz, Edificio Esperanza, 10th floor, La Paz (☎ 358676); open by appointment only
Italy
  Avenida 6 de Agosto 2275, La Paz (☎ 323597); 9 am to 2 pm
Japan
  Calle Rosendo Gutiérrez 497, esquina Sánchez Lima, La Paz (☎ 373152); 9 am to noon
Netherlands
  Avenida Arce 2031, Edificio Victoria, 2nd floor, La Paz (☎ 392064); 9 am to 12.30 pm
Paraguay
  Avenida Arce, Edificio Venus, 7th floor, La Paz (☎ 322018); 8 am to 1 pm
Peru
  Avenida 6 de Agosto, Edificio Alianza 110, La Paz (☎ 352031); 9 am to 1 pm
South Africa
  Calle Rosendo Gutiérrez 482, La Paz (☎ 367754); 9 am to noon
Switzerland
  Avenida 16 de Julio, Edificio Petrolero, 6th floor, Office 1, La Paz (☎ 353091); 9 am to noon
UK
  Avenida Arce 2732, La Paz (☎ 357424); 9 am to noon and 1.30 to 4.30 pm
USA
  Avenida Arce 2780, esquina Cordero, La Paz (☎ 430251); 9 am to noon

Venezuela
Avenida Arce 2678, Edificio Illimani, 4th and 5th floors, La Paz (☎ 432023); 9 am to 2 pm

MONEY

Costs

Overall, prices for food, services, hotels and transportation are slightly higher than in Ecuador and Peru, but lower than in Brazil, Argentina and Chile. When converted to US dollars, prices for most items, including lodging, are now actually lower than they were in the late 1980s. Budget travellers can get by on as little as US$10 to US$15 a day, while upmarket visitors won't have to spend more than US$150 a day.

One practice you may run across, especially in cities and tourist areas, is 'gringo pricing', a deliberate overcharging of foreigners. An attitude somewhere between acceptance and paranoia is advised. In restaurants, ask for the Spanish version of the menu (if you can read it) and check the bill carefully; if you suspect a problem, request an itemised bill (*cuenta detallada* or *cuenta elaborada*). Before hailing a taxi or setting off to buy something, try to ask locals for a ballpark idea of what you can expect to pay. To avoid unpleasant scenes, agree on food, accommodation and transport prices before the goods or services are consumed.

Currency

Bolivia's unit of currency is the boliviano, divided into 100 centavos. After catastrophic inflation during the first half of the 1980s, austerity measures were undertaken. 'Every Bolivian is a millionaire', one La Paz resident quoted before six zeros were lopped off the massively inflated peso denomination on 1 January 1987. Today, the boliviano is one of Latin America's most stable currencies, with an annual inflation rate of about 10%.

Bolivianos come in two, five, 10, 20, 50, 100 and 200 denomination notes, two, five, 10, 20 and 50 centavos, and one boliviano coins. Bolivian currency is practically worthless outside Bolivia, so don't change more than you'll need.

Currency Exchange

Exchange rates as of June 1996 were as follows:

USA	US$1	=	B$5.00
UK	UK£1	=	B$7.69
Australia	A$1	=	B$3.95
New Zealand	NZ$1	=	B$3.36
Canada	C$1	=	B$3.65
Germany	DM1	=	B$3.27
France	FFr1	=	B$0.96
Switzerland	SF1	=	B$3.97
Japan	¥100	=	B$4.59
Brazil	BrR$1	=	B$4.90
Argentina	Arg$1	=	B$5.00
Peru	PerSol 1	=	B$2.06
Chile	Chil$100	=	B$1.22

Changing Money

The black market in currency was abolished in late 1985, and because the official exchange rate represents the currency's actual value, there's no need for a parallel market in currency.

As a rule, visitors fare best with US dollars, which is the only foreign currency accepted throughout Bolivia. Currencies of neighbouring countries may be exchanged in border areas and at some La Paz *casas de cambio* (exchange houses) (see the Money section in the La Paz chapter). American Express travellers cheques seem to be the most widely accepted brand, but you shouldn't have problems with other major brands.

The rate for cash varies little from place to place, although rates may be slightly lower in border areas.

The rate for travellers cheques is best in La Paz, where it nearly equals the cash rate; in other large cities it's 3 to 5% lower, and in smaller towns it may be impossible to change travellers cheques at all. Some La Paz casas de cambio change travellers cheques for cash dollars for a 1to 3% commission.

Casas de cambio usually open at about 9 am and close at 6 pm, with a two to three-hour lunch break beginning at noon. Many Bolivian banks now offer currency exchange services, and some even change travellers cheques. La Paz, Cochabamba, Santa Cruz and Sucre all have casas de cambio that change both notes and travellers cheques. In smaller towns, you can't count on being able to change travellers cheques; carry enough cash to get back to a larger city.

You can often change money in travel agencies, jewellery or appliance shops, pharmacies, and any other establishment that carries on international business. Those that do change travellers cheques usually offer 5 to 10% less than for cash. In La Paz and Cochabamba, several merchants and casas de cambio exchange travellers cheques for US dollars cash, but they take 1 to 3% commission.

Notes & Change When exchanging money, ask for the cash in as small denominations as possible, as there is a chronic shortage of change. If the amount due you is small, you may receive your change in boiled sweets or other token items, but just *try* to use a B$10 or larger note to buy a B$2 bottle of soda! *'No tiene sencillo?'* (Don't you have change?) has become a sort of national mantra, and is invariably uttered anytime customers fail to produce exact change for their purchase.

There are several theories to explain the change shortage. The most plausible one suggests that certain vendors hoard change in order to create an artificial shortage – and the opportunity to charge a commission for changing larger denomination currency for smaller.

Another problem concerns mangled notes. Worn out small denomination notes, which tend to disintegrate quickly, aren't accepted back by banks on the grounds that corrupt bank managers pocket them before they can be destroyed, thereby increasing inflation. Unless both halves of torn and repaired notes bear identical serial numbers, the note is worthless. Also, don't accept any B$2 notes; they're worthless too and merchants may try to pawn them off on unknowing foreigners.

Street Moneychangers Street moneychangers operate virtually around the clock in most cities and towns, but usually they only change cash dollars, paying the same or only slightly higher rates as casas de cambio.

Most street moneychangers are legitimate, but there are some sleight-of-hand artists out there, so you must guard against rip-offs. The established method is to first say how much you want to change. They'll then tell you the rate, which should be slightly higher than in casas de cambio (unless it's after hours, in which case the rate will be lower).

If you agree with their rate, it's wise at this stage to tell them you want the cash in as small denominations as possible. They'll count out the money, then hand it to you to be re-counted. When you're satisfied, you should produce your dollar notes and count them out. The changers will then recount the dollars and if they are happy, the transaction is ended.

Credit Cards

Major cards, such as Visa, MasterCard and American Express, are useful for regular purchases and in emergencies. They may be used in larger cities at first-rate hotels, restaurants and tour agencies. Because travellers cheques may be difficult to change in some places, there's a good case for carrying a Visa or MasterCard credit card. Visa, and often MasterCard, cash withdrawals of up to US$300 per day are available with no commission and a minimum of hassle, from branches of the Banco de Santa Cruz, Banco Mercantil and the Banco Nacional de Bolivia in La Paz, Sucre, Cochabamba and Santa Cruz. Banco de La Paz charges 1.75% commission on cash withdrawals.

Alternatively, credit card cash withdrawals are available at ENLACE automatic teller machines, which may be found around La Paz and in all larger cities and towns. Commission is charged at the time of billing by the bank issuing the card. The exchange rate used is the one applicable on the date the transaction is posted.

Have on hand the number to call if you lose your credit card, and be quick to cancel it if it's lost or stolen. To guard against surreptitious duplication of your credit card, don't let it out of your sight. Carbonless credit-card coupons offer some protection against misuse but old style coupons are still in use, so ask for the carbon inserts and destroy them after use. Similarly, destroy any coupons that have been filled out incorrectly.

Tipping & Bargaining
Tipping Except in four and five-star hotels and exclusive restaurants or clubs, tipping is uncommon. Most formal restaurants add a 10% service charge to your bill anyway, so further tipping is unnecessary. As a rule, bus and taxi drivers are not tipped.

Bargaining In Bolivia, as in most of Latin America, few prices are fixed. Almost everything is negotiable, not only for artesanía, but also for food, transport and even lodging. (Note, however, that prices in formal shops or finer restaurants are generally fixed, although upmarket hotels may offer price reductions during slow periods.) On some buses, for example, high competition or low ticket demand may mean that discounts of up to 10% are available for the asking. In the case of accommodation, artesanía and market goods, you'll normally wind up paying about 80% of what is initially quoted.

Bolivians expect to haggle over prices and much of the so-called 'gringo pricing' is inspired by foreigners who pay the first price asked. If you do – whether out of ignorance or guilt feelings about how much cash you have on hand relative to the local economy – you'll not only be considered silly, but you'll be doing fellow travellers a disservice by creating the impression that foreigners will pay any price named. What's more, in well-touristed areas, visitors who voluntarily pay higher than market value actually cause market price increases. They thereby put some items and services out of reach of locals who generally have less disposable

cash. And who can blame the vendors; why sell to a local when foreigners will pay twice as much?

If you don't want to appear ripe for exploitation, play the game as the Bolivians do. Bargaining is normally conducted in a friendly and spirited manner. The vendor's aim is to identify the highest price you're willing to pay. Your aim is to find the price below which the vendor will not sell.

Even if you find precisely the item you're after, avoid becoming visibly attached to it or enthusiastic about it, as this will hinder your ability to bargain. Decide what you want to pay or what others have told you *they've* paid; your first offer should be about half this. At this stage, the vendor may laugh or feign outrage, but the price will quickly drop from the original quote to a more realistic level. When it does, begin making better offers until you arrive at a mutually agreeable price.

A distinctly Bolivian alternative to bargaining over small market items is to ask for *llapa*, a price that's agreeable if the vendor throws in additional goods. If you're haggling over a mound of oranges, for example, saying 'llapa' means that you want them to add an extra orange or two for the price. If you're buying a trinket or minor household item, they may throw in a few boiled sweets or other low-value extra.

Having said all that, no matter how adept your bargaining skills, you probably won't get things as cheaply as the locals can and there may be times when you cannot get a vendor to lower the price to anywhere near what you know the item should cost. This probably means that many tourists have passed through and if you refuse to pay the inflated prices, some other fool will.

There's no reason to lose your temper when bargaining. If the vendor appears to be intransigent or the effort seems a waste of time, politely take your leave. Sometimes vendors will change tack and call you back if they think their stubbornness may be losing a sale. If not, you can always look for another vendor or try again the following day.

POST & COMMUNICATIONS

All major and minor cities have both ENTEL (Empresa Nacional de Telecomunicaciones) and post offices (Correos de Bolivia).

Postal Rates

Airmail postcards *(postales)* or letters weighing up to 20g cost US$0.08 (B$0.70) locally, US$0.20 (B$1) to elsewhere in Bolivia and US$0.38 (B$1.90) to the rest of Latin America. To North America, they're US$0.60 (B$3), to Europe, they cost US$0.75 (B$3.50) and to anywhere else in the world, they are US$0.85 (B$4.10. Letters between 20 and 40g to North America cost US$1.75 (B$8.50) and to Europe they're US$2.40 (B$11.50), meaning that anything up to 40g will be cheaper if it's sent in two envelopes!

A one-kg airmail parcel costs US$12.75 (B$61.80) to North America, US$16 (B$77.50) to Europe and US$20.50 (B$98.70) elsewhere. Certification is recommended and costs an additional US$0.20. Express mail service to all overseas destinations costs US$20 for the first 500g and US$4 for each additional kg.

For US$0.20 extra, any piece of mail may be certified. Special precautions are taken to ensure these items aren't lost or pilfered and locals reckon it's worth it. Within Bolivia, Express Mail (Expreso) is available for an extra US$0.20.

Sending Mail

From major towns, the post is generally reliable, but when posting anything important, it's still wise to send it by certified post. The only posting boxes are inside post offices.

It's best not to mail anything from small town post offices; sacks of mail have been known to lie around for months awaiting vehicles to carry them to larger postal centres.

Parcels *Encomiendas* (parcels) to be sent overseas must weigh under two kg and are a bit more tricky to send. Firstly, the unwrapped parcel must be taken to the *aduana* (customs office) for inspection.

You'll have to wrap and seal the parcel in the presence of a customs official, so carry along a box, paper, tape, string and the address. Once the parcel is ready, the customs official stamps it and it's ready for the post office.

Some post offices have an in-house customs agent, but in some cities, such as Oruro, the customs office is across town. The most straightforward procedures exist at the new main post office in La Paz, where onsite inspectors check the parcel, oversee the wrapping and point you toward the proper window for posting. It couldn't be easier.

Although Bolivia's postal system is relatively reliable, don't post anything you can't risk losing. The chances of any posted parcel's arrival at its destination are inversely proportional to its value and to the number of 'inspections' to which it is subjected.

La Paz courier services, including UPS and DHL, ship parcels under one kg to Europe or North America for about US$30.

Receiving Mail

Poste restante (occasionally called *lista de correos*) is available in larger cities and towns. Letters sent to poste restante should include the name of the addressee followed by 'Poste Restante, Correo Central', then the city and country. Poste Restante letters are delivered to the city's main post office and are held for 90 days, more or less, before being returned to the sender. Recipients must present a passport when collecting post.

Names in Bolivia, as in all Spanish-speaking countries, are constructed of any number of given and acquired names followed by the father's family name and the mother's maiden name. The *apellido*, or surname, is therefore not the 'last' name used. This can lead to confusion in receiving mail filed or listed alphabetically. For instance, a letter to the president of Bolivia, Gonzalo Sánchez de Lozada, would be filed under 'S' for 'Sánchez'. Although most postal clerks are aware of the Western convention of placing the surname last, a letter addressed to Mary Ann Smith may still end up in the 'A' pigeonhole. Given the way things tend to work, however, Mary would be wise to check under 'M', as well. Although capitalising and underlining the surname won't always alleviate the confusion, it may help.

Post may also be received through American Express representatives. You must show your passport and proof that you're an American Express customer – a few travellers cheques or an American Express card will suffice. In La Paz, the representative is Magri Turismo Limitada (☎ 341201) at Avenida 16 de Julio 149, 5th floor, Edificio Avenida.

If you're having anything shipped to Bolivia, it's helpful to declare the lowest possible value at the point of origin. Otherwise, you'll find yourself in a quagmire of red tape and owing an import duty of up to 100% of the item's declared value.

Addresses
In this guidebook, the mailing address is often included with the street address. A post office box is called a *casilla*.

Telephone
Local Calls Local telephone calls can be made from ENTEL offices and only cost a few centavos. Trunk calls to locations within Bolivia are also inexpensive; when using trunk dialling codes, include the leading zero. The number for the operator is 101 and directory assistance is 118.

In La Paz and in some remote villages, you'll find pay telephone boxes. Alternatively, small street kiosks are often equipped with telephones that may be used for brief local calls. These cost between US$0.20 and US$0.30. ENTEL now produces telephone cards in denominations of B$10, B$20 and B$50, but as yet, card phones are available only at ENTEL offices and airports. For most public phones, you must use *fichas* (tokens), which are available at ENTEL or from vendors on the streets (this provides employment for many disabled Bolivians). Note that fichas from one city may not fit phones in another city.

In this guide, Bolivian telephone numbers are given as local numbers only. To call these numbers from elsewhere in the country, precede the local number with the relevant telephone code, provided in the introductory information for that town or city. Drop the zero when you're phoning from outside Bolivia. Where the phone number given is in another town or city (eg some rural hotels have La Paz reservation numbers), the name of the town or city is provided.

International Calls Bolivia's country code is 591. The international direct dialling access code is 00. For reverse charge calls from a private line, dial the International Operator (☎ 356700, La Paz) and explain that the call is *por cobrar*. Note, however, that ENTEL offices do not accept reverse charge calls and rates from private phones can be excessive; I made a 40-second reverse charge call from Bolivia to the UK (via the British Telecom operator) and was billed nearly US$20.

At ENTEL offices, a three-minute call to North America costs about US$8 station-to-station and US$10 person-to-person. To Europe and elsewhere, you'll pay at least 30% more.

Fax
ENTEL offices in most major Bolivian cities have a fax desk, and although the service still has some rough edges, it works surprisingly well. Oddly enough, Entelitos (small urban ENTEL offices) appear to offer more efficient fax services than main offices. Fax charges to Europe, Central America and the Caribbean are US$5 per minute; to the USA and Canada, US$4 per minute; and to Asia, Africa and Australasia, US$6 per minute.

Faxes may be received at public fax numbers in most cities. If the document includes the name, address and telephone number of the recipient's hotel, ENTEL will deliver the fax. Where applicable, public fax numbers are listed under Post & Communications for the respective city.

BOOKS
Most books are published in different editions by different publishers in different countries. As a result, a book might be a hardcover rarity in one country while it's

readily available in paperback in another. Fortunately, bookshops and libraries search by title or author, so your local bookshop or library is best placed to advise you on the availability of the recommendations in this book.

English, German and French language publications are available from Los Amigos del Libro, with outlets in La Paz, Cochabamba and Santa Cruz. They're quite pricey (due mostly to a weighty import duty), but they do offer a good selection of popular paperbacks, Latin American literature, magazines, dictionaries and histories, as well as glossy coffee-table books dealing with the anthropology, archaeology and scenery of Bolivia. The Librería del Turista on Plaza San Francisco in La Paz sells a limited range of books and maps on Bolivia and its history.

Some *librería* (bookshops) have a shelf or a box of used English-language paperbacks stashed away in a corner. It's worth asking.

Lonely Planet

The regularly updated *South America on a shoestring* (Lonely Planet, 1996) is a thoroughly researched general guide for travellers of all budgets in South America. It contains lots of maps and information in a well-organised format. If you're travelling overland, see also Lonely Planet's *Mexico – a travel survival kit* and *Central America on a shoestring*.

If you're travelling in other South American countries, Lonely Planet also has guides for *Brazil, Colombia, Peru, Ecuador & the Galápagos, Argentina, Uruguay & Paraguay, Chile & Easter Island* and others. For a full rundown, see the back of this book.

Guidebooks

The humorous but outdated budget guide, *Along the Gringo Trail*, by Jack Epstein (And/OR Press 1977), covers the eponymous 'Gringo Trail', the well-worn route from the US/Mexico border to Tierra del Fuego. The emphasis is on 1960s ideals.

A Traveller's Guide to El Dorado and the Inca Empire, by Lynn Meisch (Penguin Books, 1980) is a timeless treatise on Colom-

bia, Ecuador, Peru and Bolivia, especially their weaving and textiles traditions. It's highly recommended!

Adventuring in the Andes, Charles Frazier (Sierra Club Books, 1985) offers sparse coverage of off-the-beaten-track travel in Bolivia, Ecuador and Peru, with most of the space devoted to Peru. Bolivia gets a mere 18 pages.

Hikers and trekkers will want to pick up *Backpacking and Trekking in Peru & Bolivia*, by Hilary Bradt, Jonathon Derksen and Petra Schepens (6th edition, Bradt Publications, 1995), which covers major hikes in the Cordillera Real and the Yungas, as well as snippets on the lowland regions. Bolivia gets second billing, but there's lots of good route information and advice for keen ramblers…and the latest edition reveals a clear fascination with guinea pigs!

South American River Trips (Bradt Publications, 1982) and *Up the Creek* (Bradt Publications, 1986) are aimed at travellers planning river trips on their own. They offer useful practical advice, especially if you're skipping the cities.

The voluminous and pricey *South American Handbook*, edited by John Brooks (Trade & Travel Publications), covers everything between the Darién Gap and Tierra del Fuego.

Field Guides

Rainforests – A Guide to Tourist and Research Facilities at Selected Tropical Forest Sites in Central and South America, by James L Castner, is full of information and is especially worthwhile for researchers and rainforest visitors.

The beautifully-illustrated *In Search of the Flowers of the Amazon Forest*, by Margaret Mee, comes highly recommended for anyone (not only botanists) interested in the Amazon.

Neotropical Rainforest Mammals: A Field Guide, by Louise Emmons & François Feer, contains colour illustrations to identify mammals of the rainforest. For a reference work (as opposed to a field guide) consult the *World of Wildlife: Animals of South*

A	B
C	D
E	F

A: (RS) D: (RS)
B: (RS) E: (RS)
C: (DS) F: (DS)

On the road in Bolivia

Top Left: La Diablada mask, Oruro (MT)
Top Right: Mercado de Hechicería, La Paz (MT)
Bottom: La Diablada, Oruro (MT)

America by F R de la Fuente (Orbis Publishing, 1975).

Bird-watchers in the Amazon region of Bolivia often use field guides for other South American countries – many species overlap. Amateur interests should be satisfied with titles such as *South American Birds: A Photographic Aid to Identification* by John S Dunning; *A Guide to the Birds of Colombia*, Stephen L Hilty & William L Brown; and *A Guide to the Birds of Venezuela*, Rodolphe Meyer de Schauensee & William Phelps.

A more comprehensive tome is *A Guide to the Birds of South America*, Rodolphe Meyer de Schauensee (Academy of Natural Science, Philadelphia). The high-priced reference work, *The Birds of South America*, R S Ridgley & G Tudor (University of Texas Press, 1989), comes in several extremely detailed and technical volumes. Also definitive is *Birds of the High Andes*, by Jon Fjeldså & Niels Krabbe (Apollo Books, Denmark).

For some fascinating oddities, dip into *Ecology of Tropical Rainforests: An introduction for Eco-tourists* by Piet van Ipenburg & Rob Boschhuizen (Free University Amsterdam, 1990). This booklet is packed with intriguing and bizarre scientific minutiae about sloths, bats, the strangler fig and other extraordinary bits of rainforest ecology. It's available in the UK from J Forrest, 64 Belsize Park, London NW3 4EH; or in the USA from M Doolittle, 32 Amy Rd, Falls Village, CT 06031. Proceeds from its sales support the Tambopata Reserve Society, which funds rainforest research in south-eastern Peru's Reserva Tambopata.

A useful book for botanists is the 1000-page illustrated guide, *Guía de Árboles de Bolivia (Guide to Bolivia's Trees)*, published in 1993 by the Bolivian National Herbarium and the Missouri Botanical Garden. It's available from the Instituto de Ecología, Casilla 10077, La Paz.

In the UK, a good source for books on wildlife, vegetation and geology is the *Subbutteo Natural History Books, Ltd* (☎ (0352) 770581, fax (0352) 771590), Treuddyn, Mold, Clwyd CH7 4LN.

Travel & Narrative

The classic *Exploration Fawcett* by Colonel Percy Harrison Fawcett (Century, 1988) haphazardly follows the quirky travels of the unconventional explorer, including details of his term as a surveyor for the Bolivian government.

In Quest of the Unicorn Bird by Oliver Greenfield (HB Michael Joseph, 1992) offers a simply written but appealing narrative tracing the 19-year-old author's journey through Bolivia in search of the blue-horned curassow.

Wildlife of the Andes (formerly entitled *Land Above the Clouds*), by Tony Morrison (Nonesuch Press, 1988) is a well-observed study of the land and wildlife of the Andes. Unfortunately, it's rather hard to find.

The Old Patagonia Express, by Paul Theroux (Pocket Books, 1980) recounts a rail odyssey from Boston to Patagonia. The author takes a sniffy attitude toward budget travellers and doesn't seem to enjoy his trip, but it's still an interesting tale, and Bolivian rail travellers will certainly recognise some of the misadventures.

An intrepid sailor's journeys through landlocked Bolivia are recorded in *The Incredible Voyage*, by Tristan Jones (Sheed, Andrews & McNeel, Inc, 1977). It includes narrative about several months' sailing and exploring on Lake Titicaca and a complication-plagued haul across the country to the Paraguay River.

Sons of the Moon – A Journey in the Andes, by Henry Shukman (Charles Scribner & Sons, 1989), is a well-written account of a fairly unremarkable journey from northwestern Argentina, across the Bolivian Altiplano and on to Cuzco, Peru. It does, however, include superb observations of typically introverted Altiplano cultures.

The humorous and well-written *Inca-Kola* by Matthew Parris (Orion Books, 1993) follows the ramblings of several Englishmen on a rollicking circuit through Peru and parts of Bolivia. It would be an excellent read on a journey through the region.

The pleasantly readable *Passage through*

El Dorado, Jonathon Kandell (William Morrow & Company, 1984) describes a journalist's travels through the boom-and-bust country of the Amazon Basin. Interesting and well written, it flows along on an optimistic current that, with the benefit of hindsight, now seems sadly inappropriate for many areas, particularly Rondônia (Brazil). However, Kandell's assessment of the beautiful Río Mamoré as a 'vast, uninteresting, mainstream Amazon sort of waterway' does seem odd. He must only have seen its lower reaches, or visited when it was in flood.

The light travelogue, *Journey along the Spine of the Andes*, Christopher Portway (Oxford Illustrated Press, 1984), describes the author's travels from Bolivia to Colombia. As the narrative begins in La Paz, Bolivia is left behind in the first couple of pages.

The Cloud Forest, by Peter Mathiessen (Collins Harill, 1960), isn't exclusively about Bolivia, but this account of his 30,000-km journey across the South American wilderness from the Amazon to Terra del Fuego, is well worth a read. The descriptions of the South American environment are extraordinarily adept.

The Saddest Pleasure: A Journey on Two Rivers, by Moritz Thomsen (Graywolf Press, 1990) is a highly recommended and competently written book – skip the sickly introduction – about the author's experiences in South America, including expeditions around the Amazon region.

Let Me Speak, by Domitila Barrios de Chungara, is a Bolivian's compelling and touching account of life in the Siglo XX mine. It was originally published in Spanish as *Si Me Permite Hablar*. Another perspective is offered in *We Eat the Mines and the Mines Eat Us*, by June Nash (Columbia University Press, 1979). This anthropologist's study of life and death in the Bolivian tin mines is recommended for anyone interested in the harsh conditions faced by Bolivian miners.

Highways of the Sun – A Search for the Royal Roads of the Incas, by Victor W von Hagen (Victor Gollancz, 1956, or Plata Press, 1975) is an interesting treatise about a 1950s expedition along ancient Inca roads, and it will fascinate fans of ruins and pre-Columbian paving.

An interesting and offbeat historical character is portrayed in *Lizzie – A Victorian Lady's Amazon Adventure*, by Tony Morrison, Ann Brown & Anne Rose (BBC Books, 1985), which was compiled mostly from letters. It chronicles the experiences of a Victorian woman, Lizzie Hessel, in the Bolivian Amazon settlement of Colonia Orton during the rubber boom. Characters in the book read like a litany of modern Amazon history: Colonel Fawcett, Carlos Fermín Fitzcarrald ('Fitzcarraldo'), Dr Edwin Heath, Francisco and Nicolás Suárez, Henry Alexander Wickham and Dr Antonio Vaca Diez. The book is the companion volume to the BBC film production *Letters from Lizzie*.

The classic *Brazilian Adventure*, by Peter Fleming (Penguin, 1957), is the story of the author's 1930s expedition across the Mato Grosso and down to the Amazon to track down the missing explorer, Colonel Percy Harrison Fawcett. It's not about Bolivia, but it's one of the funniest and most entertaining travel books around, and Fleming's descriptions and impressions of the Brazilian Amazon are equally applicable to the Bolivian rainforests.

Touching the Void, by Joe Simpson (Pan Books, 1989), isn't about Bolivia, either, but this riveting tale of an ill-fated ascent of Peru's Siula Grande may well be the most (or, in a sense, least!)gripping climbing book ever written, and will affect non-climbers as much as it does experienced alpinists. The sequel, *This Game of Ghosts* (Vintage/Random House, 1994), carries the story both forward and backward and is also destined to become a climbers' classic.

History & Politics

The biography, *Ché Guevarcz*, Daniel James (Stein & Day, 1969), is a fascinating, slightly right-leaning biography of the folk hero, with emphasis upon his activities and ultimate demise in Bolivia. Perhaps better insight into Ché's thinking is available straight from the horse's mouth in *Bolivian Diary* by Ernesto Ché Guevara (Jonathan Cape/Lorrimer, 1968). This book traces the revolutionary's ill-fated travels through Bolivia, while struggling to bring the campesinos to an awareness – and defiance – of their downtrodden status.

The concise and extremely informative *Bolivia in Focus* by Paul van Lindert and Otto Verkoren (Latin American Bureau, 1994) provides an excellent synopsis of Bolivia's history, economics, politics and culture. It provides the best and most up-to-date background information available on the country and should be requisite reading for anyone wanting to familiarise themselves before a trip to Bolivia.

The modern classic on Bolivian social issues is *Rebellion in the Veins*, by James Dunkerly (Verso Editions, 1984), which chronicles Bolivian political and social struggles from 1952 to 1982. It's heavy going but full of facts and insights that are unavailable elsewhere. If you can't find a copy, order it directly from the publisher: Verso Editions, 6 Meard St, London W1V 3HR, UK.

Economists will be particularly interested in *Silent Revolution – The Rise of Market Economics in Latin America* by Duncan Green (Latin America Bureau, 1995). It outlines the causes and effects – and particularly the hardships – imposed by the International Monetary Fund's economic structural adjustment programmes in Latin America.

Despite its title, *The Great Tin Crash & the World Tin Market* by John Crabtree (Latin American Bureau, 1987) quite readably recounts the fascinating story of the Bolivian tin industry. It ties the current slump in tin prices to fluctuations in the valuation of the dollar and the pound, as well as poor infrastructure, lack of maritime access and the shortage of smelters.

The Incredible Incas & Their Timeless Land, by Loren McIntyre (National Geographic Society Press, 1975), is an easily digestible account of Inca history and description of Inca lands in modern times by one of the last South American explorers. It's written in typically informal *National Geographic* style and has lots of colour photos and illustrations.

Kingdom of the Sun God – A History of the Andes & Their People, by Ian Cameron, is an illustrated history of the Andes covering pre-Inca, Inca, colonial and modern developments in western South America.

The hard-to-find anthology, *Tales of Potosí*, Bartolomé Arzáns de Orsúa y Vela (Brown University Press, 1975), chronicles a city whose history reads more like fiction than fact. It offers good insights into colonial life in Bolivia.

Miners of Red Mountain, by P Bakewell, outlines the treasures and tragedies of Potosí's silver boom days. The book is now out of print, but may be available in libraries.

For everything you've ever wanted to know about the Andean wonder drug – and more – read the cult classic *The History of Coca – The Divine Plant of the Incas*, by W Golden Mortimer (And/OR Press, 1974), originally published in 1901. A more up-to-date assessment of Bolivia's relationship with the coca leaf is found in *Bolivia and Coca – A Study in Dependency*, by James Painter (Lynne Reiner Publishers, 1994).

John Hemming's *The Conquest of the Incas* (Harcourt, Brace, Jovanovich, 1970), is the definitive work on the Spanish takeover of the well-established Inca empire. A good companion book is *Monuments of the Incas*, by John Hemming and Edward Ranney (University of New Mexico Press, 1990), with illustrations and explanations of major Inca-era sites. A similarly comprehensive work is *The Conquest of Mexico & Peru* by Walter Prescott.

The 16th-century work, *Royal Commentaries of the Incas*, by Garsilaso de la Vega, details the history, growth and influence of the Inca Empire, as well as a first-hand account of its decline and demise.

Fiction & Literature

The novel *At Play in the Fields of the Lord*, by Peter Mathiessen, is a strong and well-written tale of missionaries in the Amazon rainforests.

The classic tale of South American life, *One Hundred Years of Solitude*, Gabriél Garcia Márquez (Picador, 1978), won the Nobel Prize for literature in 1982. Although it's considered by critics to reflect more fantasy than realism, it's actually based on acute observation and reflects South America's pervading surrealism as much as the author's vivid imagination.

The fictional classic, *The Bridge of San Luis Rey* by Thornton Wilder (Grosset & Dunlap, 1927), tells the story of a bridge that collapses into the Río Apurímac in Peru, focussing on the character and traditional Andean values of the victims.

The rollicking science fiction tale, *The Lost World*, by Sir Arthur Conan Doyle (Buccaneer Books, 1977; originally published 1912), describes a prehistoric world in the rainforested mountains of South America. The inspiration for this book was the Serranía de Huanchaca in what is now Noel Kempff Mercado National Park in north-eastern Bolivia.

Some of the finest Bolivian literature is discussed in the Arts & Culture section in the Facts About the Country chapter.

Ecology & the Amazon Region

In *Amazonia* (1991), the renowned explorer and photographer Loren McIntyre, has recorded on film the gradual demise of the Amazon region and its original inhabitants. To learn more about McIntyre's many journeys in search of the source of the Amazon and his extraordinary psychic experiences with indigenous tribes, have a look at *Amazon Beaming* (1991) by Petru Popescu.

You may be able to find a second-hand copy of George Woodcock's *Henry Walter Bates, Naturalist of the Amazons* (Faber & Faber, 1969), a fascinating account of the many years Bates spent in pursuit of plant life during the mid-19th century.

For a popularised vision of Amazonian wildlife and some good background material, see *Amazon Wildlife* (Insight Guides, 1992). It's full of fabulous photos of endear-

ing faces and the text provides an overview of tourist opportunities in the Amazon.

Wizard of the Upper Amazon – The Story of Manuel Córdova-Ríos (Houghton Mifflin, 1975) and the sequel *Río Tigre and Beyond*, by F Bruce Lamb, are worthwhile reading for insight into *yagé*, the hallucinogenic drug used by certain tribes of the upper Amazon.

The Fate of the Forest: Developers, Destroyers, and Defenders of the Amazon, by Susanna Hecht and Alexander Cockburn (Verso, 1989), provides one of the best analyses of the complex web of destruction of the Amazon, as well as ideas on ways to mend the damage.

Tropical Rainforest: A World Survey of Our Most Valuable and Endangered Habitat with a Blueprint for its Survival, by Arnold Newman, is a massive analysis of rainforest destruction and possible alternatives for sound forest management.

The compilation, *People of the Tropical Rainforest* (University of California Press & Smithsonian Institute, 1988), includes essays by rainforest experts. Augusta Dwyer also delivers a fierce indictment of corruption and mismanagement of the region in *Into the Amazon: The Struggle for the Amazon*.

The Rainforest Book, by Scott Lewis (Living Planet, 1990), is a concise analysis of rainforest problems and remedies. It's packed with examples that link consumer behaviour with rainforest development, and includes lists of conservation organisations and advice on individual involvement. A similar publication compiled by the Seattle Audubon Society and the Puget Consumers Co-operative is the booklet entitled *Rainforests Forever: Consumer Choices to Help Preserve Tropical Rainforests* (1990).

Emperor of the Amazon (Avon Bard, 1980) is by modern satirist Márcio Souza, who is based in Manaus (Brazil). His biting humour captures some of the greater horrors of the Amazon region and the absurdity of personal and governmental endeavours to conquer the rainforest. Both this and his other work, *Mad Maria* (Avon Bard, 1985), which deals with the abortive Madeira-

Mamoré railway between Pôrto Velho, Guajará-Mirim (Brazil) and Riberalta, should be of interest to travellers around Bolivia's northern frontiers.

Coffee-Table Books

Exploring South America, by Loren McIntyre, is the best of its kind, a compilation of photos from McIntyre's nearly 60 years in South America. The coffee-table study of Bolivia, *Lungo i Sentieri Incantati*, by Antonio Paolillo (Centro Studi Ricerche Liqabue di Venezia, 1987), is also full of lovely photos and is worth a look, even if you can't read the Italian text.

Language

The *Latin American Spanish phrasebook* (Lonely Planet, 1991) is handy for travellers to most of Latin America. The *University of Chicago Spanish-English/English-Spanish Dictionary* (Pocket Books 1972), which emphasises Latin American usage and pronunciation, is highly recommended.

The *Quechua phrasebook* (Lonely Planet, 1989) provides useful phrases and words in the Cuzco dialect, which is also spoken in the central Bolivian highlands.

ONLINE SERVICES

Lonely Planet's home page (http://www.lonelyplanet.com/dest/sam/bolivia.htm) has an overview of Bolivian culture, general information, travel suggestions and much more.

Bolivia Web (http://larch-www.lcs.mit.edu:8001/evs/bolivia/bolivia.html) includes maps, transport details and hotel suggestions, mostly in Spanish. Bolivia's World Wide Web Site (http://jaguar.pg.cc.md.us/bolivia.html) has brief essays on culture and history, as well as daily news (in Spanish).

NEWSPAPERS & MAGAZINES

The national daily newspaper is *La Razón*, but the major cities all have daily newspapers. They include *Presencia, El Diario, Hoy, Última Hora*, in La Paz; *La Patria* in Oruro; *El Mundo* and *El Deber* in Santa

Cruz; *El Correo del Sur* in Sucre; and *Los Tiempos* in Cochabamba. Of these, *Presencia, La Razón* and the two Santa Cruz papers generally provide the best coverage.

There's also an English-language weekly, the *Bolivian Times*, which is published on Friday and is sold at newsstands and bookshops in major cities. Overseas subscriptions cost US$111.50/131 in North America/Europe. For further information, contact The Editor, Bolivian Times (fax 390700), Pasaje Jáuregui 2248, Casilla 1696, La Paz.

Time, Newsweek, the *International Herald Tribune, The Economist*, the *Financial Times* and the *Miami Herald* are sold at some street kiosks in the major cities and at Los Amigos del Libro in La Paz, Cochabamba and Santa Cruz.

You may also want the latest copy of the monthly *Guía Boliviana de Transporte y Turismo*, which contains airline schedules and directories of services in major cities. It's available for US$5 per issue from GBT (☎ 327278; fax 391641), Oficina Receptora, Calle Fernando Guachalla, Edificio Guachalla, ground floor, Local 8, Casilla 128, La Paz. GBT also has branch offices in other major cities.

RADIO & TV

Bolivia has 125 radio stations broadcasting in Spanish, Quechua and Aymara. The seemingly inordinate number may be explained by the mountainous nature of the terrain – signals don't reach very far. Recommended listening includes FM-96.7 in La Paz, which plays classic American and English rock and pop music, and Radio Latina in Cochabamba, at the upper end of the FM band, which plays a mix of Andean folk music, salsa and local rock.

The country has two government and five private TV stations operating in La Paz, Cochabamba, Trinidad, Oruro, Potosí, Tarija and Santa Cruz, which are watched on the country's 650,000-odd TV sets. Most of the programming is foreign.

PHOTOGRAPHY & VIDEO

Photographers will find plenty of fodder in

Bolivia. Points worth remembering include cold, heat, humidity, sand, and tropical sunlight and shadows. Don't leave your camera for long in direct sunlight, and don't store used film for long in the humid conditions as it could fade.

On sunny days or at high altitudes, the best times to take photos are the first two hours after sunrise and the last two before sunset. This brings out the best colours and takes advantage of the colour-enhancing long red rays cast by a low sun. At other times, colours may be washed out by harsh sunlight and if you're shooting on sand or near water, it's important to adjust for glare. The worst of these effects can be countered by using a polarising (UV) filter. Remember to keep your photographic equipment well away from sand and water.

As in most places, the quest for the perfect 'people shot' will prove a photographer's greatest challenge. The average Bolivian doesn't indulge in photography as a hobby but does recognise the inherent value of camera equipment. If you carry a camera, especially a swanky model, you'll inevitably be branded with the 'wealthy foreigner' label. This isn't necessarily a problem, but it does set you apart. If you carry a camera, more people will try to sell you things, and those who are superstitious about photography will react differently towards you.

Film & Equipment

Cameras are available in Bolivia but import duties are high, so photographers should bring all necessary equipment from home. Certain types of film, such as Kodachrome or Polaroid, are difficult or impossible to find, but Fujichrome, Agfachrome and print film are available at reasonably low prices in some markets and from street vendors.

If you're shooting transparencies, you'll probably get the best results with Fujichrome 100, Sensia, Velvia or Kodachrome 64. La Paz is generally the best place to pick up film. In La Paz, Fujichrome 100 costs about US$6 per 36-exposure roll; Fujichrome Velvia is available only at the Fuji Centre on Plaza Pérez Velasco and costs US$10 for 36 expo-

sures. Agfachrome costs around US$4 per 36-exposure roll, and is found at the Agfa Centre at Calle Loayza 250 in central La Paz. Kodak products are available at Casa Kavlin at Calle Potosí 1130. Film prices sometimes include processing and you can post the exposed film to the labs in the envelopes provided. It's wise, however, to rewrap the package to disguise it and send it via registered post.

Useful photographic accessories include a small flash, a cable release, a polarising filter, a lens cleaning kit, and silica-gel packs to protect against humidity. Also, remember to take spare batteries for cameras and flash units and make sure your equipment is insured.

Repairs & Processing

Casa Kavlin at Calle Potosí 1130 in La Paz is reputable for repair and servicing of Kodak products. Take Japanese cameras to the Fuji Centre, two blocks away on Plaza Velasco. Technicians tend to be available only in the morning.

The quality of Bolivian film processing is generally poor; your best option at present is probably Foto Linares, in Edificio Alborada on the corner of Calles Loayza and Juan de la Riva in La Paz, which offers decent European standards at good European prices. Prints cost around US$1 for a 36-exposure roll, plus US$0.20 per print. You may want to pay only for the negatives and wait to have the prints done at home. To keep costs down on slide processing, ask for *solo revelado*, which means the slides are developed but not mounted. This costs between US$2 and US$2.50 for a 36-exposure roll. For mounted slides, you'll pay US$7 to US$8, including scratches. Alternatively, you can buy your own slide mounts at Casa Kavlin for US$7.50 per 100.

Photographing Scenery

Bolivian landscapes swallow celluloid, so don't be caught out without a healthy supply of film. Keep in mind, however, that the combination of high-altitude ultraviolet rays and light reflected off snow or water will conspire to fool both your eye and your light meter. A polarising filter is essential when photographing the Altiplano and will help to reveal or emphasise the dramatic effects of the exaggerated UV element at high altitude.

Unless there's a haze to filter sunlight, avoid taking photos during the brightest part of the day when the rays are short, the light is harshest and the shadows are blackest.

In the lowland rainforests, conditions include dim light, humidity, haze and leafy interference. For optimum photos, you need either fast film (200 or 400 ASA) or a tripod for long exposures.

Photographing People

While some Bolivians will be willing photo subjects, others – especially traditional women – may be superstitious about your camera, suspicious of your motives, or simply interested in whatever economic advantage they can gain from your desire to photograph them.

Whatever the case, be sensitive to the wishes of locals, however photogenic they are. Ask permission to photograph if a candid shot can't be made and if permission is denied, don't insist or snap a picture anyway. There will be plenty of willing subjects who can provide equally interesting 'people shots'.

Often, people will allow you to photograph them provided you give them a copy of the photo, a real treasure in rural Bolivia. Understandably, people are sometimes disappointed not to see the photograph immediately materialise. If you don't carry a Polaroid camera, take their address and make it clear that you'll send the photo by post once it's processed.

Photographing Wildlife

For serious wildlife photography, you'll need a single lens reflex camera and telephoto or zoom lenses. If all you have is a little 'point and shoot' camera, don't bother. The more sophisticated cameras may have a maximum focal length of 70 mm or so, but that's still not sufficient for decent wildlife shots.

Zoom lenses work best for wildlife pho-

tography since you can frame your shot easily and work out the optimum composition. This will be particularly useful when wildlife is on the move. You'll need at least 200 mm for good close-up shots; 70 to 300 mm zoom lenses are popular. The main problem with long lenses is that the excess of glass inside absorbs about 1.5 f-stops and necessitates higher ASA film (200 to 400) for photos in anything but broad, bright daylight.

A straight telephoto lens will yield better results and greater clarity than zoom lenses, but you're limited by having to carry a separate lens for each required focal length. A 400 or 500 mm lens will bring the action up close but you'll still need fast film.

Another option is a 2x teleconverter, a small adapter that fits between the lens and camera body and doubles the focal length of the lens. This is a good, cheap way of getting a long focal length without having to purchase expensive lenses. It does, however, have a couple of disadvantages: it requires fast film and, depending on the camera and lens, can be difficult to focus quickly and precisely, which is naturally a major drawback when it comes to wildlife photography.

When using long, heavy lenses, tripods are very useful, and they're essential for anything greater than about 300 mm unless you have an exceptionally steady hand.

TIME

Bolivian time is four hours behind Greenwich Mean Time. When it's noon in La Paz, it's 4 pm in London, 11 am in New York, 8 am in San Francisco, 4 am the following day in Auckland and 2 am the following day in Sydney.

ELECTRICITY

Bolivia uses a standard current of 220 volts at 50 cycles except in La Paz and a few selected locations in Potosí, which use 110 volts at 50 cycles. Ask before you plug in. In some areas, particularly smaller towns and villages, demand for power exceeds the power stations' ability to supply it and water and power services are routinely turned off at certain times of day and/or at night. If you're a night owl, have a torch on hand.

Most plugs and sockets in use are of the two-pin round prong variety, but in some places (particularly La Paz), you may encounter American-style two-pin parallel pronged sockets.

WEIGHTS & MEASURES

Like the rest of South America, Bolivia uses the metric system except, strangely, when weighing vegetables at the market; these are sold in *libras*, which are equal to imperial pounds. Uniquely South American measurements, which are used occasionally, include the *arroba*, which is equal to 11.25 kg, and the *quintal*, which equals four arrobas.

For converting between metric and imperial units, refer to the table at the back of the book.

HEALTH

General travel health depends on predeparture preparations, day-to-day attention to health-related matters, and the correct handling of medical emergencies if they do arise. Although the following health section may seem like a who's who of unpleasant diseases, your chances of contracting a serious illness in Bolivia are slight. You will, however, be exposed to environmental factors, foods and sanitation standards that are probably quite different from what you're used to, but if you take the recommended jabs, faithfully pop your antimalarials and use common sense, there shouldn't be any problems. However, people with a history of cardiac, pulmonary or circulatory problems should consult a physician before travelling to Bolivia, as they may be at risk of experiencing acute mountain sickness.

Travel Health Guides

There are a number of books on travel health, and if you intend to get anywhere off the beaten track on your travels, you should prepare yourself by referring to a selection of these.

Bites, Bugs & Bowels, by Jane Wilson Howarth (Cadogan, 1995). A compact, witty and practical guide to many of the developing world's health snags – both mundane and serious – is a useful companion for travel in the developing world.

Staying Healthy in Asia, Africa & Latin America by Dirk Schroeder (Moon Publications, 1995). Probably the best all-round guide to carry, as it's compact but very detailed and well organised.

Travellers' Health by Dr Richard Dawood (Oxford University Press, 1995) Comprehensive, easy to read, authoritative and also highly recommended, although it's rather large to lug around.

Where There is No Doctor by David Werner (Macmillan, 1994). A very detailed guide intended for someone such as a Peace Corps worker, who is going to work in an undeveloped country, rather than for the average traveller.

Wilderness Medical Society Practice Guidelines for Wilderness Emergency Care by William W Forgey (ICS Books, 1995). Has the best available wilderness medical guidelines, including information on how to deal with all sorts of natural hazards: altitude, frostbite, water purification, animal hazards, lightning and a host of other problems.

Mountain Sickness: Prevention, Recognition and Treatment by Peter Hackett (AACP, 1992). Practical, field-oriented and easy to carry.

Travel with Children by Maureen Wheeler (Lonely Planet, 1995). Includes basic advice on travel health for younger children.

Predeparture Preparations

Health Insurance A travel insurance policy to cover theft, loss and medical problems is a wise idea. A wide variety of policies are available; ask your travel agent for recommendations. The international student travel policies handled by STA Travel or other student travel organisations are usually good value. It's always important, however, to check the small print:

1. Some policies specifically exclude 'dangerous activities', which can include whitewater rafting, motorcycling, climbing with a rope (as if it would be less dangerous without a rope!), or even trekking. If these activities are on your agenda, such a policy would be of limited value.

2. You may prefer a policy that pays doctors or hospitals directly rather than requiring you to pay first and claim later. If you must claim after the fact, however, be sure you keep all documentation. Some policies ask you to phone (reverse charges) to a centre in your home country where an immediate assessment of the problem will be made.

3. Check on the policy's coverage of emergency transport or evacuation back to your home country. If you have to stretch out across several airline seats, someone has to pay for it!

Travel Health Information Health care services in Bolivia are very limited, so it's worth informing yourself about health-related matters before you go.

In the USA you can contact the Overseas Citizens Emergency Center and request a health and safety information bulletin on foreign countries by writing to the Bureau of Consular Affairs Office, State Department, Washington, DC 20520. There's also a special telephone line (☎ (202) 632 5525) for emergencies while abroad.

Check the home pages of the World Health Organization and the Center for Disease Control for current health and vaccine information. You can access these pages via Lonely Planet's Web site (see the Online Services section earlier in this chapter). The Center for Disease Control also has a free fax-back service in the USA (fax (404) 332 4565).

The International Association for Medical Assistance to Travellers (IAMAT) (e-mail iamat@sentex.net) at 417 Center St, Lewiston, New York, NY 14092 can provide you with a list of English-speaking physicians in South America. In Canada, its address is 40 Regal Rd, Guelph, Ontario N1K 1B5. The European office is at Voirets 57, 1212 Grand Lancy, Geneva, Switzerland.

In the UK, contact the Medical Advisory Services for Travellers Abroad (MASTA), Keppel St, London WC1E 7HT (☎ (0171) 631 4408). MASTA provides a wide range of services including health briefs and a range of medical supplies. Another source of medical information and supplies is the British Airways Travel Clinic (☎ (0171) 831 5333). The Department of Health publishes leaflets SA40/41 on travellers' health requirements, and operates a Freephone service (☎ 0800 555777).

In Australia, contact the Traveller's Medical & Vaccination Centre in any capital city for general health information pertaining to South America, and for IAMAT directories and publications. MASTA (toll-free ☎ 1800 269 917) will provide an up-to-date country-specific health brief for about A$10.

Medical Kit It's wise to carry a small, straightforward medical kit, which may include:

- Aspirin or paracetamol (called acetaminophen in the USA) – for pain or fever
- Antihistamine (such as Benadryl) – useful as a decongestant for colds and allergies, to ease itching from insect bites, or to prevent motion sickness. Antihistamines may cause sedation and interact with alcohol so care should be taken when using them.
- Antibiotics – useful if you're travelling off the beaten track. Most antibiotics are prescription medicines, so carry the prescription along with you. Some individuals are allergic to commonly prescribed antibiotics such as penicillin or sulpha drugs. It is sensible to always carry this information when travelling.
- Kaolin and pectin preparation such as Pepto-Bismol for stomach upsets and loperamide (eg Imodium or Lomotil) to bung things up in case of emergencies during long-distance travel.
- Rehydration solution – for treatment of severe diarrhoea; particularly important when travelling with children. These preparations are available from Bolivian pharmacies.
- Antiseptic liquid or cream and antibiotic powder for minor injuries.
- Calamine lotion or Stingose spray – to ease irritation from bites and stings
- Bandages and band-aids (plasters).
- Scissors, tweezers, and a thermometer – note that mercury thermometers are not permitted on airlines.
- Insect repellent, 15+ sunblock (sunscreen), sunchap stick and water purification tablets (or iodine).
- Sterile syringes recommended for travel in Amazonia. Have at least one large enough for a blood test as those normally used for injections are too small.

When buying drugs anywhere in South America, check expiry dates and storage conditions. Some drugs available there may no longer be recommended, or may even be banned, in other countries.

Health Preparations Make sure you're

healthy before embarking on a long journey, have your teeth checked and if you wear glasses or contacts, bring a spare pair and a copy of your optical prescription. Losing your glasses can be a real problem, although in larger Bolivian cities, you can have a new pair made with little fuss.

At least one pair of good quality sunglasses is essential, as the glare can be terrific, particularly on the Altiplano, and dust and blown sand can get into the corners of your eyes. A hat, sunscreen lotion and lip protection are also important.

If you require a particular medication, take an adequate supply as it may not be available locally. Take a prescription with the generic rather than brand name so it will be universally recognisable. It's also wise to carry a copy of the prescription to prove you're using the medication legally. Customs and immigration officers may get excited at the sight of syringes or mysterious powdery preparations. The organisations listed under Travel Health Information can provide medical supplies such as syringes, together with multilingual customs documentation.

Immunisations Vaccinations provide protection against diseases you may be exposed to during your travels. Currently yellow fever is the only vaccine subject to international health regulations, and a yellow-fever vaccination and related documentation is strongly recommended for every traveller in Bolivia. It's technically required for travel in Santa Cruz department, and Brazilian authorities will not grant entrance from Bolivia without it. The vaccination remains effective for 10 years.

Seek medical advice about vaccinations at least six weeks prior to your departure: some vaccinations require an initial shot followed by a booster, and some should not be given together.

The possible list of vaccinations includes:

Cholera Although some border officials may ask to see evidence of this vaccine – often unofficially as a means of extracting bribes – it is of limited effectiveness, lasts only three to six months and is not recommended for pregnant women. There have been no recent reports of cholera vaccine requirements in Bolivia or neighbouring countries.

Infectious Hepatitis Hepatitis A is the most common travel-acquired illness but it may be prevented fairly reliably by vaccination. Protection can be provided in two ways – either with the antibody gammaglobulin or with a new vaccine called Havrix. Havrix provides long-term immunity (up to 10 years or more) after an initial dose and a booster at six or 12 months.

Polio A booster of either the oral or injected vaccine is required every 10 years to maintain immunity.

Smallpox Smallpox has now been wiped out worldwide, so immunisation is no longer necessary.

Tetanus DPT Boosters are necessary at least every 10 years and are highly recommended as a matter of course.

Typhoid Fever Available as either an injection or a course of capsules. Protection with the injectable vaccine lasts three years; capsules require boosting annually. Useful if you are travelling for long periods in rural, tropical areas.

Yellow Fever Protection, available from yellow-fever vaccination centres, lasts for 10 years and is highly recommended. Vaccination is contraindicated during pregnancy but if you must travel to a high-risk area it is probably advisable.

Basic Rules

Bolivia is not a particularly unhealthy country, but sanitation and hygiene are generally poor, so you should pay attention to what you eat. Stomach upsets are the most common travel health problem (30% to 50% of people travelling outside their home country for two weeks or less can expect to experience them) but the majority of these upsets are minor. Don't be paranoid about sampling local foods – it's all part of the travel experience and shouldn't be missed. If an inexpensive restaurant or market stall is popular with locals, chances are it's a good choice.

Water Purification Some Bolivian tap water is safe to drink, but much of it isn't. The simplest way to purify suspect water is to boil it for eight to 10 minutes, but remember that at high altitudes water boils at a lower temperature and germs are less likely to be killed. Simple filtering won't remove all dangerous organisms, so if you can't boil suspect water, treat it chemically. Chlorine tablets (eg Puritabs or Steritabs) will kill many, but not all, pathogens. Micro-Pure and other silver-based tablets don't kill giardia. Iodine is very effective and is available in tablet form (such as Potable Aqua) but follow the directions carefully and remember that too much iodine is harmful.

If you can't find iodine tablets, use either 2% tincture of iodine or iodine crystals. Add four drops of tincture of iodine per litre or quart of water and let it stand for 30 minutes. (Preparation of iodine crystals is a more complicated and dangerous process, as you first must prepare a saturated iodine solution.) Iodine loses its effectiveness if exposed to air or damp, so store it in a tightly sealed container. Flavoured powder will disguise the normally foul taste of iodine-treated water and is especially useful when travelling with children.

Reputable brands of bottled water or soft drinks are usually fine, although mineral water bottles are sometimes refilled and resold, so check the seals before buying. The most widely available brand is Viscachani, but unfortunately, its mineral content appears to be salt. If you can find them, Salvietti from Sucre and Vertiente from Cochabamba are better choices.

In rural areas, take care with fruit juices and licuados, since water may have been added. Milk should be treated with suspicion as it is often unpasteurised. Boiled milk is fine if it's kept hygienically and yoghurt is always good. Tea or coffee should also be OK because the water used was probably boiled.

Food Vegetables and fruit should be washed with purified water or peeled where possible. Ice cream is usually OK but beware of ice cream that has melted and been refrozen. Thoroughly cooked food is safest but not if it has been left to cool or if it has been reheated. Take great care with shellfish or fish, and avoid undercooked meat. If a place looks clean and well run and the vendor also looks clean and healthy, then the food is probably all right. In general, places that are packed with travellers or locals will be fine. Busy restaurants mean the food is being cooked and eaten quite quickly with little standing around and is probably not being reheated.

To clean fruit and vegetables without adding undesirable flavours, you can use Bolivia's own choice, D-6 germicide, which is available at local pharmacies. Mix 25 to 30 drops in one litre of water and place the vegetables in the solution for 20 minutes.

Nutrition If your food is poor or limited in availability, if you're travelling hard and fast and therefore missing meals, or if you simply lose your appetite, you can soon start to lose weight and place your health at risk.

Make sure your diet is well balanced. Eggs, tofu, beans, lentils and nuts are all safe ways to get protein. Fruit you can peel (bananas, oranges or mandarins for example) is always safe and a good source of vitamins. Try to eat plenty of grains (rice) and bread. Remember that although food is generally safer if it is cooked well, over-cooked food loses much of its nutritional value. If your diet isn't well balanced or if your food intake is insufficient, it's a good idea to take vitamin and iron supplements.

Everyday Health A normal body temperature is 98.6°F or 37°C; more than 2°C (4°F) higher is a 'high' fever. A normal adult pulse rate is 60 to 80 per minute (children 80 to 100, babies 100 to 140). You should know how to take a temperature and a pulse rate. As a general rule the pulse increases about 20 beats per minute for each °C (2°F) rise in fever.

An abnormal respiration rate is also an indicator of illness. Count the number of breaths per minute: between 12 and 20 is normal for adults and older children (up to 30 for younger children, 40 for babies). People with a high fever or serious respiratory illness (such as pneumonia) breathe more quickly than normal. More than 40 shallow breaths a minute usually means pneumonia.

Medical Problems & Treatment
Self-diagnosis and treatment of medical problems can be risky, so wherever possible seek qualified help. Although we do give treatment dosages in this section, they are for emergency use only. Medical advice should be sought where possible before administering any drugs.

An embassy or consulate can usually recommend a good place to go for such advice. So can five-star hotels, although they often recommend doctors with five-star prices. (This is when that medical insurance really comes in useful!) In some places standards of medical attention are so low that for some ailments the best advice is to get on a plane and go somewhere else.

Pharmacies & Medications It's not necessary to take with you every remedy for every illness you might conceivably contract during your trip. Just about everything available in your home country can also be found in Bolivian pharmacies, and pharmaceutical drugs are available without a prescription. They are a bit lax about storage, however, so be sure to check expiry dates before buying. It's also a good idea to take a sufficient supply of vitamin tablets and any prescriptions that you must take habitually, including contraceptive pills.

Pharmacies in Bolivia are known as *farmacias* and medicines are called *medicamentos*. The word for doctor is *médico* and medicine tablets are known as *comprimidos*. *Farmacias de turno* are pharmacies that take turns staying open 24 hours a day. Those currently on duty are listed in daily newspapers.

Environmental Hazards
Altitude Sickness (Soroche) Much of Bolivia lies at high altitude and most of the country's population lives above 3000m. The atmospheric density at Potosí, the most lofty city at 4070m, is less than two-thirds its value at sea level; and at 5345m Chacaltaya, near La Paz, it's only about half. Water in La Paz boils at about 88°C (as opposed to 100°C), and planes landing at the city's airport reach stall speed at nearly twice the velocity as in Santa Cruz, which has an altitude of only 437m. Drivers from Santa Cruz to La Paz must let air out of their tyres; in the opposite direction, they must add air.

The human body is also affected by an increase in altitude and in much of the highland and Altiplano regions of Bolivia, travellers may experience altitude-related sickness.

On a rapid ascent to high altitude, say a flight from Lima at sea level to El Alto airport in La Paz at 4010m, your body isn't given time to adapt to the lower pressure and consequent lack of oxygen. Newly arrived visitors invariably experience a condition known as *soroche* or simple altitude sickness, and should take it easy for the first few days until their bodies have acclimatised.

In an attempt to compensate for the decreased availability of oxygen, the heart and lungs work harder. Symptoms of altitude sickness include breathlessness, a racing pulse, lethargy, tiredness, insomnia, loss of appetite, headache and dehydration. These symptoms are sometimes accompanied by nausea and vomiting.

There is no medical evidence that chewing coca leaves or drinking *mate de coca* (coca leaf tea) – the traditional remedy – works beyond deadening some of the body's senses. Rural Bolivians also make tea from other high-altitude plants – the leaves of *pupusa* and *chachakoma* and the flower of *flor de puna* – to counter soroche. The best remedy is a day or two of rest while the body begins its acclimatisation process. In any case, drinking large quantities of water – about two or three litres daily – is essential.

For altitude-related discomfort, especially on brief ascents to over 4500m, mild pain-killers can be taken. For headache, a non-aspirin pain-reliever such as paracetamol (called acetaminophen in North America) may be used.

Some local soroche remedies, such as Micoren (or the popular Sorojchi – a blend of Micoren, caffeine and aspirin), actually slow the heart rate, forcing you to breathe more deeply, thereby kicking off the acclimatisation process. Using this rather drastic approach can do more harm than good – it's akin to stopping your car by hitting a wall. Rather than take chances with your health, it's probably better to allow your body to make its own adjustments.

If you're ascending quickly to high altitudes (eg from Lima to La Paz), acetazolamide (Diamox) – available only by prescription – has been recommended as a prophylactic to help with acclimatisation. It should be taken in 250-mg doses four times daily starting 24 to 48 hours before your arrival at high altitude. Note, however, that acetazolamide can mask the warning signs of acute mountain sickness, and because it's a diuretic, it may cause dehydration. To compensate loss of liquid, drink at least three to four litres of water daily. Another side-effect is tingling in the fingers and toes. People with sulpha allergies should not take acetazolamide.

Acute Mountain Sickness (AMS) Acute mountain sickness (AMS) is a more serious condition than soroche. It is experienced by climbers and hikers who climb too high too quickly, and it can also strike visitors to La Paz.

There are two forms of malignant AMS: High Altitude Pulmonary Oedema (HAPE), and High Altitude Cerebral Oedema (HACE). Both are fatal if unrecognised and untreated. The only treatment is immediate descent to a lower altitude before someone with a bad headache becomes an unconscious stretcher case.

There is a great variation in susceptibility to AMS. Some people start feeling ill at altitudes as low as 2450m; others feel fine at 6000m. In general, AMS is rare below 2450m. To ascend to altitudes of over 5000m for any length of time (longer than a few hours at Chacaltaya), first spend a week at the altitude of La Paz or the Altiplano. Climbers and hikers going seriously high should seek medical advice and be familiar with expedition rules and methods for dealing with AMS.

Even with acclimatisation you may still have trouble adjusting. Breathlessness; a dry irritative cough (which may progress to the production of pink, frothy sputum); severe headache; loss of appetite; nausea; and sometimes vomiting, are all danger signs. Increasing tiredness, confusion, lack of coordination and balance, vision problems (including blindness), speech difficulties and irrational behaviour are real danger signs. Any of these symptoms individually, even just a persistent headache, can be a warning, and if it persists, or becomes worse, get the sufferer down to a lower altitude immediately – even in the middle of the night! Every minute counts and it is easier to assist an unwell person who can still walk than to carry someone who is unconscious. If someone is unconscious and vomiting, place them on their side to prevent the vomit entering their lungs. If someone is suffering from severe AMS in La Paz or elsewhere on the Altiplano, seek hospital treatment or descend to a lower altitude immediately.

Minimising Risk The best way to minimise the risk of AMS is to ascend slowly. Ascending to about 3000m normally presents no problem, but above that, the body needs time to acclimatise. A gain of about 300m per day is recommended but since that may be impractical (using that guideline, it would take three days to cross La Paz, from the Zona Sur to El Alto!), the best advice is to follow the climbers' adage: climb high, sleep low.

Dehydration can result from increased sweating and loss of moisture through accelerated respiration in cold, dry air, so when you trek at high altitude, increase your intake of liquids. Eat light meals high in energy-rich carbohydrates and avoid smoking, which reduces the amount of oxygen the blood can carry. Alcohol should also be avoided since it increases urine output and results in further dehydration. Furthermore, avoid sedatives as they may mask symptoms of AMS.

Most importantly, do not trek alone. AMS reduces good judgement and symptoms are often ignored or not perceived by the victim. If you are suffering from any symptoms of AMS, don't go higher, and avoid exertion until the symptoms have disappeared. Light outdoor activity is better than bed rest.

Doctors and climbers who want to keep up with the latest research on high-altitude medicine may want to contact the International Society for Mountain Medicine (fax (41 36) 553852), Dr Bruner, Membership Secretary, Arztpraxis, CH-3822 Lauterbrunnen, Switzerland. Its newsletter is available by subscription for SF50 per year.

Hypothermia Hypothermia is a dangerous lowering of the body temperature. It is caused by exhaustion and exposure to cold, damp, wet or windy weather, which can occur anywhere in Bolivia. Hypothermia is a threat whenever a person is exposed to the elements at temperatures below 10°C.

Symptoms of hypothermia include exhaustion, numbness (particularly of the toes and fingers), shivering, slurred speech, irrational or violent behaviour, lethargy, stumbling, dizzy spells, muscle cramps and violent bursts of energy. Irrationality may take the form of sufferers claiming they are warm and trying to take off their clothes.

The best treatment is of course to get the sufferer to shelter and give them warm drinks and a hot bath if possible (which it probably won't be in Bolivia). Wet clothing should be changed or removed – no clothing at all is better than wet garments. The sufferer should lie down, wrapped in a sleeping bag or blanket to preserve body heat. Another person may lie down with them in order to provide as much warmth as possible. If no improvement is noticed within a few minutes, seek help but don't leave the victim alone while doing so. The body heat of another person is of more immediate importance than medical attention.

Sunburn The Altiplano and much of the highland regions of Bolivia lie within the tropics at elevations greater than 3000m. In many areas, the atmosphere there is too thin to screen out much of the dangerous ultraviolet radiation that is absorbed and deflected at lower altitudes. The use of a strong sunscreen is essential: serious burns can occur after even brief exposure. Don't neglect to apply sunscreen to any area of exposed skin, especially if you're near water or snow. On Lake Titicaca and in the high mountains, reflected rays can burn as severely as direct rays.

Sunscreen is unfortunately quite expensive in Bolivia, and it's also difficult to find one with a rating high enough for fair skin, so you may want to bring some from home. A hat is also essential to shade your face and protect your scalp, and sunglasses will prevent eye irritation (especially if you wear contact lenses). At higher altitudes (over about 2500m), you'll need sunglasses such as those used by mountaineers, which screen 100% of incoming UV.

Some people also experience a rash caused by photosensitivity in high altitudes. This can be treated with light applications of cortisone cream to affected areas (never use cortisone near your face, however).

Prickly Heat Prickly heat is an itchy rash caused by excessive perspiration trapped under the skin. It usually strikes those newly arrived in a hot climate whose pores have not opened enough to accommodate profuse sweating. Frequent baths and application of talcum powder will help relieve the itch.

Heat Exhaustion In the tropical lowlands, Yungas and Chaco regions, heat combined with humidity and exposure to the sun can be oppressive and leave you feeling lethargic, irritable and dazed. A cool swim or lazy afternoon in the shade will do wonders to improve your mood. You'll also need to drink lots of liquids and eat salty foods in order to replenish what you've lost during sweating.

Serious dehydration or salt deficiency can lead to heat exhaustion. Take time to acclimatise to high temperatures, and make sure you drink sufficient liquids – don't rely on feeling thirsty to indicate when you should drink. Always carry a bottle of water with you on long trips. Salt deficiency, which can be brought on by diarrhoea or nausea, is characterised by fatigue, lethargy, headaches, giddiness and muscle cramps. Salt tablets will probably solve the problem.

Fungal Infections Hot weather fungal infections are most likely to occur on the scalp, between the toes or fingers (athlete's foot), in the groin (jock itch) and on the body (ringworm). You get ringworm (which is a fungal infection, not a worm) from infected animals or by walking on damp areas, such as shower floors.

To prevent fungal infections wear loose, comfortable clothes, avoid artificial fibres, wash frequently and dry carefully. If you do get an infection, wash the infected area daily with a disinfectant or medicated soap and water, and rinse and dry well. Apply an antifungal medication (eg Tinaderm). Try to expose the infected area to air or sunlight as much as possible and change your towels and underwear often, washing them in hot water.

Motion Sickness If you're susceptible to motion sickness, come prepared, because Bolivian roads and railways aren't exactly velvety smooth. If an antihistamine such as Dramamine works for you, take some along. Eating very lightly before and during a trip will reduce the chances of motion sickness. Try to find a place that minimises disturbance, near the wing on aircraft or near the centre on buses. Fresh air almost always helps but reading or cigarette smoking (or even being around someone else's smoke) normally makes matters worse.

Commercial motion sickness preparations (eg Scopolamine or Dramamine), which can cause drowsiness, have to be taken before the trip; after you've begun to feel ill, it's too late. Ginger can be used as a natural motion sickness preventative and is available in capsule form.

Infectious Diseases

Diarrhoea Sooner or later – unless you're exceptional – you'll get Montezuma's (or Atahuallpa's) Revenge, Turista or any of a dozen other names for plain old travellers' diarrhoea, so you may as well accept the inevitable. The problem is caused not so much by poor sanitation or 'bad' food but by dietary changes and lack of resistance to local strains of bacteria. Your susceptibility will depend largely on how much you've been exposed to foreign bacteria and what your guts are used to.

The first thing to remember is that every case of diarrhoea is not dysentery, so don't panic and start stuffing yourself with pills. A few rushed toilet trips with no other symptoms isn't usually indicative of a serious problem. Moderate diarrhoea, involving half-a-dozen loose movements in a day, is more of a nuisance. Dehydration is the main danger with any diarrhoea, particularly in children, where dehydration can occur quite quickly.

Fluid replacement remains the mainstay of management. Try to starve out the bugs. If possible, eat nothing, rest and avoid travelling. Weak black tea with a little sugar, soda water, or flat soft drinks diluted 50% with bottled water are all good. If you can't hack that, keep to dry toast, biscuits and black tea.

With severe diarrhoea a rehydration solution is necessary to replace minerals and salts. Commercially available oral rehydration salts (ORS) is very useful; add the contents of one sachet to a litre of boiled or bottled water. In an emergency you can make up a solution of eight teaspoons of sugar to a litre of boiled water and provide salted cracker biscuits at the same time. Stick to a bland diet as you recover; try some yoghurt but stay away from other dairy products, sweets and fruit.

Loperamide (Lomotil or Imodium) can be used to temporarily 'plug the drain' but they do not actually cure the problem. Only use these drugs if absolutely necessary (for example, if you *must* travel) and under all circumstances, remember that fluid replacement is the most important thing. In certain situations antibiotics may be indicated:

- Watery diarrhoea with blood and mucus. (Avoid gut-paralysing drugs such as Imodium or Lomotil.)
- Watery diarrhoea with fever and lethargy.
- Persistent diarrhoea for more than 48 hours.
- Severe diarrhoea, if it is logistically difficult to stay in one place.

The recommended drugs (adults only) would be either norfloxacin 400 mg twice daily for three days or ciprofloxacin 500 mg twice daily for three days. Bismuth subsalicylate has also been used successfully (it's unavailable in Australia). The dosage for adults is two tablets or 30 ml and for children it is one tablet or 10 ml. This dose can be repeated every 30 minutes to one hour, with no more than eight doses in a 24-hour period.

The drug of choice in children would be co-trimoxazole (Bactrim, Septrin, Resprim). A five-day course is given but dosage is dependent on weight. Ampicillin has been recommended in the past and may still be an alternative.

If you don't recover after a couple of days, it may be necessary to visit a doctor to be tested for other problems which could include giardia, dysentery, cholera and so on.

Giardiasis Giardia is prevalent in tropical climates and is first characterised by a swelling of the stomach, pale-coloured faeces, diarrhoea, frequent gas, headache and later by nausea and depression. Symptoms will appear after a 14-day incubation period, but may later disappear for a few days and then return; this can go on for several weeks.

Many doctors recommend 250 mg metronidazole (Flagyl) twice daily for three days. Metronidazole however, can cause side effects and some doctors prefer to treat giardiasis with two grams of tinidazole (Fasigyn or Tinaba), taken in one fell swoop to knock the bug out hard and fast. If it doesn't work the first time, the treatment can be repeated for up to three days.

Dysentery This serious illness is caused by consumption of contaminated food or water and is characterised by severe diarrhoea, often with blood or mucus in the faeces, and painful gut cramps. There are two types: bacillary dysentery, which is uncomfortable but not enduring, and amoebic dysentery which, as its name suggests, is caused by amoebas. This variety is much more difficult to treat and is more persistent.

Bacillary dysentery is characterised by a high fever and rapid onset; symptoms include headache, vomiting and stomach pains. It doesn't generally last more than a week, but it is highly contagious, and because it's caused by bacteria, it responds well to antibiotics.

Since the symptoms of bacillary dysentery themselves are actually the best treatment – diarrhoea and fever are both trying to rid the body of the infection – you may just want to hole up for a few days and let it run its course. If activity or travel is absolutely necessary during the infection, you can take either Imodium or Lomotil to keep things under control until reaching a more convenient location to R & R (rest and run).

Often recommended is norfloxacin, which should be taken in 400 mg doses twice daily for seven days, or ciprofloxacin, 500 mg twice daily for seven days. If you're unable to find either of these drugs, an alternative is co-trimoxazole (Bactrim, Septrin, Resprim) twice daily for seven days. This is a sulpha drug (each tablet contains 400 mg sulphametoxozole and 160 mg trimethoprim) and must not be used in people with a known sulpha allergy. For children, co-trimoxazole is a reasonable first-line treatment.

Amoebic dysentery, or amoebiasis, builds up more slowly and is more dangerous. It is caused by protozoans, or amoebic parasites (Entamoeba histolytica), which are also transmitted through contaminated food or water. Once they've invaded, they live in the lower intestinal tract and cause heavy and often bloody diarrhoea, fever, tenderness in the liver and intense abdominal pain. If left untreated, ulceration and inflammation of the colon and rectum can become very serious. If you see blood in your faeces over two or three days, seek medical attention.

A stool test is necessary to diagnose which kind of dysentery you have, so you should seek medical help urgently. In case of an emergency, norfloxacin or ciprofloxacin (for doses, see the Diarrhoea section above) can be used as presumptive treatment for bacillary dysentery, and metronidazole (Flagyl) for amoebic dysentery.

For amoebic dysentery, the recommended adult dosage of metronidazole is one 750 mg to 800 mg capsule three times daily for five to 10 days. Children from eight to 12 years old should have half the adult dose; the dosage for younger children is one-third the adult dose. Metronidazole should not be taken by pregnant women. An alternative is tinidazole (Tinaba or Fasigyn), taken as a two gram daily dose for two to three days. Alcohol must be avoided during treatment and for 48 hours afterwards.

The best method of preventing dysentery is, of course, to avoid eating or drinking contaminated items.

Cholera The bacteria responsible for cholera are waterborne, so attention to the rules of eating and drinking should protect you. The cholera vaccine is between 20 to 50% effective and short lived (three to six months) according to most authorities, and it can have some side effects. Vaccination is recommended, but is not legally required by Bolivian authorities. The risk is low to moderate.

Cholera is characterised by a sudden onset of acute diarrhoea with 'rice water' stools, vomiting, muscular cramps and extreme weakness. You need medical attention but your first concern should be rehydration. Drink as much water as you can – if it refuses to stay down, keep drinking anyway. If there is likely to be an appreciable delay in reaching medical treatment, begin a course of tetracycline which, incidentally, should not be administered to children or pregnant women (be sure to check the expiry date, since old tetracycline can become toxic). An alternative drug would be Ampicillin. Remember that although antibiotics might kill the bacteria, a toxin produced by the bacteria causes the massive fluid loss. Fluid replacement is by far the most important aspect of treatment.

Viral Gastroenteritis This is not caused by bacteria but, as the name implies, a virus. It is characterised by stomach cramps, diarrhoea, and sometimes by vomiting and a slight fever. All you can do is rest and keep drinking as much water as possible.

Hepatitis This incapacitating disease is caused by a virus that attacks the liver. Hepatitis A, which is the most common strain in South America, is contracted through contact with contaminated food, water, cutlery, toilets or individuals. It is a very common problem among travellers to areas with poor sanitation.

Symptoms include fever, chills, headache, fatigue, feelings of weakness and aches and pains, followed by loss of appetite, nausea, vomiting, abdominal pain, dark urine, light coloured faeces and jaundiced skin, and the whites of the eyes may turn a sickly yellow. You should seek medical advice, but in general there is not much you can do apart from rest, drink lots of fluids, eat lightly and keep to a diet high in proteins and vitamins. Avoid fatty foods, alcohol and cigarettes. People who have had hepatitis must forgo alcohol for six months after the illness, to allow the liver time to recover.

If you contract hepatitis A during a short trip to South America, you might want to make arrangements to go home. If you can afford the time, however, and have a reliable travelling companion who can bring food and water, the best cure is to stay where you are, find a few good books and only leave bed to go to the toilet. After a month of so, you should feel like living again.

The best preventative measures available are either the recently introduced long-term hepatitis A vaccine (Havrix); or a gamma globulin jab before departure and booster shots every three or four months thereafter (beware of unsanitary needles!). A jab is also in order if you come in contact with any infected person (that is, if you haven't had a hepatitis A vaccine); and if *you* come down with hepatitis, anyone who has been in recent contact with you should have a shot too. However, if symptoms of hepatitis are already present, do not get a shot.

Hepatitis B, formerly known as serum hepatitis, can only be caught by sexual contact with an infected person, unsterilised needles, blood transfusions or by skin penetration – such as tattooing, shaving or having your ears pierced. If type B is diagnosed, fatal liver failure is a real possibility and the victim should be sent home and/or hospitalised immediately. Gamma globulin is not effective against hepatitis B.

The symptoms of type B are much the same as type A except that they are more severe and may lead to irreparable liver damage or even liver cancer and fatal liver failure. Although there is no treatment for hepatitis B, an effective prophylactic vaccine is readily available in most countries. The immunisation schedule requires two injections at least a month apart followed by a third dose five months after the second. If you anticipate contact with blood or other bodily secretions, perhaps as a health care worker or through sexual contact with the local population, you should get a hepatitis B vaccination.

Other strains of hepatitis are fairly rare (so far) and following the same precautions for hepatitis A and B should be all that's necessary to avoid them.

Typhoid Contaminated food and water are responsible for typhoid fever, another gut infection that travels the faecal-oral route. Vaccination against typhoid isn't 100% effective. Since it can be very serious, medical attention is necessary.

Early symptoms are like those of many other travellers' illnesses – you may feel as though you have a bad cold or the flu combined with a headache, sore throat and a fever. The fever rises slowly until it reaches 40°C or more, while the pulse slowly drops, unlike a normal fever, in which the pulse increases. These symptoms may be accompanied by nausea, diarrhoea or constipation.

In the second week, the fever and slow pulse continue and a few pink spots may appear on the body. Trembling, delirium, weakness, diarrhoea, weight loss and dehydration set in. If there are no further complications, the fever and symptoms will slowly fade during the third week. Medical attention is essential, however, since typhoid is extremely infectious and possible complications include pneumonia or peritonitis (perforated bowel).

When feverish, the victim should be kept cool. Watch for dehydration. The drug of choice is ciprofloxacin at a dose of one gram daily for 14 days, but it's expensive and may not be available. The alternative, chloramphenicol, has been the mainstay of treatment for many years. In many countries it's still the preferred antibiotic but Ampicillin has fewer side affects. The adult dosage for chloramphenicol is 500 mg, four times a day for 14 days. Children aged between eight and 12 years should have half the adult dose; younger children should have one-third the adult dose. People who are allergic to penicillin should not be given Ampicillin.

Tetanus This potentially fatal disease is found in undeveloped tropical areas and is difficult to treat, but it's easily prevented by vaccination (which is highly recommended). Tetanus occurs when a wound becomes infected by a bacterium that lives in soil and in human or animal faeces. Clean all cuts, punctures and bites. Tetanus is also known as lockjaw and the first symptom may be difficulty in swallowing, a stiffening of the jaw and neck followed by painful convulsions of the jaw and whole body.

Rabies This is a fatal viral infection. A prophylactic rabies vaccination should be considered if you intend to travel to places more than two days away from medical help, or if you anticipate spending a lot of time around animals.

Throughout Bolivia, but especially in the humid lowlands, rodents and bats carry the rabies virus and pass it on to larger animals and humans. Avoid any animal that appears to be foaming at the mouth or acting strangely. Stray dogs are particularly notable carriers, as are bats, especially vampire bats, which are common in the Amazon Basin. Make sure you cover all parts of your body at night, especially your feet and scalp.

Any bite, scratch or even lick from a mammal should be cleaned immediately and thoroughly. Scrub with soap and running water for at least five minutes and then clean with iodine or an alcohol solution. This greatly reduces your risk of contracting rabies, but if there's any possibility that the animal is infected with rabies, you must still seek medical help. (Even if the animal isn't rabid, all bites should be treated seriously as they can become infected or result in tetanus.)

If you're bitten or scratched by a suspicious animal, you must have a booster or, if you're not immune, a course of vaccine and immunoglobulin. The virus is incurable and fatal if it reaches the brain and the symptoms appear, but it moves very slowly; although you should seek medical treatment as quickly as possible, there's no reason to panic.

Rabies vaccinations and treatment are available at the Unidad Sanitario Centro Piloto in La Paz (see the Medical Services section in the La Paz chapter).

Meningococcal Meningitis This very serious disease is spread by close contact with people who carry it in their throats and noses. They probably aren't aware they are carriers and pass it on through coughs and sneezes. Meningococcal meningitis attacks the brain and can be fatal. A scattered blotchy rash, fever, severe headache, sensitivity to light and stiffness in the neck preventing forward bending of the head are the first symptoms. Death can occur within a few hours, so immediate treatment with large doses of penicillin is vital. If intravenous administration is impossible, it should be given intramuscularly. Vaccination offers reasonable protection for over a year, but you should check for reports of recent outbreaks and try to avoid affected areas.

Tuberculosis If you will be travelling for more than three months in South America, you should consider TB risk. As most healthy adults do not develop symptoms, a skin test before and after travel to determine whether exposure has occurred is recommended. Vaccination for children who will be travelling for more than three months is recommended.

Insect-Borne Diseases

Malaria This serious disease is spread by mosquito bites. The areas of greatest risk include the Amazon Basin, the Chaco and the eastern lowlands.

Symptoms include loss of appetite, fever, chills and sweating, which may subside and recur. Without treatment malaria can develop more serious, potentially fatal effects.

There are a number of different types of malaria. The one of most concern is *Plasmodium falciparum*. This is responsible for the very serious cerebral malaria.

Malaria is curable, as long as you seek medical help when symptoms occur, either at home or overseas.

Prevention The most effective form of malaria prevention, of course, is to avoid being bitten by mosquitoes. The mosquitoes that transmit malaria bite from dusk to dawn but you can avoid bites by covering bare skin with trousers and long-sleeved shirts and using an insect repellent. It helps to wear light-coloured clothing, and use a repellent containing DEET (diethylmetatoluamide) on exposed areas of skin (overuse of DEET may be

Area of Malaria Risk

harmful, especially to children, but its use is considered preferable to being bitten by disease-transmitting mosquitoes). An alternative would be Mosi-Guard Natural, which matches the efficacy of DEET but isn't so harsh on the skin. Avoid strongly scented perfumes or aftershave, and sleep under a mosquito net.

Next best – but hardly 100% effective – is a course of antimalarials, which is normally taken two weeks before, during and several weeks after travelling in malarial areas.

The drug-resistant status of different malarial strains is constantly in flux. Expert advice should be sought regarding your choice of antimalarials, as there are many factors to consider, including the area to be visited, the risk of exposure to malaria-carrying mosquitoes, your medical history, and your age and pregnancy status. It is also important to discuss the side-effect profile of the medication, so you can work out some level of risk versus benefit ratio, and it's very important that you be sure of the correct dosage of the medication prescribed to you.

A commonly recommended prophylaxis for lowland areas of South America is chloroquine, although local strains are growing increasingly resistant to it. As a result, many doctors are recommending newer drugs, such as doxycycline (Vibramycin, Doryx) and mefloquine (Lariam). Don't switch to chloroquine, however, if you've been taking mefloquine previously; they make a potentially dangerous combination. Note also that Lariam has been associated with serious and distressing side effects.

Diagnosis & Treatment Malarial symptoms include (in this order) gradual loss of appetite, malaise, weakness, alternating shivering and hot flushes, diarrhoea, periodic high fever, severe headache, vomiting and hallucinations.

If you develop malarial symptoms, seek medical advice immediately. Diagnosis is confirmed by a simple blood test.

Chagas' Disease There is very little possibility of contracting this disease, which is caused by a parasite (*Trypanosoma cruzi*) transmitted through the bite of the ominously-named assassin bug – locally known as the *vinchuca* beetle. This beetle mainly inhabits thatch and daub huts at up to 2800m elevation.

The parasite causes progressive constriction and hardening of blood vessels, swelling of internal organs and increasing strain on the heart. At present there is no cure and Chagas' is fatal over a period of years. Mind-boggling estimates suggest that at least 25% of Bolivia's population suffers from this disease.

The best prevention is to avoid thatched-roof huts and to use a mosquito net or a hammock if you sleep in a thatched building. Bites are generally painful, and may cause a slight, hard violet-coloured swelling at the site of the bite or around the eyes. If you are bitten, wash the affected area well and don't scratch the bite or the parasite may be rubbed into the wound. The disease is only treatable if caught early, so if you are bitten, seek medical attention or perhaps even visit the Chagas Institute at the University of San Simón in Cochabamba. A blood test six weeks after the bite will confirm whether or not the disease is present.

Dengue Fever Incidences of dengue fever have been reported in low-lying jungle areas, especially in Beni and Pando departments. There is no prophylactic available for this mosquito-transmitted disease; the main preventative measure is to avoid mosquito bites. A sudden onset of fever, headaches and severe joint and muscle pains are the first signs before a rash starts on the trunk of the body and spreads to the limbs and face. After another few days, the fever will subside and recovery should begin. If it doesn't, professional attention, preferably in a hospital, should be sought immediately.

Leishmaniasis This disease – which can become truly horrible if untreated – is a protozoan transmitted at night in the bite of the Amazonian blood-sucking sandfly. These flies are ubiquitous throughout lowland Bolivia, particularly in moist forest. The first symptom is a bug bite that won't heal (it's easy to confuse with an infected tick bite). The external version of the disease attacks the skin and may leave severe scarring; the internal form, known as kala-azar, attacks the liver, spleen or bone marrow and can cause infection, organ enlargement and anaemia.

If left untreated, the infection will become systemic and begin to attack the body's cartilage, and eventually lead to death by gangrene. Not pleasant at all. The prescribed treatment is a course of drugs containing antimony.

Worms Worms are common throughout the humid tropics. They can live on unwashed vegetables or in undercooked meat, or you can pick them up through your skin by walking barefoot. Infestations may not be obvious for some time and although they aren't generally serious, they can cause health problems if left untreated. If there's a chance you have contracted them, take a stool test when you return home. Once confirmed, over-the-counter medication is available to clear it out.

Myiasis This very unpleasant affliction is caused by the larvae of tropical flies, which lay their eggs on damp or sweaty clothing. One of the most common offenders in lowland Bolivia is the botfly. The eggs of this fly hatch and the larvae burrow into the skin, producing a painful lump (or, if it becomes infected, an ugly boil) as they develop. To kill the invader, place drops of hydrogen peroxide, alcohol or oil over the boil to cut off its air supply, then squeeze the lump to remove the bug. However revolting the process, at this stage the problem is solved.

Yellow Fever Yellow fever is endemic in much of South America, including the Amazon Basin and southern lowland areas. This viral disease, which is transmitted to humans by mosquitoes, first manifests itself with fever, headache, abdominal pain and vomiting. There may appear to be a brief recovery before it progresses into its more severe stages when liver failure becomes a possibility. There is no treatment apart from keeping the fever as low as possible and avoiding dehydration. The yellow-fever vaccination, which is highly recommended for every traveller in South America, offers good protection for 10 years.

Cuts, Bites, & Stings

Cuts & Scratches The warm, moist conditions of the tropical lowlands invite and promote the growth of 'wee beasties' that would be thwarted in more temperate climates. As a result, even a small cut or scratch can become painfully infected and lead to more serious problems.

The best treatment for cuts is to frequently cleanse the affected area with soap and water and apply an antiseptic cream. Where possible, avoid using Band-aids and bandages, which keep wounds moist. If, despite this, the wound becomes tender and inflamed, then use of a mild, broad-spectrum antibiotic may be warranted.

Snakebite Although threat of snakebite is minimal in Bolivia, you may wish to take precautions if you're walking around the forested northern areas. The most dangerous snakes native to Bolivia are the bushmaster and the fer-de-lance, which inhabit the northern and eastern lowlands. To minimise chances of being bitten, wear boots, socks and long trousers when walking through undergrowth. A good pair of canvas gaiters will further protect your legs. Don't put your hands into holes and crevices and be careful when collecting firewood. Check shoes, clothing and sleeping bags before use.

Snakebites do not cause instantaneous death and antivenenes are usually available, but it is vital that you make a positive identification of the snake in question, or at the very least, have a detailed description of it. Keep the victim calm and still, wrap the bitten limb as you would for a sprain and then attach a splint to immobilise it. Tourniquets and suction on the wound are now comprehensively discredited. Seek medical help immediately, and if possible, bring the dead snake along for identification (but don't attempt to catch it if there is even a remote chance of being bitten again). Bushwalkers who are (wisely) concerned about snakebite should carry a field guide with photos and detailed descriptions of the possible perpetrators.

Insects Ants, gnats, mosquitoes, bees and flies will be just as annoying in Bolivia as they are at home. Cover yourself well with clothing and use insect repellent on exposed skin. Burning incense and sleeping under mosquito nets in air-conditioned rooms or under fans also lowers the risk of being bitten. If you're going to be walking in humid or densely foliated areas, wear light cotton trousers and shoes, not shorts and sandals or thongs. Regardless of temperature, never wear shorts or thongs in the forest, and remember to carry an effective insect repellent. Astringent Australian tea-tree oil works remarkably well on non-infected bites, to dry up the bite and minimise the itching.

Unless you're allergic, bee and wasp stings are more painful than dangerous. Calamine lotion offers some relief and ice packs will reduce pain and swelling. Anyone with bee-sting allergy should avoid parts of the Amazon Basin – particularly Noel Kempff Mercado National Park – during the enormous bee hatch-outs, which can occur anytime between September and December.

If you're camping in the northern bush, check your socks, shoes, hat and sleeping bag before inserting any part of your body. Scorpions and centipedes are particularly unpleasant and although their stings aren't normally fatal, the effects can be quite painful. Also, large and hairy spiders – as well as several smaller black ones – may deliver a painful bite.

Body lice and scabies mites are also common, and a number of shampoos and creams are available to eliminate them. In addition to hair and skin, clothing and bedding should be washed thoroughly to prevent further infestation.

Sexually Transmitted Diseases

Gonorrhoea & Syphilis Sexual contact with an infected partner can spread a number of unpleasant diseases. Abstinence is the only guaranteed preventative measure, but if this isn't for you, use of a condom will considerably lessen your risks. The most common of these diseases are gonorrhoea and syphilis, which in men first appear as sores, blisters or rashes around the genitals and pain or discharge when urinating. Symptoms may be less marked or not evident at all in women. The symptoms of syphilis eventually disappear completely but the disease continues and may cause severe problems in later years. Antibiotics are used to treat both syphilis and gonorrhoea.

HIV/AIDS HIV, the Human Immunodeficiency Virus, may develop into AIDS, Acquired Immune Deficiency Syndrome. Although HIV/AIDS hasn't yet reached staggering proportions in Bolivia, it is prevalent in neighbouring Brazil to a degree unfamiliar to most Western travellers, and should be a concern to all visitors.

Any exposure to blood, blood products or bodily fluids may put the individual at risk. Although in developed countries it's most commonly spread through intravenous drug abuse and male homosexual activity, in South America it is transmitted primarily through heterosexual activity. Apart from abstinence, the most effective preventative is always to practise safe sex using condoms. It is impossible to detect the HIV-positive status of an otherwise healthy-looking person without a blood test.

HIV/AIDS can also be spread through infected blood transfusions. If you must have an emergency transfusion, private clinics are generally a better option than public hospitals but if you're able, you should still try to make absolutely certain that the blood in question is safe.

HIV is also spread by dirty needles – vaccinations, acupuncture, tattooing and ear or nose piercing are potentially as dangerous as intravenous drug use if the equipment isn't clean. If you do need an injection, ask to see the syringe unwrapped in front of you, or buy a new syringe from a pharmacy and ask the doctor to use it. You may also want to carry a couple of syringes, in case of emergency.

Fear of HIV infection should never preclude treatment for serious medical conditions. Although there may be a risk of infection, it is very small indeed.

Women's Health
Gynaecological Problems Poor diet, lowered resistance due to use of antibiotics, and even contraceptive pills can lead to vaginal infections when travelling in hot climates. To prevent the worst of it, maintain good personal hygiene, wear cotton underwear and skirts or loose-fitting trousers.

Yeast infections, characterised by a rash, itch and discharge, can be treated with a vinegar or lemon juice douche or with yoghurt. Nystatin, micronazole or clotrimazole suppositories are the usual medical prescription. Trichomoniasis and gardnerella are more serious infection that cause a smelly discharge and sometimes a burning sensation when urinating. Male sexual partners must also be treated and if a vinegar and water douche is not effective, medical attention should be sought. Metronidazole (Flagyl) is the most frequently prescribed drug.

Pregnancy Most miscarriages occur during the first trimester of pregnancy, so this is the most risky time to be travelling. The last three months should also be spent within reasonable reach of good medical care since serious problems can develop at this stage as well. Pregnant women should avoid all unnecessary medication, but vaccinations and malarial prophylactics should still be taken where possible. Additional care should be taken to prevent illness and particular attention to diet and proper nutrition will significantly lessen the chances of complications.

TOILETS & PLUMBING
Much Bolivian plumbing is jerry-built or poorly installed and inferior to what you're probably used to. Bathtubs and hot and cold running water are rare outside upmarket tourist hotels, but you can still have hot (or tepid) showers, thanks to a deadly-looking device that attaches to the shower head and electrically heats the water as it passes through. Bare wires run from the ceiling into the shower head (if they're dangling from the ceiling, you won't have a hot shower because the device is broken).

On the wall, you'll find a lever that suspiciously resembles an electrocutioner's switch, sometimes known as a 'Frankenstein switch'. Fortunately, later models of the device allow the switch to remain permanently engaged, so you don't actually have to flip it when the water is running. When the water is turned on – leave your shoes on for this – the heater is activated, and will begin to emit an electrical humming sound. Normally, the lights in the room will dim or go out altogether due to the great deal of electricity required to operate the contraption effectively.

The water temperature can then be adjusted by increasing or decreasing the flow. However, because a large volume of water cannot be adequately heated in the time it spends passing through the shower head, a shower of a bearable temperature is often little more than a pressureless drip. Don't touch the metal valves during your shower; few of these devices are properly earthed (grounded) and you may get an electric shock. When you're finished, don't touch the valves until you're dry and have your shoes on. (This may be tricky, especially if the shower cubicle is small.)

The toilet or WC is commonly called *el baño*, or it may be misnamed *servicio sanitario* or *servicio higiénico*. Usually neither sanitary nor hygienic, facilities can be unspeakable. In markets and transport terminals, you'll pay US$0.10 to US$0.20 to use them. This investment typically yields two sheets of one-ply toilet paper, which, if you're normal, won't do the job. Most

Bolivians carry a roll of toilet paper wherever they go.

Since water pressure is typically weak, few toilets can even choke down shit, let alone toilet paper, so a wastebasket is usually provided; if there's no receptacle or if it's full, toss the used paper on the floor and someone will clean it up. In rural areas, toilets tend to be more basic; for example, a hole in a corner of the pig sty.

WOMEN TRAVELLERS

Bolivia is still very much a man's country, and for a woman travelling alone, this can prove frustrating. Things are changing – Bolivia has had a woman president, Lidia Gueiller Tejada (1979-80), and from 1993 to 1995, Mónica Medina de Palenque served as mayor of La Paz. Even so, the machismo mind-set remains and the mere fact that you appear to be unmarried and far from your home and family may cause you to appear suspiciously disreputable.

Because many South American men have become acquainted with foreign women through such reliable media as girlie magazines and North American films and TV, the concept of *gringa fácil* ('loose foreign woman'), has developed. Since Bolivia has cultural roots in southern Europe, it has been subjected to over four centuries of machismo and many men consider foreign women – especially those travelling alone – to be fair and willing game. Fortunately, the recent increase in tourism to Bolivia has meant that locals are becoming more accustomed to seeing Western travellers, including unaccompanied women. This has significantly reduced the amount of sexual harassment you're likely to encounter – it was much worse 10 years ago – but in some places, you may still have to contend with uncomfortable attention.

It may be useful to remember that at least some of the time, problem behaviour is the consequence of simple ignorance. Unequivocal insults or blatant arrogance on a woman's part may derail obnoxious suitors, but more often, it will simply amuse them and may even reinforce the undesirable behaviour. If you can't ignore the comments – as well-bred Bolivian women would be expected to do – it may help to convey (in Spanish) that you expect to be treated with more respect. Uttering a thinly veiled insult, such as *hombres civilizados respetan mas a las mujeres* ('civilised men have more respect for women') may hit the mark.

For your part, bear in mind that modesty is expected of women in much of Spanish-speaking Latin America. Short sleeves are more or less acceptable but hemlines shouldn't be above knee level and trousers should be loose-fitting. In general, the lower the altitude in Bolivia, the more liberal the dress code. The best advice is to watch the standards of well-dressed Bolivian women in any particular area and follow their example.

A 100% effective alternative is to find a male travelling companion, but then you may have to contend with being ignored while Bolivians direct their comments to your companion – even if you speak Spanish and he doesn't! In any case, if you prefer to travel alone, it's wise to avoid such male domains as bars, sports matches, mines, construction sites and the like. It's all right to catch a lift on a *camión* (truck), especially if there are lots of other people waiting, but otherwise, women shouldn't hitch alone.

GAY & LESBIAN TRAVELLERS

Naturally, homosexuality exists in Bolivia and is fairly widespread among rural indigenous communities. It's also perfectly legal (though the constitution does prohibit same-sex marriages), but the overwhelmingly Catholic society tends to both deny and suppress it, and to be openly gay in Bolivia limits vocational and social opportunities and may cause family ostracism. Government attitudes are equally draconian, and describe homosexuality as 'a problem'. Bolivia currently has three active gay rights lobby groups: MGLP Libertad, Casilla 10471, La Paz; Dignidad, in Cochabamba; and UNELDYS, in Santa Cruz. They are working to launch a national newspaper and take their cause to the government.

Gay bars and venues are limited to the larger cities, but because of problems with bashings and police raids, they come and go with some regularity. The only one I'm currently aware of is Cherry, in the north of La Paz, but I suspect there must be several in liberal Cochabamba and refreshingly cosmopolitan Santa Cruz. As for hotels, sharing a room is no problem as long as you don't request a double bed. The bottom line is that discretion is probably in order – at least for a while!

DISABLED TRAVELLERS

Bolivian businesses and services make very few concessions to disabilities; wheelchair ramps are available only at a few upmarket hotels and restaurants, and most Bolivian public transport will be especially challenging for anyone with mobility problems.

You may also want to prepare for image problems. The relatively enlightened attitudes toward disability that prevail in most Western countries haven't yet taken hold in Bolivia. Here, as in much of the developing world, people with visible disabilities may be expected to turn to professional begging or selling telephone tokens, and are often exploited by unscrupulous characters. Launching a personal crusade to set everyone straight probably won't do much good, but disabled travellers who can discuss their jobs, educational background, opportunities – and even problems – at home may well inspire some Bolivians to rethink their society's attitudes toward disability.

Organisations

For assistance and advice specific to individual needs, disabled travellers in the USA might like to contact the Society for the Advancement of Travel for the Handicapped (☎ (212) 447-SATH); fax (212) 725 8253), 347 Fifth Ave, Suite 610, New York, NY 10016. A one-year subscription to its quarterly magazine, *Access to Travel*, costs US$13. In the UK, a useful contact is the Royal Association for Disability & Rehabilitation (☎ (0171) 242 3882), 25 Mortimer St, London W1N 8AB.

USEFUL ORGANISATIONS

One of the most useful resources for visitors to South America is the South American Explorers Club (☎ (607) 277 0488, fax (607) 277 6122), 126 Indian Creek Rd, Ithaca, NY 14850, USA. This organisation provides information and support to travellers, researchers, mountaineers and explorers; sells a wide range of books, guides and maps for South America; and publishes a quarterly journal and a mail order catalogue.

The club also maintains clubhouses in Ecuador (☎ & fax 225228, e-mail explorer@saec.org.ec), at Jorge Washington 311 and Leonidas Plaza Gutiérrez, Mariscal Sucre, Quito, and in Peru (☎ (014) 314480), at República de Portugal 146, Casilla 3714, Lima. Considering the substantial package of benefits offered, membership is quite a bargain.

The counterpart in Germany is the Lateinamerikanischer Freundeskreis e.V. (☎ (0421) 239245, fax (0421) 234267), Schwachhauser Heerstrasse 222, D-28213, Bremen, Germany.

The Latin American Travel Consultants, PO Box 17-17-908, Quito, Ecuador (fax (02) 562566, e-mail rku@pi.pro.ec) publishes a quarterly news bulletin, *The Latin American Travel Advisor*, which features news on travel, public safety, health, climate, costs and so on for travellers in the region. Books, maps and videos are available by mail order. For WWW internet access, visit http://www.amerspan.com/latc.

A useful contact in the UK is the Latin American Bureau (☎ (0171) 278 2829, fax (0171) 278 0165), 1 Amwell St, London EC1R 1UL, which keeps up to date with all Latin American happenings, and publishes a growing list of titles dealing with politics, culture and travel throughout the region. The organisation is also an active proponent of political fairness and human rights issues in the region.

Hostelling International

For information about Bolivia's hostelling organisation, Asociación Boliviana de Albergues Juveniles, contact Valmar Tours, (☎ 361076, fax 328433), Edificio Alborada,

1st floor, Oficina 105, Juan de la Riva 1406, Casilla 4294, La Paz.

DANGERS & ANNOYANCES
Security

Although many visitors are apprehensive about security in Bolivia, it is in fact one of the safest – if not *the* safest – of Latin American countries. Bolivians habitually refer to their country as *muy tranquilo* ('very calm') and serious or violent crime is extremely rare – and is almost always perpetrated by foreigners (most often Peruvians) who regard Bolivians as naïve about security. In fact, violent crime elicits the same incredulous lament in Bolivia that it does in some Western countries.

In all my travels in Bolivia, I've never had anything of value stolen (touch wood!). One exception was in the first few moments of my first touchdown in Bolivia, when an airline baggage handler apparently rifled through my pack and removed what appeared to be a chocolate bar. It was in fact a laxative bar, so it can be assumed that justice was served shortly thereafter.

On my most recent trip, a friend and I were waiting for a minibus when he discovered that his wallet, which contained his passport and several hundred dollars, was missing. Assuming that it had been pinched on an earlier minibus trip, he began planning a trip to the British embassy to replace the passport. As a precaution, however, we decided to retrace our steps and see whether he'd left it somewhere. Sure enough, when we walked into the shop where he'd made several photocopies an hour earlier, he saw the wallet lying on the shelf behind the desk, unopened and with all its contents intact.

As a traveller, the biggest worries you're likely to encounter will be petty thievery and the odd crooked official. Foreigners, who may be visibly unfamiliar with the turf and possibly the language, are quite easy to pick out in a crowd, and even if you consider yourself an impecunious traveller, people may assume you're carrying an expensive camera and lots of money.

The detail in the following sections is aimed mainly at readers with limited experience in Latin America, and offers suggestions for mitigating or foiling attempted theft or the irregular conduct of officials. The intent isn't to inspire paranoia, which is certainly unwarranted in Bolivia, but to demonstrate that there are many things travellers can do to reduce the minimal risks. It may also contain useful advice for travellers approaching Bolivia through areas that do pose greater risks, such as parts of Colombia, Peru and Brazil.

Predeparture Precautions If you work on the elements of vulnerability, risks can be minimised. For starters, only take items you are prepared to lose or replace. Travel insurance is essential for replacement of valuables and the cost of a good policy is worthwhile if it limits disturbance to or abrupt termination of your travel plans. Loss through violence or petty theft can be an emotional and stressful experience, and an insurance policy can relieve some of the sting.

The less you carry, the less you have to lose. Don't travel with jewellery, gold chains or expensive watches; if you need a watch, wear a cheapie.

Precautions on the Road There are key things you can do to reduce attention from unsavouries. Before arriving in a new place, have a map or at least a rough idea about orientation. Plan your schedule so you don't arrive at night, and use a taxi if you're unsure about security. Most of all, stay observant and learn to move like a street-smart local. Also, the extra pair of eyes provided by a travelling companion is an obvious asset.

Your style of dress should be casual and inexpensive. If you carry a daypack, secure the zips with safety pins and wear it on your front. Whenever you have to put your daypack down, put your foot through the strap.

If you have a camera, don't wander around with it dangling over your shoulder or around your neck – keep it out of sight as much as possible. It's also unwise to keep it in a swanky camera bag as this will attract attention. It may help to carry your camera gear in a sturdy plastic bag from a local supermarket.

If you must carry valuables, for example if you're on your way to the bus station, don't keep them all together. Distribute them about your person and baggage to avoid having all your eggs in one basket, so to speak. Leather or cotton money belts can be worn around the waist, neck or shoulder, but competent thieves know all about them and they'll be a prime target. In any case, a money belt will provide some measure of protection only if it's worn *under* clothing; external pouches attract attention and are easy prey. An alternative would be to use cloth pouches sewn into trousers or attached under clothes with safety pins. Other methods include belts with concealed zipper compartments, and bandages or pouches worn around the leg.

Keep small change and a few banknotes in a shirt pocket, to pay for bus tickets and small expenses without having to extract large amounts of money. This small and easily accessible stash would also be useful if you're assailed by a mugger. If you carry a wallet, keep it in a zippered or buttoned inside pocket and don't use it on public transport or in crowded places.

When changing money on the street, follow the advice given in the Money section earlier in this chapter.

Favourite Scams

Distraction is a common tactic employed by street thieves. The simple 'cream technique' is now common throughout South America, including Bolivia. The trick commences when you're on the street or standing in a public place, and someone surreptitiously slops a substance on your shoulder, back or daypack. It can be anything from mustard to chocolate or even dog muck. An assistant (young or old, male or female) then taps you on the shoulder and amicably offers to clean off the mess...if you'll just put down your bag for a second. If you foolishly agree, the bag disappears. Ignore any such attempt or offer and simply endure your mucky state until you can find a safe place to wash.

Druggings have also been reported in neighbouring countries, but I've never heard of an instance in Bolivia. You may still want to be wary of cigarettes, beer, sweets etc proffered by strangers. If the circumstances appear suspicious, the offer can be gently refused by claiming medical problems.

Also beware of scams involving travellers claiming to have had all their money and belongings stolen, and asking for handouts from other travellers. However tempted you are to donate ('There but for the grace of God...' syndrome), first try to ascertain the validity of the appeal. This practice is particularly rife around Santa Cruz.

Scams are continuously being developed and transmutated across borders. Stay aware of changes by talking to other travellers, but don't let the stories get to you. Theft and security are sources of endless fascination for travellers; some of the stories are true, some are incredible, and some are taller than Illimani!

Streets & Public Transport

Follow the general guidelines outlined in the Security Precautions section above.

Thieves watch for people leaving hotels, bus terminals, railway stations, banks, casas de cambio, tourist sights – places with lots of foreigners – then follow their targets. If you notice you're being followed or closely observed, it may help to pause and look straight at the person(s) involved. You can also simply point out the person(s) to a travelling companion. The element of surprise favoured by petty criminals will then have been lost.

Long-distance bus and train travel is usually well organised. If you hand over luggage to be placed in the baggage compartment, make sure you receive and keep your receipt. If you give your luggage to a baggage handler, make sure it goes into the hold or onto the roof – and that it stays there. On my recent update trip, a Villazón baggage handler, who assumed that I'd already got on the bus, was caught trying to disappear with my pack into a warehouse across the street. It may help to padlock two or more items together in the hold or on the roof of a bus or on a rack in the train, making them awkward to carry off. If you place luggage on overhead racks, watch it closely or padlock it to the rack.

Taxis Although Bolivian taxi drivers are no different than their counterparts worldwide when it comes to arbitrary fare augmentation, more serious taxi problems are very rare in Bolivia.

Unless you are somewhere where taxis use a set fare (which is standard in Bolivian cities) and you know what it is, ascertain the price before climbing into a taxi. A disinterested party, such as a shopkeeper, will naturally provide better information than a taxi driver. Around large hotels or bus and railway stations, quoted fares are likely to be triple the actual standard rates. It's better to walk 200m down the road and start your haggling there.

When entering or leaving a taxi, keep a passenger door open during the loading or unloading of luggage – particularly if this is being done by someone other than the driver. This reduces the ease with which a taxi can drive off with the luggage, leaving the passenger behind! If there's space, try to fit luggage inside the taxi rather than in the boot (trunk). If you're not travelling alone, have at least one person remain close to the open passenger door or inside the taxi whenever luggage is still inside.

On Hiking Trails While most hikes in Bolivia can be considered safe, over the past few years, there has been an escalation in theft and robbery on a couple of Bolivia's hiking trails. The country's most popular route, La Cumbre to Coroico, has seen an upsurge in problems and a few violent robberies. There have also been several rather distressing attacks on the El Camino del Oro between Sorata and Guanay. The latter, however, have been distinctly 'un-Bolivian' in nature and it's assumed that they've been imported from across the Peruvian border.

Fortunately, most trail robberies involve relatively innocuous techniques – mainly

tent-slashing – which occurs while the victims are asleep. The best prevention for this sort of thing is to keep everything inside your tent and camp well off the trail and out of sight. Potential troublemakers know all the best camp sites and the only way to foil them is to select an improbable spot.

Perhaps the best advice for worry-free hiking is to leave your valuables elsewhere and carry only what cash you need for the trip. In the unlikely event that you do meet with threatening demands on the trail (in the absence of a serious weapon, of course), it may help to feign ignorance of Spanish – just shrug your shoulders and keep on walking – or simply ignore the crisis at hand and do something totally unexpected. For example, laugh and ask for the time, pick up three stones and start to juggle, start babbling in Spanish about some unrelated topic or simply smile and extend your hand in friendly greeting. Unless the would-be perpetrator is a real professional, they'll probably be thrown off balance long enough for you to make a polite exit.

There has been a recent increase of equipment theft from climbers' camps. If you're on an expedition, particularly on popular peaks such as Illimani and Huayna Potosí, always leave someone in camp to look after your gear.

In Hotels If you consider your hotel to be reliable, place valuables in the hotel safe and get a receipt. Pack your valuables in a small zippered bag and padlock it, or use a signed seal that will easily reveal tampering. Count money and travellers cheques before and after retrieving them from the safe.

In dodgy hotels, check the door, doorframe and windows of your room for signs of forced entry or unsecured access. To decrease the number of people with access to your room, it's better to use your own combination lock (or padlock) than the hotel padlock. Although you'd be ill advised to leave valuables in your hotel room, some travellers padlock baggage to room fixtures or tape items in concealed places. If you take the tape route, however, don't leave your valuables behind as a windfall for the cleaner!

Police & Fake Police Scams

If you have something stolen, report it to the police. No big investigation is going to occur, but you will get a police statement for your insurance company. Unfortunately, Bolivian police often attempt to extract 'fees' from individuals – particularly foreigners, whom they assume are trying to scam their insurance companies – for such statements.

However, there is a series of more mundane scams associated with police and characters purporting to be police or other law enforcement officials. Foreigners may be stopped by someone claiming to be a police officer who asks to see their money and passport. This often happens shortly after they've made the acquaintance of a stooge, a 'fellow traveller' from Peru, Chile or elsewhere, and have become engaged in conversation. The 'fellow traveller' immediately complies with the 'police officer's request as if it were routine. When the foreigner follows suit, the accomplices clean them out and disappear.

In my case, the 'stooge' was a 'Chilean tourist', who I ran into...After we'd chatted for a couple of minutes – he was carrying a small shoulder bag and said he was en route to the railway station to catch the train to La Paz – we were stopped by a gentleman who claimed to be a police officer and asked us to show him our passports. Before I could even glance at the ID card he was waving, the so-called Chilean had grabbed hold of it, made a show of perusing it quickly, nodded his approval and gave it back. After that, the 'policeman' looked at our passports and asked us to follow him to the 'oficina'. Of course, the Chilean tourist pretended that this was a routine procedure and that he didn't see any reason not to comply with this request.

As we followed the 'police officer' he continued talking to me, probably in order to prevent me from thinking and deciding upon a course of action. It wasn't until the alleged police officer flagged down a taxi that I came to my senses and decided that the time for action had arrived. The only thing I could think of was waving a finger at the police officer and grabbing my passport, which he had been holding all along. As I walked away, he made no attempt to stop me, but

jumped into the taxi, followed by the Chilean tourist. Another police officer – presumably a real one this time, since he wore a uniform – stopped another taxi and asked the driver to follow it.

The timing was so perfect that for a moment I was tempted to think that the second police officer was also in on the conspiracy, though I haven't the faintest idea what the point of such a conspiracy would have been!

Martin Bottenberg, Netherlands

This 'friendly fellow tourist' scam is a current favourite and is popping up all over South America (one wonders if there's a training school for this sort of thing). Although this incident happened in Oruro, the worst places appear to be La Paz, Cochabamba and Sucre. As the story reveals, real police are starting to crack down on these fraudulent characters.

Another common scenario proceeds as follows: a traveller is stopped on the street by a 'plainclothes police officer' with a fake ID, who asks the traveller to accompany them in a taxi to the police station. Once inside the taxi, the traveller's belongings are 'inspected' and valuables 'confiscated'. If you're stopped, insist upon full proof of their identity and *never* get into a taxi with anyone claiming to be a police officer, as it will invariably be a setup. If they don't back off, make a note of their ID and insist on phoning the station or going on foot. At this stage, they'll probably take off in search of an easier target.

In most parts of Bolivia you can contact the Radio Patrulla (Police Radio Patrol) by dialling 110.

Border Crossings

Travellers crossing the Peru-Bolivia border at Yunguyo/Copacabana have reported that their Bolivian entry stamp had been dated one day *ahead* of the day of entry. This was simply a set-up for a 'fine' later in the day. The obvious advice is to check your date stamp carefully at the border and, if incorrect, insist that it be corrected.

Villazón is particularly notorious for uniformed police who stop foreigners, alleging that they must confiscate any 'illegal' US dollar notes the travellers may be carrying. (Of course, dollars are not illegal anywhere in Bolivia.) Hide your cash well, leave it in your hotel or tell the offender you only carry travellers cheques (this worked for me).

Drugs

Bolivia may be the land of cocaine, but rumours that a cheap and abundant supply is readily available to the general public are unfounded. Refined cocaine is highly illegal in Bolivia – the standard sentence for possession of cocaine in Bolivia is eight years – so it's clearly best left alone.

The big guys get away with processing and exporting because they're able to bribe their way around the regulations. Backpacking foreigners and coca-producing Indians become statistics to wave at foreign governments (particularly the USA) as proof, if you will, that Bolivia is doing something about its drug problem. Although foreign travellers are only rarely searched these days, it's still unwise to carry drugs of any kind, even in small quantities. The consequences are too costly.

If you choose to ignore this advice and the worst happens – you're caught with drugs and arrested – the safest bet is to pay off the arresting officer(s) before more officials learn about your plight and want to be cut in on the deal. It's best not to call the payoff a bribe per se. Ask something like: *¿Como podemos arreglar este asunto?'* ('How can we put this matter right?'). They'll understand what you mean. If this seems unethical, you've never seen the inside of a Bolivian prison.

If the officer refuses, then you're on your own. As in the case of drug plants (see earlier in this section), foreign embassies are powerless and in most cases, they simply don't want to know.

Begging

For many, one of the most disconcerting aspects of travel in Bolivia is the constant presence of beggars. With no social welfare system to sustain them, elderly, disabled,

mentally ill and jobless people take to the streets, hoping to arouse sympathy.

Since donating even a pittance to every beggar encountered would be financially impossible for most visitors, each traveller has to make an individual decision about what constitutes an appropriately humanitarian response. Some choose to give only to the most pathetic cases or to those enterprising individuals who provide some value for money, such as by singing or playing a musical instrument. Others simply feel that contributions only serve to fuel the machine that creates beggars, and ignore the whining cries that haunt Bolivian streets.

The best I can offer on this issue is a couple of guidelines. Mentally indigent or elderly people who would appear to have no other possible means of support may be especially good candidates. For anyone who appears truly hungry, an offer of food will go a long way. The physically disabled are always underemployed, often relegated to selling lottery tickets or telephone tokens, but they do manage to earn something. Keep in mind, however, that many families simply set their older members on the pavement with a tin bowl hoping to generate extra income.

One ethnic group in Potosí department has even organised a begging syndicate that sends brown-clad older women into larger cities, provides them with accommodation and supplies them with suitably grubby-looking children. If I could make only one recommendation, it would be against fuelling this scam machine when there are so many genuinely needy and more deserving individuals out there. You'll know who these people are; they're always dressed in brown and accompanied by children who appear too young to be their own and often become extremely obnoxious and difficult to ignore.

Street children who must beg for a living will stand out clearly from those who have been taught to beg by well-meaning foreigners. If you hand out money, it stokes the begging tendency and leads to exploitation by unscrupulous adults; it also creates dissatisfaction with their own society and gives the impression that foreigners can always be tapped for goodies. Bolivians often complain that money given to child beggars too often winds up in the video game parlours. For a child who appears truly hungry, a piece of fruit or other healthy snack will be appreciated. If they refuse such gifts and demand money, it should be fairly obvious what's really going on.

Incorrect Information

If you're in need of information or directions, be aware that some Bolivians prefer to provide incorrect answers or directions rather than give no response at all. They're not being malicious: they merely want to please you and appear helpful and knowledgeable. It's therefore best not to take spontaneous answers at face value. Ask several people the same question and if one answer seems to prevail above the others, it's probably as close to correct as you'll find.

BUSINESS HOURS

Business hours in Bolivia are dictated largely by age-old southern European traditions, and while they can often be inconvenient for travellers accustomed to Australasian, North American or even northern European opening hours, they provide incentive for travellers to synchronise with the local rhythms.

Although more and more places are recognising a market opportunity in serving an early breakfast, few restaurants that serve breakfast roll up their aluminium doors before 9 or 9.30 am. If you're desperate for a caffeine fix, however, you'll usually find something, even if it's just the market food stalls. Similarly, shops, travel agencies and financial institutions open at about 9 or 10 am. Early morning shopping opportunities are limited to the street markets where dribbles of activity begin as early as 6 am.

At noon, cities virtually close down, with the

Gift Giving

When travelling around Bolivia, particularly rural areas, some visitors may be shocked by the apparently backward and often primitive living conditions they encounter. In response, some are moved to compare the locals' lot with their own, and experience pangs of conscience and outrage at inequalities. In an attempt to salve the guilt or inspire goodwill, many indiscriminately distribute gifts of sweets, cigarettes, money and other foreign items to local children and adults.

What people from Western societies may not realise is that in Bolivia and many other developing countries, the lack of money, TV, automobiles, mod cons or expensive playthings does not necessarily indicate poverty. The people of rural Bolivia have crops, animals and homes that provide sufficient food, clothing and shelter. They work hard with the land and it, in turn, takes care of them.

While it may be difficult for Westerners to become accustomed to this lifestyle, the proud and independent highland Bolivians have known nothing else for well over 1000 years and are as comfortable with it as foreigners are in their own element. When short-term visitors hand out sweets or cigarettes, they cause dental and health problems that cannot be remedied locally; when they give money, they impose a foreign system of values and upset a well-established balance.

It's undoubtedly well meaning, but the long-term consequences of indiscriminate gift giving are undeniable. As more visitors venture into traditional regions, proud and independent people come to associate the outside world with limitless bounty – which appears to be theirs for the asking. Visitors are pestered with endless requests, and locals become confused as once-generous foreigners begin to regard them with contempt. Communication breaks down and the meeting of cultures becomes a strain on everyone.

If you wish to be accepted by local people, perhaps share a conversation, teach a game from home, or show a photograph of your friends or family. If you wish to make a bigger difference, you can donate money and supplies to organisations working to improve rural conditions. Alternatively, bring a supply of bandages, rehydration mixture or other medicines and leave them with the local health-care nurse (larger rural villages have a clinic), or buy a handful of pens and a stack of exercise books and give them to the school teacher. When a personal gift becomes appropriate – if you're invited for a meal, for example, or someone goes out of their way to help you – share something that won't disrupt or undermine the local culture or lifestyle, such as a piece of fruit, a bread roll or a handful of coca leaves. ■

exception of markets and restaurants serving lunch-hour crowds. The afternoon resurrection begins at around 2 pm but some businesses may remain closed until as late as 4 pm. They normally then stay open until 8 or 9 pm. Many bars and restaurants close at 10 pm, although some serve until midnight and beyond.

On Saturdays, shops, services and even some eateries close down at noon but street markets remain open at least until mid-afternoon, and often into the evening. On Sundays, nearly everything – except those businesses and snack restaurants catering to families – remains dead until evening, when a few places open.

Most post offices are open from 9 am (8.30 am for some services) to noon and 2.30 to 7 pm. Some also open on Saturdays and the GPO in La Paz opens for some services from 9 am to noon on Sundays. Most banks open from 9 to 11.30 am and 2.30 to 5 pm.

PUBLIC HOLIDAYS

Bolivian public holidays include: New Year's Day (1 January); Carnaval (February/March); Semana Santa (Easter Week: March/April); Labour Day (1 May); Corpus Christi (May); Independence Days (5-7 August); Columbus Day (12 October); All-Souls' Day or Día de los Muertos (2 November); and Christmas (25 December).

In addition, each department has its own holiday: La Paz (16 July); Tarija (15 April); Cochabamba (14 September); Santa Cruz (24 September); Pando (24 September); Beni (18 November); Oruro (22 February); Chuquisaca (25 May).

SPECIAL EVENTS

Fiestas Bolivian fiestas are invariably of religious or political origin, usually commemorating a Christian or Indian saint or god, or a political event such as a battle or revolution. They can be lots of fun and they're a chance for a home-grown experience of Bolivian culture. Fiestas typically feature lots of folk music, brass bands, dancing, processions, food and ritual, as well

as generally unrestrained merrymaking involving alcohol, water balloons (tourists are especially vulnerable!) and fireworks.

Bolivian towns stage fiestas whenever an excuse arises – mainly in the winter months. The entire month of August seems to be devoted to one fiesta or another, so at that time, you'll probably catch two or three during even a short stay. The following is a partial list of the major Bolivian festivals; listed dates are subject to change.

6 January
> *Día de los Reyes* 'Kings' Day' is celebrated as the day the three wise kings visited the baby Jesus after his birth. The largest celebrations are in Reyes (Beni); Sucre; Tarija; and rural villages in Oruro, Cochabamba and Potosí departments.

24 January
> *Alasitas* The Festival of Abundance dates from Inca times and is dedicated to Ekeko, the little household god of abundance. It's celebrated in La Paz.

February (first week)
> *La Virgen de Candelaria* This week-long festival is held in honour of the Virgin of Candelaria in Aiquile (Cochabamba); Samaipata (Santa Cruz); Angostura (Tarija) and Cha'llapampa (Oruro). The biggest celebration, however, is at Copacabana in La Paz department.

February/March (week before Lent)
> *Carnaval* Celebrations are held nationwide, but the most spectacular event is *La Diablada*, which is staged in Oruro.

March (date varies)
> *Fiesta de la Uva* This Tarija festival is dedicated to grapes, wine and the spirits derived from them.

March (2nd Sunday)
> *Phujllay* The name of this festival, which takes place in Tarabuco (Chuquisaca), means 'play' in Quechua. Phujllay (pronounced 'POOKH-yai') commemorates the Battle of Lumbati. It's one of Bolivia's largest festivals.

March or April
> *Semana Santa* One of the most impressive of the nationwide Holy Week activities is the Good Friday fiesta in Copacabana, when hundreds of pilgrims walk from La Paz to Copacabana.

15 & 16 April
> *Efemérides de Tarija & Rodeo Chapaco*; Tarija's town anniversary celebrations commemorate the battle of La Tablada culminate in a rodeo recalling the city's gaucho and Argentine connections.

3 May
> *Fiesta de la Cruz* Commemorates the cross on which Christ was crucified, and despite the sombre theme, the celebrations are quite upbeat.

The greatest revelry takes place in Tarija, with 15 days of music, parades, and alcohol consumption. The fiesta is also held in Vallegrande (Santa Cruz), Cochabamba and Copacabana (both in La Paz).

27 May

Día de la Madre Mother's Day celebrations are held nationwide. In Cochabamba, the festivities are known as *Heroínas de la Coronilla* in honour of the women and children who defended their cities and homes in the battle of 1812.

May/June

Festividad de Nuestro Señor Jesús del Gran Poder This animated festival, one of Bolivia's most lively, is held in La Paz in late May or early June. It's dedicated to the 'great power of Jesus Christ'.

June (date varies)

La Santísima Trinidad The festival of the Holy Trinity takes place in Trinidad with music, dancing and a bullfight.

24 June

San Juan Batista Held nationwide, but the largest bash takes place in Santa Cruz.

31 July

Fiesta del Santo Patrono de Moxos This unique local festival in the lovely Indian community of San Ignacio de Moxos is lively, colourful and highly worthwhile.

6 August

Independence Day Fiesta This event provides inspiration for excessive raging nationwide! The largest celebration is held at Copacabana.

10-13 August

San Lorenzo Tarija department's largest fiesta is celebrated in San Lorenzo. It features traditional Chapaco dances and musical instruments.

15-18 August

La Asunción de la Virgen de Urcupiña This festival, the largest held in Cochabamba department, is staged at Quillacollo. Other celebrations commemorating the Assumption of the Virgin Mary into Heaven are held around the country, including the famous *Virgen de Chaguaya*, which is held in Chaguaya (Tarija department).

August (last week)

Chu'tillos This festival in Potosí is dedicated to the wealth of music and dance traditions from around Bolivia and throughout South America. In recent years, music and dance troupes have come from as far away as China and the USA.

September (1st Sunday)

San Roque Although San Roque's feast day is 16 August (when canine revellers honour San Roque, the patron saint of dogs), the main Tarija celebration begins a couple of weeks later. Participants wear brightly coloured clothing, feathers and belts and the unique Chapaco music features prominently.

October (1st week)

Virgen del Rosario This celebration is held on different days in different locations, including Warnes (Santa Cruz), Tarata, Morochata and Quillacollo (Cochabamba), Tarabuco (Chuquisaca), and Viacha (La Paz) and Potosí.

1 & 2 November

Día de Todos los Santos Cemetery visits and decoration of graves nationwide.

25 December

Christmas Christmas is celebrated throughout Bolivia, but some of the most unique and colourful festivities take place in San Ignacio de Moxos (Beni) and Sucre.

The Morenos dance at the Carnaval de Oruro

ACTIVITIES
Hiking & Trekking

Hiking and trekking are among the most rewarding ways to gain an appreciation for the Andes and their many moods. Although Bolivia rivals Nepal in terms of its trekking potential, it has only recently been discovered by trekking enthusiasts.

Because so much of the country is rural, lightly populated and far from main transport routes, opportunities for trekking through wild or little-visited areas are practically limitless. A glance at a topographical sheet of any highland area will reveal a host of crisscrossing footpaths. These routes, some ancient, are used by the campesinos as links with the outside world.

As with the Himalaya, the mountain backbone of South America is not a wilderness area and has been inhabited for thousands of years by farmers and herders. Most of the popular hikes and treks in Bolivia begin near La Paz, traverse the Cordillera Real along ancient Inca routes, and end in the Yungas, but many other areas of the country are also suitable for hiking. This book includes most of the popular alternatives, but doesn't begin to exhaust the possibilities.

Most of the possible routes are traversed by outsiders very infrequently, if ever, so

High Highways

Many of the finest hiking and trekking routes in the Bolivian Andes – Taquesi, La Cumbre to Coroico, Yunga Cruz, El Camino del Oro, Chataquila to Chaunaca – follow ancient routes laid down by the Incas and their predecessors. At the height of the Inca empire, the mountain landscape was crossed with a network of routes that radiated out from Cuzco and provided administrative, trade and communications links with the rest of the empire.

For their day, these roads were marvels of engineering. In fact, explorer Alexander von Humboldt said 'The roads of the Incas were the most useful and stupendous works ever executed by humanity'. They wound up and down over some of the most rugged terrain imaginable, striking a balance between the shortest and easiest routes. Across flat or open ground, they were often wide, paved thoroughfares. On steep land, they narrowed into stone stairways or followed cobbled switchbacks up the slope. Great river gorges were spanned by spindly suspension bridges, which were constructed with the twisted fibres of the cactus-like maguey plant and maintained by nearby villages. The most famous was, of course, the bridge over the roiling and fearsome Río Apurímac in Peru, which was built around 1350 and allowed the empire to expand northward. Its cables reportedly had the thickness of a man's body, and it was supported by great stone towers erected on either rim. Over the 500 years that it hung across that deep abyss, millions of people crossed over in terror of plunging to the roaring waters below. In 1927, the bridge – and the fears – were immortalised in *The Bridge of San Luis Rey* by Thornton Wilder.

Along the roads there was a series of wayside inns known as *tambos* (the New World counterpart of the caravanserai) which were built every 20 km or so along the way. These roads weren't used only by travellers and soldiers. Because the Inca lacked the wheel or a written language, communications were handled by long-distance relay runners called *chasqui* who carried messages to and from the emperor in Cuzco. These robust lads were normally sons of officials and had to run for 14 days per month for up to a year as a portion of their taxes to the empire. A strong chasqui could run from one relay station to the next, a distance of just over three km, in under 20 minutes, which meant that even faraway Quito lay only five days from the capital at Cuzco. In *Highway of the Sun*, Victor W von Hagen wrote 'At his palace in Cuzco, the Inca dined off fresh fish delivered from the coast, a distance of 200 miles (320 km) over the highest Andes, in two days.'

As a chasqui approached a station, he'd blow a conch shell, warning the next runner to prepare to receive the message and carry it on. Messages were handed over either verbally or on chains of knotted and coloured wool known as *quipus*. This system, developed and standardised by the record-keeping caste, the *quipucamaya*, became quite sophisticated over time and facilitated communications throughout the empire. With only coloured, knotted wool, they kept records of disputes, mines, population, taxes, tribute, land distribution etc.

A useful book to read on this subject is the hard-to-find *Highway of the Sun* by von Hagen (Victor Gollancz, 1956; Plata Press, 1975), which chronicles a research journey through Peru following and studying the ancient roads. ∎

people living along them may be extremely surprised – and perhaps even frightened – at the sight of foreign trekkers. In remote areas, a Quechua or Aymara-speaking guide is essential in order to reassure the campesinos that you mean no harm. A good guide doesn't necessarily have to know the terrain in question; once you've made contact, locals will almost invariably be friendly and happy to help with directions.

If you're looking for pure Andean culture and interaction with the locals, choose your trip carefully. In the more popular trekking areas, many well-meaning visitors who have passed before have indiscriminately bestowed gifts, and as a consequence, foreigners are often pestered with persistent and sometimes even threatening demands for material goods by both adults and children. For guidelines, see the Gift Giving aside in the Dangers & Annoyances section in this chapter.

For details on major trekking routes, refer to the Cordilleras & Yungas chapter. Serious hikers and trekkers should pick up the 6th edition of *Backpacking and Trekking in Peru & Bolivia* by Hilary Bradt, Jonathan Derksen and Petra Schepens.

Mountaineering

Climbing in Bolivia, like the country itself, is an exercise in extremes. It can be as uncomfortably wet as in any range in the world, and dry-season (May to October) temperatures may fluctuate over 40°C in a single day. But during the dry southern winter (May to September) the weather is better than can be expected in any other mountain range in the world.

A second plus point for climbing in Bolivia is ease of access. Although public transport may not always be possible, roads pass within easy striking distance of many fine peaks.

Most people who wish to explore Bolivia's mountains will find that the 160-km-long range to the north-east of La Paz offers the easiest access and most spectacular climbing in the country. Providing delightful contrast, this range separates the stark Alti-plano on its west from the fertile green Yungas falling away to the Amazon on its east. Six peaks of the Cordillera Real rise above 6000m and there are many more gems in the 5000m range. Due to the altitude, glaciers and ice or steep snow, few are 'walk-ups', but most are well within reach of the average climber and many can be done by beginners with a competent guide.

During the winter dry season, the Cordillera is blessed with some of the most stable weather a hiker or climber could ask for. Precipitation is minimal and winds are mild. However, temperatures are extreme, with daytime highs of up to 30°C at the lower elevations and nighttime lows of -15°C above 5000m. These conditions lead to incredibly stable snow conditions, so the peaks of the Cordillera Real are a good place to learn snow climbing, or you can perfect your technique on one of the steeper faces or gullies.

To the north of the Cordillera Real lies the less accessible Cordillera Apolobamba and to the south, the Quimsa Cruz, which boasts Bolivia's best climbing rock.

The dangers of climbing in Bolivia mainly relate to the altitude and the difficulties in mounting any sort of rescue. Avalanches present only a minimal threat. Because the Cordillera Real is relatively easy to access, there isn't sufficient time to acclimatise on the approach and potentially fatal acute mountain sickness is a threat. *Mountain Sickness*, by Peter Hackett, is one of the most practical books available, as it's field-oriented and easily transportable. It's worth carrying when you climb to high altitude.

Those spending much time in Bolivia before climbing will have a head start on acclimatisation. If you're a newly arrived climber, however, you'd do well to spend a week in La Paz or the Altiplano or hiking in the surrounding area, staying as high as possible.

Once you're acclimatised to the Altiplano's relatively thin air, remember there are still 2500 more metres of even thinner air lurking above, so climb smart. Drink plenty of fluids, sleep as low as possible and descend at any sign of serious altitude sickness *before* a headache, troubled breathing or lethargy turn into life-threatening pulmonary or cerebral oedema. Read the discussion on acute mountain sickness in the Health section earlier in this chapter.

Don't forget to treat your water with a suitable filter or with iodine or chlorine-based purifiers. Llamas are perfectly happy up to 5000m and giardia is well worth avoiding. When collecting snow or ice to melt for water on popular routes such as Huayna Potosí and Illimani, keep your eyes open for other people's waste.

A mountain rescue services is being set up but currently, if you get sick or injured, rescue cannot be expected. Many of the routes are frequently climbed, solitude is still one of the joys of Bolivian alpinism, so be prepared to get yourself out of trouble. Helicopters do not, on the whole, fly above 5000m and Bolivia is not well-endowed with helicopters, in any case. Transport difficulties and the absence of telephones mean any rescuers not already on the mountain will take many hours to arrive.

Mountaineering insurance is essential to cover the high costs of rescue and to ensure medical evacuation out of Bolivia in the event of a serious accident.

Maps Historically, maps of Bolivian climbing areas have been of poor quality, and difficult to obtain. Even now, elevations of peaks are murky with reported altitudes varying as much as 600m.

An excellent new map of the entire *Cordillera Real*, at a scale of 1:135,000, shows mountains, roads and pre-Hispanic routes. It uses Aymara names according to the current official orthography, which can be confusing (for example, the peak commonly known as Ancohuma may be labelled 'Janq'uma' or 'Chearoco Ch'iyaruq'u'). It's available directly from Liam O'Brien, 28 Turner Terrace, Newtonville, MA 02160 USA, or from map distributors in the USA, UK and La Paz.

Roughly 70% of Bolivia is covered by 1:50,000 topo sheets produced by the Instituto Geográfico Militar (IGM). Notable exceptions include the areas north of Sorata, the entire Cordillera Apolobamba and Parque Nacional Noel Kempff Mercado. IGM maps are relatively accurate on altitudes and topographical details, but their spelling of names may be inconsistent and inaccurate. When you're route-finding, bear in mind that on most maps, only major paths are marked, while other perfectly feasible routes are omitted (this is often due to the lack of map updating). For information on purchasing IGM mapping, see the Planning section earlier in this chapter.

Walter Guzmán Cordova produces colour maps of *Choro-Takesi-Yunga Cruz, Mururata-Illimani, Huayna Potosí-Condoriri* and *Sajama*, which are sold at Los Amigos del Libro and the Librería del Turista, both in La Paz, amongst other places.

The Deutscher Alpenverein (German Alpine Club) produces the excellent and accurate 1:50,000-scale maps, *Alpenvereinskarte Cordillera Real Nord (Illampu)*, which includes the Sorata area, and *Alpenvereinskarte Cordillera Real Süd (Illimani)*, which centres on Illimani. Both are occasionally available in La Paz.

Guidebooks & Magazines Michael Kelsey's *Guide to the World's Mountains* (310 East 950 South, Springville, UT 84663 USA) has helpful maps and trip descriptions. The *American Alpine Club Journal* and *Alpine Journal* are essential reading for detailed and new route information in conjunction with *Mountaineering in the Andes* by Jill Neate (2nd edition) published by the Expedition Advisory Service of the Royal Geographic Society, London, which lists every mountain in Bolivia for which there is a written record. *Summit* magazine also has some useful features, especially in the July-August 1982 to July-August 1983 issues.

There are two mountaineering guidebooks to Bolivia. *La Cordillera Real de los Andes, Bolivia* by Alain Mesili (Los Amigos del Libro, La Paz, 1984), in Spanish, is currently out of print, but photocopied editions are sometimes available at Librería Don

Bosco, on the Prado in La Paz. In German, there's *Die Königskordillere – Berg-und Skiwandern in Bolivien* by Robert Pecher & Walter Schmiemann (C & M Hofbauer-Verlag, Jutastrasse 41, 8000 Munich, 1983). It describes treks, climbs and ski tours in the Southern Cordillera Real, including Condoriri, Huayna Potosí, Illimani, Mururata and Chacaltaya.

In April 1997, The Mountaineers in the USA and Cordee in the UK are publishing the new *Climber's Guide to Bolivia*, by Yossi Brain. The British author works as a climbing guide in La Paz and is the climbing secretary of the Club Andino Boliviano.

For the alpine history of the area look for *The Bolivian Andes: a record of climbing and exploration in the Cordillera Real* by W M Conway published in London and New York in 1901.

Technical information for climbers in Bolivia is available from Yossi Brain, climbing secretary of the Club Andino Boliviano. Contact him either through the club or through the Ozono agency (for contact addresses, see later in this section).

Equipment Scrambling in the Bolivian Andes can be done with little more than what the average traveller normally carries – a sturdy pair of shoes, a good layering of clothes, hat and gloves, plastic, aluminium or neoprene water bottle, daypack etc. If higher peaks beckon, however, more serious equipment is essential. Bring climbing gear with you as that found in Bolivia is generally expensive or of poor quality, or you have to rely on buying second-hand kit from other climbers and hikers. Remember, you'll have to carry this stuff on the plane, bus, camión, mule or on your back, so 'light is right'. When you're not climbing, your gear can be left with your tour agency or a reliable hotel. The following is a list of general recommendations for clothing and gear:

Clothing
    Loose fitting layers are best for the constantly changing temperatures. A sturdy wind coat that can take the abuse of buses, camiones, mules and the constant dust is important. Bolivia is one of the few places in South America where down is practical.

Camping Gear
• sleeping mat – important for insulating from cold or rocky ground
• sleeping bag – down or synthetic, good to -5°C (you can always put on more clothes if it gets colder!)
• tent – useful for occasional snotty weather; adds warmth
• backpack – a large capacity (60 litres plus), internal frame (external frames exposed to Bolivian buses don't last long)
• water bottles – at least two one-litre containers. Avoid aluminium bottles, as they crack at sub-freezing temperatures
• headlamp – important for those pre-dawn starts; bring an adaptor as round cell batteries are available everywhere, while flat batteries are only available at a couple of specialist shops and are expensive

Food
    Dried foods such as soups, rice, instant coffee etc, can be bought locally. If you're visiting Bolivia only for a few weeks climbing, you may want to bring freeze-dried food; otherwise, buy your food at the markets. Instant rice and packet pasta meals are available in La Paz at Zatt, on Avenida Sánchez Lima near Plaza Avaroa.

Cooking
    For cooking stoves, leaded petrol, kerosene and methylated spirits *(alcohol antiséptico,* available in pharmacies, works in Trangia stoves) are available in Bolivia. White gas (shellite/Coleman fuel) is available in portable quantities only at the YPFB in Cochabamba; in La Paz, you must buy a minimum of 250 litres. Epigaz and Camping Gaz canisters are expensive but available in La Paz. No type of stove fuel or canister may be carried on aircraft anywhere in the world, and not even clean, empty aluminium fuel bottles are permitted on flights originating or stopping in the USA. Currently, flights originating or passing through New Zealand restrict both fuel bottles and camp stoves.
    Useful utensils include a large pot for melting snow and another for cooking (mixing the two can produce some pretty odd-looking water, which means you probably drink less, which may lead to dehydration, which can lead to acute mountain sickness, which…you get the picture). A Teflon frying pan is a nice luxury for frying up the ubiquitous eggs and potato.

Water Purification
    Remember giardia, dysentery, hepatitis and all their ilk lurk in the mountains, too. See the Health section earlier in this chapter.

Climbing Gear

The amount and type of gear you'll need will obviously depend on just how serious you want to get, but the following recommended equipment would suffice for the standard routes on almost any peak in the Cordillera Real. Remember, most routes are over snow and/or ice, often in glacier form. This gear won't do you any good if you don't know how to use it. Climbing and camping gear can often be sold to locals or other travellers for more than you could get back home.

- plastic ice boots – heavy and expensive but how much do you value your toes?
- crampons and protectors
- ice axe and protector
- harness
- three to five karabiners, at least one locking
- nine or 11-mm rope
- two or three ice screws and snow pickets, flukes or stakes (essential earlier in the season)
- ice hammer – particularly for the more difficult climbs (Cabeza del Condor, Illampú, Ancohuma)
- prusiks – and practice in using them – for crevasse rescue
- sun protection – top-quality sunscreen and 100 per cent UV proof glasses are essential (don't scrimp here!) and aren't readily available in Bolivia; a baseball hat with bandana makes an effective 'Lawrence of Arabia' sun shield

Buying & Hiring Equipment Condoriri (☎ & fax 319369), at Local 8, Galería Sagárnaga 339, La Paz, is run by José Miranda, a paraglider and qualified mountaineering guide who also speaks German. The shop offers the widest selection of new and second-hand climbing and camping equipment. This includes clothing, ropes, backpacks, tents, boots, paragliders, compasses, Camping Gaz, Epigaz, headtorch batteries, plus a selection of climbing hardware. It also hires out equipment and has a repair service. At the time of writing, Condoriri was also applying to become a tourist agency, specialising in mountaineering and paragliding trips.

If you can't carry everything you'll need from home – or you don't have it – climbing equipment and clothing can be hired in La Paz from any specialist agency: Colibri has the biggest selection. Some examples of daily rental charges: plastic ice boots US$3.80, crampons US$2.70, ice axe US$2.50, two-person tent US$5.70. New equipment, including headtorch batteries, ropes, backpacks and clothing can be bought at several La Paz shops.

Agencies & Guides Many La Paz travel agencies offer to organise climbing and trekking trips in the Cordillera Real and other parts of the country. Not all, however, are all they claim to be. One agency sent two tourists to Huayna Potosí with a 'guide' who couldn't even find the first camp. Others have strung up to 10 climbers on the same rope (any more than four climbers on one rope is extremely dangerous). These sort of things aren't uncommon, so it's worth sticking to reputable specialist climbing agencies.

Trekking guides generally charge US$25 per day, plus their food. Mountain guides cost US$50 per day and also need feeding. In addition, you need your food, technical equipment and clothing and – often the most expensive part of any trip – transport to and from the start of the trek or mountain. Alternatively, you can often resort to public transport, but this will require more time and you should plan for an extra couple of days food in case of glitches.

Specialist agencies in La Paz can do as much or as little as you want – from just organising transport to a full service with guide, cook, mules, porters etc, providing a full itinerary.

In addition to the agencies, there are two sources of information about mountain guides: the Club Andino Boliviano (☎ 324682), Calle México 1638, Casilla 1346, La Paz (lower Prado), which is mainly a ski organisation and runs the ski piste at Chacaltaya but also has a number of top climbers as members. The national guiding association is the Bolivian Association of Mountain Guides (☎ & fax 317497), Andean Summits, Calle Sagárnaga 189, Casilla 6976, La Paz; however, not all Bolivian mountain guides belong to the association.

The following specialist agencies are all run by mountain guides and organise both trekking and climbing trips:

Andean Summits

Calle Sagárnaga 189, Casilla 6976, La Paz (☎ & fax 317497). Run by two excellent guides, José Camarlinghi and Javier Thellaeche, who speak both English and French. A good selection of new camping and climbing gear is sold here: headtorch batteries, Camping Gaz and Epigaz etc.

Colibri

Calle Sagárnaga 309, Casilla 7456, La Paz (☎ 371936, fax 355043). Run by Oscar Sánchez who speaks French and English. It offers the greatest selection of climbing and trekking gear for hire, and German or Italian-speaking guides are available. If you're buying a trip that includes meals, discuss in advance what sort of meals you'll be getting; groups have complained their main meals consisted only of coca tea and powdered soup!

Colonial Tours

Expediciones Bolivia, Calle México 1733, Casilla 5108, La Paz (☎ & fax 316073) Specialises in mountaineering and trekking expeditions, with as few as two or three participants. The Curva to Pelechuco trek in the Cordillera Apolobamba and the Huayna Potosí expedition are both especially good value.

Guarachi Andes Expeditions

Plaza Alonzo de Mendoza, Edificio Santa Anita 314, Casilla 12287, La Paz (☎ 320901, fax 392344). Specialises in trekking and climbing in the Cordillera Apolobamba, Sajama and the Cordillera Real.

Huayna Potosí Tours

Hotel Continental, Calle Illampu 626, Casilla 731, La Paz (☎ 323584, fax 378226). The owner of this agency Dr Hugo Berrios, built and operates the relatively luxurious mountain hut Refugio Huayna Potosí, which serves as a base camp for Huayna Potosí expeditions. He also organises good value treks and climbs in areas such as the Cordilleras Real and Apolobamba, and sells maps and hires out climbing equipment.

Ozono

Office 101, 1st floor, Edificio Guanabara, Avenida Arce esquina Calle Cordero, Casilla 7243, La Paz (☎ & fax 722240). An adventure travel company that offers mountaineering, treks, 4WD tours, rock climbing, extreme skiing and lowland expeditions. Mountaineering advice and information is available, as are French and German-speaking guides.

Transamazonas

Office 3C, 3rd floor, Edificio V Centenario, Avenida 6 de Agosto, Casilla 14551, La Paz (☎ 350411, fax 360923). Covers the top end of the adventure tourism market, offering well-organised hiking, climbing and 4WD expeditions. English, French, German and Spanish are spoken.

WORK

There is a vast number of volunteer and non-governmental organisations at work in Bolivia, and quite a few international companies have offices there, but travellers looking for paid work on the spot probably won't have much luck. Medical students usually have no problem picking up work experience, but it's likely to be on a volunteer basis. Geologists probably have the best chance of paid work through the many mining and exploration companies based in La Paz, but it's worth arranging contacts before you arrive.

Teaching English

Qualified English teachers interested in working in La Paz and several other cities may want to try the professionally run Centro Boliviano Americano (☎ 351627), Avenida Aniceto Arce at Parque Zenón Iturralde, La Paz. Bear in mind, however, that you'll be required to forfeit two months salary in order to pay for your training whether you're already qualified or not.

Alternatively, phone the very amiable Señor Emo Alandia at the Pan American English Centre (☎ 340796), Edificio Avenida, 7th floor, Avenida 16 de Julio 1490, Casilla 5244, La Paz, to arrange an interview. This friendly institution is almost always looking for native English speakers (preferably qualified) to work as teachers.

There are many other English-teaching schools and universities in La Paz – ask working teachers for guidelines and recommendations.

Voluntary Organisations

If you prefer voluntary work with an emphasis on environmental protection, contact Earthwatch (☎ (617) 926 8200), 680 Mt Auburn St, Box 403, Watertown, MA 02272, USA. It currently sponsors a project to study forest habitats in the Reserva Biosférica del Beni.

Another worthwhile volunteer option is the Street Kids Project operated by ENDA Bolivia, a Swiss-sponsored project that provides food and shelter for street children while offering an education and teaching them useful skills. Among its more successful endeavours is a highly-acclaimed street theatre troupe. If you're interested in volunteering, contact Señor Hugo Montecinos (☎ 811695, fax 811446), Casilla 9772, La Paz.

ACCOMMODATION

In general, the prices and value of accommodation are not uniform throughout Bolivia. The cheapest accommodation is found in Copacabana, and the Amazon region is generally the most expensive. All accommodation rates are negotiable, especially during slow periods.

In this book, Places to Stay sections are divided into bottom-end, middle and top-end accommodation. Anything charging under US$15 for a double is typically considered bottom end. Mid-range accommodation runs from approximately US$15 to US$30 for two people, whether the rate is charged per person or per room. Top-end places typically start at US$30 for a double and include most places rated with three or more stars on the Bolivian rating scale. These categories may be adjusted slightly to account for regional price differences. Hotels that are recommended or represent particularly good value for money – or are frequented by budget-conscious travellers – are identified as such.

Camping

Bolivia offers excellent wild camping, especially along trekking routes and in remote mountain areas. Bolivia has few organised camp sites (I'm aware of only a handful in the entire country), but with the right gear – a tent, sleeping bag, light source and perhaps even a stove and fuel – you can set up camp almost anywhere outside population centres. Remember, however, that highland nights can be freezing.

Although there's often a place where you can melt into the hills near larger cities, there's rarely a safe and reliable water supply nearby, so you must carry sufficient water.

If you are hiking or trekking along mountain routes, you'll find that camping is possible just about anywhere except in someone's pasture or potato field. Ask around in villages – locals may put travellers up or allow them to camp in their garden for a small fee. Rural schools are also good – and normally clean – alternatives. If you're sleeping in thatched huts, particularly in the lowlands or the highland valleys, see the Health section for warnings about Chagas' disease.

Hotels

The Bolivian hotel rating system divides accommodation into categories that, from bottom to top, include *posadas*, *alojamientos*, *residenciales*, *casas de huéspedes*, *hostales* and *hoteles*. This rating system reflects the price scale and, to some extent, the quality.

Fortunately for travellers, most Bolivian hotel owners are friendly, honest people and demand the same of their staff. Competition is such that places can't afford a bad reputation, so unless you're staying in a hotel that already has a dodgy reputation, your belongings should be relatively safe, at least in upper bottom-end to top-range places. Still, use common sense and don't leave valuables in sight. Money or jewellery may be checked at the hotel desk, but package it well and get a receipt; in the end, it may be just as secure stashed in some obscure corner of a locked pack.

In some lower priced hotels, doors don't lock from either side and there may even be a window beside the door that can be easily opened from the outside. Decide whether you can trust the proprietor to keep an eye on things while you're away.

If you'll be away for a few days, most hotels will watch luggage free of charge. This service ranges from an informal area behind the counter to a locked baggage room; naturally, the latter is preferable.

Note that in some establishments, *simples* (single rooms), are unavailable, or cost only slightly less than a *doble* (double room). In some cases, if you're given a double you'll be expected to pay for both beds. In cheaper places, *camas matrimoniales* (double beds), are also scarce. Triple or quadruple rooms are frequently available, but they cost the same per bed as smaller rooms unless you can negotiate a high-occupancy discount.

Water and electric utilities throughout the country can be sporadic, and some inexpensive hotels only turn on the water and power for several hours in the morning and evening (see the Toilets & Plumbing section earlier in this chapter). Some establishments expect you to advise them when you want a shower so that they can make the necessary arrangements.

Some final advice – never accept a room without inspecting it first. The most cheery reception areas can shelter some pretty dank and dingy rooms, some without windows. If you're not satisfied with the room you're first shown, ask to see another. Most proprietors are eager to please.

Posadas Posadas are the bottom end – the cheapest basic roof and bed available; they're frequented mainly by campesinos visiting the city. They cost between US$1 and US$2.50 per person and vary in quality, normally from bad to worse. In most posadas, you could scrape off the scum with a putty knife. Hot water is unknown, and most even lack showers.

Alojamientos A step up are the alojamientos, which are also generally quite basic, but are considerably better and cost a bit more. Shower and toilet facilities are almost always communal, but some do offer hot showers. The value varies widely – some are clean and tidy, others are disgustingly seedy. Rates are normally charged per person rather than per room so there's no advantage in turning up as a group. Double beds can be hard to find. Prices range from US$1.20 per person in Copacabana to about US$6 in some Amazon Basin towns.

Residenciales, Casas de Huéspedes & Hostales Residenciales, casas de huéspedes and hostales all serve as finer budget hotels, but their quality also varies and some alojamientos have taken to calling themselves 'residenciales' to improve their image. Still, most are acceptable and you'll often have a choice between a baño privado (private bath with a sink and flush toilet, and a shower with a hot water attachment on the shower head), or baño común (shared toilet and shower). Many places also provide a laundry sink or reasonably priced laundry services, and there's often a restaurant or snack bar where you can buy coffee, breakfast or sandwiches. These places charge US$8 to US$20 for a double with private bath, and about 30% less without.

Other Hotels Moving upmarket, there's a whole constellation of hotels, which vary in stand-ard from literal dumps to five-star luxury. The lower-range hotels can be amazingly cheap while the most expensive hotels top US$100 per person.

In general, Bolivia is not a country for accommodation snobs. There are only a handful of five-star hotels in the country, and some of these would rate only three or four stars on an international scale. Nevertheless, you can expect clean rooms, acceptable restaurants with bars, entertainment, room service, laundry service (albeit expensive), hot and cold running water, a telephone, bar fridge and all the usual amenities – for about half the price you'd pay in New York, London or Sydney.

A one-star hotel, on the other hand, may offer only cold water – possibly with a hot-shower attachment, a snack bar, shabby but clean linen and often a rather seedy appearance. Two to four-star hotels, of course, fall somewhere in between. No stars indicate that the establishment is called a hotel but may actually belong in a lower category. Heating or air-con are unheard of below the three-star level.

Another type of hotel, exclusive to La Paz department, is the *hotel prefectural*. The idea behind these government-run hotels was to provide minimal luxury in small towns of tourist interest. Most of them have now been privatised and are becoming more mainstream and less sterile-looking than in earlier times.

Reservations

Although most top-end hotels in Bolivia will expect you to have room reservations, room availability is rarely a problem. The main exception is during major fiestas, when prices double and rooms are occupied by visiting nationals. At such times, private home owners will often let rooms. On weekends, you may have problems finding a room in Coroico, and during the winter months, Uyuni also experiences accommodation shortages. Some rural places have La Paz reservation phone numbers; this is indicated where relevant.

FOOD

Bolivian cuisine is as diverse as its regions and their many climatic zones. It may not win any international awards, but an admirable versatility has been derived from a few staple foods. The fare of the Altiplano tends to be starchy and loaded with carbohydrates, while in the lowlands, fish, vegetables and fruits feature more prominently.

Meat invariably dominates the typical Bolivian meal, and is usually accompanied by rice, potatoes (or another starchy tuber such as oca) and shredded lettuce. Sometimes the whole affair is drowned in *llajhua*, a hot sauce made from tomatoes and *locotos* (small, hot pepper pods) or another spicy sauce. In the lowlands, the potato and its relatives are replaced by steamed or fried plantain or *yuca* (cassava), and other vegetables are more prevalent than in the highlands.

Meals

Breakfast is known as *desayuno* and often consists of little more than coffee and a bread roll or some kind of pastry. Around midmorning, many Bolivians eat a snack of *salteñas*, which are described under Fast Foods later in this section.

Lunch is the main meal of the day and most restaurants offer an *almuerzo*, which means simply 'lunch', but here it refers to a set lunch served at midday (à la carte lunches aren't usually called almuerzos). For almuerzo, many restaurants, ranging from backstreet cubbyholes to classy establishments, offer bargain set meals consisting of soup, a main course, and tea or coffee. In some places, a salad starter and a simple dessert are included. Almuerzos cost roughly half the price of à la carte dishes – from US$1 to US$3, depending on the class of restaurant. If you don't want the almuerzo, you can order something from the regular menu for about twice the price of the special.

The evening meal, *la cena*, is similar to lunch, but normally less elaborate. It's invariably eaten after 7 pm.

Fast Foods

For a mid-morning snack, highland and lowland Bolivians eat *salteñas*, delicious rugby-ball-shaped meat and vegetable pasties, which originated in Salta (Argentina). They're stuffed with beef or chicken, olives, eggs, potatoes, onions, peas, carrots, raisins and whatever else might have been on hand. They're guaranteed to dribble all over the place and make a mess on your clothing, so have a supply of napkins. A similar but even juicier incarnation is the *tucumana*, which is roughly cube-shaped and packed with spicy egg, potatoes, chicken and onions. Both varieties are normally heavily spiced and are absolutely delicious.

Empanadas, ubiquitous throughout South America, are filled with varying quantities of beef *(empanadas de carne)*, chicken *(empanadas de pollo)* or cheese *(empanadas de queso)*, and are either baked or deep-fried. Sometimes other ingredients, such as those that go into salteñas, are added to the meat varieties. A variation is the *pukacapa*, a circular empanada filled with cheese, olives, onions and *ají* (hot pepper sauce) and baked in an earth oven.

The name of the *llaucha paceña*, a type of doughy cheese bread, would imply that it's a speciality of La Paz, but in fact, it appears to be more popular in Cochabamba. *Papas rellenas*, stuffed potatoes, are also delicious, especially served piping hot. They're a speciality in the central highlands around Cochabamba and Sucre.

Tamales are cornmeal dough filled with spiced beef, vegetables and potatoes.

They're wrapped in a maize husk and fried, grilled or baked. *Humintas* (sometimes spelt *humitas*), which are similar, are filled with cheese only. A related concoction, called a *relleno*, resembles a corn fritter.

A popular way of preserving vegetables – mainly carrots, onion and peppers – is to pickle them in vinegar; the result is called *escabeche*. It's eaten as a snack or an accompaniment to meals. In some markets and stands, you can get *chola* sandwiches, bread rolls filled with meat, onion, tomato and escabeche.

A common snack that is an acquired taste is *pasankalla*, puffed *choclo* (a type of maize) with caramel, which normally sits out on the street long enough to go sticky and very chewy.

Soup

Every almuerzo or cena in Bolivia is prefaced by a large bowl of soup, of which there are three main types. *Chupe* is a thick meat, vegetable and grain soup with a clear broth flavoured with garlic, ají, tomato, cumin or onion. *Chaque* is similar, but is much thicker and contains more grain. *Lawa* has a broth thickened with corn starch or wheat flour. Two delicious popular soup bases are quinoa and peanuts *(maní)*.

The type and amount of meat that appears in the soup will depend on where you get it. In markets, small eateries and bus stops, you'd be lucky to get more than a scrap of bone and gristle, usually beef or llama, in the bottom of the bowl. In more upmarket restaurants, you may get chicken or a bit of bone with some tough but edible meat attached. Look at the positive side – it's easy to remove this item and turn any Bolivian soup into a marginally vegetarian dish.

Meat & Fish

Most Bolivian dishes are derived from beef, chicken or fish and every region has its own cuisine and specialities. Poorer campesinos eat *cordero* or *carnero* (mutton), *cabrito* or *chivito* (goat) or llama.

Pork *(carne de chancho)* is considered a delicacy and is usually eaten only on special occasions; *lechón* (suckling pig) is a speciality of Cochabamba, but may also be served elsewhere as a fiesta dish. Another pork delicacy is *fritanga*, spicy hot pork with mint and maize hominy.

Typical beef dishes include barbecued or grilled beef *(parrillada* or *asado)* in various cuts *(lomo, brazuelo* and *churrasco)*. Jerked beef is called *charque*; when served with mashed maize hominy, it's known as *charque kan*. In the lowlands, charque with mashed plantain and/or yuca is known as *masaco*. In the Beni, beef may be served as *pacumutus*, enormous chunks of grilled meat accompanied by yuca, onions and other trimmings.

Other meat variations include *thimpu*, spicy lamb and vegetable stew, and *falso conejo* (which, oddly enough, means 'false rabbit'), a greasy, glutenous substance that appears to be animal-based. Another popular way to serve meat or chicken is in *milanesa*, a greasy schnitzel. When the meat is pounded even thinner and allowed to absorb even more grease, the result is known as *silpancho*, which is a speciality of Cochabamba department and other areas. It's said that a properly prepared silpancho could be used to view a solar eclipse!

The dish called *pique a lo macho* (chunked grilled beef and sausage served with chipped potatoes, lettuce, tomatoes, onions, capsicum and locoto is popular in central Bolivia. *Rostro asado*, or sheep's head, is a favourite in Oruro. *Anticuchos* (beef-heart kebabs) and *fricasés* (pork or chicken stews with maize grits) are specialities in La Paz and Cochabamba. Other Cochabamba favourites include *jolque* (kidney soup), *ranga* (potato soup with chopped liver), *witu* (beef stew with pureed tomatoes), *chajchu* (beef with *chuño* – freeze dried potatoes – hard-boiled egg, cheese and hot red pepper sauce) and *tomatada de cordero* (lamb stew with tomato sauce).

Chicken is either fried *(pollo frito)*, cooked on a spit *(pollo al spiedo)* or broiled *(pollo asado* or *pollo dorado)*, or any combination of the above (yielding *pollo a la broaster, broasted* or even *broasterd)*. It's commonly served as *pollo a la canasta* – 'chicken-in-a-basket', with mustard, chips and ají. A more sophisticated chicken concoction is Potosí's own (bizarrely-named) *ckocko* – spicy chicken cooked in wine or chicha and served with choclo, olives, raisins, grated orange peel and other aromatic condiments.

On the Altiplano, the most popular fish *(pescado)* is trout *(trucha)* from Lake Titicaca. The lowlands have a wide variety of other freshwater fish, including *sábalo*, *dorado* and the delicious *surubí*. Surubí, a kind of catfish caught throughout the lowlands, is arguably the best of the lot.

In addition, *tatu* (armadillo), *jochi* (or agouti), monkeys, alligators and other endearing rainforest critters are eaten to the brink of extinction in some lowland areas.

Dairy Foods

Fresh milk is available through agencies of the national dairy PIL in most cities and towns, but in smaller places, it may be difficult to find. Any shop displaying a picture of a happy cow licking its lips will have milk for sale. Some markets also sell raw (unpasteurised and unhomogenised) milk.

Sheep's milk cheese is made all over the Altiplano and is delicious provided it doesn't contain too much salt. Vendors will usually let you sample it before buying. It's cheaper and arguably better than cow's milk cheese, which is considered more prestigious among campesinos.

Chaco cheese from eastern Tarija and western Santa Cruz departments is coveted all over Bolivia as the finest produced in the country. The Mennonite colonies of Santa Cruz department also make some good European-style cheeses.

Tubers

Tuberous plants make up a large percentage of most Bolivians' vegetable diet. Potatoes come in nearly 250 mostly small and colourful, varieties. Freeze-dried potatoes, which are known as chuños or *tunta*, are rehydrated, cooked and eaten as snacks or as

accompaniment to meals. Chuños are made by leaving potatoes out in the winter cold for four consecutive nights. They're then pressed to extract the water, peeled and dried. Tunta, or bleached chuño, is a little more complicated and requires the chuño to be packed in straw and left in running water for at least a month before drying. Most foreigners don't find either particularly appealing because they have the appearance and consistency of polystyrene when dry, and are tough and tasteless when cooked. A favourite dish featuring chuños is *chairo*, a mutton or beef soup with chuños, potatoes and *mote* (dried maize, prepared in the same way as the chuños).

Ocas are tough, purple, potato-like tubers. They taste pretty good fried or roasted, but boiled ocas will take some getting used to (the flavour has been described as a cross between skunk spray and potato). Another tuber sold in markets everywhere is the *añu*, a tiny purple, yellow and white stalagmite-shaped thing that tastes like a cross between a swede (rutabaga) and a parsnip, and is usually served boiled.

In the lowlands, the potato and its relatives are replaced by plantain or the root of the ubiquitous yuca (manioc or cassava), which is good (if rather bland) when it has been cooked long enough.

Cereals

Two other common foods include choclo, a large kernel maize, which is eaten everywhere on the Altiplano, and *habas*, the beans of the *palqui* plant, which grow wild and are eaten roasted or added to stews. They are also used to make a coffee-like beverage. In Potosí and Sucre, a particularly appealing dish is *kala purkha*, a delicious soup made from maize that is cooked in a ceramic dish by adding a steaming chunk of heavy pumice. Another popular legume is *tarhui*, which is grown in diminishing quantities mainly around Sucre.

Quinoa, a grain unique to the area, is high in protein and is used to make flour and thicken stews. It's similar in most respects to sorghum or millet, but grows on a stalk and resembles caviar when it's in the field. Quinoa was first cultivated in the Andes several thousand years ago but the Spanish conquistadores forced the Indians to adopt European grains and thereafter, quinoa was rarely used.

This nutritious grain has recently been rediscovered, however, and analysis has revealed that it contains a unique balance of fat, oil and protein. It is the only edible plant that contains all essential amino acids in the same proportions as milk, making it especially appealing to vegans. Among the best strains are *quinoa blanca*, or *quinoa real*, which is produced on the Southern Altiplano in Potosí and Oruro departments.

Fruit

In addition to familiar fruits such as oranges and bananas, many other varieties are cultivated, some of which are unfamiliar outside South America. *Chirimoya*, or custard apple, is a green, scaly looking fruit that is sold in markets around the country. The flesh looks and tastes like custard. The fruit of the prickly pear cactus *(tuna)* is eaten in the highlands. Unripe *maracuya* (passion fruit) is known as *tumbo* and makes an excellent juice. Variations on the banana – *plátanos* (plantains) and *guineos* (finger bananas) – are available practically everywhere.

In the lowlands, scores of exotic tropical fruits defy the imaginations of visitors from the middle latitudes. Among the more unusual are *ambaiba (Cecropia sp)*, which is shaped a bit like a hand; the small, round, green and purple *guaypurú (Myrciaria cauliflora)*; the spiny yellow *ocoro (Rheedia madruno)*; lemon-like *guapomo (Silacia elliptica)*; bean-like *cupesi (Prosopis chilensis)*; the *marayau (Batris major)*, which resembles a bunch of giant grapes; the *nui (Pesudolaredia laevis)*, a berry that is similar to a currant; the *sinini (Annoru muricata)*, which resembles a scaly onion; and the stomach-shaped *paquio (Hymenaea courbaril)*. You can sample some of the more exotic fruit at Mercado Los Pozos in Santa Cruz.

Sweets

Perhaps the most interesting Bolivian sweets are *confites*, which are associated with holidays and offerings. These festive candies may only be made by traditional rural confectioners after performing a *cha'lla* (offering) to Pachamama, the earth mother. The candies are made of blue, pink, red or green boiled sugar syrup, hardened around a filling of nuts, aniseed, fruits, biscuit or desiccated coconut. Ceremonial confites are intended as religious offerings and are not meant to be eaten.

Another sweet popular with children is *tojorí*, an oatmeal-like concoction of mashed corn, cinnamon and sugar. In Potosí, you can get *tawa-tawas*, relatives of the doughnut, and delicious *sopaipillas*, sweet fried breads. The similar *buñuelos* are available around Bolivia.

For a real treat, Bolivia's own Breick chocolate rivals that of Switzerland and some say it's better than Cadbury. Judge for yourself!

Restaurants

Restaurants serving typical European or North American foods are often found around larger hotels or in middle-class districts of larger cities. There are also several fast-food joints in La Paz and Cochabamba, including a couple that try very hard to look like some popular US-based chains.

Italian restaurants are increasingly popular, *chifas* (Chinese restaurants) exist in most major cities, and even more exotic cuisines, such as vegetarian, Mexican, Swiss and Japanese, are represented.

Local restaurants range from street stalls selling quick bites to classy sidewalk cafés where you can sit beside a palm-lined boulevard and eat steak. In a *confiterías* or *pastelería*, you find little more than snacks and a cup of coffee. *Heladerías*, or ice cream parlours, are becoming increasingly sophisticated, offering pizza, pasta, doughnuts, salteñas, and coffee specialities, in addition to ice cream. They're open daily, including Sunday afternoons.

There are also hundreds of backstreet cubbyholes, greasy-spoon truckstops and hundreds of family-run operations of varying quality in every population centre. This is the sort of place where wall space is shared by Swiss chalets, Jesus Christ, the Pope, and bikini-clad babes suggesting you enjoy a beer with your lunch.

Smaller informal establishments have no menus. The day's offerings, which frequently depend upon what was bargain-priced in the market that morning, are usually written on a blackboard posted at the entrance. If there is a menu, it's probably just a list of what someone wishes were available rather than a true representation of what's cooking. In some cases, it's more efficient to ignore the menu and ask what's on offer.

Food stalls in the market *comedores* (dining halls) sell cheap and filling – and usually tasty. They're found in every city and town, and are viable and convenient if you're travelling on limited funds or enjoy sampling a bit of local culture. Keep in mind, however, that your internal plumbing may need time to adjust; don't give up on market food just because you got the runs the first time you tried it.

DRINKS
Nonalcoholic Drinks
Beyond the usual black tea, coffee and chocolate, typical local hot drinks include *mate de coca* (coca leaf tea), *mate de manzanilla* (chamomile tea) and *api* (which is described under Chicha, later in this section).

Common soft drinks are available, as are locally produced soft drinks of varying palatability. Locals have also been known to enjoy a Peruvian sugar rush known as Inca Kola (immortalised in the book by Matthew Parris), a piss-yellow soft drink that tastes like liquefied bubble gum. It's too disgusting for words.

A favourite that you'll find at bus stops and railway stations is *refresco* (refreshment), an anonymous fruit-based juice, often with a fuzzy ball in the bottom of the glass. The fuzzy ball, known as *despepitado* or *mocachinchi*, is actually a dried and shrivelled peach.

Other favourite drinks include *tostada* (known as *aloja* in southern Bolivia), which is made of corn, barley, honey, cinnamon and cloves. A delicious walnut-based drink, which was originally made popular in Central America, is known as *horchata*. Many markets and restaurants serve up licuados, delicious fruit shakes made with either milk or water. *Batidas* are whipped up with milk, sugar and a nonalcoholic beer known as *bi-cervecina*.

Alcoholic Drinks
When imbibing stronger alcoholic beverages, keep in mind that altitude intensifies the effects. In La Paz, you can be good and laid out after three bottles of beer and practically unconscious after the fourth. Also remember that when Bolivians gather to drink alcohol – whether it's beer, wine, *chicha* or whatever – it's serious; they intend to get plastered. Before accepting an invitation to drink with locals, consider that you'll be expected to do the same. In fact, Bolivians seem to take offence if any person in their party is able to walk out of a bar under their own steam.

Beer Bolivian lagers generally aren't bad. Popular brands include the fizzy and strange-tasting Huari, and the good but rather nondescript Paceña, both from La Paz; the pleasant but weak-flavoured Sureña from Sucre; refreshing Taquiña from Cochabamba; Astra, from Tarija, which is available as lager or malt; robust Potosina from Potosí; and the slightly rough Ducal, and cold and tasty Tropical Extra – arguably the best of the lot – both from Santa Cruz. Note that at higher altitudes, beer (particularly Huari) tends to froth more than you're probably used to.

Wine & Singani Most of Bolivia's wine is produced around Tarija with varying degrees of success. The best – and most expensive – is Concepción San Bernardo de la Frontera, which sells for about US$5 a bottle. San

Appeasing the Spirits

The world of the Andean Indians – Quechua and Aymara – is populated by hosts of well-respected spirits, the *apus* and *achachilas* (mountain spirits believed to be ancestors of the people). They mainly pervade wild areas and are prone to both favourable behaviour and fits of temper. The people also believe they themselves are literally descended from the earth mother, Pachamama, who is also respected and venerated.

In order to demonstrate respect and keep on the better side of all these entities, people take them into consideration in facets of everyday life. Before a person takes the first sip of alcohol from a glass, it is customary to make an offering, or *t'inka*, to Pachamama. This is done by spilling a few drops from the glass onto the floor or ground, thus demonstrating to Pachamama that she takes precedence over her human subjects. When an object such as a home or vehicle needs to be blessed by Pachamama, the apus and/or achachilas, a glass of alcohol is splashed over the object. This is known as a *cha'lla*. When it's sprinkled with the fingers, it's called a *chu'ra*.

These rituals are readily observed by visitors on weekends in Copacabana, when cars and trucks are blessed with a cha'lla, and at La Cumbre near La Paz, in preparation for the treacherous descent into the Yungas. ■

Pedro, which is produced in beautiful Camargo, also costs US$5 a bottle and isn't bad.

The same wineries also produce *singani*, a spirit obtained by distilling poor-quality grapes and grape skins, and in fact, some products labelled as 'wine' are actually singani mixed with grape juice. The three main brands of singani – San Pedro, Rujero and Casa Real – all employ grading systems. The finest quality singani are San Pedro de Oro, Rujero Etiqueta Negra and Casa Real Etiqueta Negra Merillada. Cheaper and harsher are San Pedro de Plata and Casa Real Etiqueta Negra Común. For the real rotgut stuff, go for San Pedro Cinteña, Rujero Etiqueta Roja or Casa Real Etiqueta Roja.

A favourite singani-based cocktail is *chuflay*, a pleasant blend of singani, 7-up, ice and lemon. Around Cochabamba, you can sample such alcoholic concoctions as *guarapo*, a speciality in Sipe-Sipe, and *garapiña*, which is popular in Quillacollo.

Imported wines are also available and if you buy them at small street stalls, *tiendas* or *almacenes*, they can be excellent value. The popular Chilean wine, Undurraga (white or red), costs only US$2 for a 750 ml bottle in La Paz. Even better is the Argentine Toro Viejo, which costs from US$1.50 to US$2.50 for a 750 ml bottle. The red is particularly good. More expensive wines –

mainly Chilean, Argentine and Californian – are also available for considerably less than you'd pay in Europe or North America.

Chicha The favourite alcoholic drink of the Bolivian masses is a maize liquor known as *chicha cochabambina*, obtained by fermenting maize. It's quite good and is guaranteed to produce an effect, but there are a lot of rumours flying around Bolivia concerning additional ingredients, which are best ignored if you plan to drink it.

Although chicha is made all over Bolivia, production is concentrated in the Cochabamba region. Those white plastic flags you see flying on long poles indicate a *chichería*, a place where chicha is sold.

Considerably milder are the numerous other incarnations of chicha, which are made from a variety of items and may or may not contain alcohol. In Copacabana and La Paz, *api* is served at breakfast or after meals. Usually served hot, api is a very syrupy form of chicha made from *kulli* or *maíz morada* (sweet purple maize), lemon, cinnamon and staggering amounts of white sugar. A less sweet and lightly alcoholic form of *chicha de maíz* is made from *maíz blanco* (white maize). *Chicha de maní* is made from peanuts. In the Amazon region, a favourite drink is *chicha de yuca*, a light and refreshing yuca beverage that tastes like an Indian lassi.

In San Ignacio de Moxos, *chicha de camote*, sweet potato chicha, is served as an accompaniment to meals. Rich and not too sweet, it's actually a lot better than it sounds.

Poorer campesinos rarely consider such trifles as taste or personal health when looking for a cheap and direct route to inebriation, and many favour an especially head-pounding swill known simply as *alcoól*. This fiery, gut-wrenching stuff is essentially pure potable alcohol, so if you're offered a glass, you may wish to make a particularly generous offering to Pachamama (see the Appeasing the Spirits aside earlier in this section).

ENTERTAINMENT
Cinema
Every Bolivian city has at least one cinema. Most films are shown in English with Spanish subtitles, but sound systems are poor and crackly and nobody bothers to keep quiet for the foreign dialogue, anyway, so a knowledge of Spanish will help.

The movies shown aren't typically of top quality, but if you happen to enjoy the likes of *Girls' Dorm, Ninjas from Space and Rocky Meets Rambo* sort of pictures, you can spend a lot of time in Bolivian cinemas. In all fairness, some cinemas do screen better films, but they're the exception.

Admission to a film or double feature averages US$1.50, although in some places, you can opt to sit on the concrete bleachers in the *galería* for a 30% reduction.

Theatre
Bolivia's most renowned theatre group is Sucre-based Teatro de los Andes (fax 31642 or 30535), Casilla 685, Sucre, which was begun in 1991 by Argentine-born César Brie. Brie studied and worked in Italy and Denmark before returning to South America and settling in Bolivia because of its rich indigenous traditions. His aim is to combine 20th century European theatre with Andean themes and traditions. The troupe now consists of seven members – Argentine, Bolivian and Italian – who are based at Brie's *finca*

(country retreat) in Yotala, occasionally offering theatre workshops.

Over the past few years, the group has performed a range of European, Bolivian and original works, from *Don Quixote* and *Romeo and Juliet* to *Ubu* and *Legend of a People who Lost the Sea*. They perform not only in the cities – which pays the expenses – but also in rural areas, where they hope to spread an appreciation of theatre not only to the urban middle classes, but to the campesinos, as well.

Traditional/Folk Music
If you want a taste of Bolivian folk music, try to attend at least one peña, an Andean or highland Bolivian folk music show that may include dancing. The music is usually played on typical Andean instruments such as *quenas*, *zampoñas* and *charangos*. Shows featuring only guitars, singing, comedy or a combination of these are also common. In all cases, the music gets better as the bottles get emptier, and to get you started the admission charge will generally include your first drink. Although most peñas ambitiously advertise action six nights a week, when there aren't enough patrons they scale them back to two or three nights a week, most often Thursday to Saturday.

Pubs/Bars
Don't expect much from local bars in Bolivian cities. They're frequented almost exclusively by men who go there not to dance or carry on conversation, but to drink and get drunk. Once that goal is met, anything can happen. Most patrons are already past sobriety by 6 pm and the next six hours until closing do nothing to improve their condition (to avoid trouble, most local bars stop serving at midnight or earlier).

In Bolivia, as elsewhere, drink tends to bring out a measure of brutal honesty and intense emotion in people, and things could become uncomfortable. Reactions toward foreigners may go either way, but will rarely be neutral. If you're a male, there's a chance you'll have an interesting experience, but you'll also run the risk of being regarded in a less-than-friendly manner. For example, just try to reason with someone who's been seized with the notion that all foreigners are Drug Enforcement Agency (DEA) agents. Unaccompanied women would be wise to avoid local male bars altogether, lest they be misconstrued.

Classier drinking dens are sometimes known as *wiskerías*. La Paz and Santa Cruz – and on a lesser scale Sucre and Cochabamba – also have a slew of reputable bars which draw most of their clientele from the local middle class and substantial expat-riate communities.

THINGS TO BUY
Although prices will be lower at the point of original production, any type of artesanía available in Bolivia can also be found somewhere in La Paz, which is the artesanía capital of Bolivia. Most of this shopping action focuses on the steep Calle Sagárnaga hill, between Avenida Mariscal Santa Cruz and Calle Isaac Tamayo, where expensive

---

Buying a Charango
Professional musician Daniel Harvey tramped around La Paz in search of the perfect charango. Here's what he found:

Although it's rumoured that Bolivia's best charango makers reside in central Bolivia, La Paz offers the widest variety of fine instruments. Once you wade past the herd of made-for-tourist charangos, two classes of instruments remain.

In the US$100 to US$200 category, the work of Juan Achá Campo stands out. His one-piece constructions of fine materials and consistent quality can be found at either of the two shops of La Casa de Charangos at Calle Sagárnaga 177 and 213 in La Paz. Also at Calle Sagárnaga 213 at locale #10, are René Gamboa's charangos, which play well although their necks are of two-piece construction. At Galería Artesanal #3 near the Iglesia de San Francisco, a charango maker called Rumillajta sells fine one-piece, squarish-necked instruments.

If you're looking to spend less money and are willing to invest more time, it's possible to buy a charango directly off the workbench. The quality of charangos in made-to-order shops varies greatly. Unlike the work of Achá and Rumillajta, these artesans utilise two-piece construction, which may not offer the durability of one-piece instruments; however, a fine instrument at one of these shops may be obtained for as little as US$35.

The most common complaint with smaller shops is their reluctance to tune instruments. Most artesans prefer building instruments to tuning them and because new strings stretch so much, tuning them is very time consuming. The conventional tuning is D (re), G (sol), B (ti), E (mi) and B (ti). The B strings are tuned one octave apart. Once a charango is to pitch, listen carefully to determine whether the frets are placed at proper intervals.

The brothers Bernardino and José Torrico work at Calle Linares 818 (Arte Aiquileño) and 820 (Yachay) in La Paz. José produces the most amazing small charangos called *hualaichos*, as well as fine larger instruments. Bernardino's charangos are labelled *sumakj llajta* and consist of some of the most beautiful woods to be found, but watch their intonation. Bernardino carves interesting and elaborate designs on the backs of some of his soundboxes, and both brothers are also adept at charango repair and reconstruction.

Only 30m away at 270 Calle Santa Cruz is the shop of Phuju Pampa. Sadly, most of his instruments are constructed with *quirquinchos* (armadillos), which are an endangered species in Bolivia. This type of instrument is less sonorous and more fragile than the wooden ones, so try out Phuju Pampa's wooden charangos; his work may appear sloppy but the charango I tested had exceptional voice.

Daniel Harvey, USA

All sorts of clothing, including ponchos, *chompas* (jumpers), *chullos* (woollen hats), vests, jackets and mufflers, are available in wool, llama and alpaca, or any combination of the three. Alpaca is the finest and most expensive. Some pieces are hand-dyed and woven or knitted, but others are obviously machine-made. Learn to tell the difference and never take an overzealous shopkeeper's word for it. Some would tell you it was made of solid gold if it would result in a sale.

Prices vary, of course, depending on quality, but expect to pay about US$15 to US$17 for a passable alpaca sweater and up to US$25 for a good one. A chullo costs about US$3 and a very nice poncho, up to US$16 to US$18. Prices for most things will be slightly higher in La Paz than in Puno or Cuzco (Peru) or directly from the artesans around the country, but this is justified by the quality and variety of items available.

Altiplano campesino wearing a chullo

shops compete with street vendors. As a general rule, the lower their elevation, the higher their prices. As a rule, shopkeepers are less willing to haggle over prices than are street vendors, whose prices are lower to begin with.

Some shops specialise in woodcarvings and ceramics from the Oriente, and silver items from Potosí. Others deal in rugs, wall-hangings, woven belts and pouches. Music tapes and recordings are available in small shops and stalls along Calle Evaristo Valle.

Quite a few shops sell tourist kitsch, an art form unto itself. You'll find ceramic ashtrays with Inca designs, fake Tiahuanaco figurines, costume jewellery, T-shirts and all manner of mass-produced woollens.

Buying Musical Instruments

Many La Paz artesans specialise in quenas, zampoñas, *tarkas* and *pinquillos*, among other traditional woodwinds. There's a lot of low quality or merely decorative tourist rubbish around; visit a reputable workshop where you'll pay a fraction of gift-shop prices and contribute directly to the artesan rather than to an intermediary.

There are clusters of artesans working along Calle Juan Granier near Plaza Garita de Lima in La Paz, not far from the cemetery. Other recommended shops in La Paz include those on Calle Isaac Tamayo near the top of literally breathtaking Calle Sagárnaga, and those at Calle Linares 855 and 859.

For information on buying a charango, see the boxed aside on the previous page.

Getting There & Away

AIR

South America isn't exactly a hub of international travel nor is it an obvious transit point along the major international routes. Air fares to or from Europe, North America and Australia often reflect this. There are some bargain fares to Quito (Ecuador), Lima (Peru) and Rio de Janeiro (Brazil), from where you can travel overland or find decent short-haul flight deals to La Paz or Santa Cruz.

You'll also get some relief with low-season fares and fortunately, the low season partially coincides with the best times to visit the region. Low and shoulder-season fares from Europe and North America typically apply from April to June. High season is between July and September and the several weeks around Christmas. The rest of the year falls into the shoulder-season category.

Buying Tickets

Your plane ticket will probably be the single most expensive item in your budget, and buying it can be an intimidating business. There is likely to be a multitude of airlines and travel agents hoping to separate you from your money, and it is always worth putting aside a few hours to research the current state of the market. Start early: some of the cheapest tickets have to be bought months in advance, and some popular flights sell out early. Talk to other recent travellers – they may be able to stop you making some of the same old mistakes. Look at the ads in newspapers and magazines (not forgetting the press of the ethnic group whose country you plan to visit), consult reference books and watch for special offers. Then phone around travel agents for bargains. (Airlines can supply information on routes and time-tables; however, except at times of inter-airline war, they do not supply the cheapest tickets.) Find out the fare, the route, the duration of the journey and any restrictions on the ticket. Then sit back and decide which is best for you.

You may discover that those incredibly cheap deals are 'fully booked, but there's another one that costs a bit more...' Or the flight is on an airline notorious for its poor safety standards and leaves you in the world's least favourite airport in mid-journey for 14 hours. Or the agent may claim to have the last two seats available for that country for the whole of July, and will hold them for you for a maximum of two hours. Don't panic – keep ringing around.

Use the fares quoted in this book as a guide only. They are approximate and based on the rates advertised by travel agents at the time of going to press. Quoted airfares do not necessarily constitute a recommendation for the carrier.

If you are travelling from the UK or the USA, you'll probably find the cheapest flights advertised by obscure bucket shops whose names haven't yet hit the telephone directory. Many such firms are honest and solvent, but there are a few rogues who'll take your money and disappear, only to reopen elsewhere a month or two later under a new name. If you are suspicious, don't hand over all the money at once – leave a deposit of 20% or so and pay the balance when you get the ticket. If the agent insists on cash in advance, go somewhere else. And once you have the ticket, ring the airline to confirm that your booking has actually been made.

You may opt to sacrifice the bargains and play it safe with a better-known travel agent. Firms such as STA Travel, which has offices worldwide, Council Travel in the USA or Travel CUTS in Canada aren't going to disappear overnight, leaving you clutching a receipt for a nonexistent ticket, and they do offer good prices to most destinations.

Once you have your ticket, copy down the ticket number, the flight number and other details, and keep the information safe and separate from the ticket. If the ticket is lost or stolen, this will help you get a replacement. It's sensible to buy travel insurance as early as possible. Travel insurance purchased the week before you fly may not cover flight delays caused by industrial action.

Economy-Class Tickets Standard economy-class tickets probably aren't the most economical way to go, though they do allow maximum flexibility and are valid for 12 months. Also, if you don't use them, they are fully refundable, as are unused sectors of a multiple ticket.

APEX Tickets APEX stands for Advance Purchase Excursion fare. These tickets usually cost 30% to 40% less than the full economy fare but there are restrictions. You must purchase the ticket at least 21 days in advance (sometimes more) and travel for a minimum period (usually 14 days) and return within a maximum period (90 or 180 days). Stopovers aren't allowed and if you must change your dates of travel or destination, you'll incur extra charges. If you cancel altogether, you'll probably receive a refund that is considerably less than the price of the ticket.

Round-the-World Fares Round-the-world (RTW) tickets have become all the rage in the past few years. Basically there are two types: airline tickets and agent tickets. An airline RTW ticket is issued by two or more airlines that have joined together to market a ticket that takes you around the world on their combined routes. Within certain time and stopover limitations, you can fly pretty well anywhere you choose using the combined routes, as long as you keep moving in approximately the same direction east or west.

The other type of RTW ticket, the agent ticket, is a combination of cheap fares strung together by an enterprising travel agent. This can be cheaper than an airline RTW ticket but the choice of routes may be limited.

However, most RTW tickets that include South America will be of this type. If you wish to include South America on an RTW routing, you'll probably wind up flying into Rio de Janeiro from London or into Lima from Miami or Los Angeles.

Student Discounts Some airlines offer student card-holders 20% to 25% discounts on their tickets. The same often applies to anyone under the age of 26. These discounts are generally only available on ordinary economy-class fares.

Bucket Shop Tickets At certain times of the year and/or on certain sectors, many airlines fly with empty seats. This isn't profitable and it's more cost-effective for them to fly full even if that means selling drastically discounted tickets. This is done by off-loading them onto 'bucket shops', travel agents who specialise in discounted fares. The agents, in turn, sell them to the public at reduced prices. These tickets are often the cheapest you'll find, but you can't buy them directly from the airlines. Availability varies widely, of course, so you'll not only have to be flexible in your travel plans, you'll also have to be quick off the mark as soon as an advertisement hits the press.

As you can imagine, there's lots of scope in this business for shady dealings. Many bucket shops are reputable organisations but there will always be the odd fly-by-night operator who sets up shop, takes your money and then either disappears or issues an invalid or unusable ticket. Be sure to check what you're buying before handing over the dough.

Children's Fares Airlines will usually carry babies up to two years of age at 10% of the relevant adult fare, and some carry them free of charge. For children between two and 12 years of age, the fare on international flights is usually 50% of the regular fare or 67% of a discounted fare. These days, most fares are considered discounted.

Travellers with Special Needs

If you have special needs of any sort – you've broken a leg, you're a vegetarian, travelling in a wheelchair, taking the baby, terrified of flying – let the airline know as soon as possible so that the staff can make all the appropriate arrangements. Restate your needs when you reconfirm your booking and again when you check in at the airport. It may also be worth ringing around the airlines before you make your booking to find out how they can handle your particular needs.

Airports and airlines can be surprisingly

Air Travel Glossary

Baggage Allowance This will be written on your ticket: usually one 20 kg item to go in the hold, plus one item of hand luggage.

Bumped Just because you have a confirmed seat doesn't mean you're going to get on the plane – see Overbooking.

Cancellation Penalties If you have to cancel or change an Apex ticket there are often heavy penalties involved, insurance can sometimes be taken out against these penalties. Some airlines impose penalties on regular tickets as well, particularly against 'no show' passengers.

Check In Airlines ask you to check in a certain time ahead of the flight departure (usually 1½ hours on international flights). If you fail to check in on time and the flight is overbooked the airline can cancel your booking and give your seat to somebody else.

Discounted Tickets There are two types of discounted fares – officially discounted (see Promotional Fares) and unofficially discounted. The lowest prices often impose drawbacks like flying with unpopular airlines, inconvenient schedules, or unpleasant routes and connections. A discounted ticket can save you other things than money – you may be able to pay Apex prices without the associated Apex advance booking and other requirements. Discounted tickets only exist where there is fierce competition. [Full Fares] Airlines traditionally offer first class (coded F), business class (coded J) and economy class (coded Y) tickets. These days there are so many promotional and discounted fares available from the regular economy class that few passengers pay full economy fare.

No Shows No shows are passengers who fail to show up for their flight, sometimes due to unexpected delays or disasters, sometimes due to simply forgetting, sometimes because they made more than one booking and didn't bother to cancel the one they didn't want. Full fare passengers who fail to turn up are sometimes entitled to travel on a later flight. The rest of us are penalised (see Cancellation Penalties).

On Request An unconfirmed booking for a flight.

Open Jaws A return ticket where you fly out to one place but return from another. If available this can save you backtracking to your arrival point.

Overbooking Airlines hate to fly empty seats and since every flight has some passengers who fail to show up (see No Shows) airlines often book more passengers than they have seats. Usually the excess passengers balance those who fail to show up but occasionally somebody gets bumped. If this happens guess who it is most likely to be? The passengers who check in late.

Promotional Fares Officially discounted fares like Apex fares which are available from travel agents or direct from the airline.

Reconfirmation At least 72 hours prior to departure time of an onward or return flight you must contact the airline and 'reconfirm' that you intend to be on the flight. If you don't do this the airline can delete your name from the passenger list and you could lose your seat. You don't have to reconfirm the first flight on your itinerary or if your stopover is less than 72 hours. It doesn't hurt to reconfirm more than once.

Standby A discounted ticket where you only fly if there is a seat free at the last moment. Standby fares are usually only available on domestic routes.

Tickets Out An entry requirement for many countries is that you have an onward or return ticket, in other words, a ticket out of the country. If you're not sure what you intend to do next, the easiest solution is to buy the cheapest onward ticket to a neighbouring country or a ticket from a reliable airline which can later be refunded if you do not use it.

Transferred Tickets Airline tickets cannot be transferred from one person to another. Travellers sometimes try to sell the return half of their ticket, but officials can ask you to prove that you are the person named on the ticket. This is unlikely to happen on domestic flights, but on an international flight tickets may be compared with passports. ■

helpful, but they do need advance warning. Most international airports can provide escorts from check-in desk to plane where needed, and there should be ramps, lifts, accessible toilets and reachable phones. Aircraft toilets, on the other hand, are likely to present a problem; travellers should discuss this with the airline at an early stage and, if necessary, with their doctor.

Guide dogs for the blind usually must travel in a specially pressurised baggage compartment with other animals, away from their owner. All guide dogs will be subject to the same quarantine laws (six months in isolation, etc) as any other animal when entering or returning to countries currently free of rabies, such as the UK or Australia.

Deaf travellers can ask for airport and in-flight announcements to be written down for them.

Reputable international airlines usually provide nappies (diapers), tissues, talcum and all the other paraphernalia needed to keep babies clean, dry and half-happy. Airlines generally provide 'Skycots' for infants if requested in advance; they'll hold a child weighing up to about 10 kg. Pushchairs (strollers) can often be taken as hand luggage.

The USA

In the USA, the best way to find cheap flights is by checking the Sunday travel sections in major newspapers, such as the *Los Angeles Times* or the *San Francisco Examiner* or *Chronicle* on the west coast and the *New York Times* on the east coast. The student travel bureaus – STA Travel or Council Travel – are also worth a go but you may have to produce proof of student status and, in some cases, be under 26 years of age to qualify for their discounted fares.

North America is a relative newcomer to the bucket shop traditions of Europe and Asia, so ticket availability and restrictions need to be weighed against what is offered on the standard APEX or full economy (coach) tickets.

The magazines specialising in bucket shop advertisements in London (see the discussion under Europe) will post copies so you can study current pricing before you decide on a course of action.

Also recommended is the newsletter *Travel Unlimited* (PO Box 1058, Allston, MA 02134), which details the cheapest airfares and courier possibilities for destinations all over the world from the USA.

As with US-based travellers, Canadians will probably find the best deals travelling to South America via Miami. Travel CUTS has offices in all major Canadian cities. The *Toronto Globe & Mail* carries travel agents' ads.

Discount Travel Agencies Although North Americans won't get the great deals that are available in London, there are a few discount agencies which keep a lookout for the best airfare bargains.

CHA
    333 River Rd, Vanier, Ottawa, Ontario KIL 8H9
Canadian International Student Services
    80 Richmond St W #1202 Toronto, Ontario M5H 2A4 (☎ (416) 364 2738)
Council on International Educational Exchange
    205 East 42nd St, New York, NY 10017
STA Travel
    48 East 11th St, New York, NY 10017 (☎ (212) 486 0503)
    Suite 507, 2500 Wilshire Blvd, Los Angeles, CA 90057 (☎ (213) 380 2184)
    166 Geary St, Suite 702, San Francisco, CA 94108 (☎ (415) 391 8407)
Travel International
    114 Forrest Ave, Suite 205, Narbeth, PA 19072 (☎ (215) 668 2182)
Uni Travel
    PO Box 12485, St Louis, MO 63132 (☎ (314) 569 2501)
Whole World Travel
    Suite 400, 17 East 45th St, New York, NY 10017 (☎ (212) 986 9470)

Nondiscounted Tickets Flights originating in the USA are subject to numerous restrictions and regulations because of competition between carriers and governmental red tape in determining fare structures. This is especially true of bargain tickets; anything cheaper than the standard tourist or economy fare must be purchased at least 14 days, and sometimes as much as 30 days, prior to departure.

In addition, you'll have to book departure and return dates in advance and these tickets will be subject to minimum and maximum stay requirements: usually seven days and six months, respectively.

It's often cheaper to purchase a return ticket and trash the return portion than to pay the one-way fare. From the USA, open tickets, which allow an open return date within a 12-month period, are generally not available, and penalties of up to 50% are imposed if you make changes to the return booking.

From the USA the major carrier gateway cities are New York, Los Angeles and Miami. All have basically the same fare structure. The best deals are out of Miami.

Economy fares often must be purchased two weeks in advance, and usually require a minimum stay of two weeks and a maximum stay of three months.

If you want to fly directly between Miami and Bolivia, your best bets are American Airlines, which flies three times weekly to La Paz, and Lloyd Aéreo Boliviano (LAB), which flies daily between Miami, Santa Cruz and La Paz via Panama City (Panama), Caracas (Venezuela) and/or Manaus (Brazil). The cheapest one-way/return fares from Miami to La Paz or Santa Cruz are US$542/832.

Some of the cheapest flights between the USA and Brazil are charters between Manaus, Belém, Rio de Janeiro or São Paulo (all in Brazil) and Miami (the Disney World express!). Manaus, which lies halfway between Rio and Miami, is a useful gateway city for any long circuit around South America.

From the US west coast to Lima (Peru), the best fare is on Varig, which offers return-only APEX fares of US$915. Varig flies on Sunday and Wednesday. It is less expensive to travel via Miami using any Super Saver ticket from Los Angeles than to fly to South America directly from Los Angeles.

Australia & New Zealand

Travel between Australasia and South America is not cheap. It makes sense for Australasians to think in terms of an RTW ticket or a return ticket to Europe with a stopover in the USA, Rio de Janeiro, Buenos Aires or Santiago. RTW tickets can still be found for as little as A$2100, but these tend to include only northern hemisphere stopovers; surcharges are levied for inclusion of Latin America or the South Pacific.

The best publications for finding good deals are the Saturday editions of daily newspapers such as the *Sydney Morning Herald* and the Melbourne *Age*.

One option is to take advantage of Qantas or Air New Zealand's APEX fares between Sydney or Auckland and the US west coast which are about A$1500 return, with up to three stopovers. From Los Angeles or San Francisco it's a matter of overlanding or finding a cheap APEX ticket to Miami.

Aerolíneas Argentinas flies over the South Pole once a week via Sydney, Auckland, Buenos Aires and Rio de Janeiro. LanChile flies Sydney, Papeete, Easter Island, Santiago for A$2599. Qantas flies from Sydney to Rio de Janeiro via North America for A$4130, with three stopovers. Its Rio route via Johannesburg or Bangkok costs A$3304.

Discount Travel Agencies In Australia and New Zealand, inexpensive travel is available mainly from STA Travel, which has branches in all capital cities and on most university campuses.

Europe

Bucket Shop Tickets There are bucket shops by the dozen in London, Paris, Amsterdam, Brussels, Frankfurt and other places. In London, several magazines with lots of bucket shop ads can put you on to the current deals. The best ones include:

Globe BCM Roving, London WC1N 3XX. A newsletter published for members of the Globetrotters' Club. It covers obscure destinations and can help in finding travelling companions.

The Star & SA Times (☎ (0171) 405 6148, fax (0171) 405 6290, e-mail satimes@atlas.co.uk), Tower House, Sovereign Park, Market Harborough, Leics LE16 9EF, UK. Published mainly for South African visitors and expats in London, but it contains a lot of good travel advertising.

Time Out (☎ (0171) 836 4411), Tower House, Southampton St, London WC2E 7HD. London's weekly entertainment guide. It also contains travel information and advertising, and is available at bookshops, newsagents and newsstands. Subscription enquiries should be addressed to Time Out Subs, Unit 8, Grove Ash, Bletchley, Milton Keynes MK1 1BZ, UK.

TNT Magazine (☎ (0171) 937 3985), 52 Earls Court Rd, London W8, UK. Can be picked up (for free) at most London Underground stations and on street corners around Earls Court and Kensington. It caters to Aussies and Kiwis working in the UK and is therefore full of travel advertising. In these magazines, you'll find discounted fares to Lima, Quito and Rio de Janeiro, as well as other parts of South America. Many of them use AeroPerú or Varig.

Trailfinder This magazine is put out quarterly by Trailfinders (☎ (0171) 603 1515, fax (0171) 938 3305), 42-48 Earls Court Rd, London W8 6EJ, UK. It's free in London, but if you want it mailed it costs UK£6 for four issues in the UK or Ireland and UK£10 or the equivalent for four issues elsewhere (airmail). Trailfinders can fix you up with all your ticketing requirements, as well as jabs, anti-malarials, visas and travel publications. It also has a library of information for prospective travellers. It's been in business for years and the staff are friendly.

Farang (La Rue 8 à 4261, Braives, Belgium) is a newsletter that deals with exotic destinations.

You'll find the latest deals listed in the travel sections of the Saturday and Sunday editions of London newspapers. Prices for discounted flights between London and Rio start at around UK£300 one way or UK£550 return – bargain hunters should have little trouble finding even lower prices. A word of warning, however: don't take travel agency advertised fares as gospel truth. To comply with advertising laws in the UK, companies must be able to offer *some* tickets at their cheapest quoted price, but they may only have one or two of them per week. If you're not one of the lucky punters, you may be looking at higher fares. Start looking for deals well in advance of your intended departure so you can get a fair idea of what's available.

Discount Travel Agencies Especially in London, a growing number of travel agencies offer very good deals on long-haul travel. The following are good places to initiate your price comparisons:

France
> *Council Travel*, Rue St Augustine, 2ème, Paris (☎ 01 42 66 20 87)
> *Council Travel*, 22 Rue des Pyramides, 1er, Paris (☎ 01 44 55 55 44)

Germany
> *Alternativ Tours*, Wilmersdorferstrasse 94, Berlin (☎ (030) 881 2089)
> *SRID Reisen*, Bergerstrasse 1178, Frankfurt (☎ (069) 43 01 91)
> *SRS Studenten Reise Service*, Marienstrasse 23, Berlin (☎ (030) 281 5033)

Ireland
> *USIT Travel*, 19 Aston Quay, Dublin (☎ (01) 679 8833)

Netherlands
> *NBBS*, Rokin 38, Amsterdam (☎ (020) 624 0989)
> *Malibu Travel*, Damrak 30, Amsterdam (☎ (020) 623 6814)

UK
> *Bridge the World*, 52 Chalk Farm Rd, Camden Town, London NW1 8AN (☎ (0171) 911 0900, fax (0171) 916 1724)
> *Journey Latin America (JLA)*, 14-16 Devonshire Rd, Chiswick, London W42HD (☎ (0181) 747 3108, fax (0181) 742 1312); publishes a very useful *Flights Bulletin*
> *Passage to South America*, 113 Shepherds Bush Rd, London W6 7LP (☎ (0171) 602 9889, fax (0171) 602 4251
> *Quest Worldwide*, 29 Castle St, Kingston, Surrey KT1 1ST (☎ (0181) 547 3322)
> *South American Experience*, 47 Causton St, Pimlico, London SW1P 4AT (☎ (0171) 976 5511, fax (0171) 976 6908)
> *STA Travel*, 74 Old Brompton Rd, London SW7 (☎ (0171) 937 9962); 117 Euston Rd, London NW1 2SX (☎ (0171) 465 0486)
> *Trailfinders*, 42-48 Earls Court Rd, London W8 (☎ (0171) 938 3366); 194 Kensington High St, London W8 (☎ (0171) 938 3939)
> *Travel Bug*, 125A Gloucester Rd, London SW7 4SF (☎ (0171) 835 2000); 597 Cheetham Hill Rd, Manchester M8 5EJ (☎ (0161) 721 4000)
> *Travel Mood*, 246 Edgware Rd, London W2 1DS (☎ (0171) 258 0280)

Nondiscounted Tickets The cheapest direct flight from Europe to Bolivia is currently the weekly Líneas Aéreas Paraguayas (Lapsa) flight from Brussels to Santa Cruz (Bolivia), and Asunción (Paraguay).

Another possible routing is via Miami. On whatever bargain-basement trans-Atlantic carrier is currently operating, you can hop to New York for as little as US$150 in the low season. APEX return fares between New York and Miami can be as low as US$99, but if you're pressed for time, Delta, United, British Airways, Virgin Airways and others offer direct flights between London and Miami for as little as US$400 return.

Note that some US airports (such as Raleigh-Durham, North Carolina) aren't set up to handle international transit passengers. If you must transit one of these airports, you'll need to clear US immigration, even for a stay of only a couple of hours. Some European citizens, including those of Britain and Germany, can participate in the US visa waiver scheme unless they're travelling on a non-accredited airline (which includes all Latin American airlines). Transiting through major airports, such as New York (JFK) or Miami, will be no problem provided you aren't transferring to a domestic flight within the USA.

For information on flights between Miami and South America, see the USA section earlier in this chapter.

Asia

From Asia, the hot tickets are on Japan Airlines (JAL) and Singapore Airlines. JAL flies from Tokyo to Rio de Janeiro and São Paulo (Brazil) via Los Angeles and it has reasonable fares to Rio from the west coast of the USA.

Elsewhere in South America

Argentina Lloyd Aéro Boliviano (LAB) has a service from Buenos Aires to La Paz via Santa Cruz on Tuesday, Friday and Sunday. One-way/return fares are US$310/500 to La Paz and US$256/408 to Santa Cruz. On Sundays, this flight also serves Salta (Argentina). On Mondays, Aereolíneas Argentinas

(☎ 375711, fax 391059, La Paz) flies between Buenos Aires and Santa Cruz via Salta and Córdoba, and on Thursday and Saturday, between Buenos Aires and La Paz.

Brazil LAB has flights between Rio de Janeiro, São Paulo and La Paz via Santa Cruz four times weekly. One-way/return fares from Rio are US$341/517 to La Paz and US$273/412 to Santa Cruz. From São Paulo, they're US$317/479 to La Paz and US$262/397 to Santa Cruz. Varig/Cruzeiro (☎ 314040, La Paz) flies the same route on Tuesday, Thursday, Friday and Saturday. On Friday AeroPerú (☎ 370002, La Paz) flies between La Paz, Santa Cruz, Rio de Janeiro and São Paulo. In addition, LAB does a Thursday run between Manaus and Santa Cruz for US$207/414 one-way/return. There is a US$18 departure tax on international flights originating in Brazil.

Chile LanChile (☎ 358377, La Paz) and LAB both fly daily between La Paz, Arica (US$92/147 one way/return), Iquique (US$119/203) and Santiago (US$215/329). Passengers departing Chile are subject to a departure tax of US$15.

Paraguay LAB flies between Asunción, Santa Cruz and La Paz on Tuesday and Friday. One-way/return fares from Asunción are US$168/291 to Santa Cruz, US$215/385 to La Paz.

Peru LAB, KLM (☎ 323965, La Paz), AeroPerú and Lufthansa (☎ 372170, La Paz) all fly between Lima and La Paz. LAB has a service on Tuesday, Thursday, Saturday and Sunday for US$180 one way. To Cuzco, AeroPerú flies daily except Sunday (about US$100 one way) and KLM flies twice weekly. Peru levies an air-ticket tax of 21% for Peruvian residents and 7% for non-resident tourists.

LAND

The popular and inexpensive route between North and South America along the 'Gringo Trail' includes eight fascinating countries between the Río Grande (Mexico-US border) and the Colombian border. Belize and Costa Rica are currently at the top of the tourist heap.

Because the Pan-American (or Inter-american) Highway is broken in Eastern Panama, travellers are obliged to either fly into Colombia or travel overland past the Darién Gap (Panama) using a combination of methods, all of which include at least a seven to 14 day slog through the rainforest. For details on this route, see Lonely Planet's *Central America on a shoestring*.

Argentina

There are two major land crossings between Bolivia and Argentina – at Pocitos and between Villazón and La Quiaca – as well as a minor crossing between Bermejo and Aguas Blancas.

Argentine officials are extremely vigilant about drugs and no one entering from Bolivia escapes suspicion. Expect thorough searches by customs and police at the frontier and 20 km down the road, inside Argentina.

Via La Quiaca From Salta or Jujuy in north-western Argentina, buses leave every couple of hours during the day for La Quiaca, opposite the Bolivian town of Villazón. It takes about 20 minutes to walk between the Argentine and Bolivian bus terminals, excluding immigration procedures, but taxis are available.

From Villazón, buses run to Tupiza and Potosí, and trains leave for Tupiza, Uyuni, Oruro and La Paz on Monday, Tuesday, Thursday and Friday; an express train runs on Saturday.

La Quiaca and Villazón are covered in the Southern Altiplano chapter.

Via Pocitos The border crossing at tiny Pocitos is just a short distance south of Yacuiba (Bolivia), and north of Tartagal (Argentina). The walk across the border between Pocitos (Argentina), and Pocitos (Bolivia), takes about 10 minutes. There are taxis between Pocitos and Yacuiba and buses to and from Tartagal.

From Tucumán in north central Argentina, take a bus to Embarcación (Argentina) and Tartagal, and from there to Pocitos on the frontier. There are trains from Yacuiba to Santa Cruz daily except Wednesday and Sunday, as well as daily buses to and from Tarija, Santa Cruz and Sucre. See the Pocitos and Yacuiba sections in the South Central Bolivia & the Chaco chapter for further information.

Via Orán This is a minor border crossing with immigration formalities in the hamlet of Aguas Blancas, one hour by bus from Orán. Aguas Blancas lies on the Río Bermejo opposite Bermejo (Bolivia). Access across the river is by ferry. From Bermejo, several bus companies do daily runs to Tarija. See the South Central Bolivia & the Chaco chapter for details.

Brazil

Via Corumbá Corumbá, opposite the Bolivian border town of Quijarro, has both train and bus connections from São Paulo, Rio de Janeiro, Cuiabá and southern Brazil. It is the busiest port of entry along the Brazil-Bolivia border.

Once in Corumbá, take a bus to the frontier and from there go by taxi to the Quijarro railhead (US$1 per person). From Quijarro, passenger trains leave for Santa Cruz on Monday, Tuesday, Thursday and Saturday. The more frequent freight trains will also accept passengers in the *bodegas* (boxcars), but they may be less comfortable. During the wet you may face waits of several days.

From Cáceres, south-west of Cuiabá, you can cross to San Matías in Bolivia and from there either take a bus to San Ignacio de Velasco or fly to Santa Cruz (via Roboré).

For further information, see the Santa Cruz, Quijarro and Corumbá sections.

Via Northern Brazil From Brasiléia, in Acre state, you can cross into Cobija, Bolivia. Only a short time ago, it was necessary to fly from there to other Bolivian cities, but now

Cobija is connected to the rest of the country by road, and buses run to Riberalta at least three times weekly during the dry season. From there, dry-weather roads run to La Paz and Guayaramerín.

A more popular crossing is by ferry from Guajará-Mirim, across the Río Mamoré in Brazil, into Guayaramerín, which is on the Bolivian bank of the river. From there, you can travel the long and dusty bus routes to Riberalta and on to Cobija, Rurrenabaque or La Paz.

From Guayaramerín, it's also possible to take a 10 day (or longer) river trip up the Río Mamoré and Río Ichilo to the highway at Puerto Villarroel, which has a highway link with Cochabamba, or, when the water is high, from Riberalta up the Río Beni to Rurrenabaque. Alternatively, LAB has flights from Guayaramerín and Riberalta to cities in central and southern Bolivia.

For further details, see the Guayaramerín, Guajará-Mirim, Cobija and Brasiléia sections in the Amazon Basin chapter.

Chile

It's worth noting that meat, fruit and vegetables cannot be carried from Bolivia into Chile and will be confiscated at the border. You will, however, be issued with a receipt.

Via Arica Ferrobuses run between La Paz and Arica, with immigration formalities at the Visviri/Charaña border crossing. They leave Arica on Tuesday and Saturday mornings, as well as on Thursday in the summer. This trip gets extremely cold, especially in the border area. In fact, Bolivians have a saying '...mas frío que Charaña', 'colder than Charaña', which indicates serious cold, so carry warm clothing.

Flota Litoral and Geminis both have two buses weekly between Arica and the main La Paz bus terminal, via the Chungará/Tambo Quemado border crossing. This formerly character-building route is currently being paved and when it's finished, the 18 hour trip will be shortened to as little as seven hours. Trans-Sabaya also has a twice-weekly service between Oruro and Chungará (Lauca

National Park), with direct connections to Arica. For more information, see the La Paz and Oruro Getting There & Away sections.

Agencia Martinez, also in Arica, runs a Wednesday bus service from Arica to Visviri to meet the Bolivian train that connects Viacha (south of La Paz) with the frontier at Charaña.

Via Iquique Both Flota Litoral and Geminis each have three buses weekly between Iquique and La Paz, via the Colchane border crossing. Their offices are at the main La Paz bus terminal.

Via Antofagasta/Calama Coming from Antofagasta, you must first take a bus from the Tramaca bus terminal to Calama (US$3, two hours). From there, a Wednesday evening train goes to Ollagüe on the Bolivian border, eight hours uphill from Calama. In Ollagüe, passengers cross the border to Avaroa on foot to connect with the Bolivian train to Uyuni and Oruro. Although this connection does work occasionally, it may also entail waits of up to 12 hours for the Bolivian train to arrive (as one reader put it 'time enough to get to know all the Ollagüe pigs by their first names'). As on all routes between Chile and Bolivia, warm clothes are vital. For details, see the Southern Altiplano chapter.

Paraguay

The three-day overland route between Bolivia and Paraguay is extremely rough and sandy, but the trip is now negotiated by hardy camiones (trucks) and buses during the winter dry season. To go from Asunción to Santa Cruz, Flota Santa Ana leaves the main bus terminal on Monday, Wednesday and Friday, and STEL Turismo (☎ 26059, Asunción) leaves on Friday. The fare is US$72. Camiones run every few days between Filadelfia (Paraguay), and Boyuibe (Bolivia), charging US$10 to US$15 per person.

Coming from Paraguay, it's easier to cross into Brazil at Ponta Porã from Pedro Juan Caballero and travel by bus or train to

Corumbá in Brazil (18 hours with a change at Campo Grande). At Corumbá you can cross to Quijarro (Bolivia).

Peru

Via Puno There are two routes from Puno, which is Peru's main access point for Bolivia. The quicker but less interesting route is by *micro* (minibus) from Puno to the frontier at Desaguadero (US$2, two hours), where you can connect with several daily micros to La Paz (US$2, 4½ hours).

The more scenic and interesting route is via Copacabana and the Estrecho de Tiquina (Straits of Tiquina). Micros leave from Puno and enter Bolivia at Yunguyo, about 11 km from Copacabana. There you connect with another minibus, or with a bus company, for the four to five hour trip to La Paz, including the boat across the straits. The entire run from Puno to La Paz can be done in a day, but the Copacabana area merits a couple of days exploration. See the Copacabana section in the Lake Titicaca chapter for more information.

Via Other Destinations There are other obscure border crossings, such as the one from Puerto Acosta north of Lake Titicaca, and a couple of ports of entry along the rivers of the north, but they require some effort and no public transport is available. Details on crossings from far northern Bolivia are under Cobija in the Amazon Basin chapter.

Car & Motorcycle

An explanation of how to take your own vehicle to South America is beyond the scope of this book. Suffice it to say that you can enter Bolivia by private vehicle from any of the neighbouring countries – Chile, Peru, Brazil, Argentina or Paraguay. The routes from Brazil and Chile are poor, and the one from Paraguay should be considered only with 4WD and careful preparation. For details about driving within Bolivia, see the Car & Motorcycle section in the Getting Around chapter.

RIVER

Brazil

Information on boats between Asunción (Paraguay) and Corumbá (Brazil), just over the Brazilian border from Quijarro, is available at the Porto Geral in Corumbá. Now that the regular riverboat service is in mothballs and no longer runs between Asunción and Corumbá, river transport between Paraguay and Bolivia is likely to involve a series of shorter river journeys and informal arrangement with individual boat captains.

Paraguay

From Asunción, there's a regular river service to Concepción (Paraguay), which costs US$8 (Gs 14,000) in a hammock on deck and US$11 (Gs 19,000) for a cabin. Make arrangements with the captain of the boat, which moors one long block west of the main port area in Asunción. To travel from Concepción on to Corumbá by river isn't particularly difficult, but it will involve making informal arrangements with boat owners. You'll probably wind up doing it in two stages: Concepción to Bahía Negra (northern Paraguay) and then Bahía Negra to Corumbá.

DEPARTURE TAXES

A US$20 departure tax is charged on international flights for those who have spent less than 90 days in Bolivia. Those staying longer than 90 days must pay an additional US$30. The tax is payable to the aviation authority, AASANA, after check in.

ORGANISED TOURS

There are literally hundreds of tour companies out there, and a growing number are adding South America to their lists of itinerary offerings.

There are basically two types of tour companies. Overseas agents book transport and hotels, and cobble together a range of itineraries, and locally based operators actually provide the tours. Within Bolivia, there are quite a few of these tour companies, most of which run their trips in small coaches, minibuses or 4WD vehicles.

This sort of tour is less prevalent in Bolivia than in neighbouring Peru, where 'checklist sites' such as Cuzco and Machu Picchu serve as mass tourism magnets. As yet, Bolivia has few such sites, and it hasn't really entered into the mass tourism consciousness. A typical Bolivia package tour booked entirely overseas will probably include some sort of hydrofoil excursion on Lake Titicaca, a stop on Isla del Sol, a visit to the Tiahuanaco ruins, perhaps a drive to Chacaltaya, and museum visits and shopping in La Paz. Some tours also include Sucre or Potosí and increasingly, a circuit through the far south-west. Although this is a comfortable way to check off the sites, it's also a confining and expensive way to travel, and it isn't for everyone.

Considerably more appealing for most people are adventure tour packages, which feature activities more than sightseeing and are usually designed with some sort of ecotourism angle in mind. These may include anything from treks in the Cordillera Real or ascents of 6000m peaks to wildlife expeditions in the Bolivian Amazon, and you'll find them advertised mainly in hiking, mountaineering and wildlife magazines.

If you're going the package route, it always pays to shop around for deals; especially in Europe, it's becoming increasingly popular to look for late bookings, which are available at a fraction of the normal price. The best place to start looking is the travel sections of weekend newspapers. In some cases, there are special late bookings counters at international airports.

If you prefer not to organise all your time beforehand, you can always book just your flights and your first few nights' accommodation, then take your chances on joining a tour locally (lists of local operators are provided in the Organised Tours section in the Getting Around chapter). Naturally, time flexibility is essential, but you'll often find some very good deals.

The following list will give you an idea of the range of packages available, including some of the more creative and offbeat offerings. These tours can be booked directly or through a travel agent.

UK

Exodus Walking Holidays, 9 Weir Rd, London SW12 0LT (☎ (0181) 675 5550; fax (0181) 673 0779). Exodus, which is better known for its overland trips, also does hiking and trekking excursions. Its best Bolivian programme is probably the seven day Inca Llama Trek, which traverses the northern end of the Cordillera Real.

High Places Ltd, Globe Works, Penistone Road, Sheffield S6 3AE (☎ (0114) 275 7500; fax (0114) 275 3870). This hiking and trekking specialist offers walking itineraries around Lake Titicaca and the Cordillera Apolobamba.

Journey Latin America, 14-16 Devonshire Rd, Chiswick, London W4 2HD (☎ (0181) 747 8315; fax (0181) 742 1312). This popular company is better known for good airline deals, but it also organises highlights trips around Latin America. In Bolivia, the focus is on La Paz, Potosí, Lake Titicaca and the Yungas.

South American Experience, 47 Causton St, London SW1P 4AT (☎ 0171) 976 5511; fax (0171) 976 6908). Basic tours all over the continent, with catchy names including the Llama, the Potato and the Coffee Bean; several of these include Bolivian highlights. A plus point is that the airfare portion of the tour is likely to be the lowest available.

Wildwings, International House, Bank Rd, Bristol BS15 2LX (☎ (0117) 984 8040; fax (0117) 967 4444). If you've always wanted a bird-watching holiday in the mountains and rainforests, here's your opportunity. Wildwings concentrates on birds and if you see larger animals as well, they're frosting on the cake!

USA

Focus Tours, Inc, 14821 Hillside Lane, Burnsville, MN 55306 (☎ 612) 892 7830; fax (612) 892 0900. Operates bird-watching tours from the Andes to the Amazon, and other natural-history excursions in Bolivia and other countries.

Myths & Mountains, Inc, 976 Tee Ct, Incline Village, NV 89451 USA (☎ (702) 832 5455; fax (702) 832 4454). Organises small-group tours that focus on natural folk medicine, archaeology and indigenous arts and crafts. It aims to emphasise socially and ecologically responsible tourism, and use local guides and encourage cultural interaction. Offerings include trips in the Cordillera Apolobamba and Kallahuayas country, the Yunga Cruz trek, archaeology trips around south-western Bolivia, and arts and crafts tours in both the highlands and lowlands.

Rainforest Expeditions, PO Box 2242, Nevada

City, CA 95959 (☎ (916) 265 0958). Runs exciting camping, canoeing and kayaking trips in the rainforests of northern Bolivia. It's a good choice if you really want to get off the trampled track.

Sobek Mountain Travel, 6420 Fairmount Ave, El Cerrito, CA 94530 (☎ (510) 527 8100 or toll-free (800) 227 2384; fax (510) 525 7710). This well-known adventure travel company operates a range of climbing and trekking trips in the Cordillera Real.

Wilderness Travel, 801 Allston Way, Berkeley, CA 94710 (☎ toll-free (800) 368 368 2794). The speciality of this firm is guided hiking, trekking and other adventure activities in the Cordillera Real and beyond.

Overland Trips

Overland trips are very popular, especially with UK and Australasian travellers. They're designed mainly for first-time travellers who feel uncomfortable striking out on their own or for those who prefer guaranteed social interaction to the uncertainties of the road. If you have the slightest inclination towards independence or would feel confined travelling with the same group of 25 or so for most of the trip, think twice before booking something like this.

For information or a list of agents selling overland packages in your home country, contact one of the following South America overland operators, all of which are based in the UK (Exodus and Encounter also have offices in Australia, New Zealand, the USA and Canada, which are contactable through the UK offices).

Dragoman, Camp Green, Kenton Rd, Debenham, Stowmarket, Suffolk IP14 6LA (☎ (01728) 861133; fax (01728) 861127)

Encounter Overland, 267 Old Brompton Rd, London SW5 9JA (☎ (0171) 3706845)

Exodus Overland Expeditions, 9 Weir Rd, London SW12 0LT (☎ (0181) 673 0859; fax (0181) 675 7996)

Guerba Expeditions, 101 Eden Vale Rd, Westbury, Wiltshire BA13 3QX (☎ (01373) 826689; fax (01373) 838351)

Hann Overland, 201/203 Vauxhall Bridge Rd, London SW1V 1ER (☎ (0171) 834 7337; fax (0171) 828 7745)

Kumuka Expeditions, 40 Earls Court Rd, London W8 6EJ (☎ (0171) 937 8855; fax (0171) 937 6664)

Top Deck, Top Deck House, 131/135 Earls Court Rd, London SW5 9RH (☎ (0171) 244 8641; fax (0171) 373 6201)

World Tracks Ltd, 12 Abingdon Rd, London W8 6AF (☎ (0171) 937 3028; fax (0171) 937 3176)

WARNING

The information in this chapter is particularly vulnerable to change: prices for international travel are volatile, routes are introduced and cancelled, schedules change, special deals come and go, and rules and visa requirements are amended. Airlines and governments seem to take a perverse pleasure in making price structures and regulations as complicated as possible. You should check directly with the airline or a travel agent to make sure you understand how a fare (and ticket you may buy) works. In addition, the travel industry is highly competitive and there are many lurks and perks.

The upshot of this is that you should get opinions, quotes and advice from as many airlines and travel agents as possible before you part with your hard-earned cash. The details given in this chapter should be regarded as pointers and are not a substitute for your own careful, up-to-date research.

Getting Around

AIR

Air travel in Bolivia is inexpensive and is the quickest and most reliable means of reaching out-of-the-way places. It's also the only means of transport that doesn't wash out during the wet season, and although schedule disruption does occur, planes can get through even during summer flooding in northern Bolivia.

Bolivia's national carrier is Lloyd Aéreo Boliviano (LAB), which flies to the major cities and remote corners of Bolivia, as well as to Miami, Panama and most major South American cities. Fares are quite reasonable, and during the dry season, flights run more or less on schedule.

LAB offers rudimentary but adequate service and is proud of its skilled pilots, who are familiar with Bolivia's difficult terrain, and its near-perfect safety record (a DC-6 did go down in the Cordillera Quimsa Cruz in 1969, but this was because of a politically motivated bombing). LAB has ticket offices in every town it serves and, except around holidays, seats are usually available the day before the flight.

LAB offers a special LABpass, an air pass that allows four flights between any of the main cities served by LAB: La Paz, Cochabamba, Sucre, Santa Cruz, Tarija and Trinidad. It costs US$150 and is available from LAB offices and travel agents.

Bolivia's other domestic airline, AeroSur, generally offers better service than LAB, including snacks and in-flight meals on longer flights. It's mostly competitive with LAB between the major cities, but fares to Amazon Basin towns are notably higher. In general, AeroSur covers the profitable runs (eg La Paz-Cochabamba and La Paz-Santa Cruz) more frequently than LAB and also fills in gaps in LAB's schedules (such as Camiri, Yacuiba and San Borja), but it doesn't serve Tarija or smaller towns in the northern lowlands.

The military airline, Transportes Aéreos Militares (TAM), also operates domestic flights. (Its logo – a lost pelican in a thunderstorm over Illimani – isn't so much a comment on the operation as a political statement on Bolivia's lost seacoast.) TAM uses small planes, such as the Fairchild F27, which fly closer to the ground than the big jets and allow better aerial viewing and photography. As with most military operations, schedules can change, flights may be cancelled and reservations may dematerialise. Perhaps as a result of its poor public image, TAM appears to be winding down its passenger operations and it isn't a viable alternative unless you are really stuck.

All airlines allow passengers to carry 20 kg of luggage, excluding hand luggage, without additional charges. If your flight isn't full, you might get away with a bit more.

Fares

The following are sample one-way LAB fares (all include a 4.2% domestic tax):

From La Paz to:	US$
Cochabamba	41
Puerto Suárez	145
Riberalta	128
Santa Cruz	91
Sucre	56
Tarija	88
Trinidad	57

Domestic Air Taxes

AASANA, the government agency responsible for airports and air traffic, charges a US$1.20 to US$2 domestic airport departure tax (*derecho del aeropuerto*) on domestic flights, which is payable at the AASANA desk on check-in for the flight. Some airports also charge a municipal airport tax on internal flights, which is not included in the ticket price and must also be paid when checking in.

See Departure Taxes in the Getting There & Away chapter for details about international departure taxes.

BUS

For the most part, bus travel in Bolivia is inexpensive and is the favoured form of transport among the Bolivian middle classes. If you're interested in meeting the Bolivian people, their children, their luggage and sometimes even their animals, buses are the way to go. Long-distance bus lines in Bolivia are called *flotas*. Large buses are known as *buses* (BOO-says) and small ones are called *micros* (MEE-cros). If you require directions to a bus terminal, ask for *la terminal terrestre*.

Bolivian buses range from sagging, sputtering, dilapidated wrecks to large, modern and increasingly comfortable coaches with video machines, *pullman* (1st class) seats and ample leg room for the average foreigner. The good news is that the vast majority of flotas now operate the latter type. Gone are the days when a Bolivian bus trip almost invariably meant a long, stiff journey aboard an ancient Bluebird school bus salvaged from a US scrap yard after 500,000 km of faithful service. Some Bolivian roads, however, remain so wretched that companies will only run expendable equipment over them, providing these older buses with a continued sense of purpose.

Having said that, even the plushest Bolivian coaches are subjected to a lot of hard use, and true to local standards, they enjoy only a minimum of non-essential repairs. This leaves many with sprung seats, jammed windows and non-functioning heaters – and a conspicuous (and merciful) absence of on-board toilets, which would require more maintenance that anyone wants to commit to. In all my experience on Bolivian buses, I've never encountered a reading light that actually worked or a window that would remain in the position I wanted it. However, most flotas do proudly keep video machines in tip-top repair.

Between any two cities, you should have no trouble finding at least one bus leaving every day. On the most popular routes, such as La Paz-Oruro, La Paz-Cochabamba or Cochabamba-Santa Cruz, some flotas may offer as many as 15 runs daily.

There are, however, a few things you should know about bus travel in Bolivia.

If you can manage to travel by daylight, you'll be treated to an eye-level view of the spectacular Bolivian landscapes. Unfortunately, most flotas depart in the evening and travel through the night to arrive in the wee hours of the morning. Except on the three most popular runs – La Paz-Oruro, La Paz-Cochabamba and Cochabamba-Santa Cruz, all the flotas depart around the same time of day – regardless of how many companies service that run.

Although most buses travel at night, conditions aren't optimum for sleeping. If you have a seat – and fortunately, most flotas do accept advance seat reservations – you'll soon discover buses were designed with capacity rather than comfort in mind. Even if a flota limits the number of passengers to the number of seats available, children aren't counted as passengers, and wind up wherever they find room to stretch out – whether on the floor, on the luggage, or on the laps of their parents or other passengers. On buses where seating capacity is ignored, the floors, racks and roof may be packed to overflowing with bags, boxes, tins, animals and Bolivians. Using simple arithmetic, you can calculate that the locals travel with an average of 16 pieces of luggage per person, which leaves pitifully little room for anyone's feet.

Then there's the obligatory radio or tape player – or increasingly, video machine – that typically blares insipid Latin pop music at concentration-shattering volumes through the night. Add to that the screaming children, the highway *trancas* (police check points), the meal and toilet breaks and, of course, the inevitable breakdowns, and you'll be lucky to even close your eyes.

Compared to the highway systems of other South American countries, Bolivia's is rather poor, but given their inhospitable terrain and limited resources, the Bolivians have done an admirable job of highway construction.

Although the Bolivian government is currently upgrading several main routes, work is progressing rather slowly and construction crews have converted many main routes into sand traps and mud holes. Even if you're stifling or suffocating from lack of air or heat exhaustion, people will insist on trying to keep the windows shut tight, lest they invite the swirling Sahara that's outside into the bus.

During the November to March rainy season, and particularly in lowland regions, any or all modes of public transport, including airlines, may suspend service for weeks at a time.

A good rule of thumb is that any bus journey over unsurfaced roads, even under optimum conditions, can take up to a quarter again as long as scheduled. During the rainy season, anticipate spending at least double the time.

Drunken driving is as serious a problem in Bolivia as it is elsewhere. It's officially prohibited (of course) but don't be surprised to see drivers swill a drink or two during rest stops.

The Journey

It's wise to take along food and something to drink on long bus journeys, especially if you're travelling through remote areas. Rest stops are unscheduled and depend largely upon the whims and bodily necessities of the driver. When you do stop, ask the driver or assistant when the bus will leave; stops rarely allow time for a leisurely meal and passengers are expected to attend to ablutions and eat their food as quickly as the driver does, or risk being left behind.

On some overnight routes, there may be no rest stops at all; on the infamous 12 hour run from Santa Cruz to San Ignacio de Velasco, the only stop is at Cotoca, just an hour outside Santa Cruz. The obvious advice is to use the toilet before you leave and drink as little as possible along the way.

Just a few years ago, at any sort of stop – trancas, intermediate stations and toll posts – buses were invaded by vendors selling anything from parrots to shish kebab to shampoo. These days, most of the vendors are required to remain outside the buses,

forcing them to carry on their awkward business through the windows. Nowadays, most vendors offer only edibles, which may include anything from soda pop, bread, fruit or potatoes to complete meals. Refresco is available everywhere; for an oily and spotty glass full, you'll pay just a few cents.

Changes in altitude often necessitate addition and subtraction of clothing, and even in lowland areas, nights get surprisingly cold. Once it gets dark or you climb into the highlands, you'll quickly work out why the Bolivians seemed so overdressed when they boarded the bus in 30°C heat, and you'll sorely miss that fuzzy alpaca pullover packed safely away on the roof of the bus.

Don't be lulled into a false sense of security by flotas that advertise heating systems; I've yet to see one actually working, and buses are usually rattled so badly on the unpaved roads that it's impossible to keep the windows latched anyway.

Major Routes

Flotas offer long-distance services between the following: La Paz and Oruro, Copacabana, Cochabamba, the Yungas (Coroico, Chulumani and Sorata), Rurrenabaque, Riberalta and Guayaramerín; Cochabamba and Sucre, Santa Cruz and Oruro; Potosí and Sucre, Uyuni, Oruro, Tupiza and Tarija; Tupiza and Villazón, Uyuni and Tarija; Tarija and Yacuiba; Santa Cruz and Trinidad, Camiri, Yacuiba and the Jesuit Missions; Guayaramerín and Riberalta; and Riberalta and Cobija. Other long-distance routes are constructed with connections between one or more of these and may require waits and changing buses.

CAMIÓN

The majority of the Bolivian population, especially the lower economic classes, use the *camión* (flat-bed truck) as their primary means of long-distance transport, while camión owners use passengers as a means of lowering their costs. Often the number of passengers loaded onto the camiones far exceeds the practical – and the comfortable – capacity of the vehicle, but if you want to get off the main routes, camiones make an excellent option.

For their part, drivers usually charge about 75% of the standard bus fare on the same run. It's wise to ask fellow passengers what a reasonable fare would be. Drivers may assume you're rich and adjust the price accordingly, apparently unaware that rich people rarely climb onto rattle-trap trucks loaded with chickens, oil drums, noodles and 42 other passengers.

Every town has a market, street or plaza where camiones await passengers. When they're full by the driver's definition, they leave, and it can be quite a contest. Once a few passengers have assembled, the driver announces that the vehicle will leave *ahorita* – 'right away'. If the passengers feel ahorita isn't soon enough, they may shift to another waiting vehicle. At this point, all other passengers in all other waiting vehicles also shift to this vehicle. The lucky driver of the nearly 'full' vehicle keeps trying to recruit a few more for as long as the passengers will tolerate it. As soon as they begin to climb down, imminent departure is announced and, wonder of wonders, the vehicle begins to move. After a spin around the block, however, the vehicle returns to the spot where it was waiting before the 'departure'. When collective patiences again begin to wear thin, the vehicle actually departs.

A less trying method is to take a taxi or micro to the tranca, the highway police post outside every entrance to every town. All vehicles are required to stop at these posts, and it's a convenient place to ask drivers where they're headed. The drawback is that at this point you've lost the option of choosing a place to sit.

While most Bolivians ride in the back of camiones because of the economic savings, foreigners (especially women) may be accorded VIP treatment and invited to ride in the cab. Failing that, you can pay 30% or so more and ride inside anyway. This isn't nearly as interesting as riding *atrás* (in the bed of the camión), but if it's raining, you'll appreciate the option.

This brings up another point: rain damages cargo, so every camión carries a large sheet of heavy canvas tarpaulin known as *la carpa*, which is draped over the truck bed during rainstorms. Passengers are required to either bear the weight of it on their heads or hunker down in the dark, claustrophobic and fume-filled space below. When diesel exhaust and carbon monoxide have turned the experience into a literal hell on wheels, your only option is to confront the elements face on and escape to the rear bumper of the vehicle to contemplate the joys of independent travel.

Even if you're sitting atop your luggage, it may be wedged inaccessibly beneath cargo, luggage and other passengers. When riding atrás, have a variety of clothing at hand, especially on journeys that involve altitude gain.

TRAIN

The Bolivian national railroad, ENFE (Empresa Nacional de Ferrocarriles), has 4300 km of rail lines in two networks. The Red Occidental (Western Network) has its nerve centre in Oruro with services to La Paz, Cochabamba, Sucre, Potosí, Villazón (on the Argentine border), Avaroa and Charaña (both on the Chilean border). The Red Oriental (Eastern Network) focuses on Santa Cruz, with lines to Quijarro on the Brazilian border, and Yacuiba on the Argentine border.

Since it was created from an amalgamation of four private railways in 1964, ENFE has suffered from chronic inefficiency, mainly as a result of top-heavy administration, outdated equipment and, thanks to political interference, a lack of focus (every time the government changed, an entirely new staff came on board). It's hoped that the current privatisation process will solve some of these problems, but also that it won't create a new set of problems by cutting passenger services or placing rail fares out of reach of the people.

Reservations & Tickets

ENFE is Bolivia's national showcase of disorganisation; although there's an official

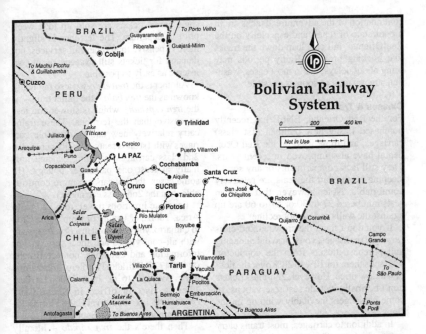

printed timetable, it bears little resemblance to reality, and arrival and departure times may be written on a chalkboard at the station (*la estación de ferrocarriles* or just *la estación*) as soon as it appears something may happen. In small stations – where things rarely happen – tickets aren't even available until the train has arrived, causing delays at nearly every stop. Even in major towns, tickets can be reserved only on the day of expected departure. The best information is usually available from the *jefe de la estación* (stationmaster).

Intermediate stations are allotted only a few seat reservations (although most smaller stations receive no seats at all) and they go on sale quite literally whenever ENFE employees decide to open up. When the window does open, however, the only sense of urgency is with the folks clamouring to buy tickets.

The obvious result of ENFE's efficiency crisis has been a move by the general public away from rail travel and towards the more convenient bus and airline services. (Perhaps as a ploy to lure back lost custom, sparkling pork-barrel railway stations have been built in Santa Cruz and Uyuni.) In turn, lower demand has led to a decrease in the frequency of rail services and has done away with the worst of the queueing nightmares. People no longer have to queue for days waiting for the *boletería* (ticket window) to open – or hoping that it won't slam shut before they've secured a ticket.

As a prospective rail traveller, you may still be faced with a bit of scuffling to secure and defend your place in a ticket queue, but once the boletería opens, you'll rarely wait more than an hour or two. Make sure you have on hand the personal documents of each person for whom you're buying tickets. This is a remnant from the days when ticket scalping was profitable.

If you do get a seat reservation and the train does arrive, the trip itself will be a continuation of the adventure. Tracks are in a poor state of repair and especially on the Red Oriental, rail cars leap down the tracks like bucking broncos. Rainy periods may bring about delays, but in most cases, washouts are repaired as soon as possible.

Classes & Trains

For the Red Oriental, ENFE has recently purchased flashy new pullman (1st class) carriages, and those used on the Red Occidental have also improved in recent years. They still lack compartments or any sort of sleeping berths, but the seats are relatively comfortable. Note, however, that pullman seats numbered 27 to 30 or 57 to 60 are up against the walls and do not recline.

If you don't mind the crowded 2nd-class (*especial*) carriages, you can avoid queueing and purchase tickets from the conductor, who sells them for 10% to 20% over the ticket window price. However, 2nd-class tickets don't normally include seat reservations, so some passengers inevitably wind up on the floor.

In addition to carriages, most trains carry empty *bodegas* (boxcars), which may be occupied by 2nd-class passengers. On most runs, there is space to spread out and relax, adequate ventilation and, because the doors are left open, a good view of the passing scenery. However, prepare for extreme heat and cold, and carry something to sit or sleep on, as the bodegas are cleaned only by the bottoms of passengers. If you're travelling from the Brazilian or Argentine frontiers, be on hand when the cars open and stake out a place to sit. These runs are often crowded with merchants and their wares – often harmless contraband (noodles, wine, flour etc) – being imported unofficially.

There are four sorts of trains. The best is usually the *ferrobus*, which is currently available between La Paz and Arica; La Paz, Potosí and Sucre; and Oruro and Cochabamba. This 'bus on bogies' is a relatively comfortable and punctual alternative to regular rail services. It's reasonably comfortable, and ticket sales are limited to available seats in both 1st and 2nd class. In some cases, tickets are sold up to a week prior to departure. The ferrobus is slightly more expensive than other rail services, but demand for tickets still exceeds supply, so reserve as early as possible.

Another is the *tren expreso* (also farcically known as the *tren bala* – the bullet train – or the *tren especial*), which is slower and less expensive than the ferrobus. These trains carry relatively new and comfortable carriages with 1st class seats, as well as crowded 2nd class carriages, a dining car and normally at least one passenger bodega. (In some cases, the boxcars are more comfortable than the 2nd class carriages.)

For more luxurious travel from La Paz to Arica, Tupiza or Uyuni, or from Santa Cruz to Quijarro, you can travel in a *Bracha* coach, with air-con, videos and meal service. For information and bookings, contact Bracha (☎ 327472), Edificio Petrolero, mezzanine floor, Avenida 16 de Julio 1606, La Paz. There's also an office in Santa Cruz (☎ 366640, fax 322209) at Calle Florida 11, near the corner of 24 de Septiembre.

Then there's the *tren rápido* – literally 'fast train', though it is actually very, very slow and stops at every station – and finally, the *tren mixto*, an excruciatingly slow mixed goods train that has no delusions about its velocity. Only 2nd class is available and most passengers ride in bodegas.

Because of their low fares, these last two types are principally used by campesinos and all their attendant children, luggage and animals, so you'll have lots of company. The trenes mixtos don't run to a fixed schedule and may well hold the low speed record for the continent.

Travelling by train in Bolivia is still a great adventure. We wanted to get from Río Mulatos to Potosí, and the official told us the train would leave at 5 am the next morning. So we got out of our sleeping bags at 4 am, trying not to freeze to the -20°C ground and ran to the station. NOTHING! No train, no official, no passengers, no lights. A couple of hours later, the official arrived and told us the train would leave around 11 am, but at 1 pm we learned that the locomotive had to be repaired first. At 9 pm, there was still no train in sight, so we lay down in the unheated *sala de espera* ('waiting room'; better would be *sala de esperanza* – 'hoping room'). While cold winds were blowing into our hoping room, we tried to catch a little sleep.

The train finally arrived at 3 am and left one hour later. The shock was great when we saw the wagon – a nice brown bodega. We were allowed to lie down on the floor together with some Bolivians and tonnes of grime. Unfortunately, the doors didn't close so we had a persistent -20° C storm inside. The trip took 8½ hours to go 160 km. There were no tunnels and [there was] a great view most of the way. En route, the train stopped at El Condor, one of the world's highest railway stations at 4786m.

Evangelos Kotsopoulos, Germany

Don't believe anyone who tells you there will be no train, or when it might come if there is one. We were told in La Paz that there was a train on Wednesday night from Uyuni to La Paz (el rápido!). Tuesday night in Uyuni they said no, no train at that time. By mid-morning Wednesday, they had changed their mind and said, oh, yes, in fact there was a train. I talked with an Aussie who had spent two days trying to get a train in the opposite direction. One night at midnight, they told him 'no train' so he went back to his hotel; the train arrived at 4 am. The next day they told him 11 am. He turned up to find it had left a half hour earlier. The woman at one travel agency helped us make bookings when the ticket office was closed – her brother worked for the railway and made our booking – but it turned out that he was the guy who gave us the first false information that there wouldn't be a train...Once we got on, it was fine – even heated – and we understand that it's the best train in Bolivia!

Anne Burrill, Italy

CAR & MOTORCYCLE

The advantages of using a private vehicle are, of course, schedule flexibility, access to remote areas and the chance to seize photographic opportunities. However, driving as an exclusive means of transport in Bolivia is not recommended. Only a few Bolivian roads are sealed and others are in varying stages of decay, so high speed travel is impossible (unless, of course, you're a Bolivian bus driver) and the typically narrow and winding mountain roads meander along contours and rocky riverbeds rather than following the shortest route.

If you are undaunted, prepare your expedition carefully. Bear in mind that auto parts are a rare commodity outside cities and that many Bolivian mechanics simply gerry-rig repairs well enough to render the vehicle

functional by local definition. A 4WD high-clearance vehicle is essential for travel off major routes. You'll need a set of tools, one or two good spare tyres, a puncture repair kit, extra petrol, oil and water, and as many spare parts as possible – as well as the expertise to diagnose problems and install the parts. For emergencies, carry camping equipment and plenty of food and drinking water.

Low-grade (85-octane) petrol and diesel fuel are available at *surtidores de gasolina* (petrol dispensers) – also known as *bombas de gasolina* (petrol pumps) – in all cities and major towns. At the time of writing, petrol costs about US$0.50 (B$2.20) a litre.

Road Rules

An international driving licence is required to operate a motor vehicle in Bolivia (motorcycles excluded). When entering Bolivia, a circulation card, or *hoja de ruta*, must be obtained from the Servicio Nacional de Tránsito at the frontier or in the Bolivian city where your trip begins. This document must be presented and stamped at all police posts, variously known as trancas, *tránsitos* and *controles*, along the routes.

Peajes or 'tolls' are sometimes charged at these checkpoints and vehicles and luggage may be searched for contraband, although fortunately this practice is becoming quite rare. If you're an obvious foreigner, the police may not be able to resist stopping you, so expect to pay a few bogus fines for alleged infringements.

Traffic regulations don't differ greatly from those in North America or Europe. Speed limits are infrequently posted, but in most cases, the state of the road will prevent you from exceeding them anyway. As in most of the Americas, Bolivians keep to the right. On the Yungas road between La Paz and Coroico, however, downhill vehicles are required to keep to the outside, whichever side of the road that happens to be. For the nail-biting lower half of the trip (the half nearest Coroico), this means traffic must pass on the left side of oncoming traffic. This way the driver, who sits on the left side of the vehicle, has a better idea of where the left side tyres are.

In the cities, most of the cacophonous horn-honking isn't to get traffic moving or to intimidate pedestrians; when two cars approach an uncontrolled intersection (ie one with no police officer or functioning signal) from different directions, the driver who honks first has right of way if intending to pass straight through. Turning vehicles, of course, must wait until the way is clear before doing so. Keep in mind that this system doesn't always work in practice. While timidity may cost some time, it may be better for your sanity until you're accustomed to local driving habits.

When two vehicles meet on a mountain road too narrow for both to pass, the vehicle headed downhill must reverse until there's enough room for the other to overtake. Again, this works better in theory than in practice.

Rental

Given the state of roads and services in Bolivia, and the convenience of public transport, few travellers hire self-drive vehicles. Although things are improving, it's best not to put much faith in Bolivian hire vehicles. Only the most reputable agencies service vehicles regularly and insurance bought from rental agencies may cover only accidental damage. This means that breakdowns may be considered the renter's problem, but even where they are covered, the logistics of having repairs done must be handled by the driver. Sort out the policy and get details in writing before accepting the vehicle!

Minimum ages for most rental agencies are between 21 and 25 years. You need a driving licence from your home country (or in some cases, an international driving licence), a major credit card or cash deposit and, usually, you'll need accident insurance. You'll be charged a daily rate and a per km rate (some agencies allow a set number of free km, after which the rate applies). They'll also want you to leave your passport or *cédula de identidad* as a deposit.

Prices vary widely between agencies and

areas. The average daily rate for a small Volkswagen or Toyota is between US$20 and US$35, plus an additional US$0.20 to US$0.35 per km. Many agencies also offer up to 100 km per day for a slight discount on the per km rate. For its least expensive 4WD vehicle, Imbex charges as little as US$25 per day plus US$0.25 per km, but most places charge between US$35 and US$50 per day, plus US$0.35 to US$0.50 per km. Lower daily rates are available for rentals of a week or more. Collision damage waiver insurance is included in the rental fees.

If you plan on a lot of driving, go with an agency that offers unlimited km. The best deals are with Save Rent-a-Car in Santa Cruz, which hires 4WD vehicles starting at US$50/300 per day/week with unlimited km. International, Oscar Crespo Maurice and Imbex, all in La Paz, offer unlimited km only on rental periods of a month or more. The best prices are from Imbex, which charges US$1099/1299 per month for the cheapest car/4WD.

Here's a listing of some of the better known agencies in Bolivia, but inclusion in this list doesn't necessarily constitute a recommendation:

AB Rent-a-Car, Avenida Alemana y Segundo Anillo, near Rotonda Willy Bendeck, Santa Cruz (☎ 420160, fax 423439)
  Calle Sucre E-0727 esquina Antezana, Cochabamba (☎ 22774)
Adventures Rent-a-Car, Hotel Plaza, Area Comercial, Local 10, Casilla 2411, La Paz (☎ 378301, fax 785759)
American Rent-a-Car, Avenida Mariscal Sucre 1423, La Paz (☎ 361666, fax 328635)
Barron's Rent-a-Car, Avenida Cristóbal de Mendoza 286, Zone El Cristo, Segundo Anillo, Santa Cruz (☎ 333886)
Imbex Rent-a-Car, Avenida Montes 522, Casilla 13400, La Paz (☎ 795790, fax 379884)
  Calle Bolívar 790, Potosí (☎ 22184)
  Calle Potosí 499, Sucre (☎ 31222)
International Rent-a-Car, Calle Colombia 361, near 25 de Mayo, Cochabamba (☎ 26635)
  Calle Federico Zuazo 1942, La Paz (☎ 342406)
  Rotonda Avión Pirata esquina Avenida Uruguay, Santa Cruz (☎ 344425)
Kolla Motors, Calle Rosendo Gutiérrez 502, La Paz (☎ 341660; fax 391189)

Avenida Sánchez Lima 2321, La Paz (☎ 341660, fax 391189)

Oscar Crespo Maurice Rent-a-Car, Avenida Símon Bolívar 1865, Miraflores, La Paz (☎ 350974, fax 326298)

Save Rent-a-Car, Avenida Suárez Arana 700, Santa Cruz (☎ 340828, fax 338516)

Calle Murillo 242, Santa Cruz (☎ 321077)

Aeropuerto de Viru Viru, Santa Cruz (☎ (mobile) (013) 93777)

Drivers

Rather than a tour, many people just want transport to trailheads or base camps. Examples of one-way transport prices from La Paz, regardless of the number of passengers, include the following: Refugio Huayna Potosí – US$70; Estancia Una (for Illimani climb) – US$140; Curva, for the Cordillera Apolobamba trek – US$325; Chuñavi or Lambate, for the Yunga Cruz trek – US$150; Sajama – US$300; and Rurrenabaque – US$325. For return rates, double these figures. Salar de Uyuni and South-West Circuit tours cost from US$180 per day.

The following La Paz drivers/owners can carry up to nine people in Toyota Land Cruisers, including kit (on the roof rack): Ramon Flores (☎ 721789); Vitaliano Ramos (☎ 416013, fax 722240), Casilla 1472, La Paz; Oscar L Vera Coca (☎ & fax 230453), Casilla 13667, La Paz (speaks some English and French).

Motorcycle

In lowland areas where temperatures are hot and roads are scarce, motorcycles are popular around towns. They're also great for exploring areas not served by public transport and can be hired for about US$18 (B$90) per day from motorbike taxi stands on or near the main plaza in northern Bolivian towns.

Motorcycle taxi drivers can make a lot more money by hiring out their bikes than by working, and while you're using their bike, they have the day off. As a result, there's lots of competition, so negotiate the price – which should be payable upon return of the vehicle.

No special licences or permits are required, but you do need a driving licence from your home country. Bear in mind that many travel insurance policies will not cover you for injuries arising from motorbike accidents; check your policy carefully.

BICYCLE

For cyclists who can cope with the challenges of steep terrain, cold winds, poor road conditions and high altitude, Bolivia is a paradise. In this vast and breathtaking country of back roads and remote villages, a mountain bike will bring within reach local culture and magnificent scenery inaccessible to travellers confined to public transport.

Fortunately, traffic isn't a serious problem because there's so little of it. On main routes, however, large, loud and intimidating buses and *camiones* (trucks) may leave cyclists lost in clouds of dust and sand, or embedded in mud. Where there's a parallel rail line, you may prefer to abandon the road and follow the typically less-used footpath alongside the tracks. On minor roads and tracks, however, apart from foot and animal traffic, cyclists will have the roads largely to themselves.

Naturally, finding supplies – particularly off the beaten track – may prove difficult. Few small villages have even a tiny provisions shop, so cyclists in remote areas must carry ample food and water to reach the next city or town.

Transporting a Bicycle

As far as I'm aware, all international airlines accept bikes as checked baggage. Some airlines may charge a standard rate – say US$25 – to transport a bike, but most will simply apply their excess baggage charge if you're over your allowed weight limit. You'll probably be required to decrease the space required (and the risk of damage to the bike) by removing the pedals and handlebars, and locking the front wheel. You should also deflate the tyres to prevent an explosion in the event of depressurisation. Usually, it isn't strictly necessary to pack your bike in a bike bag or encase it in plastic or cardboard, but those items would serve as a thin line of protection against the inevitable bumps and scratches it will receive in the care of under-conscientious baggage handlers.

In Bolivia, there's no problem transporting bikes on camiones (unless the camión is already packed to the gills with passengers and/or cargo). Most flotas are equally amenable, which isn't surprising considering that a bicycle takes up much less space than the luggage carried by an average Bolivian person. Similarly, Lloyd Aéreo Boliviano and AeroSur are not averse to carrying bikes as checked baggage provided they don't exceed your 20 kg weight limit.

Equipment

Outside La Paz, bicycle spares and tools are for the most part unavailable, although most towns do have bicycle repair shops, which can manage emergency or gerry-rigged repairs. However, not even in La Paz will you find parts for state-of-the-art or complicated brake and gearing systems, or non-standard sized tyres (you'll probably be limited to 27 and 28-inch tyres). The best place for cycle parts is the lowly shop at Avenida Buenos Aires 606 in La Paz.

Unless you're willing to forego familiarity, versatility and durability, think about carrying your equipment from home. Although some people do purchase bikes in Latin America, those available in Bolivia generally won't stand up well to the rigours of touring there. To minimise maintenance, you'll need a strong but stable traditional mountain bike. For the hills, you'll fare best with cantilever brakes and a low-gear ratio.

For detailed advice and recommendations on equipment options – bike models, features, panniers, spare parts, tools, clothing and so on – a good source of information is *Latin America by Bike* by Walter Sienko (The Mountaineers, Seattle, 1993). It contains gear and parts checklists, offers hints on bicycle security and even contains a handy Spanish-English vocabulary of cycle parts.

HITCHING

Thanks to relatively easy access to camiones and a profusion of buses and other long-distance public transport, hitching isn't really popular in Bolivia (although it could be argued that passengers riding in the backs of camiones are in fact hitchhikers). Still, it's not unknown and drivers of *mobilidades – carros* (cars), *camionetas* (pick-up trucks), NGO vehicles, petrol trucks and other vehicles – are usually happy to pick up passengers when they have space. Always ask the price, if any, before climbing aboard; if they do charge, it should amount to about half the bus fare for the equivalent distance.

Please note that hitching is never entirely safe in any country in the world. If you decide to hitch, you should understand that you are taking a small but potentially serious risk. Travel in pairs and let someone know where you're planning to go.

WALKING

At its best, walking can be a very appealing way of seeing Bolivia, and for those who can't (or prefer not to) splash out on tours, air charters or 4WD hire, many of the country's best and most beautiful places are accessible in no other way. For information on hiking, trekking and mountaineering in Bolivia, see Activities in the Facts for the Visitor chapter.

BOAT
Cargo Boats

The most relaxing way to get around in the Amazon region is by river. You can lie in a hammock for days on end and read, sleep, relax and watch the passing scene. Adventurous types may even build a raft or hire a dugout canoe to explore under their own steam, but they'd need either a local river guide or a measure of expertise in wilderness survival and familiarity with navigation along multi-channelled tropical waterways.

There's no scheduled passenger service in the Bolivian Amazon, so river travellers almost invariably wind up on some sort of cargo vessel, but the quality, velocity and price will largely depend on luck. Passenger comfort is probably the last thing Amazonian cargo boat builders have in mind, but accommodation standards in Bolivia are still superior to those on many of the 'cattle-boats' that ply the Amazon proper.

While the riverside scenery can be mesmerising, it changes little, so bring along a couple of books, but don't expect to be bored. Shipboard acquaintances develop quickly and on some routes, you'll have good chances of seeing wildlife both in the water and on the riverbanks.

Wildlife Viewing Bolivia's portion of the Amazon Basin is probably more interesting than the Amazon proper. For a start, the rivers are narrower so the boats travel nearer the shore, allowing better observation. The area is also relatively little developed and has a much lower population density, so wildlife viewing is considerably better than along the heavily populated Brazilian rivers.

The Río Beni isn't much of a wildlife river – nor is it well covered by cargo vessels – but along the Mamoré and Ichilo you'll almost certainly see sloths, monkeys, capybaras, rheas, turtles and hundreds of species of birds and butterflies. On the Mamoré, you have a good chance of seeing giant river otters, alligators, anacondas and countless pink river dolphins, and if you're very lucky, even a tapir or an anteater.

Food & Accommodation River passages typically include food and although onboard cooks tend to show little imagination, the fare is life sustaining. Breakfast invariably consists of *masaco*, a mash of *yuca*, plantain, *charque* (dried meat), oil, maize and salt – which is definitely an acquired taste. Other meals usually consist of rice or noodles, more charque and fried or steamed plantains. Many boats transport lemons, bananas, grapefruits and oranges, so fruit is often plentiful. Coffee is made from river water and sugar is added unsparingly until it reaches a syrupy consistency. Take along a supply of goodies to complement your diet and relieve your taste buds.

On some runs, passengers may be offered turtle eggs or soup made from turtle meat. In the interest of the turtles, which are threat-ened throughout the Bolivian Amazon, you may wish to avoid partaking and express concern about their diminishing numbers. This won't stop anyone eating turtles or turtles' eggs, but it may introduce an entirely new perspective.

On some boats, you'll need a hammock for sleeping. On others, you can roll out a sleeping bag on the deck, the roof or even on the cargo. On one trip between Puerto Barador and Guayaramerín, the decks were full and I was permitted to sleep on the roof of the boat, witness to the sunset, stars and the raucous night-long jungle symphony. All these magical things were missed by passen-gers sleeping under the roof and nearer to the noisy engines.

Even the jungle gets chilly at night, and there's always a heavy dew, so you do need a sleeping bag. Some sort of mosquito pro-tection (a net or a good repellent) is also essential, especially if your boat ties up at night. If you must spend a lot of time outside, use a strong sunscreen. You're also advised to carry either bottled drinking water or water purification tablets, preferably iodine-based, to treat the murky water, which is typically drunk straight from the river.

Most boats are equipped with toilet facili-ties, but bathing and laundry are done in the river. Piranhas and alligators appear to pose little threat – everyone swims – but just the same, check with locals before jumping in.

Routes The most popular routes are from Puerto Villarroel to Trinidad and Trinidad to Guayaramerín. There's also the less fre-quented route from Rurrenabaque to Riberalta. All these trips require a minimum of three to five days.

Lake Titicaca

Water travel is not limited to the rivers. Lake Titicaca, which straddles Bolivia's boundary with Peru, is traditionally known as the highest navigable lake in the world. At an altitude of 3810m, it bustles with all sorts of watercraft including the world-famous totora reed boats, which Thor Heyerdahl used on his Ra II Expedition from North

Africa. These sturdy canoes have plied the waters of Titicaca since pre-Columbian times.

In the more recent past, steamers, which were carried piece by piece from the sea to landlocked Bolivia, ferried passengers between Guaqui and the Peruvian ports, linking the railroad terminals of the two countries. This service was discontinued in 1985, however, when its home port of Guaqui disappeared under the waters of the rising lake.

Currently, the only public ferry service operates between San Pedro and San Pablo, across the narrow Estrecho de Tiquina (Straits of Tiquina). This is along the well-travelled route between La Paz and Copacabana, Puno and Cuzco (these last two are in Peru, of course).

To visit the several Bolivian islands of Lake Titicaca, there are launches, sailing boats and rowing boats for hire. To the Huyñaymarka islands in the lake's southern-most extension, hire boats in Huatajata. To visit Isla del Sol, you can hire a launch or sailing boat in Copacabana (US$2 per person), or a rowboat in Yampupata (US$1 per person). To visit Isla de la Luna, look for a sailing boat or rowboat from either Isla del Sol or Yampupata.

Cruise ship service is provided by Transturin Ltda, of La Paz, but it's expensive compared to other modes of lake transport. There are daily bus departures at 6 am, arriving in Huatajata at 7.30 and leaving at 8 am for Isla del Sol, Copacabana and Puno. In the opposite direction, they leave Puno at 6.30 am and arrive back in Huatajata at 4.30 pm and La Paz at 6.30 pm.

Crillon Tours, which is also in La Paz, offers hydrofoil excursions between Huatajata, Copacabana, Isla del Sol and the Peruvian ports of Juli and Puno. For further information, see the Organised Tours section later in this chapter; other details are provided in the Lake Titicaca chapter.

LOCAL TRANSPORT
Micro
Micros – half-size buses – are used in larger cities and serve as Bolivia's least expensive form of public transport, ranging in price from US$0.10 (B$0.50) per ride in Sucre to US$0.18 (B$0.90) in La Paz. Few micros are in optimum condition – at least from the exterior – but mechanically, they seem to go on forever and make remarkably easy work of steep hills.

Micros follow set routes, and the route numbers or letters are usually marked on a placard behind the windscreen. This is often backed by a description of the route, including the streets that are followed to reach the end of the line. They can be hailed anywhere along their routes. When you want to disembark, move towards the front and tell the driver or assistant where you want them to stop.

Trufi
Colectivos, or *trufis*, are prevalent in both La Paz and Cochabamba and may be either cars or minibuses. They follow set routes, which are numbered and described on placards either in the front window or on the roof. For the benefit of nonreaders, they often employ a child who calls (or screams) out the destination whenever the trufi passes a group of potential customers. They are always cheaper than taxis – the set fare in La Paz is currently US$0.20 (B$1) – and they're nearly as convenient. As with micros, you can board or alight anywhere along their route. Drivers of car trufis may even deviate slightly from their set route in order to drop you at your destination.

Taxi
Urban taxis in Bolivia are relatively inexpensive. Few are equipped with meters, but in most cities and towns there are standard per person fares for short hauls – in La Paz it's currently US$0.40 (B$2). When you first arrive in a city, ask a merchant or other local what the usual taxi fare is to your destination before you agree on a price with the driver. Outside bus terminals, railway stations and larger hotels, taxi drivers will initially quote inflated fares, particularly if you appear to be a newly arrived foreigner. In these cases,

walk down the street 200m or so before hailing a taxi.

In most places, taxis are collective and charge a set rate per person, but if you have three or four people all headed for the same place, it's worthwhile negotiating a reduced rate for the entire group. Radio taxis, on the other hand, always charge a set rate for up to four people; if you squeeze in five people, the fare increases by a small margin. When using taxis, try to have enough change to cover the fare; drivers often like to plead a lack of change in the hope that you'll give them the benefit of the difference.

Taxis may also be chartered for longer distances. They're particularly handy if, as a group, you want to visit places near major cities, which are outside local transport areas but too near to be covered by long-distance bus networks.

ORGANISED TOURS

A growing number of foreign and Bolivian tour operators are cashing in on the country's appeal and organising excursions to places that would otherwise be difficult to reach. Note, however, that most operators will only run a tour if a specified minimum number of people are interested, so keep this in mind when considering out-of-the-way destinations. If you can't muster a group of the requisite size, you may have to pay at least partial fares for the number lacking.

Options range from half-day familiarisation tours in or near major cities to fully guided, multi-week excursions that include food, transport, accommodation, transfers etc. The latter are 'classical' tours, which include organised excursions by bus, jeep or boat to the classic tourist sites, such as Isla del Sol, Tiahuanaco or the Salar de Uyuni. Agencies specialising in this sort of tour cater mainly to the top end of the market. They take the uncertainties out of accommodation, transport and sightseeing. Such tours are usually purchased outside Bolivia.

Shorter day tours, on the other hand, are typically organised locally through hotels or agencies. If you're short on time, they provide a convenient way to quickly visit a site you'd otherwise miss. They're also relatively inexpensive, averaging about US$25 for a day trip, and less for a half-day trip.

For the more adventurous, who nevertheless don't want to strike out into the wilderness alone, there are lots of outfits offering adventure tours, including mountaineering, trekking, jungle tours, mountain biking, kayaking, parapente, extreme skiing, canyoning, sailing on Lake Titicaca, and any other hands-on or adrenalin-inducing activity you can name. Prices vary between agencies, but well-established companies generally charge considerably higher prices. The best agencies will be able to organise speciality tours and draw up customised itineraries for you or your group. On request, they'll also be able to provide English, French or German-speaking guides (but often at a higher price).

For mountain trekking or climbing in the Cordilleras, tour operators mainly offer customised expeditions, and can arrange anything from just a guide and transport right up to camping and mountaineering equipment, porters and even a cook.

The majority of Bolivia's tour operators are concentrated in La Paz and other large cities. The most popular short options from La Paz, for example, include city sightseeing and half-day or full-day tours to nearby attractions, such as Chacaltaya or Tiahuanaco (where an English-speaking guide can turn the ruins into more than an impressive heap of rocks!). Inexpensive tour agency transfers to Puno provide the most straightforward access to Peru, and longer excursions to hard-to-reach destinations, such as the Far South-west or the Cordillera Apolobamba are most conveniently done through agencies. These tours are more comfortable than crowded local buses, but they do encourage you to pack more sights into less time.

If you have only a short time in Bolivia, don't set out on a whirlwind circuit through the main cities without first checking with adventure offerings. If you're up to it, a trek through the Cordillera Apolobamba or a climb up Illimani or Huayna Potosí would almost certainly be more rewarding than Oruro, Cochabamba and Santa Cruz combined!

Note that not all Bolivian travel agencies are local tour operators or agents. Some concentrate only on flights or external tourism and earn their keep by selling airline tickets and Disney World tours to Bolivian holidaymakers.

The following is a list of La Paz agencies offering organised tours around Bolivia. Agencies that concentrate only on a specific area appear under Organised Tours for the respective city or town.

Abotours
Calle Ayacucho 378, Casilla 11133, La Paz (☎ 329707, fax 391225). Adventure, natural history, geology and cultural tours with a focus, for example Andean weaving, Andean astronomy, Amazonian national parks and wildlife, anthropology and archaeology, Andean natural medicine, and Bolivian music.

America Tours
Avenida 16 de Julio 1490, ground floor, Casilla 2568, La Paz (☎ 328584, fax 374204). Small group (two to six people) cultural and ecotourism trips to Sajama, the Salar de Uyuni, Potosí, Sucre and the Beni via the Yungas and Rurrenabaque; also trips to the Jesuit Missions in Santa Cruz. English, French and German-speaking guides.

Andean Summits
Calle Sagárnaga 189, first floor, Casilla 6976, La Paz (☎ & fax 317497). Mountaineering and trekking in all parts of Bolivia plus rock climbing, mountain biking, jungle trips, paragliding and archaeological tours. Run by two top Bolivian mountain guides José Camarlinghi and Javier Thellaeche, who speak English and French. One of the best selections of new climbing and camping equipment for sale.

Balsa Tours
Avenida 16 de Julio 1650, Edificio Alameda, Casilla 5889, La Paz (☎ 356566; fax 391310). Cruise excursions around the Islas Huyñaymarkas, Isla del Sol, Isla de la Luna and Copacabana; also operates the Complejo Nautico Las Balsas, a resort hotel at Puerto Pérez, on the shores of Lago Huyñaymarka.

Colibri
Calle Sagárnaga 309, Casilla 7456, La Paz (☎ 371936, fax 355043). Comprehensive adventure travel service, including trekking, mountaineering, mountain biking, jungle trips and 4WD tours; the greatest selection of climbing and trek-

king gear for hire. French and English are spoken; German and Italian-speaking guides.

Colonial Tours
Expediciones Bolivia, Calle México 1733, Casilla 5108, La Paz (☎ & fax 316073). Mountaineering and trekking, as well as classical and cultural tours. Run by friendly María Laura Prömmel, who speaks English and publishes a calendar of mountaineering and trekking departures. Scheduled trips run with as few as two participants. Horse-riding, including a half day in La Paz's Zona Sur and four days to Illimani base camp. Curva to Pelechuco trek in the Cordillera Apolobamba costs a very reasonable US$280 per person, including transport, equipment, meals, a guide and porters. Three-day expedition up Huayna Potosí costs US$156 per person, with transport, climbing equipment, meals, a cook, guide, porters and, if required, a day of predeparture climbing instruction.

Crillon Tours
Avenida Camacho 1223, Casilla 4785, La Paz (☎ 374566; fax 391039). Upmarket hydrofoil trips between Huatajata and Puno on Lake Titicaca (takes three hours); also runs a five-star hotel in Huatajata. Transfers between La Paz and Puno by bus and hydrofoil cost US$160 per person each way. A rushed return day tour from La Paz to Huatajata, Isla del Sol (a quick run up and down the Escalera del Inca) and Copacabana 'packaged right down to the campesino paid to stand with his llamas on the dock for the tourists to take photos', costs US$130 per person.

ECOlogical Expeditions
Calle Sagárnaga esquina Murillo 189, Galería Dorian 13, La Paz (☎ & fax 314172). Enthusiastic and highly recommended for its friendliness and sincere ecological angle. Programmes around the country, including Rurrenabaque, Parques Nacionales Amboró and Noel Kempff Mercado, the Río San Julián, Sucre/Potosí, Torotoro, Lake Titicaca, the South-West Circuit and the Jesuit Missions Circuit.

Fremen Tours
Calle Belisario Salinas 429, La Paz (☎ 327073); Casilla 1040, Calle Tumusla 245, Cochabamba (☎ 59392, fax 59686); and Loreto esquina Riberalta, Trinidad (☎ 22276). Tours of the Amazon area, as well as around Cochabamba, including Torotoro, Incallajta and Cerro Tunari. For more information, see the Cochabamba chapter, and Villa Tunari and Trinidad in the Amazon Basin chapter.

Guarachi Andes Expeditions
Plaza Alonzo de Mendoza, Edificio Santa Anita 314, Casilla 12287, La Paz (☎ 320901, fax 392344). Adventure tours to out-of-the-way destinations, including hikes along the El Camino del Oro, Taquesi and Yunga Cruz trails, and in the

Cordillera Apolobamba; climbing Volcán Sajama and the peaks of the Cordillera Real; and exploration of the Far South-west.

Huayna Potosí Tours

Hotel Continental, Calle Illampu 626, Casilla 731, La Paz (☎ 323584, fax 378226). Operates the Refugio Huayna Potosí mountain hut at Paso Zongo, at the foot of Huayna Potosí (US$7 per night). Run by Dr Hugo Berrios Martín, a great character who speaks both English and French, and organises what are probably the least expensive Huayna Potosí climbs; also organises trekking and climbing expeditions in the Cordillera Real, Cordillera Apolobamba, the Yungas and areas. Try a 42-km downhill mountain bike ride from Zongo to Cahua!

Ozono

Office 101, 1st floor, Edificio Guanabara, Avenida Arce esquina Calla Cordero, Casilla 7243, La Paz (☎ & fax 722240, e-mail ozono@bolivia.com). New and recommended adventure travel company, run by two British mountain and trekking guides, and a *paceño* who has worked in Canada as a ski instructor. Ecotourism and activities and destinations off the trodden track, including mountaineering, trekking, rock climbing and extreme skiing, 4WD trips, and lowland expeditions with the Foundation for Trekking, Research and Exploration (Trex). French and German-speaking guides, as well as mountaineering advice and information, and an e-mail post restante service (via ozono.pr@bolivia.com).

Paititi

Calle Hermanos Manchego 2469 (☎ 353558, fax 329625) or Camino Real Aparthotel, Calle Capitán Ravelo 2123, La Paz (☎ & fax 342759). Tours and treks around La Paz, in the Yungas, Amazonia and south-western Bolivia. Recommended trips include the four-day trek through the little-known Ciudad de Piedra (US$224 per person) and white-water rafting on the Río Coroico (US$67); also offers three-day treks on the Choro (US$109) and Taquesi (US$128) routes. Can arrange hire of camping and mountaineering equipment.

Tauro Tours

Avenida 16 de Julio 1566, 1st floor, Casilla 11142, La Paz (☎ 322370, fax 392549. Combines classical tourism with a wide range of upmarket adventure activities, including 4WD tours to the Far South-west, Lake Titicaca, Rurrenabaque, Pando, the Beni, archaeological trips, and 'total adventure tours' that combine fast-paced 4WD tours with rafting, climbing and parapenting. Mountaineering, trekking and adventure activities are run by the experienced guide Carlos Aguilar, who is qualified with the German Alpine Club.

TAWA Tours

Calle Sagárnaga 161, 1st floor, Casilla 8662, La Paz (☎ 325796, fax 391175). Adventure tourism, including mountaineering, cross-country skiing, jungle trips, trekking, horse riding and mountain biking in all parts of Bolivia. Specialities include trekking and 4WD tours through the Cordilleras Real and Apolobamba, plus trips into the lowlands where TAWA Tours maintains its own resorts and camp sites. French, English, Italian and German-speaking guides.

Transturin

Avenida Mariscal Santa Cruz 1295, 3rd floor, Casilla 5311, La Paz (☎ 320445, fax 391162). Enclosed catamaran cruises around the Lake Titicaca highlights, including Copacabana, Isla del Sol and Puno, Peru. The focus is on responsible tourism and to a point, they succeed in providing visitors with an appreciation of local culture. La Paz to Puno, with stops at Copacabana and Isla del Sol, costs US$127 per person. Return trips to Isla del Sol are US$70 and to Copacabana, US$90. Isla del Sol with an overnight at Hotel Titicaca costs US$130 per person. Prices include meals.

Transamazonas

Office 3C, 3rd floor, Edificio V Centenario, Avenida 6 de Agosto, Casilla 14551, La Paz (☎ 350411, fax 360923). Covers the top end of the adventure tourism market, offering well organised hiking, climbing and 4WD expeditions. English, French, German and Spanish are spoken.

La Paz

The home of more than a million Bolivians, over half of whom are of Indian heritage, La Paz is the country's largest city and its centre of commerce, finance and industry. Although Sucre remains the judicial capital, La Paz has usurped most government power and is now the de facto capital.

A visitor's first view of La Paz (alas, except for those sneaking in from the Amazon Basin via the Yungas) will never be forgotten. La Paz belongs in the same scenic league as Rio, Cape Town, San Francisco and Hong Kong, but you wouldn't know it as you approach through the grey, littered and poverty-plagued sprawl of El Alto, on muddy streets that appear to have escaped attention since Inca times. Once merely a La Paz suburb, El Alto has now burgeoned into a separate entity where unkempt children play in expanding potholes; Indian women pound laundry in a sewage-choked stream; streets are lined with sparsely-stocked market stalls; and every second business appears to be an auto repair shop or a scrap-yard.

At the edge of El Alto, however, the earth drops away as if all the poverty and ugliness has been obliterated, and there, 400m below, is La Paz, filling the bowl and climbing the walls of a gaping canyon nearly five km from rim to rim. On a clear day, the snow-capped triple peak of Illimani (6402m) towers in the background. If you're fortunate enough to arrive on a dark night, La Paz may appear like a mirrored reflection of a glittering night sky.

Since La Paz is nearly four km above sea level, warm clothing is needed through much of the year. In the summer, the climate can be harsh: rain falls on most afternoons, the canyon may fill with clouds, or the steep streets may become torrents of run-off. In the winter, days are slightly cooler, but the crisp, clear air is invigorating. Occasionally, rain and even snow fall during spring and autumn.

Highlights

- Admire the mestizo architecture of Iglesia San Francisco
- Discover Bolivian history and culture at the four museums – Museo de Metales Preciosos Pre-Colombinos, Museo del Litoral, Museo Casa Murillo and Museo Costumbrista Juan de Vargas – on colonial Calle Jaén
- Catch a *peña* for a taste of traditional folk music
- Shop for *artesanía* on and around Calle Sagárnaga
- Stroll through the Mercado Negro and other sprawling markets to see and experience indigenous La Paz
- Spend a day exploring the ruins of Tiahuanaco
- Hike through the dramatic Cañón del Huaricunca (Palca Canyon)

History

La Paz was founded on 20 October 1548 by a Spaniard, Captain Alonzo de Mendoza (under orders of Pedro de la Gasca, to whom the Spanish king had entrusted rule over the former Inca lands), and named La Ciudad de Nuestra Señora de La Paz – The City of Our Lady of Peace. The first site chosen by Mendoza was at present-day Laja on the Tiahuanaco road. Shortly after its founding, La Paz was shifted to its present location, the valley of the Chuquiago Marka. Until then, the site had been occupied by a community of Aymara miners and goldsmiths.

The 16th-century Spanish historian Cieza de León remarked of the new city:

This is a good place to pass one's life. Here the climate is mild and the view of the mountains inspires one to think of God.

In spite of León's rather lofty assessment, the reason behind the city's founding was much more terrestrial. The Spanish had always had a weakness for shiny yellow metal and the now fetid Río Choqueyapu, which these days flows beneath La Paz, seemed to be full of it. The Spaniards didn't waste any time in seizing the gold mines, of course, and shortly thereafter, Mendoza was installed as the new city's first mayor. The conquerors also imposed their religion and lifestyle on the Indians, and since most of the colonists' women remained in Spain, unions between Spanish men and Indian women eventually gave rise to a primarily mestizo population.

If the founding of La Paz had been based on anything other than gold, its position in the depths of a rugged canyon probably would have dictated an unpromising future. However, the protection this setting provided from the fierce Altiplano wind and weather – and its convenient location on the main trade route between Lima and Potosí – did also offer the city some hope of survival and prosperity once the gold had played out. Much of the Potosí silver bound for Peruvian ports on the Pacific passed through La Paz, and by the time the railway lines were built, the city was well enough established to command continuing attention.

On 1 November 1549, Juan Gutiérrez Panaigua was given the task of designing an urban plan. He was to lay out plazas and public lands and designate sites for public buildings. La Plaza de los Españoles, now known as Plaza Murillo, was selected as the future site of the cathedral, royal homes and government buildings.

The logo on La Paz's coat of arms, commissioned in 1555 by King Carlos V, lauds the city's peaceful beginnings, but in subsequent years, the City of Our Lady of Peace would know precious little of it. Spain controlled La Paz with a firm grip and the Spanish king had the last word in all matters political. He once denied the job of La Paz mayor to a certain petitioner named Miguel Cervantes de Saavedra. It was probably just as well; the rejected candidate stayed in Spain and wrote *Don Quixote* instead. Some Bolivians, however, feel that given the opportunity, he would have written it anyway, but to the glory of Bolivia rather than Spain.

Twice in 1781, for a total of six months, a group of Aymara under the leadership of Tupac Katari laid siege to La Paz, destroying public buildings and churches before the uprising was quelled. Another period of unrest erupted 30 years later when Altiplano Indians laid a two-month siege on La Paz. Since Bolivian independence in 1825, Plaza Murillo (the main square in La Paz) has been centre stage for other revolutions and protests.

An abnormally high mortality rate once accompanied high office in Bolivia, and with the job of president came a short life expectancy. In fact, the presidential palace on the plaza is now known as the Palacio Quemado (Burnt Palace), due to its repeated gutting by fire. As recently as 1946, the then president of Bolivia, Gualberto Villarroel, was publicly hanged in the Plaza Murillo by 'distraught widows'.

Orientation

It's almost impossible to get lost in La Paz. There's only one major thoroughfare, which follows the canyon of the Río Choqueyapu (fortunately for people's olfactory systems, the river flows mostly underground these days). The main street changes names several times from top to bottom: Avenidas Ismael Montes, Mariscal Santa Cruz, 16 de Julio (the Prado) and Villazón. At the lower end, it splits into Avenida 6 de Agosto and Avenida Aniceto Arce. If you find you become disoriented and want to return to this main street, just head downhill.

On Sunday afternoon, the lower Prado is closed to traffic to make way for promenading families, and the pavements fill up with balloon, candy floss and soft-drink sellers, and people hiring kites, bicycles and little cars. Especially when the sun shines, there's a pleasantly festive atmosphere, and it may recall a bit of lost childhood.

Away from the Prado and its extensions, streets climb steeply uphill, and many are cobbled or unpaved. Above the downtown skyscrapers, the adobe neighbourhoods and the informal commercial areas climb toward the canyon's rim.

Contrary to US and European standards, the business districts and wealthier neighbourhoods occupy lower altitudes. The most prestigious suburbs are found far down in the canyon in the generically-named Zona Sur (Southern Zone, which includes the suburbs of Calacoto, Cotacota, San Miguel, La Florida and Obrajes), while above, cascades of cuboid mud dwellings and makeshift neighbourhoods spill over the canyon rim and down the slopes on three sides. The best preserved colonial section of

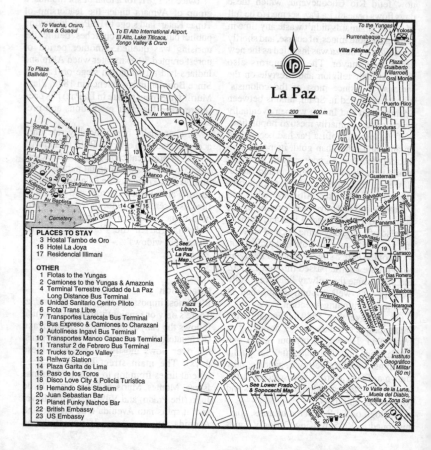

PLACES TO STAY
3 Hostal Tambo de Oro
16 Hotel La Joya
17 Residencial Illimani

OTHER
1 Flotas to the Yungas
2 Camiones to the Yungas & Amazonia
4 Terminal Terrestre Ciudad de La Paz
    Long Distance Bus Terminal
5 Unidad Sanitario Centro Piloto
6 Flota Trans Libre
7 Transportes Larecaja Bus Terminal
8 Bus Expreso & Camiones to Charazani
9 Autolíneas Ingavi Bus Terminal
10 Transportes Manco Capac Bus Terminal
11 Transtur 2 de Febrero Bus Terminal
12 Trucks to Zongo Valley
13 Railway Station
14 Plaza Garita de Lima
15 Paso de los Toros
18 Disco Love City & Policía Turística
19 Hernando Siles Stadium
20 Juan Sebastian Bar
21 Planet Funky Nachos Bar
22 British Embassy
23 US Embassy

town is near the intersection of Calles Jaén and Sucre, where narrow cobbled streets and colonial churches offer a glimpse of early La Paz.

Maps The best city maps are *La Paz Información* and *La Paz – the Map & Guide* (but it doesn't really merit the US$2 price), which are sold at the tourist office and several bookshops. The tourist office also sells simple route maps of hiking areas in the valley below La Paz.

For information on buying topo sheets and climbing maps, see Planning in the Facts for the Visitor chapter.

Information

Tourist Office Senatur (☎ 367442, fax 374630) has its La Paz office at Plaza del Estudiante, on the corner of Calle México and Avenida 16 de Julio. It's open Monday to Friday from 8.30 am to 8 pm and on Saturday from 8.30 am to 1 pm. They distribute brochures in English, French and German, but the original Spanish versions may make more sense than the often amusing translations. (This was partially explained by a brochure from a La Paz translation service that was advertising 'accurate traductions' into English – in Spanish, 'translation' is *traducción*. They must do a booming business with the tourist office!)

Foreign Consulates Embassies and consulates are listed in the Facts for the Visitor chapter.

Money Most of the *casas de cambio* are found in the central area of the city. Casa de Cambio Sudamer, on Calle Colón, changes travellers cheques for a 1% commission and is open on weekdays from 8.30 am to noon and 2 to 6 pm, and on Saturday from 9 am to noon. It also sells currency from neighbouring countries (when it's available). Some casas de cambio also change travellers cheques into cash for a 1% commission, which is worth considering, as outside La Paz you'll get 3 to 10% less for cheques than

for cash. Both Sudamer and Casa de Cambio Silver, at Calle Mercado 979, have been recommended. Check carefully for counterfeit US dollar notes, which have been surfacing with increasing frequency.

On Saturday, casas de cambio are open in the morning only. To change travellers cheques on Sunday or after hours, go to the Hotel Gloria, the Residencial Rosario or the El Lobo Restaurant. Around the intersections of Calle Colón, Avenida Camacho and Mariscal Santa Cruz, *cambistas* (street moneychangers) change cash for slightly lower than casa de cambio rates, but stay attentive during the transaction.

Visa and MasterCard cash withdrawals of up to US$300 daily are available with no commission and a minimum of hassle from the Banco de Santa Cruz, at Calle Mercado 1077, Banco Mercantil, on the corner of Calles Mercado and Ayacucho, and Banco Nacional de Bolivia, on the corner of Calle Colón and Avenida Camacho. Banco de La Paz charges 1.75% commission on cash withdrawals; the aforementioned Casa de Cambio Silver charges only 1%. Cash withdrawals on Visa cards are also available at ENLACE automatic teller machines dotted around the city.

The American Express representative is Magri Turismo (☎ 341201, fax 366309), Avenida 16 de Julio 1490, Edificio Avenida, 5th floor.

Post & Communications The main post office, on the corner of Avenida Mariscal Santa Cruz and Calle Oruro, is open Monday to Friday from 8.30 am to 8 pm, Saturday from 9 am to 7 pm and Sunday from 9 am to noon. Poste restante is free, but you must present your passport when collecting post. It's sorted into foreign and Bolivian stacks; check the Bolivian stacks as well if your surname is Latin.

To post an international parcel, take it downstairs to the customs desk and have it inspected before sealing it up and taking it to the parcels desk. Parcels to Bolivian destinations should be taken to the desk marked Encomiendas. A large notice board in the main hall lists airport departure times for post to various destinations.

Magri Turismo (☎ 341201, fax 366309) will hold mail for travellers carrying an American Express card or travellers cheques (see Money in this chapter).

The main ENTEL telephone office, at Calle Ayacucho 267, is open daily from 7.30 am to 10.30 pm for national and international telephone calls. Public telephones are found in the ENTEL lobby and in hotels, restaurants, street stalls and in telephone boxes along the Prado. There is also an increasing number of convenient Entelitos (little ENTELS) scattered around the city. ENTEL also provides telegram and telex services and has recently opened a convenient but rather inefficient fax office. The public fax numbers are 811 2760 and 811 9121. The telephone code for La Paz is 02.

Bookshops La Paz has quite a few bookshops but most sell only comics, trashy novels or Bolivian school texts. Gisbert & Cia, Calle Comercio 1270, has a good selection of Spanish-language literature and reference books.

Los Amigos del Libro, near the corner of Calles Mercado and Colón, has a selection of popular English and German-language paperbacks and souvenir books, as well as dictionaries, Spanish-language books and foreign news magazines: *Time*, *Newsweek* and the *Economist*. The Librería del Turista (Tourist Bookshop) on Plaza San Francisco sells a limited selection of books on Bolivian topics, English-language novels and several hiking and trekking maps, but also at premium prices.

For popular used paperbacks in English, check out the street stall of friendly Señor Raúl Salmón, opposite the intersection of Avenidas Ismael Montes and Uruguay.

Immigration Extensions to visas and lengths of stay are normally processed with little ado

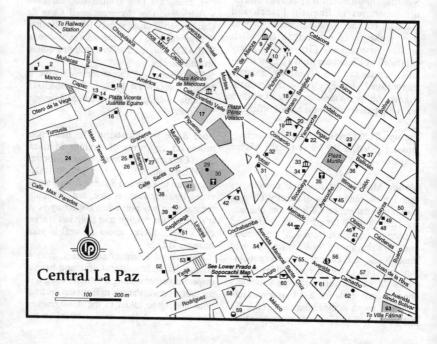

Central La Paz

0   100   200 m

at the immigration office (☎ 370475), at Avenida Camacho 1433. It's open weekdays from 9 am to noon and 2.30 to 6 pm.

Cultural Centres Three international centres offer cultural programmes and reading rooms with films, magazines, books and news from their sponsoring countries: Centro Boliviano Americano (☎ 351627) on Avenida Aniceto Arce at Parque Zenón Iturralde; Goethe Institut (☎ 391369) at Avenida 6 de Agosto 2118; and Alliance Française (☎ 325022), at Fernando Guachalla 399, near Avenida 20 de Octubre.

Laundry Most middle and high-range hotels offer laundry services. A recommended laundry is Express Lavandería, at Aroma 720, just around the corner from the Residencial Rosario. It charges by the kg. There's a coin-operated laundrette at Avenida Ecuador and Calle Rosendo Gutiérrez.

Film Fujichrome colour slide film is widely available for about US$6 per roll; be cau-tious about buying film at street markets where it is exposed to strong sun all day. Fujicolour is the most widely available print film and costs as little as US$2.50 for a roll of 36 exposures.

For processing of both slides and print film, two reliable laboratories are Casa Kavlin at Calle Potosí 1130 and Foto Linares in Edificio Alborada on the corner of Calles Loayza and Juan de la Riva. The latter is the better choice for specialist processing.

If you have camera problems, the man to see is Rolando Calla. You'll find him in Idem-Fuji Color (☎ 327391) at Calle Potosí 1316 between 10.30 am and noon, and at his home (☎ 373621) at Avenida Sánchez Lima 2178 from 3 to 7 pm.

Camping Equipment Bolivia's widest selection of new and second-hand climbing, trekking and camping equipment is at Con-doriri (☎ & fax 319369), at Local 8, Galería Sagárnaga 339. It sells everything from ropes and backpacks to boots, compasses and headtorch batteries, plus a selection of

PLACES TO STAY		PLACES TO EAT			
1	Hostal Cris	4	El Palacio de Pescado		Costumbrista Juan de Vargas; Museo Casa Murillo
2	Hotel Panamericano	11	La Casa de los Paceños		
3	Hostería Florida			10	Peña Marka Tambo
5	Alojamiento Universo	20	Pensión Otto	12	Cinemateca Boliviana
6	Hotel Oruro	27	La Hacienda	17	Mercado Lanza
8	Hostal Ingavi	36	Chifa Ballivián	18	Teatro Municipal
13	Hotel Andes	37	Confitería Paris	19	Museo de Etnografía y Folklore
14	Alojamiento Metropoly	38	El Lobo		
15	Hotel Italia	42	Peña Naira	24	Mercado Negro
16	Hotel Continental	43	Restaurant Veg-etarianista Lila Vaty	29	Librería del Turista
21	Hostal Austria			30	Iglesia de San Francisco
22	Hostal Yanacocha	45	Pollo Copacabana		
23	Gran Hotel Paris	46	Boutique del Pan	33	Museo Nacional del Arte
25	Residencial Rosario	48	El Vegetariano		
26	Residencial Copacabana	51	Snack El Montañés	35	Cathedral
		54	La Fiesta	41	Mercado de Hechicería
28	Hostería Blanquita	55	Confitería Club de La Paz & Los Escudos		
31	Hotel Presidente			44	ENTEL
32	Hotel Gloria & Café Pierrot	58	Acuario II	47	Los Amigos del Libro
		61	Café Verona	56	Casa de Cambio Sudamer
34	Hotel Torino				
39	Hotel Alem		**OTHER**	57	Immigration
40	Hotel Sagárnaga	7	Museo Tambo Quirquincho	59	Plaza Belzu (micros to Ventilla)
48	Hotel Neumann				
49	Hotel Viena	9	Museo de Metales Preciosos Pre-Columbinos; Museo del Litoral; Museo	60	Post Office
50	Hostal República			62	LAB (Airline)
52	Hotel Milton			63	Mercado Camacho
53	Alojamiento Colonial				

climbing hardware. It also hires out equipment and has a repair service. You'll also find camping equipment at Caza y Pesca on the ground floor of the Handal Centre on the corner of Socabaya and Mariscal Santa Cruz. It's a good place to pick up gas canisters for Bleuet stoves. If you prefer to hire equipment, see Cordillera Real, No 30 Galería Doryan, at the corner of Sagárnaga and Murillo.

Medical Services The Unidad Sanitario Centro Piloto (☎ 369141), near the brewery just off upper Avenida Ismael Montes, is open from 8.30 am to noon and 2.30 to 6.30 pm. Anyone heading for the lowlands can pick up yellow-fever vaccinations, and free chloroquine to be used as a malaria prophylaxis. Don't take chloroquine, however, if you've previously been taking Lariam (mefloquine); they make a potentially dangerous combination.

Rabies vaccinations are available for US$1. Anyone bitten or scratched by a suspect animal should seek medical attention (see the Health section in the Facts for the Visitor chapter).

If you're in need of an English-speaking doctor, try Clínica Americana (☎ 783509), at 5809 Avenida 14 de Septiembre, Calle 9, in Obrajes (Zona Sur). The sign outside says 'Hospital Metodista'. The German clinic, Clínica Alemana (☎ 329155), is at Avenida 6 de Agosto 2821.

Pharmacies that are open on weekends and public holidays are listed in the newspaper El Diario.

Emergency Robberies and other problems may be reported to the Policía Turística (☎ 225016) at Disco Love City on Plaza del Estadio in Miraflores. They won't recover any stolen goods but will take an affidavit (*denuncia*) for insurance purposes. The phone number for Radio Patrulla (Radio Patrol), as in all major Bolivian cities, is 110.

Dangers & Annoyances La Paz is a great city to explore on foot, but don't be in too much of a hurry or the altitude might take its toll, especially when you're walking uphill. If you're arriving in La Paz from the lowlands, read the section on Environmental Hazards under Health in the Facts for the Visitor chapter.

Churches

Iglesia de San Francisco The hewn stone basilica of San Francisco, on the plaza of the same name, reflects an appealing blend of 16th-century Spanish and mestizo trends. The church was founded in 1548 by Fray

---

The Río Choke

If recent statistics are anything to go by, the name of the Río Choqueyapu, which flows through La Paz, might as well be shortened to the Río Choke. This fetid stream, which provided the gold that gave La Paz its present location, is now utterly dead and beyond help. According to one source, 'the Río Choqueyapu receives annually 500,000 litres of urine, 200,000 tonnes of human excrement and millions of tonnes of garbage, animal carcasses and industrial toxins'. These include cyanide from leather factories and a cocktail of chemicals and dyes from textile and paper industries, which cause the river to flow bright orange in places, or red topped with a layer of white foam.

The Choqueyapu fortunately flows underground through the city, but as it emerges in the Zona Sur, it's used by campesinos, who must make their way around heaped trash and animal carcasses to take water for washing, cooking and drinking. Most people heat the water before drinking it, but few boil it, and even boiling wouldn't eliminate chemical pollutants from industrial wastes. The potential for future health problems is staggering.

Currently, no-one can be fined or cited for dumping waste into the river because – incredibly – the city has no laws or regulations against it. In 1994, the Municipal Environmental Office outlined 48 projects aimed at controlling water pollution, vehicle emissions, rubbish dumping and noise. As always, the problem with implementation is funding, and still, the foul flood continues to flow. ∎

Francisco de los Ángeles and construction began the following year. The original structure collapsed under heavy snowfall in about 1610, but it was reconstructed in the eight years between 1744 and 1753. The second building was built entirely of stone quarried at nearby Viacha. The façade is decorated with stone carvings of natural themes such as *chirimoyas* (custard apples), pine cones and tropical birds.

After looking at the church, turn towards the bizarre and ambitious sculpture on the upper portion of Plaza San Francisco. This mass of rock pillars and stone faces in suspended animation is intended to represent and honour Bolivia's three great cultures – Tiahuanaco, Inca and modern.

Cathedral Although it's a recent addition to La Paz's collection of religious structures, the 1835 cathedral on Plaza Murillo is an impressive structure – mostly because it is built on a steep hillside. The main entrance on Plaza Murillo is 12m higher than its base on Calle Potosí. The sheer immensity of the building, with its high dome, hulking columns, thick stone walls and high ceilings, is overpowering, but the altar is relatively simple. Inside, the main attraction is the profusion of stained-glass work throughout; the windows behind the altar depict a gathering of Bolivian generals and presidents being blessed from above by a flock of heavenly admirers.

Beside the cathedral is the Presidential Palace, and in the centre of Plaza Murillo, opposite, stands a statue of ex-president Gualberto Villarroel. In 1946, he was dragged from the palace by vigilantes and publically hanged from a lamppost in the square. Don Pedro Domingo Murillo, for whom the plaza was named, had met a similar fate there in 1810.

Iglesia de Santo Domingo Like the Iglesia de San Francisco, the exterior of the Iglesia de Santo Domingo, at nearby Yanacocha and Ingavi, shows evidence of Baroque and mestizo influences. The rest of the structure, however, is of limited interest.

Museums
La Paz, as Bolivia's de facto capital, has its share of cultural and historical museums. Four interesting museums – the Museo de Metales Preciosos Pre-Colombinos, the Museo del Litoral, the Museo Casa Murillo and the Museo Costumbrista Juan de Vargas – are clustered together along Calle Jaén, a beautifully restored colonial street, and can easily be bundled into one visit. The museums are open Tuesday to Friday from 9.30 am to noon and 2.30 to 6.30 pm, and on weekends from 10 am to 12.30 pm. Foreigners pay US$2 for a combination ticket that covers admission to all four. On Saturday, admission is free for everyone.

Museo de Metales Preciosos Pre-Columbinos Also known as the Museo del Oro, this museum houses three impressively presented salons of pre-Conquest silver, gold and copper works. A fourth salon in the basement has examples of ancient pottery.

Museo del Litoral Sometimes called Museo de la Guerra del Pacífico, this small exhibit incorporates relics from the 1884 war in which Bolivia became landlocked after losing its Litoral department to Chile. The collection consists mainly of historical maps that defend Bolivia's emotionally charged claims to Antofagasta and Chile's Segunda Región.

Casa de Don Pedro Domingo Murillo Once the home of Pedro Murillo, a leader in the La Paz Revolution of 16 July 1809, the house now displays collections of colonial art and furniture, textiles, medicines, musical instruments and household items of glass and silver that once belonged to Bolivian aristocracy. Other odds and ends include a collection of Alasitas miniatures (see Special Events later in this section). Murillo was publically lynched by the Spanish on 29 January 1810, in the plaza now named after him. Oddly enough, one of the paintings on display in the house is entitled *The Execution of Murillo*.

LA PAZ

Museo Costumbrista Juan de Vargas
This contains art and photos of old La Paz,
as well as some superb ceramic figurine dio-
ramas of old La Paz. One of these is a
representation of *akulliko*, the hour of coca-
chewing; another portrays the festivities
surrounding the Día de San Juan Bautista on
June 24; another depicts the hanging of
Murillo in 1810. Also on display are colonial
artefacts and colourful dolls wearing traditional costumes.

Museo de Etnografía y Folklore The Ethnography and Folklore Museum, on the

corner of Ingavi and Calle Genaro Sanjinés,
is a must for anthropology buffs. The building, which is itself a real treasure, was
constructed between 1776 and 1790, and
was once the home of the Márquez de
Villaverde.

Exhibits cover the customs and artistry of
two of the more obscure Bolivian ethnic
groups, the Chipayas of western Oruro
department and the Ayoreos of the Beni lowlands. It has a fine collection of photos,
weavings and artefacts from the Chipayas, a
group whose language, rites and customs
differ greatly from those of neighbouring

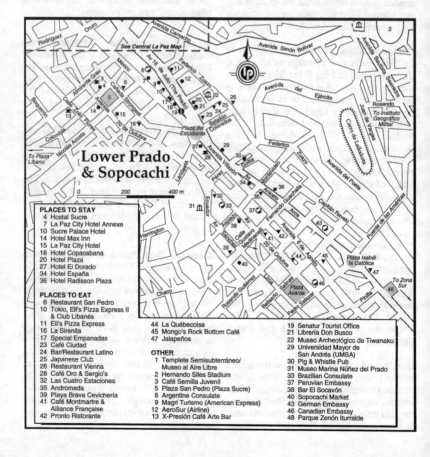

Lower Prado & Sopocachi

0   200   400 m

PLACES TO STAY
4 Hostal Sucre
7 La Paz City Hotel Annexe
10 Sucre Palace Hotel
14 Hotel Max Inn
15 La Paz City Hotel
18 Hotel Copacabana
20 Hotel Plaza
27 Hotel El Dorado
34 Hotel España
36 Hotel Radisson Plaza

PLACES TO EAT
6 Restaurant San Pedro
10 Tokio, Eli's Pizza Express II
     & Club Libanés
11 Eli's Pizza Express
16 La Sirenita
17 Special Empanadas
23 Café Ciudad
24 Bar/Restaurant Latino
25 Japanese Club
26 Restaurant Vienna
28 Café Oro & Sergio's
32 Las Cuatro Estaciones
35 Andromeda
39 Playa Brava Cevichería
41 Café Montmartre &
     Alliance Française
42 Pronto Ristorante

44 La Québecoise
45 Mongo's Rock Bottom Café
47 Jalapeños

OTHER
1 Templete Semisubterráneo/
    Museo al Aire Libre
2 Hernando Siles Stadium
3 Café Semilla Juvenil
5 Plaza San Pedro (Plaza Sucre)
8 Argentine Consulate
9 Magri Turismo (American Express)
12 AeroSur (Airline)
13 X-Presión Café Arte Bar

19 Senatur Tourist Office
21 Librería Don Busco
22 Museo Arqueológico de Tiwanaku
29 Universidad Mayor de
     San Andrés (UMSA)
30 Pig & Whistle Pub
31 Museo Marina Núñez del Prado
33 Brazilian Consulate
37 Peruvian Embassy
38 Bar El Socavón
40 Sopocachi Market
43 German Embassy
46 Canadian Embassy
48 Parque Zenón Iturralde

cultures. Some anthropologists have suggested that the Chipayas are descendants of the vanished Tiahuanaco culture. The museum is open weekdays from 8.30 am to noon and 2.30 to 6.30 pm. Admission is free.

Templete Semisubterráneo Also known as the Museo al Aire Libre, this open pit opposite the stadium is a replica of the Templete Semisubterráneo at Tiahuanaco. It contains restorations of statues found at Tiahuanaco, and if you aren't visiting the actual site, it's worth a quick look.

Museo Arqueológico de Tiwanaku The Museo Nacional de Arqueología, also known as the Museo Arqueológico Tiwanaku (both 'Tiwanaku' and 'Tiahuanaco' are correct), is on Calle Tiwanaku just two blocks from the Prado. It holds a small but well-sorted collection of artefacts that illustrate the most interesting aspects of Tiahuanaco culture's five stages (see Tiahuanaco later in this chapter).

Most of Tiahuanaco's treasures were stolen or damaged during the colonial days, so the extent of the collection isn't overwhelming and can be easily digested in an hour. Some of the ancient stonework disappeared into Spanish construction projects, while valuable artwork – gold and other metallic relics and artwork – found their way into European museums or were melted down for the royal treasuries. Most of what remains in Bolivia – pottery, figurines, trepanned skulls, mummies, textiles and metal objects – is housed in this one room.

It's open Tuesday to Friday from 9 am to noon and 2.30 to 6.45 pm, and on Saturday from 10 am to 12.30 pm and 2.30 to 6.30 pm. Admission for foreigners is US$1. Official guides are free, so don't let them charge you after the fact.

Museo de la Catedral The Cathedral Museum at Calle Socabaya 432, is open Tuesday to Friday from 9.30 am to noon and 3 to 5.30 pm, and on Saturday from 10 am to 12.30 pm. Foreigners pay US$1 admission. The museum consists mostly of typical religious paraphernalia, but there are two unusual mother-of-pearl coffins and well-executed portraits of the 12 Apostles.

Museo Tambo Quirquincho Tambo Quirquincho on the corner of Plaza Alonzo de Mendoza and Calle Evaristo Valle once served as a *tambo*, which in Quechua refers to a wayside inn and market. It has been converted into a museum housing an exhibit of weird and colourful Diablada masks, drawings of 1845 Bolivia by Neman Regendas, old-time clothing, silverware, paintings, sculptures, photos and festive items. It's open Tuesday to Friday from 9.30 am to 12.30 pm and 3.30 to 7 pm, and on weekends from 10 am to 12.30 pm. Admission is US$.50 on weekdays and Sunday, and free on Saturday.

Museo del Charango Also known as the Museo de Instrumentos Nativos, the Museo del Charango (☎ 355776) at Calle Linares 900, near the corner of Calle Sagárnaga, is the home of *charango* master Ernesto Cavour. Here he displays all possible incarnations of charangos and other indigenous instruments. Phone in advance to arrange a visit and when you arrive, speak with the friendly woman who keeps the music shop on the premises, and she'll show you where the displays are.

Museo de la Historia Natural La Paz's Natural History Museum on the university campus on Calle 16, Cotacota (Zona Sur), has exhibits on Bolivia's geology, palaeontology, botany and zoology. The location is a bit inconvenient, but it's worthwhile if you're in the area. It's open Tuesday to Sunday from 10 am to 5 pm, and admission is free. From the Prado, take *micro* 'Ñ' or *colectivo* 21 headed downhill (south-east).

Museo Nacional del Arte The National Art Museum, on the corner of Calles Comercio and Socabaya near Plaza Murillo, is housed in the former Palacio de Los Condes de Arana. The building was constructed in 1775 of pink Viacha granite, and was restored to

Marina Núñez del Prado

Bolivia's foremost sculptor, Marina Núñez del Prado, was born on 17 October 1910 in La Paz. From 1927 to 1929, she studied at the Escuela Nacional de Bellas Artes (National School of Fine Arts) and from 1930 to 1938 worked there as a professor of sculpture and artistic anatomy.

Her early works were in cedar and walnut, and represented the mysteries of the Andes: indigenous faces, groups and dances. From 1943 to 1945, she lived in New York and turned her attentions to Bolivian social themes, including mining and poverty. She later went through a celebration of Bolivian motherhood with pieces depicting indigenous women, pregnant women and mothers protecting their children. Other works dealt largely with Andean themes, some of which took appealing abstract forms. She once wrote 'I feel the enormous good fortune to have been born under the tutelage of the Andes, which express the richness and the cosmic miracle. My art expresses the spirit of my Andean homeland and the spirit of my Aymara people'.

During her long career she held over 160 exhibitions, which garnered numerous awards and received international acclaim from the likes of Pablo Neruda, Gabriela Mistral, Alexander Archipenko and Guillermo Niño de Guzmán. In her later years, Marina lived in Lima, Peru, with her husband, Peruvian writer Jorge Falcón. She died there in September 1995 at the age of 84. ■

its original grandeur by Bolivian architects Teresa Gisbert and José de Mesa.

In the centre of a huge courtyard, surrounded by three storeys of pillared corridors, is a lovely alabaster fountain. The various levels are dedicated to contemporary artists: Marina Núñez del Prado, the late-Renaissance works of Melchor Pérez de Holguín and students of his Potosí school, and works of other Latin American artists. Visiting exhibitions are shown in the outer salon.

It's open Tuesday to Friday from 9.30 am to 12.30 pm and 3 to 7 pm, and on Saturday from 9.30 am to 1.30 pm. Admission is US$0.20.

Museo Marina Núñez del Prado This museum (☎ 324906) is dedicated to the work of the late Marina Núñez del Prado, whose sculptures focus on subjects from the Quechua and Aymara cultures. Located in her former home at Avenida Ecuador 2034, in Sopocachi, it contains her personal collection of cultural paraphernalia and numerous examples of her work. It's open weekdays from 10 am to 1 pm and 3 to 7 pm and on Saturday from 10 am to 1 pm. Phone ahead if you wish to visit at any other time.

Cemetery

As in most Latin American cemeteries,

bodies are first buried in the traditional way, but within 10 years they're disinterred and cremated. Families then purchase or rent glass-fronted spaces in walls for the ashes and affix plaques and mementos of the dead, and place flowers behind the glass door. Each wall has hundreds of these doors and some of the walls have been expanded upwards to such an extent that they resemble three or four-storey apartment blocks. As a result, the cemetery is an active place. People are constantly passing through to visit relatives and leave or water fresh flowers. On 1 November, the Día de los Muertos (Day of the Dead), half the city turns out to honour their ancestors.

There are also huge family mausoleums, as well as sections dedicated to mine workers and their families, and common graves for soldiers killed in battle. You may even see the black-clad professional mourners who provide suitable wails and tears during burials.

Markets

If you want to meet people or just observe the rhythms of local life, an ideal place would be one of the city's dozen or so markets. There's an artesans' market, a witchcraft market, a flower market, a black market and several food markets. Anything from cassette tapes and washtubs to toothpaste and strawberry jam is available somewhere in the markets of La Paz.

Mercado de Hechicería The city's most unusual market lies along Calle Linares between Sagárnaga and Santa Cruz, amid lively tourist *artesanía* shops. In Spanish, it's known as the Mercado de Hechicería or Mercado de los Brujos (the Witches' Market), and in Aymara, it's called *laki'asina catu*. What they're selling isn't exactly witchcraft as depicted in horror films and Hallowe'en tales; the merchandise includes mainly herbs and folk remedies as well as a few more unorthodox ingredients intended to manipulate and supplicate the various malevolent and beneficent spirits that populate the Aymara world.

If you're constructing a new home or office building, for example, you can buy a dead llama foetus to bury beneath the cornerstone as a *cha'lla* (offering) to Pachamama, encouraging her to inspire good luck therein. This practice is strictly for poor campesinos, however; wealthier Bolivians are expected to sacrifice a fully functioning llama. If someone is feeling ill, or is being pestered by unwelcome or bothersome spooks, they can purchase a plateful of colourful herbs, seeds and assorted critter parts to remedy the problem. As you pass the market stalls, watch for wandering *yatiri* (witch doctors) who wear dark hats and carry coca pouches, and circulate through the area offering fortune-telling services. Foreigners, however, don't seem to be accepted as clients.

In general, photography is discouraged around this market, although it largely depends on who you ask and whether you're a customer or just an observer.

Mercado Negro & Upper Market Areas
The entire section of town from Plaza Pérez Velasco uphill (west) to the cemetery – past Mercado Lanza and Plazas Eguino and Garita de Lima – has a largely indigenous population, and is always bustling. The streets are crowded with traffic honking its way through the narrow cobbled streets,

cholas rushing about socialising and making purchases, and pedestrians jostling with sidewalk vendors and market stalls, which sell all manner of practical items from clothing and fast foods to groceries, health-care products and cooking pots. The focus of activity is near the intersection of Calles Buenos Aires and Max Paredes, especially on Wednesday and Saturday.

The Mercado Negro, or 'Black Market', along upper Calle Graneros and Eloy Salmón, is the place to pick up undocumented merchandise and just about anything else you may hope for. Most of it isn't stolen, exactly, although some of it is bootlegged, and in the case of music tapes, vendors make no effort to conceal the fact; the covers are merely photocopied. It's also good for electronic goods, imitation designer clothing and inexpensive Fuji and Agfa film, including slide film. Be especially careful when wandering around this part of town; it's notorious for rip-offs and light fingers.

Between Plaza Pérez Velasco and Calle Figueroa is Mercado Lanza, one of La Paz's main food markets (the other major one is Mercado Camacho). It sells all manner of fruits, vegetables, juices, dairy products, breads and tinned foods. There are also numerous stalls where you can pick up a sandwich, soup, *salteña*, empanada or full meal.

The Flower Market, appropriately located opposite the cemetery at the top of Avenida Tumusla, is a beautiful splash of colour amid one of the city's drabber areas. Unfortunately, it also sits alongside a festering open sewer and garbage dump, which make it rather confusing to the nostrils.

El Alto At first glance, it would seem that the entire city of El Alto is one big market. From the canyon rim at the top of the El Alto Autopista (Motorway) or the top of the free route at Plaza Ballivián, the streets hum with almost perpetual activity. In the lively La Ceja (eyebrow) district you'll find a variety of small electronic gadgets such as tape recorders, and mercantile goods. Try the Thursday and Sunday Mercado La Ceja (also known as Mercado 16 de Julio), which stretches along the main thoroughfare and across Plaza 16 de Julio. If you keep your wits about you, speak Spanish and bargain politely, you're sure to have an excellent time, meet some friendly, down-to-earth Bolivians, and find some great deals. The activity starts at about 6 am and peters out after 3 pm.

Botanical Gardens

The botanical gardens are in Cotacota, down in Zona Sur. Set around an artificial lake, they were established in 1991 and include mainly Andean vegetation, as well as sections with cacti and medicinal herbs. For information, contact Señora Esther Valenovela (☎ 792582).

Activities

Hiking & Climbing Established in 1939, the Club Andino Boliviano (☎ 324682) is an organisation of climbers, skiers and other outdoor enthusiasts. It's responsible for organising club mountaineering trips and running the Chacaltaya ski area (there are plans to split the club into skiing and climbing sectors).

The club offers climbing advice and runs weekend trips to Chacaltaya, as well as special monthly activities – off-piste skiing, climbing, slide shows etc – which are open to anyone. From January to March it organises ski competitions, and in April and May it runs snow-climbing courses. The office is at Calle México 1638, Casilla 1346.

Another La Paz organisation is Club de Excursionismo, Andinismo y Camping (☎ 783795), a society of outdoor enthusiasts who organise excursions to natural venues around the country. The club is currently going through a thin patch and in any case, isn't really geared toward travellers. Nevertheless, anyone is welcome to participate in its outings and if you're going to be around for a few months, it may be worth getting in touch. Contact the club through its postal address Casilla 8365, La Paz, or through Plaza Tours (☎ 378322), Avenida 16 de Julio 1789.

Rock Climbing The rocky Amor de Dios area in the Choqueyapu valley near La Florida (Zona Sur) offers excellent day climbing and bouldering. The routes, which are graded from IV to VII-C on the French scale, are all bolted. You can hire shoes, ropes, harnesses, carabiners etc from Colibri (☎ 371936, fax 355043), Calle Sagárnaga 309, and from Andean Summits, at Calle Sagárnaga 189.

To get there, take a *trufi* or micro from the lower Prado going to La Florida, Aranjuez or Mallasa and get off at the Amor de Dios bridge over the Río Choqueyapu. The most easily accessible rock, El Peñón (literally, 'large rock') sits behind the Amor de Dios football ground.

If you're a beginner or prefer an organised trip, Ozono Tours (☎ 722240) offers rock-climbing courses and day tours from May to September. They cost US$25 per day, including your transport, equipment and teacher/guide. Discounts are available for groups.

Golf & Tennis Golf and tennis buffs interested in some high-altitude practice must join a club because public facilities do not exist. La Paz has two major tennis clubs: the Club de Tennis La Paz (☎ 793930), on Avenida Arequipa in La Florida; and the La Paz Sucre Tennis Club (☎ 324483) at Avenida Busch 1001. If you just want to get in a couple of games, you should be able to arrange a few hours access to the courts for a reasonable price.

If you'd like to hone your driving and putting skills at the world's highest golf course in Malasilla, you'll pay about US$10 for a caddy and a round of 18 holes. Bring your own equipment.

Skiing Skiing is possible at Chacaltaya during the season. See Around La Paz in this chapter for details.

Language & Music Courses

Spanish language courses are available at the Centro Boliviano Americano (see Cultural Centres under Information in this chapter).

The unfortunately-named Fastalk Language School (☎ 340676) on the 2nd floor of Edificio Jazmin, Calle 20 de Octubre 2019, offers seven and 10-day Spanish courses, with instruction for three hours per day. Fees are about US$5 per classroom hour. The Carrera Lingüística, on the 13th floor of the Universidad Mayor de San Andrés (UMSA) on Villazón also offers language courses.

Not everyone advertising language instruction is accredited or even capable of bringing you to grips with their language, however well they speak it, so seek recommendations and examine credentials before signing up. A recommended teacher is Señora Zenaida Gutiérrez, Casilla 11134, La Paz. She charges US$300 for two-week courses, including room and board. Prospective students – particularly women – should approach with caution any La Paz courses advertised by 'Gonzalez'.

For musical instruction (in Spanish) on traditional Andean instruments – *zampoña*, *quena*, charango etc – see Professor Heliodoro Niña at the Academía de Música Helios, Calle Illampu 816. He charges about US$4 per hour.

Organised Tours

Most of Bolivia's tour operators are based in La Paz – the city has at least 100 of them. Some are clearly better than others and many specialise in particular interests or areas.

Most day tours are moderately priced and provide easy sightseeing in the city's environs, including such popular destinations as Tiahuanaco, Copacabana, Zongo Valley, Chacaltaya, Valle de la Luna etc. Inexpensive agency transfers to Puno are the most straightforward way of getting to Peru, and they allow a stopover in Copacabana en route. Tour operators can also take you climbing in the marvellous snow-capped cordillera peaks. If you lack hiking or trekking equipment, many will hire out whatever is necessary. For mountaineering and trekking agencies, see Activities in the Facts for the Visitor chapter.

The following companies run short tours around La Paz, Lake Titicaca and environs.

For a list of La Paz agencies offering similar tours around La Paz and further afield – Cordillera Apolobamba, the Far South-west (these tours are more economically arranged in Uyuni), Rurrenabaque, Potosí, Sucre and so on – see Organised Tours in the Getting Around chapter.

Diana Tours
    Hotel Sagárnaga, Calle Sagárnaga 328 (☎ 358757). This popular agency does city tours, and tours to Tiahuanaco, Valle de la Luna, Chacaltaya and the Yungas. The guides certainly aren't top quality but it does have some of the cheapest transfers to Copacabana (US$4) and Puno (US$8). From La Paz to Cuzco, using minibuses to Puno and rail from there to Cuzco, cost US$35/40 in tourist/luxury class.
Turisbus
    Residencial Rosario, Calle Illampu 704, (☎ 325348). Turisbus, which is slightly more expensive than its main rival, Diana Tours, runs day tours around La Paz and also does trips to the Salar de Uyuni, Laguna Colorada and Laguna Verde. Day tours from La Paz to the Huyñaymarka Islands in Lake Titicaca cost US$41 per person with two participants and US$27 with four or more people. It also offers one-day trekking on Isla del Sol, day tours to Copacabana and transfers between La Paz, Puno and Cuzco.

Special Events

La Paz enjoys several local festivals and holidays during the year. Of particular interest for visitors are Alasitas, held in late January, and El Gran Poder, which takes place in late May or early June.

Alasitas The origin of the festival of abundance, or Alasitas (oddly, 'buy from me' in Aymara), dates back to Inca times when it coincided with the spring equinox on 21 September. During the colonial period, the fair was moved from the equinox to 20 October in honour of the city's founding. Historians generally agree that the current 24 January Alasitas Fair, though based on the original, began in La Paz around the time of Tupac Katari, who led the siege of the city in 1781. At this time, Governor Sebastián Segurola again changed the date, this time to 24 January, which previously had been the date of the Festividad de Nuestra Señora de La Paz.

Traditionally, the Alasitas Fair was intended to demonstrate the abundance of the fields. The campesinos weren't pleased with the changes nor with the January date imposed by the Spanish, and in effect, decided to turn the celebration into a corny mockery of the original. 'Abundance' was redefined to apply not only to crops, but also to homes, tools, cash, clothing and lately, cars, trucks, aeroplanes and even 12-storey buildings. The little god of abundance, Ekeko, made his appearance and the modern Alasitas traditions began.

Ekeko, whose name means 'dwarf' in Aymara, is the household god and the keeper and distributor of material possessions. During the Alasitas Fair, his devotees collect miniatures of those items they'd like to acquire during the following year and heap them on small plaster images of the god. He's loaded down with household utensils, baskets of coca, airline tickets, wallets and trunks full of miniature US dollars, lottery tickets, liquor, chocolate and other material goods. The more optimistic devotees buy

A statue of Ekeko, the god of abundance, loaded down with blessed miniatures

buses, Toyota 4WDs, airline tickets to Miami, Volkswagen beetles and three-storey suburban homes! Once purchased, all items must be blessed by a certified yatiri before they can become real.

If this apparent greed seems not to be in keeping with Aymara values – the community and balance in all things – it's worth noting that Ekeko is also charged with displaying that which a family is able to share with the community.

El Gran Poder La Festividad de Nuestro Señor Jesús del Gran Poder began in 1939 as a candle procession led by an image of Christ through the predominantly campesino neighbourhoods or upper La Paz.

The following year, the local union of embroiderers formed a folkloric group to participate in the event. In subsequent years, other festival-inspired folkloric groups joined in and the celebration grew larger and more lively. It has now developed into a strictly *paceño* festival (a paceño is a resident of La Paz), with dancers and folkloric groups participating from around the city. The embroiderers prepare elaborate costumes for the event and the performers practice for weeks in advance.

El Gran Poder is a wild and exciting time in La Paz and offers a glimpse of Aymara culture at its festive finest. A number of dances feature, such as the *suri sikuris*, in which the dancers are bedecked in ostrich feathers, the lively *kullasada*, and the *inkas*, which duplicates Inca ceremonial dances.

If you'd like to catch the procession, go early to stake out a place along the route (see map), keeping a lookout for stray or unruly water balloons. The tourist office can provide specific dates and details about a particular year's celebration.

Places to Stay – bottom end
La Paz has dozens of low-cost hotels and residenciales, the vast majority of which lie in the area between Calle Manco Capac and Avenida Ismael Montes, but others are scat-

Fiesta del Gran Poder

0   200   400 m

········ Procession Route

tered around the city. Most bottom-range hotels have a midnight curfew.

A cheap, clean, secure and friendly place, with hot showers, is *Alojamiento Universo* (☎ 340341), at Calle Inca Mayta Capac 175, which charges just US$2.25 per person. Ground-floor rooms are nicer than those upstairs. Similar quality rooms but at a higher price are found at *Alojamiento Colonial* on Calle Tarija, which is actually a stairway in these parts. Rooms without bath cost US$4 per person.

A favourite with Peace Corps volunteers – and a very friendly digs – is the *La Paz City Hotel* (☎ 322177), near Plaza San Pedro. Singles are US$5.50; larger rooms cost US$4 per person. It also has an *annexe* (☎ 36380) on Calle México. A slightly more upmarket place in the same neighbourhood is *Hostal Sucre* (☎ 328414), on Plaza San Pedro, which has singles/doubles with bath for US$11.50/18.60 and US$7.20/12.50 without bath.

If being central is a concern, the convenient *Hotel Torino* (☎ 341487), at Calle Socabaya 457 is a good bet. Its demeanour has grown a bit surly – an unfortunate by-product of its former reputation as *the* travellers crash pad. It's still quite popular with mountaineers. Services for guests include a book exchange and a free left-luggage service. The attached bar/restaurant serves good almuerzos for under US$2 and offers live music on weekends, but it's mainly synthesised pop that most people would rather be without. Singles/doubles without bath cost US$8/11; with bath, they're US$16/21.

The current backpackers' favourite – and rightfully so – is the friendly and centrally located *Hostal Austria* (☎ 351140), at 531 Yanacocha. It has safe gas-heated showers and cooking facilities. One to four-bed rooms with shared bath cost US$5 per person. Although several basic rooms lack windows, it's always full. When booking, be clear about when you expect to arrive, and don't be late otherwise your booking might disappear.

In the same area is *Hostal Ingavi* (☎ 323645), Calle Ingavi 727, which charges a negotiable US$6.50 per person with shared bath. Although it's a bit noisy and less than sparkling clean, it is recommended by the Hostal Austria when they're full.

From the outside, the one-star *Hotel Italia* (☎ 325101), Calle Manco Capac 303, looks more expensive than it is. The toilets aren't the best and the nicer rooms at the front are subject to lots of street noise. Almuerzos in its restaurant are a bargain at US$0.80 and there's a folk music peña on Friday night at 9 pm. Singles/doubles with shared bath cost US$5.20/8; with private bath, they're US$9.30/11.20.

Just over the street at Calle Manco Capac 364 is the *Hotel Andes* (☎ 323461), with large rooms and rarely-functioning lifts. It's friendly, however, and marginally popular with budget travellers. A single/double room will cost you US$10.30/14.50 with bath or US$5.80/9.50 without. Hostelling International members receive 20% discount. The most pleasant rooms are 402 to 405, which have balconies.

A good huff and puff from the centre is the *Hotel Panamericano* (☎ 340810) at Calle Manco Capac 454, near the railway station. It's clean and is still good value for money, catering mainly to organised groups that don't want to pay for the Sheraton. Clean singles/doubles with private baths and hot water cost only US$6.60/10.80.

Just up the hill, towards the railway station, is the cheaper *Hostal Cris* (☎ 365837), which charges US$3 per person for rooms without bath. Double-bedded rooms with bath are good value at US$8.25.

A new option is the relatively elegant *Hotel La Joya* (☎ 324346, fax 350959), near Plaza Garita de Lima near the Mercado Negro. The official single/double rates of US$13/17 without bath and US$21/28 with bath, place it in the three-star mid-range, but when space is available (especially in low season), backpackers can stay for US$6.50 per person. It's away from the centre of town but it's on numerous micro and trufi lines. The proprietor is friendly, there's room service, and the rooms are cleaned on a daily basis.

A pleasant inexpensive place is the quiet and friendly *Residencial Illimani* (☎ 325948), at Avenida Illimani 1817, not far from the stadium. There's hot water a few hours a day, a laundry sink and a patio sitting area where cooking is allowed. The señora will pleasantly admit you if you arrive or return after lock-up time at midnight. It's away from the centre of action but it's quiet, friendly and popular with laid-back travellers. Singles/doubles without bath cost US$5/7.50.

Handy to the bus terminal, at Avenida Armentia 367, is the pleasantly quiet, cosy and colonial-looking *Hostal Tambo de Oro* (☎ 322763). Nice carpeted single/double rooms with private bath are good value at US$10.50/14.50; without bath they're US$6.20/8.30.

Also acceptable is the rather aloof *Hostería Florida* (☎ 363298), at Calle Viacha 489. The street outside unfortunately smells of piss, but the hotel rooms are clean and comfortable, and cost only US$6 per person with private bath. Upper-floor rooms may offer excellent views of the city and proximity to the TV lounge, but the lift is (apparently permanently) broken. Breakfast costs extra.

The *Hostal Yanacocha*, at Yanacocha 540, is a boarding-house-style hotel (fortuitously opposite the chronically full Hostal Austria), but it has water only occasionally and is frequented by questionable characters. The basic *Alojamiento Metropoly* (☎ 353731), on Manco Capac, has a friendly owner and offers hot water all day, but even travellers accustomed to rough accommodation may waver at the sight of the toilets. Rooms with shared bath cost US$4.80. Another marginal place is *Alojamiento Illampu* at Calle Illampu 635, but at US$2.20 per person, it's economical and there's an especially good view from the top floor.

Places to Stay – middle

It seems the much lauded *Residencial Rosario* (☎ 325348, fax 375532), at Calle Illampu 704, has let success go to its top floor. The staff have become a bit blasé, prices have risen and all available space has been converted into a rabbit warren of stairways and passages to accommodate its enormous popularity. Still, it remains ultra-clean and pleasantly quiet: a sort of travellers capsule with Bolivia just outside the door. Plus points include a sunny courtyard, a sauna (open Tuesday to Sunday from 3 to 9 pm), a travel agency on the ground floor and an excellent café and restaurant serving such gringo-trail specialities as crêpes, oatmeal, granola, cream of asparagus soup and banana pancakes.

Advance booking is essential these days, but the reservation system has a few holes – don't even think about getting a double bed. Singles/doubles/triples without bath cost US$14/18/25. Rooms with private bath are reserved primarily for tour groups and are priced accordingly at US$24/30/38.

A couple of doors away is the recently upgraded *Residencial Copacabana* (☎ 367896). With private bath, it's US$21 per person and with shared bath, US$11.50 per person. Rates include a continental breakfast.

The sparkling and ultra-friendly *Hostal República* (☎ 357966), at Calle Comercio 1455, is in a lovely historic building that was once home to a Bolivian president. It has two large courtyards, a garden and a warm reception area with a small library of foreign-language books for guests' use. The staff really aim to please. Singles/doubles cost US$16/21 with private bath, US$9.50/13 without. Triple and quadruple rooms are also available.

At Calle Illampu 626, on Plaza Eguino, is the two-star *Hotel Continental* (☎ & fax 378226), which is in direct competition with the Residencial Rosario. It's good value at US$13.50/17.50 for singles/doubles without bath and US$21/28 with bath. Beware of the raucous disco on the 2nd floor.

The clean *Hotel Milton* (☎ 368003, fax 365849), at Calle Illampu 1224, is a two-star hotel in the heart of the market area. The gas showers are an attraction for any who fear the standard Frankenstein switch system. Singles/doubles/triples with telephone and TV cost US$21/28/36, including breakfast. Laundry services and *cajas de seguridad* (safe boxes) are available.

On Plaza San Pedro, a relatively quiet part of town, is the recommended three-star *Hotel Max Inn* (☎ 374391, fax 341720). For large, bright singles/doubles with bath, it charges US$30/42. The attached restaurant serves marginal meals.

Overlooking 'artesanía alley' on steep and bustling Calle Sagárnaga is the recommended *Hotel Sagárnaga* (☎ 350252, fax 360831). Rooms cost US$21/28 for a single/double with bath, and US$13/17 without. All rates include a continental breakfast and discounts of 10% are available during periods of low occupancy. Peñas are held on Wednesday and Sunday from 8 to 11 pm. Next door at Calle Sagárnaga 334 is the pleasant *Hotel Alem* (☎ 367400), with singles/doubles for US$7/11 without bath and US$13.50/18.50 with bath; all rates include breakfast. It's so clean that the floors squeak and it smells of disinfectant!

On Plaza Alonso de Mendoza, opposite the trufi terminus, is the *Hotel Oruro* (☎ 325893). It's of somewhat limited character, but does attract lots of wedding parties at weekends. At US$6/11 for a single/double without bath and US$10/13.50 with a private bath, it is decent value for money.

An interesting lower mid-range place is *Hotel Viena* (☎ 326090), at Calle Loayza 420, a Baroque-style building with immense high-ceiling rooms; it could be the set for a horror film. Room 113 is especially pleasant. Singles/doubles with private bath cost US$9/13.50. For something more plush, next door at Loayza 442, the three-star *Hotel Neumann* (☎ & fax 369814)42, charges US$20/30 for singles/doubles.

At the lower end of the centre, at Avenida 6 de Agosto 2074, you'll find the comfortable *Hotel España* (☎ 345643, fax 342329), a friendly and helpful place with a lovely courtyard that receives direct sun most of the day and is ideal for writing letters. It's also near most of the city's best restaurants. Singles/doubles, with breakfast and private bath, cost US$16.50/21.70. You can opt for a room with shared bath, including breakfast, for US$10 per person.

A new place is the neo-Baroque *Hostería Blanquita* (☎ 352933), on Calle Santa Cruz just above Calle Murillo. If you can get past the sensation that you've dived into a sweet and sticky European pastry, it's comfortable and friendly. Singles/doubles with hot showers and breakfast cost US$18.50/22. A gym and a jacuzzi are on the cards.

See also *Hotel La Joya* under bottom-end options.

Places to Stay – top end

The number of top-end options in La Paz is growing all the time. If you're after a bit of luxury, they're bargains considering the prices of comparable accommodation in most other world capitals! Expect such amenities as health clubs, spas, swimming pools, pubs, coffee shops and discos.

At the bottom of the top end is the *Hotel Gloria* (☎ 370010, fax 391489) at Calle Potosí 909, towering above the snarling traffic of the Prado. Singles/doubles cost US$40/50. Breakfast is included, but is widely bemoaned as not up to scratch for a hotel in this price range.

The *Hotel Copacabana* (☎ 352244, fax 327390), on the Prado (not to be confused with Residencial Copacabana on Calle Illampu), offers comfortable accommodation and good value for money. Singles/doubles with TV, bath and continental breakfast cost US$30/40. If you stay more than three days, a 10% discount is applied. For the same price, you can also stay in a heated room at the *Sucre Palace Hotel* (☎ 363453, fax 390251), just a block farther up the Prado.

Another recommended place is the popular *El Rey Palace* (☎ 393016, fax 367759), at Avenida 20 de Octubre 1947. This pleasant four-star hotel offers all Euro-

pean-standard services, including telephones, air con and cable TV. All rooms from the 4th floor up have private jacuzzis. The 80-seat restaurant serves à la carte dishes and does executive almuerzos for US$6. There's also a restaurant, El Rey Arturo (King Arthur) and a bar called Enrique VIII (Henry the Eighth). Singles/doubles cost US$70/80, which is very good value given what's on offer. Additional beds cost US$15 and suites are US$85 to US$105.

The *Gran Hotel Paris* (☎ 319170, fax 372547), on Plaza Murillo on the corner of Calle Bolívar, sits on the corner of La Paz's main plaza. This relatively small hotel has the elegant Café Paris, which offers full restaurant service. Singles/doubles cost US$70/US$90, and a double suite is US$100. All prices include American breakfast and 34 cable TV channels.

The *Hotel El Dorado* (☎ 363355, fax 391438), on Avenida Villazón, just below the Plaza del Estudiante, is a well-located three-star option. The rates, US$29/36 for single/double rooms with breakfast, represent quite good value. The Skyroom Grill on the top floor affords a spectacular view over the city.

The *Hotel Plaza* (☎ 378317, fax 343391), at Avenida 16 de Julio 1789, is one of the few places that still employs a dual pricing system in which foreigners pay up to 50% more than Bolivian residents (whatever their national origin). Singles/doubles with cable TV and a continental breakfast included cost US$100/120.

The *Hotel Radisson Plaza* (☎ 316163, fax 343391), at Avenida Aniceto Arce 2177, is a contender for La Paz's most upmarket option. It has everything you'd expect in a five-star hotel, including cable TV, but the cold and impersonal atmosphere isn't for everyone. Standard singles/doubles with breakfast cost US$130/150, but there is also a range of more luxurious options, from executive suites for US$150/170 up to the presidential suite for US$550.

The *Hotel Presidente* (☎ 368601, fax 354013), Calle Potosí 920, bills itself as the highest five-star hotel in the world, which is

Hillside neighbourhoods, La Paz (RS)

Top: Accounting Bolivian style, La Paz (WH)
Left: Young girl, La Paz (WH)
Right: Aymara women on Calle Graneros, La Paz (WH)

The World's Highest Street Kids

You'll see street kids everywhere in La Paz – shining shoes, selling sweets, yelling out minibus destinations or doing any other work they are offered. There are an estimated 500,000 working children in Bolivia and their numbers are increasing because of Bolivia's poor economic situation – it is the third poorest Latin American country after Haiti and Guyana and, according to UNICEF, 80% of its population lives below poverty level.

One survival strategy employed by Bolivian families is to send as many children as possible to work as early as possible. Children often begin working at the age of five, and often bring home more money than both their parents. According to the Bolivian Institute of Statistics, an average El Alto family earns about US$31 per month, which doesn't cover 10% of basic living costs. Meanwhile each working child – who will typically work up to 12 hours a day – can earn up to US$60 a month.

While struggling to survive, they soon realise that one job isn't enough to support themselves, and therefore grab every money-making opportunity offered, including theft and organised crime.

Of the children living on the street, 80% are male. Girls are usually kept at home to do the housework and look after their younger sisters and brothers, or are given to wealthy families to work as maids. Those who do turn to the street survive mainly by prostitution – which is the easiest way to get (pathetically little) money quickly. Pregnancy is common and they either attempt to get an abortion (which is illegal) or they have the children and are unable to provide them with basic necessities. This merely perpetuates the vicious cycle of destitution.

There are several private and state institutions in La Paz that provide street kids with food, dormitories and bathrooms. Only a few, however, offer psychological help, workshops and a route back to 'normal' life. One of these is HAPMA (Hogar Albergue Para Menores Abandonados – 'Home Hostel for Abandoned Children'), the main aim of which is to teach the children self-esteem and help them to take responsibility for their own lives. For more information write to HAPMA, Casilla 9343, El Alto, La Paz. ∎

Ulli Schatz, Germany

accurate since the equally five-star Hotel Plaza and Hotel Radisson Plaza are a few metres lower, farther down the Prado. Standard singles/doubles with heating and TV, as well as a buffet breakfast and airport transfers, cost US$100/120. Executive suites with private jacuzzi cost US$150/170. Weekend specials will get you a double room for Friday and Saturday nights for just US$150.

Places to Eat

La Paz's wealth and quality of restaurants – from street kiosks to fine dining – is generally good and whatever the standard, they're quite reasonable compared to what you'd probably pay at home.

In the cheapest ranges, don't expect much variation from the local standards. Nearly all specialise in – or serve exclusively – some sort of beef or chicken. Most offer set meals (mainly almuerzo but sometimes also cena) and a short list of the most common dishes and sometimes regional specialities.

The mid-range and upmarket restaurants are concentrated at the lower end of town: around Avenidas 20 de Octubre, 6 de Agosto and 16 de Julio (it's easy to remember historical dates in La Paz!) and in the Zona Sur.

Breakfast Few places that serve breakfast open before 8.30 or 9 am, but early risers desperate for a caffeine jolt before they can face the day will find bread rolls and riveting coffee concentrate at the markets for about US$0.40.

An exception to the late-opening rule is *La Fuente* at the Residencial Rosario, and nothing beats its fresh fruit, juices, delicious bread and all the other elements of continental and American breakfasts: ham, eggs, cheese, pancakes and excellent cocoa and cappuccino. Another good breakfast spot is the *Café Torino*, beside the Hotel Torino, which opens at 7.30 am every day and serves breakfasts of rolls, salteñas and fruit juices. Both almuerzos and cenas are available at good prices. Intending trekkers can buy large bags of granola here for less than US$1.

Another good place for American or continental breakfasts and salteñas is the *Tokio* (not to be confused with the New Tokyo), on the Prado, which opens at 8 am. It's pricey, however, and the salteñas sold in the markets for a third the price are often just as good; try the street stalls opposite the cemetery. Other great salteña options are *San Luis*, on Calle Socobaya near Potosí – it also sells cookies by the kg – and *Salteñas Filippo* on Calle 20 de Octubre at Plaza Avaroa.

For healthy vegetarian breakfasts of porridge, yoghurt, juice, granola and crêpes, try *El Vegetariano*, on Calle Loayza between Calles Obispo Cárdenas and Illimani. Breakfast is available from 9.15 am. If you prefer a quick coffee and a roll or salteña, go to *Confitería Club de La Paz*, a literary café and haunt of politicians (and formerly, of Nazi war criminals – I've reluctantly dined alongside Klaus Barbie here – but they're a dying breed these days) at the sharp corner of Avenidas Camacho and Mariscal Santa Cruz. It's known especially for its strong espresso and lemon meringue pie. Anyone hankering after sticky doughnuts and rich hot cocoa can resort to *California Donuts* on Avenida Camacho near Coló.

Snacks If you don't mind its hectic setting, the cheapest food scene is the markets. Unfortunately, the most central, *Mercado Lanza*, off Plaza Pérez Velasco, has a rather dirty, unpleasant comedor. Better is the *Mercado Camacho*, at Camacho and Bueno, where takeaway stalls sell empanadas and chicken sandwiches, and comedores dish up filling meals of soup, main course, rice, lettuce and oca or potato for less than US$1. You'll find other cheap and informal meals in the areas around Calle Buenos Aires and the cemetery.

On Avenida Simón Bolívar is *Las Velas*, a warren of smoky cubicles where vendors whip up everything from burgers to kebabs, sausages, sandwiches and other fast delights for an utter pittance. It's very good and is open until late.

Empanada aficionados should head for the first landing on the steps between the Prado and Calle México, where US$0.50 buys an enormous and excellent beef or chicken *empanada especial* smothered in your choice of sauces.

Opposite Hostal Ingavi on Calle Ingavi, you'll find great fruit shakes and yogurt drinks at *Vigor*. Near the cem-etery is *El Palacio de los Helados*, which is locally popular for ice cream, has some strange colourful murals outside and lacks the carnival atmosphere of most ice-cream places in the centre.

The *Boutique del Pan* on Calle Obispo Cárdenas is a bakery selling any imaginable bread concoction: brilliant fruit bread, rolls, sweet breads, brown bread and so on. The oddly named *Industria Alimentar El Luis* on Calle Socabaya is actually a bakery shop selling good bread and pastries.

If you're a fan of sweet biscuits, make a pilgrimage to *The Hutch* near Calle 21, just below the Ketal Supermarket in San Miguel (Zona Sur). I could wax poetic about the soft chocolate chips and awe-inspiring peanut butter cookies. The Hutch also does American-style burgers and especially generous portions of other fast foods. It's open daily except Sunday from 10.30 am to 9 pm.

A favourite for sweet snacks is *Kuchen Stube*, at Calle Rosendo Gutiérrez 461; you can stuff yourself with decadent European coffee, pastries, biscuits and other sweets. Some of the best coffee in town – including gourmet blends – is served up at *Café Oro* on Avenida Villazón below Plaza del Estudiante. Another friendly coffee shop is the *Pierrot*, on the ground floor of Hotel Gloria.

For a reasonable burger, *California Burgers* on Avenida Camacho, or *Denny's* at Mariscal Santa Cruz 1605, are two possibilities. Alternatively, there's the unfortunately named *Clap*, which has two locations – Avenida Aniceto Arce and Belisario Salinas, or the new and ominously named chain, *Baby Burger (la de pura carne* – 'the one with pure meat'), with several outlets around town. The latter is reportedly very good.

For quick chicken, try *Pollo Copacabana*, where you'll find roast chicken, chips and fried plantain smothered in ketchup, mustard and ají for US$2. There are locations on Calle Potosí and on Calle Comercio. Beside the former is a wonderful *sweets shop* selling great chocolates.

A good choice for Italian ice cream is *Heladería Napoli* on Plaza Murillo. In addition to ice-cream concoctions, it serves breakfasts, pastry, cakes and other snacks. There are also several popular ice-cream parlours along the Prado, such as *Unicornio*.

Lunch Lunch options are numerous and limited only by what you're prepared to pay. For the strictest budgets, the markets are naturally the cheapest options. They have takeaway snack stands selling empanadas and chicken sandwiches, and restaurant stalls with covered sitting areas. If you don't expect too much in the way of sanitation, a filling meal of soup, a meat dish, rice, lettuce and oca or potato will cost about US$0.60.

In addition, there are plenty of family-run cubbyhole restaurants displaying blackboard menus at their doors; you can assume that these places are really cheap. As a general rule, the higher you climb from the Prado, the cheaper the meals will be.

There are lots of acceptable budget restaurants on Evaristo Valle, where an almuerzo or cena can cost as little as US$1. Try the *Pensión Yungueña*, at Evaristo Valle 155 or the recommended *Snack El Diamante*, at Calle Manco Capac 315. *La Hacienda*, diagonally opposite the Residencial Rosario on Calle Illampu, is known for its home-made chicken soup. *Snack El Montañés*, directly opposite Hotel Sagárnaga, has good light meals and desserts. *Restaurant Un Camino* on Calle Murillo, near where it becomes Calle México, has a lively local atmosphere and serves almuerzos and cenas for under US$0.50. Also cheap are the several places along the lower (eastern) end of Calle Rodríguez, which offer almuerzos for about US$0.50.

Calle Rodríguez also boasts a handful of excellent ceviche places, where a bowl of Peruvian-style ceviche costs about US$1.50. The best is *Acuario II* (no sign), opposite the Acuario I (which does have a sign). A bit more sophisticated for ceviche is the nearby *Portales*, on Avenida Mariscal Santa Cruz a block uphill (north-west) from the post office. An oft-recommended ceviche place is the *Playa Brava Cevichería* on Fernando Guachalla two blocks above (south-west of) Calle 6 de Agosto, opposite Sopocachi market. Yet another option for ceviche, as well as all sorts of fish and shellfish, is the *Pescadería y Marisquería La Sirenita* on the corner of Otero de la Vega and Cañada Strongest near Plaza San Pedro.

Such Bolivian specialities as charque kan, chorizo, anticuchos and chicharrón are available at *Típicos*, on the 6th level of the Shopping Norte arcade, on the corner of Calles Potosí and Socabaya. In a more hectic setting, amid the lively market atmosphere of Calle Buenos Aires, is *Paso de los Toros*. Lake Titicaca trout costs US$2 to US$3, depending on the size of the fish, and standard Bolivian dishes are also prepared. It's open for Sunday lunch.

On weekdays, *Restaurant San Pedro*, near Plaza San Pedro, serves good value four-course almuerzos for US$1. On Sunday it offers an elaborate 'executive lunch' special, with wine, for just US$1.75. Pensioners get 10% discount. A cosy little place that's popular with locals is *Pension Otto*, on Calle Ingavi near the Hostal Austria. It serves snacks and inexpensive almuerzos and cenas, and is open on Sunday.

The *Confitería Paris*, on Calle Ballivián at Plaza Murillo, serves an odd combination of dishes, including ceviche, charque kan and Lake Titicaca trout, in a nice atmosphere. Just opposite is *Chifa Ballivián*, which serves basic Chinese meals as well as trout and Bolivian standards.

La Fuente at the Residencial Rosario is recommended, especially for the cream of asparagus and french onion soup, crumbed chicken and pasta dishes.

A convenient fast food venue is *Eli's Pizza Express*, with locations at 1491 and 1800

Ave 16 de Julio, and at Avenida Mariscal Montenegro 1431 in San Miguel, Calacoto (Zona Sur). You can choose between pizza, pasta, pastries and some rather unusual tacos. The food is only mediocre – the pizza is greasy and the pasta just bordering acceptable – but there's no wait.

Nicer pizza, as well as pasta and fish dishes – including trout and steamed surubí – are available at *Mamma Mia*, at 20 de Octubre 2030, near the corner of Aspiazu. In the same area, on 20 de Octubre between Pérez and Aspiazu, is the similarly recommended *Luigi's Pizza*.

Arguably the best pizzas in town come from *Sergio's*, a hole-in-the-wall place on Avenida Villazón near the Aspiazu steps. Don't miss it! The *Roma Café Restaurant* at Avenida Villazón 1970, near the university, serves almuerzos and a variety of pastas, hot sandwiches and fondues, among other things, for mid-range prices. On Friday and Saturday, it offers ceviche. It's open Monday to Saturday from 11 am to 11 pm.

Café Verona, on Calle Colón near Avenida Mariscal Santa Cruz, is recommended for its US$1.50 sandwiches, US$3 pizzas and US$3.50 almuerzos.

For a taste of Empire, climb up to La Paz's socially impeccable bastion of Victorian romance, *Club Libanés*, at Avenida 16 de Julio 1698. The restaurant features smoked-glass chandeliers, wrought-iron balustrades, gold spiral staircases and stately portraits of 'old money' peering down from the walls. Almuerzos are surprisingly good value at US$1.50 and the atmosphere simply must be experienced.

Another good lunch choice is French-oriented *Café Montmartre*, at Alliance Française on Calle Fernando Guachalla. Lunch specials, with some vegie choices, cost US$3. There's a range of crêpes and salads, and coq au vin becomes pollo al vino. It's open Monday to Friday for lunch and dinner. Just opposite is *Don Francisco*, serving good French and Italian dishes. An excellent choice for lunch is *Andromeda*, at the bottom of the Aspiazu steps on Avenida Arce. It serves vegetarian almuerzos on Monday and Wednesday, and meat dishes and vegetarian options on other days. On Friday, the almuerzo is always a fish dish.

At *Café Ciudad*, on Plaza del Estudiante, service is slow and the food ordinary – the coke is warm and the fettucine alfredo (which is actually carbonara) is cold – but the full menu is available 24 hours a day, every day, and you're free to linger over its two redeeming features, coffee and apple pie. Just down the hill, on Batallón Colorados, is *Bar/Restaurant Latino*, which does good but more down-to-earth almuerzos for US$1.50.

The very popular *La Fiesta*, on Mariscal Santa Cruz opposite the bottom of Calle Socabaya, has lunches for US$1.75, but the breakfasts are slightly overpriced. For good but relatively expensive German-style lunches – sausages, smoked pork chops, sauerkraut and the like – try *Max Bieber* at Avenida 20 de Octubre 2080. Plan on paying US$3 to US$4 per person. It's closed on Tuesday.

Tiny *El Vegetariano*, beside Hotel Viena, serves good breakfasts and great vegetarian almuerzos for about US$1, but it's often packed out. You can also pick up delicious vegetarian salteñas for US$0.40. Another recommended vegetarian restaurant – which claims to be the most popular eatery on the Gringo Trail – is at *Hotel Gloria*, Calle Potosí 909. Almuerzos cost US$2.50 but arrive before 12.30 pm or you risk missing out. The informal *Gringo Limón* on Plaza Avaroa, on the corner of Calles Salazar and 20 de Octubre, does Bolivian and European specialities, including a lunchtime bufé de verduras (vegetable buffet).

On Calle Sagárnaga near Plaza San Francisco and at Calle Santa Cruz 266 are branches of the *Restaurant Vegetarianista Lila Vaty* (☎ 325372), serving vegetarian and macrobiotic meals. Almuerzos, including salad bar, soup, main course, sweet and mate (tea), cost US$1.75. To reach the Calle Santa Cruz place, you pass through a shop selling leather clothing and beneath a poster of leather-clad Megadeth – perhaps the cows were vegetarians. It's open Monday to Saturday, from 10 am to 10 pm. You'll also find health foods and courses in yoga and vegetarian cuisine.

Nearby, in an arcade off Sagáranga, between Linares and Murillo, is the recommended *Imperial*, which emphasises Indian vegetarian cuisine and also has muesli and vegie burgers. It's open daily from 10 am to 9 pm. Another vegetarian possibility is *Natur Center*, on Cañada Strongest.

Dinner Many of the suggested lunch places also serve dinner.

The *Tambo Colonial*, in the Residencial Rosario, is known for its salad bar and excellent dishes such as trout in white wine sauce, steak with bacon and mushroom sauce, as well as assorted pasta dishes. Afterwards, indulge in what may be the best chocolate mousse south of the equator. There are live music performances on Thursday, Friday and Saturday nights.

The repeatedly recommended *Pronto Ristorante*, at Pasaje Jáuregui 2248, a small alley off Fernando Guachalla near Avenida 6 de Agosto, serves delicious homemade pasta. Although fairly posh, it's very good value and there's no fuss about appearances.

For fish, go to the quirky *El Palacio de Pescado* on Avenida Muñecas América, where you'll pay about US$4 for surubí, pacu, trucha, pejerrey, sábalo etc. When I was there, the day's catch, which had been flown in from the Beni, was stacked on the floor in the middle of the dining room!

Inexpensive almuerzos and cenas are also available at the popular but aloof *El Lobo*, on the corner of Calle Santa Cruz and Illampu. The curry and chicken are particularly nice but the chips should come with a grease warning. Ask to see their books of travellers' recommendations in both English and Hebrew if you want to find out where everyone else is going or avoiding, or which places are turning into a travellers' ghetto.

The *Nuevo Oruro*, upstairs at Ingavi 773, near the Pichincha steps, has been recommended but it's not for vegetarians:

Inside are fantastic ceiling murals and good views from the window tables. We had the Plato de la Casa, which was a platter with steak, chicken, blood sausage, chorizo, intestines, kidneys, whole potatoes and a large salad. Easily a meal for two, but we didn't know this so we also ordered *brazuelo de cordero*, which was a huge roast shoulder of mutton on top of creamed chuño and potatoes. We ate leftovers all the way to Potosí.

Tom Harriman & Jan King

The odd combination in the plato de la casa is known as *El Intendente* after the finicky government official who habitually requested this bizarre ensemble from restaurant owners.

An exceptional choice is *La Casa de los Paceños*, at Calle Sucre 856, near Pichincha. In addition to set almuerzos for US$1.50, this friendly family-run place serves typical La Paz dishes, including saíce, sajta, fricasé, chairo paceño and fritanga (fried pork). It's open for lunch daily except Monday, and for dinner from Tuesday to Friday. For a similar range – plus charque kan, rabbit and grilled llama – in an international setting, try *Bar-Restaurant El Príncipe* (☎ 230123) at Calle Simón Aguirre 105, between Ballivián and Las Casas in relatively remote Villa Copacabana.

La Québecoise (☎ 361782), at 20 de Octubre 2355, features Canadian and American cuisine. It's not cheap at about US$7 per person, but the food and atmosphere are top quality.

Mongo's Rock Bottom Café (☎ 353914), at Hermanos Manchego 2444 above (west of) Plaza Isabél la Católica, is open every day of the week. The specialities of this American-style bar & restaurant include onion rings, nachos, enormous burgers, Budweiser beer and even US football on a big-screen TV.

The German restaurant *Zur Mönchsklause* (☎ 721249), on Calle 13 on the corner of Ovando Candia in Irpavi, Zona Sur, is open for lunch and dinner from Friday to Sunday and on public holidays. It isn't easy to reach but it's definitely worth the effort. The menu includes a huge selection of meat and fish, and a meal outside at their garden tables is a great way to spend a sunny Sunday afternoon.

For a strange Middle Eastern-Bolivian-New York hybrid, try the *Wall Street Café* (☎ 316090) at Avenida Camacho 1363, which is open 8 am to midnight Monday to Saturday. Specialities include Greek gyros, kepi, felafels, a range of sandwiches and Yungas coffee. It's very good.

The *New Tokyo*, at Avenida 6 de Agosto 2932, serves decent Japanese Bolivian food, but it's not cheap (from US$10 per person). The main problem is the obnoxious big-screen entertainment system, showing videos that are typically less than palate-inspiring. Perhaps a better and cheaper place for Japanese cuisine is the *Japanese Club*, on the 3rd floor of the Japanese club near the corner of Batallón Colorados and Federico Zuazo. It's open daily from 11.30 am to 2.30 pm and from 6.30 to 10 pm.

El Viejo Tonel near the corner of 20 de Octubre and Calle Gustavo Medinacelli is an expensive but recommended Brazilian-style churrasquería (steak house). It's not to be confused with the related *El Viejo Tonel III* (☎ 796539), which is a Mexican-theme restaurant, bar and disco in Calacoto, Zona Sur. On Calle Landaeta near 20 de Octubre is the tasteful *El Batán*, which serves excellent Chuquisaqueña (Sucre) specialities for US$5 to US$6 per person. Regional fare is also available at the more basic, pub-like *Comida Camba*, also on Landaeta. As the name would imply, specialities hail from Santa Cruz department and include a range of dishes based on beef, cassava, plantain and other tropical favourites. Plan on US$1.50 to US$2 for à la carte dishes.

Restaurant Vienna, which many expatriates believe is the best restaurant in La Paz, serves traditional central European cuisine in an antique atmosphere. It serves both lunch and dinner, but there's no set almuerzo. You'll find it at Federico Zuazo 1905, near Batallón Colorados.

Rumors, on the corner of Avenida Ballivián and Calle 9 in Calacoto, is on the expensive side, but serves excellent Mexican dishes in a pleasant restaurant/bar setting. It's particularly popular with the affluent youth of Zona Sur. Also in Calacoto, at Avenida Montenegro 5B, is *Super Mex* (☎ 795696). It's owned and run by people from Guanajuato, Mexico, and as the name suggests, it's a super Mexican restaurant. A more central Mexican place is the upmarket but very nice *Jalapeños*, on Avenida Arce near Plaza Isabél la Católica. On Wednesday to Saturday evenings, the *Planet Funky Nachos Bar*, on Calle Montículo near Calle Ecuador, serves up great Mexican choices.

Sunday evening meals may be difficult because few places are open. *Café Verona* is well-attended on Sunday evenings, when it's the only light on in this part of town. In Calacoto, between Calles 15 and 16 in Zona Sur, is *Abracadabra*, accessible by micro or minibus trufi. It's good, but unfortunately falls short of its aim to turn standard American fare – steaks, ribs, pizza and salads – into trendy haute cuisine. Check your bill carefully, especially if you're in a large group.

Self-Catering The markets – *Mercado Lanza* and *Mercado Camacho* – are the place to find staple foods at good prices. If you're after sweet snacks, go to Calle Isaac Tamayo, near Manco Capac. On the corner of 20 de Octubre and Belisario Salinas is *ZAT*, an enormous and expensive US-style supermarket, selling just about everything, including dehydrated pasta meals for trekking.

If you're just looking for an inexpensive bottle of wine – Chilean Undurraga and Argentine Toro Viejo are both recommended and cost US$2 for 750 ml – try the *street stalls* on Calle Manco Capac, just above the Isaac Tamayo stairway.

Entertainment

Peñas Typical of La Paz (and all Bolivia) are folk music venues known as peñas. Most present traditional Andean music, rendered on zampoñas, quenas and charangos, but also often include guitar shows and song recitals. Some peñas play six days a week, while others have shows only on Friday and Saturday nights. They all start at around 10 pm and last until 1 or 2 am. Admission ranges from US$5 to US$6 and usually includes the first drink.

The best known is *Peña Naira* (☎ 325736), at Calle Sagárnaga 161, just above Plaza San Francisco, but it's aimed at foreign tourists and Bolivian business people. It plays nightly except Sunday from 10.30 pm to 2 am and costs US$6. The attached restaurant does good but overpriced fondues, but it does have better value options. Note the remarkable table settings.

A less expensive – and some claim more traditional – peña is the *Marka Tambo* at Calle Jaén 710. Although the food is poor, the music is great and costs only US$5. Another popular peña is staged at *La Casa del Corregidor* (☎ 363633), a beautiful colonial building at Calle Murillo 1040. It plays Monday to Saturday at 9 pm and costs US$3 per person, but come earlier to enjoy a meal at its recommended lunch and dinner restaurant, El Horno, which serves delicious trout, chicken and vegetable dishes. Dinners average about US$6.

Also good for its restaurant as well as its Friday and Saturday night peñas is *Las Cuatro Estaciones*, on the corner of Calles 20 de Octubre and Pérez, which serves almuerzo for US$1.50, delicious sopa de marisco (seafood soup) for US$3 and ceviche for US$2.50 to US$3.

The peña at *Los Escudos* (☎ 322028) on Avenida Mariscal Santa Cruz (in the same building as Café Club de La Paz) rounds out the list of larger tourist peñas. It plays Monday to Saturday and the cover charge is low at US$5, including the first drink. The set meal costs US$10.

You may also want to check the La Paz paper for advertisements and details about smaller unscheduled peñas and other musical events.

Bars & Pubs There are scores of inexpensive local drinking dens scattered around the city, but unaccompanied women should steer clear and no-one should sit down to drink with Bolivians in one of these unless they intend to pass out later in the evening. A tame local option is the informal *Café Semilla*

Juveníl, Almirante Grau 443, with weekend talks and music events.

You'll also find lots of more elegant bars, which are frequented by foreigners and middle-class Bolivians. Highly recommended are the two British-style pubs. The *Pig & Whistle* on Calle Goitia, near Avenida Arce, is a pleasant but slightly-too-refined Tudor-style pub where you can drink, snack and chat. There are also darts, backgammon, rather expensive pub meals and a variety of imported European beer. (It's currently for sale, so there may be substantial changes.) The *Britannia* between Calles 15 and 16 in Calacoto is the place to go if you can't live without a game of darts or a bottle of imported (and expensive!) Bateman's bitter. During the Friday happy hour (7 to 8 pm) it's crowded with Bolivians and foreigners taking advantage of the free pub snacks and half-price drinks. It's open Tuesday to Sunday nights.

Café Montmartre, at Alliance Française, stages live bands on weekend evenings. At the new *Bavaria*, on 20 de Octubre at Plaza Avaroa, you get a predictable Teutonic slant. It has four German beers and good but expensive meals. It's open Tuesday to Saturday from 6.30 pm (and for lunch on Sunday) and is a good place to begin a cruise around the Sopocachi bar scene, since everything else opens later.

Side by side on Calle Montículo, near Calle Ecuador, are the agreeably tame *Juan Sebastian Bar* and the pleasantly spacey *Planet Funky Nachos Bar*. The latter, which does indeed serve nachos, is a hangout for mountaineers and rock climbers and features a useful climbers notice board. (Note the relevant gecko theme by local climber Andy St Pierre.) It's open evenings from Wednesday to Saturday.

Mongo's, at Calle Hermanos Manchego 2444, serves up both American beer and the Sports Channel on big-screen TV. It's open every night. Happy hours, which feature half-price drinks, are on Friday from 5 to 7 pm and Saturday from 6.30 to 8.30 pm. On Tuesday, women pay half price for drinks from 6.30 pm onward.

The *X-Presión Café Arte Bar*, at Calle Zoilo Flores 1334, offers live music on Friday and Saturday, and a Brazilian night on Wednesday. Another basic place with live music is the locally popular *La Luna* (☎ 320523) at Calle Oruro 197; there's a US$3 cover charge.

The *Resolana Piano Bar* (☎ 350530), upstairs at Calle Sagárnaga 161, is a real hybrid and can't really decide whether it's a bar or a restaurant. You'll enjoy the live jazz performances on weekends, but it also serves fine pizza, pasta and fish dishes, and even makes free pizza deliveries.

A lively hangout is the Chilean-run *La Cueva* on Calle México, just uphill (west) from the main post office. It hops to the beat of salsa and rock music and has become quite popular with foreign travellers. If you'd like to hear Bolivian bands attempt Pink Floyd, here's your opportunity.

There's also a lively pub/bar/café scene in and around Sopocachi: the *Carcajada* at Calle Almirante Grau 525; *Bar El Socavón* at 20 de Octubre 2180 (US$1.50 cover charge); *Caras y Caretas* at Belisario Salinas 380, which offers live bands and pool tables; *Matheus* on the corner of Fernando Guachalla and 6 de Agosto; *Equinoccio* at Calle Belisario Salinas 380, which regularly offers live entertainment; and just opposite, the *Ritz*, which also stages live performances and isn't as trendy or upmarket as its name would suggest.

A more upmarket choice is *El Bodegón de Cinti* at La Casa del Corregidor, Calle Murillo 1040; it opens at 10 pm. The chuquis-aqueño theme dictates southern specialities and drinks based on singani from Cinti province in Chuquisaca department.

Discos La Paz has several discos that appeal to the young and restless at heart. *Forum* at Calle Víctor Sanjinés 2908 near Ricardo Mujía in Sopacachi has been recommended for its diversity; each night of the week it focuses on different musical themes. Other discos include two local teenage favourites near the stadium: the optimistically named *Disco Love City* and, opposite it, *Disco Papillón*.

Cinema Your best chances of catching a quality film are at the *Cinemateca Boliviana*, on the corner of Pichincha and Indaburo. It shows subtitled foreign films daily at 4 and 7.30 pm for the same US$1.50 admission price charged by other cinemas. Other La Paz cinemas show first-run films (many of which deserve to be last-run), and most are presented in English with subtitles.

Theatre The Teatro Municipal, on the corner of Sanjinés and Indaburo, has an ambitious programme of folklore shows, folk music concerts and foreign theatrical presentations. It's a great old restored building with a round auditorium, elaborate balconies and a vast ceiling mural. The newspapers and tourist office have information about what's on. The average ticket price is about US$4.

Spectator Sport

The popularity of *futbol*, professional football (soccer), in Bolivia is comparable to that in other Latin American countries. Matches are played at Hernando Siles Stadium on Sunday year-round, as well as on Thursday evening during the winter. You can imagine what sort of advantage the local teams have over mere lowlanders; players from elsewhere consider La Paz games a suicide attempt! Check newspapers for times and prices.

Getting There & Away

Air El Alto airport sits on the altiplano at 4018m, 10 km from the city centre. It's the world's highest international airport; larger planes need five km of runway to lift off and must land at twice their sea-level velocity to compensate for the lower atmospheric density. Stopping distance is much greater, too, and planes must be equipped with special tyres to withstand the extreme forces involved.

Airport services include a newsagent, souvenir shops, a tiny bookshop, a coffee shop and an upstairs bistro. The currency exchange facilities offer poor rates on travellers cheques – if possible, wait until you're in town. The duty-free shop is available to passengers departing internationally.

Domestic flights are serviced by LAB and AeroSur. LAB has the widest network and flies to just about every corner of the country. Some sample fares are: Cochabamba (US$41), Sucre (US$56), Santa Cruz (US$90.50), Puerto Suárez (US$145), Yacuiba (US$172), Tarija (US$87.50), Trinidad (US$62), Guayaramerín (US$132) and Cobija (US$144). TAM is a bit cheaper but is generally unreliable and flights must be booked well in advance.

The following is a list of some airline offices in La Paz. Specific schedules and fares change regularly so it's best to contact individual carriers for details.

Aerolíneas Argentinas
Avenida 16 de Julio 1486, Banco de la Nación Argentina, ground floor (☎ 351711, fax 391316)
AeroPerú
SKORPIOS, Avenida 16 de Julio 1490, Edificio Avenida, (☎ 370002, fax 291313)
Aerosur
Avenida 16 de Julio 1607 (☎ 371833, fax 390457)
American Airlines
Plaza Venezuela 1440, Edificio Herrmann P Busch (☎ 351360, fax 391080)
British Airways
Edificio Mariscal Ballivián, 12th floor (☎ 373857, fax 391072)
Faucett Peruvian Airlines
Edificio Cámara de Comercio Office 4, ground floor (☎ 325764, fax 350118)
Iberia
Avenida 16 de Julio 1616, Edificio Petrolero, 2nd floor (☎ 358605, fax 391192)
KLM
Plaza del Estudiante 1931, (☎ 323965, fax 362697)
LanChile
Avenida 16 de Julio, Edificio Mariscal de Ayacucho, Suite 104, ground floor (☎ 358377, fax 392051)
LAB (Lloyd Aéreo Boliviano)
Avenida Camacho 1460 (☎ 367710)
Lufthansa
Avenida Mariscal Santa Cruz, Edificio Hansa, 7th floor (☎ 372170, fax 391026)

TAM (Transportes Aéreos Militares)
Avenida Ismael Montes 728 (☎ 379285, fax 390705)
United Airlines
Calle Mercado 1328, Edificio Ballivián 1606 (☎ 328397, fax 391505)
Varig/Cruzeiro
Edificio Cámara de Comercio, Avenida Mariscal Santa Cruz 1392 (☎ 314040, fax 391131)

You can fly to Potosí on the plane that delivers newspapers from La Paz, departing daily at about 9 am (US$65, 2 hours). Book through Transamazonas (☎ 3504111, fax 360923) Office 3C, 3rd floor, Edificio V Centenario, Avenida 6 de Agosto, Casilla 14551.

For information on international flights, see the Getting There & Away chapter.

Bus The main bus terminal (☎ 367275), the Terminal Terrestre Ciudad de La Paz, is at Plaza Antofagasta, a 15-minute walk from the city centre. Bus fares are relatively uniform between companies, but competition on most routes is such that discounts are available for the asking. Some destinations – among them Copacabana, Sorata, Guaqui and the Yungas – are served only by private operators whose terminals are scattered around the cemetery and Villa Fátima districts. Most of these companies run micros or minibuses.

Southern & Eastern Bolivia Buses to Oruro run about every half-hour (US$2.20, three hours). Flota Bustillo has direct services to Llallagua several times daily. To Uyuni, Panasur departs on Tuesday and Friday at 5.30 pm for US$10. Plenty of *flotas* go to Cochabamba, leaving either in the morning or between 8 and 9 pm (US$5, six hours). Many of these continue on to Santa Cruz or connect with a Santa Cruz bus in Cochabamba.

Buses to Sucre (US$12) normally pass through Cochabamba, and some require an eight to 10-hour layover there. Numerous flotas go to Potosí daily (US$8, 12 hours), leaving between 6 and 6.30 pm. Have warm clothes handy for this typically chilly trip.

Some Potosí buses, including San Lorenzo and Velóz del Sur, continue on to Tarija, Tupiza, Yacuiba or Villazón.

Lake Titicaca & Peru Transportes Manco Capac (☎ 350033), Calle José Maria Aliaga 670, and Transtur 2 de Febrero (☎ 377181), Calle José Maria Aliaga 287, run to Copacabana (US$3, five hours) several times daily. Both are just off Avenida Baptista near the cemetery and quite a long way from the hotel areas. Fares are US$2. At Copacabana, you'll find *camiones* and colectivos to Puno and beyond. Flota Trans Libre has frequent micro services to Huatajata from its terminal on Calle Cardona.

Alternatively, for US$6, there are more comfortable tourist minibuses, which provide the easiest way to Peru. From Copacabana, lots of minibuses and micros run to Puno (Peru). Most companies offer daily services to Puno (with a change in Copacabana) for about US$10, including hotel pick-up. The trip takes nine to 10 hours, including lunch in Copacabana. If a company doesn't fill its bus, passengers are shunted to another company so no-one runs half-empty buses. In this case, passengers may not actually travel with the company that issued the ticket. All companies allow stopovers in Copacabana.

Autolíneas Ingavi (☎ 328981) has four buses daily along the relatively uninteresting southern route to Desaguadero, on the Peruvian border, via Tiahuanaco and Guaqui. They depart from Calle José María Asín, near the cemetery (US$1.50, about three hours).

Buses to Huatajata and other eastern Lake Titicaca towns and villages leave daily approximately every half-hour from 4 am to 5 pm (to Huatajata: US$1, about two hours). The terminal is on the corner of Calles Manuel Bustillos and Kollasuyo, also in the cemetery district. To return to La Paz from these places, flag the bus down on the highway.

The Yungas & the Amazon Basin A number of flotas in Barrio Villa Fátima,

steeply uphill (north) from the stadium (reached by micro or trufi from the Prado or Calle Camacho), offer daily bus and minibus services to the Yungas and beyond: Coroico, Chulumani, Caranavi, Guanay, Rurrenabaque, Reyes, Santa Rosa, San Borja, Trinidad, Riberalta (with connections to Cobija) and Guayaramerín. It's wise to reserve seats in advance. Camiones to the Yungas and Amazonia leave from near the petrol station, just off Avenida Las Américas in Villa Fátima.

From Calle Ángel Babia in the cemetery district, Transportes Larecaja and Flota Unificado Sorata operate daily morning and early afternoon buses to Sorata. Seats are in short supply, so book your ticket at least the day before.

Chile Warm clothing is essential for any land crossing between Bolivia and Chile! To Arica (Chile), Flota Litoral (☎ 358603) leaves on Tuesday and Friday at 8.30 pm, from the terminal terrestre, travelling via Tambo Quemado and Lauca National Park. Géminis, also at the bus terminal, leaves on Wednesday and Saturday. From Arica, they leave at 1 am on Tuesday and Friday. With either flota, the trip costs US$33 and takes from 18 to 22 hours, depending on the delay at the Tambo Quemado immigration post (this trip will be greatly improved and shortened with the completion of the new Arica-La Paz highway).

Flota Litoral also has a Tuesday, Thursday and Saturday service to Iquique (Chile) at 5 pm for US$35. Géminis, which is slightly more expensive, has a direct service to Iquique on Tuesday, Thursday and Saturday, and also offers daily connections to Calama, Antofagasta and Santiago. Buses usually reach the Colchane border at about 3.30 am, but passengers must endure typically icy conditions until immigration opens at 7.30 am. Fortunately, the coffee and empanada vendors, as well as moneychangers, arrive at about 6.30 am.

Train The Estación Central (☎ 373068) is on upper Manco Capac, steeply uphill (north-west) from the city centre. Three railway lines run out from La Paz. One goes southward to Oruro, Uyuni, Tupiza and Villazón. Branches from this line cut off at Uyuni for Calama (Chile), at Río Mulatos for Potosí and Sucre, and at Oruro for Cochabamba. Another line goes to Arica in Chile; and the third, which is not currently in use, goes to Guaqui on Lake Titicaca.

Note that arranging rail tickets from La Paz is somewhat less than straightforward, and may waste lots of time. In most cases, it's better to take a bus to Oruro and arrange onward rail transport there.

Ferrobuses leave for Potosí and Sucre on Tuesday and Saturday at 5 pm. The 1st class fares are US$11/13 to Potosí/Sucre. The ferrobus to Arica (Chile) departs on Monday and Friday at 7.15 am and costs US$52. In summer, there's an additional departure on Wednesday at 8 am. The train to high, cold and windy Charaña, on the border, departs from Viacha (a railway station on the Altiplano south-east of La Paz) on Wednesday at 3 pm. It costs US$3 in 2nd (especial) class. Agencia Martínez, in Arica, runs a Wednesday bus from Arica to Visviri, to connect with this train.

Trains to Avaroa, where you'll find rail connections to Calama, depart only from Oruro; expect delays in Uyuni and bring warm clothing and a sleeping bag to cope with the typically subzero temperatures on this journey.

To Villazón, the *Expreso del Sur* runs on Friday at 1 pm (US$19/17 1st/2nd class, 18 hours). The 1st/2nd class fares to Uyuni and Tupiza, which are intermediate stops, are US$11.50/13 and US$15/17, respectively. Don't count too heavily on the timetable, however, and bring warm woolly clothing for the journey. Other trains to Uyuni, Tupiza and Villazón run only from Oruro. This service formerly continued to Buenos Aires, but passenger services within Argentina have been suspended and are unlikely to resume.

Tickets for rail services within Peru are available at the ENAFER office in the terminal terrestre. The tourist class (one step above 1st class) fare from Puno to Cuzco is US$22. From Puno to Arequipa costs US$19. For slightly more, you can opt for the even more plush Inca class. Reserve and purchase Bracha class tickets at Bracha (☎ 327472), Edificio Petrolero, mezzanine, Avenida 16 de Julio 1606.

Car & Motorcycle Driving the steep, winding and one-way streets of La Paz may be intimidating for the uninitiated, but for longer daytrips into the immediate hinterlands, hiring a car isn't a bad idea. For information on agencies and prices, see Car & Motorcycle in the Getting Around chapter.

Motorcycles may be hired from Moto-Rent (☎ 366234) at Avenida Busch 1255. The charge is about US$20 per day with unlimited km.

Getting Around
The Airport El Alto International Airport is on the Altiplano 10 km from the city centre. There are two roads to the airport, the *autopista* or toll road, which costs US$0.75, and the sinuous free route, which issues you into El Alto's Plaza Ballivián.

The cheapest but least convenient way to El Alto airport is on the La Ceja micro (US$0.18), which will drop you at the brow of the canyon; from there, it's a level two-km walk to the airport.

Much easier is the minibus trufi 212, which runs between Plaza Isabél la Católica and the airport, and costs US$0.75. Heading into town from the airport, catch trufi 212 outside the terminal. It will drop you anywhere along the Prado.

Radio taxis for up to four passengers cost US$6 from the city centre to the airport, and will pick you up at your door. Confirm the price with the dispatcher when booking and pay only what you're quoted. Coming from the airport, taxi drivers lie in wait for arriving foreigners, hoping to charge unrealistic fares; the current standard fare is US$6 (B$30) for up to four passengers. For a fifth person, they charge an additional US$1.

TAM flights leave from the military

airport in El Alto, accessible on the micro marked Río Seco, which you can catch on the upper Prado.

Around Town La Paz is well served by its public transport system. Basically, you can choose between micros (small buses), which charge US$0.18 (B$0.90); trufis – either cars or minibuses – which charge US$0.20 (B$1) around town, US$0.60 (B$3) to the airport and US$0.40 (B$1.70) to Zona Sur; shared taxis, which charge US$0.40 (B$2) per person around the centre, although this may be a bit more for long uphill routes; and radio taxis, charging US$1.20 (B$6) around the centre, US$1.60 (B$8) to the cemetery district, US$2.20 (B$11) to Zona Sur and US$7.20 (B$35) to the airport. Radio taxi charges are for up to four passengers and include pick-up, if necessary.

Any of these vehicles can be waved down anywhere, except near intersections or in areas cordoned off by the police. In the case of micros and trufis, destinations are identified on placards on the roof or windscreen.

Micro La Paz's sputtering and smoke-spewing micros mock the law of gravity and defy the principles of brake and transmission mechanics as they grind up and down the city's steep hills. You'd be forgiven for assuming they somehow missed their appointment with the scrap dealer, but they do provide cheap, coronary-free transport for the city's masses.

In addition to a route number or letter, micros plainly display their destination and route on a signboard posted in the front window. You'll see micro stops, but they're superfluous; micros will stop wherever you wave them down.

Trufi & Colectivo Trufis and colectivos are small cars or minibuses, which ply set routes and provide reliable and comfortable transport that falls somewhere between the taxis and micros. For the benefit of nonreaders, colectivos often carry small urchins with big lungs who cry out the destinations.

Taxi Although most things worth seeing in La Paz lie within manageable walking distance of the centre, both the rail and bus terminals are rather steep climbs from the main hotel areas. Especially considering the altitude, struggling up the hills through traffic beneath a heavy pack isn't fun.

Fortunately, taxis aren't expensive, but if the journey involves lots of uphill travel, drivers may expect a bit more. Most regular taxis – as opposed to radio taxis, which carry roof bubbles advertising their telephone numbers – are actually collective taxis. Don't be concerned if the driver picks up additional passengers and don't hesitate to flag down a taxi already carrying passengers. If you're travelling beyond the city centre or your journey involves a long uphill climb, arrange a fare with the driver before climbing in and if possible, pay the fare in exact change. As a general rule, taxi drivers aren't tipped, but if an individual goes beyond the call of duty, a tip of US$0.20 or US$0.40 or so (B$1 or B$2) wouldn't be amiss.

Taxi drivers may not always be well versed in city geography, so have a map handy to explain roughly where you want to go.

Long-distance taxis gather at the Centro de Taxis on Avenida Aniceto Arce near Plaza Isabél la Católica. Prices are negotiable; as a general rule, plan on US$40 to US$50 per day.

Around La Paz

VALLE DE LA LUNA
The Valle de la Luna (Valley of the Moon) is a pleasant and quiet half-day break from urban La Paz and may be visited easily in a morning or combined with a hike to Muela del Diablo, for example, to fill an entire day. It isn't a valley at all, but a bizarre eroded hillside maze of canyons and pinnacles technically known as badlands. It lies about 10 km down the canyon of the Río Choqueyapu from the city centre. This desert-like landscape and its vegetation inspire the

imagination and invite exploration. Several species of cactus grow here, including the hallucinogenic *choma*, or San Pedro cactus.

The route is badly eroded and unconsolidated silt makes it slippery and dangerous; the pinnacles collapse easily and some of the canyons are over 10m deep. Be cautious, carry drinking water and wear a good pair of hiking shoes.

Getting There & Away

If you visit Valle de la Luna as part of an organised tour, you'll have only an unimpressive five-minute photo stop. On your own, however, you'll have time to explore the intriguing formations on foot.

Catch any Mallasa-bound micro or trufi from the Prado. Continue past Calacoto and Barrio Aranjuez and up the hill to the fork in the road; the right fork goes to Malasilla Golf Course. After you see a sign announcing Valle de la Luna, get off at the first football ground on your left. This is at the top of Valle de la Luna.

Alternatively, get off at Barrio Aranjuez, cross the Río Choqueyapu bridge to your right, cross the ditch to your left and follow the nondescript track up the hill. After 10 minutes, you'll reach the *cactario* or cactus garden. It's not marked as such but is easily identifiable as a slightly artificial-looking stand of cacti. From there, a badly eroded and dangerous track winds up through Valle de la Luna to emerge at the aforementioned football ground near Mallasa. Since the rains drastically alter this fragile landscape, portions of the track may wash out in coming years and the route may change.

MALLASA

After a traipse around Valle de la Luna, you can also visit the blossoming resort village of Mallasa. La Paz's spacious new Vesty Pakos Zoo, just east of Mallasa, is open daily from 8.30 am to 3.30 pm. Admission is US$0.70. Guides are available only on weekends.

Places to Stay & Eat

Several shops in Mallasa sell snacks, beer and soft drinks; the restaurant at the zoo serves meals only on weekends.

The *Hotel Oberland* (☎ 796818, fax 796389), Casilla 9392, La Paz, is a well-designed luxury country-style hotel 30

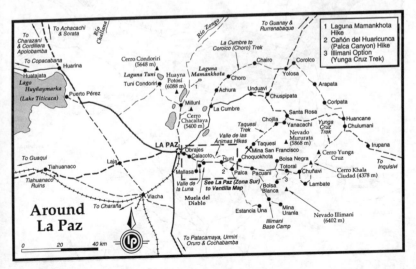

1	Laguna Mamankhota Hike
2	Cañon del Huaricunca (Palca Canyon) Hike
3	Illimani Option (Yunga Cruz Trek)

Around La Paz

0   20   40 km

minutes by trufi from the centre of La Paz. It sits at an altitude of just 3200m, so it's a good 5°C warmer than central La Paz. Cacti grow in the garden, which is frequented by butterflies and dragonflies, and guests have use of the swimming pool and sauna, and squash, racquet ball and volleyball courts. Double rooms are US$38 per night; honeymoon suites, US$60; one/two/three/four-bedroom self-catering flats, US$60/75/90/120.

The restaurant is also lovely, with tables in the garden – try the pacu, a large freshwater fish from Beni department. The hotel is run by a Swiss-German man named Walter Schmid, who also speaks English and French.

Getting There & Away

From La Paz, take any micro or trufi marked 'Mallasa' or 'Zoológico'. From the top of Valle de la Luna, you can either hop on one of these or simply go on foot; it's only a couple of km.

MUELA DEL DIABLO

The prominent rock outcrop known as the Muela del Diablo (Devil's Molar) is actually an extinct volcanic plug rising between the exceedingly smelly Río Choqueyapu (or 'Omo River', after the laundry soap flowing in it) and the recently established outer suburb of Pedregal. A hike to its base makes a pleasant half-day trip from La Paz, and can be easily combined with a visit to Valle de la Luna.

From the cemetery in Pedregal, the trail climbs steeply, affording increasingly fine views over the city and the surrounding tortured landscape. After a breathless hour or so, you'll reach a pleasant grassy swathe where the Muela del Diablo comes into view, as well as some precarious pinnacles farther east.

At this point, the route turns sharply left, descends through a hamlet and then circles around and resumes its climb towards the base of the Muela. This final bit takes about

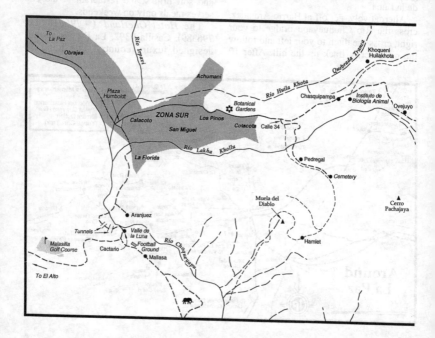

half an hour. With extreme caution, you can pick your way up to the cleft between the double summit, where someone planted a large cross in 1994, but without technical equipment and expertise, it's inadvisable to climb further.

At this point, either return the way you came or pick your way down one of the three steep routes that descend to the Río Choqueyapu (any of which will turn the hike into a full-day trip). One takes off from the grassy spot half an hour back towards Pedregal and the other two descend from the Muela itself.

The map *Trekking en La Paz*, which shows the latter two routes, costs US$1 at the La Paz tourist office.

Getting There & Away

To reach the start of the hike from La Paz, it's best to take minibus trufi 288, marked 'Comunidad Pedregal', from Calle Murillo or the lower Prado (US$1.50). The end of the

line is the parking area about 100m below the cemetery in Pedregal. Alternatively, take micro 21, which is marked Los Rosales. It will drop you at a murky rivulet (the ambitiously named Río Lakha Khollu) from where it's a 600m uphill climb to the cemetery.

If you don't mind walking further, you can take any Cotacota, Chasquipampa or Ovejuyo micro or minibus trufi from Calle Murillo, near the corner of Calle Sagárnaga, or anywhere on the lower Prado. Get off at the sign identifying Calle 34, where the main road swings sharply to the left, and head downhill, through the apparently half-constructed village. After crossing the aforementioned Río Lakha Khollu, follow the maze of well-worn trails uphill, bearing left up the slope, until you strike the main road. This road climbs straight to the Pedregal cemetery, where the hike begins.

Coming from Valle de la Luna, you can board the micros or trufis at Plaza Humboldt.

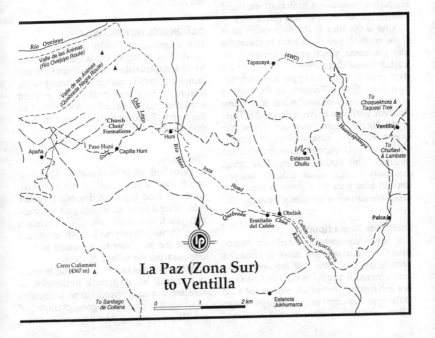

La Paz (Zona Sur) to Ventilla

VALLE DE LAS ÁNIMAS

The name Valle de las Ánimas (Valley of Spirits) is used roughly to describe the eerily eroded canyons and fantastic organ-pipe spires to the north and north-east of Chasquipampa, Ovejuyo and Apaña (which are rapidly being absorbed into the Zona Sur neighbourhoods of La Paz). The scenery resembles that of Valle de la Luna, but on a grander scale.

There are two walking routes through the Valle de las Ánimas; for either, you need an early start from La Paz.

Río Ovejuyo Route

The Río Ovejuyo route begins at Calle 50, near the Instituto de Biología Animal in Chasquipampa. This point is accessible on any micro or minibus trufi marked Chasquipampa or Ovejuyo. From the northern side of the road, the route descends slightly through desultory development. When you reach the diminutive Río Ovejuyo, turn right and follow its southern bank north-eastward past the spectacularly eroded formations.

After about six km, the river valley turns to the north. If you don't want to return the way you came, you'll need a compass, the 1:50,000 topo sheet *5944-II* and, for a very short section along the upper Río Ovejuyo, topo sheet *5944-I*. Traverse up the slope to your right and head southward, over Cerro Pararani, until you arrive at the head of Quebrada Negra. Here, you can follow the Quebrada Negra route (described below) either back to Ovejuyo or down to the village of Huni. This option can be challenging, especially because of the altitude, and you have to take your own water as there's no drinkable surface water along the way.

Quebrada Negra Route

The seven-km route up Quebrada Negra, over Cerro Pararani and down to Huni is a demanding day hike that requires six to seven hours. It begins at the obvious Quebrada Negra ravine, which crosses the road at the upper (eastern) end of Ovejuyo village. Micros and trufis simply marked 'Ovejuyo'

stop about half a km short of this ravine, but micro 'Ñ' and minibus trufi 385, marked 'Ovejuyo/Apaña', both continue right past the ravine mouth.

The easy-to-follow four-km route up Quebrada Negra will take you through the most dramatic of the eroded Valle de las Ánimas pinnacles. Near the head of the ravine, you need to traverse south-eastward around the northern shoulder of Cerro Pararani until you strike the obvious route that descends steeply to Huni village (*not* Huni chapel, which is also marked on the topo sheet). In fine weather, you'll have good views of Illimani along this section.

To return to La Paz, follow the road for two km up over Paso Huni and thence another 1.5 km downhill to Apaña, where you'll catch up with regular micros and trufis returning to the city.

For this route, you'll need a compass and either the tourist office *Trekking en La Paz* map, or the 1:50,000 topo sheets *5944-I* and *6044-III*.

CAÑÓN DEL HUARICUNCA

The magnificent Cañón del Huaricunca (marked on the topo sheet as Quebrada Chua Kheri and often called simply Palca Canyon) brings a slice of grand canyon country to the dramatic badland peaks and eroded amphitheatres east of La Paz. A walk through this wonderful gorge makes an ideal day hike from La Paz.

The Route

At Paso Huni, about two km above Ovejuyo, you'll pass a small rubbish-rimmed lake where the road begins to descend the other side. Several hundred metres past the summit, you'll see some magnificent 'church choir' formations on your left. About two km beyond the pass, turn right (south) along a side road into the village of Huni.

After less than one km, the road deteriorates into a walking track impassable to vehicles. It actually appears to be the remains of an ancient road, with good examples of pre-Hispanic paving. As it descends, running parallel to the Río Huni, the scenery becomes increasingly dramatic.

With sensational views all along, the route drops slowly towards the gravelly canyon floor. The approach to the canyon is dominated by a prominent 100m-high obelisk, and in the opposite wall is the rock formation Ermitaño del Cañón, which resembles a reclusive human figure hiding in an enormous rock niche. The route then winds along the usually diminutive Río Palca for about two km between spectacular vertical walls. Upon exiting the canyon, you'll end up back on the road for a gentle three-km climb through green farmland to the former gold-mining village of Palca.

If you don't find transport back to La Paz on the same day, you can stay at the alojamiento in Palca. If you have camping equipment, look for a site around Palca or nearby Ventilla. However, beware of the surface water, which is badly polluted, and ask permission before you set your tent up in a field or pasture.

Getting There & Away

For the start of this hike, you need to reach Huni, which is served only by micros and minibus trufis headed for Ventilla and Palca. These leave at least once daily from Plaza Belzu, two blocks above (south-west of) the main post office in La Paz. They run to no set schedule, but usually go in the morning. You'll have the most luck on Saturday and Sunday, when families make excursions into the countryside. Alternatively, take micro 'Ñ' or minibus trufi 385, marked 'Ovejuyo/Apaña', get off at the end of the line, and slog the 1.5 km up the road to Paso Huni.

From Palca back to La Paz, you'll find occasional camiones, micros and minibus trufis, particularly on Sunday afternoon, but don't count on anything after 3 or 4 pm. Alternatively, you can hike an hour uphill, through a pleasant eucalyptus plantation, to Ventilla and try hitching from there.

If you arrive in Palca geared up for more hiking, you can always set off from Ventilla along the Taquesi Trek, a two-day route over a pre-Hispanic road into the Yungas. For a

map and description of this hike, see the Cordilleras & Yungas chapter.

CHACALTAYA

The world's highest developed ski area (the term 'developed' is used loosely) lies at an altitude of over 5000m, atop a dying glacier on the slopes of 5345m Cerro Chacaltaya. The name is derived from the Aymara words *chaka* meaning 'bridge' and *thaya* meaning 'cold'. It's only a 90-minute ride from central La Paz, and the accessible summit is an easy hike from there.

If you've flown into La Paz from the coast or lowlands, wait a few days before attempting a visit to Chacaltaya or other high altitude places; otherwise, you're at serious risk of high altitude cerebral oedema. See Health in the Facts for the Visitor chapter for information on ways to avoid or cope with altitude mountain sickness.

Snacks and hot drinks are available at the lodge; if you want anything more substantial, bring it from town. Bring warm (and windproof) clothing, sunglasses (100% UV proof) and sunscreen.

A number of La Paz tour agencies take groups to Chacaltaya. Club Andino Boliviano will be your best bet if you're planning to ski (see the the La Paz Activities section). During periods of heavy snow, especially from March to May, the Chacaltaya road may become impassable, so check the situation before deciding on a tour that can't arrive at its destination!

Skiing

The steep, 700m ski piste runs from 5320m (25m below the summit of the mountain) down to about 4900m. The ski season is January to March but it's often possible to ski on snow rather than ice even later in the year. There is no 'bunny hill', but even as a beginner you can have a good time if you aren't afraid of a few bumps. The major problem is the lift; real beginners often spend the entire day at the bottom of the hill because they can't get to grips with the utterly confounding cable tow. The club has long intended to replace it, but the project has been less than successful (see the Skiing in Bolivia aside). Wear expendable clothing; it will suffer if you do manage to hook up to the cable.

The Club Andino Boliviano (☎ 324682) organises transport to Chacaltaya on Saturday and Sunday throughout the year, as long as there are sufficient takers to justify sending a minibus. The ski lift only operates when snow conditions are favourable. To reserve a spot, ring or drop by the office at Calle México 1638. It's open weekdays from 9.30 am to noon and 3 to 7 pm. Ski trips leave from the club office at 8.30 am and arrive at Chacaltaya sometime before 11 am. You ski until 4 pm and are back in La Paz by 6.30 pm.

Transport alone costs US$9.25 per person; equipment rental is an additional US$15 including a tow hook *(gancho)* for the ski tow. The equipment rental shop is in the warm-up hut. When you're choosing equipment, make sure that your gancho has a

complete U-shaped curl, otherwise it won't clip onto the cable tow.

Hiking

If you're a non-skier – or it's out of season – a trip to Chacaltaya can still be rewarding. The views of La Paz, Illimani, Mururata and 6088m Huayna Potosí are spectacular, and it's a relatively easy (but steep) one-km high-altitude climb from the lodge to the summit of Chacaltaya. Remember to carry warm clothing and water and take plenty of rests, say a 30-second stop every 10 steps or so and longer stops if needed, even if you don't feel tired. If you begin to feel light-headed, sit down and rest until the feeling passes. If it doesn't, you may be suffering from mild altitude sickness and the only remedy is to descend.

From Chacaltaya it is possible to walk to the Refugio Huayna Potosí, at the base of Huayna Potosí, in half a day. Climb to the second false summit above the ski slope and

---

Skiing in Bolivia – Thin Air & Thin Ice

The improvement of the Chacaltaya ski lift, the highest in the world, has been on the Club Andino Boliviano agenda for almost as long as the club has been in existence (since 1939). Built in 1940, it was South America's first ski lift, and it hasn't changed much since then. An automobile engine in an aluminium hut turns a steel cable loop. Skiers clip on to the cable at the bottom of the slope using a length of steel fashioned into a hook (gancho), which is attached to a short length of rope and bit of wood. This fits between the skiers' legs and acts as a seat that theoretically drags them to the top of the hill where they disengage from the cable. As you can imagine, there's lots of scope for complications.

In 1994, a retired – but still relatively modern – ski lift (25 years old) was shipped to Chacaltaya from the ski resort of Sestriere in northern Italy. Until two engineers were flown over from Sestriere to install it nearly a year later, it languished in an El Alto warehouse as a rather large and formidable jigsaw puzzle. The engineers determined that, yes, the jigsaw puzzle could be reassembled but, because the piste was on a glacier (that is, slowly moving ice), the lift would have to be re-erected every year to make adjustments for glacial motion. It was decided that this would make it uneconomic, and in 1995 the old steel cable was replaced and bits of the Sestriere lift were cannibalised to improve the existing lift.

More bad news for Chacaltaya lies in what is popularly called 'global warming', which is causing the glacier to recede at a rate of six to 10m per year. Glacial shrinkage is not new at Chacaltaya – Club Andino Boliviano helped pay to construct the road to the piste by selling chunks of the glacier – but this time it's terminal. According to current estimates, unless there's a change in current world climatic trends, the Chacaltaya glacier will completely disappear within 30 years.

As a result, the search is on for another piste but all of Bolivia's glaciers are shrinking (as they are all over the world – only the Patagonian ice cap is expanding) and there's very little permanent ice left on any Bolivian peak under 5000m. Higher glaciers still have a long way to go before the big melt-down, but they're so high that day-trippers from La Paz would risk cerebral or pulmonary oedema. The future of skiing in Bolivia looks bleak, so enjoy it while you can. ■

then wind your way down past a turquoise lake, to meet up with the road just above the abandoned mining settlement of Milluni. Turn right on the road and follow it past Laguna Zongo to the dam, where you'll see the refugio on your left and the trailhead for Laguna Mamankhota on your right (see Milluni & the Zongo Valley later in this section).

Places to Stay

For overnight stays at Chacaltaya, you can either crash in Club Andino's well-ventilated mountain hut or ask at the La Paz UMSA research laboratory, about 200m downhill from the warm-up hut. The latter is heated, and the friendly scientific personnel welcome visitors. A warm sleeping bag, food, and some sort of headache/soroche relief are essential for an overnight stay in either location.

Getting There & Away

There's no public transport to Chacaltaya; you'll have to go with either Club Andino Boliviano or a La Paz tour operator (see Organised Tours in the Getting Around chapter). Unless you have a very good 4WD vehicle and excellent driving skills, you'd be ill-advised to attempt the road on your own.

If you go to Chacaltaya with the club on Saturday and want to stay overnight, there should be no problem catching a lift back down with the Sunday day trip, if the bus isn't full. On other days, tour groups will probably have space for an extra person, but you may have to pay at least half the tour price to join them.

MILLUNI & THE ZONGO VALLEY

Dramatic Zongo Valley plunges sharply down from the starkly anonymous mining village of Milluni – from 4624m to 1480m within 33 km. At its head, between Chacaltaya and the spectacular peak of Huayna Potosí, is the Laguna Zongo hydro-electric power station.

Laguna Mamankhota Hike

Once upon a time, a lovely set of ice caves high above the valley floor provided a good excuse for day hikes and tours. However, in 1992 they melted away, leaving not even an ice cube; now, the best excuse to climb to the former site is the impressive views of Huayna Potosí across ice-blue Laguna Mamankhota (which is also known as Laguna Cañada).

To reach the trailhead, continue for about five km north-east of Milluni, which will be visible downhill on your left. You may want to have a look at the interesting miners' cemetery on the roadside, overlooking Milluni. If you're travelling by vehicle, you'll reach Laguna Zongo, an artificial lake with milky blue-green water, and the Companía Minera del Sur gate a few minutes later. On your right you'll see a trail climbing up the hillside to meet with an aqueduct. From there, the road winds steeply downward into Zongo Valley.

The hike begins at 4600m. From the parking area, strike off uphill to the right. After about 100m, you'll reach an aqueduct, which you should follow for about 50 minutes along a rather treacherous precipice. Watch on your left for the plaque commemorating an Israeli's final motorbike ride along this narrow and vertigo-inspiring route. The plaque marks the spot where he plunged over the precipice.

About 20m after you cross a large bridge, turn right along a vague track leading uphill, following the cairns that mark the way. After a short climb, you'll reach Laguna Mamankhota, and stunning views of Huayna Potosí, Tiquimani, Telata and Charquini – if the peaks aren't shrouded in clouds. A further 25 minutes up the vague trail will bring you to the site of the former ice caves.

Places to Stay & Eat

At Paso Zongo, above the dam at the head of Zongo Valley, the mountain hut *Refugio Huayna Potosí* provides accommodation for US$7 per person; meals are available. Hikers will find an incredible number of day hikes and long-distance trekking possibilities in

LA PAZ

the area. Contact Huayna Potosí Tours (☎ 323584) at the Hotel Continental on Plaza Eguino in La Paz for information or reservations. See the Climbing in the Cordillera Real section, in the Cordilleras & Yungas chapter also.

Getting There & Away

A camión leaves for Zongo Valley from Plaza Ballivián in El Alto at about noon on Monday, Wednesday and Thursday, and usually returns the following day. It's an uncomfortable ride, but the fare from La Paz to Paso Zongo is only US$1 per person. Micros, which cost slightly more, leave from the same place on Monday, Wednesday and Friday at around 6 am.

By hired taxi, the half-day trip will cost about US$40 for up to five people. Make sure the driver understands that you want the Zongo valley via Milluni. Drivers may expect you to ask for Chacaltaya and try to take you there anyway. At the trailhead, ask the driver to wait while you walk up the mountain to the lake; allow a minimum of three hours for the return walk.

To hire a 4WD and driver from La Paz to Paso Zongo costs about US$70 for up to nine people.

LAJA

The tiny village of Laja, formerly known as Llaxa and Laxa, lies about midway between La Paz and Tiahuanaco. In 1548, the Spanish captain Alonzo de Mendoza was charged with founding a city and rest stop along the route from Potosí to the coast at Callao, Peru. On 20 October 1548, he arrived in Laxa and declared it his chosen location. He soon changed his mind, however, and the site was shifted to the gold-bearing canyon where La Paz now stands.

Over Laja's plaza towers a grand church built in commemoration of Spanish victories over the Incas. The interior is ornamented with gold, silver, wooden carvings and colonial artwork. Most organised Tiahuanaco tours make a brief stop here.

TIAHUANACO

Little is actually known about the people who constructed the great Tiahuanaco ceremonial centre on the southern shore of Lake Titicaca over 1000 years ago. Archaeologists generally agree that the civilisation that spawned Tiahuanaco rose around 600 BC. Construction on the ceremonial site was underway by about 700 AD, but around the year 1200 AD the group had melted into obscurity, becoming another 'lost' civilisation. Evidence of its influence, particularly in the area of religion, has been found throughout the vast area that later became the Inca empire.

The treasures of Tiahuanaco have literally been scattered to the four corners of the earth. Its gold was looted by the Spanish, and early stone and pottery finds were sometimes destroyed by religious zealots who considered them pagan idols. Some of the work found its way to European museums; farmers destroyed pieces of it as they turned the surrounding area into pasture and cropland; the church kept some of the statues or sold them as curios; and the larger stonework went into Spanish construction projects, and even into the bed of the La Paz-Guaqui rail line that passes just south of the site.

Fortunately, a portion of the treasure has been preserved and some of it remains in Bolivia. A few of the larger anthropomorphic stone statues have been left on the site, or are displayed in the Museo al Aire Libre and the Museo Arqueológico de Tiwanaku in La Paz. Pieces from the earliest Tiahuanaco periods are kept in an onsite museum, which is opened infrequently to the public. Pieces from the three later epochs may be found scattered around Bolivia, but the majority are housed in archaeological museums in La Paz and Cochabamba. The ruins themselves have been so badly looted, however, that much of the information they could have revealed about their builders is now lost forever.

Tiahuanaco is open daily from 9 am to 5 pm. Foreigners pay US$2 admission, including entrance to the tiny visitor centre at the ticket office. Guides and people selling

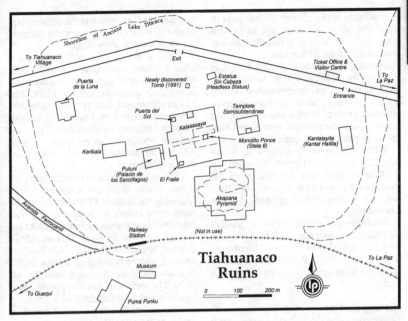

Tiahuanaco Ruins

Labels on map: Shoreline of Ancient Lake Titicaca; To Tiahuanaco Village; Exit; Ticket Office & Visitor Centre; To La Paz; Puerta de la Luna; Newly discovered Tomb (1991); Estatua Sin Cabeza (Headless Statue); Entrance; Puerta del Sol; Templete Semisubterráneo; Kalasasaya; Monolito Ponce (Stela 8); Kantatayita (Kantat Hallita); Kerikala; Putuni (Palacio de los Sarcófagos); El Fraile; Akapana Pyramid; Avenida Ferrocarril; Railway Station; (Not in use); To La Paz; Museum; To Guaqui; Puma Punku; 0 100 200 m

cheap clay trinkets (fortunately all fake; don't pay more than about US$0.20 for a small one) are no longer permitted inside the ruins area. Guides are available outside the fence for about US$2, but you'll have to bargain.

History

Although no-one is certain whether or not it was the capital of a nation, Tiahuanaco undoubtedly served as a great ceremonial centre. At its height, the city had a population of as many as 20,000 inhabitants, and encompassed approximately 2.6 sq km. Although only a very small percentage of the original site has been excavated – and what remains is less than overwhelming – Tiahuanaco represents the greatest megalithic architectural achievement of pre-Inca South America.

The development of Tiahuanaco civilisation has been divided by researchers into five distinct periods, numbered Tiahuanaco I through V, each of which has its own outstanding attributes.

The Tiahuanaco I period falls between the advent of the Tiahuanaco civilisation and the middle of the 5th century BC. Significant finds from this period include multicoloured pottery and human or animal effigies in painted clay. Tiahuanaco II, which ended around the beginning of the Christian Era, is hallmarked by ceramic vessels with horizontal handles. Tiahuanaco III dominated the next 300 years, and was characterised by tricolour pottery of geometric design, often decorated with images of stylised animals.

Tiahuanaco IV, also known as the Classic Period, developed between 300 and 700 AD. The large stone structures that dominate the site today were constructed during this period. The use of bronze and gold is considered evidence of contact with groups farther east in the Cochabamba valley and farther west on the Peruvian coast. Tiahuanaco IV pottery is largely anthropomorphic; pieces uncovered by archaeologists include some in the shape of human heads and faces with bulging cheeks, indicating that the coca leaf was already in use at this time.

Tiahuanaco V, or the Expansive Period, is marked by a decline that lasted until Tiahuanaco's utter disappearance around 1200 AD. Pottery grew less elaborate, construction projects slowed and stopped, and no large-scale monuments were added after the early phases of this period.

When the Spanish arrived in South America, local Indian legends recounted that Tiahuanaco had been the capital of the bearded white god Viracocha, and that from his city Viracocha had reigned over the civilisation.

For further information on the rise and fall of Tiahuanaco, you may want to pick up the English translation of the book *Discovering Tiwanaku* by Hugo Boero Rojo, which is available from Los Amigos del Libro in La Paz.

Visiting the Site

Scattered around the Tiahuanaco site, you'll find heaps of jumbled basalt and sandstone slabs weighing as much as 175,000 kg each. Oddly enough, the nearest quarries that could have produced the basalt megaliths are on the Copacabana peninsula, 40 km away over the lake. Even the sandstone blocks had to be transported from a site more than five km away. It's no wonder, then, that when the Spanish asked local Aymara how the buildings were constructed, they replied that it was done with the aid of the leader/deity Viracocha. They could conceive of no other plausible explanation.

Tiahuanaco's most outstanding structure is the **Akapana pyramid**, which was built on an existing geographical formation. At its base, this roughly square 16m hill covers a surface area of about 200 sqm. In the centre of its flat summit is an oval-shaped sunken area, which some sources attribute to early, haphazard Spanish excavation. The presence of a stone drain in the centre, however, has led some archaeologists to believe it was used for water storage. Because much of the

original Akapana went into the construction of nearby homes and churches, the pyramid is now in a rather sorry state.

North of the pyramid is **Kalasasaya**, a ritual platform compound with walls constructed of huge blocks of red sandstone and andesite. It measures 130 by 120m. The blocks are precisely fitted to form a platform base three metres high. Monolithic uprights flank the massive entrance steps up to the restored portico of the enclosure, beyond which is an interior courtyard and the ruins of priests' quarters.

Other stairways lead up to secondary platforms where there are other monoliths including the famous **El Fraile**. At the far north-west corner of Kalasasaya is Tiahuanaco's best known structure, **Puerta del Sol** (Gateway of the Sun). This megalithic gateway was carved from a single block of andesite and archaeologists assume that it was associated in some way with the sun deity. The surface of this fine-grained, grey volcanic rock is ornamented with low-relief designs on one side and a row of four deep niches on the other. Some believe these may have been used for offerings to the sun, while others maintain that the stone served as some kind of a calendar. The structure is believed to weigh at least 44,000 kg.

There's a smaller, similar gateway carved with zoomorphic designs near the western end of the site, which is informally known as **Puerta de la Luna** (Gateway of the Moon).

Near the main entrance to Kalasasaya, a stairway leads down into the **Templete Semisubterráneo**, a red sandstone pit structure measuring 26 by 28m with a rectangular sunken courtyard and walls adorned with small carved stone faces.

West of Kalasasaya is a 55 by 60m rectangular area known as **Putuni** or Palacio de los Sarcófagos, which is still being excavated. It is surrounded by double walls and you can see the foundations of several houses.

The heap of rubble at the eastern end of the site is known as **Kantatayita**. Archaeologists are still trying to deduce some sort of meaningful plan from these well-carved slabs; one elaborately decorated lintel and some larger stone blocks bearing intriguing geometric designs are the only available clues. It has been postulated – and dubiously 'proven' – that they were derived from universal mathematical constants, such as pi; but some archaeologists simply see the plans for a large and well-designed building.

Across the railway line south of the Tiahuanaco site, you'll see the excavation site of **Puma Punku** (Gateway of the Puma). In this temple area, megaliths weighing over 440,000 kg have been discovered. Like Kalasasaya and Akapana, there is evidence that Puma Punku was begun with one type of material and finished with another; part was constructed of enormous sandstone blocks, and during a later phase of construction, notched and jointed basalt blocks were added. Unfortunately, the site museum here opens only sporadically.

Special Events

On 21 June, when the rays of the rising sun shine through the temple entrance on the eastern side of the complex, the Aymara New Year is celebrated. Special buses leave La Paz at 4 and 5 am to arrive in time for sunrise. Visitors are invited to join the party, drink singani, chew coca and dance, but bundle up, because the pre-dawn hours are bitterly cold at this time of year. Local artesans are also establishing an annual *feria de artesanía* (crafts fair), to be held on this day.

Organised Tours

Dozens of La Paz tour agencies offer reasonably priced guided full and half-day tours to Tiahuanaco. Daytrips are remarkably inexpensive – about US$12 per person, including transport and guide – and are probably worth it to avoid the crowded local buses. A list of tour agencies can be found in the Organised Tours section in the Getting Around chapter.

Places to Stay & Eat

Tiahuanaco village, one km west of the ruins, has several marginal restaurants and an incredibly colourful Sunday market. As a tour participant, you may want to carry your own lunch; otherwise, you'll be herded into a restaurant and charged three times the going rate to cover the tour guide's kickback. The museum snack shop opposite the ruins sells soft drinks and chips, but as you'd expect, prices are elevated.

For overnight stays, the basic but fairly clean *Hostal*, at the La Paz end of Tiahuanaco village, charges US$3 per person. Simple but decent meals in the attached restaurant cost from US$0.50 to US$1.

Named after a Bolivian archaeologist, the Ponce Monolith dates back to the 7th century AD and stands just inside the Kalasaya

Getting There & Away

Bus Flota Ingavi leaves for Tiahuanaco (and sometimes Guaqui – see the Lake Titicaca chapter) about eight times daily from Calle José María Asín in La Paz. The trip to Tiahuanaco costs US$1 each way. Buses are crowded beyond comfortable capacity, so go early and try to get a seat reservation; even when passengers are hanging out the windows and doors, drivers still call for more.

To return to La Paz, just flag down a micro. They'll already be filled to overflowing by the time they pass the ruins, so it may be worth walking into Tiahuanaco village to catch one there. Micros to Guaqui and the Peruvian border leave from the plaza in Tiahuanaco village, or may be flagged down just west of the village. Again, expect crowds.

Taxi Taxis to Tiahuanaco from La Paz cost anywhere from US$40 to US$50 return for up to four people.

URMIRI

Urmiri lies at an elevation of 3800m, in the Valle de Sapahaqui, 30 km east of the La Paz-Oruro highway and three hours southeast of La Paz. Here, the La Paz departmental government runs the basic resort-style Hotel Prefectural, which owes its existence to the **Termas de Urmiri** (Urmiri Hot Springs). It boasts two outdoor pools, one lukewarm and another smaller, warmer one.

Places to Stay & Eat

Camping is possible outside the village and, although it can get chilly, those luscious hot springs are never far away.

Rooms at the two-star *Hotel Prefectural*, each with an adjoining hot bath, cost US$12.50 per person, including three basic meals and use of the hot springs. Non-guests may use the pools for US$3 per person. Make accommodation and transport reservations at least two days in advance. The hotel office (☎ 374586 or 328584) is on the 7th floor of the building overlooking Plaza San Francisco in La Paz.

Getting There & Away

The easiest way to reach Urmiri is with the hotel shuttle vehicle, which charges US$6 for the return trip; make transport reservations before booking your room. The shuttle departs La Paz in the morning from Plaza Pérez Velasco.

If you want to attempt it independently, take a bus or camión from La Paz towards Oruro and get off near the bridge in Villa Loza, 70 km south of La Paz. Here, turn east along the unpaved road and pray for a lift, because if nothing is forthcoming, you're in for a very long walk. About five km along, the road passes a cluster of chullpas, and further on, as the road winds into the fruit-producing Valle de Sapahaqui, views of the Cordillera Quimsa Cruz will open up ahead. After 20 km, you'll reach the junction at Lurjavi, where you should turn right for the final three-and-a-bit km into Urmiri.

The Cordilleras & Yungas

The 200-km-long Cordillera Real, Bolivia's most prominent range, is also one of the loftiest and most imposing in the Andes. Not only is it Bolivia's best mountaineering venue, it's also popular as a trekking destination and the bulk of the country's popular walking routes follow ancient roads connecting the high Altiplano with the steamy Yungas (valleys).

North of Lake Titicaca, lies the remote Cordillera Apolobamba with scores of little-known valleys and traditional Aymara villages. Here live the renowned Kallahuaya medicine men who employ a blend of herbs and magic to cure ailments. This area also includes the Parque Nacional Ulla Ulla, a *vicuña* reserve abutting the Peruvian border. Access to the Apolobamba, which is well off the beaten track, is difficult and tourism is still relatively unknown. It does, however, offer some wonderful trekking opportunities.

The wild and untouristy Cordillera Quimsa Cruz, the beautifully glaciated southern extension of the Cordillera Real, also holds promise as a trekking and mountaineering destination. It has long been a major tin mining area, but only recently has it been discovered by anyone else.

To the north of the Cordilleras are the misty, jungle-filled valleys and gorges known as the Yungas, which form a distinct natural division between the cold, barren Altiplano and the rainforested Amazon lowlands of northern Bolivia. The relatively short trip from 4600m La Cumbre passing down into the Alto Beni region entails a loss of 4343m elevation.

The first settlers of the Yungas were inspired by economic opportunity. In the days of the Inca empire, gold was discovered in the valleys of the Río Tipuani and Río Mapiri and the gold-crazed Spanish immediately got in on the act. To enrich the royal treasury, they forced local people to labour for them along the Yungas streams

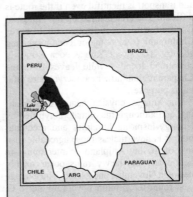

Highlights

- Follow the pre-Inca paving on the Taquesi trek
- Lounge, hike and eat your fill in cloud-wreathed Coroico
- Survey the spectacular scenery on the Lambate route of the Yunga Cruz trek
- Visit medieval-looking Sorata and enjoy its fabulous hiking opportunities
- For the really keen, climb the 6088m Huayna Potosí
- Hike the Curva to Pelechuco trek in the wild Cordillera Apolobamba

and the region became one of the continent's most prolific sources of gold. Today, the rivers of the lower Yungas are being ravaged by hordes of wildcat prospectors and a growing number of multinational mining concerns who have apparently perfected the art of large-scale environmental devastation. A distressing side effect is water pollution from the mercury used to recover fine particles from gold-bearing sediment; in parts of Brazil, the extent of water pollution poses a major health hazard and could also affect northern Bolivia.

Agriculture has also played a part in the development of the Yungas. Today, most of the farmland in the Yungas occupies the intermediate altitudes, roughly between 600 and 1800m. Sugar, citrus fruits, bananas and coffee are grown in sufficient quantities to supply the highlands with these products, and transport is plentiful even if the route is difficult. The area centred on the village of Coripata and extending south towards Chulumani is also major coca-producing country. The sweet Yungas coca is mostly consumed locally, while leaves from the Chapare region farther east serve more infamous purposes.

The Yungas' physical beauty is astonishing, and although the climate is typified by lethargy-inspiring humidity and precipitation, it is nevertheless more agreeable than that of the icy Altiplano. Winter rains are gentle and the heavy rains occur mainly between November and March. The average year-round temperature hovers around 18°C, but summer daytime temperatures in the 30s aren't uncommon, especially in the Alto Beni. As a result, the region provides a lowland retreat for chilly highlanders, and is also a favourite of foreign travellers.

The Yungas is composed of two provinces in La Paz Department, Nor and Sud Yungas (oddly, most of Sud Yungas lies well to the north of Nor Yungas!), as well as bits of other provinces. Transport, services, commerce and administration focus on Coroico and Chulumani, while outlying towns such as Sorata, Caranavi and Guanay function as regional commercial centres.

LA CUMBRE TO COROICO (CHORO) TREK

The La Cumbre to Coroico (or Choro) trek, north-east of La Paz, is now the premier hike in Bolivia. It begins at La Cumbre, the highest point on the La Paz-Coroico highway, and climbs to Abra Chucura (Chucura Pass) at 4859m before descending 3250m into the steaming Yungas to the village of Chairo. Along the route there are distinct differences in the people and their dress, herds, crops and dwellings.

Energetic hikers can finish the trek in two days, but it's more comfortably done in three days, and many people allot even more time to appreciate the incredible variety of landforms and vegetation across the various altitude zones.

Prepare for a range of climates. On the first day you'll need winter gear, but on the second and third days, it will be peeled off layer-by-layer. For the lower trail, light cotton trousers or similar will protect your legs from sharp vegetation and biting insects.

Dangers & Annoyances

Since the first edition of this book (1988), this route has seen a marked increase in begging (a real annoyance), theft and robbery, and in 1990, a robbery-motivated murder near Choro brought brief media attention to the problems. Although the frequency of aggressive or violent robbery has since declined, petty theft remains rife. Camp away from the trail – out of sight if possible – and don't leave anything outside your tent. I've had quite a few reports of theft from tents, even when the occupants were sleeping inside, so at night, valuables should be ensconced inside your sleeping bag. Most thefts occur between Achura and Choro.

Organised Tours

If you're looking for hiking companions, a growing number of companies offer organised treks along this route for very reasonable prices. Most include meals, guides and camping equipment, and some also include the services of pack animals or porters. For a list of agencies and their offerings, see Organised Tours in the Getting Around chapter.

Access

The La Cumbre to Coroico trek is easy to access and follow. From the Villa Fátima area of La Paz, there are several companies running buses and minibuses to the Yungas. The first daily departure is usually around 7 or 8 am. If there's space (Yungas-bound passengers naturally take first priority), you'll pay US$1 per person to be dropped at La Cumbre, the high point of the Yungas road, where the trek begins.

Alternatively, *camiones* leave for the Yungas from behind the Villa Fátima petrol

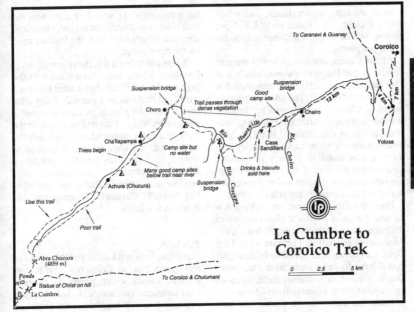

La Cumbre to Coroico Trek

To Caranavi & Guanay

Coroico

Suspension bridge

Choro

Trail passes through dense vegetation

Suspension bridge

Good camp site

Chairo

12 km

7 km

4 km

Yolosa

Cha'llapampa

Trees begin

Camp site but no water

Casa Sandillani

Drinks & biscuits sold here

Achura (Chucura)

Many good camp sites below trail near river

Suspension bridge

Use this trail

Poor trail

Abra Chucura (4859 m)

Ponds

Statue of Christ on hill

La Cumbre

To Coroico & Chulumani

0   2.5   5 km

station between about 7 am and early after-noon. They charge US$0.75 per person to La Cumbre.

The road climbs steeply out of Villa Fátima and less than an hour out of La Paz at the 4725m crest of the La Paz-Yungas road is La Cumbre, marked by a statue of Christ. This is the trailhead. For the best chances of good clear views of the stunning scenery, start as early as possible, before the mist rises out of the Yungas.

The Route

From the statue of Christ, follow a well-defined track to your left for about one km. There you should turn off onto the smaller track that turns right and passes between two small ponds. Follow it up the hill until it curves to the left and begins to lose altitude.

At this point, follow the light track that leads up the gravelly hill to your right and through an obvious notch in the barren hill before you. This is Abra Chucura, and from

here, the trail trends downhill all the way to its end at Chairo. At the high point is a curious pile of stones called Apacheta Chucura. For centuries, travellers have marked their passing by tossing a stone atop it (preferably one that has been carried from a lower elevation), as an offering to the mountain *apus* (spirits). An hour below the *abra* lie the remains of a *tambo* (wayside inn), which dates from Inca times.

The best first-night camp sites are found along the river, an hour's walk below the village of Achura (also known as Chucura). Tentless travellers may see the schoolteacher about accommodation in the school, which should be about US$1 per person. It's likely that an 'official' will turn up later and demand more as a tribute for village 'hospitality'; it's probably best to explain that you've already agreed on an unspecified rate, and suggest the official take up the matter with the schoolteacher. At Cha'llapampa, between Achura and Choro, a local woman, Señora Juana, has established a camp site, which costs US$1 per person, and basic guest accommodation for US$2 per person.

Above Choro, many stretches of the trail consist of pre-Hispanic paving, which is at once beautiful and difficult to negotiate due to its state of disrepair. The good suspension bridge at Choro was destroyed by flooding several years ago. After the two twig-and-vine structures that replaced it also headed downstream, a tenuous cable and pulley contraption was installed to ferry people and cargo across the river. A new wooden bridge has now been constructed and will hopefully withstand the elements for years to come.

From the crossing, bear left. After a few metres, the route begins to climb steeply to the ridge above town, then enters dense trail-swallowing vegetation. There are several dry camp sites between this point and Chairo, but you'll have to carry water from elsewhere. Due to the risk of nocturnal theft, try to set up camp as far as possible from Choro.

From the ridge above Choro, the trail plunges and climbs alternately from sunny hillsides to vegetation-choked valleys. It passes streams and waterfalls and at one point, crosses the deep gorge of the Río Coscapa with the help of a crude but effective suspension bridge.

Near the trail's end, about 2½ hours from Chairo, you'll encounter the curious and unexpected Casa Sandillani, an Oriental home surrounded by beautifully manicured gardens. The friendly Japanese owner, Mr Tamiji Hanamura de Furio, is full of trail news and enjoys having visitors stop by to chat and sign his guestbook. He's happy to let you camp in his garden; you may want to bring some stamps or postcards from home to augment his now extensive collections. In this area, you'll also encounter a number of snack and soft drink stalls set up by enterprising locals for hungry and thirsty hikers.

From Casa Sandillani, it's seven easy downhill km to Chairo, where you'll find occasional camiones to Yolosa or Coroico, as well as other intermittent traffic. If you must stay over in Chairo, you can sleep on the verandah of the school or camp near the trail across the suspension bridge. Meals and supplies are available from the friendly shop on the main street.

If you can't find a lift, the relatively level four-hour 12-km walk from Chairo to the highway isn't difficult, but it does involve a river ford that can be especially hairy after rain. If the water is too high, there is a spindly suspension bridge. Plan on four hours for the walk and carry water. Once you reach the main road, it's easy to find a camión to Yolosa, four km away (which is just seven km from Coroico). There's also lots of traffic heading back up to La Paz or farther downhill towards Caranavi, Guanay and the Amazon lowlands.

YOLOSA

Travelling between La Paz and the Beni – or from anywhere to Coroico – you'll pass through Yolosa, which guards the Coroico road junction. The *tranca* at Yolosa closes between 1 and 5 am, impeding overnight traffic between the Yungas and La Paz. Pick-up trucks awaiting passengers to Coroico queue up on the hill at the road junction. The standard fare is US$0.40 (B$2) per person.

Places to Stay & Eat

If you're planted overnight here, you can crash at *Alojamiento El Conquistador*, which charges just US$1.50 per person. Alternatively, there's the *Balneario la Macarena*, which is five minutes on foot uphill from the pick-up stop. Simple but adequate rooms cost US$5 per person, plus US$2 for a continental breakfast. The appeal is the pleasant natural river swimming hole.

Near Chairo, about five km from the end of the La Cumbre to Coroico trek, is the newish *Río Selva Resort* (☎ & fax 327561, La Paz), a rather posh five-star option, right on the riverside. Single or double rooms cost US$52, triples are US$60 and cabañas accommodating up to six people cost from US$95 to US$105. Peripheral amenities include racquetball courts, aerobics, a sauna and a swimming pool. Three-day river rafting packages cost from US$155 to US$220 per person, including two nights accommodation, four meals and one day's rafting on the Río Huarinilla. You can choose between three possible runs, which are ranked from beginner to expert. The resort also organises four-day trekking packages along the Choro Trail (US$165 to US$225), with a big finish at the resort and transport back to La Paz.

Along with rows of street stalls selling fast snacks to truckers, there's the *Spaguetti Restaurant*, which doesn't serve spaghetti, but can rustle up chicken and chips.

COROICO

Serene little Coroico, the Nor Yungas provincial capital, sits at the pleasantly tropical altitude of 1750m. Perched eyrie-like on the shoulder of Cerro Uchumachi, it commands a far-ranging view across forested canyons, cloud-wreathed mountain peaks, patchwork agricultural lands, citrus orchards, coffee plantations and dozens of small settlements. When the weather clears, the view stretches to the snow-covered summits of Huayna Potosí and Tiquimani, high in the Cordillera Real.

The town's most appealing attraction is its tranquillity and slow pace, which allow plenty of time for relaxing, swimming, lying in the sun or walking in the surrounding hills. Coroico stays relatively warm year-round, but rain is frequent at any time of the year and summer storms can bring some mighty downpours. Because of its ridge-top position, fog is common, especially in the afternoon when it rises from the deep valleys and swirls up through the streets and over the rooftops.

Information

Money The only place to change travellers cheques is the Hotel Esmeralda, but several businesses change US dollars cash.

Post & Communications The post office is open Tuesday, Thursday, Friday and Satur-day from 9.30 am to noon and 2.30 to 5 pm. On Sunday, it's open from 9.30 am to noon.

Coroico now has a telephone service and direct dialling. The ENTEL office on the plaza can make connections anywhere in the world. The local telephone network, COTEL is open Monday to Saturday, from 8 am to noon and 2 to 10 pm. The telephone code for Coroico is 0811.

Laundry Laundry services are available at Lavandería Benedita, Avenida Monsignor Thomas Manning, near the Hotel Prefectural.

Walks

Cerro Uchucachi For a good panoramic view of Coroico and the surrounding countryside, walk up to the Iglesia Calvario (Calvario Church) on the hill. From there, it's a 2½-hour climb along the partially-wooded ridge to the summit of Cerro Uchumachi. Wait for a fine day, however, or the spectacular view will be irrelevant.

Waterfall Walk Alternatively, turn left at Iglesia Calvario and follow the trail that winds around the hillside. It follows a route across some flowery hillsides, occasionally plunging into mini-rainforests. After five km – about two hours – you'll reach a waterfall above a picturesque village, with lovely views down the valley. Since the stream supplies water to lower villages, bathing is forbidden. If you climb higher up, you'll reach two more waterfalls. Wear sturdy shoes, as the track is overgrown in places.

Río Coroico The tracks leading down to the Río Coroico are more complicated and difficult to follow because part of the trip involves road walking. The easiest one leads from the north-west corner of the plaza. When you reach the very bottom of the village, you'll see a track winding downhill. This will take you to the main road about nine km from Yolosa towards Caranavi. Turn right on the road and continue along it until you reach Puente Mururata. Here you'll find

CORDILLERAS & YUNGAS

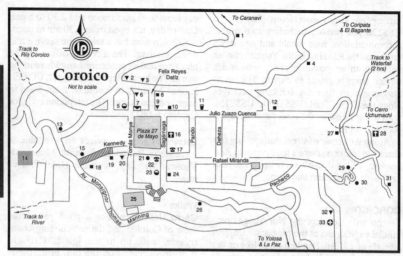

Coroico
Not to scale

To Caranavi
To Coripata & El Bagante
Track to Río Coroico
Track to Waterfall (2 hrs)
Felix Reyes Datiz
To Cerro Uchumachi
Julio Zuazo Cuenca
Plaza 27 de Mayo
Rafael Miranda
Kennedy
Av Monseñor Thomas Manning
Tomás Monye
Sagárnaga
Pando
Dehesa
Pacheco
Track to River
To Yolosa & La Paz

PLACES TO STAY
1   Hotel El Viejo Molino
4   Hotel Don Quixote
8   Hotel Lluvia de Oro
10 Alojamiento de la Torre
12 Hostal & Restaurant Don Pesante
14 Hotel Prefectural
18 Hostal & Restaurant La Casa
19 Hostal Kory
24 Residencial 20 de Octubre
27 Hotel Esmeralda
31 Hostal Sol y Luna

PLACES TO EAT
2   Reddy's
3   Bamboo's & Los Jasmines
6   Comedor Municipal
9   Daedalus Pub & Pizzería
10 Safari Restaurant & Disco
20 Back-Stube Konditorei
32 Ranch Beni Café & Horse Rental

OTHER
5   Yungueñita & Candelaria Bus Terminals

7   Post Office
11 Taurus Pub
13 Lavandería Benedita
15 Madres de Clarisa Convent
16 Church
17 COTEL
21 Artesanías Arco Irís
22 ENTEL
23 Totaí Bus Terminal
25 Market
26 Tranca
28 Iglesia Calvario
29 Military Base
30 Cemetery
33 Hospital

some lovely swimming holes just upstream from the bridge.

You can also continue walking up to the African-Bolivian village of Tocaña. Cross Puente Mururata and follow the road for about 500m to the Tocaña track, which turns off to the left. The village is about 2.5 winding km uphill from there.

Around the bush near the river, use insect repellent and wear long trousers as protection against the nasty yellow flies that can make your life miserable for several days

after an encounter. On the brighter side of the insect world are the blue morphos and other butterfly species that are frequently observed there. Watch also for toucans and other colourful tropical birds.

El Bagante A good day walk will take you to El Bagante, an area of natural stone swimming holes in the Río Santa Bárbara. Follow the road towards Coripata to Miraflores Hacienda, about half a km beyond the Hotel Don Quixote. Here you should turn left at a fork in the road and head steeply downhill. After two hours along this route, you'll reach a cement bridge; from there, continue up the other side for 20 minutes and you'll arrive at a series of natural swimming holes and waterfalls. The water isn't drinkable, so carry all you'll need for the hike, and bear in mind that the return route is uphill all the way.

Horse Riding

French folk Dany and Patricio at Ranch Beni (see also Places to Eat) hire horses for US$5 per hour, including a guide, but don't accept horses that appear to be less than fit and healthy.

Organised Tours

For organised walks and trips into the Coroico hinterlands, contact M César Argandoña (☎ 6005) at Snack Paola Denisse, Calle Pacheco 56. He runs excursions to sites of natural interest as well as several nearby villages, including Tocaña, which is home to much of the Yungas' African-Bolivian community.

Places to Stay – bottom end

Secluded camp spots may be found near the church on the hill above town. *Hostal Sol y Luna* has camp sites for US$2 per person. *Hostal Don Pesante* also has camping.

Hotels are completely booked out on Friday and Saturday nights, so make reservations in advance. Prices also jump for as much as 100% on weekends. On Monday, however, the town closes down to recover from the Sunday tourist rush.

The cheapest acceptable place is the clean and sunny *Alojamiento de la Torre*, beside the Safari Restaurant, which charges US$2 per person. A pleasant Mediterranean-style spot is the leafy *Hostal Don Pesante*, on the main uphill road. Rooms with shared baths cost only US$2.75 per person on weekdays and US$4 per person on weekends and during fiestas. You can also camp. The attached restaurant has fine food and plays videos and mellow folk music.

Although its standards are sliding downhill, the *Hotel Lluvia de Oro* still hangs in there with its sundeck, patio, green pool, mediocre restaurant and faded garden. Rooms cost US$5 per person without bath or US$10.50 for a room with a double bed and bath. A bit better is the friendly *Residencial 20 de Octubre*; rooms with shared bath are US$4.20 per person and double beds with private bath cost US$10.50.

One of Bolivia's most appealing backpackers' haunts is the friendly, family-run *Hotel Esmeralda* (☎ & fax 6017), which sits amid the clouds, 300m from the centre. The restaurant is equal to the indescribable view; don't miss the vegetarian dishes and excellent Yungas coffee (even espresso). Rooms cost US$7/10 per person, without/with bath. Peripheral amenities include a pool, tropical garden, pleasant video lounge and sunny patio overlooking the universe. If you can't climb the hill with luggage, phone for a free pick-up from the plaza.

The popular *Hostal Kory* (the name means 'gold' in Quechua) is also a good bet. For US$5 per person, you get a restaurant, a swimming pool and good hot showers, and the view, which takes in everything from the valleys to the Cordillera peaks, makes it a travellers' standard. From the number of letters I've had about clothing going missing from the laundry line here, it can be safely assumed that someone in Coroico has a substantial backpacking wardrobe by now. If you have a favourite T-shirt or pair of jeans, dry them in your room or just let them keep on reeking.

The *Hostal La Casa*, down the stairs from the Hostal Kory, is as clean and tidy as you'd expect from a German-run establishment. Rooms with shared baths and swimming pool access cost US$3 per person and a double bed with private bath costs US$9.50.

Another German-run favourite is the friendly and very quiet *Hostal Sol y Luna*, which sits in a luxurious garden setting, high on the hillside a 20-minute walk from town. Double cabañas cost US$4 per person with private bath and fireplace; rooms cost US$3 per person; and camp sites are US$2 per person. For full board, add US$5. Plus points include the novel open-air showers, the swimming pool, the breezy vegetarian restaurant and the home-grown, home-roasted Yungas coffee. The owner, Sigrid Fronius, will provide 50 minutes of Japanese massage (nirvana for weary bones coming off the Choro trek!) for US$12. For bookings, contact Chuquiago Turismo (☎ 362099), Avenida Mariscal Santa Cruz 1364, Edificio La Primera, Ground floor, La Paz.

Places to Stay – middle

Downhill from town near the football grounds is the red-roofed *Hotel Prefectural* (☎ 212604, La Paz). It gets two stars under the Bolivian rating system and the view is undeniably superb. Unfortunately, there are two rooms per bath and the room doors don't lock, and I've had reports of problems. With a three-meal plan, rooms cost US$15.20/18 per person on week-days/weekends; without meals, the charge is US$8.50/10.

The exceptionally friendly and good value *Hotel Don Quixote* (☎ 6007), 800m from the plaza, is popular with Bolivians. It looks more expensive than it is and makes an excellent alternative to staying in town. Ultra-clean rooms with all the amenities of a solid mid-range option cost only US$8.25/7.25 per person on weekends/weekdays, but also ask about backpacker discounts. Don't miss out on meeting Casildo the monkey, who is a permanent fixture there, as well as parrots Paco and Matías.

Places to Stay – top end

As you'd expect, the top end in Coroico is very nice indeed, and it's represented by *El Viejo Molino* (☎ & fax 6004), a five-star hotel one km from the centre on the road towards the Río Santa Bárbara. Standard single/double rooms with TV and private bath cost US$35/50, including a buffet breakfast and access to the swimming pool, sauna, jacuzzi and gym. Book through Valmar Tours (☎ & fax 328433), Casilla 4294, La Paz.

Places to Eat

For its size, Coroico offers a boggling variety of excellent eateries; in fact, few people can stick around long enough to exhaust the possibilities.

An inexpensive local place with acceptable food and an ordinary menu is the *Safari Restaurant & Disco* at the Veloz del Norte bus terminal. This establishment serves mainly chicken and burgers and has a video bar as well as a disco. Alternatively, make a selection from the crop of food stalls in the Comedor Municipal, where you'll find good vegetarian food as well as standard Bolivian favourites.

Hotel Esmeralda and Hostal Kory also have recommended restaurants. The former offers a good range of vegetarian options accompanied by great 60s and 70s music. For tasty Mexican dishes, try *Bamboo's*, just north of the plaza. *Los Jasmines* next door has an extensive menu and good food. Two notable pizzerias are *Reddy's*, just below the main plaza, and the *Daedalus Pub & Pizzería*. The former is also excellent for pizza, pasta dishes and cakes, and has live music on weekends. The funky *Taurus Pub* is fun for a drink or snack.

The *Back-Stube Konditorei*, run by friendly Hans and Claudia Hellenkamp, serves excellent European-style breakfasts with Yungas coffee from 6.30 to 11.30 am. The rest of the day, they do unbeatable pizza, pasta, soups, omelettes, vegetarian dishes and German-style cakes and pastries. You'll even find that ubiquitous travellers icon, the banana pancake.

European cuisine is also available at the German/Bolivian-run *Hostal La Casa*, down the stairs from the main plaza. For breakfasts, fondues, coffee, chocolate, pancakes, and local or continental dishes, it's hard to beat. If you're geared up for fondue, you'll need a minimum of two people and an advance booking. A wonderful fondue bourguignonne or raclette costs only US$5 per person, including a range of salads and appetisers. Like most things in Coroico, La Casa is closed on Monday.

An extraordinary treat if you have a group

Top: Guaqui, Lake Titicaca (TM)
Left: Horca del Inca observatory, Copacabana (DS)
Right: Totora reed boat, Huatajata, Lake Titicaca (WH)

Top: Entrance to Moorish cathedral, Copacabana (DS)
Bottom Right: Huayna Potosí, Cordillera Real (RS)
Bottom Left: Coroico (DS)

The Yungas Road

Although rumour has it that a road more terrifying than the one between La Paz and the Yungas exists somewhere in Zanskar or Bhutan, I'd have to see it to believe it. Several apparently courageous readers have written to complain that I've exaggerated the dangers of this route, but given the phenomenal number of fatal accidents that occur on it, I remain unswayed. In 1994, 26 vehicles went over the edge – an average of one every two weeks – and the following year, a report from the Inter-American Development Bank listed this as the most dangerous road in the world.

So, if you're up to an adrenalin rush, you'll be in your element, but if you're unnerved by unsurfaced roads just wide enough for one vehicle, sheer 1000m drops, hulking rock overhangs and waterfalls that spill across and erode the highway, your best bet is either to walk to Coroico or to bury your head and don't look until it's over. There may be some comfort in taking a minibus: they're smaller and presumably safer than camiones or even buses.

The trip starts off innocuously enough. Upon leaving La Paz to cross La Cumbre, you'll notice a most curious phenomenon: dogs are posted like sentinels at 100m intervals, presumably awaiting handouts. Camión drivers feed them in the hope that the *achachilas* (ancestor spirits who dwell in the high peaks) will encourage gravity to be merciful during their trip down. At La Cumbre, drivers also perform a cha'lla for the *apus* (mountain spirits) and achachilas, sprinkling their vehicle's tyres with alcohol or methylated spirits before beginning the descent.

A number of crosses, described as 'Bolivian *Caution* signs', line the way and testify to frequent tragedies. The most renowned took place on 24 July 1983, when driver Carlos Pizarroso Inde drove his camión over the precipice, killing himself and more than 100 passengers. It was the worst accident in the history of Bolivian transport.

However, if you do take an open camión and keep your eyes open, you'll be rewarded with some of the most stunning vertical scenery South America has to offer. Carry an arctic-to-tropical range of clothing and raingear for drenching mists and waterfalls; the road drops 3000m in the two-hour trip from La Cumbre to Coroico!

Note: Although Bolivian traffic normally keeps to the right, downhill traffic on the Yungas road passes on the outside, whether that's the right or the left side of the road. That is, vehicles heading downhill must manoeuvre onto the sliver-like turnout ledges bordering the big drop and wait while uphill traffic squeezes past, hugging the inside wall. While it may seem unpleasant, it makes eminent sense, as it ensures that the risk is taken by the driver with the best possible view of the outside tyres. ■

– or can muster one – is the *luna llena*, an Indonesian buffet for eight to 20 people at German-run *Hostal Sol y Luna* on the hill. It costs an affordable US$4.20 per person, but must be booked a day in advance.

The *Madres de Clarisa Convent*, opposite La Casa, is renowned for its delicious brownies, orange cakes, peanut butter, biscuits (chocolate, vanilla, coconut, honey and peanut butter!) and local wines. It's open from 8 am to 8 pm; knock on the door to get into the shop area.

For a snack in a verdant open-air setting, with an inspiring view, go to the French-run *Ranch Beni*, where Dany and Patricio serve up superb Yungas coffee, chocolate mousse, cakes and other goodies. You'll find them beside the hospital, a 20-minute walk uphill from the town centre.

Entertainment

Coroico's novel and fun outdoor cinema, near the market, shows films nightly at 9 pm. Take a warm jacket and a pillow to cushion your backside on the hard benches.

Things to Buy

For quality handmade jewellery, visit Artesanías Arco Irís, on the plaza. It isn't cheap, but you'll find some very nice things.

Getting There & Away

Bus Buses and minibuses to Coroico leave from the Villa Fátima neighbourhood of La Paz, and camiones leave regularly from the Villa Fátima petrol station. Given the road conditions, the minibuses are the best way to go. There's now a lot of competition on this route – the three main companies are Totaí,

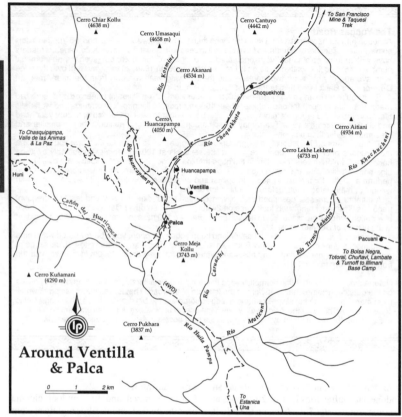

Around Ventilla & Palca

0   1   2 km

Yungueñita and Candelaria – so you'll have no problem finding transport. Most weekday departures are in the morning; there are extra runs on weekends. Transportes Totaí (☎ 6016) has an efficient, direct service.

For Yolosa, seven km downhill from Coroico, catch buses and camiones going north to Guanay and Rurrenabaque, and farther into Bolivian Amazonia.

Camión Camiones from La Paz to Coroico leave until mid-afternoon from the street behind the Villa Fátima petrol station.

From Coroico, the first step is getting to Yolosa. All vehicles headed down the hill must stop at the tranca office near the town entrance so it's best to wait there for a lift. Drivers all seem to stop for a snack in Yolosa, so if your lift isn't continuing on to your destination, this is a good opportunity to chat with other drivers about onward lifts. There should be no problem finding transport to Caranavi, Guanay or La Paz, but to Puerto Linares you'll first have to go to Caranavi and then find another vehicle from there.

To reach Chulumani, head back towards La Paz and change vehicles at Unduavi (there's also a scenic but little-travelled route from bleak Chuspipata). For a trip through Bolivia's main coca-growing region, take a camión from Yolosa to Arapata, another from Arapata to Coripata, and yet another to Chulumani. Don't be in too much of a hurry.

Walking Many people walk to Coroico from La Cumbre, the summit of the Yungas road, near La Paz. For details, see the description of the trek from La Cumbre to Coroico, earlier in this chapter.

TAQUESI TREK

Also known as the Inca Trail or Inca Road, the Taquesi trek is one of the most popular walks in the Andes. The route was used as a highway not only by the early Aymara but also by the Incas and the Spanish, and it still serves as a major route to the humid Yungas over a relatively low pass in the Cordillera Real. Nearly half the trail's 40 km consists of expertly engineered pre-Inca paving, more like a highway than a walking track. The walk itself takes only 12 to 14 hours, but plan on several days due to transport uncertainties to and from the trailheads.

Naturally, the May to October dry season is best for this trip. In the rainy season, the wet and cold combined with ankle-deep mud may contribute to a less-than-optimum experience. Since the trail's end is in the Yungas, however, plan on some rain at any time of year.

As for maps, you're in luck here because the entire route appears on a single 1:50,000 IGM topo sheet: *Chojlla – 6044-IV*.

Access

On public transport, your first destination will be Ventilla. There's a micro that leaves for Bolsa Negra, via Ventilla, between 9 and 9.30 am from Plaza Belzu in La Paz. There are also minibus trufis going from the same place to Ventilla and Palca at least once daily on weekdays and several times daily on weekends. There aren't any signs marked 'Ventilla', which is little more than a road junction, so make sure the driver – and

anyone else you may want to tell – knows that that's where you want to get off.

You can also take an urban micro or minibus trufi from La Paz centre to Chasquipampa or Ovejuyo, then either hitch along the road or trek through the beautiful Cañón del Huaricunca (and the Valle de las Ánimas, if you like) from Ventilla and thence to Ventilla. This will add at least one extra day to the trip, but will be a fitting run-up to the longer trek. For details, see Around La Paz in the La Paz chapter.

Transport between Ventilla and the San Francisco mine, where the trek begins, is sparse. If you're extremely lucky, a vehicle may pass and offer a lift, but otherwise, you should probably resign yourself to the four-hour slog to the trailhead.

Long-distance taxis from the taxi centre near Plaza Isabél la Católica in La Paz charge about US$50 for up to four people to the San Francisco Mine trailhead. A 4WD and driver will cost around US$100 for up to eight or nine people.

The Route

About 150m beyond Ventilla, turn left and follow the rough road uphill. After climbing for 1½ hours, you'll reach the village of Choquekhota, which may remind you of something in the remotest bits of North Wales. On foot, it's another two to 2½ hours of climbing to the trailhead, which is marked by a rock depicting a praying campesino. Shortly after a stream crossing, the main road continues another km to the San Francisco mine, but hikers should turn right here onto a smaller track.

After an hour climbing, you'll reach the final ascent, a switchbacking half-hour climb, partly on superb pre-Inca paving, to the 4650m pass. There, you'll find the *apacheta* (pile of stones) and a spectacular view of 5868m Nevado Mururata. Just beyond you'll see a mine tunnel; it's best not to enter, as there's always a danger of collapse, but it can be explored with a torch from outside.

If you've walked all the way from Ventilla, you may want to camp the first

CORDILLERAS & YUNGAS

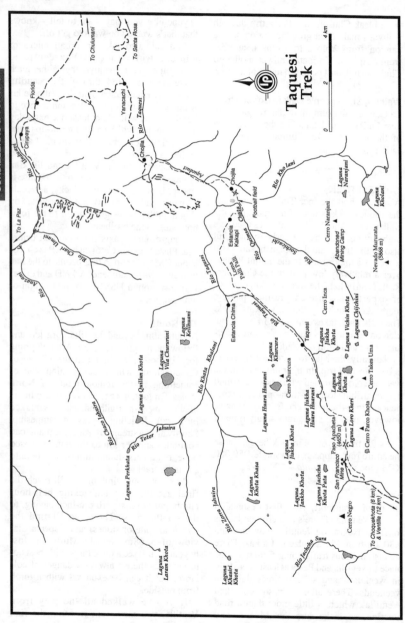

night at Laguna Loro Kheri, a quarter of the way between the pass and the village of Taquesi. If daylight is on your side, there's another lake, Laguna Jiskha Huara Huarani, to the left of the trail midway between the pass and Taquesi. This stretch contains some of the finest examples of Inca paving in Bolivia. At the ancient-looking village of Taquesi, there's a hut where you can sleep on the floor for US$0.50, but if you want to explore the village, watch out for vicious dogs.

Beyond Taquesi, the trail crosses a bridge over the Río Taquesi and continues downhill along the beautiful churning waters before moving upslope from the river and traversing a long way around Loma Palli Palli where you're protected from steep dropoffs by a pre-Columbian wall. As you descend, the country becomes increasingly vegetated. In the village of Estancia Kakapi you can purchase beer and perhaps soft drinks and see the pretty little Capilla de las Nieves church.

Beyond Kakapi, the track drops sharply to a bridge over the Río Quimsa Chata (which suffers varying degrees of damage each rainy season) climbs up past a football ground on the left to a pass at the hamlet of Chojila, before reaching the final crossing of the Río Taquesi, on a concrete bridge, where you can wash off some of the dirt. From there, it's a 1½-hour trudge along an aqueduct to the horridly ramshackle mining village of Chojlla at 2280m. If you don't mind staying in such a drab place, you can sleep in the basic alojamiento for US$1 or on the floor of the schoolhouse for US$0.50. Almost in compensation, the village bakery is turning out fresh bread by about 6.30 am.

From Chojlla, a crowded micro leaves for La Paz around 7 am; tickets go quickly, so purchase yours (US$2.50) upon your arrival in Chojlla. If you can't endure a night in Chojlla (and few people can), continue five km along the road to the more pleasant village of Yanacachi where there's a simple alojamiento owned by a greengrocer who charges US$1.50 per person, and a hotel costing US$4 per person. You can either catch up with the morning micro from Yanacachi to La Paz or walk an hour down the mountain to Santa Rosa. Here you'll find plenty of traffic to either La Paz or Chulumani.

YUNGA CRUZ TREK

This relatively little-trodden trek, with good stretches of pre-Hispanic paving, connects the village of Chuñavi with the Sud Yungas provincial capital of Chulumani. There are a couple of variations to the standard trek, including a pass over the northern shoulder of Illimani to get you started, as well as an alternative – and considerably more spectacular – route over Cerro Khala Ciudad, which starts beyond Lambate. Expect to see lots of condors, eagles, hawks, vultures and hummingbirds along the route.

The map in this book is intended as a route-finder only; you'll need to carry the 1:50,000 topographic sheets *Palca – 6044-I*, *Lambate – 6044-II* and *Chulumani – 6044-III*. The walk takes at least four days, not including the Illimani option or transport time to and from the trailheads.

Access

There's a good case for laying out the money to hire a 4WD and driver to take you to the trailhead at Tres Ríos, Chuñavi or Lambate. On your own, you'll first have to get to Ventilla (see the Taquesi Trek), which is a bit of a transport cul-de-sac. Beyond there, the road is poor and vehicles are scarce.

The Bolsa Negra micro from Plaza Belzu in La Paz will get you all the way to Tres Ríos, 40 km from Ventilla, where the vehicle turns north towards the Bolsa Negra mine. From Tres Ríos, you can either continue walking (or hitching) along the road towards Chuñavi or walk over the northern shoulder of Illimani to Estancia Totoral (not to be confused with Totoral Pampa three km west of Tres Ríos). See the Illimani Option, later in this section.

Alternatively, you can go straight to Chuñavi by micro, which is an all-day trip from La Paz. Buses leave from Calle

Venancio Burgoa, near Plaza Líbano, at least twice weekly at 9 am. Advance information is hard to come by and no reservations are taken; you'll just have to turn up early (around 7 to 7.30 am) and see if a micro is leaving. Friday is a good day to try. Failing those options, go to Ventilla and wait for an eastbound camión, or begin walking along the road, over 4700m Abra Pacuani.

Taxi access from La Paz isn't good due to the distance and condition of the road – at least five hours to the Chuñavi trailhead and six or more to Lambate. It would be preferable to hire a 4WD and driver from La Paz (see Drivers in the Getting Around chapter).

The return to La Paz is straightforward; just catch one of the many daily camiones from the tranca at Chulumani or go with one of the flotas.

The Route

Illimani Option If you're taking the Illimani option and have made it as far as Tres Ríos, cross the bridge over the Río Khañuma and follow the Río Pasto Grande uphill towards Bolsa Blanca mine, on the skirts of Illimani. After two km, a track leads downhill and across the river (it traverses around the northernmost spur of Illimani), but it's better to continue along the western bank of the river to some abandoned buildings (a good camp site) at the head of the valley. From here begins a steep and direct huff and puff up the valley headwall to the 4900m pass below Bolsa Blanca mine, which is overlooked by the triple-peak of Illimani. From the valley floor to the pass takes the better part of two hours.

From the pass, the route becomes more obvious as it descends steeply into the Quebrada Mal Paso. Once you've entered the valley, cross to the southern bank of the Río Mal Paso as soon as possible and follow it steeply down to the village of Estancia Totoral, back on the Lambate road, where there's a small *tienda* (small shop).

Even strong hikers will need two days from Tres Ríos to Estancia Totoral, owing to the altitude as well as the several exhausting climbs and treacherous descents. The best camp site is at the Pasto Grande valley headwall below Bolsa Blanca.

Chuñavi Trailhead Approximately five km east of Estancia Totoral, turn north-east (left) along the track that descends through the village of Chuñavi. Beyond the village, the track traverses a long steady slope, high above the Río Susisa, and keeps to about 4200m for the next 30 km. It passes the westernmost flank of Cerro Khala Ciudad, but the spectacular views of the mountain's cirques and turrets are hidden from view.

Two km beyond Cerro Khala Ciudad, the track joins up with the Lambate Trailhead route and four km later, skirts the peak of Cerro Yunga Cruz before trending downhill along a ridgeline through heavy cloud forest. Just below the tree line is a prominent camp site – the last before the trail's end – but unfortunately it's dry, so fill your water bottles at every opportunity. Despite the dampness and vegetation, the track stays above the watershed areas and running water is scarce unless it has been raining. In 1990, there was a massive landslide on the main track through this section. An alternative route around cuts to the right past a stagnant pool, but it's difficult to follow.

After the track narrows and starts to descend steeply, the vegetation thickens and often obscures the way. Three hours below the tree line, the trail forks in a grassy saddle between two hills. The right fork climbs up the shoulder of Cerro Duraznuni before descending anew. After approximately two hours, you'll pass through a steep plantation to the hillside village of Estancia Sikilini, a citrus estate across the Huajtata Gorge from Chulumani. When you hit the road, turn left and continue along it for about two hours into Chulumani.

Lambate Trailhead This route is more difficult but also more beautiful than the Chuñavi route. Lambate is approximately 2½ hours on foot east of Estancia Totoral, and two km beyond the Chuñavi cut-off. Lambate, which enjoys a commanding view,

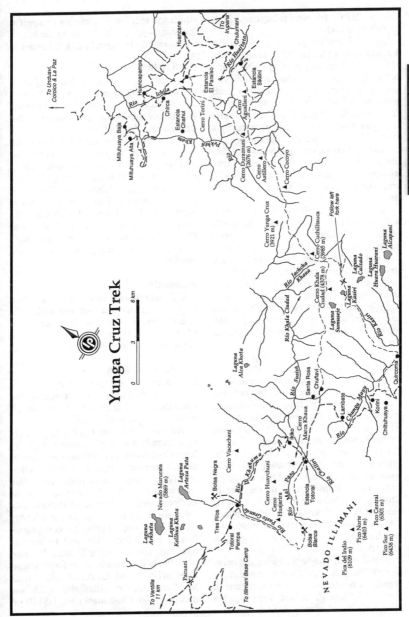

Yunga Cruz Trek

has a tienda – the last place to buy a soft drink or pick up snacks.

Beyond Lambate, you descend into the dramatic Chunga Mayu Valley, losing nearly 1500m elevation and gaining quite a few degrees in temperature. After a steep descent, turn downstream onto a path beside a small house and follow it for about one km to the bridge over the Chunga Mayu. On the other side, you'll be on a track that traverses up a steep hillside to Quircoma (Ranchería).

From Quircoma, which is the last possible camp site for awhile, the route is fairly straightforward but a real struggle – it's a 10 km, 2000m climb past Laguna Kasiri to the pass.

After the first couple of hours, the heat will back off a bit and two hours later, you'll reach a well-watered meadow with good camp sites beside the Río Kasiri, which you've been following. From here, the track steeply ascends the prominent mountain spur to the west, then levels off before the final short climb to Laguna Kasiri, which is said to be haunted by an evil spirit. This lovely and mysterious spot lies in a cirque surrounded by the snowy peaks of Cerro Khala Ciudad.

At the lake, you still have a steep 2½-hour climb to the 4300m pass on Cerro Khala Ciudad where there's an apacheta and a predictably incredible view from the Cordillera Real right down into the Yungas. Immediately after the pass, take the obvious left fork or you'll wind up in the wrong valley. Traverse along the hillside; after two km, you'll meet up with the Chuñavi Route. From this point, the increasingly forested route trends downhill – with a couple of minor uphill blips – most of the way to Chulumani. When you reach a small meadow before Cerro Duraznuni, continue directly across it, then take the right fork, which climbs the hill but skirts the right side of the peak.

At this point, you begin a long and occasionally steep descent through increasingly populated countryside to the citrus farm at Estancia Sikilini. From here, you can either take a short cut across Huajtata Gorge –

which will seem an excruciating prospect at this stage – or just lumber along the longer but mercifully level road into Chulumani.

CHULUMANI

Chulumani, the capital of Sud Yungas, is another relaxing town with a view. It lies at a subtropically warm and often wet altitude of 1700m, and is a centre for growing coffee, bananas and Yungas coca.

Rebels during the 1781 La Paz revolt escaped to the Yungas and hid out in the valleys around Chulumani until things calmed down. There is a large population of African-Bolivians living in the Chulumani area, descendants of the slaves brought to work in the Potosí mines. Locals claim the town's name is derived from *Cholumanya* (Tiger's Dew), to commemorate a jaguar's visit to the town well; it's a good story, anyway.

Information

There's no official tourist office, but there's a good area map painted just inside the church doors. The telephone code for Chulumani is 0811 and the telephone service in this area is provided by COTEL.

Things to See & Do

Chulumani sees few visitors, but it is a good base for several worthwhile excursions and when the going gets too hot, you can cool off in the municipal pool for US$0.20.

The most interesting day trip is probably to the **Apa Apa ecological forest**, eight km from Chulamani. The 800-hectare forest is the last remnant of primary humid montane forest in the Yungas, and is rich in tree, orchid and bird species. In fact, a 10-year scientific study revealed the presence of 16 previously unknown plants. It's a beautiful place for day hikes, and a camping ground is being established. For information and to arrange transport, contact Señor Ramiro Portugal (☎ 6106) in Chulumani, or the forest administration (☎ 790381, La Paz), Casilla 10109, Miraflores, La Paz. Admission, guide and transport from Chulumani costs US$10 per person.

A pleasant day walk will take you to the unpolluted and swimmable **Río Solacama.** In three or four hours, you can also walk to the lovely village of **Ocabaya,** which claims to have Bolivia's second-oldest church. Nearby **Chicaloma** has lots of Afro-Bolivian residents, and during celebrations they dance the traditional *saya*.

Special Events
The only time Chulumani breaks its pervasive *tranquilidad* is during the week following 24 August, when it stages the riotous four-day Fiesta de San Bartolomé. Lots of winter-weary highlanders turn up to join in the festivities.

Places to Stay
A good cheap option is *Alojamiento Dion* – the entrance is through a paint shop. Rooms on the lower floors cost US$3.75 per person and on the higher floors, US$4.10. If you're staying at *Hotel Garcia* on Friday or Saturday night, you'll have to either go dancing in the disco or bring earplugs. Rooms cost US$4.10 per person with bath; US$3 per person with shared bath; and US$2 per person for rooms on the lower level. *Alojamiento Daniel* is now in the process of renovation and expansion into a larger building; rooms cost US$2 per person. The standard *Alojamiento Chulumani* also charges US$2 per person.

Hotel Huayrani, a complex of self-catering flats with a large garden and a small pool, is run by the friendly and knowledgeable Ximena Tetard. Rates are US$6.20 per person on weekdays and US$10.50 on weekends. The quiet and good value *Los Jazmines* has a pool with a view. *La Hostería*, with the best restaurant in town, charges US$4.10/6.20 per person without/with private bath. It's a lovely wooden building with a charming sort of colonial air about it.

The friendly little *Hotel Panorama* has a nice garden, a restaurant and a small swimming pool. The charge is US$6.20 per person, with private bath. The similarly amenable *Residencial El Milagro* is also fine, with a beautiful garden, an antique-furnished

reception area and a great view. A one or two-bed double costs US$6.20 with a private bath and a room with six beds and a bath costs US$4.10 per person. There are no single rooms.

The mid-range *Hotel Monarca* – formerly Hotel Prefectural – is laid out like a holiday camp and lacks much character, but it has an enormous swimming pool to help you cope with the subtropical stickiness. The five-star *Hotel San Bartolomé* has everything you'd expect from a hotel of this standing, including an odd Z-shaped swimming pool. Rooms start at about US$50 per person. For weekend guests, the hotel organises minibus transport from La Paz. Book through the Hotel Plaza (☎ 378314) in La Paz.

Out of Town Along the route to Chulumani, 20 km from Unduavi, is the relaxing two-star *El Castillo* (☎ 392184, fax 356573), Casilla 13732, La Paz. This private castle, Castillo el Chaco, now functions as a hotel and restaurant with its own swimming pool, river bank and waterfall. It's only two hours from La Paz and its subtropical climate and oxygen-rich 1934m altitude make it an appealing weekend getaway from the highlands. Rooms cost US$12.50 per person, including breakfast. To get there, take a Chulumani minibus from La Paz and get off 20 km past Unduavi.

Near Puente Villa, 30 km towards La Paz from Chulumani at the intersection of the La Paz and Coripata roads, is the relatively posh *Hotel Tamampaya*. This affordable place is perfect for soaking up serenity. To make a reservation, contact Safra Limitada, Casilla 1314, La Paz.

Places to Eat
The market in Chulumani may well be the cleanest in Bolivia. It's especially good for breakfast, as local coffee is available but you'll also enjoy their delicious cocoa.

Your choice of eateries in Chulumani is limited, and coming directly from nosh-rich Coroico you may feel deprived. The best cheap place is probably the *Restaurant Garcia*, with *almuerzos* for US$1. The

CORDILLERAS & YUNGAS

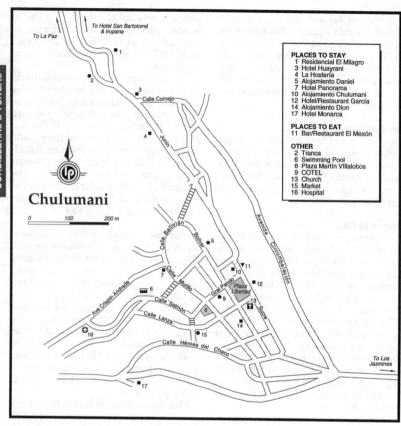

Chulumani

```
0        100        200 m
```

PLACES TO STAY
1 Residencial El Milagro
3 Hotel Huayrani
4 La Hostería
5 Alojamiento Daniel
7 Hotel Panorama
10 Alojamiento Chulumani
12 Hotel/Restaurant García
14 Alojamiento Dion
17 Hotel Monarca

PLACES TO EAT
11 Bar/Restaurant El Mesón

OTHER
2 Tranca
6 Swimming Pool
8 Plaza Martín VIllalobos
9 COTEL
13 Church
15 Market
16 Hospital

quality is decent and the patio dining room overlooks a pastoral slice of the Yungas. Several small cafés are scattered around and just uphill from the Plaza Libertad; for Bolivian stand-bys, try *Bar El Mesón*, which also has a good view over the surrounding countryside.

Unless you can afford the posh five-star Hotel San Bartolomé, the only choice with a varied menu is *La Hostería*. Main courses range from US$3 to US$4.

Entertainment
On Friday and Saturday nights, *Hotel Garcia*

stages a cacophonous disco. Next door to the Alojamiento Dion is the *micro-cine*, which runs daily video presentations – don't expect anything more highbrow than Bruce Lee.

Getting There & Away
The beautiful route from La Paz to Chulumani, which extends on to Irupana, is wider, less unnerving and statistically safer than the road to Coroico. Trekkers on the Yunga Cruz trek from Lambate or Chuñavi finish up in Chulumani and the town is easily accessible from Yanacachi, at the end of the Taquesi trek. From Yanacachi, walk down to

the main road and wait for transport headed downhill; it's about 1½ hours to Chulumani.

Buses, micros and minibuses leave for Chulumani from Calle Yanacochi in Villa Fátima, La Paz, several times daily and there's no problem finding a camión to Chulumani from behind the Villa Fátima petrol station any day of the week. Most traffic departs between 5 am and 2 pm. By minibus, the trip takes four hours and costs US$2.75.

From Chulumani, buses leave regularly and minibuses irregularly from Plaza Libertad. To assure a seat, book with Trans San Bartolomé or Yungueña Tours.

You can wait for camiones to La Paz or other Yungas towns at the tranca near Residencial El Milagro. To La Paz by camiones takes up to eight or nine hours. Camiones also run irregularly to neighbouring villages; ask around local transport firms or hotels, or wait beside the appropriate road in the morning.

If you're coming from Coroico or Guanay, get off at Unduavi and wait for another vehicle. Clothing suggestions for the Yungas road (see The Yungas Road aside earlier in this chapter) apply here, too. Between Unduavi and Chulumani, watch for the wispy Velo de la Novia (Bridal Veil Falls) beside the road, and the unusual Castillo El Chaco, a castle-like hotel 20 km from Unduavi.

SORATA

Lovely, medieval-looking Sorata, with its steep stairways and maze of narrow cobblestone streets, may well have the finest setting of any town in Bolivia. Perched on a hillside at an elevation of 2695m in a valley beneath the towering snowcapped peaks of 6362m Illampu and 6427m (more or less) Ancohuma, it's a popular getaway for urban Bolivians and also attracts growing numbers of hikers and mountaineers.

Tourists aren't the only ones enchanted with Sorata. Bolivian writer Don Emiterio Villamil de Rada was so inspired by the bountiful greenery and clear rivers that he used Sorata as the setting for the Garden of Eden in *La Lengua de Adán* (Adam's Tongue). Aymara, he postulated, was the language of Adam and Cerro Illampu was the true Mt Olympus.

In colonial days, Sorata provided a link to the goldfields and rubber plantations of the Alto Beni and a gateway to the Amazon Basin. In 1791 it was the site of a distinctly unorthodox siege by indigenous leader Andrés Tupac Amaru and his 16,000 soldiers. They constructed dykes above the colonial town and when these had filled with runoff water from the slopes of Illampu, they opened the floodgates and the town was washed away.

Now that commercial traffic moves into the Yungas from La Paz, Sorata has slipped into comfortable obscurity. Today, it's best known to travellers and paradise-seekers who've re-routed the Gringo trail to include this formerly off-the-beaten-track destination. For mountaineers, it's the base to use for scaling Illampu (also called Kun-Tixi-Wiracocha, 'the giver of water', or Hualpacayo, 'the hen's foot' in Aymara), and Ancohuma, which is also spelt Jankhouma and a variety of other renditions. You'd be hard-pressed to find anyone who doesn't like the place.

Information

Sunday is Sorata's market day, and Tuesday, when many businesses are closed, is considered the *Domingo Sorateño* (Sorata's Sunday). Tourist information is available at both the Residencial Sorata and the Hotel Copacabana.

Although tourism is increasing in Sorata, it's difficult to change money. The only place to change travellers cheques is Artesanía Sorata, which pays 15% less than official bank rates. The telephone code for Sorata is 0811.

Things to See

There isn't much of specific interest in Sorata itself – the town's main attractions are its noncommercial medieval feel (when the mist rolls in, this effect is accentuated), its narrow cobblestone streets, which are suit-

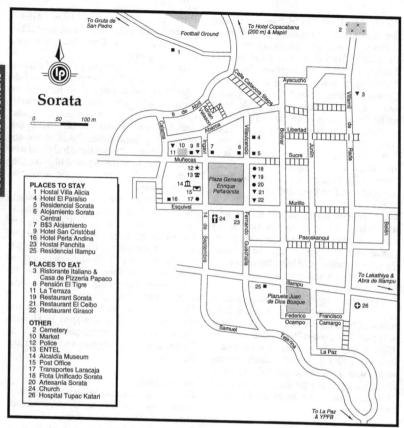

Sorata

0   50   100 m

PLACES TO STAY
1 Hostal Villa Alicia
4 Hotel El Paraíso
5 Residencial Sorata
6 Alojamiento Sorata
   Central
7 BS3 Alojamiento
9 Hotel San Cristóbal
16 Hotel Perla Andina
23 Hostal Panchita
25 Residencial Illampu

PLACES TO EAT
3 Ristorante Italiano &
   Casa de Pizzería Papaco
8 Pensión El Tigre
11 La Terraza
19 Restaurant Sorata
21 Restaurant El Ceibo
22 Restaurant Girasol

OTHER
2 Cemetery
10 Market
12 Police
13 ENTEL
14 Alcaldía Museum
15 Post Office
17 Transportes Laracaja
18 Flota Unificado Sorata
20 Artesanía Sorata
24 Church
26 Hospital Tupac Katari

able only for foot traffic and its convenience
as a base for hiking amid the peaks.

It's worth taking a look at **Casa Günther**,
a historical mansion that now houses the
Residencial Sorata. It was built in 1895 as
the home of the Richters, a trading family. It
was later taken over by the Günthers, who
were involved in rubber extraction until
1955.

The main square, **Plaza General Enrique
Peñaranda**, is Sorata's showcase. With the
town's best view of the nevados, it's graced
by towering date palms and immaculate
gardens. Unfortunately, it's fenced off and is

open to the public only on Wednesday, Saturday and Sunday. Upstairs in the *alcaldía*,
on the plaza, there's a small **town museum**
containing artefacts from the Inca Marka site
near Laguna Chillata (see under Hiking in
this section) and an exhibit of old festival
clothing. It's open on weekdays (except
Tuesday) from 8 am to noon and 2 to 5 pm.

Hiking

The Sorata area offers fit and enthusiastic
trekkers some of Bolivia's finest hiking and
trekking. Options range from half-day jaunts

to San Pedro Cave (Gruta de San Pedro), to 24-day expeditions to Rurrenabaque, following the route used by Colonel Fawcett in the early part of this century.

For independent trekkers, the best advice is available at Residencial Sorata, where you'll find maps, suggestions and directions and freelance guides for hire. Guides for groups of four or five people will typically charge about US$7 per day, plus their food.

If you prefer an organised trek, with food, camping gear, a guide, porters, mules and muleteers, see the Club Sorata Travel Agency at Hotel Copacabana. Residents of Hotel Copacabana who wish to go independently may also hire camping and climbing gear there.

Hikers should carry the *Alpenvereinskarte Cordillera Real Nord (Illampu) 1:50,000* for all except the Gruta de San Pedro, which is off the map. For that walk, use the rather outdated 1:50,000 IGM sheet *5846-I*. Basic information on climbing Ancohuma is included under Climbing in the Cordillera Real near the end of this chapter.

The following popular hikes pass through quite traditional areas so try to stay tuned to local sensitivities. Unless you're invited, don't set up camp anywhere near a village and if you're not made to feel welcome, try to move on quickly.

Gruta de San Pedro Most visitors make a daytrip of the 12-km hike to the Gruta de San Pedro near the village of San Pedro, two to 2½-hours from Sorata. Begin by descending the Calle Catacora steps. Take the shortcut down past the Hostal Villa Alicia to meet up with the road to San Pedro. If you turn left here and head down the valley, it's 10 km to San Pedro; you'll see the village church and football ground. The cave is 15m above the end of the road, less than one km beyond the village and just past the cutoff towards Consata.

Alternatively, follow a parallel track along the Río San Cristóbal. Start with the shortcut to the San Pedro road via the Hostal Villa Alicia as described above, turn left, and look for the sign to the *seminario* (seminary, of course), which sits on the river bank. From there, just pick your way downstream; the path is fairly clear most of the way. After 2½ to three hours, you'll reach a large flat area and a steep track that leads uphill past the top of a prominent landslide to the football grounds in San Pedro village.

Admission to the cave is US$0.60, and there's usually someone on hand to crank up the generator, to power the lights (although given the cave's current condition, it may be better left in the dark), so you may have to wait for enough people to make it worth their while. Several hundred metres in is a cold underground lake that impedes further exploration but makes a novel swimming hole. With luck, you'll see some of the cave's batty residents.

It's worth continuing about ten minutes along the track past the cave, then turning right on the steep uphill track. After another 20 minutes, you'll reach a prominent ridge, where there's a great lunch spot, a camp site and excellent views down the valley. There's also a decent camp site on the river bank, accessed by a track leading directly down from the cave.

Lakathiya & Abra de Illampu A hike to the village of Lakathiya, high above Sorata at an elevation of about 3950m, makes a good grunt of a day hike for the very fit. For a longer overnight trek, you can climb up into the Abra de Illampu, a dramatic pass on the northern shoulder of Cerro Illampu. This route is also the start of the Illampu Circuit and provides convenient access to Ancoma, at the start of the Camino del Oro trek, detailed later in this chapter, (obviating the need to hire a 4WD in Sorata).

To get started, take the track uphill at the northern end of the hospital to the aqueduct, where you should turn right and follow the aqueduct. After about 500m, the route slopes uphill to the left, away from the aqueduct. (Don't be tempted to take the trail that turns left immediately after the first ridge, which is a longer and more difficult route to Lakathiya.) After about one km, there's a trail fork just below the crest of an obvious ridge. Don't cross the ridge, but follow the route to the left, which traverses the ridge and crosses it a few minutes later.

Two hours further along, you'll pass through the tiny village of Quilambaya, which should exit on the track up the slope to the north. Then follow the obvious route up and over a ridge and along the slope to cross the Río Lakathiya before zigzagging uphill into the village of Lakathiya, about 2½ hours beyond Quilambaya.

In a large open meadow about 100m higher than the village, you'll find ample camp sites. Three hours and 800m of climbing will take you to the 4741m Abra de Illampu, where it's possible to make a cold and windy camp.

Laguna Glacial The rather generically-named Laguna Glacial lies at an altitude of 5038m, below a glacier separating Cerros Ancohuma and Illampu. The route begins on the same track as the one to the village of Lakathiya and Abra de Illampu, but when you reach the fork one km above the aqueduct, just below the obvious ridge, bear right rather than left. The route continues to climb, following the northern slopes of the Río Tucsa Jahuira valley for another 1.5 km before crossing the river and climbing through the village of Kolani, at 3000m elevation.

At the junction about 500m beyond Kolani, take the left turning and follow the steadily climbing route. At 3600m, about 2.5 km from Kolani, note the field of dug-out tombs. This is Inca Marka, which is believed to belong to the Tiahuanaco-period Mollu culture. Although the site has suffered at the hands of amateur pot hunters, it remains an important burial site, so avoid camping in the area.

From the trail fork four km above Kolani, the left turning goes past some ruins to Laguna Chillata while the right fork heads towards the Titisani Khollu tin mine and eventually, Laguna Glacial. Beyond the mine, follow the stock tracks southward for about 2.5 km, roughly following the 4450m contour, or take the shortcut over a promi-

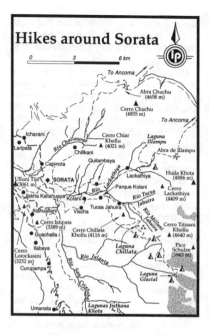

Hikes around Sorata

nent rocky ridge. When you reach an obvious gravel moraine, turn left uphill; the lake lies about 1.75 km up this moraine.

Most people take three days for this trip, which involves a very taxing 2500m elevation gain from Sorata. The first day is a climb to the Titisani mine, where there's good camping at 4450m elevation. There are also two natural caves at the 4300m level, about 30 minutes before Titisani mine, but you'll probably need a guide to find them. They're suitable for camping – one sleeps three people and the other accommodates one person.

On the second day, most people hike from Titisani to the lake and back, to avoid having to spend the night at over 5000m in a very exposed area subject to glacial blasts. The final day is for the descent to Sorata.

Laguna Chillata If you have only limited time, an exhausting but recommended 12-hour return hike will take you to the beautiful

Laguna Chillata, with views up to the surrounding peaks and glaciers. Several decades ago, this eerie and mysterious-looking lake was the focus of an irrigation project, and elicited all sorts of offerings to the traditional Bolivian earth mother deity Pachamama, in the hope of inspiring her to provide abundant water for fields lower down. The lake water is now quite clean and safe to drink.

The route to Laguna Chillata begins the same as for Laguna Glacial, but instead of crossing the Río Tucsa Jahuira into Kolani, continue upstream along the northern bank of the river for about 1.5 km and cross on the bridge about 300m below the confluence of the Río Lakathiya. From there, the path climbs through some trees, trending east along the southern slopes of the Tucsa Jahuira valley and through the village of Tucsa Jahuira itself.

About 1.5 km above the village, beyond the Río Milluni Jahuira, the route bears sharply uphill and climbs very steeply to an abandoned mine at 4000m, where you'll cross the river. If you're not doing the trip as a day hike, this area offers adequate camp sites. Laguna Chillata is about a km away, in a hollow over the next ridge to the south. Near the top of the ridge above the lake is a warm spring and several ruins, which include an old house foundation. This may have been used as a ceremonial centre and is believed to date from pre-Inca times, but was probably also used by the Incas.

From Laguna Chillata, you can conveniently continue to Laguna Glacial or return via the Kolani route, which is described under Laguna Glacial.

Cerro Istipata & Untuma Warm Springs A walk along the ridge opposite Sorata, across the Río San Cristóbal, makes an excellent day hike, and may be extended to include two sets of warm springs in the Chilabaya Valley. From Sorata, the walk begins at the YPFB station just south of town; take the obvious downhill path to reach a bridge over the Río San Cristóbal, then climb up the

other side, following established footpaths to the ridge.

An easier alternative is to start by taking a La Paz-bound bus and get off at the road crest just south of the 3061m peak of Cerro Ulluni Tijka, which bears a statue of Christ. From there, you can start your walk south along the prominent ridge (this ridge adds a good 10 km of road distance along the main route to La Paz). The next summit you reach will be 3252m Cerro Lorockasini, which once bore a large cross on its summit. It was removed when Ilabaya residents blamed a spate of crop failures on the fact that the cross faced Sorata and not Ilabaya.

Continuing south, roughly following the main ridge, you'll reach the next peak, flat-topped Cerro Istipata, which rises to 3389m. On its summit, locals make offerings to Aymara gods and leave coins, in the belief that they'll multiply. Cerro Istipata also offers excellent views of the Cordillera Real peaks. From there, walking tracks descend to the main road, near where it crosses the Río San Cristóbal.

If you don't want to return directly to Sorata, it's also possible to descend the western slopes of the ridge to the village of Ilabaya. From there, a track descends into the valley of the Río Chilabaya, where you'll find the 32°C Untuma warm springs. There's also a set of 35°C springs about a km upstream, along a tributary stream.

Illampu Circuit To get started on this rewarding seven or eight-day circumambulation of the Illampu-Ancohuma massif, follow the instructions to Lakathiya and Abra de Illampu. The best map is the *Alpenvereinskarte Cordillera Real Nord (Illampu)*, which includes much of the route. To my knowledge, however, there's no map available that covers the entire trek. For general route finding, you can refer to the Illampu Circuit map in this book, but it's not detailed enough to use as a sole source of direction.

A short but interesting diversion on the third day of this route is to Laguna Subirana

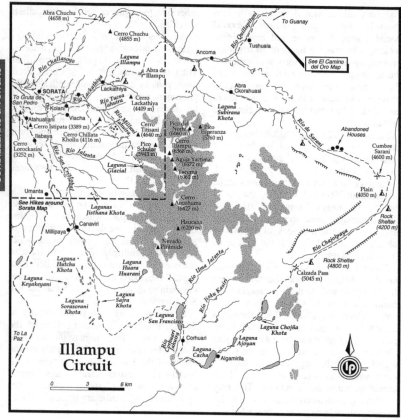

Illampu Circuit

0   3   6 km

Khota, at 4433m, which serves as the climbers' base camp for 5760m Pico Esperanza. There's a particularly beautiful camp site and a bizarre legend that the lake is responsible for swallowing both people and their cattle.

Organised Tours

The Club Sorata Travel Agency (☎ & fax 5042) at Hotel Copacabana organises a range of challenging trekking options from Sorata. A three-day trek to Lakathiya/Laguna Chillata or Laguna Glacial costs US$48 per person. The Illampu Circuit costs US$130 per person. For an organised trek along the Mapiri Trail, you'll pay US$190 per person; the six-day Camino del Oro route costs US$150. A hike from Sorata up through Aymara country to the shores of Lake Titicaca, via the hot springs at Mina Mathilde, costs US$110. If you prefer to walk the entire length of the Cordillera Real, you can opt for the 12-day trek from Sorata to Laguna Tuni, near Condoriri, which involves crossing more than a dozen passes over 4000m. This one costs US$260.

The most ambitious possibility, however,

is the 24-day route from the shores of Lake Titicaca to Rurrenabaque, via Sorata, Mapiri and Apolo. This route combines the best of Bolivia, from the high Altiplano to the Amazon lowlands and costs US$900 per person, which isn't bad considering it's all-inclusive. If you're not up to the entire route, you can opt for the Apolo to Rurrenabaque segment for US$240. All prices include a guide, transport, porters, mules, muleteers, food and any hotel costs. Camping equipment hire may cost extra.

Special Events
Sorata's main annual fiesta, which can be a riotous affair, is held on 14 September.

Places to Stay
The cheapest formal accommodation is the *Hotel Perla Andina*, a block west of the main plaza, where basic rooms accommodating two, five or six people cost US$1 per person. Hot water is available in shared facilities. Around the plaza, however, there are a couple of crash pads where you'll pay only US$0.60 for a spot to throw a sleeping bag.

The quirky *Alojamiento Sorata Central*, run by the friendly Miguel Coromi, is also cheap at US$2 per person but the showers may be a problem. Note the interesting shields and the jungle scene in the courtyard. The spartan *Hotel San Cristóbal* charges US$2.50 per person, with cold water only.

For its clean, friendly atmosphere and brilliant flower garden (complete with hummingbirds), the Canadian-run *Residencial Sorata* (☎ 5044, Sorata; ☎ 793459, La Paz) is an accommodation highlight. Grand antique rooms in this colonial-style mansion, known as Casa Günther, cost US$4/6 per person without/with bath; smaller rooms at the back are US$3 per person. Other amenities include a restaurant, a spacious lounge, table tennis and a novel book exchange where you can trade a book for two beers or various pastries. Videos are shown nightly at around 8.30 pm. The Québecois manager, Louis, who speaks French, English and Spanish, has made a hobby of the building's history, and has lots of interesting data about

the days of the quinine and rubber booms, and early mining activities around Mapiri and Tipuani.

Another popular spot is the German-run *Hotel Copacabana* (☎ & fax 5042), seven to 10 minutes from the plaza on the route towards San Pedro. Rooms with shared bath cost US$4/3 per person in high/low season, and doubles with bath cost US$18.50. Owners Eduard and Diana are video fiends, and their growing collection is available to guests.

The exceptionally friendly *Hostal Villa Alicia*, five minutes downhill from the plaza, is also a worthy choice. They have eight rooms, which cost US$5 per person, including a buffet breakfast. The only drawback is its position opposite the school, which gets a bit noisy during the day. You can make reservations through the COTEL office (☎ 3234) in the plaza.

The more upmarket *Hotel El Paraíso* (☎ 5043), with lots of flowers and a good restaurant, has comfortable rooms with private bath for US$6.20 per person. Another choice is the peach-coloured *Hostal Panchita* (☎ 364919, La Paz), which has a nice clean courtyard and a rather aloof demeanour. Pleasant single/double rooms cost US$3/5. At the front is a tiny ENTEL desk.

Places to Eat
The best place to eat is the irresistible *Casa de Papaco*, signposted as 'Ristorante Pizzería Italiano'. Run by a 'gentleman from Bologna', it offers genuine Italian cuisine – as well as good beer, wine and espresso – set in a paradise-like garden with orange trees and grape vines. Specialities include pizzas (US$4 for a small one and US$7 to US$10 for a medium), pastas, vegetarian dishes, beef dishes and sweets. The spinach and ricotta cannelloni (US$5), comes especially recommended and the home-made gelato is superb.

If your budget doesn't stretch that far, go for the small, inexpensive restaurants around the plaza, where filling almuerzos cost as little as US$1. The *Restaurant El Ceibo* serves breakfasts, vegetarian dishes, sandwiches, typical Bolivian dishes and a few marginal international ones; on Sunday you can get salteñas and tucumanas. The *Restaurant Girasol* does breakfast and good-value almuerzos, but à la carte dishes are overpriced.

The recommended *La Terraza*, just down from the market, serves three meals daily, including almuerzo and cena specials. With advance notice, it also does vegetarian meals. *Pensión El Tigre*, upstairs on the corner of the plaza, is another lunch choice.

The decent restaurants at the Residencial Sorata and Hotel Copacabana serve three meals daily and offer more elaborate fare. Basic breakfasts at the Residencial Sorata are quite good at US$0.80; juice or eggs cost extra. The US$3 evening set menu at the Hotel Copacabana includes salad, soup, main course, dessert and a hot drink. The restaurant attached to Hotel San Cristóbal serves unexciting but good value meals: breakfast (US$0.50), almuerzo (US$0.85) and cena (US$0.80).

Things to Buy
Artesanía Sorata, on the plaza, was founded by Diane Bellamy, who has spent two decades in Sorata. It sells a range of locally produced crafts and material arts, including unique hand-knitted woollens, dyed with natural materials, as well as dolls, wall-hangings, carved wooden articles and other traditional gifts.

Getting There & Away
Sorata is a long way from the other Yungas towns and there's no road connecting it directly with Coroico; you must go through La Paz. The route is now being paved but at the current pace, the project could extend beyond the turn of the century.

From La Paz, Transportes Larecaja and Flota Unifacado Sorata leave two to six times daily (from 6 am to 2 pm) from Calle Angel Babia, near the cemetery. Buses get crowded, so book tickets the previous day and note that there's limited service on Tuesday. The trip costs US$2 and takes 4½

hours; foreigners must register at the military post near Achacachi, so have your passport handy. Micros from Sorata to La Paz leave from the plaza any time after 5 am; the last departure may be as late as 5 pm. To travel between Copacabana and Sorata, alight at Huarina and wait for another bus (you'll probably have to pay the full fare between Copacabana and La Paz).

The only road route between Sorata and the lowlands is a rough 4WD track that connects Sorata with the gold-mining settlement of Mapiri. It strikes out from Sorata, and passes through Quiabaya, Tacacoma, Itulaya and Consata (also called Santa Rosa), roughly following the courses of the Ríos Llica, Consata and Mapiri all the way to Mapiri. The biggest drawbacks are horrendous mud, road construction and some hairy unbridged river crossings that can only be made by 4WD. *Camionetas* leave Sorata more or less daily for the gruelling 10-hour journey to Consata (US$10 per person) and on to the Sorata Limitada mine (US$12 per person), four to five hours further along. From Sorata Limitada, you'll find camionetas on to Mapiri, which is another three hours or so away.

ISKANWAYA
The major but near-forgotten ruins of Iskanwaya, on the western slopes of the Cordillera Real, sit at 1700m in a cactus-filled canyon above the Río Llica. They're attributed to the Mollu culture and are thought to date from between 1145 and 1425.

While Iskanwaya isn't exactly the 'Machu Picchu of Bolivia', the 13-hectare site is outwardly more impressive than Tiahuanaco. This large city-citadel, perched on the side of a small valley, was built on two platforms and flanked by agricultural terraces and networks of irrigation canals. It contains more than 100 buildings, plus delicate walls, narrow streets, small plazas, storerooms, burial sites and niches. If you're fortunate enough to visit Iskanwaya, take special care not to alter anything.

In the nearby village of Aucapata, there's

a small museum of artefacts excavated at the site. Admission is free, but donations are expected. For more information on the ruins, ask around for Señor Jorge Albaracin, or look for the book *Iskanwaya: La Ciudadadela que Solo Vivía de Noche* by Hugo Boero Roja (Los Amigos del Libro, La Paz, 1992), which contains photos, maps and diagrams of the site, plus background on area villages.

Organised Tours

The Ozono agency in La Paz (see the Organised Tours section in Getting Around chapter) runs all-inclusive two-week tours taking in Iskanwaya, as well as trekking on Isla del Sol and the La Cumbre to Coroico Trek, for US$1250 per person.

Places to Stay & Eat

Aucapata has no formal accommodation, but you can probably arrange something informally. Contact the Asociación de Residentes de Aucapata (☎ (0811) 5059) and ask for Señor Luis Clavel. Neither are there any shops or restaurants, so carry all your food and provisions from elsewhere.

Getting There & Away

Iskanwaya lies about 20 km north-east of Quiabaya, 50 km north-west of Sorata and an hour's walk (four km) down the canyon from the end of the 4WD track in the remote village of Aucapata. The only road access is via Aucapata (sometimes spelt Ancopata), at the end of a long and roundabout 26-hour 4WD trip from La Paz.

Public transport isn't really practical, but if you want to have a go, begin by taking a minibus to Achacachi from above the cemetery in La Paz; they leave more or less hourly through the day. In Achacachi, you'll have to find a camión – or anything – heading for Escoma (or beyond), and then look for something heading towards Ulla Ulla, Charazani or Pelechuco. Get off at the village of Wilacala, 53 km west of Escoma, and either start walking the 63 km to Aucapata or prepare to hang around for days, if necessary, waiting for a lift.

With a car and driver from La Paz, you'll pay about US$400 for up to five or more people. One driver who knows the route is Oscar L Vera Coca (see the Drivers section in the Getting Around chapter).

There's also a rather difficult access from Sorata, which involves a four-day hike via Pulliyunga. Another option is to find transport from Sorata to Consata (see the Sorata Getting There & Away section) and get off above the Boca del Lobo bridge over the Río Llica. Descend, cross the river and climb up the other side to Iskanwaya. In the rainy season, hiking in is dangerous and not recommended. There's no accurate map, but Louis at Residencial Sorata can offer directions.

EL CAMINO DEL ORO (THE GOLD TRAIL)

If the current road-building trend continues, the popular trek between Sorata and the Río Tipuani goldfields may last only a few more years. This Inca road has been used for nearly 1000 years as a commerce and trade link between the Altiplano and the lowland goldfields. Indeed, the Tipuani and Mapiri valleys were major sources of the gold that once adorned the Inca capital, Cuzco.

Today, however, the fields are worked primarily by bulldozers and dredges owned by mining cooperatives. They scour and scrape the landscape for the shiny stuff and dump the detritus, which is picked over by out-of-work Aymara refugees from the highlands. Squalid settlements of plastic, banana leaves and sheet aluminium have sprung up along the rivers, the banks of which are staked out for panning by wildcat miners. It's projected that gold will soon replace tin as Bolivia's greatest source of mineral export income.

Fortunately, the upper part of the route remains magnificent and nearly everything above Chusi has been left alone, including some wonderfully exhausting Inca staircases and dilapidated ancient highway engineering. This trek is more challenging than the Taquesi, La Cumbre to Coroico, or Yunga Cruz routes; if you want to get the most from it, plan on six or seven days to walk between Sorata and Llipi, less if you opt for a jeep to Ancoma. At Llipi, find transport to Tipuani or Guanay to avoid a walking-pace tour through the worst of the destruction.

Although it's unlikely the road will push up the valley as far as Ancoma, the aesthetics of the lower valley have already been scarred and eroded by large-scale mining and road building.

Access

Nearly everyone does the route from Sorata down the valley to Tipuani and Guanay, simply because it trends downhill. It's a shame, because the final bits pass through devastated landscapes and some of the ugliest settlements imaginable. Nevertheless, I'll be true to tradition and describe the walk from the top down.

For the route between Sorata and Ancoma there are three options. First, you can hire a 4WD in Sorata and cut two days off the trek. After bargaining, you'll pay US$5 per person or US$50 to hire the entire vehicle. A challenging alternative is the steep route that ascends from near the cemetery in Sorata. It roughly follows the Río Challasuyo, passing through the village of Chillkani and winding up on the road just below 4658m Abra Chuchu (this is also the access to the Mapiri Trail), which is four hours walking from Ancoma. The third option, which is shorter and more scenic, is to follow the route through the village of Lakathiya and over the 4741m Abra de Illampu, to meet up with the road about 1½ hours above Ancoma (see Lakathiya & Abra de Illampu under Sorata). Foreigners are charged US$2 per person to camp anywhere in the vicinity of Ancoma, and US$0.50 to cross the bridge there.

Allow two days for either of the abras, and before setting out, see the Residencial Sorata or Hotel Copacabana for advice on routes and conditions.

The Route

Once you're in Ancoma, the route is fairly straightforward. Leave the 4WD track and follow the southern bank of the Río Quillapituni (which eventually becomes the Río Tipuani). At a wide spot called Llallajta, about 4½ hours from Ancoma, it crosses a bridge and briefly follows the north bank before recrossing the river and heading towards Sumata. Another Inca-engineered diversion to the north bank has been avoided by bridge washouts, forcing hikers to follow a spontaneously constructed but thankfully brief detour above the southern bank.

Just past the detour is the village of Sumata, and just beyond it, a trail turns off to the north across the river and heads for Yani (which is the start of the Mapiri Trail). A short distance farther along is Ocara, where there's a small shop. From here, the path goes up the slope – don't follow the river. After 1½ hours, you'll reach Lambromani, where a local has set up a toll gate and demands that foreigners pay US$0.40 (B$2) per person to pass. Here you can camp in the schoolyard.

An hour past Lambromani you reach Wainapata, where the vegetation grows thicker and more lush. Here, the route splits (to rejoin at Pampa Quillapituni); the upper route is very steep and dangerous, so the lower one is preferable. A short distance along, the lower route passes through an interesting tunnel drilled through the rock. There's a popular myth that it dates from Inca times, but it was actually made with dynamite and probably blasted out by the Aramayo mining company early in the present century to improve access to the Tipuani goldfields. At Pampa Quillapituni, half an hour beyond, is a favourable camp site. Just east of this spot, a trail branches off to the right towards Calzada Pass, several days away on the Illampu Circuit.

Four hours after crossing the swinging bridge at the Río Coocó, you'll reach the friendly new settlement of Mina Yuna where the trail is routed through an uninspiring mine pit. Here you can pick up basic supplies and it's possible to camp on the football grounds.

An hour further down is Chusi, which lies just four hours before your first encounter with the road. There's no place to camp here, but you can stay in the school for US$0.80 per person. Puente Nairapi, over the Río Ticumbaya, is a good place for a swim to take the edge off the increasing heat.

Once you reach the road, the scene grows increasingly depressing. For a final look at relatively unaffected landscape, follow the shortcut trail, which begins with a steep Inca staircase and winds up at Baja Llipi and the Puente de Tora toll bridge US$0.40 (B$2) over the Río Santa Ana. In 1992, Llipi experienced one of Bolivia's worst ever natural disasters when a massive mudslide broke loose from the hillside and killed 74 people.

The US$200,000 of foreign aid money intended for disaster relief mysteriously disappeared before hitting its mark and the village still hasn't recovered.

After crossing the bridge, climb up the hill and hope for a camioneta or 4WD to take you to Tipuani and Guanay. Camionetas between the Río Santa Ana bridge and Unutuluni cost about US$1 per person; to continue on to Tipuani or Guanay costs an additional US$3.

You can pick up basic supplies at Ancoma, Wainapata, Mina Yuna, Chusi and Llipi, as well as all the lower settlements along the road. Spartan accommodation may be found

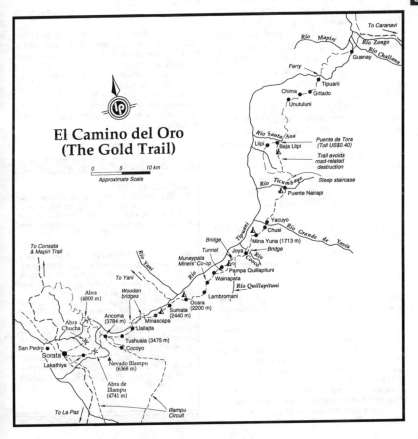

El Camino del Oro
(The Gold Trail)

0   5   10 km
Approximate Scale

in Unutuluni, Chima (more rough and ready than most and not recommended!), Tipuani and Guanay, all of which are along the road.

MAPIRI TRAIL

A longer and more adventurous alternative to the Camino del Oro trek is the pre-Hispanic Mapiri Trail, which was upgraded 100 years ago by the Richter family in Sorata to connect their headquarters with the cinchona (quinine) plantations of the upper Amazon Basin.

This unspoilt route begins over 4658m Abra Chuchu, then climbs and falls among the open grassy flanks of the Illampu massif to the village of Ingenio. For the next three days, it descends along one long ridge through grassland, dense cloud forest and pampa to the village of Mapiri. It takes anywhere from six to eight days, depending on the weather, your fitness and whether you reach the trailhead at Ingenio on foot or by motor vehicle.

Unfortunately, due to mining sensitivity in the area, no government mapping is available for this trek. The sketch map in this book (which is based on several sources) will head you in the right direction, but independent trekkers should speak with Louis at the Residencial Sorata in Sorata for the most up-to-date details. This is also offered as an organised trek by Club Sorata Travel Agency in Sorata.

Another Inca route followed the Río Khobi Jahuira from present-day Tacacoma to the village of Chiñijo. It's now overgrown and largely impassable, but may open up in the future.

This must be one of the world's most staggering walks – in every sense. It is wildly beautiful and unremittingly tough. It follows a 1000-year-old pre-Inca track, remarkable not so much for its stonework (Taquesi is better) as for the feat of engineering that accommodated this 3000m drop into the jungle and for its millennium of human uphill and downhill traffic. In 1903, the entire Bolivian army went down it to lose a war with Brazil. It has been overgrown since the 1950s, but in 1990, the Club Sorata Travel Agency in Sorata hacked back the worst obstructions.

You'll almost certainly need a guide and a porter, which can be arranged in Sorata. Believe me, every kg of your load soon becomes a very personal matter. Travel light – never more than a 10-kg pack including food and water. Water is available in places en route, but is a constant problem. Take bottles and purification for at least three litres per person (unless you have porters, there goes your 10-kg limit!). Camps must be waterproof and insect-excluding: flies, wasps, bees and ants make themselves very much a part of the experience. And don't suppose that because the route drops overall, there aren't many arduous climbs!

The way is rough and you'll spend much of the week cursing yourself, your guide and God. Much of the time is spent crawling over rocks, along branches and under logs, but you'll be rewarded with parrots, butterflies, flowers, tree-ferns, millions of tonnes of moss and unbelievable views over vast vertical cloud forest, unpenetrated by humans but for this single trail.

Matthew Parris, UK

This is an excellent way down to the Amazon Basin. The track is completely deserted as it isn't used by locals any more. It travels through dense cloud forest for two days and in places, a machete may be necessary. There can also be problems obtaining water as most of the route follows a ridge line. It's physically tough and it can rain a lot (it certainly did on us). However, there are fantastic views and great walking, and there's the chance of seeing a lot of wildlife, including spectacled bears.

James A Lind, UK

An Enigmatic End

In 1906 Colonel Percy Harrison Fawcett followed the Mapiri Trail and in his diary, recounted the tale of an odd occurrence that had taken place several years earlier at an inn in Yani:

About the turn of the century, two Bolivian army officers arrived here late one night...and seeing a handsome girl in the doorway of a house adjoining the *tambo*, tossed up to decide who should try his luck at courting her. The loser stayed with the village headman – the *Corregidor* – and next morning to his horror discovered his brother officer dead on the broken stone floor of a ruined house, which he could have sworn was not only whole but occupied on the previous night.

'The house has been a ruin for years,' declared the Corregidor. 'There was no maiden and no doorway, *mi capitán*. It was a...ghost you saw.' ■

Access

The Mapiri Trail begins at the village of Ingenio, which can be reached either by 4WD from Sorata (four hours) or on foot over the 4658m Abra Chuchu. For the latter, start at the cemetery in Sorata and follow the track up past the tiny settlements of Manzanani and Huaca Milluni to the larger village of Chillkani, about three hours from Sorata. From there, you have five hours of fairly relentless climbing up the semi-forested slopes to the Abra Chuchu. You'll meet up with the road about four twisting km below the pass.

Shortly after the crest, take the left turning (the route straight on leads to Ancoma and the Camino del Oro trek) down towards a small lake. This route will take you over 4750m Lechasani Pass and down past the Mina Suerte mine to Ingenio and the start of the Mapiri Trail at 3550m elevation.

The Route

Past Ingenio, you'll cross the Río Yani. Here the trail starts downstream but half an hour later, cuts uphill along a side stream; there's a good camp site where it crosses the stream. The way then twists uphill for 1½ hours over a 4000m pass. In the next two hours, you'll cross three more ridges and then descend past a cave known as Cueva Cóndor, which is a good camp site, to a small lake. From the lake, the route ascends 3940m Apacheta Nacional pass and then twists down El Tornillo, a corkscrew track that drops 150m. After less than an hour, you'll cross the Río Mamarani, where there's a good camp site.

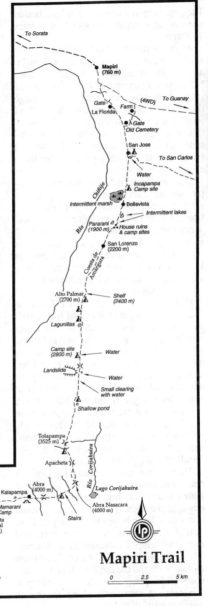

Mapiri Trail

0   2.5   5 km

The next camp site is three hours later, beside a stream crossing at the foot of yet another 4000m pass.

At the next stream, half an hour later, is another streamside camp site and a climb up a long staircase and down into another valley before you again ascend to 4000m. At this point, Abra Nasacara, you're on the ridge that dominates most of the Mapiri Trail route. For the next three days, you'll follow this ridge up and down, slowly losing altitude and passing through mostly lush and jungly vegetation; fill your water bottles at every opportunity here.

Six hours beyond Abra Nasacara is a very pleasant ridgetop camp site, with water in a shallow pond 50m away. About three hours later, just before a prominent landslide, watch for the water three metres off the track to the right. Four hours and three crests beyond that is a permanent water source at Lagunillas (where there's also a camp site), and an hour later, you'll find good camp sites on the hill Alto Palmar.

From Alto Palmar, the trail follows the Cuesta de Amargura ('Ridge of Bitterness', so-called because it's devoid of water sources) for nine hours to Pararani at 1900m, where you'll find water in a small pond near the ruins of an old house. An hour later, there's a semi-permanent lake. Just beyond here, the trail leaves the dense vegetation and issues onto a grassy ridge. Then it's 4½ hours to Incapampa, with a semi-permanent marsh and a camp site. Along this stretch, wildlife is rife – mainly in the form of bees, ants, ticks, flies and mosquitoes – but you should also see plenty of butterflies.

Three hours beyond Incapampa, you'll reach the settlement of San José, where there's a camp site. Water can be found 300m down to the right of the route. Four more hours of walking brings you to Mapiri. Here you'll find a simple alojamiento and motorised canoes downstream to Guanay, which is also on the bus routes. They leave around 9 am and the thrilling three-hour trip costs US$5 per person. Alternatively, you can catch a camioneta along the rough 4WDtrack uphill to Sorata.

GUANAY

Isolated Guanay makes a good base for visits to the gold-mining operations along the Río Mapiri and Río Tipuani. If you can excuse the utter rape of the landscape for the sake of gold, the down-to-earth miners and panners, known as *barranquilleros*, can make a visit to Guanay a singularly interesting experience. This area and points upriver are frontier territory, and you may be reminded of the USA's legendary Old West. Gold is legal tender in shops, and saloons, gambling, prostitutes and large hunks of beef appear to form the foundations of local culture.

Information

There's no place to change travellers cheques, but everyone displaying *Compro Oro* signs (which is just about everyone in town) changes US dollars cash. The ENTEL office is in the entrance to the Hotel Minero.

River Trips

Access to the mining areas is by jeep along the Llipi road, or by motorised dugout canoes up the Río Mapiri. The Mapiri trip is easier to organise because boats leave more or less daily. The trip to Mapiri takes five hours upstream and costs about US$7 per person. The exhilarating three-hour downstream run back to Guanay costs US$5. Although the forest has been decimated in some places, bugs are still a nuisance and you'll need repellent. If you want to spend the night, Mapiri has a marginal alojamiento.

Places to Stay & Eat

The *Hotel Pahuichi*, one block downhill from the plaza, is by far the best value in town, and also has Guanay's best and most popular restaurant. A good, friendly alternative is the *Hotel Minero* next door. Both these places charge US$2 per person. *Alojamiento Plaza* and *Alojamiento Santos*, both on the plaza, are also recommended and charge just US$1.60 per person.

For large steaks and fresh juices, try *Las Parrilladas*, on the road leading down to the port. The *Fuente de Soda Mariel*, on the plaza, does empanadas, cakes, ice cream, licuados and other snacks.

Getting There & Away

Bus & Camión The bus offices are all around the plaza, but buses actually depart from a block away, towards the river. Four companies offer daily runs both to and from La Paz, via Caranavi and Yolosa; Flota Yungueña, Turbus Totaí and Trans Trópico all leave Guanay between 4.30 and 5 pm. Only Trans Totaí has a morning departure, at 8 am.

Micros to Caranavi take four hours; daily at about 7 am, they rush around Guanay honking and looking for passengers. From Caranavi, it's seven more hours to La Paz.

Camiones to Caranavi, Yolosa and La Paz are also plentiful and cheaper, but the trip takes longer. To reach Coroico, you'll have to alight at Yolosa (unfortunately, most buses pass Yolosa in the wee hours of the morning) and catch a camioneta up the hill. If you're heading for Rurrenabaque, Trinidad or Riberalta, get off in Caranavi and connect with a northbound bus.

Walking For information on walking routes from Sorata, see the Camino del Oro and Mapiri trek descriptions earlier in this chapter. A 4WD track has been bulldozed from Mapiri through to Consata and Sorata but the route is rough and transport is unreliable.

Boat Alternatively, you can travel by canoe along the Río Beni to or from Rurrenabaque. There is plenty of interest along the way and it's a relaxing way to go.

For the first three hours from Guanay, you'll pass through mine-ravaged landscapes, dotted with toiling barranquilleros and spoilt by the heaps of mining detritus. At one point, the river squeezes between two large rocks and drops over a two-metre waterfall, which is quite a rush in a large wooden canoe. In several places, you pass between high and narrow canyon walls, including the dramatic Beú Gorge. Three hours from Rurrenabaque, a more lethargic

river slides past the 'Campamento de Papagayos', the nesting site of the brilliant and now endangered scarlet macaw. All along, you'll see the camps of *cazadores* (hunters), *pescadores* (fisherfolk) and *madereros* (woodcutters), who are taking the once pristine environment into their own hands and re-creating it in their own image.

Make arrangements at the Agencia Fluvial in either Guanay or Rurrenabaque. The canoes comfortably hold 10 people and their luggage. Foreigners are usually expected to pay US$20 per person or US$150 per boat, but you may be able to negotiate a better rate with someone who's going anyway. If you don't want the driver to crowd in more passengers along the way, you may want to pay only half the agreed fare in advance and hold back the rest until you arrive.

PUERTO LINARES

Although it was once a jumping-off point for river trips along the Río Beni to Rurrenabaque and Riberalta, cargo transport from Puerto Linares is now cut off by the Sapecho bridge near Caranavi. You can still arrange motorised canoe trips down the river from Puerto Linares, but otherwise, there's little reason to visit. To get there from La Paz, take a bus or camión to Caranavi, then another camión to Puerto Linares.

CARANAVI

All buses between La Paz and the lowlands pass through uninspiring little Caranavi, midway between Coroico and Guanay. There's little for visitors, but you may want to look at the Untucala suspension bridge, which spans a crossing used since Inca times.

Caranavi has several inexpensive hotels, among them *Hotel Avenida*, *Residencial México*, and the basic but economical *Residencial Caranavi*. The nicer *Hotel Landivar*, with a pool, charges US$7 per person. More sophisticated is the *Caturra Inn* (☎ 374204, fax 328584, La Paz), which has single/double rooms with private baths, hot showers and fans for US$13/22. It's set in lovely gardens and has a good restaurant and clean pool. For meals, *El Tigre* does basic *cenas* for US$0.75.

Climbing in the Cordillera Real

The Cordillera Real has more than 600 peaks over 5000m, all of which are relatively accessible. They're also free of the growing bureaucracy attached to climbing and trekking in the Himalaya. The following section is a rundown of the more popular climbs in the Cordillera Real, but this is by no means an exhaustive list. There are many other peaks to entice the experienced climber and whether you choose one of those described here or one of the lesser known and less travelled ones, climbing in the Bolivian Andes is always an adventure.

Note that the climbs described here are technical and require climbing experience, a reputable climbing guide and proper technical equipment. For information on Bolivian mountaineering, see Activities in the Facts for the Visitor chapter.

HUAYNA POTOSÍ

Huayna Potosí, at 6088m, is the most popular major peak in Bolivia because of its imposing beauty and ease of access, as well as the fact it is over the magic 6000m figure (but 26 feet under the magic 20,000-foot figure). It's also appealing because it can be climbed by beginners with a competent guide and technical equipment.

Some people attempt to climb Huayna Potosí in one day, but this cannot be recommended. It's a 1500m vertical climb from the Paso Zongo and 2500m vertical altitude gain from La Paz to the summit, and to ascend in one day would pose a great risk of potentially fatal cerebral oedema.

Access

Access is by taxi, which costs about US$26 (B$125) – make sure your driver knows the

way – or by the camión from Plaza Ballivián in El Alto at around midday on Monday, Wednesday and Friday. It may be difficult to squeeze on and the ride is dusty and uncomfortable, but it's cheap at US$1 (B$5) as far as Paso Zongo. A 4WD from La Paz to the trailhead costs about US$70 for up to nine people.

As Huayna Potosí is so popular, lots of climbers are headed out that way during the climbing season. If you only want a lift, check with specialist climbing agencies. Someone will probably have a 4WD going on the day you want, and you can share costs for the trip.

The Route

From the *refugio* (mountain hut), cross the dam and follow the aqueduct until you reach the third path taking off to your left. Follow this to a useful signpost that says 'Huayna Potosí Glaciar' and points right across a glacial stream. Follow this path through and across the rocks to reach the ridge of a moraine. Near the end of the moraine, descend slightly to your right and then ascend the steep scree gullies. At the top, you should bear left and follow the cairns to reach the glacier.

The glacier is crevassed, especially after July, so rope up while crossing it. Ascend the initial slopes, then follow a long gradually ascending traverse to the right before turning left and climbing steeply to a flat area between 5500 and 5700m known as Campo Argentino. To this point will take you about four hours. Camp on the right of the path, but note that the area farther to the right is heavily crevassed, especially later in the season; in 1995, an Israeli climber was killed falling into a crevasse here.

The following morning, you should leave between 4 and 6 am. Follow the path/trench out of Campo Argentino, then head uphill to your right until you join a ridge. Turn left here and cross a flat stretch to reach the steep and exposed Polish Ridge (named in honour of the Pole who fell off it and died while soloing in 1994). Here, you cross a series of rolling glacial hills and crevasses to arrive below the summit face. Either climb straight up the face to the summit or cross along the base of it to join the ridge that rises to the left. This ridge provides thrilling views down the 1000m-high West Face. Either route will bring you to the summit in five to seven hours from Campo Argentino.

Descent to Campo Argentino from the summit takes a couple of hours; from there, it's another three hours or so back to the refugio at Paso Zongo.

Places to Stay

Dr Hugo Berrios, who speaks Spanish, English and French, owns and runs a luxury refugio in Paso Zongo and also guides climbs on the mountain (as well as treks to the Yungas and in the Cordillera Apolobamba). Accommodation in the refugio costs US$7 per person per night; meals are extra. Dr Berrios can also organise transport to the hut, mountain guides and food rations, as well as porters to carry your kit up to first camp. Contact him at Huayna Potosí Tours (☎ 323584), Hotel Continental, Calle Illampu 626, Casilla 731, La Paz.

ILLIMANI

Illimani, the 6439m giant overlooking La Paz, is probably the most renowned of Bolivia's peaks. It was first climbed by a party led by W M Conway, a pioneer 19th-century alpinist. Although it's technically not a difficult climb, the combination of altitude and ice conditions warrants serious consideration and caution. Technical equipment is essential above the snow line; caution is especially needed on the section immediately above Nido de Condores where six Chileans died on the descent in 1989.

Access

The easiest way to reach first camp, known as Puente Roto, is via Estancia Una, a three-hour trip by 4WD from La Paz costing about US$150. It is then a three to four-hour hike to reach Puente Roto. You can hire mules for US$7.20 (B$35) from Estancia Una to Puente Roto. In theory it is possible, but not

recommended, to catch the buses and camiones which leave several times weekly from Plaza Belzu to Estancia Una or Cohoni at around 6 am. Expect to pay about US$2 (B$10) per person. However, don't go with any vehicle that stops at Quilibaya, the village before Estancia Una, unless you are a masochist and fancy slogging up an extra 400 vertical metres to reach the start of the walk-in. If you're arriving by public transport, remember to carry enough food to spend up to a couple of days waiting for a return truck.

You can hire porters in Estancia Una or Pinaya for US$10 each. They'll carry rucksacks from Puente Roto to the high camp at Nido de Condores.

The Route

The normal route to Pico Sur, the highest of Illimani's five summits, is straightforward but heavily crevassed. You'll either have to have technical glacier experience or hire a competent professional guide.

The route to Nido de Condores, a rock platform beside the glacier, is a four to six-hour slog up a rock ridge from Puente Roto. There's no water at Nido de Condores so you'll have to melt snow – bring sufficient stove fuel.

From Nido de Condores, you need to set off at about 2 am. Follow the path in the snow leading uphill from the camp; this grows narrower and steeper, then flattens out a bit before becoming steeper again. It then crosses a series of crevasses before climbing up to the right to reach a level section. From here aim for the large break in the skyline to the left of the summit, taking care to avoid the two major crevasses, and cross one steep section that is iced over from July onwards. After you pass through the skyline break, turn right and continue up onto the summit ridge. The final three vertical metres to the highest point involve walking 400m along the ridge at over 6400m elevation.

Plan on six to 10 hours for the climb from Nido de Condores to the summit and three to four hours to descend back to camp.

If possible, continue down from Nido de

Condores to Puente Roto on the same day. The 1000m descent is not appreciated after a long day, but your body will thank you the following day and will recover more quickly at the lower altitude. You'll also avoid having to melt snow for a second night.

On the fourth day, you can walk back out to Estancia Una in about two to three hours from Puente Roto.

CONDORIRI MASSIF
The massif known as Condoriri is actually a cluster of 13 peaks ranging in height from 5100 to 5648m. The highest of these is Cabeza del Condor (literally, 'head of the condor') which has twin wing-like ridges flowing from either side of the summit pyramid. Known as 'Las Alas' ('the wings'), they cause the peak to resemble a condor lifting its wings on takeoff.

Cabeza del Condor is a challenging climb following an exposed ridge and should only be attempted by experienced climbers. However, a number of other peaks in the Condoriri Massif, including the beautiful Pequeño Alpamayo, can be attempted by beginners with a competent guide.

Access
There is no public transport to Condoriri. A 4WD to the start of the walk-in at the dam at Laguna Tuni costs US$70. If you don't want to use a 4WD transfer, you can trek the 24 km from Milluni into Laguna Tuni dam on the road to Paso Zongo (see under Huayna Potosí earlier in this section).

From Laguna Tuni, follow the rough road that circles south around the lake and continues up a drainage trending north. Once you're in this valley, you'll have a view of the Cabeza del Condor and Las Alas.

It isn't possible to drive beyond the dam because there's a locked gate across the road. Some drivers know a way round it, but if you need to hire pack animals you'll have to do so before the dam, anyway. For mules, locals charge US$8 (B$40) per day and for llamas, which can carry less, they charge US$6 (B$30) per day.

The Route
From the end of the road, follow the obvious paths up along the right side of the valley until you reach a large lake. Follow the right shore of the lake to arrive at the base camp, which is three hours from Laguna Tuni.

Leave base camp at about 8 am, following the path up the north-trending valley through boulders and up the slope of a moraine. Bear to the left here and descend slightly to reach the flat part of the glacier, above the seriously crevassed section. You should reach this point in about 1½ hours from base camp.

Here you should rope up and put on crampons. Head left across the glacier before rising up to the col (lowest point of the ridge), taking care to avoid the crevasses. Ascend to the right up the rock-topped summit called Tarija – which affords impressive views of Pequeño Alpamayo – before dropping down a scree and rock slope to rejoin a glacier on the other side. From there, either climb directly up the ridge to the summit or follow a climbing traverse to the left before cutting back to the right and up to the summit. The summit ridge is very exposed.

ANCOHUMA
Ancohuma is the highest peak in the Sorata massif, towering 6427m on the remote northern edge of the Cordillera Real. It was not climbed until 1919 and remains very challenging.

No-one seems to know how high Ancohuma is. At present, the generally accepted height is 6427m, but the *Times World Atlas* has it at 7012m, the map in the *South American Handbook* says its 7014m high, and various tourist board publications put it at 7002m. In 1994, a satellite picture suggested it was in fact nearly 7000m high. If that's correct, Ancohuma would not only be higher than the 6542m volcano Sajama (which is currently believed to be Bolivia's highest peak) but also the highest peak in the world outside the Himalaya. It would also mean that all those climbers who've slogged up Argentina's Aconcagua, believing it to be

South America's highest summit, would have to come to Bolivia and try again.

A 1995 attempt to make an accurate measurement with two Global Positioning Systems could not establish the height after one of the GPSs failed. However, the expedition leader, Dennis Moore, is certain that Ancohuma is over 6500m high and is determined to climb it again and settle the matter conclusively.

Access

The peak is accessed via Sorata, which is accessible by public transport. From this lovely little town, you can hire a 4WD for the long traverse to Cocoyo, where the fun begins. (It's also possible to hire a 4WD all the way from La Paz to Cocoyo, which is more convenient, but extremely expensive.) If you have a serious amount of gear, you can hire a mule train to carry it from Sorata to base camp, in the lake basin east of the peaks at about 4500m. Plan on at least two days for these various transport arrangements to get you to the lakes. Alternatively, Ancohuma can be climbed from the west, using Laguna Glacial as a base camp (see Hiking under Sorata). Further advice and information are available in Sorata (see earlier in this chapter).

The Routes

From the lakes, head west up to the glacier following the drainage up through loose moraine. Make camp below the north ridge, the normal route. After a circuitous path through a crevasse field, a steep pitch or two of ice will gain the north ridge. An exposed but fairly easy ridge walk will take you to the summit.

If you've opted for the more easily accessed western route, hike from Sorata to base camp at Laguna Glacial. From there, the route climbs the obvious moraine and thence ascends the glacier, over fields of extremely dangerous crevasses to a bivouac at 5800m. From there, it climbs to the bergschrund and across a relatively level ice plateau to the summit pyramid. This is most easily climbed via the north ridge; the first part is quite steep and icy, but it gets easier towards the summit.

Cordillera Quimsa Cruz

The Cordillera Quimsa Cruz, an as yet undiscovered gem for mountaineers, was once described by the Spanish climbing magazine *Pyrenaica* as a 'South American Karakoram'. Granite peaks, glaciers and lovely lakeside camp sites make Quimsa Cruz arguably the most scenically spectacular of Bolivia's four main cordilleras. It lies to the south-east of Illimani and geologically speaking, is actually a southern outlier of the Cordillera Real.

The Quimsa Cruz is not a large range – it's only 50 km from end to end – and the peaks are lower than in other Bolivian ranges. The highest peak, Gigante Grande, rises to 5748m, but the rest average about 5300m.

The Quimsa Cruz lies at the northern end of Bolivia's tin belt and tin has been exploited here since the late 1800s. However, with lowering prices and increased competition from elsewhere, many of the miners remaining in the Quimsa Cruz are either self-employed or members of cooperatives. Most of the mining activity is divided between Mina Caracoles and Viloco.

Trekking is possible throughout the range, which is covered by IGM mapping. A popular route is the three-day hike from Viloco to Mina Caracoles. Villages offer only very limited supplies, so take all your food and fuel from La Paz.

Getting There & Away

Access is relatively easy due to the number of mines in the area. It's possible to drive to within 30 minutes of some glaciers, but on public transport, it's still a challenge. There's a lorry from Río Seco in El Alto, which takes seven to ten hours to reach Viloco, the starting point for most trips. Alternatively, take an Oruro bus from La Paz and get off at the village of Panduro, about 70 km short of

Oruro, and wait there for a bus or truck heading towards Mina Caracoles.

If you have more money, you can hire a 4WD and driver for a five-hour journey, but make sure the driver is familiar with the terrain. A reputable driver who knows the area is Vitaliano Ramos (☎ 416013, fax 722240), Casilla 1472, La Paz.

The only flota into the region is Trans Rosario, which serves several communities on the northern slopes of the Quimsa Cruz. From La Paz, the buses leave for Quimé, Inquisivi, Cajuata, Circuatu and Suri on Wednesday and Friday at 11 am and on Sunday at 10.30 am. On Wednesday, they also go to Licoma. On Monday at 6.15 am, they leave for Cajuata and on Tuesday at the same time, there's a departure for Yacopampa and Frutillani.

Cordillera Apolobamba

The remote Cordillera Apolobamba, flush against the Peruvian border north of Lake Titicaca, is gradually opening up as a popular hiking, trekking and climbing venue. Mountaineers, in particular, will find a wonderland of tempting peaks, first ascents and new routes to discover.

It must be stressed that although things are changing rapidly, this region remains remote and isn't set up for tourism. There are few services, transport isn't reliable and the people maintain a fragile traditional lifestyle. Sensitivity to local sentiments will help keep its distinctive character intact.

If you're in the area around 5 August, you may want to visit the village of Italaque, north-east of Escoma, for the Fiesta de La Virgen de las Nieves. It features a potpourri of traditional Andean dances: Quena Quenas, Morenos, Llameros, Choquelas, Kapñis, Jacha Sikuris, Chunchos etc.

Organised Tours

Individualised tours may be organised through any of the La Paz travel agencies that know the Cordillera Apolobamba. For suggestions, see Organised Tours in the Getting Around chapter and Activities in the Facts for the Visitor chapter.

CHARAZANI

Charazani, also known as Villa General José Pérez, is the administrative town of Bautista Saavedra province. The surrounding area of the upper Charazani valley is the home of the Kallahuaya, the wandering medicine men who are versed in the art of natural healing with herbs, potions, amulets and incantations.

Despite the number of foreign researchers passing through, few locals speak Spanish and sensitivity to local culture is requisite in this highly traditional area.

Places to Stay & Eat

There's an alojamiento on the plaza beside the church. Basic food supplies are usually available but they arrive only sporadically, so carry reserves.

Getting There & Away

From Mercado Tejar in the cemetery district of La Paz, a weekly camión leaves for Charazani on Tuesday at 2 pm and arrives 15 to 20 hours later. The dusty and bumpy trip, which costs from US$2 to US$3 per person, isn't the most pleasant journey on earth – you'll be cold and rattled at the end – and you'll still face a long day walk on to Curva.

Micros to Charazani leave from the street four blocks above the cemetery in La Paz on Friday, Saturday and Sunday at 6 am (US$4.50, 10 hours). On Saturday, the micro continues to Curva, two hours away, for an additional US$1.20. These micros leave Charazani for La Paz on Sunday, Monday and Tuesday.

Alternatively, you can take the Pelechuco micro (see Pelechuco later in this section) and get off at Abra Pumasani (the Charazani turn-off). From there, you can walk the long and winding 30 or so km to Charazani or try for a lift with the occasional camiones carrying supplies to Charazani and on to Curva.

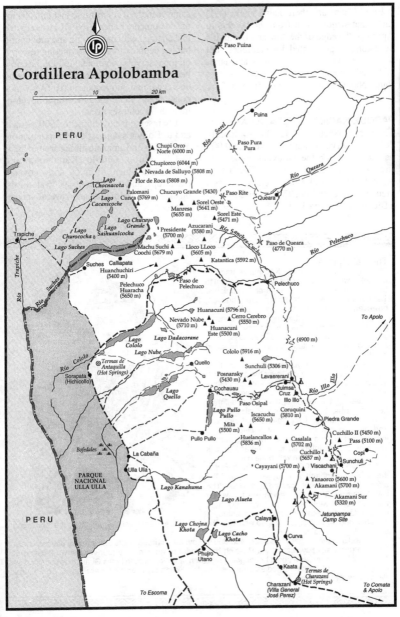

CORDILLERAS & YUNGAS

From Charazani, there's also a new 4WD route that winds down from the heights to Apolo, at the edge of the Amazon Basin. It's occasionally negotiated by camiones, but several serious stream crossings and landslide risks mean it's strictly a fair-weather route. Naturally, it can also be done on foot.

PARQUE NACIONAL ULLA ULLA

The Parque Nacional Ulla Ulla is a loosely defined reserve of approximately 200,000 hectares between the Peruvian border and the western slopes of the Cordillera Apolobamba. It was established in 1972 as a vicuña reserve, and in 1977 was upgraded to a Biosphere Reserve by UNESCO. Later the

same year, the wool institute Instituto Nacional de Fomento Lanero (INFOL) was created and charged with monitoring and preventing habitat degradation and conducting research on the reserve's cameloids. INFOL has now been transformed into the Instituto Boliviano de Tecnología Agropecuaria (IBTA), which concentrates more on agricultural development and social services.

The reserve is now home to 3000 vicuñas and to Bolivia's densest condor population. You'll also find amazing hiking around lagos Cololo, Nube, Quello, Kanahuma and Pullopullo, which all enjoy snow-covered backdrops and populations of waterbirds: black ibises, flamingos and several species of geese.

The Kallahuaya

The origins and age of the Kallahuaya tradition are unknown, although some Kallahuaya claim to be descended from the apparently vanished Tiahuanaco culture. The Kallahuaya language, however, which is used exclusively for healing, is derived from Quechua, the language of the Incas. Knowledge and skills are passed down through generations, although it's sometimes possible for aspiring healers to study under acknowledged masters.

The early Kallahuaya were known for their wanderings and travelled all over the continent in search of medicinal herbs. The most capable of today's practitioners will have memorised the properties and uses of 600 to 1000 different healing herbs, but their practices also involve magic and charms. They believe that sickness and disease are the result of a displaced or imbalanced *ajallu* or 'life force'. The incantations and amulets are intended to encourage it back into a state of equilibrium within the body.

Hallmarks of the Kallahuaya are the *huincha*, the woven headband worn by women, and the *alforja* (medicine pouch) carried by the men. The Kallahuaya of Charazani region are known for their colourful weavings, which typically bear natural designs, both zoomorphic and anthropomorphic, and for their llijllas, striped women's shawls with bands of colour representing the landscape of the village of origin.

The Kallahuaya's legacy has been recorded by several anthropologists and medical professionals; German university psychiatrist Ina Rössing has produced an immense four-volume work called *El Mundo de los Kallahuaya* about her ongoing research, and Frenchman Louis Girault has compiled an encyclopaedia of herbal remedies employed by the Kallahuaya, entitled *Kallahuaya, Curanderos Itinerantes de los Andes*. ■

Information

For predeparture information, contact IBTA (☎ 316230, fax 315794), Dirección Nacional de Conservación de la Biodiversidad. The IBTA office in Ulla Ulla is also a source of hiking and wildlife information.

Dangers & Annoyances There have been reports of Pervuian banditry in this area, including incursion by Sendero Luminoso guerrillas, so keep tabs on the latest news.

Places to Stay

Noncampers will normally find accommodation in local homes for about US$2 per person, and there's a tiny tienda in Ulla Ulla village. At the park headquarters at La Canaña, five km from Ulla Ulla village, IBTA runs a small, inexpensive hostel and can also provide simple meals for guests. Ask anyone in Ulla Ulla how to get there.

Getting There & Away

The micro to Pelechuco passes through Ulla Ulla. For details, see Getting There & Away under Pelechuco, later in this section.

CURVA TO PELECHUCO TREK

If you're up to a fantastic trek through splendid and largely uninhabited wilderness, do the four-day trek from Curva to Pelechuco, which stays mostly above 4000m and includes two high passes. There's arguably no better scenery in the Andes and along the way, you're sure to see llamas and alpacas, as well as more elusive Andean wildlife, such as viscachas, vicuñas and condors.

The trek may be done in either direction, as both Charazani and Pelechuco have public transport. Most people do the route from south to north, but starting in Pelechuco would mean an additional day of downhill walking and a grand finish at the hot springs near Charazani.

If you need pack mules and an *arriero* (muleteer), contact Alcides Imaña in Pelechuco, who charges US$6.25 per mule per day, plus US$6.25 per day per mule driver. Clients must carry their own stove

and food, and also provide meals for their guides, porters and muleteers.

If possible, bring all your trekking food from La Paz, as Curva and Pelechuco have only basics – fresh fruit and vegetables, bread, tins, pasta and drinks.

Access

For information on public transport, see Getting There & Away under Charazani and Pelechuco, elsewhere in this section.

A more expensive but considerably easier and more comfortable way to go is by 4WD. The trip from La Paz to Curva takes about 10 hours and costs US$300, but may be worthwhile because it allows daylight travel through the incomparable scenery. Be sure to fit in a diversion to the Valle de Amarete, where the scenery takes on Himalayan proportions. All the way to Pelechuco by 4WD costs US$350 one way.

Alternatively, you can pay to leave the logistics to someone else and do the trek with a tour agency (see Organised Tours in the Getting Around chapter).

The Route

Because most people do the trek from south to north – Curva to Pelechuco – that's how it's described here.

From Curva, head towards the cross on the hill north of the village and skirt around the right side of the hill. About an hour from Curva, you'll cross a stream. Continue uphill along the right bank of the stream. When you reach a patch of cultivated field, cross the stream to join a well-defined path into the valley on your left. If you follow this path, you'll reach an excellent camp site in a small flat spot beside a stream. Alternatively, you can keep following this trail for another 1½ hours to the ideal 4200m-high camp site at Jatunpampa.

From Jatunpampa, head up the valley and across a small flat area to the col with a cairn. From the 4700m pass immediately above it, you'll have fabulous views of Akamani off to the north-west. Downhill and to the southeast of the col, you'll find a nice camping spot near the Incachani waterfall at 4100m.

The ascent that will face you the next morning may appear a bit daunting, but it isn't that bad. Cross the bridge below the Incachani waterfall and take the zigzag path up the scree gully. As you ascend, you'll have distant views of Ancohuma and Illampu, and after two hours or so, you'll reach the pass at 4800m.

From the pass, traverse gently uphill to the left until you join the ridge, where you'll have great views of Ancohuma, Illampu and the Cordillera Real to the south and Cuchillo II to the north. From there, the obvious trail descends past a small lake before arriving at a larger lake with a good view of Akamani.

Climb from here up to the next ridge before descending to the small mining settlement of Viscachani, where you strike the 4WD track towards Illo Illo. In an hour, this road ascends to a 4900m pass, where you'll have views of the Cordillera Real to the south and Cuchillo II and the Sunchuli Valley to the north and west.

At the pass, the road drops into the valley; at the point where it bears right, look for a path turning off to the left. This will take you to a point above the Sunchuli gold mine, which reopened in 1992 and is worked by up to 100 miners. From Sunchuli, follow a contour line above the aqueduct for about an hour, until you see an ideal 4600m high camp site below Cuchillo I.

The fourth day of the hike is probably the finest, as it includes sections that have been used for centuries by gold miners and campesinos. From the camp site below Cuchillo I, the road ascends to a 5100m pass via a series of switchbacks. From the pass, you can scramble up to a cairn above the road for excellent views dominated by Cololo, the highest mountain in the southern Cordillera Apolobamba.

Descend along the road for a few minutes, then turn right down a steep but obvious path, which crosses a stream opposite the glacier lake below Cuchillo II before descending to the valley floor. Turn right here to rejoin the road a couple of minutes above the picturesque stone and thatch village of Piedra Grande.

Keep on the road for an hour or so, follow the pre-Hispanic road turning off downhill to your right. After you cross a bridge, you should follow the obvious path to the right, which will conduct you into the village of Illo Illo. Here you'll find small shops selling beer and basics – biscuits, pasta, tuna, soft drinks, and even candles and batteries.

When leaving Illo Illo, don't be tempted onto the path to the left, which leads west to Ulla Ulla and the Altiplano (although this is also a viable trek). The correct route leaves the village above the new school, between the public facilities and the cemetery. From there, cross the fields and llama pastures until the path becomes clear again. After crossing a bridge and beginning up a valley with a sharp rock peak at its head, you'll stumble on an ideal camp site. It lies at a bend in the valley, where there are a number of large fallen rocks.

From the camp site, head up valley for about half an hour until you reach a bridge over the stream. At this point, the route begins to climb up to the final pass at 4900m, which you should reach in 1½ hours or so.

From the pass, the route descends past a lake, crossing llama and alpaca pastures and following some pre-Hispanic paving. Less than two hours later, you'll arrive in Pelechuco, at 3500m.

PELECHUCO

The lovely colonial village of Pelechuco nestles beneath the snowy peaks of the Cordillera Apolobamba. It's most often visited as a trailhead on the Curva to Pelechuco trek or as a staging point for the much longer and more challenging trek from Pelechuco down to Apolo in the northernmost reaches of the Yungas. Meals are available from Señora Alvarez on the plaza and staple supplies are sold at a couple of small tiendas.

Places to Stay

Pelechuco has two alojamientos. *Alojamiento Rumillajta*, behind the church, charges US$1.50 per person and *Chujlla Wasi*, on the plaza, costs only US$1 per person.

Getting There & Away

From Mercado Tejar in La Paz, the Bus Expreso micro leaves La Paz on Wednesday at 11 am and provides 15 to 24 hours of bumping and jostling pleasure for just US$6. This micro leaves Pelechuco for La Paz on Friday at 8 pm. This is also the transport to use for Parque Nacional Ulla Ulla, Termas de Putina (Putina Hot Springs) or the areas around the Lagos Cololo, Nube and Quello.

If you're hiking into Pelechuco and aren't being met by a 4WD, it's worth hiking west along the road for two hours. Just beyond Antaquilla, you'll find luscious open-air bathing in the thermally heated adobe brick swimming pool. It's worth camping at the baños because there's nowhere to eat before Escoma (five hours away by 4WD) and the views through Parque Nacional Ulla Ulla are superb. From Escoma it's another five hours by 4WD to La Paz.

If you do have a 4WD, try to approach or leave Pelechuco as early as possible, so you can enjoy the incredible mountain views to the west and over the 5000m pass, as well as on the drive along Lago Cololo.

Lake Titicaca

Lake Titicaca is an incongruous splash of blue amid the parched dreariness of the Altiplano, with clear sapphire-blue waters reminiscent of the Aegean Sea. Set in the rolling, scrub-covered hills in the heart of the Altiplano north-west of La Paz, it straddles the Peru-Bolivia border like a bridge between the two countries. At its present lake level of 3820m, it's one of the world's highest navigable lakes (there are higher lakes in both Peru and Chile that can be navigated by small craft). The lake was long thought to be 'bottomless', but its depth was recently measured at 457m.

With a surface area of over 9000 sq km, Lake Titicaca is South America's second-largest lake, after Venezuela's Lake Maracaibo. It's a remnant of the ancient inland sea known as Lago Ballivián, which covered much of the Altiplano before geological faults and evaporation caused the water level to drop. The lake's average dimensions are 230 km long and 97 km wide, but during the flooding of 1986, the water level rose several metres and inundated an additional 1000 sq km.

History

When you first glimpse the gem-like waters of Lake Titicaca, beneath the looming backdrop of the Cordillera Real in the clear Altiplano light, you'll see why early peoples connected it with mystical events. The pre-Inca peoples of the Altiplano believed that both the sun itself and their bearded, white leader/deity, Viracocha, had risen out of its mysterious depths, while the Incas believed it was the birthplace of their civilisation.

Titicaca Island, renamed Isla del Sol (Island of the Sun) by the Spanish, lies in Bolivian waters near the mainland village of Yampupata.

When the Spanish arrived in the mid-16th century, legends of treasure began to surface, including the tale that certain Incas, in des-

Highlights

* Watch the sun set over Lake Titicaca from a hilltop around the charming lakeside village of Copacabana
* Visit Copacabana's impressive Moorish-style cathedral
* Walk the lakeshore from Copacabana to Yampupata and take a magical spin around the bay in a reed boat
* Watch the Saturday *cha'lla* (vehicle blessing) in Copacabana
* Hike Isla del Sol from end to end and enjoy spectacular lakeshore views, ancient ruins and lovely Mediterranean-like landscapes
* Join the revelry of a Copacabana fiesta

peration, had flung their gold into the lake to prevent the Spanish carting it off. Because of the obvious fluctuation in the water level, other rumours alleged that entire ruined cities existed beneath the surface.

Although evidence of submerged cities is inconclusive, archaeologists have turned up interesting finds around Isla Koa, north of Isla del Sol. These include 22 large stone boxes containing a variety of artefacts: a silver llama, some shell figurines and several types of incense burners. They haven't, however, revealed much evidence of an underwater city.

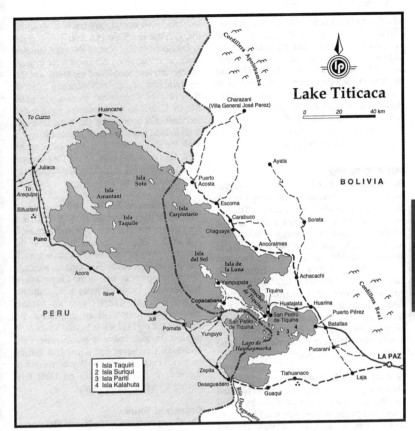

Water level changes from year to year are not uncommon and previous fluctuations may have inundated other ruins and artefacts. In the floods of 1985-86, highways, docks, fields, and streets disappeared beneath the rising waters; adobe homes turned to mud and collapsed, and 200,000 people were displaced. It took several years for the Río Desaguadero, the lake's only outlet, to drain off the flood waters.

Organised Tours

You can choose from several guided lake excursions that begin in La Paz and include a stop in Copacabana, usually around lunch time (for a complete list of tour companies, see the Organised Tours section in the Getting Around chapter). Tours are best arranged from La Paz but if you're already in Copacabana and there's space, Copacabana agencies may let you join a tour when the boat stops for lunch. There's a choice of hydrofoils, catamarans, launches and land transport of all descriptions. Given limited time and unlimited funds, this is a quick way to 'do' Titicaca.

The most popular companies are Balsa Tours, with motor excursions around the lake (see Puerto Pérez below); Crillon, which has a hydrofoil service; and the recommended Transturin, with covered catamarans. The largest, Transturin catamaran, accommodates 150 passengers and charges US$130 per person for a day of cruising, stopping at a combination of the following: Suriqui, Huatajata, Isla del Sol, Copacabana, Puno and possibly one of the Peruvian islands. Travellers required to have Peruvian visas must have a visa for this trip.

PUERTO PÉREZ

Puerto Pérez, only 67 km from La Paz, was the port established in the 1800s by English entrepreneurs as a home for the Lake Titicaca steamship service. Today, it's the site of a future 'eco-friendly' housing development for the wealthy and the home port of Balsa Tours (☎ 356566, fax 391310, La Paz) and its five-star lake resort, *Complejo Náutico Las Balsas* (☎ & fax 813226, La Paz). Amenities include a health and fitness centre, racquetball, massage, sauna and five restaurants of varying emphasis. Using the hostel at the resort as a base, it operates day tours to the islands of Kalahuta, Suriqui and Pariti for US$30 per person.

Getting There & Away

Most people arrive at the Complejo Náutico Las Balsas on a transfer arranged by Balsa Tours. On public transport, get off any lakeshore micro at Batallas and walk the last seven km to the shore, following the signs to the resort.

HUATAJATA

The tiny community of Huatajata lies midway between Copacabana and La Paz beside Lago Huyñaymarka, the southern extension of Lake Titicaca. Huatajata itself is mostly just a jumping-off point for trips to the Islas Huyñaymarkas and tourist cruises on Lake Titicaca. The lake's only yacht club – once a stronghold of relocated WWII-era Germans – is open to members only. Crillon Tours (see the Organised Tours section in the Getting Around chapter) bases its hydrofoil

services in Huatajata, and has also installed the five-star Hotel Inca Utama.

Life around this part of the lake remains much as it was when the Incas were capturing the imaginations – and the lands – of the Aymara inhabitants with dazzling tales of their origins. The tourist scene aside, daily life in Huatajata is dominated by age-old routines. Each morning the men take out their fishing boats and each afternoon, return with the day's haul. Women mostly spend their days repairing nets, caring for children, weaving, cooking, cleaning and selling the previous day's catch.

Museo Altiplano Eco

This set of displays at the Hotel Inca Utama focuses on the anthropology and archaeology of the Altiplano cultures as well as the natural history of the Lake Titicaca region. It features aspects of the Tiahuanaco, Inca and Spanish empires as well as the Chipayas and Kallahuayas (visitors meet a Kallahuaya medicine man). There's also an Aymara observatory, known as an *alajpacha*, for viewing the night skies. It's quite a nice little production and makes a worthwhile visit. Although I've never had a problem getting in, travellers have reported that admission to the museum is contingent on their first having a meal at the restaurant.

Organised Tours

The Catari brothers at the Hostal-Restaurant Inti Karka (see Places to Stay) run relatively informal day trips to the Islas Huyñaymarka – Suriqui, Pariti and Kalahuta – for US$45 for groups of up to five people. For more information, see the Islas Huyñaymarka section later in this chapter.

Crillon Tours operates rather rushed hydrofoil cruises on Lake Titicaca for US$130 per person. The standard tour entails a bus trip from La Paz to Huatajata and a visit to the Museo Altiplano Eco before hitting the water. The cruise stops at the Estrecho de Tiquina (Straits of Tiquina), then continues to Isla del Sol to spend 30 minutes at Pilko Kain, halts for lunch and sightseeing in Copacabana, then returns to Hotel Inca

Utama and La Paz. Crillon Tours also offers transfers between La Paz and Puno (Peru) by bus and hydrofoil for US$160 per person, and longer tours taking in Puno, Cuzco and Machu Picchu (Peru).

Special Events

In late spring or early summer, depending on the year, the small lakeside community of Compi, midway between Huatajata and the Estrecho de Tiquina, stages a folk festival with dancing, feasting and, oddly enough, bicycle racing.

Places to Stay

The well-situated *Hostal-Restaurant Inti Karka* (☎ 813212, La Paz), run by the Catari brothers, has basic rooms for US$4 per person. It's overpriced, but it's right on the shore and has magnificent views of the lake, especially at sunset. Unfortunately, there's no running water. There's a sign for the hotel on the main highway but not on the building itself; just look for a three-storey white house on the waterfront. (This is also the place to find out about the brothers' excursions to the Islas Huyñaymarka.) A step up is the *Hostal Lago Azul* next door, which charges US$9.50 for doubles with bath.

Crillon Tours' perpetually expanding five-star *Inca Utama* (☎ 350363, fax 391039, La Paz) resort provides a posh alternative for tour groups to Lake Titicaca and features prominently in the agency's Lake Titicaca hydrofoil cruise programs. Amenities include conference rooms, a health spa, dining room and bar; there are also programs dealing with lake ecology, natural healing and Aymara religious traditions.

Midway between Huatajata and Huarina, nearer La Paz, is the similarly upmarket *Hotel Titicaca* with an indoor heated pool, sauna and racquetball courts. You can make reservations through Transturin (☎ 320445, fax 391162, La Paz).

Places to Eat

The Hostal Restaurant Inti Karka on the main road sells inexpensive meals and the speciality is – you guessed it – trout. It also

prepares chicken and typical Bolivian dishes. Alternatively, the inexpensive *Wiñay Marca* in Huatajata village offers a similar menu.

Beyond that, there is a whole slew of more elegant tourist-oriented restaurant choices along the shore, all serving trout and other standard fare, and there's not much to choose between them: *Las Playas*, *La Kantuta*, *La Casa Verde*, *Inti Raymi*, *Lago Azul*, *Ollantay*, *Panamericano* and *Huatajata Utama*. The last four have been recommended. The hotel Inca Utama adds to the choices with its upmarket *Jaipuru* dining room and *Musiña* lounge-bar.

At nearby Chúa is the beautiful colonial-style *La Posada del Inca* restaurant, which is open for lunch on weekends and holidays, and whenever it's booked by tour groups.

Getting There & Away

Even if you're getting off at Huatajata most companies will charge a full La Paz-Copacabana fare. Lakeside communities between Puerto Pérez and Achacachi (including Huatajata) are served by micros, which leave roughly every half-hour between 4 am and 5 pm from the corner of Calles Manuel Bustillos and Kollasuyo in the La Paz cemetery district.

To return to La Paz, just flag down any bus heading east along the main highway. The last one runs at about 6 pm.

ISLAS HUYÑAYMARKA

The three most visited islands in Lago de Huyñaymarka – Kalahuta, Pariti and Suriqui – are easily visited in a few hours. It's also possible to camp overnight, especially on the more sparsely populated islands of Pariti and Kalahuta.

Isla Kalahuta

The island of Kalahuta, which translates as 'stone houses' in Aymara, served as an Inca-era cemetery and is dotted with stone *chullpas* (funerary towers) several metres high. Legends abound about the horrible fate that will befall anyone who desecrates the cemetery. Locals refuse to live outside Queguaya, the island's only village, and are also reluctant to venture anywhere at night. If you dare to camp on Kalahuta, you'll have most of the island to yourself.

The shores of Kalahuta are lined with beds of *totora* reed, the versatile building material for which Titicaca is famous. By day, fisherfolk ply the island's main bay in totora reed boats; others paddle in to the shoreline to gather reeds for canoe construction.

Isla Pariti

Like Kalahuta, much of Pariti is surrounded by marshes of totora reed. This small and friendly island provides a view into the tranquil lifestyle of its inhabitants. The Indians there trade cheese, fish and woollen goods in Huatajata for items from the Yungas and La Paz. Their sailing boats, which are used for fishing, are beautiful to watch as they slice through the Titicaca waters in search of a bountiful catch.

Isla Suriqui

Suriqui, the best known of the Huyñaymarka islands, is world-renowned for the totora reed boats that are still constructed there and used by many islanders in everyday life. The construction process is relatively simple. Green reeds are gathered from the lake shallows and left to dry in the sun. Once they're free of all moisture, they're gathered into four fat bundles and lashed together with strong grass. Often a sail of reeds is added. These bloated little canoes don't last very long as far as watercraft go; after six months of use, they become waterlogged and begin to rot and sink. In order to increase their life span the canoes are often stored away from the water.

In the early 1970s Dr Thor Heyerdahl, the unconventional Norwegian explorer and scientist, solicited the help of the Isla Suriqui shipbuilders, the Limachi brothers and Paulino Esteban, to design and construct his vessel the *Ra II*. Dr Heyerdahl wanted to test his theory that early contact and migration occurred between the ancient peoples of North Africa and the Americas. He planned

to demonstrate the feasibility of travelling great distances using the boats of the period. Four Aymara shipbuilders accompanied him on the expedition from Morocco to the Barbados.

Near the dock is the small museum, Museo de Balsas Trans-Oceánicas, which was first established as the Museo San Pablo. It contains all sorts of paraphernalia about *Ra II* and the other Heyerdahl expeditions that employed ancient design watercraft, such as the *Ra I, Tigris* and the *Kon Tiki*. Displays also include the various types of reed boats used on the lake and small, meticulously constructed models are for sale. Señor Demetrio Limachi Corani will construct full-size totora reed canoes to order for about US$20.

Tourism has become an island mainstay but unfortunately, once-proud Suriqui has been sadly corrupted by outside influences. Mindless tourists rush around poking cameras in peoples' faces while whining locals besiege them for sweets, money and other gifts. Everyone winds up in a bad mood and it's depressing to see how unpleasant it can become for all concerned. If you go, please try to behave sensitively!

Isla Incas

Legend has it that this tiny, uninhabited island near Suriqui was part of an Inca network of underground passageways, reputed to link many parts of the Inca empire with the capital at Cuzco.

Getting There & Away

Often, Aymara fisherfolk in Huatajata are willing to take a day off to informally shuttle visitors around the islands. The most experienced guides are the Catari brothers from the Hostal Restaurant Inti Karka (see the Huatajata Places to Stay section), who will take up to five people to Kalahuta, Pariti and Suriqui for about US$45, or just to Suriqui for US$25. They can provide informative commentary on the legends, customs, people, history and natural features of the lake. You're allowed as much time as you'd like on each island and they'll introduce you to friends who can offer insights into Aymara traditions and lifestyle. If you'd like to camp overnight on one of the islands, you can arrange to be picked up the following day.

All-inclusive organised cruises to the islands by covered catamaran or hydrofoil are available through Balsa Tours, Transturin and Crillon Tours (see the Organised Tours section in the Getting Around chapter) and Turisbus in La Paz (see the Organised Tours section in the La Paz chapter).

COPACABANA

The bright town of Copacabana on the southern shore of Lake Titicaca was established around a splendid bay between two hills. As a stopover along the Tiquina route between La Paz and Cuzco, it served as a site of religious pilgrimage for centuries, beginning with the Incas.

Copacabana is still well known for its fiestas, which bring this ordinarily sleepy place to life with pilgrims and visitors from all over Bolivia. At other times, it's a sleepy little place visited mainly as a pleasant stopover between La Paz and Puno (Peru). It's also a convenient base for visits to Isla del Sol.

From February to November, the climate is mostly pleasant and sunny, but there's often a cool wind off the lake, and nights at this 3800m altitude can be bitterly cold. Most of the rainfall occurs in mid-summer (December and January).

History

After the fall and disappearance of the Tiahuanaco culture, the Kollas or Aymara rose to become the dominant population group in the Titicaca region. Their most prominent deities included the sun and moon (who were considered husband and wife), the earth mother Pachamama, and the ambient spirits known as *achachilas* and *apus*. Among the idols erected on the shores of the Manco Capac peninsula was *Kota Kahuaña* or *Copacahuana* (which sounds exotic, but means simply 'lake view' in Aymara), an image with the head of a human and the body of a fish. It stood at the site now known as Asiento del Inca.

Once the Aymara had been subsumed into the Inca empire, Emperor Tupac Yupanqui founded the settlement of Copacabana as a wayside rest for pilgrims visiting the *huaca* (shrine). This site of human sacrifice (gulp!) was at the rock known as *Titicaca* (Rock of the Puma), at the northern end of Isla del Sol.

Before the arrival of the Spanish Dominican and Augustinian priests in the mid-16th century, the Incas had divided local inhabitants into two distinct groups. Those faithful to the empire were known as Haransaya and were assigned positions of power. Those who resisted, the Hurinsaya, were relegated to manual labour. This went entirely against the grain of the community-oriented Aymara culture, and the floods and crop failures that befell them in the 1570s were attributed to this social aberration.

A direct result was the rejection of the Inca religion and the partial adoption of Christianity and establishment of the Santuario de Copacabana. This developed into a syncretic mishmash of both traditional and Christian premises. As its patron saint, the populace elected La Santísima Virgen de Candelaria, and established a congregation in her

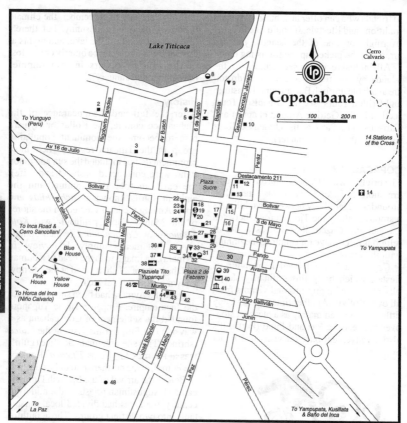

honour. Noting the lack of an image for the altar, Francisco Tito Yupanqui, a direct descendant of the Inca emperor, fashioned an image of clay and placed it in the church. However, the rude effort was deemed unsuitable to represent the honoured patron of the village, and was removed.

The sculptor, who was humiliated but not defeated, journeyed to Potosí to study arts and find the perfect model for the image he wanted to create. In June 1582 he was feeling suitably inspired, and began carving a wooden image that took eight months to complete. On 2 February 1583 La Virgen Morena del Lago (The Dark Virgin of the Lake) was installed on the adobe altar at Copacabana and shortly thereafter the miracles began. The number of early healings was reportedly 'innumerable' and Copacabana quickly developed into a pilgrimage site.

In 1605, the Augustinian priesthood advised that the community construct a cathedral commensurate with the power of the image and architect Francisco Jiménez de Sigueza was commissioned to design it. The altar was completed in 1614 but work on the building continued for 200 years. It wasn't until 15 April 1805 that the *mudéjar*

PLACES TO STAY		PLACES TO EAT		OTHER	
2	Residencial Rosario del Lago	35	Residencial Boston	1	Bolivian Customs
3	Hotel Prefectural	36	Hospedaría	5	Bicycle Rental
4	Alojamiento Kota Kahuaña	37	Residencial Imperio	8	Boat Landing & Tickets to Isla del Sol
6	Alojamiento Las Playas	42	Residencial Rosario		
		43	Alojamiento Illimani	14	Church
10	Alojamiento Aroma	44	Alojamiento Cochabamba	19	Banco Bidesa
11	Alojamiento San José			23	Wiñay Marka Tours
12	Alojamiento Urinsaya	45	Residencial Sucre	30	Market
13	Hotel Ambassador	47	Alojamiento Emper- ador	31	Transportes Manco Capac Bus Termi- nal
15	Residencial Solar				
16	Residencial Copacab- ana			32	Artesanías Virgen de Copacabana
		PLACES TO EAT		38	Moorish Cathedral
18	Hotel Playa Azul	7	Café Video	39	Transtur 2 de Febrero Bus Terminal
21	Residencial Casa Blanca	9	El Rey		
		17	La Merced	40	Post Office
24	Residencial & Pensión Aransaya	20	Puerta del Sol	41	Museo en Miniatura
		22	Fantástico	46	ENTEL
26	Alojamiento Oasis	25	Restaurant Snack 6 de Agosto	48	Intikala (Tribunal del Inca)
27	Alojamiento Solar				
29	Residencial Porteñita	28	Tito Yupanqui		
		33	Tourist Palace		
		34	Napoles		

(Moorish-style) cathedral was consecrated; construction wasn't completed until 1820. On 10 August 1925 Francisco Tito Yupanqui's image was canonised by the Vatican.

Information

Money The Banco Bidesa, beside the Hotel Playa Azul, changes both cash and travellers cheques. It's open Wednesday to Sunday from 8.30 am to noon and 2.30 to 5 pm. Artesanías Virgen de Copacabana also changes travellers cheques, but charges a commission of US$1 per cheque.

The Hotel Playa Azul changes Peruvian *soles* and will cash US dollars, but rates are normally better around the plaza in Yunguyo, just beyond the Peruvian frontier.

Post & Communications The new post office is on Plaza 2 de Febrero. It's open Wednesday to Sunday only. ENTEL, with a modern new office on Plazuela Tito Yupanqui, is now open daily. The public fax number in Copacabana is 2144. The telephone code is 0862.

Film With a constant influx of tourists, both national and foreign, Copacabana is a good

place to buy film. The vendors in front of the cathedral sell 36-exposure Kodak, Fuji or Agfa print film for US$2.50 per roll, and 36-exposure Fujichrome Sensia 100 or 200 for US$6.

Dangers & Annoyances Police and *tranca* (highway police post) officials sometimes try to extract an unofficial 'tax' from arriving tourists and pilgrims, ostensibly for upkeep of the sanctuary and the Virgin. In reality, anything you pay is pocketed – neither the church nor the sanctuary see any of it. Sometimes, travellers (mainly those entering from Peru) have been spontaneously 'fined' for a variety of 'infractions', including taking photos without a permit and carrying US dollars.

During festivals, be particularly wary of light-fingered revellers. Foreign tourists are prime targets and nearly everyone experiences at least one robbery attempt. Also, stand well back during fireworks displays; when it comes to explosive fun, crowd safety takes rather low priority.

The thin air and characteristically brilliant sunshine in this area combine to admit scorchingly high levels of ultraviolet radiation. Remember to wear a hat, especially when you're out on the water, and use a reliable sunscreen.

Hikers in the hills may want to watch what their brushing against; there's a particularly insidious variety of thorn bush that shreds skin on contact.

Cathedral
Built between 1605 and 1820, the sparkling white Moorish-style cathedral, with its mudéjar domes and colourful *azulejos* (blue Portuguese ceramic tiles), dominates the town. Its beautiful courtyard is usually ablaze with the colours of wild and domestic flowers.

Virgen de Candelaria The cathedral is a repository for both European and local religious art, including the Virgen de Candelaria. The black statue was carved in the 1580s by the Indian artist Francisco Yupanqui, grandson of the Inca emperor Tupac Yupanqui (see the Copacabana History section). It's encased in glass above the altar upstairs in the cathedral; follow the signs to the Camarín de la Virgen. The statue is never moved from the cathedral, as superstition suggests that its disturbance would precipitate a devastating flood of Lake Titicaca. The *camarín* (niche in which the statue is displayed) is open daily from 9 am to noon and 2 to 6 pm; admission is US$0.40.

Museo de la Catedral The cathedral museum contains some interesting articles. Don't miss the ostrich vases or the hundreds of paper cranes donated by a Japanese woman hedging her bets with the Virgin in the hope of bearing an intelligent child. It's open Sunday only from 8.45 am to noon; admission is US$0.50.

Museo en Miniatura
On one corner of the Plaza 2 de Febrero is the Museo en Miniatura, a large collection of tiny miniatures – bottles, dolls, furniture and even ceramic Bolivian market scenes. It's open daily from 9 am to 5 pm. Admission is US$0.50.

Cerro Calvario
Copacabana is set between two hills that offer bird's-eye views over both the town and the lake. The summit of Cerro Calvario can be reached in half an hour and is well worth the climb, particularly in the late afternoon, to see the sunset over the lake. The trail to the summit begins near the church at the end of Calle Destacamento 211 and climbs past the 14 Stations of the Cross.

Niño Calvario & Horca del Inca
The small but prominent hill east of town is called Niño Calvario (Little Calvary), also known as Seroka and by its original name, Kesanani. Its weirdly rugged rock formations and oddly-arranged boulders merit a couple of hours exploration. From the end of Calle Murillo, a trail leads uphill to the Horca del Inca (Inca Gallows), an odd trilithic gate perched on the hillside. This pre-Inca observatory, which was never used for stringing up disobedient Incas, is surrounded by pierced rocks that permit the sun's rays to pass through onto the lintel at the solstices.

The higher hill behind Niño Calvario, Cerro Sancollani, is flanked by Inca-era *asientos* (seats), agricultural terraces and numerous unrestored and little-known ruins. To get there, follow Calle Murillo to its end where, between two brightly coloured houses, it becomes a cobbled road. Fifty metres or so beyond this point, a crumbling stone route (probably an aqueduct) leads off to the left about a metre above the road level. The easiest access to the summit of Cerro Sancollani is from the saddle between it and Niño Calvario.

Intikala (Tribunal del Inca)
North of the cemetery on the south-eastern outskirts of town is a field of artificially sculpted boulders known as the Tribunal del Inca (Inca Tribunal). Its original purpose is unknown, but there are about seven carved stones with asientos, basins and *hornecinos* (niches), which probably once contained idols. During the rainy season, the place hops with thousands of tiny frogs.

LAKE TITICACA

Kusillata & Baño del Inca

A two-km walk along the Titicaca shoreline from the end of Calle Hugo Ballivián will bring you to a colonial manor building known as Kusillata, which has been converted into a small museum. Beside the manor is a pre-Columbian tunnel that was used to access the underground water supply. The carved stone water tank and spigot are known as the Baño del Inca (Inca Bath).

Organised Tours

Several tour agencies around town organise tours around Copacabana's environs. Wiñay Marka Tours, on Calle 6 de Agosto, does a US$5 half-day tour. The trip takes in the route to Isla del Sol via Yampupata, and includes a stop at the Gruta de Lourdes (a cave said to evoke images of its French namesake), a quick spin in a totora reed boat and 2½ hours on Isla del Sol.

The less formal agency at the Alojamiento San Jose (see Places to Stay) runs all-day tours by launch to Isla del Sol, taking in Pilko Kaina, the Escalera del Inca and Palacio del Inca at the Chincana ruins (see the Isla del Sol section) for US$5 per person. Half-day tours to only the southern end of Isla del Sol – returning in time for the buses to La Paz or Puno – cost US$4.

Special Events

Copacabana hosts three major annual fiestas. From 2 to 5 February, the town celebrates the Fiesta de la Virgen de Candelaria, in honour of the Dark Virgin of the Lake. Although the date is celebrated to varying degrees around Bolivia, Copacabana stages an especially big bash, and pilgrims and dancers come from Peru and around Bolivia. Traditional Aymara dances are performed and there's much music, drinking and feasting. On the third day, celebrations culminate with the gathering of 100 bulls in a stone corral along the Yampupata road. The braver (and drunker) of the town's citizens jump into the arena and try to avoid attack.

On Good Friday the town fills with *peregrinos* (pilgrims) who have travelled to Copacabana to do penance at the Stations of the Cross on Cerro Calvario. Many of them journey on foot from La Paz, 158 km away. Once on the summit, they light incense and purchase miniatures representing material possessions in the hope that the Virgin will bless them with the real thing during the year of their pilgrimage. Beginning at dusk from the cathedral, pilgrims join a solemn candlelit procession through town, led by a statue of Christ in a glass coffin and a replica of the Virgen de Candelaria, the patron saint of Copacabana and all Bolivia. A local priest relates the significance of the holiday through a microphone, a military band plays dirges and city hall's audio system broadcasts *Ave Maria* for all to hear.

Copacabana stages its biggest bash during the week of Bolivian Independence Day (the first week in August). The most animated of the town's annual festivities, it's characterised by pilgrimages, dancing, around-the-clock music, parades, brass bands, flute and panpipe ensembles, fireworks and staggeringly high – and continuous – consumption of alcohol. Although Copacabana is relatively free of petty thievery, this is a time to beware of light-fingered types who may prey on careless celebrants.

> ### Cha'lla
>
> The word *cha'lla* is used for any ritual blessing, toasting or offering to the powers that be, whether Inca, Aymara or Christian. On weekend mornings in front of the cathedral in Copacabana, cars, trucks and buses of pilgrims, visitors and even flota companies are decked out in garlands of real or plastic flowers, coloured ribbons, model reed boats, flags and even stuffed ducks. Petitions for protection are made to the Virgin and a ritual offering of alcohol is poured over the vehicles' tyres and bonnets, thereby consecrating them for the journey home. The vehicle cha'lla is especially popular with pilgrims visiting Copacabana between Good Friday and Easter. On one of my visits, one La Paz flota had brought a newly purchased fleet of buses for the spiritual baptism to prepare them for the Bolivian highways. ■

LAKE TITICACA

Places to Stay

For a town of its size, Copacabana is well-endowed with hotels, residenciales and alojamientos and is the least expensive town in Bolivia for accommodation. During fiestas everything fills up and prices increase up to three-fold, but at other times, you'll have no trouble finding a choice of inexpensive accommodation.

Despite its proximity to the lake, Copacabana's water and electric utilities are unpredictable. Many accommodation places – even budget places – commendably go to extreme efforts to fill water tanks in the morning (the supply is normally switched off at 11 am), so showers are available to guests at all hours.

Places to Stay – bottom end

Camping Although the slopes around Copacabana are generally steep and rocky, there are several excellent camp sites in the area. The field opposite the beach is fairly private and comfortable and the summits of both Niño Calvario and Cerro Sancollani have smooth, grassy saddle areas suitable for tent camping. They also provide magnificent views of the lake, the surrounding farms and villages, and the Andean Cordillera. Another pleasant camp site is the high point of the Inca road toward Yunguyo (Peru) at the foot of Cerro Sancollani, one km from the end of Calle Murillo.

Hotels For something different and extremely cheap, try the *Hospedaría*, in an old mansion with plenty of rooms overlooking a marvellous flowery courtyard. The gloomy medieval cells lack beds, but with a sleeping bag and ground protection, you can stay for as little as US$0.50 per person.

The small *Alojamiento Urinsaya* may look a bit shabby, but it's friendly and good value. Rooms cost US$1.50 per person; try for one of the clean, airy rooms upstairs (one is a six-bed dormitory). Hot water is available in the morning and there's a laundry sink and sundeck. The *Alojamiento San José* (☎ 2066) next door has hot water from 7 to 11 am and costs US$2 per person.

The budget travellers' choice is currently the *Alojamiento Emperador*, at Calle Murillo 235. This upbeat and colourfully speckled place charges US$1.50 per person with shared bath, and there's a sunny mezzanine ideal for lounging. The helpful staff happily provide visitor information. If you're in need of reading material, check out the travellers book exchange. For more speckled rocks, try out the nearby *Alojamiento Cochabamba*, which charges US$1.50 per person.

At the comfortable *Residencial Aransaya* (☎ 2229), single rooms without/with bath are US$4/5. Doubles are US$6/8. The sunny patio is especially inviting and if you crave conversation, turn to Carlos, their chatty bird-brained parrot who entertains diners with acrobatics above the patio.

The oddly designed but friendly and expanding *Alojamiento Aroma* (☎ 2004) may seem a construction zone dump from the ground floor, but the clean, cosy double rooms on the top floor cost only US$2 per person and open onto a sunny patio with tables and the best view in town. Viewless rooms cost US$1.60. Refreshments are available on the patio and you'll get hot showers all day.

Another excellent choice is the equally friendly – and ultra clean – *Alojamiento Oasis* (☎ 2037), on Calle Pando, which is dominated by a multicoloured pastel paint job. Rooms, some with carpeting, cost US$1.20 per person on weekdays and US$2 on Saturday night. Hot water in the communal showers is available at all hours. This place is destined to become a Copacabana favourite. If it's available, request room 14.

Nearer the lake is the basic and friendly *Alojamiento Kota Kahuaña*, which charges US$1.20/2 per person without/with bath. Seven-bed dormitory rooms with a private bath cost US$1.50 per person. There's hot water all day, guests have access to kitchen facilities and some upstairs rooms have a lake view.

If you don't mind tiny rooms, the friendly *Residencial Solar* is a good choice. The spacious rooftop patio has lake views and full exposure to the sun. Singles/doubles/triples with bath cost US$5/8.40/10.50. Without bath, singles are US$4 and triples, US$9.40. Rooms with both a single and double bed (no bath) cost US$6.20 and with two double beds, US$8.40. Watch your head on the stairways! The annexe *Alojamiento Solar*, around the corner, has acceptable accommodation for US$2 per person.

The refurbished *Hotel Ambassador* (☎ 2216) has comfortable rooms with bath for US$6.20 per person. Space heaters are available upon request. This is the acting youth hostel in Copacabana.

The friendly *Residencial Porteñita* (☎ 361431, La Paz), with clean rooms, a very leafy patio and some lovely trees, charges US$2/3 per person without/with private bath.

Residencial Sucre (☎ 2080), on Calle Murillo, seems more like a mid-range hotel than a budget place, and has been recommended for its friendliness, washing facilities and good-value accommodation. Rooms without/with private bath cost US$2/3 per person. Colour TV costs an additional US$2 per person.

Places to Stay – middle

Most organised tour groups wind up at *Hotel Playa Azul* (☎ 2227). Single/double rooms cost US$22/31 with bath and an obligatory three-meal plan, which is a shame, as Copacabana has several restaurants worth trying. Triple and quadruple rooms are also available.

A nicer alternative with a good lake view is the new three-star colonial-style *Residencial Rosario del Lago* (☎ 325348, fax 375532, La Paz), which is owned by the same folks who run Residencial Rosario in La Paz. Single/double rooms without bath cost US$14/18; with bath they're US$23/32 and family rooms accommodating two adults and two children cost US$36. All rates include a buffet continental breakfast.

The *Hotel Prefectural* (☎ 2002), near the beach, affords a lovely view of the lake and surrounding mountains. It's utterly dead during the week but springs to life on weekends. Upstairs you'll find table tennis and billiards tables, and there's a decent dining room with live entertainment on weekends. A few rooms even have lake-view sundecks. Clean but stark rooms cost US$12 per person.

Places to Eat

The local speciality is trucha criolla (salmon trout) from Lake Titicaca, which may be the world's largest and most delicious trout. The fish were introduced in 1939 by foreign pisciculturists in order to increase the protein content in the local diet. For years the trout were also tinned and exported, but that ended when fish stocks became severely depleted. Otherwise, there's little gastronomic originality in Copacabana; everything is served up with greasy rice, fried potatoes and lettuce.

As usual, the bargain basement is the market food hall, where numerous small operations compete fiercely for your business. You can eat a generous meal of trout or beef for a pittance, while a contingent of the town's canine population patiently awaits handouts. If you're up to an insulin shock in the morning, treat yourself to a breakfast of hot api morado and syrupy buñuelos.

A favourite restaurant that is pleasantly accessible to slim budgets is *Pensión Aransaya* on Calle 6 de Agosto. The food is especially good and the service friendly. Plan on about US$4 for a meal of trout, trimmings and a tall, cold beer.

At *Snack 6 de Agosto*, the service may be crusty, but the exceptionally well prepared food is probably the best in town and the patio seating area can be heavenly on a typically sunny day. The milanesa napolitana is especially recommended, as are the breakfasts, chicken dishes, pique a lo macho, pejerrey, and the speciality, suckling pig. A meal of trout prepared to order costs US$3.50.

The snazzy exterior of *Puerta del Sol*, on Calle 6 de Agosto, unfortunately belies its rather comatose service and mediocre food. (The spaghetti I ordered here was the second-worst meal I've had in Bolivia!) and the market meals are better at a fraction of the cost. Just opposite is the quite acceptable and less pretentious *Restaurant Fantástico*, which specialises in good breakfasts, trout and suckling pig.

Don't be fooled by the name of the *Restaurant Napoles*; the original chef left so it no longer serves Italian cuisine. It's still friendly, however, and serves good American and continental breakfasts, and a large range of Bolivian dishes, including (of course) trout. *Snack Cristal* on Calle Murillo also specialises in trout and is repeatedly recommended for inexpensive meals.

Restaurant *Tito Yupanqui* at Calle General Gonzalo Jáuregui 119 is known for its vegetable soup. *Café Video*, half a block from the beach opposite Alojamiento Las Playas, is best known for nightly showings of videos about Copacabana. They begin at 8 pm.

The Tourist Palace on Calle 6 de Agosto has an extensive menu. It serves continental and English breakfasts as well as trout dishes, delicious pejerrey and other standards, and an unnamed parrot provides background sound effects.

On Calle General Gonzalo Jáuregui near 3 de Mayo is *La Merced*, a lovely courtyard restaurant with friendly owners. It's a great place to spend a mellow afternoon drinking a *Paceña* or two over some journal or letter writing. And of course, they serve trout.

On sunny days, *El Rey* and other beachfront restaurants have tables outside where you can have a drink and observe quintessential Bolivian beach life, such as it is.

Things to Buy

Local specialities include handmade miniatures of totora reed boats, enormous peanuts, unusual varieties of Andean potatoes, and *pasankalla* (puffed *choclo* with caramel). This last item is a South American version of popcorn which, if crispy, can be quite tasty. You'll also find shops that produce the dark-coloured felt derby hats worn by local women. Vehicle adornments used in the cha'lla, miniatures and religious paraphernalia are sold in stalls in front of the cathedral.

Miniatures are also sold en masse atop Cerro Calvario.

Getting There & Away

The impressive journey between La Paz and Copacabana follows a scenic route across the Altiplano and along the shoreline to the Estrecho de Tiquina(Straits of Tiquina). Vehicles are ferried by barge across these straits, between San Pedro and San Pablo, while passengers ride in launches. These cost a very reasonable US$0.20 per person, which is payable at the dock ticket offices. Even passengers on public buses must pay for the ferry. A bridge across the straits is now in the planning stages.

Bus Two major bus companies also run between La Paz and Copacabana. Both Transportes Manco Capac (☎ 350033, La Paz) and Transtur 2 de Febrero (☎ 377181, La Paz) have three to four daily connections to La Paz, with extra departures on Sunday. The spectacular trip costs US$2 and takes four hours. Buses to Yunguyo (Peru) cost US$0.30 and depart when full – approximately every half-hour – from customs at western end of town.

The cheapest way to reach Puno (Peru) is to catch a bus or minibus from Plaza Sucre to the border at Yunguyo (US$0.40), about 15 km away. From Yunguyo, you'll find frequent onward transport to Puno (two hours). In the opposite direction, most transport from Puno to Copacabana departs between 8 and 9 am. If you require a visa to enter Bolivia, you'll find consulates in both Puno and Yunguyo (the former is not recommended). Non-Bolivian Latin Americans entering Bolivia here must register with the police in Yunguyo before crossing the border. See Peru in the Getting There & Away chapter for more information.

Minibus Tourist micros and minibuses between Puno and La Paz provide the best sightseeing opportunities along the dramatic road between Tiquina, Copacabana and Peru. When buying a ticket from a minibus/

travel agency, you can arrange to break the journey in Copacabana, then continue to La Paz or Puno with the same agency. If there's space available, casual travellers can catch them in Copacabana.

Any minibus with Peruvian number plates will be headed to either Yunguyo or Puno. The US$2 to US$2.50 trip takes two or three hours, depending on the whims of the Peruvian and Bolivian immigration offices.

Most micros and minibuses gather in front of the Pensión Aransaya and Hotel Ambassador between noon and 2 pm. The fare to either La Paz or Puno is US$5. Although there are plenty of them, many arrive full, so if you want to be sure of a seat, book tickets in advance through the Pensión Aransaya, the Hotel Playa Azul or one of the tour agencies around town. On Saturday and Sunday, services are crowded so try to book in advance. Note that Peruvian time is one hour behind Bolivian time.

Boat The days of haggling over transport to Isla del Sol are effectively over. Now all you have to do is go down to the beach in the morning and buy a US$2 ticket from one of the two cooperative offices to be on the next boat going. Some boat drivers, however, may still try to gain advantage with foreigners if they think they'll get away with it.

If you're going round-trip with the same boat, arrange your length of stay with the driver in advance or you may find yourself with just 15 minutes on the island. Once you strike a deal, stand your ground. Attempts to add on extra charges and decrease your time on the island are almost standard practice.

Getting Around
Bicycles can be hired at Calle 6 de Agosto 125 or on the beach, but by local standards, foreigners are charged relatively high rates: US$1.25 per hour, US$5 for six hours and US$8 for 12 hours (6 am to 6 pm).

COPACABANA TO YAMPUPATA TREK
From Copacabana, a particularly enjoyable way of reaching Isla del Sol is to trek along the lake shore to the village of Yampupata, which lies just a short rowboat ride from the ruins of Pilko Kaina on Isla del Sol. If you're arriving from La Paz, this four to five-hour walk will help accustom your lungs to the altitude, and the glorious scenery along the way presents a suitable prologue to a couple of days trekking around Isla del Sol.

For a longer trek, you can also opt to walk the pre-Hispanic route from Cruce Paquipujio, near the Estrecho de Tiquina. This route passes through the village of Chisi, where there's a Templete Semi-subterráneo that dates back to the pre-Tiahuanaco Chavín culture. It then continues through San Francisco, Chachacoyas, Kollasuyos, Santa Ana and the lovely cobblestoned village of Sampaya, which lies on the hill top about five km from Yampupata. This route joins up with the Copacabana to Yampupata trek at Titicachi.

Access
The route starts along Calle Pando in Copacabana.

The Route
From Copacabana, strike out north-east along the road running across the flat plain. After about 40 minutes, the road turns sharply left and climbs gently onto a ledge overlooking the lake. About one to 1½ hours from Copacabana, you'll pass the isolated Hinchaca fish hatchery and reforestation project on your left. Beyond the hatchery, you should cross the stream on your left and follow the obvious Inca road up the steep hill. Just above the stream, you'll pass what is variously called the Gruta de Lourdes or Gruta de Fátima, a cave that for locals evokes images of its French or Portuguese namesake, respectively. This stretch shows some good stone paving and makes a considerable short cut, rejoining the road at the crest of the hill.

From here, the road passes through more populated areas. At the fork just below the crest, bear left and descend to the shore and into the village of Titicachi, where there's a shop selling overpriced soft drinks and staple items.

In and around Titicachi are several sites of interest, among them the Tiahuanacota Inca cemetery, some pre-Inca walls and on the offshore islet of Jiskha Huata, the Museo de Aves Acuáticos (Museum of Aquatic Birds). This small display of Lake Titicaca birdlife, is reached only by boat. While you're in the area, watch in the reeds for the real things: the black duck-like bird known as *cho'k'a*; the grey-coloured, blue-beaked water bird *pan'a*; and a small dark-brown bird with tiny eggs, the *solojita*, among others.

At the next village, Sicuani, José Quispe Mamani and his wife, Margarita Arias, and daughter Rosemeri, run the *Hostal Yampu* (the name is Aymara for 'reed boat'). You can't miss it – just look for the bright rose-coloured house. Basic accommodation with bucket showers costs US$1 per person; breakfast and lunch cost US$1 each and dinner is US$0.50. Hikers can pop in for a beer or soft drink and for US$0.75, you can take a magical spin around the bay in a totora reed boat. José is a very amenable character and asserts that his prices are 'economical and within reach of all travellers'.

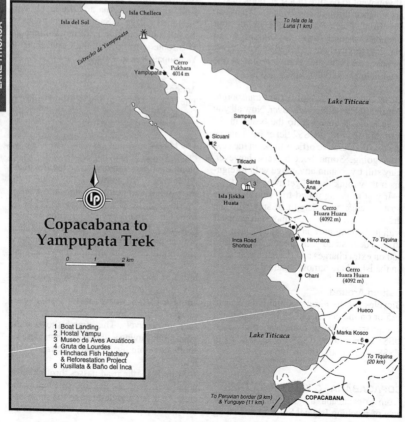

Copacabana to Yampupata Trek

0   1   2 km

1 Boat Landing
2 Hostal Yampu
3 Museo de Aves Acuáticos
4 Gruta de Lourdes
5 Hinchaca Fish Hatchery
   & Reforestation Project
6 Kusillata & Baño del Inca

To Isla de la Luna (1 km)

Isla Chelleca

Isla del Sol

Estrecho de Yampupata

Cerro Pukhara 4014 m

Yampupata

Lake Titicaca

Sampaya

Sicuani

Titicachi

Isla Jiskha Huata

Santa Ana

Cerro Huara Huara (4092 m)

Inca Road Shortcut

Hinchaca

To Tiquina

Cerro Huara Huara (4092 m)

Chani

Hueco

Marka Kosco

To Tiquina (20 km)

Lake Titicaca

To Peruvian border (9 km) & Yunguyo (11 km)

COPACABANA

Between four and five hours walking from Copacabana, you'll reach Yampupata, a collection of adobe houses on the lake shore, where you can hire a rowboat to take you across the Estrecho de Yampupata to Pilko Kaina for US$1 per person and to the Escalera del Inca (see the Isla del Sol section) for US$1.70. If you opt for the Escalera del Inca, make sure that's where you're dropped off; some boat owners will assume you don't know any better and try to drop you off at Pilko Kaina, anyway. Also, resist attempts to add extra charges, such as invented 'landing fees'.

Getting There & Away

The easiest way to and from Yampupata and Copacabana is on the daily minibus, which leaves Copacabana at around 8 am and from Yampupata at 9.30 am. There are also boats leaving Copacabana between 8 and 9 am every Thursday, Saturday and Sunday (US$2 per person), and a Saturday *camión* (open truck), which costs US$0.75 per person and leaves in the early to mid-afternoon (the trip may be slow, since it stops to sell produce). Or you can walk, of course.

ISLA DEL SOL

Isla del Sol (Island of the Sun) was known to early inhabitants as Titicachi, from which Lake Titicaca takes its name. This island has been identified as the birthplace of several revered entities, including the sun itself. There the bearded white leader/deity Viracocha and the first Incas, Manco Capac and his sister/wife Mama Ocllo, mystically appeared under direct orders of the sun. Modern-day Aymara and Quechua peoples of Peru and Bolivia accept these legends as their creation story.

The 5000 people of Isla del Sol are distributed between the main settlements of Cha'llapampa, near the island's northern end; Cha'lla, which backs up a lovely sandy beach on the central east coast; and Yumani, which occupies a hill top above the Escalera del Inca.

Exploring the Island

With a host of ancient ruins, tiny traditional villages, beautiful walking routes and a distinctly Aegean look, Isla del Sol merits a couple of days. Visitors can wander through the ruins at the island's northern and southern ends; explore its dry slopes, covered with sweet smelling *koa* (incense) brush; and hike over the ancient *pampas* (terraces), which are still cultivated by island families.

There are no vehicles on Isla del Sol, so visitors are limited to hiking or travelling by boat. The main ports are at Pilko Kaina, the Escalera del Inca and Cha'llapampa. There's also a small port at Japapi on the south-west coast.

Networks of walking tracks make exploration easy, but the altitude may take a toll. You can do a walking circuit of the island sites in a long day, but you'd be happier devoting a day each to the northern and southern ends.

Most people stay either in Yumani, where there are three decent guesthouses, or in Cha'lla, where Juan Mamani runs a basic guesthouse on the wide and lovely beach.

Southern End

Pilko Kaina Near the southern tip of the island is the prominent ruins complex Pilko Kaina, which sits well camouflaged against a steep terraced slope. The best known site is the two-level Palacio del Inca. The rectangular windows and doors taper upward from their sill and thresholds to narrower lintels that cover them on top. The arched roof vault was once covered with flagstone shingles and reinforced with a layer of mud and straw.

Here you'll find a tourist-oriented restaurant and a basic hostel. Foreigners pay US$1 per person to visit the ruins complex.

Escalera del Inca & Fuente del Inca About an hour's walk north of Pilko Kaina you'll reach the Escalera del Inca/Fuente del Inca complex. Here, streams of fresh water gush from a natural spring and pour down three artificial stone channels alongside a beautifully constructed Inca-era staircase. Early

LAKE TITICACA

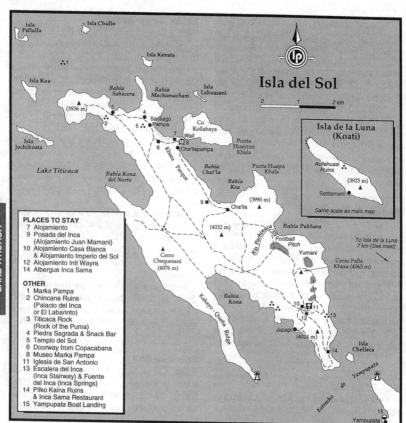

Isla del Sol

Isla de la Luna (Koati)

Same scale as main map

PLACES TO STAY
7   Alojamiento
9   Posada del Inca
     (Alojamiento Juan Mamani)
10 Alojamiento Casa Blanca
     & Alojamiento Imperio del Sol
12 Alojamiento Inti Wayra
14 Albergue Inca Sama

OTHER
1   Marka Pampa
2   Chincana Ruins
     (Palacio del Inca
     or El Labarinto)
3   Titicaca Rock
     (Rock of the Puma)
4   Piedra Sagrada & Snack Bar
5   Templo del Sol
6   Doorway from Copacabana
8   Museo Marka Pampa
11 Iglesia de San Antonio
13 Escalera del Inca
     (Inca Stairway) & Fuente
     del Inca (Inca Springs)
14 Pilko Kaina Ruins
     & Inca Sama Restaurant
15 Yampupata Boat Landing

Spaniards believed it was a Fountain of Youth. This incongruous water has inspired a lovely terraced and cultivated water garden on either side of the staircase. The fountain provides a bountiful source of water for Yumani people, who come with their donkeys to fetch water and carry it up the steep trail to their homes on the ridge.

Yumani In Yumani, near the ridge, you'll see the small Iglesia de San Antonio, which serves the southern half of the island. Here you'll find three guesthouses and fabulous views over the water to Isla de la Luna. You

can also climb up onto the ridge for a view down to the deep sapphire-coloured Bahía Kona on the western shore. From the crest, you'll find routes leading downhill to the village of Japapi and north along the ridge to Cha'llapampa and the Chincana complex at the island's northern end.

Kakayo-Queña Ridge With extra time, you can make your way over the isthmus and up onto the Kakayo-Queña Ridge, which is the island's south-western extremity. This prominent feature slopes more gently on the east than it does in the west. A walk along the ridge to the lighthouse on the southern end can be quite serene, but will require at least a half-day from Yumani.

Northern End

There are two major routes between the northern and southern ends of Isla del Sol. One winds scenically through the fields, hamlets and villages and around the bays and headlands above the coast. The shorter and more dramatic route begins on the ridge in Yumani and heads north, roughly following the almost uninhabited ridge north to the Chincana complex. The views down to both coasts of the island are nothing short of spectacular and you'll encounter few people.

About half an hour from Yumani, you'll reach a four-way trail junction: the track to the left leads to the shore at Bahía Kona; the one to the right descends to Bahía Kea; and straight ahead it continues along the ridge to Cha'llapampa and the Chincana ruins complex.

Cha'llapampa Most boat tours visiting the northern ruins land at Cha'llapampa, which straddles a slender isthmus. The wall dividing the village from the Kollabaya peninsula was designed to keep people out of the planted area; in the growing season, children aren't allowed onto the peninsula, lest they trample the precious crops.

The attraction is the well-presented museum of artefacts excavated in 1992 from Marka Pampa, an underwater archaeological site in eight metres of water, at the centre of a triangle formed by the islands of Chullo, Koa and Pallalla. It's fancifully referred to by locals as *la ciudad submergida*, the 'sunken city', in reference to a legend that a city and temple existed between the islands of Koa and Pallalla in an age when the lake level was lower than today.

This small museum displays a boggling variety of interesting stuff: ancient spoons, blades, anthropomorphic figurines, stone tools, shells, animal bones, pot shards, Tiahuanaco-era artefacts, pots found in chullpas, vases, pitchers, bowls, skull parts,

Medallion from Marka Pampa

a jaguar statue, puma-shaped ceramic koa censors and cups resembling Monty Python's Holy Grail. Most interesting, however, are the Marka Pampa stone boxes and their contents: a medallion, a cup, a puma and a woman, all made of gold. The boxes were so expertly carved and capped that their contents remained dry until their modern discovery. For foreigners, admission is US$1 (unless you've already paid for a Chincana ticket). If there's no attendant, ask around for Señor Hiriberto Ticoma, who has the key.

Piedra Sagrada & Templo del Sol From Cha'llapampa, the Chincana route parallels the beach, climbing gently along an ancient route to the isthmus at Santiago Pampa (Kasapata).

Immediately east of the trail, an odd artificially carved boulder stands upright in a small field. This is known as the Piedra Sagrada (Sacred Stone). There are theories that it was used as an execution block for those convicted of wrongdoing or as a huaca, a rainmaking stone, but no-one is entirely certain of its purpose. Today, its main function seems to be dragging flagging tourists off their feet and onto the picnic bench for cold beers and sandwiches, which are served up by an enterprising local. Considering the location, they're good value.

Over the track, just south-west of the Piedra Sagrada, are the ancient walls of the complex known as the Templo del Sol, the purpose of which is also unknown. Although little remains, it contains the only Bolivian example of expert Inca stonework comparable with that of Cuzco.

Chincana Ruins Chincana, near the northern tip of Isla del Sol, is the island's most spectacular ruins complex. The main feature is the Palacio del Inca, also known as El Labarinto (Labyrinth) or by its Aymara name, Incanotapa. This maze of stone walls and tiny doorways overlooks a lovely white beach lapped by deep blue waters.

Backing up the ruins, about 150m southeast, is the Mesa Ceremónica (Ceremonial Table), which appears to be a conveniently-placed picnic spot – and indeed, it's often used as such. It's thought to have been the site of human and animal sacrifice. Behind (east of) the table stretches the large rock known as Titicaca – or more accurately, Titi Khar'ka, the Rock of the Puma – which features in the Inca creation legend. It's likely that the name derives from its shape which, when viewed from the south-east, resembles a crouching cat.

Three natural features on the rock's western face also figure in legend. Near the northern end is one dubbed the Cara de Viracocha (Face of Viracocha – or is it the face of a puma?), which takes some imagination to distinguish. At the southern end are four distinctive elongated niches. The two on the right are locally called the Refugio del Sol (Refuge of the Sun) and those on the left, the Refugio de la Luna (Refuge of the Moon).

In the surface stone immediately south of the rock, you'll pass the Huellas del Sol (Footprints of the Sun). These natural markings resemble footprints and have inspired the notion that they were made by the sun after its birth on Titicaca rock.

Admission to Chincana is US$1 per person for foreigners; a ticket from the museum in Cha'llapampa also covers entry to Chincana.

Most north-end tours begin at the boat landing in Cha'llapampa, and follow the prominent Inca route past the Piedra Sagrada and Templo del Sol to Chincana. Another access route is along the ridge from Yumani. When you reach a point directly above Cha'llapampa, leave the main trail and continue straight ahead along a jumble of light tracks for two km, picking your way over shrub-covered slopes (mostly below the ridge) and around bizarre rock outcrops.

Cha'lla The agreeable village of Cha'lla, the site of the island's secondary school, stretches along a magnificent sandy beach that appears to be taken straight out of a holiday brochure for the Greek islands. It's a great place to soak up the sun and watch people playing football and families strolling. Literally one metre off the sand is the popular restaurant and Posada del Inca guesthouse, run by the friendly Juan Mamani.

Places to Stay

You can camp just about anywhere on the island but it's best to set up away from villages, avoiding cultivated land. There are plenty of deserted beaches and the wild and practically uninhabited western slopes of the island are particularly secluded.

One of the friendliest hostels is the basic but popular *Posada del Inca*, also known as *Alojamiento Juan Mamani*, right on the beach near the school at Cha'lla. Juan is among the best sources of information on island ruins and hiking routes, and the colourful garden and outdoor tables tempt non-guests to stop for snacks and conversation. For beds, blankets and use of a stove, Juan charges US$1.20 per person.

Near the ridge top in Yumani village, above the Fuente del Inca, are three nice options. The modern-looking *Casa Blanca*, has two rooms upstairs: a double and a dorm room that accommodate up to five people for US$1.50 per person. Meals are available on request. However, the outdoor facilities are straight out of the Middle Ages.

Nearby, on the same ridge, is the beautiful

and amicable *Hostal Inti Wayra* (☎ 355222, La Paz), which dominates one of the island's finest vantage points. You'll have a great view from any room, but those upstairs are more open and spacious (they aren't for sleepwalkers!), and there's an unsurpassed rooftop vista over the water to Isla de la Luna (the full moon rises behind the island). Rooms with communal facilities cost US$1.50 per person; American breakfasts are US$1 and other meals (including vegetarian options) are US$1.20 each. Negative points include the pair of unhappy caged pumas, which screech through the night (and have been known to get rough with their keeper); and a tendency toward convenient mistakes on final accounts.

A third option is the new *Imperio del Sol*, run by Gualberto Mamani, with seven rooms and space for 18. As with anywhere in Yumani, there's a great view. Rooms cost US$1.50 per person.

The *Albergue Inca Sama* at Pilko Kaina offers very simple accommodation for US$1.50. You can prebook through Playa Azul in Copacabana.

In Cha'llapampa, an aid project is building a *comedor popular* (public dining room) with alojamiento accommodation upstairs. When it's finished, you'll find a bed for about US$1.20. Also in Cha'llapampa, Señor Lucio Arias Ticoma runs an eight-bed *alojamiento*. He charges US$1 for camping and US$1.50 for beds, and can also provide meals. It has received mixed reviews; take special care with your valuables.

Places to Eat

The Posada del Inca in Cha'llapampa and the three Yumani guesthouses prepare meals and snacks for about US$1.20 per meal. The only restaurant is *Albergue Inca Sama*, beside the Pilko Kaina ruins, which specialises in trout; for anything else, establish prices beforehand. It caters mainly to day-trippers visiting the ruins. Cooked snacks, such as potatoes, eggs and so on, are sold to arriving tours near the Escalera del Inca, in lower Yumani.

The lake water is generally clean, but should be boiled or purified before drinking.

Getting There & Away

Boat From Copacabana, there are numerous launches and sailing boats available for the journey to Isla del Sol. The set rate for boat transport between Copacabana and Isla del Sol is US$2 per person each way. Tickets may be purchased at the ticket offices on the beach or at agencies in Copacabana (see Organised Tours in the Copacabana section). Boats to the northern end of the island land at Cha'llapampa, while those going to the southern end land at either Pilko Kaina or the Escalera del Inca.

Charter If you have a group or there aren't enough people to justify a departure, individual charter is also available. To hire a launch, you'll pay about US$30 per day for up to 12 passengers. Sailing boats cost about US$15, but the journey takes up to four hours each way, and you may end up rowing. From Isla del Sol to Isla de la Luna, you'll pay US$12 return for a launch charter and US$8 for a sailing boat. In a sailing boat, the trip can be done in four hours each way, but allow longer, as the wind can be fickle.

The main drawback to return trips with the same boat is that your desire to explore the island will normally conflict with the driver's aim to get home as quickly as possible. When negotiating rates, make it clear how much time you'll be spending on the island, then politely demand that the driver honour the agreement and resist any attempts at collecting more money.

It's wise to carry your lunch and ample water, since it's not possible to visit the ruins *and* the villages in a half-day trip. Also, remember that the sun was born here and he's still going strong: a good sunscreen is essential, particularly on the water.

If you're staying overnight on the islands, return transport will normally be a matter of hit or miss, but there are boats every day from Cha'llapampa and the Escalera del Inca. Any of the island guest houses can help with information.

Organised Tours Titicaca Tours offers US$4 return tickets that are good for three days on the island. Boats leave from Copacabana at 8 am daily and return from the Escalera del Inca at 10.30 am and from Cha'llapampa at 2.30 pm. Buy tickets at the beach office in Copacabana or Hostal Inti Wayra on the island.

The standard rate for guided day tours, including return transport from Copacabana and stops at the northern or southern ruins complexes, is US$5 per person, excluding admission to the ruins.

Walking Although there have been lots of miracles at Lake Titicaca, you can't really walk to Isla del Sol. It is possible, however, to walk from Copacabana to the village of Yampupata on the mainland, just a short distance by rowing boat from the island's southern tip. For details, see the Copacabana to Yampupata Trek section, earlier in this chapter.

ISLA DE LA LUNA

Legend has it that the Island of the Moon, or Koati, was the place where Viracocha commanded the moon to rise into the sky. This peaceful little island is surrounded by clear aquamarine water and a walk up to the summit eucalyptus grove, where shepherds graze their flocks, is rewarded by a spectacular vista of Cerro Illampu and the entire snow-covered Cordillera Real.

The ruins of an Inca nunnery for the Vírgenes del Sol (Virgins of the Sun), known as Iñak Uyu (or Acllahuasi), occupies an amphitheatre-like valley on the north-eastern shore. It's constructed of well-laboured stone seated in adobe mortar. Foreigners pay US$1 admission to the temple.

Places to Stay

It's possible to camp anywhere on the small island away from the settlement but expect a bit of attention.

Getting There & Away

From the Escalera del Inca, you can charter launches to Isla de la Luna for US$12.50 return, for up to 12 people. Sailing boats or rowboats, with sailors or rowers, respectively, cost US$8.50 return. Either will hold up to about six people.

THE NORTH-EASTERN SHORE

If you're heading north-west from Huatajata toward the Peru-Bolivia border area at Puerto Acosta, you may be delayed by a couple of sites of minor interest.

About 90 km north of La Paz, along the road to Sorata, is the large and aloof market town of Achacachi where you'll find a couple of less than welcoming alojamientos. The church in Ancoraimes, about 20 km north of Achacachi, features a lovely ornamental screen above the altar. In the colonial township of Carabuco is a colourful Sunday market. From Escoma (165 km north-west of La Paz) you can strike off toward the Cordillera Apolobamba.

Just offshore near Puerto Acosta are a couple of submerged stone piers and breakwaters that may date from pre-Inca times. In 1980, however, diver and underwater researcher Carlos Ponce suggested that they may have been constructed as recently as 1900. There's little solid evidence for either notion.

Getting There & Away

Inexpensive micros run occasionally from the cemetery district in La Paz to Puerto Acosta, near the Peruvian border, but beyond there, you'll probably have to rely on camiones. For information on the Cordillera Apolobamba region, see the Cordilleras & Yungas chapter.

GUAQUI

Three hours by bus from La Paz, Guaqui sits beside, and partially beneath, Lago Huyñaymarka, the southern extension of Lake Titicaca. It lies only 20 minutes by micro beyond Tiahuanaco, near the Peruvian frontier at Desaguadero. This tranquil little Altiplano town has a truly beautiful church with a silver altar and some colonial artwork inside. Most of the excitement Guaqui ever sees is during the riotous Fiesta de Santiago in the final week of July.

Evidence of the 1986 flooding, which left half the town in ruin, is still apparent. There's no longer a train service from La Paz, and the famous Guaqui-Puno lake steamer was discontinued when the lake port disappeared beneath rising flood waters.

Places to Stay & Eat

The *Residencial Guaqui*, near the port, is really the only accommodation in town. It was damaged in the flooding but has since undergone repairs. Rooms, which aren't terribly secure, cost US$2 per person. There's a pleasant courtyard and the friendly attached restaurant is the best option in town.

Getting There & Away

Most of the Tiahuanaco buses from La Paz continue to Guaqui. The first micros from Guaqui back to Tiahuanaco and La Paz leave at 5.30 am and there's something at least every hour until about 4 or 5 pm. They leave from the main avenue in the lower part of town.

There's also Espreso Desaguadero, on Calle Isaac Tamayo, near the corner of Manco Capac; minibuses leave for Guaqui and Desaguadero at 9.30 am and 2 and 5.30 pm. The fare is US$2.20. Espreso Desaguadero is also establishing direct services between La Paz and Puno, which will run hourly from 7 am.

From Guaqui, you'll find minibuses to Desaguadero, on the Peruvian border, for US$1. After completing the normally quirky immigration formalities at Desaguadero, you'll find lots of Peruvian services along the lake shore to Puno and Yunguyo (from where you can cut back into Bolivia at Copacabana).

LAKE TITICACA

Southern Altiplano

Stretching southward from La Paz to the Chilean and Argentine frontiers and beyond is a harsh, sparsely populated wilderness of scrubby windswept basins, lonely peaks and glaring, almost lifeless salt deserts. This is the archetypal Altiplano, a Tibet-like land of lonely mirages, indeterminable distances and an overwhelming sense of solitude. Though the air retains little warmth, the land and sky meet in waves of shimmering reflected heat and the horizon disappears. Stark mountains seem to hover somewhere beyond reality, and the nights are just as haunting, with black skies and icy stars. The moment the sun sets – or even passes behind a cloud – you'll realise this air has teeth.

During the Cretaceous period some 100 million years ago, the vast Altiplano plateau was a deep intermontane valley. Erosion in those mountains filled the valley with a 15,000m-deep deposit of sediment to create the base for the present-day Altiplano. With such porous alluvial soil, the basin's fertility might seem predictable, but the presence of salts, lack of adequate moisture and a rocky surface character make agriculture a challenging venture.

The relatively few inhabitants of the Southern Altiplano are among the world's hardiest souls, and many live at the ragged edge of human endurance. They contend with wind, drought, bitter cold and high altitude with few modern conveniences to make the harsh conditions more bearable. The *campesino* miners, farmers and herders of the Altiplano labour throughout their lives to wrest an existence from this land, and deserve a great deal of respect for their accomplishments.

Even given the opportunity of relative prosperity in the developing lowlands, few Aymara people have chosen to leave their ancestral homes. This is the same hardy culture that managed to resist efforts by the Incas to assimilate it, body and soul, into the empire. The Aymara refused the Quechua

Highlights

- Feel small at the foot of Parque Nacional Sajama's hulking Nevado Sajama volcano
- Follow in the footsteps of Butch Cassidy and the Sundance Kid in the hills and cactus-spiked canyons and *quebradas* around Tupiza
- Experience the unearthly geology of Bolivia's remote south-west highlands with their brine-splashed landscape of steaming volcanos, hot springs and flamingo-filled lakes
- See the enormous spikes of Comanche's 12m *Puya raimondii* erupt into flower for the first and only time in its 60 to 100-year life cycle
- Join in Oruro's wild annual La Diablada carnival celebration or scale nearby Rumi Campana with local rock climbers

language and the Inca culture, and was the only conquered tribe to get away with it.

The sheltered and spectacular red rock country around the peaceful town of Tupiza represents a gentler side of south-western Bolivia, but over the years, its population has swelled with *mineros despedidos* (laid-off miners), victims of privatisation and labour strife in the mines of Oruro and Potosí.

Economically, this mineral-rich region

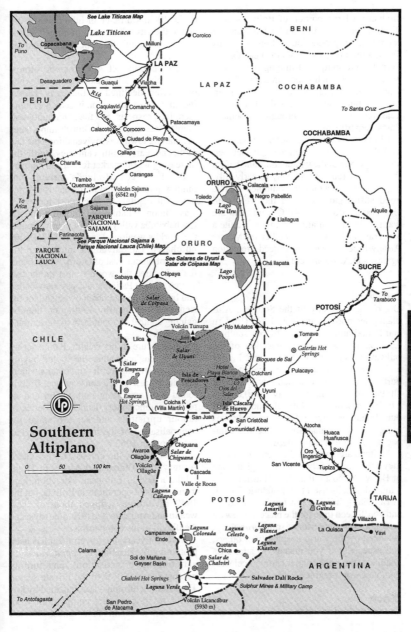

Southern
Altiplano

produces a large portion of Bolivia's non-illicit exports. Oruro and Llallagua are centres of tin production and an enormous tin smelter operates at Vinto, near Oruro. Remote and antiquated mining operations, which dip into rich concentrations of antimony, bismuth, silver, lead, zinc, copper, salt, sulphur, magnesium and other buried treasures, are scattered throughout southern Potosí department.

Climatically, the best months to visit are probably August, September and October, after the worst of the winter chills and before the summer rains. From May to early July, night time temperatures combined with a good stiff wind can bring the wind chill temperature down to -40°C. Summers are warmer, but for an arid area, there's quite a lot of rainfall between November and March. At any time of year, you'll need protection against sun, wind and cold.

ORURO

Oruro, the only city of the Southern Altiplano, lies north of the salty lakes Uru Uru and Poopó and three hours by bus south of La Paz. It sits at the intersection of the railway lines between Cochabamba, La Paz and Chile/Argentina, crowded against a colourful range of mineral-rich low hills at an altitude of 3702m. The city's 150,000 to 170,000 inhabitants, 90% of whom are of pure Indian heritage, refer to themselves as *quirquinchos* (armadillos), after the carapaces used in their *charangos*.

Visitors are rarely indifferent to Oruro; they either love it or hate it. Although it's one of Bolivia's most culturally colourful cities – indeed, it calls itself the 'Folkloric Capital of Bolivia' – there are few tourist attractions and you'll need time for the place to grow on you. The crusty exterior of some *orureños* is balanced by the warm hospitality of others, and especially if you manage to attend La Diablada, the wild annual carnival celebration, you won't regret a visit.

History

Oruro, founded in 1606, owes its existence to the 10-sq-km range of hills rising 350m above the city. Chock full of copper, silver and tin, these hills form the city's economic backbone.

Early mining activities focused almost exclusively on silver extraction, but when production declined in the early 1800s, Indian workers moved on in search of more lucrative prospects, and the community was more or less abandoned. Oruro's importance as a mining town was revived during the late 19th and early 20th centuries, with the increasing world market for tin and copper.

By the 1920s, Bolivia's thriving tin-mining industry rested in the hands of three powerful capitalists. The most renowned was Simon I Patiño, an Indian from the Cochabamba valley who disputedly became the world's wealthiest man. In 1897, Patiño purchased La Salvadora mine near the village of Uncia, east of Oruro, which eventually became the world's most productive source of tin. Patiño's success snowballed and by 1924, he had taken ownership of the rich mines at nearby Llallagua, thereby gaining control of about 50% of the nation's tin output.

Once secure in his wealth, Patiño set up house in England, where he started buying up European and North American smelters and tin interests. As a consequence, Bolivia found itself exporting both its tin and its profits. Public outcry launched a series of labour uprisings and set the stage for nationalisation of the mines by Victor Paz Estenssoro in 1952.

The two other 'tin barons', Carlos Victor Aramayo of Tupiza and Mauricio Hothschild, a Jew of European extraction, kept their centres of operations in Bolivia, but the 1952 revolution stripped them of their wealth and Aramayo fled to Europe to escape the ill will of his compatriots.

In recent years, the government has been promoting fiscalisation, or *capitalización* (a variation on privatisation), and turning mining interests over to the private sector. The resulting turmoil – accompanied by low world tin prices, stiff competition from abroad and turbulent labour unrest – has left the already fluctuating population of Oruro in a state of uncertainty.

Information

Tourist Office The helpful but poorly funded tourist office (☎ 51764) on the plaza is open weekdays from 9 am to noon and 2 to 6 pm, and weekends from 9 am to noon.

The booklet *Carnaval de Oruro Bolivia – Guía Turística 1991,* by Elias Delgado Morales, is a source of information for those who read Spanish. It's available in Oruro bookshops.

Foreign Consulate For some unfathomable reason, there's a German Consulate on Adolfo Mier, near the main plaza. It's open weekday mornings until 11 am.

Money The Banco Boliviano Americano and the Banco de Santa Cruz both change cash and travellers cheques, but they charge an extortionate 4% commission, with a minimum commission of US$8. You may also be able to change them for a lower rate at the Farmacia Santa Marta, on Calle Bolívar, or the Ferretería Findel, on the corner of Adolfo Mier and Pagador. You can change cash at any shop displaying 'Compro Dólares' signs. Street moneychangers mill around the corner of 6 de Octubre and Aldana, near Plaza Ingavi.

Post & Communications The post office lies just off the plaza. Parcels must first be inspected by the Aduana Nacional on Velasco Galvarro between Ayacucho and Calle Junín.

The ENTEL office, one of the nicest modern buildings in Oruro, is near the corner of Soria Galvarro and Bolívar, just below Plaza 10 de Febrero. The public fax number in Oruro is 50574. The telephone code is 052.

Laundry Laundry service is available at Lavandería Alemana, on Calle Aldana.

Dangers & Annoyances Pickpocketing and bag-slashing are particularly rife at the Mercado Campero and around the railway station.

Mines

Most of the old mines in the hills behind Oruro have now been closed, and are dangerous to enter. Among them is Mina San José, high on the mountain behind the city, which claims to have operated for over 450 years. If you wish to hike around the colourful tailings heaps, take a yellow *micro* 'D', marked 'San José', which leaves from the north-west corner of Plaza 10 de Febrero near the tourist office.

The main mining operation in Oruro now is the gold mine, Inti Raymi. Prospective visitors will need to muster a group, arrange for a guide and obtain permission from EMUSA in La Paz. Information is available at the German Consulate in Oruro.

Churches

The cathedral just below the main plaza has fine stained glass work above the altar. The Santuario de la Virgen del Socavón, on Cerro Píe de Gallo (Cock's Foot Hill), offers a view over the city and figures prominently in the Diablada as the site where good ultimately defeats evil (see Special Events). For the energetic, there's also a good view from the Capilla de Serrato, a steep climb from the end of Calle Washington. Iglesia de Conchupata at the top of Avenida Presidente Montes is easier to reach for a great view over the town.

Museo Patiño (Casa de la Cultura)

The university-administered Museo Patiño, in the Casa de la Cultura on Calle Soria Galvarro, is a former residence of tin baron, Simon I Patiño. Exhibits include his furniture and personal effects, and an ornate stairway. Visiting exhibitions are featured in the downstairs lobby. It's open Monday to Friday from 9 am to noon and 2.30 to 6 pm. Admission for foreigners is US$1.50.

Museo Etnográfico Minero

The Museo Etnográfico Minero (Mining Museum), adjacent to the Santuario de la

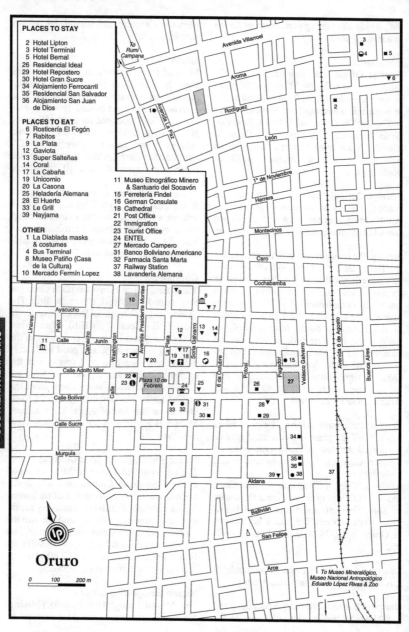

PLACES TO STAY

2 Hotel Lipton
3 Hotel Terminal
5 Hotel Bernal
26 Residencial Ideal
29 Hotel Repostero
30 Hotel Gran Sucre
34 Alojamiento Ferrocarril
35 Residencial San Salvador
36 Alojamiento San Juan
   de Dios

PLACES TO EAT

6 Rosticería El Fogón
7 Rabitos
9 La Plata
12 Gaviota
13 Super Salteñas
14 Coral
17 La Cabaña
19 Unicornio
20 La Casona
25 Heladería Alemana
28 El Huerto
33 Le Grill
39 Nayjama

OTHER

1 La Diablada masks
  & costumes
4 Bus Terminal
8 Museo Patiño (Casa
  de la Cultura)
10 Mercado Fermín Lopez
11 Museo Etnográfico Minero
   & Santuario del Socavón
15 Ferretería Findel
16 German Consulate
18 Cathedral
21 Post Office
22 Immigration
23 Tourist Office
24 ENTEL
27 Mercado Campero
31 Banco Boliviano Americano
32 Farmacia Santa Marta
37 Railway Station
38 Lavandería Alemana

Oruro

0   100   200 m

Virgen del Socavón, is housed in an actual mine tunnel. It reveals various aspects and methods of Bolivian mining: tunnels, 'mailboxes', tailing dumps, chimneys, El Tío (the devilish character who owns the minerals) etc. It's open daily from 9 am to noon and 3 to 5.30 pm. Admission is US$0.75.

Museo Nacional Antropológico Eduardo López Rivas

This museum, at the south end of town, has been newly remodelled and upgraded with local contributions and the help of the German government. The focus is on the Oruro area and displays include artefacts and information on the early Chipayas and Uros tribes. It's open Tuesday to Sunday, 10 am to noon and 3 to 6 pm and admission is US$0.75. Take the orange micro 'C', marked 'Sud' from the north-west corner of the plaza or opposite the railway station, and get off just beyond the tin-foundry compound.

Museo Mineralógico

The Museo Mineralógico, on the university campus south of the city centre, has worthwhile exhibits of minerals, precious stones, fossils and crystals from around the world. It's open Monday to Friday from 8 am to noon and 2.30 to 5 pm and admission for foreigners is US$0.60. If the door is locked, visit the Departamento de Minas at the university and ask to be allowed in. From the patio outside there's a nice view of Lago Uru Uru, several km away.

To get to the museum, catch a green micro 'A' marked 'Sud' from the YPFB petrol station opposite the railway station and get off at the end of the line.

Zoo

Oruro's nauseatingly unkempt zoo lies near the children's playground opposite the Museo Antropológico. Its most interesting feature is the large aviary where you'll have close-up views of Andean condors, but interest pales when you realise such large and stately birds would prefer to be soaring over remote Andean crags. It's open Tuesday to Sunday from 10 am to noon and 3 to 6 pm and costs US$0.50. From the plaza, take the orange micro 'C', marked 'Sud'.

Old Trains

There are dozens of old and decomposing steam locomotives and rail cars moored along the tracks at the north end of town. The railyards are off limits to outsiders, but you can catch a glimpse of them through the fence.

Activities

Rock climbers will enjoy the area known as Rumi Campana (Bell Rock), after an unusual acoustic phenomenon. It lies about two km north-west of town. (On the way, note the brilliantly coloured mine tailings heaped around the hills.) On weekends, you can practice your skills with the friendly and enthusiastic local climbing club, Club de Montañismo Halcones. There's some excellent rock and a range of routes with protection already in place. Try your hand with the challenging overhanging route, *Mujer Amante*, or the wonderful '7'-rated route known as *Sueño*. For information, contact Edgar Martinez (☎ 50793).

Organised Tours

If you want to travel into the farther reaches of western Oruro department, where there's a wealth of natural interest – wildlife, volcanoes, hot springs and colourful lakes and lagoons – ask around hotels or at the tourist office for the private guide, Juan Carlos Vargas, who can arrange custom trips.

Special Events

La Diablada The Diablada (Dance of the Devils) has become the most renowned and largest annual celebration held in Bolivia.

In the broad sense, the *Carnaval* festivities can be described as a re-enactment of the triumph of good over evil, but the festival is so interlaced with threads of both Christian and Indian myths, fables, deities and traditions that it would be inaccurate to oversimplify it in that way.

The origins of a similar festival may be

traced back to 12th-century Cataluña (Spain), although orureños maintain that it commemorates an event that occurred during the early days of their own fair city. Legend has it that one night a thief called Chiruchiru was seriously wounded by a traveller he'd attempted to rob. Taking pity on the wrongdoer, the Virgin of Candelaria gently helped him reach his home near the mine at the base of Cerro Pié del Gallo and succoured him until he died. When the miners found him there, over his head hung an image of the Virgin. Today, the mine is known as the Socavón de la Virgen (Grotto of the Virgin). This legend has been combined with the ancient Uros tale of Huari and the struggle of Michael the Archangel against the seven deadly sins into the spectacle that is presented during the Oruro carnival.

The design and creation of Diablada costumes has become an art form in Oruro and several Diablada clubs consisting of members from all levels of Oruro society are sponsored by local businesses. Groups number anywhere from 40 to 300 dancing participants. Costumes, which may cost several hundred dollars each, are owned by individual dancers, and rehearsals of their diabolical dances begin on the first Sunday in November, several months in advance of the carnival.

Festivities begin the first Saturday before Ash Wednesday with a glorious *entrada* or opening parade led by the brightly costumed Michael the Archangel character. Behind him, dancing and marching, come the famous devils and a host of bears and condors. The chief devil, Lucifer, wears the most extravagant costume, complete with a velvet cape and an ornate mask. Faithfully at his side are two other devils, including Supay, the Andean god of evil that inhabits the hills and mineshafts.

The procession is followed by vehicles adorned with jewels, coins and silver service (in commemoration of the *achura* rites in which the Incas offered their treasures to Inti – the sun – in the festival of Inti Raymi), and the miners offer the year's highest quality

The Diablada mask is worn by dancers in the opening parade of Carnaval

mineral to El Tío, the devilish character who is owner of all underground minerals and precious metals.

Behind them follow the Incas and a host of conquistadores, including Francisco Pizarro and Diego de Almagro. When the Archangel and the fierce-looking devilish dancers arrive at the football stadium, a series of dances unfold the ultimate battle between good and evil. When it becomes apparent that good has triumphed, the dancers retire to the Santuario de la Virgen del Socavón and a mass is held in honour of the Virgen del Socavón, who pronounces that good has prevailed.

For three days following the *entrada*, other dance groups perform at locations throughout the city. Each group has its specific costume and performs its own dance. For a brief rundown of the dances, refer to the discussion of Dance in the Arts section of the Facts about the Country chapter.

Left: Moon over Salar de Uyuni (DS)
Right: Salt extraction, Salar de Uyuni (DS)
Bottom: Salar de Uyuni from Isla de Pescadores (RS)

Top: Church, San Juan (DS)
Bottom: Jesuit Mission church, San José de Chiquitos (DS)

Places to Stay – bottom end

Accommodation is booked out during La Diablada, so make your reservations early or contact the tourist office about accommodation in local homes. Note that prices climb considerably during the festivities and 'gringo pricing' adds to the toll.

Camping There aren't any organised sites, but it is possible to camp in the low hills immediately behind the university where it shouldn't be too difficult to find a secluded place to pitch a tent with views of the city and Lago Uru Uru. There's no surface water so carry what you'll need.

Hotels Most of the accommodation in Oruro falls into the bottom-end range. The best seems to be *Alojamiento Ferrocarril* (☎ 60079), at Velasco Galvarro 6278. *Alojamiento San Juan de Dios* (☎ 53083), at Velasco Galvarro 6344, makes a rather poor alternative. A step up is *Residencial San Salvador* (☎ 30771), near the railway station, which charges US$3 per person with communal facilities. Slightly better, but far from ideal, is the *Residencial Ideal* (☎ 52863), at Calle Bolívar 386, which charges US$5/7 for a single/double.

The main advantage of *Hotel Lipton* (☎ 41583), on the corner of Avenida 6 de Agosto and Rodríguez, is its proximity to the bus terminal. Spartan rooms without bath cost US$4 per person but the shared loos don't receive much attention. Rooms with double beds, private bath and TV cost US$10 for two people.

Much better value – in fact, the best value in town – is the warm and welcoming *Hotel Bernal* (42468), opposite the bus terminal. Quality-wise, it's actually a solid mid-range hotel, complete with a dining room, but clean single/double rooms with bath cost just US$5/8.25.

The relaxed *Hotel Repostero* (☎ 50505), at Calle Sucre 370, charges a negotiable US$5 per person for rooms with bath and hot showers. With a youth hostel card, you're eligible for a 10% discount.

Places to Stay – middle

More upmarket is the *Hotel Gran Sucre* (☎ 53838), at Calle Sucre 510. Single/double rooms with private bath and hot showers cost US$12.50/21. Rooms without hot water are slightly less and those with TV, slightly more. They seem to have a thing about Charlie Chaplin.

As far as amenities go, the *Hotel Terminal* (☎ 53127, fax 53187), literally on top of the terminal, is the top of the range in Oruro. Singles/doubles with private baths, hot showers, heating, TV and a garage cost US$16/22. Rooms with a double bed are US$25.

Places to Eat

If you're hoping for anything but a market breakfast, your Oruro mornings may be disappointing. Most places don't open until 11 am or later. The best salteñas are found at *La Casona*, on Avenida Presidente Montes, just off the main plaza, and *Super Salteñas*, on Soria Galvarro. Both these places serve sandwiches at lunch time and pizza in the evening. *Heladería Alemana* serves snacks of ice cream and empanadas for less than US$0.50.

Market food stalls in both the *Mercado Campero* and *Mercado Fermín Lopez* feature noodles, falso conejo, mutton soup, beef and thimpu de cordero (boiled potatoes, oca, rice and carrots over mutton, smothered with hot llajhua sauce).

For bargain lunch specials, check out the small eateries around the railway station or at *Coral* on Calle 6 de Octubre, *Rabitos* on Ayacucho; *Gaviota* on Calle Junín, which has especially good value almuerzos and cenas; and the reasonable and recommended *Le Grill*, on Calle Bolívar. *Unicornio* is good for snacks and lunches, and it's even open Sunday afternoon.

Nayjama, on the corner of Pagador and Aldana, has good lunches and typical dishes for under US$4. Poor vegetarian dishes are available at *Restaurant Vegetariano El Huerto*, on Calle Bolívar; almuerzos cost from US$1 to US$1.50. Beware of overcharging.

El Fondito, on Avenida Villarroel near the bus terminal, specialises in pork dishes, including quintas (pork fricasee) and chicharrón de cerdo (fried pork). For typical Bolivian dishes, there's *La Cabaña* on Calle Junín and *Restaurant La Plata* on Calle La Plata. The latter specialises in charque kan, thimpu and chairo served in traditional ceramic bowls. Another recommended place specialising in local cuisine is *El Conquistador* on Calle 6 de Octubre; the menu includes pictures for those who don't read Quechua.

Out near the bus terminal is the odd *Rostería El Fogón*, specialising in wat'iya a la piedra, which sounds more exotic than it is: potato and oca baked in a clay oven and served with plantains, chicken (or pork) and a mixed salad.

If you're after something totally unexpected in Oruro, check out *Pub the Alpaca* at Avenida La Paz 690, near Plaza de Ranchería. It's actually a lot like an English pub and the owners Eva and Willy speak a range of European languages: English, French, Spanish, Swedish, German, Finnish and Russian! Accommodation is also available. If it's locked, just ring the bell.

Things to Buy

The design, creation and production of Diablada costumes and masks has become an art and a small industry. On Avenida La Paz, between León and Villarroel, are small shops where artesans sell embroidered wall hangings, devil masks, costumes and other devilish things for US$2 to US$200 or more.

Llama and alpaca wool bags and clothing are sold at artesanía shops in the town centre, while less expensive articles are found around the north-east corner of Mercado Campero. Zampoñas, charangos and other indigenous musical instruments are hawked at roadside kiosks around the railway station. Tucked away in Mercado Campero is an impressive Mercado de Hechicería.

Getting There & Away

Bus All buses leave from and arrive at the bus terminal, Terminal de Omnibuses Hernando Siles, north of the centre. While you're waiting for your bus, it's worth strolling out for a look at the rainbow-coloured mural on Avenida 6 de Agosto, which welcomes visitors to Oruro.

Several different companies run buses to La Paz every half-hour or so; the trip costs US$2.20 and takes three hours. About midway into the trip, watch for a shallow lake about 100m west of the highway which normally teems with flamingos.

There are also several daily buses to Cochabamba (US$4.50, six hours) and Potosí (US$4, 7 hours) and Santa Cruz (US$12, 20 hours). Flota Universo goes to Villazón daily at 8 pm. To Sucre, you must go via either Cochabamba or Potosí. To Uyuni, 16 de Julio leaves daily at 8.30 am and to Flecha Norte at 7 pm. Flota Bustillo, Trans Minera and Conta de Oro have numerous daily runs to Llallagua for US$1.50.

For Tambo Quemado and Chungará (Chile), with connections to Arica (Chile), Trans-Sabaya leaves Tuesday and Saturday at 9.30 am. From Arica to Oruro, it leaves at 10 am Sunday and Wednesday. Flota Geminis serves Arica on Tuesday, Thursday and Saturday. The fare to Chungará (Lauca National Park) is US$8.50; to Arica, it's US$17. When the paved road is completed, this minimum 18-hour trip will take less than half the time.

Train Thanks to its mines, Oruro is a railroad centre and for what it's worth, has one of the most organised and efficient railway stations in Bolivia. In fact, the schedules for Bolivia's western rail network are devised here and the proud planners have produced an impressive printed timetable – the only one found anywhere in the country – with hopeful schedules showing precision to the minute.

Oruro marks the beginning for most rail journeys towards Chile or Argentina. Because rail service between La Paz and Oruro is slow and difficult to arrange, most people travel by bus from La Paz to Oruro and begin their rail journey there.

From Oruro, you can travel to Uyuni, where the railway line splits; one line goes to Tupiza and Villazón (on the Argentine border) and the other to Ollagüe and Calama, in Chile. Heading east, there are lines to Cochabamba, and to Potosí and Sucre via Río Mulatos.

The *ferrobus* to Cochabamba leaves on Wednesday and Friday at 2 pm (US$3.50/2.75 1st/2nd class, five hours), and the *tren rápido* goes on Thursday at 8.20 am (US$3.20/2.50 1st/2nd class, 11 hours).

To La Paz, the tren expreso leaves on Sunday at 2.45 am (US$2.50 1st class, five hours), but given the hour, it's not very popular. To Villazón, via Uyuni and Tupiza, the *tren expreso* leaves on Friday at 5.30 pm (US$17/15 1st/2nd class, 12 hours), the tren rápido goes on Monday and Thursday at 7 pm (US$7.50 1st class, 15 hours) and the *tren mixto* runs on Wednesday and Sunday at 7 pm (US$5.50 2nd class, 17 hours).

On the amazing trip to Potosí and Sucre, the railway crosses the scenic 4786m pass at El Cóndor, which is the highest point on the Bolivian railway lines and one of the highest in the world. The ferrobus does this run on Tuesday and Saturday at 9.10 pm (to Potosí US$8.60 1st class, seven hours; to Sucre US$10.20 1st class, 12 hours).

To Avaroa (US$6.50 2nd class, 12 hours) and Calama, Chile (US$15 2nd class, 22 hours), the tren rápido runs on Sunday at 7.30 pm. For Calama, you must change at the Avaroa/Ollagüe border post from the Bolivian to the Chilean train. To Antofagasta, on the coast, there's still a railway, but no rail service. Once in Calama, you can board a bus for the two to three-hour trip. You may have time to change money in Uyuni or Ollagüe, but don't count on it. Casa de Cambio Sudamer in La Paz gives the best rates on Chilean pesos (when they're available).

Getting Around

Oruro city micros and minibuses cost US$0.15 and connect the city centre with outlying areas. They're lettered A, B, C and D but each micro may do several different runs. One micro 'D', for example, goes to the Vinto smelter and is marked 'Vinto ENAF'. Another micro 'D' goes to the San José mine and is marked 'San José'. Oruro micros are

---

By Rail to Chile

The rail route between Bolivia and Chile passes through some spectacular landscapes and if you're prepared for the uncomfortable conditions, the journey is highly worthwhile. Temperatures in the coaches may well fall below zero at night so a sleeping bag or woollen blanket and plenty of warm clothing are essential. There's no dining car, so bring food as well. Any sort of fruit, meat or cheese will be confiscated at the border (you'll get a receipt), so eat it up before reaching customs at Ollagüe.

Between Uyuni and the border, the line crosses vast saltpans, deserts and rugged mountains and volcanoes. Flamingos, guanacos, vicuñas and wild burros are common, and thanks to a startling mirage effect, so are a host of other things. *Remolinos* (dust devils or willy-willys) whirl across the stark landscape beneath towering snow-capped volcanoes. One type of vegetation that flourishes is *llareta* (*Azorella compacta*), a combustible salt-tolerant moss that oozes a turpentine-like jelly and is used by the locals as stove fuel. It appears soft and spongy from a distance but is actually rock-hard. Llareta grows very slowly; a large clump may be several hundred years old. The plant is now an officially protected species in Chile and in the Reserva de Fauna Andina Eduardo Avaroa.

Bolivian exit stamps are given on the train as soon as it leaves Uyuni: passports are collected in bulk, stamped in the last coach of the train and then returned coach by coach. The Chilean immigration procedures at Abaroa/Ollagüe, a windy, dusty and unprotected outpost in a broad pass through the Andes, can be trying. You must queue up for your entrance stamp and again for a luggage search. All this takes place outside, and at night it's a miserable exercise in endurance.

At the border post, you have to change to the Chilean coaches, which are in surprisingly worse repair than their Bolivian counterparts. Oddly enough, the service is run by British-owned Ferrocarril Antofagasta-Bolivia, which loses money on the line but is required by an 1888 mineral transport treaty to keep the passenger service running indefinitely. Perhaps that explains why the windows are broken and the coaches lack light and heating, why they have wooden benches instead of seats, loose boards that allow cold winds to whistle through and toilets that are outside, exposed to the elements! ■

small and crowded so if possible, avoid carrying luggage aboard.

Taxis from the transportation terminals to the centre, or between the transportation terminals, cost US$0.30 per person. Prices aren't negotiable and some cabbies charge an additional US$0.20 if you have a lot of luggage but otherwise, don't let them convince you to pay any more.

AROUND ORURO
Complejo Metalúrgico Vinto
This US$12 million tin smelter was constructed in the early 1970s during the presidency of General Hugo Banzer Suárez. By the time it was put into operation, the Bolivian tin industry was already experiencing a steady decline.

Vinto lies eight km east of Oruro, and may be visited on weekdays from 9 am to noon. To get there, take micro 'D' marked 'Vinto ENAF' from the north-west corner of Plaza 10 de Febrero and apply at the office for permission to tour the operation.

Lago Uru Uru (Lago del Milagro)
Lago Uru Uru, a large shallow lake just south of town, offers good fishing for pejerrey and you'll also see flamingos in the shallow water. There's a small restaurant and a *cabaña* at the shore where you may hire rowboats for fishing or exploring the lake. To reach the shore, take micro 'A' marked 'Sud' to its terminus at the university. From there, it's a three-km walk along the highway to the lake.

Cha'llapata & Lago de Poopó
About 75 km south of Oruro is the large but shallow Lago de Poopó, which covers 2530 sq km but has an average depth of only six metres. This oversized puddle attracts flamingos and a host of other waders, making it an appealing spot for ornithologists and bird-watchers.

If you're interested in visiting little-known *chullpas* in the area, seek out the local indigenous leader, Juvenal Pérez in Cha'llapata. To get there, either take a micro

or hop on any south-bound train and get off at Cha'llapata, which is 110 km south of Oruro and 12 km east of the lakeshore.

The spartan alojamiento in Cha'llapata can arrange bicycle hire to the lake for US$2 per day, or you can walk. Prepare for cold, windy conditions as well as a high UV factor.

Capachos & Obrajes
The hot springs of Capachos and Obrajes are 16 and 23 km north of Oruro along the Cochabamba road. Both resorts have covered hot pools and individual baths, but Obrajes is the nicer of the two. Micros to both springs cost US$0.40 and leave when full from Avenida 6 de Agosto, near Calle Montecinos. Admission to either place is US$1 per person.

Calacala
The archaeological site at Calacala lies about 20 km east of Oruro, along the road to Negro Pabellón. The rock paintings and engravings are in a rock shelter at the base of a hulking monolith. A llama theme is most prominent, but there is also a puma and some roughly human figures painted in white and earth tones. As yet, no definitive theory of their origin has been formulated, but some investigators suggest an Inca-era cameloid cult (see the Andean Cameloids aside later in this chapter).

On Saturday and Sunday, micros run from Oruro to Calacala; at other times, you may have to take a taxi. Once in the village, you must track down the park guard, who will unlock the gate to the site and act as a guide. The paintings are about a 40-minute walk from the village, towards the old brewery.

On 14 September, the church in Calacala hosts a pilgrimage and fiesta in honour of the Señor de las Lagunas.

COMANCHE AREA
The area around Comanche, south of La Paz and north-west of Oruro, boasts several interesting natural history sites and, as yet, it lies well off the trodden track.

Reserva Natural de Comanche

The Reserva Natural de Comanche, administered as a loosely defined national park, has been set aside to protect the incredible yucca-like *Puya raimondii*, which is actually a relative of the pineapple. These gigantic plants, which grow in the hills west of the village, reach heights of 12m and their enormous spikes erupt into greenish flowers only after the plant has reached 60 to 100 years of age. Once they've flowered, they begin to self-destruct, slowly decomposing into a heap of blackened material. The best time to see one in flower is in the early summer, from November to December. The main site can be visited in a day trip from La Paz.

Also of interest are the 18th-century churches in the nearby villages of Callapa and Caquiaviri and the several burial chullpas along the route.

Corocoro

Corocoro, just east of the Río Desaguadero near the La Paz-Arica railway line, is another Southern Altiplano mining town. The Corocoro mines produce nearly all of Bolivia's copper and Corocoro is one of the two major sources of native copper in the world today, the other being on Michigan's Upper Peninsula on the US shore of Lake Superior. Since the copper is found in nugget form and not in ore, which must be smelted, the early native peoples of the Altiplano used it long before anyone knew what to do with ore copper. The Museo de Metales Preciosos Pre-Columbinos in La Paz displays some examples of their work.

Ciudad de Piedra

East of the village of Calacoto (not to be confused with the suburb of the same name in the Zona Sur of La Paz) lies the forest of natural sandstone formations known as the Ciudad de Piedra. These pinnacles were formed by wind and rain erosion and are good for day hikes.

Places to Stay & Eat

There's no formal accommodation in the area, but you can always find private accommodation in villages or camp in the hills. Caquiaviri has a small restaurant, but otherwise, you'll have to rely on stalls and small shops.

Getting There & Away

Micros from La Paz to Comanche, Callapa, Caquiaviri, Corocoro and Calacoto leave from Avenida Franco Valle 105 in the Zona 12 de Octubre, El Alto. In Viacha, they leave from behind the market. The fare from La Paz to Comanche is US$1; to Calacoto, it's US$1.50. Trains between La Paz and Oruro stop at all these villages except Caquiaviri.

LLALLAGUA

First owned by the Chilean Llallagua Company, the town of Llallagua was bought out in 1924 by tin baron Simon Patiño once he'd gained the capital from his successful operation in nearby Uncia. The area's most famous mine, Siglo XX, grew into Bolivia's most productive, and remains the largest tin mine in the country, with 800 km of underground passages.

History

With the nationalisation of mining interests in 1952, control of Llallagua passed into the hands of COMIBOL (Corporación Minera de Bolivia). It was then operated by the federal government until the mid-1980s when Victor Paz Estenssoro (the same president who had initiated the 1952 mining reform!) decided during his third non-consecutive term of office to return the project to private, miner-owned cooperatives.

A large sign posted outside Siglo XX states that visitors must obtain permission from COMIBOL headquarters in Catavi before they'll be admitted. Strikes, layoffs and the drop in tin prices have turned Llallagua into a near ghost town and often, promised severance pay hasn't materialised and many destitute, out-of-work miners have emigrated from the region en masse. Given all this, plus the confusion from transition-related strife, catering for curious tourists is the least of the miners' concerns. Having said that, most of the cooperative miners are friendly, earnest and hard-working people. They passionately try to keep abreast of the political situations that so profoundly affect their lives and are normally happy to engage willing listeners in a discussion of their favourite topic.

It is not possible to visit the town or the plant without permission granted by the COMIBOL general manager who lives near the Patiño theatre. Once you're through the security gate, there's no problem visiting. Mining methods are the same as they were centuries ago, and the cooperative miners are friendly and quite happy to tell you about their work on the tailings dumps and in the rivers. They are proud that their work is respected enough by others to ask questions.

The book by Domitila Barrios de Chungara, *Let Me Speak*, is a good description of living and working in Siglo XX.

Special Events
The fiesta of the Virgen de la Asunción, on the 14th and 15th of August, is celebrated with processions and drunken *tinku* fighting.

Places to Stay & Eat
The basic but friendly *Hotel Llallagua* charges US$1.50 per person and the restaurant cooks up anything they can find in the market. Slightly more upmarket is the *Hotel Bustillo*.

Getting There & Away
Llallagua lies 95 km by road south-east of Oruro. Several *flotas* offer service from Oruro all day long. There are also services between Llallagua and Potosí.

PARQUE NACIONAL SAJAMA
Loosely defined and undeveloped Parque Nacional Sajama occupies approximately 80,000 hectares abutting the Chilean border. It was created on 5 November 1945 for the protection of the hulking Nevado Sajama volcano and the wildlife that inhabits this northern extension of the Atacama desert. Unfortunately, depredation in the park has already eliminated the puma, Andean deer

(huemules), viscacha and guanaco; and only limited number of vicuñas, condors, flamingos, rheas and armadillos survive.

The world's highest forest covers the foothills flanking the impressive Volcán Sajama, which is disputably Bolivia's highest peak, at 6542m. The forest consists of dwarf queñua trees, a species unique to the Altiplano, but unless you're into ticking off superlatives, it's nothing to get steamed up about. The 'trees' have the size and appearance of creosote bushes.

Information
Park visitors and prospective climbers should check in with Telmo Nina at Sajama village and pay a US$1 park entry fee. This is payable even if you're just visiting the village (unless you're on the bus). If you're organising a private expedition, perhaps speak to Telmo, who keeps a log of routes up Sajama. Artesanía produced here – mostly articles of pastel-dyed alpaca wool – is sold in the shop of former Sajama resident, Peter Brunnhart, on Calle Sagárnaga in La Paz; he may be another source of information on the mountain.

Nevado Sajama
This mountain is unquestionably the centrepiece of all it surveys and is attracting increasing numbers of mountaineers who'd like to try their abilities (and luck) on its glaciers and wildly eroded slopes. There are no trails per se, so park hiking is strictly of the backcountry variety. On all hikes, remember to carry an ample supply of water.

Although it's a relatively straightforward climb, Sajama's altitude and ice conditions make the peak more challenging than it initially appears. Many of the glaciers are receding, turning much of the route into a sloppy and crevasse-ridden mess. If you're looking for an organised expedition, quite a few La Paz agencies offer organised climbs of Sajama. For suggestions, see Activities in the Facts for the Visitor chapter, or Tours in the Getting Around chapter.

Access to the mountain is from the Tambo Quemado-Patacamaya road near the village

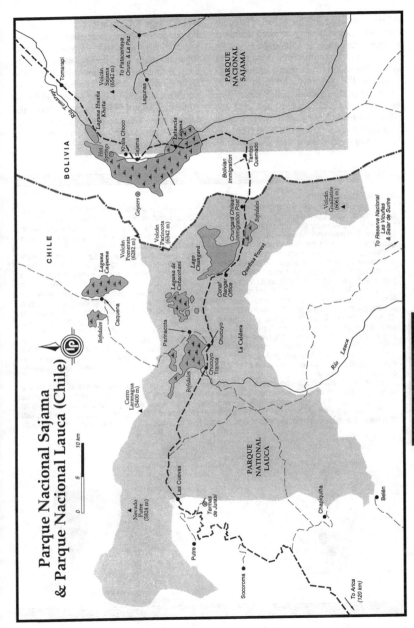

of Sajama or from the Oruro-Turco-Lagunas road near Lagunas. Experienced climbers can commence their assault on the mountain from the north, south (from Lagunas), or west (from Sajama); allow two or three days to reach the summit and prepare for extremely cold and windy conditions. When the wind really picks up, dust and sand add to the discomfort. Carry lots of water, though once on the snow cap, there'll be plenty in the form of ice and snow.

Hot Springs & Geysers

For a good warm soak, there are some lovely hot springs five km north-west of Sajama village. The springs are relatively easy to find but locals can point you in the right direction. About 1½ hours on foot due west of Sajama is a geyser field with some nice spouting hot springs. Given the temperature and the obvious risks, don't get too close and by all means, resist the temptation to swim!

Andean Cameloids

Unlike the Old World, the western hemisphere had few grazing mammals after the Pleistocene era, when mammoths, horses and other large herbivores disappeared for reasons that appear to be linked to hunting pressure by the earliest human inhabitants of the plains and pampas of North and South America. For millennia, however, the Andean people have relied on the New World camels – the wild guanaco and vicuña and the domesticated llama and alpaca – for food and fibre.

Guanaco *(Lama guanicoe)* and vicuña (*Vicugna vicugna*) are relatively rare today, but are the likely ancestors of the domesticated llama and alpaca. In fact, they were among very few potential New World domestic animals – contrast them with the Old World cattle, horses, sheep, goats, donkeys and pigs that have filled so many vacant niches in the Americas. Of the major domesticated animals from across the Atlantic, only the humped camel has failed to achieve an important role here. While the New World camels have lost ground to sheep and cattle in some areas, they are not likely to disappear.

The guanaco ranges from the central Andes to Tierra del Fuego at elevations from sea level up to 4000m or higher. In these regions, early native hunters ate its meat and dressed in its skin. In the central Andes, where the human population is small but widely dispersed and domestic livestock numerous, guanaco numbers are small. However, on the plains of Argentine Patagonia and in reserves such as southern Chile's Parque Nacional Torres del Paine, herds of rust-coloured guanaco are still a common sight. Bolivia's only guanaco population, which amounts to only a few animals, shelters in the highland plains of the Reserva de Fauna Andina Eduardo Avaroa, in the extreme south-western corner of the country.

By contrast, the vicuña occupies a much smaller geographical range, well above 4000m on the puna and Altiplano from southern central Peru to north-western Argentina. Although not as numerous as the guanaco, it played a critical role in the cultural life of pre-Columbian Peru, which assured its survival. Its very fine golden wool was the exclusive property of the Inca emperors, and the Spanish chronicler Bernabé Cobo wrote that the ruler's clothing 'was made of the finest wool and the best cloth

Alpaca

Llama

Places to Stay & Eat

Camping is fine just about anywhere in this sparsely populated region, so a tent and a good cold-weather sleeping bag are highly recommended. Otherwise, see Señor Telmo in Sajama village, who keeps a list of families offering private lodging in their homes; it's organised on a rotation basis and costs US$1 per person per night. Most homes are very modest, so you'll still need a warm sleeping bag and many layers

of clothing for the typically cold, windy nights.

About five km along the main road from Sajama towards Patacamaya, at the point nearest the hot springs, a campesino family offers clean basic lodging for US$1 per person. Meals are also available for US$1 each.

Only basic staples are sold in the village, so carry your hiking and climbing food from elsewhere.

---

that was woven in his whole kingdom...most of it was made of vicuña wool, which is almost as fine as silk'.

Strict Inca authority protected the vicuña, but the Spanish invasion destroyed that authority and over the past 500 years, the species has been under pressure from hunting. By the middle of this century, poaching reduced vicuña numbers from two million to perhaps 10,000 and caused its inclusion on Appendix I of the Endangered Species List. Conservation programmes such as that in Chile's Parque Nacional Lauca have achieved so impressive a recovery that economic exploitation of the species may soon benefit the puna communities in that country. In Lauca and surrounding areas, vicuña numbers grew from barely 1000 in the early 1970s to more than 27,000 two decades later.

The communities of the puna and Altiplano – mostly Aymara – still depend on llamas and alpacas for their livelihood. The two species appear very similar but they differ in several important respects. The taller, rangier and hardier llama has relatively coarse wool that is used for blankets, ropes and other household goods. It also works as a pack animal, but thanks to the introduction of camión traffic on the Altiplano, llama trains are becoming increasingly rare in Bolivia; the last major trade route served by llama train is the salt trail from the Salar de Uyuni to Tarija.

Llamas can survive and even flourish on relatively poor, dry pastures, whereas the smaller, more delicate alpacas aren't pack animals and require well watered grasslands to produce their much finer wool, which has a higher commercial value than that of llamas. Both llama and alpaca meat are consumed by Andean households and are sold in urban markets all over Bolivia.

In recent years, the meagre earnings from the sale of wool and meat haven't been sufficient to stem the flow of population from the countryside into such urban poverty traps such as El Alto, near La Paz. However, the commercialisation of vicuña wool might help do so, if international agreement permits it. According to a recent study by CONAF (the Chilean national parks commission), production and sale of vicuña cloth could bring a price of nearly US$290 per square metre; if local people were involved, it would also serve to diversify local economies and keep people on the land. ■

Guancaco (Huanacu)

Vicuña

Getting There & Away

All buses between La Paz and Arica (Chile) pass through Sajama National Park, but if you get off there, you'll probably have to pay the full Arica fare of US$22. The current route is excruciatingly rough; plan on eight to 12 hours from La Paz to the park, depending on road conditions. After rain, it may not be passable at all. However, a new road is currently being constructed and parts of it may be open by the time you read this.

Once you've come this far, a visit to Chile's spectacular Parque Nacional Lauca is highly recommended (see the following discussion of Parque Nacional Lauca). For onward travel into Chile, flag down a passing bus on Wednesday, Thursday, Saturday or Sunday morning. The border crossing between Tambo Quemado, Bolivia, and Chungará, Chile, is straightforward. However, no-one at the Tambo Quemado border post is in much of a hurry, so allow for delays.

Returning to La Paz, *flotas* normally pass in the early to mid-afternoon on the same days, but you probably won't get a seat. *Camiones* do pass infrequently and accept paying passengers.

PARQUE NACIONAL LAUCA (CHILE)

Across the frontier from Sajama is Chile's poodle-shaped Parque Nacional Lauca – 137,000 hectares of marvellously intact Andean ecosystems. It was declared a national park by the Chilean government in 1970 to protect its profusion of wildlife: flamingos, coots, Andean gulls, Andean geese, condors, vicuñas, guanacos, llamas, alpacas, rheas, viscachas, foxes, armadillos, Andean deer and even pumas, as well as unusual vegetation such as *queñua* trees and *llareta*.

Lago Chungará

Near the Bolivian border beneath the volcanoes Pomerata and Parinacota, known collectively as Las Payachatas (both higher than 6000m), is the lovely alpine lake, Lago Chungará. At 4517m, it's one of the world's highest bodies of water. Visitors may walk at will, but will have to reckon with the high altitude and swampy ground, and frequently fierce climatic conditions. Snow is possible at any time of year.

Because of Arica's insatiable appetite for hydroelectricity and the Azapa valley's thirst, the Chilean electric company has built an intricate system of pumps and canals which may compromise the ecological integrity of Lago Chungará. Because the lake is so shallow, any lowering of its level would drastically reduce its surface area and affect feeding and nesting sites used by wading birds, including flamingos and giant coots.

Parinacota

The lovely pre-Hispanic stone village of Parinacota sits along the Arica-Potosí silver route at an elevation of 4400m. In the background stretches the Laguna de Cotacotani and its surrounding *bofedales* (a shallow lake dotted with tussocks of vegetation and used as pasture for llamas and alpacas). The Chilean National Parks department, CONAF, operates a visitor centre and a museum at the eastern end of the village.

The imposing whitewashed stone church was originally built in the 1600s but was reconstructed in 1789. The surreal 17th-century frescoes on the interior walls, the work of artists from the Cuzco school, recall Hieronymus Bosch's *Sinners in the Hands of an Angry God*. Note also the depiction of soldiers bearing Christ to the cross as Spaniards. Ask caretaker Cipriano Morales for the key, and leave a small donation to the church.

Places to Stay & Eat

On Lago Chungará, there's a CONAF camp site and a *refugio* with a couple of beds and a warm stove. Camping costs US$4 per site and beds, when they're available, are US$10. At the CONAF visitors centre, museum and high-altitude genetic research station, at the eastern end of Parinacota village, there's a comfortable if sparsely furnished refugio. Beds cost US$10 per person, but hot-water availability depends upon the arrival of gas canisters from Arica.

At Chucuyo (the Parinacota turn-off), Matilde and Máximo Morales have two rooms to let in their home for US$1 per person. Matilde will prepare alpaca steaks or other simple meals for around US$1.50. Chucuyo also has a passable restaurant serving inexpensive set meals and selling locally produced alpaca *chompas*, gloves, hats and scarves.

At Putre, near the park's western entrance, is *Hostería Las Vicuñas* (☎ 224997), which charges US$55/70 for a single/double. The *Restaurant Oasis* (which is actually a place to stay) offers a more economical option at US$5 per person.

Getting There & Away

The road from Arica to Lauca is now paved all the way to the Bolivian border. The route follows the lovely oasis-like Lluta valley and climbs into the Atacama hills past ancient petroglyphs and the interesting adobe church and cemetery at Poconchile. Between 1300 and 1800m, you'll see the appropriately named candelabra cactus, which grows just five mm annually and flowers for only 24 hours. It virtually never rains in the Atacama so the cactus must take its moisture from the fog.

Bear in mind that the trip from Arica to Lauca involves a climb from sea level to 4500m, and there's a high risk of altitude sickness.

Independent access to Lauca isn't inordinately difficult. Buses between Arica and La Paz pass right through the park (see Parque Nacional Sajama earlier in this chapter). Buses La Paloma (☎ 222710), at Germán Riesco 2071 in Arica, serves Putre five times weekly, departing at 6.45 am and returning the following morning. To Parinacota, use Buses Martinez (☎ 232265), at Pedro Montt 620, or Transporte Humira (☎ 231891) at Pedro Montt 622, both in Arica. Both leave on Tuesday and Friday at about 10 am.

Several Arica tour operators also run guided tours to Lauca. A good one is Jurasi Tour (☎ 251696), at Bolognesi 360-A in

Arica. Alternatively, try Vicuña Tour (☎ 222971) at 18 de Septiembre 399, Arica.

South-Western Bolivia

The south-western corner of Bolivia is the most remote highland area of the country. With few roads or inhabitants, unpredictable weather conditions, only a few scattered settlements and unreliable transport, travel into and around the region becomes an exercise in patience and creativity. Its boundaries are more or less defined by the railway lines between Uyuni and the Chilean and Argentine frontiers and by the minor ranges known as the Cordillera de Lipez and Cordillera de Chichas. Nearly treeless, the country and villages south of the Salar de Uyuni are occupied only by a few miners, military personnel and some very determined Aymara.

For adventurous travellers, this is paradise. Transport is scarce and expensive and amenities few, but visitors are rewarded with a first-hand view of this unearthly geology. Bleached brine deposits provide an occasional white splash amid the prevailing browns. The surreal landscape is punctuated by steaming, towering volcanoes; dozens of hot pools and springs; flamingo-filled lakes stained by minerals and algae into a palette of rainbow hues; and the featureless salt deserts that are some of the world's flattest terrain.

History

The prehistoric lakes Minchín and Tauca, which once covered most of this highland plateau, evaporated some 10,000 years ago, leaving behind a parched landscape of brackish puddles and salt deserts. Humans haven't left much of a mark on the region; sometime in the mid-15th century, the reigning Inca Pachacuti sent his son Tupac Inca Yupanqui southward to conquer all the lands he encountered. He was apparently clever with public relations because the south-western extremes of Bolivia and deserts of northern

SOUTHERN ALTIPLANO

Chile were taken bloodlessly. The conquerors marched on across the wastelands to the northern bank of Chile's Río Maule, where a fierce band of Araucanian Indians inspired them to stake out the southern boundary of the Inca empire and turn back towards Cuzco.

Owing to the harsh conditions, the Incas never effectively colonised this desert area, and it's still sparsely populated. Beyond the towns of Uyuni, Tupiza and Villazón, most of the people cluster around mining camps, health and military outposts and geothermal projects.

Independent Travel

The remoteness of this area and the difficulties of individual travel cannot be overstressed. Flexibility is the key if you're relying on lifts in camiones or 4WDs. Days can pass without a sign of activity. Self-motivated explorers must come equipped with a tent, torch, compass, warm sleeping bag, fuel, reliable stove, , sunglasses, sunscreen, water and maps. It's also a good idea to carry twice as much food as you expect you'll need, as well as clothing for subzero temperatures. Soroche can be a problem (see Health in the Facts for the Visitor chapter), especially for hikers, and snow may fall at almost any time.

Puestos sanitarios (health posts) are dotted around for the benefit of local miners, military personnel and campesinos, but their medical supplies and expertise are basic and shouldn't be counted on. Friendly locals and miners will normally do what they can to provide a place to crash and even share their limited food, but it's unfair to rely on them. You may want to bring small amounts of coffee, fruit, magazines, coca etc – anything that isn't locally available – to offer as reciprocal gifts to helpful officials and workers.

The best time to travel in this region is from July to early October, when the days are dry and cool but not as cold as in early winter. From October to March, rainfall causes roads to deteriorate badly and snowfall is common from February to May.

Organised Tours

The easiest way to explore the region is with an organised tour. The best and most economical are those leaving from Uyuni, and a variety of itineraries are available. For recommendations, see Organised Tours under Uyuni. Further discussion of the main sites of interest is found under the Salar de Uyuni, the Salar de Coipasa and the South-West Circuit later in this chapter.

UYUNI

In politically correct terms, Uyuni is 'climatically challenged'. Mention its name to a Bolivian and the first response you're likely to hear is *mucho frío*. One tourist brochure simply describes it as *frígido* (frigid, of course). To compound things, buildings are generally draughty, indoor heating is all but unknown and the icy winds can bite through any number of clothing layers. Although the warmer summer months do bring some relief – and warm, sunny days certainly aren't unknown – this uninspiring desert community does receive more than its share of chills.

Nevertheless, Uyuni's isolated position and otherworldly outlook elicit an affectionate respect from both Bolivians and travellers. In fact, it has been generously nicknamed *La Hija Predilecta de Bolivia* (Bolivia's Favourite Daughter). This stems not from any aesthetic merits, but from its pampering of Bolivian troops returning from the Guerra del Pacífico, the war in which Bolivia lost its seacoast to Chile.

Uyuni was founded in 1889 by Bolivian president, Aniceto Arce. Most of its current 11,000 residents are employed in two major enterprises: government and mining (although tourism is up and coming as a matter to be reckoned with). The former includes railway workers, military and police personnel and city officials. The latter are almost exclusively involved in salt extraction on the Salar de Uyuni.

Information

Tourist Office The new Dirección Regional de Turismo (☎ 2098, fax 2060) can handle

SOUTHERN ALTIPLANO

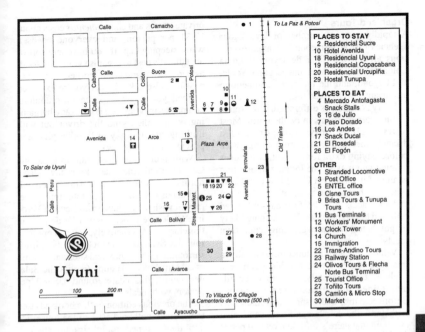

PLACES TO STAY
2 Residencial Sucre
10 Hotel Avenida
18 Residencial Uyuni
19 Residencial Copacabana
20 Residencial Urcupiña
29 Hostal Tunupa

PLACES TO EAT
4 Mercado Antofagasta Snack Stalls
6 16 de Julio
7 Paso Dorado
16 Los Andes
17 Snack Ducal
21 El Rosedal
26 El Fogón

OTHER
1 Stranded Locomotive
3 Post Office
5 ENTEL office
8 Cisne Tours
9 Brisa Tours & Tunupa Tours
11 Bus Terminals
12 Workers' Monument
13 Clock Tower
14 Church
15 Immigration
22 Trans-Andino Tours
23 Railway Station
24 Olivos Tours & Flecha Norte Bus Terminal
25 Tourist Office
27 Toñito Tours
28 Camión & Micro Stop
30 Market

all your questions about Uyuni and the entire South-West. Thanks to the enthusiastic efforts of the committed tourism director, Señor Tito Ponce Lopez, it's the best and most well-informed tourist office in Bolivia. It's open weekdays from 9 am to noon and 2.30 to 5 pm.

Money Despite Uyuni's tourism boom, the bank doesn't change money and no-one changes travellers cheques; in an emergency, you may convince the Agencia Trans-Andino, which carries on a lot of overseas trade, to change a small amount. For cash, try the Restaurant 16 de Julio on the plaza.

Post & Communications The post office lies in a surprisingly desolate part of town, several blocks from centre. The ENTEL office is a bit nearer, behind the clock tower. Uyuni's public fax number is 2121. The telephone code is 0693.

Immigration If you're travelling on to Chile from Uyuni, you must pick up a Bolivian exit stamp at the immigration office in Uyuni. Technically, you must leave Bolivia within three days of getting the stamp. Although this isn't always strictly enforced, it's still best not to pick up the stamp until you're sure about transport to the border.

Cementerio de Trenes
Uyuni's only real tourist attraction is the 'train cemetery', a large collection of historic steam locomotives and rail cars that are decaying in the yards about 500m down Avenida Ferroviaria, south-west of the station. There are now plans afoot to use them to form the basis for a railway museum, perhaps with the help of the railroad, but for a least a couple of years, they'll keep on rusting. There are also quite a few old locomotives behind the station itself, but some railway employees may ask for bribes to let you in to see them.

Organised Tours

A rapidly growing number of Uyuni tour agencies (20 at last count) arrange excursions around the Salar de Uyuni, Laguna Colorada, Sol de Mañana, Laguna Verde, and beyond, and the increased competition has meant lower priced tours.

Every company is different, but for some, cutting corners seems to be the norm. Most tours include only transport and a driver/guide, and you should think twice before paying extra for a tour that includes lodging and meals. The lodging in question is almost invariably a US$2 bed or a US$1 space on the earthen floor of an adobe hut and the meals may be four-day-old bread rolls and boiled potatoes. You're more likely to get better value organising your own meals.

Vehicles are another concern, especially in this wild region where a vehicle can be a lifeline. Unfortunately, they're often ill-maintained and breakdowns do occur. Before leaving, make sure the vehicle can withstand the harsh conditions and also ascertain that there's sufficient oil and petrol for the journey (beyond Uyuni, there's no reliable supply). Also carry enough food and water to cover days beyond the projected length of your trip.

The ease of organising an excursion from Uyuni will depend largely on the season. From July to September, you'll rarely wait more than a day or two. At other times waits may be considerably longer.

In the high season (July to early September), the popular four-day circuit around the Salar de Uyuni, Laguna Colorada, Sol de Mañana and Laguna Verde costs as much as US$450 for a 4WD tour, without food. During slower periods, the same trip may cost as little as US$280 to US$300.

For a vehicle, you can normally choose between 4WDs holding six or seven people and tour buses holding up to 30. Bus tours often work out cheaper per person and are normally more comfortable, but the smaller 4WD groups offer more group unity and flexibility.

The invariably basic accommodation in private homes and *campamentos* costs about US$1 per person, and everyone needs a warm sleeping bag. If you have any sort of appetite, it's best to organise your own food, as most companies cut corners wherever possible; also ask whether you're expected to feed your driver. (Some unscrupulous companies may say you don't – as a bargaining point – then send the driver out with nothing assuming you'll take pity and provide meals, anyway).

With more time, you can add Laguna Celeste, a chlorine-blue lake a day's drive north-east of Laguna Verde. This option will add about US$100 to your total tour price. (If you wish to continue from Laguna Verde into Chile, see under Laguna Verde later in this chapter.) Alternatively, you can opt for a four-day Salar tour that includes Llica, Jiriri, surrounding archaeological sites and a climb of 5432m Volcán Tunupa (across the Salar de Uyuni); this costs around US$80 per person, with meals.

The previous edition of this book advised travellers to withhold 50% of the tour price until they returned from their tour satisfied. Unfortunately, standards on some of these tours are below what even hard-bitten travellers expect (there are horror stories aplenty) and quite a few were unsatisfied. Rather than improving operations, some agencies simply began requiring full payment in advance. Now you'll only get away paying half in advance if a group is desperate for participants. Therefore, the importance of choosing a reputable operator cannot be overstressed; things still may not run according to plan, but there's less chance of a desert disaster.

For descriptions of these tour destinations, see the Salar de Uyuni, Los Lipez and South-West Circuit sections later in this chapter. Recommended Uyuni agencies include the following:

Brisa Tours
> Avenida Ferroviaria 320, Uyuni (☎ 2096) This recommended agency, run in league with Olivos Tours (see later in this list) by the very gregarious Amalia, also operates South-West Circuit tours.

Destinations include all the standard stops, and the five-day tour includes Quetena Chico, Tomas Laka and Laguna Celeste. Brisa also offer a particularly nice Salar de Uyuni programme, which features a climb of 5400m to Volcán Tunupa.

Cisne Tours
Avenida Arce, Uyuni (☎ 2121) This friendly, low-key agency does a pretty good job with the South-West Circuit tours from Uyuni. The tours don't appear to be terribly innovative, but they are a solid and acceptable choice.

Olivos Tours
Avenida Potosí 68, Uyuni (☎ 2173) This agency is probably the best and most innovative of any running the South-West Circuit tours from Uyuni. The friendly and knowledgeable owners, Rita and Manco de Ayaviri, are always looking for new and interesting sites to enhance their itineraries, and take pains to provide the best possible service. Its five-day tour takes in little-visited Quetena Chico, Tomas Laka and turquoise-blue Laguna Celeste.

Toñito Tours
152 Avenida Ferroviaria, Uyuni (☎ & fax 2094) Friendly, organised and environmentally conscious Toñito Tours offers two, three and four-day itineraries around the South-West Circuit – the Salar de Uyuni, the Tunupa volcano, Laguna Colorada and Laguna Verde. Another plus point with its South-West Circuit tours is that meals cost only US$15 per person for four days, and vegetarians are accommodated. It also has an office (☎ 360204) at 180 Cuba St in La Paz.

Trans-Andino Tours
Avenida Arce 2 esquina Ferroviaria, Uyuni (☎ 2132) This Italian-owned company specialises in two to five-day circuits around the south-western highlights, including the Salar de Uyuni and the lagunas. It also runs short tours around La Paz, Lake Titicaca, Potosí and Sucre.

Tunupa Tours
Avenida Ferroviaria, Uyuni (☎ 2099) Tunupa is another company offering South-West Circuit tours from Uyuni. It also does one-day trips of the Salar de Uyuni, taking in the major sites plus the little-visited Isla Cáscara de Huevo.

Special Events

Uyuni's big annual festival falls on 11 July and commemorates the town's founding. Celebrations entail torch parades, speeches, dancing, music and naturally, lots of drinking.

Places to Stay

Uyuni's recent tourism boom has meant that hotels fill up quickly, so a booking may offer some peace of mind, especially if you're chugging in on the rails at 2 am.

The most popular digs is still *Hotel Avenida* (☎ 2078), near the railway station, run by the charmingly irascible and formerly peripatetic Don Jesús Rosas Zúniga. Single/double rooms without bath cost US$2.40/4.40. Showers are available until noon for US$1. Doubles with private bath are US$12.50. The office locks up at midnight but will stay open later if there's space available. Breakfast and other meals are no longer served.

Alternatively, the marginal *Residencial Sucre* (☎ 2047) charges US$2.50 per person with shared bath. Nicer is the friendly *Hostal Tunupa* (☎ 2023), at Avenida Ferroviaria 84, south of the railway station. It's housed in a green building beneath a sign reading 'Agencia de Aduanas' (customs agency) – only in Uyuni would this seem logical). There are five rooms, which are arranged around a courtyard. Doubles or dormitory accommodation costs US$2.50 per person. Hot showers cost US$0.60 extra.

If you're really desperate, there is a trio of cheap places on Plaza Arce: the very poor *Residencial Copacabana* (no shower or sink), the filthy *Residencial Uyuni* and the better *Residencial Urcupiña*, which is considerably cleaner and friendlier than the other two. All these places charge US$1.60 per person.

In an emergency, you can crash out in the *sala de espera* at the railway station; it's free and with all the bodies normally crashed out there, it can also be good and warm. Unfortunately, some Bolivians don't appear to mind the cold, and you may be getting up and down all night to close the door. As an alternative, if you appear reputable, the friendly officials at the alcaldía (municipal hall) may allow you to spread out on the floor there.

Places to Eat

One favourite food haunt is the *Restaurant 16 de Julio*, with warming high-carbohydrate fare. It's the first place open for breakfast, but don't arrive much before 8 am. Almuerzos cost US$1.20. They leave the door open but will provide a space heater when icicles begin to form on your nose. The *Restaurant-Pizzería Paso Dorado* next door serves the good old Bolivian stand-bys, plus pizzas, pancakes, burgers and a variety of milanesa incarnations. Another good choice for burgers and standard Bolivian fare is *Los Andes*. *El Fogón* also has a relatively extensive menu, featuring sandwiches, steak and standards. It once offered an imaginative dish featuring milk soup with French fries (yes, in the soup), but it wasn't a big hit.

El Rosedal, across the plaza, also serves American breakfasts of eggs, meat, greasy fried potatoes, bread and horrible coffee for US$1.50. Other meals are more typically Bolivian. On weekend evenings, it operates as a disco. Check out the unusual kerosene drip heater in the middle of the room and watch out for lions, tigers and bears.

Economical meals are prepared at the market comedor and food stalls. For a dose of charque kan (mashed hominy with strips of dried llama meat, an Uyuni speciality) or chicken and chips, try the basic *Snack Ducal*, two blocks away. Good snacks of potato cakes and hamburgers are sold at small stands in the middle of Calle Avaroa, as is fresh bread. You'll also find snack meals at *Mercado Antofagasta* on Avenida Colón.

Entertainment
The cinema beside the Hotel Avenida shows films, mostly of the action genre, daily at 8.30 pm.

Getting There & Away
Bus Several flotas – 11 de Julio, Americano and Emperador – have daily runs to Potosí (US$3.75) and Sucre (US$7.50), departing between 10.30 am and 1 pm from their respective offices along Avenida Ferroviaria. Flota 11 de Julio also serves Tupiza (US$3) on Wednesday and Sunday at 3 pm and Emperador goes to Tarija (US$10) daily at 11 am. Panasur buses to Oruro (US$8) and La Paz (US$10) leave on Wednesday and Sunday at 6 pm from just south of the plaza. Flecha Norte leaves for Oruro (US$8) daily at 8 am.

Train Uyuni sits at the junction of the railway lines to Antofagasta (Chile), Villazón and Oruro, and lies just south of Río Mulatos, where the Potosí and Sucre line branches off the main north-south route.

Uyuni's now boasts a sparkling new railway station, and rail connections are growing more efficient every year. That's not to say they don't still arrive late (or depart even further behind schedule), but the once typical six to 12-hour delays are now more the exception than the rule.

Trains run to Oruro nightly except Wednesday and Sunday. The Friday express train continues on to La Paz. To Tupiza and Villazón, trains leave on Monday, Tuesday, Thursday and Friday, normally in the middle of the night. Trains to Avaroa, with connections to Calama (Chile), leave on Monday and Thursday at 5 am. For more information, see the Getting There & Away chapter and Getting There & Away under Oruro, earlier in this chapter.

SALAR DE UYUNI
The 12,106-sq-km Salar de Uyuni, Bolivia's largest salt pan, covers nearly all of Daniel Campos province. The Salar de Uyuni is now a centre of salt extraction and processing, particularly around the settlement of Colchani, 20 km up the railway line from Uyuni. The estimated annual capacity of the Colchani operation is 19,700 tonnes, 18,000 tonnes of which is for human consumption while the rest is for livestock.

When there's a little water on the flats, it reflects perfectly the blue Altiplano sky and the effect is positively eerie. When they're dry, the salar becomes a blinding white expanse of the greatest nothing imaginable.

History
In recent geological history, this part of the Altiplano was covered entirely by water. Around the ancient lakeshore, two distinctive levels of terraces are visible, indicating the succession of two lakes; below the lower one are fossils of coral in limestone. From 40,000 to 25,000 years ago, Lago Minchín,

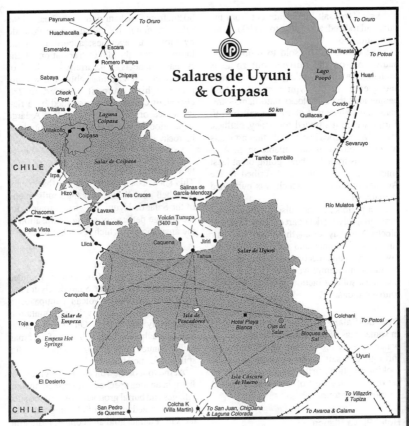

Salares de Uyuni & Coipasa

0   25   50 km

whose highest level reached 3760m, occupied much of south-western Bolivia. When it evaporated, the area lay dry for 14,000 years before the appearance of short-lived Lago Tauca, which lasted for only about 1000 years and rose to 3720m. When it dried up, it left two large puddles, Lagos Poopó and Uru Uru, and two major salt concentrations, the Salares de Uyuni and Coipasa.

This part of the Altiplano is drained internally, with no outlet to the sea; the salt deposits are the result of the minerals leeched from the mountains and deposited at the lowest available point.

Colchani

There remain at least 10 billion tonnes of salt in the Salar de Uyuni, but the only takers thus far are the Colchani campesinos who hack it out with picks and shovels. There's a salt treatment plant near the Colchani railway station, and when trains pull in, vendors board to sell small parcels of salt for domestic use.

Cooperativa Rosario

South-west of Colchani is the extraordinary Cooperative Rosario workshop, known to the tour operators as *Bloques de Sal*, 'salt blocks'. Here, salt blocks are cut from the salar and iodised, according to WHO recommendations.

Most of the salt is sold to refiners and hauled off on the railway, but some is exchanged with local villages for wool, meat and grease. In the winter months, these people load the salt blocks onto llama caravans and transport it along the salt trail to Tarija, where it's traded for honey, chillies, maize, wood, coca leaves and other products which are otherwise unavailable on the Altiplano. This trade has been going on at least since 1612, when it was described in the Aymara orthography, which was published in that year.

As a peripheral, they also produce furniture and lively works of art entirely from salt blocks. You may see anything from souvenir carvings of vicuñas and condors to blocky lawn chairs and decorative triangles. The operation now employs 60 workers and has become a solid attraction on Salar de Uyuni tourist circuits.

Ojos del Salar

In some areas of the salar, cold underground water rises to the surface and bubbles up through the salt layer, creating unusual-looking eruptions on the salt. This distinctive set of examples west of Colchani is visited on most salar tours.

Hotel Playa Blanca

Apart from its straw roof, this unusual hotel, 35 km west of Colchani, is constructed entirely of salt blocks. The exterior isn't much to look at, but its novel position in the middle of the salar and degree of relative comfort are bound to attract someone and, indeed most Salar de Uyuni tours do stop for photos. It has 15 beds costing US$20 per person, not including meals. Bookings should be made through Hidalgo Tours in Potosí.

Isla de Pescadores

For most Salar de Uyuni tours, the main destination is the lovely Isla de Pescadores,

80 km from Colchani right in the heart of the salar. (Although it's called Isla de Pescado by most tour agencies, according to the tourist office, the direct translation of the Aymara name is – bizarrely – 'Island of Fishermen'.) It's a remarkably otherworldly place, a hilly outpost covered in *Trichocereus* cactus and surrounded by a flat, white sea of hexagonal salt tiles. A large population of stranded viscachas populates its rocky slopes.

Isla Cáscara de Huevo

This small island, with a name that means 'eggshell island', lies near the southern end of the Salar de Uyuni. It's visited mainly for the strange patterns of salt crystallisation in the area, some of which resemble roses.

Jiriri & Volcán Tunupa

Diagonally opposite Colchani, a rounded promontory juts into the Salar de Uyuni and on it rises the 5400m Volcán Tunupa. Altitude aside, this hulking yellow mountain is a relatively easy climb. One legend states that Atahualpa slashed the breast of a woman called Tunupa on its slopes, and the milk that spilt out formed the salar.

At the foot of the volcano is the village of Jiriri, in an area specked with ruined ancient villages and burial grounds. Some of the sites have contained articles of clothing and artefacts in ceramic, gold and copper, indicating the presence of an advanced and little-known culture. Unfortunately, remoteness has laid the area open to amateur treasure hunters who have taken a heavy toll on its potential archaeological value.

Private accommodation in Jiriri costs US$2 for a bed and US$1 for a spot on the floor.

Llica

Directly across the Salar from Colchani is the village of Llica, the unlikely site of a teachers college (which can serve as accommodation). There's also a basic new *Alojamiento Municipal* charging US$2 per person.

Getting There & Away

From the rail line between Uyuni and Oruro, you'll glimpse the salar during the stop at Colchani, but to fully appreciate the place, you need to get out onto the salt. The easiest access is with an organised tour (see the Uyuni section) but if you prefer an independent approach, camiones leave for Colchani and Llica from Avenida Ferroviaria in Uyuni, opposite the Hostal Tunupa. You'll have the most luck between 7 and 9 am. Some salt workers living in Uyuni commute daily to Colchani in private vehicles or on motorbikes, and for a small fee you may be able to hitch along.

Alternatively, you can walk between Uyuni and Colchani, as the following letter attests.

It's possible to walk to the Salar de Uyuni over a flat but astounding landscape. Head along the railway track from Uyuni towards Colchani, past the oil depot. Walk about seven km (as measured by distance markers on the railway line) until you reach a ruined building, where the railway curves slightly. Here you'll see a dwelling to your left about three km away in the desert. Head towards it, passing it on your left. Here, take a bearing of 290 compass degrees and you may be able to make out a tiny black blob against the white of the salar. Head for it; it's only a pile of stones acting as a marker, but once you reach it, you're on the salar. This walk would alone justify a journey to Bolivia. Return to the railway line by heading towards the giant 'Z' formed by a road that goes up the mountain. Sunglasses are vital and sunscreen, too. It's about 30 km total and took about eight hours return, including time to stop and gawp at the overwhelming beauty of the place.

Tim Eyre, UK

Getting Around

Camiones from Uyuni make the trip to Llica in a couple of hours and sometimes continue further into the south-west region, carrying supplies to sulphur mines and other camps. This is an adventurous way to go, but come well prepared with food, water and camping gear.

For salar trips in your own vehicle, carry a compass, food, water, extra fuel, tools, spare parts and a means of warming up. Drivers have become lost on the white expanse, and have been known to drive in circles until the vehicle ran out of petrol, which would be a pleasant situation. Also, be sure to keep to the existing vehicle tracks on the salar; it's not only safer, but also prevents damage to this amazing natural feature.

SALAR DE COIPASA

The more remote Salar de Coipasa, the great salt desert north-west of the Salar de Uyuni, was part of the same prehistoric lakes which covered the area over 10,000 years ago. The road to the Salar de Coipasa is extremely poor and vehicles are subject to bogging in deep sand, so you'll need a 4WD. The village of Coipasa sits on an island in the middle of the salar.

Chipaya

Immediately north of the Salar de Coipasa, on the Río Sabaya delta, live the Chipaya Indians, who occupy a single desert village of circular mud huts. Some researchers believe the Chipaya may be a remnant of the lost Tiahuanaco civilisation. Much of this is based on the fact that their language, which is vastly different from either Quechua or Aymara, closely resembles Uros. Other researchers note similarities to Mayan, Arabic and North African tribal languages.

Chipaya tradition maintains that the people descend from the builders of the chullpas scattered around Lake Titicaca. Their religion, which is essentially a nature cult, deifies phallic images, stones, rivers, mountains, animal carcasses and Chipaya ancestors, among other things. Even the rather phallic village church tower is considered a revered deity, and the people also pray to the Volcán Sajama, another honoured spirit.

Within a 15-km radius of the settlement are nine whitewashed sod cones, which are receptacles for appeasement offerings to keep evil spirits from invading the village. The commemoration of the dead ancestors culminates on 2 November, All Saints' Day, when villagers make offerings of fruit, bread, grain and other items.

SOUTHERN ALTIPLANO

Visiting Chipaya In general, tourists aren't particularly welcome, but culturally sensitive visitors can still develop a rapport with the people. If you don't go to gawk or simply 'bag' photos, your chances of acceptance are much better. Traditionally, the Chipayas have been rather superstitious about cameras; although some individuals are now willing to model for a fee, in the interest of avoiding confrontation, visitors should probably abstain from photographing people here.

Visitor 'hospitality' in Chipaya currently costs US$50 per person and everyone must pay. Attempts at bargaining normally only aggravate matters and create ill will. The price only decreases if you're someone the locals want to have around, so put your best self forward.

Getting There & Away Chipaya may be reached from Llica across the Salar de Coipasa or from Oruro via Toledo, Corque and Huachacalla. Hitching from Uyuni is slow. If you're coming from Oruro, there are occasional camiones from the Plaza Walter Khon.

LOS LIPEZ & THE SOUTH-WEST CIRCUIT

The south-western 'toe' of Bolivia is comprised of the provinces of Nor Lipez, Sud Lipez and Baldiviezo, which collectively make up the region known as Los Lipez. Much of it is nominally protected in the Reserva de Fauna Andina Eduardo Avaroa, which was created in 1973 and expanded to its present size in 1981. Its current emphasis is on the vicuña and the llareta plant, both of which are threatened in Bolivia.

This high, wide and lonesome desert country represents one of the world's harshest wilderness regions and a final refuge for some of South America's hardiest wildlife. As a hotbed of volcanic and geothermal activity, the landscape literally boils with minerals. When you see the resulting spectrum of wild unearthly colours in the mountains and lakes, you'll suspect that

Pachamama occasionally takes a walk on the wild side.

Salar de Uyuni to Laguna Colorada

The normal tour route from Uyuni is via Colchani, 20 km to the north-west, then 80 km west across the salar to Isla de Pescadores (see the Salar de Uyuni section earlier in this chapter). After a stop to explore the island, the route turns south and 45 km later, reaches the edge of the salar, where there's a small house where you can buy soft drinks and biscuits.

After another 22 km you reach the village of Colcha K (pronounced COL-cha-KAH), also known as Villa Martín, where you'll pass through a military checkpoint. In the village, there's a lovely adobe church and rudimentary accommodation in a private home and shop 100m up the cobbled street.

About 15 km further along is the quinoa-growing village of San Juan, with another interesting church, a cemetery and in the vicinity, several burial chullpas. Accommodation is provided at an upmarket hostel or in several private homes.

At San Juan, the route turns west and starts across the borax-producing Salar de Chiguana, where the landscape opens up and snowcapped Ollagüe, an active volcano straddling the Chilean border, appears in the distance. There's a rough road leading to a field of steaming fumaroles and sulphur lakes at the 5000m level near the summit and it's possible to catch a ride up with miners working at the sulphur camps.

Before the Chiguana military camp, a short side trip leads to the oddly named Comunidad Amor, which subsists not on love, but on quinoa, and holds several interesting burial chullpas.

At Chiguana, across the Uyuni-Calama railway line, your passport will be scrutinised by gawking soldiers. The route then turns south and climbs into high and increasingly wild terrain, past the lagunas Cañapa, Hedionda, Chiarkhota, Honda and Ramaditas. These mineral-rich lakes are filled with Andean, Chilean and James flamingos and several are backed up by hills resembling spilt chocolate sundaes. After approximately 170 km of rough bumping through marvellous landscapes, the road winds down a hillside to Laguna Colorada.

Laguna Colorada

Fiery red Laguna Colorada, 151 km south of Chiguana, sits at 4278m and covers approximately 48 sq km. The rich red colouration is derived from algae and plankton which thrive in the mineral-rich water, and the shoreline is fringed with brilliant white deposits of sodium, magnesium, borax and gypsum. The lake sediments are also rich in diatoms, tiny microfossils used in the production of fertiliser, paint, toothpaste and plastics, and as a filtering agent for oil, pharmaceuticals, aviation fuel, beer and wine. More apparent are the flamingos that breed here, and all three local species may be

observed (see the Frozen Flamingos aside below).

On the western shore is the Campamento ENDE electric power station. Accommodation is in the squalid and waterless little refugio of Señor Bernal, where visitors now pay US$2 to sleep in draughty unheated rooms. Those relegated to the adobe floor pay half price. Some visitors report also being charged to pitch a tent at the base of the hills, ostensibly because they were within view of the refugio.

The clear air is bitterly cold and night-time temperatures can drop below -20°C. Just as well; if it ever rose much above freezing, the stench of shit and animal carcasses would probably make the place uninhabitable. Instead, the air is perfumed with llareta smoke, which seems sad and ironic given the proximity of Campamento ENDE and the region's practically limitless geothermal, wind and solar potential. There are currently

Frozen Flamingos

Three species of flamingo breed in the bleak high country of south-western Bolivia, and once you've seen these pink posers strutting through icy mineral lagoons at 5000m elevation, you'll abandon time-worn associations between flamingos, coconut palms and the hot, steamy tropics.

Flamingos have a complicated and sophisticated system for filtering the foodstuffs from highly alkaline brackish lakes. They filter algae and diatoms from the water by sucking in and vigourously expelling water from the bill several times per second. The minute particles are caught on fine hair-like protrusions which line the inside of the mandibles. The suction is created by the thick fleshy tongue which rests in a groove in the lower mandible and pumps back and forth like a piston.

The Chilean flamingo *(Phoenicopterus chilensis)* reaches heights of just over one metre and has a black-tipped white bill, dirty blue legs, red knees and salmon-coloured plumage. The James flamingo *(Phoenicoparrus jamesi)* is the smallest of the three species and has dark-red legs and a yellow-and-black bill. It's locally known as *jututu*. The Andean flamingo *(Phoenicoparrus andinus)* is the largest of the three and has pink plumage, yellow legs and a yellow-and-black bill. ■

plans to build a basic solar-powered hotel near the lake.

Sol de Mañana

Most transport you find along the tracks around Laguna Colorada will be supplying or servicing mining and military camps or the developing geothermal project 50 km south at Sol de Mañana.

The main interest is the 4850m-high geyser basin with bubbling mud pots, hellish fumaroles and a thick aroma of sulphur fumes. Approach the site cautiously; any damp or cracked earth is potentially dangerous and cave-ins do occur, sometimes causing serious burns.

Termas de Chalviri

At the foot of Cerro Polques and beside a large salt lake, you'll reach the small 28 to 30° C hot pool known as Termas de Chalviri. Although it's not bathtub temperature by any means, it's still suitable for bathing and is thought to relieve the symptoms of arthritis and rheumatism.

Laguna Verde

Laguna Verde, a stunning blue-green lake at 5000m, is tucked into the south-western corner of Bolivian territory, 52 km south of Sol de Mañana. The incredible green colour springs from high concentrations of lead, sulphur and calcium carbonates. In this exposed position, an icy wind blows almost incessantly, whipping the water into a brilliant green and white froth. This surface agitation combined with the high mineral content means that the temperature must drop well below freezing before ice can form. (I've seen it still liquid at -20° C!)

Behind the lake rises the cone of 5960m Volcán Licancábur, whose summit is said to have once sheltered an ancient Inca crypt. It's believed that on this and other peaks, young Inca men were marched to the summit, exposed to the cruel elements and allowed to freeze to death as a sacrifice to commemorate critical events in the empire. Some tours include an ascent of Licancábur and although it presents no technical diffi-

culties, the wind, temperature, altitude and ball-bearing volcanic pumice underfoot may prove too much for most people.

There are two approaches to Laguna Verde. Where the route splits about 60 km south of Sol de Mañana, the slightly shorter right fork winds along a relatively level route and around a range of caramel-coloured hills to Laguna Verde. The more scenic left fork climbs up and over a 5300m pass, then up a stark hillside resembling a freshly raked Zen garden dotted with the enormous Rocas de Dalí, which appear to have been meticulously placed by Salvador Dalí himself.

Down the far slope are two sulphur mines, a military camp and a refugio where overnight guests pay US$2 per person for a mattress on the floor and running water. Behind the military post, there's a hot spring in a creek where you can have a welcome bath.

To Chile To continue from Laguna Verde into Chile, you must first check out of Bolivia at immigration in Uyuni; the exit stamp allows three days to leave the country. Most agencies can arrange for groups to be picked up by a Chilean agency at the unstaffed Hito Cajón border crossing, seven km from Laguna Verde, for around US$50 per group (but you're still expected to pay the full Bolivian tour price). Note, however, that this system doesn't always run like clockwork, so carry extra food, water and warm gear. If your arranged pick-up doesn't appear, you can either hoof it back to the Laguna Verde refugio or cross into Chile on frozen feet and hope to find a lift.

From Laguna Verde to Hito Cajón is a bitterly cold and windy walk at a 5000m elevation. You'd be very lucky to find a lift there, but fortunately, it's only about a 10-km walk to the road, where you can hope for a camión running between one of the Chilean mining camps and San Pedro de Atacama, 35 km away. Once in San Pedro, remember to check in with Chilean immigration.

Laguna Celeste

Laguna Celeste, which translates as either

'blue lake' or – more romantically – 'lake of heaven', is still very much a peripheral trip for most Uyuni agencies, but it is bound to gain popularity as they grow increasingly competitive. A local legend suggests the presence of a submerged ruin, possibly a chullpa, in the lake.

Behind the lake, a road winds its way up the 6020m Uturuncu volcano to the Uturuncu sulphur mine, which lies in a 5900m pass between the mountain's twin cones. That means it's about 300m higher than the road over the Kardung La in Ladakh (India), making it the highest motorable road in the world.

Other Lakes
In the same region are countless other fascinating lakes which have so far escaped much attention. In the vast eastern reaches of Sud Lipez are at least three more lakes of odd colouration. The milky-looking Laguna Blanca contains water only in the summer rainy period. Laguna Amarilla is, as its name would suggest, sulphur-coloured. The wine-coloured Laguna Guinda lies astride the Bolivia-Argentina border. Some or all of these may eventually find their way onto the circuit.

Quetena Chico
About 120 km north-east of Laguna Verde and 30 km south-west of Laguna Celeste, is the squalid settlement of Quetena Chico, which subsists at the most basic of levels on the extraction of alluvial gold.

The procedure takes place in a 1000-hectare concession around the place called Orckoya, which is five km from Quetena Chico, and is overseen by the Cumbre de la Frontera cooperative. To isolate the gold, prospectors dig holes about one metre deep along the banks of Río Quetena and manually wash it through sluices, where the gold is separated from gravel. Each prospector can hope to come up with between 15 and 30g of gold per month, which is scant reward for the amount of work involved – and the living standards reflect this disheartening fact.

Tomas Laka
The site called Tomas Laka, two km from Quetena Chico, is conjectured to have been an ancient fort. Still visible are ruined walls, several incomplete chullpas and a stone hollow which is thought to have been used as a mortar for pulverising grain.

It lies in an area of bizarrely eroded rock formations which bear some equally unusual rock paintings. Subjects include the standard pumas and serpents, but there's also a line-up of bizarre-looking 'bugs' – a sort of cross between giant ants and space creatures – wearing World Cup referee uniforms.

Valles de Rocas & San Cristóbal
The route back to Uyuni turns north-east a few km north of Laguna Colorada and winds through more high, lonesome country and several valleys of bizarre eroded rock formations known as the Valles de Rocas. Petrol is available sporadically at the village of Alota, from which it's a trying six-hour jostle back to Uyuni.

If you can still cope with sightseeing at this stage, a short side trip will take you to the village of San Cristóbal, in a little valley north-east of Alota. Here you'll find a lovely 350-year-old church constructed on an age-old Pachamama ritual site. The walls bear a series of paintings from the life of Christ and the altar is made of pure silver and backed up by a beautifully preserved 17th-century organ. The site is so revered that the *llaves sagradas* – the 'sacred keys' – to the church, may only be touched by 'pure spirits', and at sowing time, there's a tradition of writing the names of one's vices on rocks from the fields and symbolically depositing them in the church.

PULACAYO
At the semi-ghost town of Pulacayo, between Uyuni and Potosí, brilliantly coloured rocks rise beside the road and a mineral-rich stream slides past, revealing streaks of blue, yellow red and green.

The Pulacayo mines, north of the village, yielded mainly silver. They were first opened in the late 17th century, but closed in 1832 on account of the Independence war. In 1873, however, the mining company Compañía Huanchaca de Bolivia (CHB) took over operations and resumed silver extraction. The grave of the company founder A Mariano Ramirez can still be seen.

The little-known Museo de Minas, the mining museum, may be an attempt at reviving Pulacayo from the dead, but it is worthwhile. You can explore nearly two km of mine tunnels (the mine's entire extent is just under six km) with local guides for US$2 per person. Pulacayo is also home to several decaying steam locomotives, which were imported to transport ore. They include Bolivia's first steam engine, *El Chiripa*, and others with such names as *El Burro*, *El Torito* and *Mauricio Hothschild*.

You can also visit the historic 1878 home of Aniceto Arce, which features lovely marble fireplaces, pianos, old telephones and period furniture imported from England.

Places to Stay & Eat

Befitting its more active past, Pulacayo has a very basic but surprisingly pleasant 100-room hotel, *Hotel El Rancho*. Rooms cost US$3 per person and meals are available.

Getting There & Away

All transport between Uyuni and Potosí passes through Pulacayo.

TOMAVE

The centrepiece of Tomave is its unusual 1530 church, which took 100 years to build and is laid out in the form of a Latin cross. The pipe organ, which is probably the original one, dates from the 16th century. The ceiling windows are made of marble, as is the beautiful baptismal font. Some of the paintings on the walls were painted by the Cuzco school, and there are at least three by the Bolivian master Pérez de Holguín.

At the village of Asientos, four km north of Tomave, is the ruin of another home of Aniceto Arce. The small village church houses a very impressive antique Bible. With a guide, visitors can enter the abandoned

gold and silver mine that spawned and once sustained Asientos. The intact chimney on the hillside also merits a look.

Getting There & Away

Camiones leave for Tomave from in front of the police station in Uyuni on Wednesday at 10 am, and return the following day at the same time. If you have a group, day tours to Tomave can be arranged through Agencia Tunupa in Uyuni.

TUPIZA

In the background looms the Tupizan range, very red, or better, a ruddy sepia; and very distinct, resembling a landscape painted by an artist with the animated brilliance of Delacroix or by an Impressionist like Renoir...In the tranquil translucent air, flows the breath of smiling grace...

Carlos Medinaceli, Bolivian writer

Tupiza, embedded in some of Bolivia's most spectacular countryside, is a real gem. The capital of Sud Chichas, a province of Potosí department, Tupiza is among Bolivia's most literate and educated cities. It's also a comparatively young city – half of its 20,000 inhabitants are under the age of 20 and its growth rate is one of the country's highest.

The city lies at 2950m in the valley of the Río Tupiza, surrounded by the rugged Cordillera de Chichas. The climate is mild year-round, with most of the rain falling between November and March. From June to August, days are hot, dry and clear, but night-time temperatures can drop to below freezing.

Economically, the town depends on agriculture and the mining of antimony, lead, silver, bismuth, and some tin. A YPFB (Yacimientos Petrolíferos Fiscales Bolivianos) refinery five km south of town provides employment, and the country's only antimony smelter operates along a dry tributary of the Río Tupiza. Although tourists have recently begun trickling into Tupiza, the Chichas area is still well off the rutted track.

The charm of Tupiza lies in the surrounding countryside – an amazing landscape of rainbow-coloured rocks, hills, mountains and canyons. The landscape is a vision from the Old West, and appropriately so. Tupiza lies in the heart of Butch Cassidy and the Sundance Kid country. After robbing an Aramayo payroll at Huaca Huañusca, about 40 km north of town, the pair reputedly met their untimely demise in the mining village of San Vicente. See the San Vicente section, later in this chapter.

History

The tribe that originally inhabited the valley and surrounding mountains called themselves Chichas. They left archaeological evidence of their existence but little is known of their culture or language. It's assumed they were ethnically separate from the tribes in neighbouring areas of southern Bolivia and northern Argentina. However, anything unique about them was destroyed between 1471 and 1488 when the Incas, under the leadership of Tupac Inca Yupanqui, annexed the region into the Inca empire. The Chichas were used by the Incas as a military nucleus from which to gather forces and organise armies to conquer the Humahuaca, Diaguitas and Calchaquíes tribes of northern Argentina.

Once the Inca empire had fallen to the Spanish, the entire southern half of the Viceroyalty of Alto Peru was awarded to Diego de Almagro by decree of King Carlos V of Spain. When Almagro and company arrived in the Tupiza valley on a familiarisation expedition in October 1535, the Chichas culture had been entirely subsumed by that of the Incas. Almagro stayed briefly in the valley, and then moved southward towards Chile, bent on exploring the remainder of his newly acquired spoils.

Officially, Tupiza was founded on 4 June 1574 by Captain Luis de Fuentes (who also founded Tarija), but this date is pure conjecture. The origin of the name is similarly hazy. The current spelling was derived from the Chichas word *Tope'sa* or *Tucpicsa*, but no-one is sure what it meant. It has been suggested that it probably referred to 'red rock' since that seems to be the area's predominant feature, but that's just a guess.

In the tumultuous Campesino Rebellion of 1781, the peasants' champion Luis de la Vega, mobilised the local militia and proclaimed himself governor of Chichas, Lipez, Cinti and Porco, and encouraged resistance against Spanish authorities. The rebellion was squashed before it really got underway, but the mob was successful in executing the Spanish *corregidor* (chief magistrate) of Tupiza and levelling his estate. At the same time, 4000 Indian troops led by Pedro de la Cruz Condori, which had been charged with organising and carrying out terrorist acts against the government, were intercepted by Spanish forces before reaching their destination.

On 7 November 1810, the first victory in Alto Peru's struggle for independence from Spain was won at the Battle of Suipacha, which took place just east of the Tupiza valley. At the end of the war, on 9 December 1824, the deciding battle took place at Tumusla in the northern Chichas.

From Tupiza's founding through the War of Independence, its Spanish population grew steadily, lured by the favourable climate and suitable agricultural and grazing lands. Later, the discovery of minerals in the Cordilleras de Chichas and Lipez attracted even more settlers, and with them came Indians to do the manual labour. In 1840, Argentine revolutionaries fleeing the dictator Juan Manuel Rosas escaped to Tupiza and were incorporated into the community. More recently, campesinos have drifted in from the countryside, and many out-of-work miners and their families have already settled. The favourable climatic and economic conditions also attract migrants from other parts of Bolivia.

Information

There's no tourist office in Tupiza, but the friendly folk at the Hotel Mitru can answer most of your questions. The telephone code for Tupiza is 0694.

Money You'll see lots of 'Compro Dólares' signs; the Cooperativa El Chorolque, on Plaza Independencia, changes cash, but at

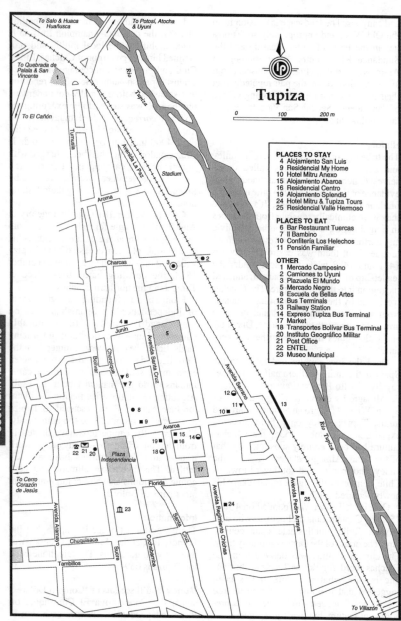

Tupiza

0   100   200 m

PLACES TO STAY
4 Alojamiento San Luis
9 Residencial My Home
10 Hotel Mitru Anexo
15 Alojamiento Abaroa
16 Residencial Centro
19 Alojamiento Splendid
24 Hotel Mitru & Tupiza Tours
25 Residencial Valle Hermoso

PLACES TO EAT
6 Bar Restaurant Tuercas
7 Il Bambino
10 Confitería Los Helechos
11 Pensión Familiar

OTHER
1 Mercado Campesino
2 Camiones to Uyuni
3 Plazuela El Mundo
5 Mercado Negro
8 Escuela de Bellas Artes
12 Bus Terminals
13 Railway Station
14 Expreso Tupiza Bus Terminal
17 Market
18 Transportes Bolívar Bus Terminal
20 Instituto Geográfico Militar
21 Post Office
22 ENTEL
23 Museo Municipal

SOUTHERN ALTIPLANO

poor rates. Better choices are the hardware stores, Ferretería Cruz, on Santa Cruz, and Ferretería Marco Hermanos, on the corner of Santa Cruz and Florida. The Manaco shoe store also changes cash at a decent rate. There's no place to change travellers cheques, but in an emergency, ask around for the very friendly Señor Umberto Bernal, who may be able to help.

Finca Chajrahuasi

Across the river, mostly overgrown with weeds, is the abandoned farmstead of tin baron Carlos Victor Aramayo. Aramayo, who had maintained his business in Bolivia using Bolivian labour, was heaped into the same category as the absentee Simón Patiño and when his mines were nationalised in 1952, the estate was confiscated and Aramayo fled to Europe to escape the backlash. Finca Chajrahuasi now serves as a rough football field but it was apparently once quite a comfy residence.

Escuela de Bellas Artes

The Escuela de Bellas Artes (School of Fine Arts) occupies the 16th-century mansion of the Eguía family. Inside is a mini art museum and a small but beautiful library of old literary works and reference books in Spanish, English and French.

Museo Municipal

Tupiza's municipal museum, just off the plaza, houses a mix of historical and cultural artefacts, including an antique cart, historical photos, archaeological relics, old weapons and historic farming implements. It's open Monday to Friday from 6 to 8 pm. Foreigners pay US$0.50.

Cerro Corazón de Jesús

The short trail to the summit of Cerro Corazón de Jesús, flanked by Stations of the Cross, is a pleasant morning or evening walk when the low sun brings out the fiery reds of the surrounding countryside. The hill, which is crowned by a statue of Christ, affords a good overall view of the town.

Markets

The Mercado de Ferias takes place on Monday, Thursday, and Saturday mornings along Avenida Regimiento Chichas. The Mercado Negro, where you'll encounter a mishmash of consumer goods, occupies the block between Avenida Regimiento Chichas, Avenida Santa Cruz, Junín and Avaroa. It's open daily.

Organised Tours

Tupiza Tours (☎ & fax 3001) at Hotel Mitru runs good value day trips exploring Tupiza's wild quebradas. It also runs tours (US$60 per person) along the trail of Butch and Sundance to Huaca Huañusca (worth it for the scenery alone!) and the bleak and lonely mining village of San Vicente where, in 1908, the outlaws' careers abruptly ended. If you have a group of at least four people, Tupiza will arrange a *peña* featuring a typical *tupiceño* ensemble known as *anatas*, with *zampoña*, *quena* and tambourine.

Tupiza Tours also organises bus, train and air tickets for a 10% commission.

Places to Stay

The friendly, bright and airy *Hotel Mitru* (☎ & fax 3001) and the affiliated *Hotel Mitru Anexo* are both excellent choices. Rooms without/with bath cost US$4.20/6.20 per person and dormitory rooms with four beds are just US$2 per person.

The comfortable *Residencial Centro* (☎ 2705), on Avenida Santa Cruz, costs US$3/5 for a single/double with private bath. It's clean but don't put too much faith in their claims about having hot water. A popular, good value option is the cosy-sounding *Residencial My Home* (☎ 2947), at Avaroa 288, charges US$4.20 per person with private bath, US$2.75 without.

Another decent place is the *Residencial Valle Hermoso* (☎ 2592), which charges US$2 per person; seven-minute showers are an additional US$0.75. A recent addition, *Alojamiento San Luis* (☎ 3040), charges US$2 per person and an additional US$0.75 for a 15-minute hot shower.

Moving even further down the scale are the alojamientos *Abaroa* and *Splendid* on Avenida Santa Cruz. Simple beds cost US$1 per person. Don't expect much and you won't be disappointed.

Places to Eat

For inexpensive almuerzos and cenas, try the small restaurants around the bus terminals; the *Pensión Familiar* is recommended. In the afternoon, stands outside the railway station serve filling meals of rice, salad, potatoes and a main dish for US$1. The inexpensive market foods are especially good for breakfast.

You'll find Tupiza's best salteñas at the friendly *Il Bambino*, which also has excellent value almuerzos for US$1.20. In the afternoon, you can snack on empanadas, pasteles and other savouries. The *Bar Restaurant Tuercas* does excellent lunches, but it's often haunted by irritating drunks. *Cremelin* on the plaza serves good inexpensive ice cream.

The dining rooms at *Residencial My Home* and the *Hotel Mitru* both serve good set meals. The latter serves continental/American breakfasts for US$1/2.20 and lunches for US$2. Residencial Centro has a pleasant-looking attached restaurant that never appears to be open.

Confitería Los Helechos at the Hotel Mitru Anexo, the only restaurant that keeps reliable hours, sets the scene with a cactus skeleton done up in coloured Christmas lights. Breakfasts are especially inviting, served with quince jam and real coffee. Later in the day they do good burgers, milanesa, chicken, licuados, and as a novelty, a variety of international cocktails involving such tipples as sake, tequila, vodka, rum and of course, singani. The associated restaurant next door serves well-prepared and filling local dishes.

Getting There & Away

Bus Most buses depart from Avenida Serrano, opposite the railway station. Several companies have morning and evening departures to Potosí (US$6.50, 12

hours). Flota Cristal and Trans Gran Chaco have evening departures to Tarija (US$4, eight hours), with connections to Yacuiba. Expreso Tupiza, which leaves from Avenida Regimiento Chichas, has buses to Villazón (US$2, two hours) several times daily, between 7 am and 5 pm.

On Monday and Thursday, Flota 11 de Julio leaves for Uyuni at 2 pm (US$3, eight hours). Trucks to Uyuni leave in the morning from Calle Charcas just east of Plazuela El Mundo, a traffic circle around an enormous globe.

Camión Thanks to mining activities on the Altiplano west of town, there's a relatively good network of crisscrossing roads. There's no public transport, but you can hitch lifts with the camiones that service the mines, foundries, geological camps and health posts scattered between Tupiza and the Chilean and Argentine frontiers.

Train The ticket window has no set opening hours, so ask for local advice regarding when to queue up. The tren expreso to Uyuni (US$10/8.50 1st/2nd class), Oruro (US$16/14 1st/2nd class) and La Paz (US$17/15 1st/2nd class) passes Tupiza on Saturday at 3.30 pm; to Villazón (US$6/5 1st/2nd class), it passes on Saturday at 4.15 am. The tren rápido to Uyuni (US$3/2.10 1st/2nd class) and Oruro (US$6/4.50 1st/2nd class) leave Tupiza on Tuesday and Friday at 4 or 4.30 pm and the tren mixto passes on Monday and Thursday at 7.15 pm.

Trains to Villazón (US$1.70/1.20 1st/2nd class), coming from either Oruro or La Paz, run on Monday, Tuesday, Thursday and Friday, passing Tupiza between 7 and 9 am.

AROUND TUPIZA

Much of Tupiza's appeal lies in the surrounding landscape. Hiking opportunities abound and even within three or four km of town, the mazes of ridges, quebradas and canyons provide a good sampling of what the country has to offer. Occasionally, the IGM office on

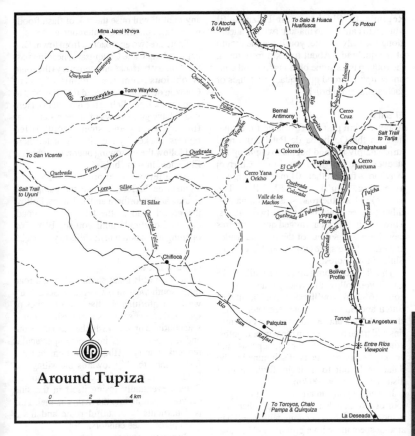

Around Tupiza

0   2   4 km

the plaza in Tupiza has topographic sheets of the area; otherwise, you can pick them up in La Paz. However, even without a map, it would be difficult to get lost.

You should carry at least two or three litres of water for each day you intend to spend hiking in this dry desert climate. It's wise to wear shoes that can withstand assault by prickly desert vegetation, and to carry a compass if you're venturing away from the tracks. Flash flooding is also a danger, especially in the summer months; avoid camping in the quebradas, especially if it looks like rain.

Quebrada de Palala

Just north of Tupiza is the broad wash known as the Quebrada de Palala, which is lined with some very impressive red conglomerate formations known as *fins*. During the rainy season, it becomes a tributary of the Río Tupiza, but in the winter months, it serves as a highway into the back country and part of the salt route from the Salar de Uyuni to Tarija. Beyond the dramatic red rocks, the wash rises very gently into hills coloured greenish blue and violet by lead and other mineral deposits.

To get started, head north on Avenida

Regimiento Chichas, past Plazuela El Mundo to campesino market; two km ahead, along the railway line, you'll see the mouth of the quebrada. About five km from town, the route passes some obvious fins and continues up the broad quebrada, past stands of cactus and scrub brush.

El Sillar

About 2.5 km past the first large fin formations in the Quebrada de Palala, the road turns sharply left and begins to climb up the steeper and narrower Quebrada Chiriyoj Waykho. After another 10 km of winding and ascending, you'll reach El Sillar (The Saddle), where the road straddles a narrow ridge between two peaks and two valleys. Throughout this area, rugged amphitheatres have been gouged out of the mountainsides and eroded into spires that resemble China's Shilin Stone Forest.

The distance from Tupiza to El Sillar is 16 km; if you follow this road for another 3½ hours (65 km), you'll reach San Vicente, of Butch and Sundance fame (see later in this chapter). This entire route is part of a centuries-old trade route and in the winter months, you'll see trains of llamas, alpacas and donkeys carrying blocks of salt mined in the Salar de Uyuni to trade in Tarija, a total distance of nearly 300 km.

In Tupiza you can arrange a taxi for up to four or five people to El Sillar or other sites in the area for US$4 per hour, which isn't bad at all, especially with a group – and because you're paying by the hour, the drivers will accommodate as many photo stops as you like. Try Radio Taxi la Joya (☎ 473) at Avenida Santa Cruz 306. Alternatively, the folk at Tupiza Tours (☎ 3001) can arrange day tours or recommend specific drivers.

El Cañón

El Cañón, a lovely walk east of Tupiza through a narrow twisting canyon past dramatic fin formations, makes a great half-day stroll from town. It gently ascends for 2.5 km along a sandy riverbed, to end at a *chacra* (cornfield) near the canyon head. There are several good camp sites along the route, but

any rainfall will raise the risk of flash flooding in this constricted watercourse.

There are two approaches from town. One begins along Calle Chuquisaca, heading past the military barracks and cemetery (the route is obvious from the summit of Cerro Corazón de Jesús). The road then narrows to a sandy track paralleling the mountains. Here you'll have good views of some spectacular fin formations and steep cactus-filled ravines, backed by red hills. Bear left here and follow the narrowing quebrada, which is El Cañón, into the hills.

An alternative approach is past the Escuela de Fátima, beyond the campesino market at the northern end of Tupiza. Follow the gravel road to the left up this broad, cluttered quebrada until you see El Cañón opening into a notch in the hills to your right.

Quebrada Seca

Near the YPFB plant south of town, a road turns south-west into Quebrada Seca ('dry wash'). Unfortunately, the lower reaches of Quebrada Seca serve as a rubbish tip but if you continue up the wash, the trash thins out and the route passes into some spectacular red rock country. At the intersection, the right fork climbs the hill towards the village of Palquiza and the left fork crosses the Río San Rafael, eventually losing itself in the side canyons opening into the main channel. This is a particularly beautiful route and it's a good place to see condors.

During the dry season, hikers can turn left just before the Río San Rafael bridge (10 km south of Tupiza) and follow the river's northern bank to Entre Ríos. If you wade the Río Tupiza at this point, you can return to town via the road coming from Villazón.

Quebrada de Palmira

Between Tupiza and Quebrada Seca lies the wonderful Quebrada de Palmira, a normally dry wash flanked by tall and precarious fin formations. The right fork of the wash is rather comically known as Valle de los Machos (Valley of Males) or the less genteel Valle de los Penes (Valley of Penises). The names stem from the crowds of exceptionally phallic pedestal formations that line it.

At the head of the main fork of the quebrada, you can ascend along a trickle of calcium-rich fresh water, up over boulders and through rock grottoes, into a hidden world beneath steep canyon walls. About 300m up the canyon you'll find several excellent camp sites with some water available most of the year.

La Angostura & Entre Ríos

Eight km south of town, the Río Tupiza narrows to squeeze through La Angostura (The Narrows), a tight opening in the rock. Here the Villazón road is conducted past it through a rock tunnel, with views through to the churning waters below.

As you approach La Angostura from Tupiza, watch along the ridge west of the river for the formation known as Bolívar, a rock outcrop resembling a profile of the liberator.

There's a nice view across the confluence of the Ríos Tupiza and San Rafael from the lay-by at Entre Ríos, 10 km south of Tupiza.

La Deseada

The name La Deseada means 'The Desired'. This shady little spot beside the Río Tupiza, 12 km south of Tupiza, has a broad flat area for tent camping near the river bank and is a favourite picnic site for Tupiza people. To get there, cross the Calle Beni bridge from Tupiza and look for a ride at the tranca on the Villazón road.

Huaca Huañusca

On 4 November 1908, Butch Cassidy and the Sundance Kid pulled off the last robbery of their career when they politely and peacefully relieved Carlos Peró of the Aramayo company payroll, which amounted to US$90,000, at the foot of a hill called Huaca Huañusca. The name, which means 'dead cow', was apparently applied because of the hill's resemblance to a fallen bovine. The site itself is nothing spectacular, but you can see the distinct *camino de radura* (saddle track) followed by the bandits and their victims.

More incredible than Huaca Huañusca itself is the route between Tupiza and the village of Salo, at the foot of the climb up to Huaca Huañusca. Red spires, pinnacles, canyons, tall cactus and tiny adobe villages create an illusion of 1890s Arizona, and appear to have been lifted straight from a John Ford Western. Almost as impressive is ENTEL's experimental rural communications programme, which is evident in the several hamlets en route. From these tiny adobe settlements, it's now possible to direct dial anywhere in the world!

SAN VICENTE

This one-mule town wouldn't even rate a mention were it not the village where the legendary outlaws Robert LeRoy Parker and Harry Alonzo Longabaugh – better known as Butch Cassidy and the Sundance Kid – met their untimely demise when cornered by a posse on 6 November 1908.

The mine in San Vicente has now been closed and the village is rapidly becoming a ghost town with a current population of around 40 and dropping. Most of those remaining are mine security people and their families.

Places to Stay & Eat

San Vicente has become a bit of a pilgrimage site for Butch and Sundance fans, as well as for travellers taken with the lure of the Old West. That still amounts to only a trickle of visitors, however, and San Vicente still lacks any semblance of tourist infrastructure.

There is a *hotel*, of sorts, and an adjoining restaurant, called *Rancho*, on the main street, but thanks to an unstable village economy, operations are rather sporadic. When they are open, beds and rather 'resourceful' meals cost about US$1 each.

Bread is available at the village *bakery*, identifiable by morning queues of san vicenteños, and you'll find grocery staples – tinned milk, sardines, biscuits, soft drinks and beer – in tiny *tiendas* along the main

SOUTHERN ALTIPLANO

The Last Days of Butch Cassidy & the Sundance Kid

Butch and Sundance came to southern Bolivia in August 1908 and took up residence with the Briton AG Francis, who was transporting a gold dredge on the Río San Juan de Oro. While casing banks to finance their retirement, the outlaws learned of an even sweeter target: a poorly guarded US$480,000 (B$80,000) mine-company payroll to be hauled by mule from Tupiza to Quechisla.

On 3 November 1908, manager Carlos Peró picked up a packet of cash from Aramayo, Francke & Compañia in Tupiza and headed north with his 10-year-old son and a servant, but they were discreetly tailed by Butch and Sundance. Peró's party overnighted in Salo, then set off again at dawn. As the trio ascended the hill called Huaca Huañusca, the bandits watched from above with binoculars. In a rugged spot on the far side of the hill, they relieved Peró of a handsome mule and the remittance, which turned out to be a mere US$90,000 (B$15,000) – the prized payroll had been slated for shipment the following week.

Dispirited, Butch and Sundance returned to AG Francis' headquarters at Tomahuaico. The following day, Francis guided them to Estarca, where the three of them spent the night. On the morning of 6 November, the bandits bade farewell to Francis and headed north-west to San Vicente.

Meanwhile, Peró had sounded the alarm, and posses were scouring southern Bolivia. A four-man contingent from Uyuni reached San Vicente that afternoon. Butch and Sundance arrived at dusk, rented a room from Bonifacio Casasola, and sent him to fetch supper. The posse came to investigate and had scarcely entered the courtyard when Butch shot and killed a soldier. During the brief gunfight that ensued, Sundance was badly wounded. Realising that escape was impossible, Butch ended Sundance's misery with a shot between the eyes, then fired a bullet into his own temple.

At the inquest, Carlos Peró identified the corpses as those of the men who had robbed him. Although buried as *desconocidos* (unknowns) in the cemetery, the outlaws fit descriptions of Butch and Sundance, and a mountain of circumstantial evidence points to their having met their doom in San Vicente. Nonetheless, rumours of their return to the USA have made their fate one of the great mysteries of the American West.

In 1991, a team led by forensic anthropologist Clyde Snow attempted to settle the question by excavating a grave indicated by an elderly San Vicenteño to be that of the Aramayo bandits. The grave's sole occupant, however, turned out to be a German miner named Gustav Zimmer.

Anne Meadows & Daniel Buck, USA
(Anne Meadows is the author of *Digging up Butch & Sundance*, Bison Books, University of Nebraska Press, 1996)

street. Occasionally, a *kiosk* on the plaza dishes up plates of llama fricassee.

Getting There & Away

There's no regular public transport to remote San Vicente, but occasionally, a camión leaves early on Thursday morning from the stop, just over the railway line from Plazuela El Mundo in Tupiza; it's mainly dependent on the current economic situation in San Vicente.

The easiest way to go is with Tupiza Tours; see Organised Tours under Tupiza, earlier in this chapter. If you prefer to reach San Vicente on your own, ask Hotel Mitru about arranging a pick-up taxi; with up to four people, you'll pay US$80 to US$100 (plus food for the driver) for the 10-hour return trip.

Access by hired vehicle from Atocha, via the colonial-era ghost town of Portugalete, takes about two hours. The longer route from Tupiza runs via El Sillar and the northward turning at the village of Nazarenito, which has a basic tienda. The scenery is more spectacular than on the Atocha route, but the trip takes about four hours. This is also part of the salt route from the Salar de Uyuni.

VILLAZÓN

Villazón, the most popular border crossing between Bolivia and Argentina, is a dusty, haphazard settlement which contrasts sharply with relatively tidy La Quiaca, Argentina, just over the border. In addition to being a point of entry, Villazón is a warehousing and marketing centre for contraband

Top Left: Travelling in south-western Bolivia (RS)
Top Right: Landscape over the horizon, south-west Bolivia (DS)
Bottom Left: Sol de Mañana geyser basin, south-west Bolivia (DS)
Bottom right: Stone pinnacle, north of Tupiza (DS)

Top: Travel by camión in the Cordillera Real (TM)
Bottom: Shepherd, south-western Bolivia near Sajama (TM)

(food products, electronic goods and alcohol) being smuggled into Bolivia on the backs of peasants, who form a human cargo train across the frontier. This is known as the *comercio de hormigos* (ant trade). Much of Argentina's Jujuy province is populated by Bolivian expats and migration into Argentina continues, lending Villazón the nickname the 'Tijuana of Bolivia'.

Information

Foreign Consulate The helpful Argentine Consulate, upstairs in the Galería Ojeda, is open Monday to Friday from 10 am to noon and 2 to 5 pm.

Money To change US cash dollars or Argentine pesos into bolivianos, you'll get reasonable rates from the casas de cambio along Avenida República Argentina. However, not all places offer the same rates, so shop around. If dollars are currently in demand, Universo Tours will change travellers cheques but at a poor rate with at least 5% commission.

Post & Communications There are post and telephone offices on both sides of the border, but the Bolivian services are generally cheaper. The telephone code for Villazón is 0696.

Time From October to April, there's a one-hour time difference between Bolivia and Argentina (noon in Villazón is 1 pm in La Quiaca). From May to September, the Argentine province of Jujuy, where La Quiaca is located, operates on Bolivian time (only a bit more efficiently).

Dangers & Annoyances For some reason, you'll need to be more on your guard in Villazón than other parts of Bolivia. I've encountered several 'fake police' scams there and on my most recent trip, a bus station baggage handler attempted to disappear with my pack into a warehouse across the street. Readers also report problems, mainly pickpockets and other sneak thieves.

Counterfeit US dollar notes are also making appearances.

Places to Stay

Villazón has a couple of economical hotels and alojamientos. An excellent choice is the clean and friendly *Residencial Martínez* (☎ 562), near the bus terminal. Singles/doubles without bath cost US$4/6. The hot showers are a real plus point, and operate without an electric attachment.

As for the *Grand Palace Hotel* (☎ 333), don't be taken in by the name – or the advertising for the *piste de patinaje* (skating rink), which appears to be used only as a disco. It's not that bad at US$3 per person without bath, but service is disinterested and the atmosphere less than friendly.

Another cheap option is *Alojamiento Quillacollo* (☎ 399), on Avenida República Argentina. It's a real dump but costs only US$2 per person. Near the railway station is *Residencial Panamericano*; rooms cost US$3 per person, without bath or hot water.

A travellers' favourite is the clean and cosy *Residencial El Cortijo* (☎ 209), two blocks from the bus terminal. Single/double rooms with shared bath cost US$4/7.

Places to Eat

For meals, there isn't much choice. Try the *Charke Kan Restaurant*, opposite the bus terminal, which is good but rather grimy. The owners are keen on music and a bizarre round record player hums in the background. There are several other less appealing restaurants near the transportation terminals. Quick chicken and Bolivian staples are on offer at *Snack El Pechegón*. The market food stalls make up in price what they lack in variety. You'll also find delicious licuados and fruit juices – incongruous treats in this climate. Alternatively, pop over to La Quiaca for meals (see La Quiaca later in this chapter).

Getting There & Away

Bus All northbound buses depart from the central terminal; tickets and reservations for

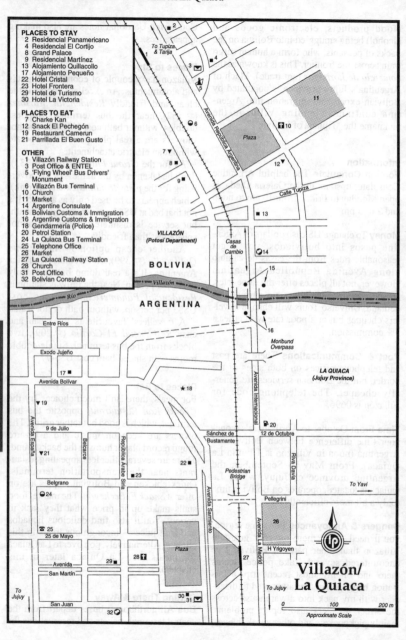

PLACES TO STAY
2 Residencial Panamericano
4 Residencial El Cortijo
8 Grand Palace
9 Residencial Martínez
13 Alojamiento Quillacollo
17 Alojamiento Pequeño
22 Hotel Cristal
23 Hotel Frontera
29 Hotel de Turismo
30 Hotel La Victoria

PLACES TO EAT
7 Charke Kan
12 Snack El Pechegón
19 Restaurant Camerun
21 Parrillada El Buen Gusto

OTHER
1 Villazón Railway Station
3 Post Office & ENTEL
5 'Flying Wheel' Bus Drivers' Monument
6 Villazón Bus Terminal
10 Church
11 Market
14 Argentine Consulate
15 Bolivian Customs & Immigration
16 Argentine Customs & Immigration
18 Gendarmería (Police)
20 Petrol Station
24 La Quiaca Bus Terminal
25 Telephone Office
26 Market
27 La Quiaca Railway Station
28 Church
31 Post Office
32 Bolivian Consulate

Argentine buses are sold at the offices opposite the main terminal entrance.

Flotas leave for Tupiza in the morning and afternoon (US$2, 2 hours). It's a beautiful trip so go in the morning (the first bus is at 6.45 am) for maximum daylight viewing. There are also at least five daily buses to Potosí via Tupiza (US$8, 13 hours), with connections to Sucre, Cochabamba and La Paz.

There are several nightly buses to Tarija, which leave daily between 7 and 8 pm (US$3, eight hours); it's too bad they travel at night, because the canyon country scenery – and the treacherous road – are exceptionally dramatic. From Tarija, Flota Trans-Yacuiba continues along the equally beautiful route to Villamontes (US$10, 20 hours) and Yacuiba (US$10, 22 hours).

Train Trains to Tupiza, Uyuni and Oruro depart on Monday, Tuesday, Thursday and Friday at 4 or 4.30 pm. There's no longer onward rail service into Argentina.

The ticket window is meant to open at 8 am on the day of departure, but tickets can be difficult to secure. If you'd rather avoid the ferrocarril frolics, see Universo Tours on Avenida República Argentina. You'll pay a commission but there's a minimum of fuss. Avoid the temptation to purchase tickets from scalpers outside the station unless you're certain they're legitimate; people often try to sell used tickets, banking that new arrivals in Bolivia won't know the difference.

Crossing into Argentina Villazón has an Argentine consulate, and La Quiaca has a Bolivian consulate. For quick trips over the border, just walk straight across the bridge; you don't have to go through immigration unless you're staying more than a couple of hours. Crossing the border is usually no problem, but avoid the contrabandistas' procession otherwise it may take you hours to get through. Bolivian immigration is open from 7 am to 7 pm and doesn't close for lunch. If the Argentine official is working

alone, the post closes for lunch between noon and 2 pm.

If you're entering Argentina, count on an exhaustive customs search about 20 km south of the border. The entry/exit tax occasionally charged by Bolivian immigration officers is strictly unofficial.

LA QUIACA (ARGENTINA)

Villazón's twin town of La Quiaca lies just across the Río Villazón in northern Argentina. The contrast between the two sides is striking; La Quiaca is a neatly groomed town with tree-lined avenues, surfaced streets, pleasant restaurants and well-stocked shops.

Information
Bolivian Consulate The Bolivian Consulate is open Monday to Friday from 8.30 to 11 am and 2 to 5 pm. On Saturday, it opens from 9 am to noon.

Money On the Argentine side, US dollars are legal tender and dollars and Argentine pesos are exchanged at a par. However, dollar notes with even the slightest flaw aren't accepted anywhere.

If you're exchanging Bolivianos for dollars or pesos here, it's a good idea to exchange just enough cash to get you to Salta or Jujuy where rates will be better.

The province of Jujuy issues its own peso banknotes, which resemble Monopoly money and may be used only within the province.

Post & Communications The post is generally more reliable than in Bolivia and reverse charge phone calls are accepted to limited areas. La Quiaca's telephone code is 0885; to dial from outside Argentina, add the country code (54) and drop the leading zero.

Iglesia de San Francisco
If you're continuing into Argentina, a visit to Yavi 15 km east of La Quiaca is recommended. Here you'll find the tiny Iglesia de San Francisco, built in 1680, which has an ornately gilded interior and translucent onyx windows. It's open Tuesday from 9 am to

noon and 3 to 6 pm, and on Saturday from 9 am to noon. Find the caretaker who can open the door and show you around. Flota La Quiaqueña departs for Yavi from the La Quiaca bus terminal.

Places to Stay

The bottom-end in La Quiaca is the basic *Alojamiento Pequeño* near the frontier. It isn't terribly friendly, but there is a pleasant parrot and lots of dogs to keep you company. Simple rooms without bath cost US$5 per person. A more expensive dump is the *Hotel La Victoria* on the main plaza, where stark rooms cost US$10 per person.

The mid-range *Hotel Crystal* (☎ 2255) at Avenida Sarmiento 539 charges US$18/28 for a single/double with bath and heat. Triples/quadruples cost US$38/46. Rooms without bath cost US$7 per person. Request the one that shares a wall with the bakery; it's almost as good as having a heater!

The *Residencial Frontera* costs US$8 per person with shared bath. There's no heating but you can get an electric shower.

Near the corner of República Arabe Siria and San Martín is the clean *Hotel de Turismo* (☎ 2243, fax 2201) which charges US$17/28 for a single/double with TV and private bath. They do have radiators but they only fire them up in July.

Places to Eat

The food is generally better here than in Villazón, and it's worth tripping across the border for a meal, but as you'd expect in Argentina, menus are heavily weighted in favour of carnivores.

The *Hotel de Turismo* has a warm dining room with a stone fireplace. An immense steak with chips goes for US$5. For parrillada, try *Camerun* and *Confitería El Buen Gusto*, both near the bus terminal. The *Restaurant Terminal*, upstairs in the bus terminal, serves almuerzos and snacks.

The pleasant *Confitería Cristal* is a good choice for snacks and light meals. The unassuming *Confitería La Frontera* at the Residencial Frontera serves nice *tortillas españolas* and luscious *tallarines al pesto*, with real pesto sauce, for US$4. Four-course set-menu almuerzos are a reasonable US$3.50. Service can be a bit surly but the food makes up for it.

Getting There & Away

Bus All buses now depart from the new central bus terminal in La Quiaca, and most long-distance services offer heat, air conditioning, video and on-board facilities.

Flota Panamericano has services to Argentina, including Humahuaca and Jujuy (or more precisely, San Salvador de Jujuy) almost hourly, with four express services daily. The trip to Jujuy, which passes through some stunningly colourful, cactus-studded landscapes, costs US$20 and takes six or seven hours by express. Otherwise, the trip takes eight or nine hours and costs US$16.

From Jujuy, Panamericano has frequent connections to Salta, Cafayate, Rosario and Córdoba, as well as the most direct service to Buenos Aires (US$85, 48 hours with a change in Güemes). Flota Atahuallpa connects La Quiaca with Jujuy at least six times daily, with connections all over the country, including frequent departures to Salta (despite what they'll tell you, they don't have direct buses from La Quiaca to Salta) and four daily to Buenos Aires. Andesmar has daily connections to Santiago (Chile) and all over Argentina, including Bariloche and Santa Cruz de Patagonia.

Flota El Quiaqueño serves Yavi, Abra Pampa and other nearby communities, as well as Jujuy.

Train There is no longer passenger rail service from La Quiaca.

Cochabamba

Cochabamba, a progressive and economically active city, has a growing population of over 400,000 and a vitality that is visibly absent from the more traditional higher altitude cities.

The saying *'Las golondrinas nunca migran de Cochabamba'* ('The swallows never migrate from Cochabamba') aptly describes what *cochabambinos* believe is the world's most comfortable climate, with warm, dry, sunny days and cool nights.

The city's name is derived by joining the Quechua words *khocha* and *pampa*, meaning 'swampy plain'. Cochabamba lies in a fertile green bowl, 25 km long by 10 km wide, set in a landscape of fields and low hills. To the north-west rises 5035m Cerro Tunari, the highest peak in central Bolivia. The area's rich soil yields abundant crops of maize, barley, wheat, alfalfa, and orchard and citrus fruits.

Apart from the climate, however, there's little for tourists. Once you've seen the museums and done some shopping, it's time to head for the hinterlands. At some point, try to sample *chicha cochabambina*, an alcoholic maize brew typical of the region.

History

Cochabamba was founded in January 1574 by Sebastián Barba de Padilla, and named the Villa de Oropeza in honour of the Count and Countess of Oropeza, parents of Viceroy Francisco de Toledo who chartered and promoted its settlement.

During the height of Potosí's silver boom, the Cochabamba Valley developed into the primary source of food for the miners in agriculturally unproductive Potosí. Thanks to its maize and wheat production, Cochabamba came to be the 'breadbasket of Bolivia'. When Potosí declined in importance during the early 18th century, so did Cochabamba, and grain production in the Chuquisaca (Sucre) area, much closer to

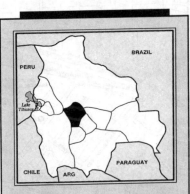

Highlights

- Tour the opulent Palacio de Portales to see the excesses of Bolivia's mining 'royalty'
- Visit one of the country's finest archaeological museums and see artefacts spanning Bolivian culture from 15,000 BC to colonial times
- Shop for just about anything imaginable at Cochabamba's vast, nerve-shattering, crowded and colourful La Cancha market
- Relax beside a waterfall in Parque Nacional Torotoro, bathe in idyllic swimming holes, and examine enormous fossilised dinosaur footprints
- Hike up through fern and butterfly-filled temperate forest in the Parque Nacional Tunari to the trout-filled Lagunas de Huarahuara
- Climb up to the immense *Cristo de la Concordia* to admire the view of Cochabamba

Potosí, was sufficient to supply the decreasing demand.

By the mid-19th century, however, the economic crisis stabilised and the city again assumed its position as the nation's granary. Elite landowners in the valley grew wealthy and began investing in highland mining ventures in western Bolivia. Before long, the

Cochabamba

PLACES TO STAY		17	Gopal	27	Post Office
12	Gran Hotel	18	La Salsa Café	28	LAB (Airline)
	Ambassador	19	Eli's Pizza Express	29	ENTEL
20	Residencial Familiar	21	Rondevu Pizzería	31	Immigration Office
	Anexo	22	Confitería Bambi	32	Tourist Office
21	Capitol Hotel	26	Tea Room Zürich	38	Iglesia & Convento
23	Hotel Boston	30	Pizza Llauchas		de San Francisco
41	Caesar's Plaza Hotel	33	Heladería Dumbo	39	Los Amigos del Libro
45	City Hotel	34	California Burgers &	42	Banco de Santa Cruz
49	Hostal Colonial		Donuts	43	Iglesia de Santo
52	Hostal Central	35	Confitería Cecy &		Domingo
53	Residencial Familiar		Kivón Helados	44	Cathedral
56	Alojamientos	36	La Vie en Rose	47	Chilean Consulate
	Cochabamba &	37	Snack Uno	48	Viajes Fremen
	Roma	40	Restaurant Lose	50	'The Big Screw'
57	Residencial Florida	46	Chifal	55	Banco BISA
58	Mary Hotel	51	Restaurant El Corso	66	Micros to Quillacollo,
59	Alojamiento Escobar	54	Café Express Bolívar		Payrumani, Sipe
61	Residencial Escobar	60	El Caminante		Sipe etc
62	Americano Hotel &	65	Bar Pensión Familiar	71	Mercado Cancha
	Rodizio Grill	67	Churrasquería Hawaii		Calatayud
	Americano	70	Pensión La Suiza	72	Flota 7 de Junio
63	Hostal Jordán			73	Bus Terminal
64	Residencial Jordán	**OTHER**		74	Heroínas de la
68	Residencial Urkupiña	1	Palacio de Portales		Coronilla
69	Residencial Elisa	3	Brazilian Consulate		Monument
		4	Argentine Consulate	75	Railway Station
PLACES TO EAT		5	US Consulate	76	Mercado de Ferias
2	IC Norte	7	Peruvian Consulate	77	Micros to Torotoro
6	Palacio del Silpancho	11	Convento de Santa	78	Micros & Buses to
8	Bibossy		Teresa		Chapare
9	La Cantonata	14	El Caminante Equipo	79	Micros to Tarata
10	El Rincón Salón de Te		de Camping	80	Micros to Cliza
13	Café Bistro El Carajillo	15	El Hospicio	81	Micros to Punata &
16	Metrópolis Bar/	24	Museo Arqueológico		Arani
	Restaurant	25	Casa de la Cultura		

Altiplano mines were attracting international capital and the focus of Bolivian mining shifted from Potosí to south-western Bolivia. As a result, Cochabamba thrived and its European/mestizo population gained a reputation for affluence and prosperity.

Orientation

Cochabamba's central business district lies roughly between the Río Rocha in the north and Colina San Sebastián and Laguna Alalay in the south-west and south-east, respectively.

The largest market areas are on or south of Avenida Aroma, sandwiched between Colina San Sebastián and Laguna Alalay. The long-distance bus terminal, the railway station and most of the intra-valley bus terminals are also in this vicinity.

Cochabamba addresses are measured from Plaza 14 de Septiembre and are preceded by 'N' (norte), 'S' (sud), 'E' (este) or 'O' (oeste – to avoid alphanumeric confusion, a 'W' is sometimes used instead). Obviously, these stand for 'north', 'south', 'east' and 'west', respectively.

Maps The Instituto Geográfico Militar (☎ 27965) has an office at Calle Antezana S-0648, which sells topo sheets from around Cochabamba department.

Information

Tourist Office The tourist office on Plaza 14 de Septiembre is open Monday to Friday from 9 am to noon and 2 to 6 pm. The staff sell photocopied town plans for US$1.20.

COCHABAMBA

Foreign Consulates Consular representatives in Cochabamba include:

Argentina
Calle Federico Blanco O-929 (☎ 29347); weekdays from 8.30 am to 1 pm.
Brazil
Edificio Banco Sur, 9th floor (☎ 55860); weekdays from noon to 6 pm.
Chile
Avenida de las Heroínas, corner of Lanza E-620 (☎ 22845); weekdays from 8.30 am to 1 pm.
Germany
Edificio Promontora, 6th floor (☎ 54024); Monday and Friday from 5 to 6.30 pm and Wednesday from 11 am to noon.
Peru
Avenida Pando 1143, Recoleta (☎ 46210); weekdays from 9 am to noon and 3 to 6 pm.
USA
Avenida Libertador Bolívar 1724 (☎ 43216); weekdays from 9 am to noon.

Money The BISA bank gives the best exchange rate in town for American Express travellers cheques; unfortunately, it doesn't change any other brands. American Exchange and Exprint-Bol usually give decent rates and also change travellers cheques. Moneychangers gather around the ENTEL office and along Avenida de las Heroínas. Their rates are competitive, but they'll only accept US dollars cash and don't give much over the official rates.

Visa and MasterCard cash advances are available at major banks and at Enlace machines around the city.

Post & Communications The post and telephone offices are both in the large complex on Avenida Ayacucho between Calle General Achá and Avenida de las Heroínas. Postal service from Cochabamba is reliable and the facilities are among the country's finest. Downstairs from the main lobby is an express post office.

The main ENTEL office is open daily from 6.30 am to 10 pm, and there's also one at the airport, which has more limited opening hours. Cochabamba's public fax number is 48500. The telephone code is 042.

Bookshops Los Amigos del Libro has several small outlets, at Avenida de las Heroínas E-311 and at Calle General Achá E-110, and in the Torres Sofer Shopping Centre. They sell some English, French and German-language paperbacks, reference books and souvenir publications. Among the *artesanía* stalls behind the post office are vendors selling Spanish-language literature and other books for reasonable and negotiable prices.

Cultural Centres Alliance Française, Calle Santivañez O-187, and the Goethe Institut, on the corner of Calles Sucre and Antezana, sponsor cultural activities and have reading rooms with current newspapers and books in French and German, respectively. The reading room of the Centro Boliviano-Americano, Calle 25 de Mayo N-365, near Plaza Colón, is open weekdays from 9 am to noon and 3 to 9.30 pm. Its library, which is open until 7 pm, is limited to American literature.

Laundry Moderna I is at Nataniel Aguirre 2-0742 and charges US$1 per kg for washing and drying. The service takes 10 hours.

Camping Equipment You'll find camping equipment at El Caminante Equipo de Camping shop at Calle 25 de Mayo N-391, near Plaza Colón.

Film & Photography Slide film is sold at Foto Broadway, Calle Colombia 283, and in the Korean-owned shops around the plaza.

Dangers & Annoyances During the Andean cholera epidemic of several years ago, Cochabamba was one of the most hard-hit areas. Although the problem now appears to be under control, visitors should be especially careful with raw produce, animal products and drinking water.

Readers have warned of impromptu passport checks and fines from fake police around the Colina San Sebastián; if you're stopped, ask to see the officer's identification. If they continue to hassle you, insist that the matter be settled at the police station.

In Cochabamba's rural hinterlands, be especially wary of vinchuca beetles, which carry Chagas' disease (see the Health section in the Facts for the Visitor chapter). The Chagas Institute at the Universidad San Simón does tests and distributes booklets about the beetle and the disease.

Churches

Cochabamba's churches are rarely open during the hours posted at the tourist office; you'll have the most luck in the early morning, late afternoon, on Saturday afternoons and on Sundays.

Cathedral The cathedral on the arcaded Plaza 14 de Septiembre was built in neo-Classical style in 1571, making it the oldest religious structure in the valley. With a myriad of architecturally diverse additions over the years, the composition doesn't hang together at all well, but the frescoes and paintings inside are worth a look.

Iglesia & Convento de San Francisco Constructed in 1581, the Iglesia de San Francisco on Calle 25 de Mayo and Avenida Libertador Bolívar is Cochabamba's second-oldest church. Major revisions and renovation occurred in 1782 and 1925, however, and little of the original structure remains. The attached convent and cloister were added in the 1600s. In appreciation of the pleasant Cochabamba climate, the cloister was constructed of wood rather than stone, as would have been customary at the time. The pulpit displays fine examples of mestizo design. San Francisco is normally open from 6.30 to 8 pm.

Convento de Santa Teresa If you can look past the kitsch halo of lights over the altar, the interior of the Convento de Santa Teresa on Calle Baptista and Plaza Granado is quite impressive. It's actually a combination of two churches, one built on top of the other. Work on the first church was begun in 1753

by Jesuits. In theory, Santa Teresa is open from 7.30 to 8 am.

El Hospicio El Hospicio on Plaza Colón combines Baroque, Byzantine and neoclassical architectural styles. It was begun in 1875 and is the valley's most recent major church.

Iglesia de Santo Domingo The Rococo-style Iglesia de Santo Domingo, on the corner of Calle Santiváñez and Avenida Ayacucho was founded in 1612, but construction wasn't begun until 1778. When its chief promoter Francisco Claros García died in 1795, construction was still underway. The intriguing main doorway is flanked by two anthropomorphic columns.

Iglesia de la Recoleta The Iglesia de la Recoleta, north of the river, is a Baroque structure started in 1654. The attraction is a wooden carving entitled *Cristo de la Recoleta*, which was hewn from a single piece of wood by Diego Ortiz de Guzmán.

Colina San Sebastián

This hill, just south of Avenida Aroma, towers over the airport and is a pleasant place to relax, read or watch the planes. There's also a nice view over the city. From San Sebastián a trail leads along a ridge to another hill, La Coronilla, with a monument dedicated to the women, children and senior citizens who courageously defended the city from the Spanish forces of José Manuel Goyeneche in 1812.

Museo Arqueológico

The Museo Arqueológico, on 25 de Mayo between Avenida de las Heroínas and Calle Colombia, is one of Bolivia's finest. Exhibits include thousands of artefacts, dating from as early as 15,000 BC and as late as the colonial period. Admission is US$1, and the excellent guided tour, conducted in English, French or Spanish, takes about 1½ hours. The museum is open Monday to Friday from 9 am to noon and 2 to 6 pm, and on Saturday from 9 am to 1 pm.

COCHABAMBA

Museo de la Historia Natural & Jardín Botánico Martín Cárdenas

The Natural History Museum, once well displayed in the Casa de la Cultura, has been transferred to its current outpost in the botanical gardens. The insect collection, with thousands of beetles, bugs and butterflies, is impressive, but as it's now crammed into an uncomfortably small room, it's difficult to appreciate. The museum also contains some colourful mineral specimens and a pathetic collection of moth-eaten stuffed animals.

The even less interesting Martín Cárdenas Botanical Gardens are little more than a four-hectare swathe of dry grass studded with sickly shrubs and eucalyptus trees (it also includes six hectares of wild bushland in the Serranía de San Pedro). If you've nothing else to do, it's open from 6 am to 6 pm. Take *micro* 'H' from Avenida San Martín to Avenida Ramón Rivero at the end of Aniceto Arce.

Casa de la Cultura

The city archives, reading room and art exhibits are on the 3rd floor of the Casa de la Cultura, on the corner of Avenida de las Heroínas and Calle 25 de Mayo. It's open Monday to Friday from 8 am to noon and 2 to 6 pm, and admission is free. Ask the curator to show you the fascinating discoveries from Omereque, a pre-Inca burial site near Aiquile, south-east of Cochabamba. The faces bear an uncanny resemblance to the 'little green men' of UFO encounters around the world!

Palacio de Portales

The Palacio de Portales, in the barrio of Queru Queru, provides more evidence of the extravagance of tin baron Simón Patiño. Construction of this opulent home began in 1915 and was completed in 1927; the final design by French architect Eugene Bliault in 1925. Except perhaps for the brick, everything was imported: the fireplaces were constructed of flawless Carrera marble; the furniture and woodwork were carved in wood imported from France; and the walls were covered with silk brocade – one intricate 'painting' is actually a woven silk tapestry. The gardens and exterior, which were inspired by the palace at Versailles, also reflect inconceivable affluence. In spite of all this extravagance, the house was never occupied, and today it is used as a teaching centre, a hall for visiting exhibitions and an arts complex.

The building is open Monday to Friday from 5 to 6 pm and on Saturday from 10 am to noon. The attached art museum is open Monday to Saturday from 2.30 to 6.30 pm. Foreigners pay US$1.50 for guided tours. Take micro 'G' from the corner of Avenida de las Heroínas and Calle San Martín.

Markets

Cochabamba is the biggest market town in Bolivia, and the formerly separate markets around San Antonio, near the railway station and bus terminal, have now coalesced into one enormous market, known simply as 'La Cancha'. This is one of the best stocked and most crowded and nerve-shattering places in the entire country.

The inordinate bustle is mostly a result of the 'New Economic Policy', which has been promoting privatisation of public services and cuts in public spending since 1985. It has resulted in massive unemployment and forced thousands of people to earn a living as street vendors or market stall holders. Around the market, you'll find just about anything imaginable, and a wander through is both worthwhile and totally exhausting.

The largest and most accessible area is Mercado Cancha Calatayud, which sprawls across a wide area in Avenida Aroma and south towards the railway station. Here is your best opportunity to see local dress, which differs strikingly from that of the Altiplano. Both Cancha Francisco Rivas and the Mercado de Ferias Central sprawl around the railway station, and other minor markets are scattered around the city. The artesanía is concentrated near the junction of Tarata and Calle Esteban Arce, near the south-western end of the market area. Here you'll find two alleys filled with friendly and reasonably priced stalls: one alley specialises in cloth and ornaments, the other has musical instruments.

Cristo de la Concordia

An immense new statue of Cristo de la Concordia (Christ of the Concordance) stands on a hill top behind Cochabamba. It's a few cm higher than the famous Cristo Redentor on Rio de Janeiro's Corcovado, which stands 33m high, or one metre for each year of Christ's life. Cochabambinos justify the one-upmanship by claiming that Christ actually lived 33 years and a bit ('33 años y un poquito').

Micros reach the foot of the statue on weekends only; look for micro 'LL' from near the corner of Avenida de las Heroínas and Calle 25 de Mayo. At other times, you'll either have to walk or take a taxi. The walk takes three hours from the city centre and half an hour on the new footpath from the base of the mountain, but beware of vicious dogs. For a small fee, you can climb to the top of the statue for a great overview of the city. Taxis charge US$5 for the return trip, including a half-hour wait while you look around the statue.

Language Courses

Cochabamba is probably the best place in Bolivia to hole up for a few weeks of Spanish or Quechua lessons. Cochabamba has a couple of language institutes, the largest of which is the Padres de Maryknoll Instituto de Idiomas, Casilla 550, Cochabamba, Bolivia. Write in advance for information.

Another option is the Instituto de Lenguaje Cochabamba (☎ 44868), at Plazuela Busch S-0826 esquina Bolívar, Casilla 2966, Cochabamba, Bolivia, which offers Spanish, Quechua and Portuguese courses.

There are also plenty of private teachers, who charge around US$5 per hour, but not all are experienced. Two of the best are Señor Reginaldo Rojos (☎ 42322) and Jaime Claros (☎ 41241), who offers intensive instruction in both Spanish and Quechua for US$5 per hour. Also recommended are Marycruz Almanza Bedoya (☎ 27923 or 87201) and Ms Haydee Lobo (☎ 41447), who has many years experience teaching both Spanish and Quechua. Alternatively, seek recommendations at the Centro Boliviano-Americano (☎ 21288), at Calle 25 de Mayo N-365.

Organised Tours

A recommended agency is Dutch-operated Viajes Fremen (☎ 59392, fax 59686), Casilla 1040, Calle Tumusla 245 (attention María de los Ángeles Ribera), which organises excursions throughout the Cochabamba area. It's not cheap, but if you have a group, the per person costs drop to quite reasonable levels. Tours are run to Chapare, Torotoro, Incallajta, Parque Nacional Tunari, Cerro Tunari and several interesting villages around the Cochabamba Valley. Other specialities include the Amazon area, particularly the Chapare region, Parque Nacional Isiboro-Sécure, Hotel El Puente (a wilderness resort near Villa Tunari) and the Reina de Enin riverboat, which is based in Trinidad. For more information, see the Villa Tunari and Trinidad sections in the Amazon Basin chapter.

Special Events

Cochabamba's major annual event is the Heroínas de la Coronilla on 27 May, a solemn commemoration in honour of the women and children who defended the city in the battle of 1812.

The fiesta of Santa Veracruz Tatala is celebrated annually on 2 May, in and around a chapel seven km down the highway towards Sucre. Farmers from around the Cochabamba Valley gather to pray for fertility of the soil during the coming season. The fiesta is accompanied by folk music, dancing and lots of raging drunken activity.

See the Quillacollo section for information on the Virgen de Urcupiña festival, which is the valley's largest celebration.

Places to Stay – bottom end

The alojamientos strung out along Avenida Aroma – *Fortaleza, Ayacucho, Miraflores, Aroma* and others – make up Cochabamba's

COCHABAMBA

grotty bottom-end lodgings. For very basic accommodation, you'll pay around US$2.

The cheapest decent accommodation is *Alojamiento Cochabamba* (☎ 25067), at Calle Nataniel Aguirre S-591. It's popular with budget travellers, but is basically a flop-house. Rooms with shared bath cost US$2.20 per person, without breakfast. *Alojamiento Roma* (☎ 58592), next door, charges US$2.20 per person single or double; there's also a triple room for US$6.

Near nerve-racking Avenida Aroma are the *Residencial Escobar* (☎ 29275), at Uruguay E-0213, which charges US$3 per person with common bath, and *Alojamiento Escobar* (☎ 25812), at Calle Nataniel Aguirre S-0749, at US$2 per person. Cleaner but a bit dingy is the *Residencial Urkupiña* (☎ 23502), at Esteban Arce 750, which charges US$3 per person.

One of Bolivia's nicest inexpensive digs is *Residencial Elisa* (☎ 27846), at Calle Agustín Lopez 834 near Avenida Aroma. Despite the dodgy location, just inside the door it's a different world, with a grassy courtyard and clean, sunny garden tables. The friendly owner can help with tourist information. A room with bath costs US$7; without bath, it's US$4.

Another excellent choice is *Residencial Florida* (☎ 57911), at Calle 25 de Mayo S-0583, which has a quiet patio and lawn furniture on the main floor and a sundeck upstairs. It's in a good location midway between the town centre and the transport terminal, and it's a good place to meet other travellers. There's hot water until 1 pm, and the friendly owner cooks up a mean break-fast for her guests. For single/double rooms, you'll pay US$6.20/11.50 with bath and US$4/7.50 without.

Residencial Familiar (☎ 27988), Calle Sucre E-554, and *Residencial Familiar Anexo* (☎ 27986), Calle 25 de Mayo N-0234, are popular with both Bolivian and foreign travellers. In the latter residencial, one of the regulations reads: 'Persons who register alone are not to be visited by persons of the opposite sex and particularly not by persons of doubtful morality or animals of any species.' The slightly overpriced rooms, arranged around a central courtyard, cost US$4 per person without bath. Note that the door locks aren't always secure.

The friendly, clean and secure *Hostal Colonial* (☎ 21791) is rapidly becoming a travellers' favourite. Try to get a room upstairs overlooking the leafy courtyard gardens. Rooms with bath cost US$6 per person.

One of the best deals around is *Hostal Central* (☎ 23622; fax 49397), on Calle General Achá, which charges US$7 per person for a room with private bath, TV and a continental breakfast. The rooms are set back from the street and are therefore quiet.

At the top of the price range is the four-star *Hostal Jordán* (☎ 25010; fax 24821), at 25 de Mayo 651. At US$9.50/15 for a single/double room it offers good value accommodation. All rooms have private bath, colour TV and phone, and there's a pool and solarium. The affiliated *Residencial Jordán* (☎ 25010; fax 24821), at Calles Antezana 671, gets three stars and costs US$8/14 for a single/double with similar amenities.

Places to Stay – middle

At Calle 25 de Mayo N-167 is the *Hotel Boston* (☎ 28330; fax 57037), a reasonable mid-range option with singles/doubles for US$20/30, including breakfast and private bath.

The clean but rather noisy *City Hotel* (☎ 22993) at Calle Jordán E-341 charges US$12.50/19 for a single/double room with bath. Rooms without bath on the upper floors are US$10.50/14.50.

The *Capitol Hotel* (☎ 24510; fax 23422), at Calles Colombia and 25 de Mayo, isn't bad at US$12/19 for a single/double with bath, but rooms are dim and merely func-tional.

A new mid-range choice within easy reach of the bus terminal is the *Mary Hotel* (☎ 52487; fax 51746), at Calle Nataniel Aguirre S-601. Carpeted rooms with bath, TV, telephone and continental breakfast cost

US$17/30 for a single/double. Double beds are US$28.

Places to Stay – top end

A prominent upmarket hotel is *Caesar's Plaza* (☎ 50045; fax 50324) at Calle 25 de Mayo S-210. Singles/doubles/triples start at US$45/55/76, including breakfast. All rooms have heating, air-con, TV, phone and frigobar (bar fridge). The front desk changes US dollars cash for a reasonable rate.

The four-star *Gran Hotel Ambassador* (☎ 48777) at Calle España N-349 has single/double rooms for US$30/45 with bath, TV, phone and breakfast included. Suites cost US$55/65.

The friendly three-star *Americano Hotel* (☎ 50552; fax 50484), on the corner of Avenida Aroma and Esteban Arce, is a highly recommended upmarket option. The rooms are all bright and clean with TV and private baths, and are good value at US$25/35 for a single/double.

Places to Eat

One of the joys of a visit to Cochabamba is its wonderful choice of quality restaurants. You can easily spend a few days munching your way around the city, and some of the best places aren't necessarily expensive.

Markets & Self-Catering The enormous *main market area* stretches northward from the Mercado de Ferias, near the railway station, to Cancha Calatayud, along Avenida Aroma between San Martín and Lanza. The most central market is on Calle 25 de Mayo between Calles Sucre and Jordán. For lunch or dinner, markets cook up inexpensive but tasty meals. They're also the cheapest places to find coffee and a roll for breakfast. Since the mild Cochabamba Valley is known for its fruit production, there's also a nice selection of orchard and citrus produce. If you're up for something more traditional, try arroz con leche, a local breakfast speciality.

If you prefer more processing and packaging, you'll be in heaven at the enormous and trendy North American-style supermarket *IC Norte*, on Avenida Pando. On Heroínas and

San Martín, the *Super-Haas* ('super rabbit', but it may not be intentional) supermarket has a good variety of expensive cheeses and lots of deli-style foreign goods. For munchies or hiking snacks, stop by *San Marcos* on Ladislao Cabrera between Calle Esteban Arce and Nataniel Aguirre where you can buy large bags of granola de tarhui (tarhui is a legume) for US$0.50.

Breakfast For breakfast, *Kivón Helados*, at Avenida de las Heroínas E-352, serves great juice, eggs, toast and chocolate, as well as Irish coffee and salteñas. It will also pile on the pancakes, French toast, eggs, ham and so on. *Pizza Llauchas*, half a block from the plaza, serves nice salteñas and llauchas (overstuffed cheese empanadas), as well as fruit juices and licuados. The coffee is a bitter brew, but it's cheap and is even available on Sunday mornings. On the corner of Calle General Achá and Avenida Villazón, street vendors sell delicious papas rellenas (potatoes filled with meat or cheese).

Snacks Avenida de las Heroínas is fast-food row. *Confitería Cecy* is good for light lunches of burgers, chips, chicken, pizza and other snacks. The friendly owner speaks English, having spent many years in the USA, and although he has North American fast-food culture down to an art, he also produces delicious award-winning salteñas, which are available mid-morning. Other similar places include *California Burgers & Donuts*, with good strong Irish coffee, the bizarrely decorated *Unicornio*, and *Kivón Helados*, which serves snack meals, pastries, flans and ice cream (the world's most superfluous public employee is the officer outside who spends the day guarding a nearby parking spot for the Bolivian navy). *Heladería Dumbo*, with its landmark flying elephant, and *Confitería Bambi*, at Calles Colombia and 25 de Mayo, may infringe Disney copyright, but both serve good light meals and ice cream. *Heladería Imperial*, on Calle Sucre, has excellent but inexpensive ice cream – a large cup costs only US$1.

For excellent Venezuelan arepas and black

beans, as well as salteñas, go to *La Cara-queña* on Plaza de Calacala, north of the centre; take micro 'A'. On street corners, you can buy delicious burgers known as porkies for US$0.60, but go easy on the chilli sauce provided – it will probably be more potent than you expect.

El Rincón Salón de Te, at Mayor Rocha 355, offers coffee, cakes and other snacks, including cheesecake and lemon meringue pie; it's recommended for afternoon tea. Alternatively, try the coffee, doughnuts and éclairs at the *Tea Room Zürich*, at Avenida San Martín 143, open daily except Tuesday from 9.30 to 11.30 am and 2 to 7.30 pm. The northern end of Calle España and neighbouring Calle Venezuela have lots of little pastelerías and confiterías serving coffee and sweet snacks.

Café Express Bolívar, on Avenida Ballivián, offers what may be Cochabamba's best espresso and cappuccino. *Pizza Llauchas* does pizza and baguette sandwiches. You'll also find excellent sandwiches, cappuccino, espresso, tea and breakfast options at the *Snack Terminal*, in the main bus terminal. It's almost the only place to go when your bus arrives in the wee hours of the morning.

Lunches & Dinners You'll find economical almuerzos just about everywhere. Try *Bar Pensión Familiar*, Avenida Aroma O-176, which does salad, soup, a main course and a dessert for US$1; the beer is also inexpensive. Other good bets are *Anexo El Negro*, on Calle Esteban Arce between Calles Jordán and Calama; *Rellenos Calama*, on Calle Calama between Calles 16 de Julio and Antezana; and *El Caminante*, on Calle Esteban Arce near Cabrera. The latter serves inexpensive lunches in a pleasant open courtyard. For an interesting local alternative, check out *El Palacio del Silpancho*, which dishes up the eponymous flattened schnitzel with egg, chips, rice and spicy onion salad.

The basic but recommended *Pensión La Suiza* at Avenida Ballivián 820, serves good cheap almuerzos, sandwiches and even that Altiplano speciality, charque kan.

Moving up in price, there's a string of sidewalk cafés along Avenida Ballivián, offering European, Bolivian and North American fare in a pleasant environment. If you're really hungry, try *Bibossy* at Avenida Ballivián N-539 near Plaza Colón – the formidable lunch portions bury the plate.

Nearer the centre is the appealing steak-oriented *Rodizio Grill Americano*, beside the Hotel Americano, which serves three meals daily, including outstanding almuerzos for US$2.50. It's a real carnivore's delight, but they do compensate with a great soup and salad bar. Just a few blocks down Avenida Aroma is the *Churrasquería Hawaii*, which also specialises in steak and is popular with locals.

More of a fish emphasis characterises the *Restaurant El Corso*, on the corner of Calles Junín and General Achá. Choices include surubí, pejerrey, parrillada and pato al horno (baked duck). For a semblance of French cuisine – as well as breakfasts, pastas and German options – try the nice but rather

---

Chicha Cochabambina

Chicha quiero, chicha busco,
Por chicha mis paseos.
Señora, deme un vasito
Para cumplir mis deseos.

This longing old Bolivian verse cries: 'I want chicha, I search for chicha, for chicha are my wanderings. Lady, give me a glass to satisfy my longing'.

To most Bolivians, Cochabamba is known for one of two things: romantics will dreamily remark on its luscious climate, whereas hardcore imbibers, such as the author of the above poem, will identify Cochabamba with its luscious chicha cochabambina. Both images of the city are well founded.

Throughout the valley and around much of southern Cochabamba department, you'll see white cloth or plastic flags flying on long poles, indicating that chicha is available. Travelling outside the town, you'll realise just how popular it is and, at 2570m elevation, it does pack a good punch! ■

pretentious *La Vie en Rose* at Avenida de las Heroínas E-452.

What may be Bolivia's finest Mexican food – tacos, enchiladas, burritos, quesadillas, nachos and other treats – is served up at the colourful *La Salsa Café*, at Calle 25 de Mayo N-217. Breakfast choices include American pancakes, omelettes and speciality coffees. La Salsa also prepares llauchas, chilli dogs, burgers, chicken, chips, pizzas, ice cream, international baguette sandwiches and Bolivian specialities. The music isn't bad, either.

A good choice for lunch or dinner is the Korean-run, Chinese-oriented *Restaurant Lose* on the plaza, which dishes up abundant Chinese-style noodles, sweet and sour and vegetable dishes, as well as pasta and inexpensive Bolivian almuerzos. It's excellent value, but don't be in too much of a hurry.

In the northern part of town, on Plaza de Calacala, is the *Club Social*, which serves tasty salteñas as well as typically spicy Cochabamba specialities: chicken in hot red sauce, beef tongue in hot yellow sauce, and picante mixto, a sort of mixed hot pot.

Cochabamba's best vegetarian food is served at *Snack Uno* on Avenida de las Heroínas. Almuerzos, including soup, salad, main course and dessert, cost US$1.20; you can also get pizza and pasta dishes. The *salteñería* next door is also recommended. An alternative is *Chifal* on Calle Jordán near Calle 25 de Mayo, which serves buffet lunches for US$1.75. An old favourite is the Hare Krishna *Gopal* vegetarian restaurant, which features a colourful sign announcing the 'Falange Socialista Boliviana'. Unfortunately, it has gone downhill, but is still an option for non-spicy Indian dishes heavy on the meat substitutes served to the tones of particularly screechy sitar music. The lassi (ask for it without sugar) and pakoras are fine, but absolutely avoid the gnocchi in white sauce. The fruit and vegies are washed in iodine so there's no risk of giardia.

Pizza fans will enjoy *Rondevu* (☎ 53937), on the corner of Calles 25 de Mayo and Colombia; the staff deliver pizzas Monday to Saturday from 10 am to midnight and on Sunday from 6 pm to midnight. A bit less appealing but still popular is *Eli's Pizza Express*, beside the Residencial Familiar Anexo. Just a block away, concealed behind rose-coloured stucco, is another Italian incarnation – and one of the city's finest restaurants – *La Cantonata*. It makes for a nice decadent splurge, and you can sip fine Chilean wine before a roaring fireplace. The menu, as the staff point out, is based on that of the *Porto Bello* in Houston, Texas. It's closed on Monday.

Diagonally across the street is the aloof *Café Bistro El Carajillo*. Foreigners are just tolerated, but it is a lively place for a drink, Spanish-style tapas, wholemeal bread sandwiches and other trendy bar snacks, as well as beer and light pub meals. The music reflects a strong taste for reggae and jazz.

The top eating, drinking and socialising spot with expats and overseas volunteer organisations is the *Metrópolis*. Specialities include soup, salad, pasta, sweet or savoury German-style pancakes and occasionally even ceviche or goulash. For afters, don't miss the fresh fruit salad with cream or ice cream.

More eclectic – but also friendly and inviting – is *Café Tío Lucas* on Calle Jordán near Calle Junín. There's no sign, but it's worth the trouble of finding it. On the other side of the glass door, the conversation will vary from music to theology to psychology in just a few minutes. The food and coffee aren't bad.

Entertainment

For information about what's on, phone or see the newspaper entertainment listings. On Avenida América, just beyond the second bridge west of town, *Peña Arahui* (☎ 40086) features live folk music shows on Friday, Saturday and Sunday evenings. To get there, take a taxi or micro 'J' from Avenida Ayacucho. There's also *Cafe Concert Cuicacalli* (☎ 49647) at Calle Junín 800 which serves meals and stages concerts, theatre, traditional music *peñas* and other cultural events.

High up on the hillside is a bar called

COCHABAMBA

Loco's, which is housed in a two-storey corner house with red curtains; to find it, follow the right arm of Cristo de la Concordia – he's pointing right at it (what a recommendation!). For something a bit more seedy, try *Arlequín*, along the river near the stadium, where on Wednesday, it's all-you-can-drink-until-midnight for US$3. It's also a disco frequented by locals. Recommended night clubs include *Demones*, *Las Brujas* and *Keops*.

Cochabamba also has eight *cinemas*, and good films quite often sneak in; watch the newspapers for listings.

Things to Buy

If you missed purchasing a locally crafted musical instrument in La Paz, visit Inti Fábrica de Instrumentos Musicales near the corner of Calles Tumusla and General Achá. It seems tourist-oriented, but may be worth a look. For inexpensive souvenirs and trinkets, ramble among the artesanía stalls behind the main post office.

Locally produced woollens are available at three main outlets: Fortrama on Avenida de las Heroínas, Asarti's at Mayor Rocha 375 and Casa Fisher's at Avenida Ramón Rivero 204. Fortrama also has a bargain factory outlet up the hill above Calacala Circle (the roundabout near the entrance to Parque Nacional Tunari). Cheaper alpaca and llama wool *chompas* (jumpers) are found in the markets.

Getting There & Away

Air Cochabamba is served by both LAB (☎ 50760) and AeroSur (☎ 28385). Fares are US$41 to La Paz, US$53 to Santa Cruz and US$64.50 (LAB only) to Tarija. To Sucre, you'll pay US$35 with LAB (AeroSur flies via La Paz and charges US$84).

The flight from La Paz to Cochabamba must be one of the world's most incredible. Sit on the left side of the plane for an incredible – and disconcertingly close-up – view of the peak of Illimani, and a few minutes later, a bird's-eye overview of the dramatic Cordillera Quimsa Cruz.

Bus Cochabamba's central bus terminal is on Avenida Ayacucho just south of Avenida Aroma. Most buses to La Paz – there are at least 20 per day – leave between 7 and 9 pm, though there are also quite a few morning departures (US$5, six hours). About 20 companies have daily services to Oruro between 7 am and 10 pm (US$3, four hours). Jumbo Bus Ballivián has a daily service to Vallegrande (US$5, eight hours) at 8.30 pm.

Most buses to Santa Cruz leave from 4 to 6 pm (US$7, 11 hours), but there are also lots of morning departures. Santa Cruz buses now follow the Chapare route rather than the more scenic route over Siberia Pass. Flotas América and Unidos go to Trinidad (US$14, 24 hours), via Santa Cruz, at 8.30 am and 7.30 pm.

Five to 10 buses leave daily for Sucre between 4.30 and 6.30 pm (US$7, 11 hours). Some then continue to Potosí (at least US$8 more). Micros to Villa Tunari (US$2, five to six hours) and Puerto Villarroel (US$3, eight hours) in the Chapare region, leave between 6 and 10.30 am near the corner of 9 de Abril and Oquendo. Flota 7 de Junio (☎ 55458) leaves for Villa Tunari (US$2.60, five hours) several times in the morning and at 1 and 4 pm. The office is on Avenida República near 16 de Julio.

Trufis and micros to eastern Cochabamba Valley villages leave from along Calle Manuripi; to the western part of the valley, they leave from the corner of Avenidas Ayacucho and Aroma. See also the Cochabamba Valley section, later in this chapter. Micros to Torotoro leave on Thursday and Sunday at about 6 am from near the corner of Avenida República and Calle Punata.

Camión *Camiones* to Sucre and Santa Cruz leave from Avenida de la Independencia, 1.5 km south of the railway station. You'll pay roughly half the bus fare. In the dry season, there are several weekly camiones to Torotoro from near the Mercado de Ferias. There's no set schedule, but they leave at about 5 am.

Train *Ferrobuses* to Oruro run on Wednesday and Friday at 2 pm (US$3.60/2.80 1st/2nd class, five hours). The *tren rápido* leaves on Sunday at 8 am (US$3.20/2.50 1st/2nd class, 11 hours).

The rail trip between Cochabamba and Oruro is one of the great rail trips of South America. It runs along the river valley for two hours past small, otherwise inaccessible, villages, then crosses the river and zigzags 5000 feet uphill onto the Altiplano. The views of the valley below and the rock formations at sunset are quite majestic.

Kevin Bell

Getting Around

The Airport The José Wilsterman Airport is accessible on micro 'B' from the main plaza. Taxis from the centre cost about US$1 per person.

Bus Micros, which run to all corners of the city, are lettered and don't display their destination, making them more difficult to use than those in other cities. Fortunately, cochabambinos are happy to help. Micros cost US$0.15 (B$0.80) per ride.

Taxi The taxi fare to anywhere south or east of the river, or north or west of Laguna Alalay is US$0.30 (B$1.50) per person. Beyond those limits, it doubles.

Around Cochabamba

PARQUE NACIONAL TUNARI

The Parque Nacional Tunari was created in 1962 to protect the forested slopes above Cochabamba. However, regulations aren't enforced, and the city has encroached so far into parkland that it's too late, anyway. In fact, parts of Parque Nacional Tunari may soon be reclassified as merely a semi-urban green area.

There's a good dirt road that zigzags its way from the park gate up the steep mountain face. If you're on foot, you'll find it more interesting to turn left 100m up the track from the entrance gate and walk up a stony avenue of eucalypts towards some farm buildings. In less than a km, you'll reach a pleasantly cool and shady woodland. There are numerous routes leading up the hill, but all will eventually rejoin the road. Three km from the gate, there's a picnic site that has barbecues and an amazing children's playground with slides, firefighters' poles, swings, mini-golf and other attractions.

Immediately beyond the playground you'll see the sign for a *sendero ecológico* (nature trail). Don't expect too much in the way of *ecología* – there is one sign announcing a type of cactus – but it's a well-made path that gains altitude rapidly, winding into thickening mature woodland. Already the views are tremendous, with Cochabamba spread out below and in the opposite direction, Cerro Tunari and other hills in the Cordillera. At the middle elevations, you'll be in temperate forest with small waterfalls, wild flowers, ferns and mosses, and a variety of colourful butterflies and moths. With an early start and plenty of water, you should be able to make it up to some of the nearer peaks on a long day hike.

Ten km up the road from the playground, at an altitude of 4000m, are the lovely Lagunas de Huarahuara, two small lakes containing trout. In a day, you can hike from here to the summit of El Pirámide, northwest of the lakes, for views down the other side of the cordillera. The area offers a choice of wild camping sites.

Getting There & Away

Take micro 'G' or trufi 35 (marked 'Temporal') from Plaza Colón. Micro 'G' terminates at the top of a steep cobbled hill in Temporal and trufi 35 passes the gate to the park. If you catch micro 'G', you need to walk 200m up the hill to the east to reach the gate, which is a big wooden archway fitted with a semicircular fire-risk indicator. You may have to show identification and sign into the park. From here, the road zigzags up to the playground and Huarahuara.

COCHABAMBA

CERRO TUNARI

Snow-dusted Cerro Tunari, at 5035m, is the highest peak in central Bolivia. Its flanks lie 25 km west of Cochabamba, along the road to Independencia. This spectacular area offers excellent camping and hiking but access can be tough.

If you're travelling independently, get started by catching a micro to Quillacollo, 13 km from Cochabamba (see the Cochabamba Valley section), then look for a camión or other vehicle heading towards Morochata and get off about five km beyond Liriuni (or you can find transport to Liriuni and walk from there; see the Cochabamba Valley section below). From there, it's a complicated four to five-hour climb to the summit.

You can manage the return trip in a long day, but the stiff high-altitude ascent will be more pleasant if you allow two days and camp overnight. A guide will be very useful to find the best route.

A longer and steeper (but more easily accessed) alternative is to follow the ravine behind Payrumani, which will take you right to the base of the peak.

Organised Tours

Another option is an organised trek with Viajes Fremen (see the Organised Tours section in the Getting Around chapter), which leads two day excursions up the mountain. With two people, you'll pay US$100 per person. Groups of four pay only US$80 per person, all inclusive.

Places to Stay

The only accommodation is at Liriuni (see the Cochabamba Valley section), or at the village school three km beyond Liriuni.

COCHABAMBA VALLEY
Quillacollo

Besides Cochabamba itself, Quillacollo is the largest and most commercially important community in the Cochabamba Valley. Its name is derived from *khella-collu* meaning 'ash hill'. Apart from the Feria Dominical (Sunday market) and the pre-Inca burial mound discovered beneath Plaza Bolívar, the main attraction is the church, which houses the shrine of the Virgen de Urkupiña. The niche lies to the right of the altar in a little side chapel, which is full of candles and commemorative plaques thanking the Virgin for blessings received. Elsewhere in the well-kept church, note the interesting religious statues. Be prepared for the squad of women who pin pilgrims' badges of the Virgin on your clothes and then ask for money.

If you're visiting the Sunday market, try to sample *garapiña*, Quillacollo's answer to the dessert drink. This deceptively strong combination is a blend of chicha, cinnamon, coconut and *ayrampo*, a local mystery ingredient that colours the drink red. In Cochabamba, you can try garapiña at the El Caminante restaurant, on Calle Esteban Arce near Cabrera.

Special Events If you're in the area around 15 to 18 August, try to catch the Fiesta de la Virgen de Urcupiña, which is the biggest annual celebration in Cochabamba department. Folkloric musicians and dancers come from around Bolivia to perform, and the chicha flows for three days.

The celebration commemorates repeated visitations of the Virgin Mary and child to a shepherd girl at the foot of the hill known as Calvario. The visits were later witnessed by the girl's parents and a crowd of village people when the shepherdess shouted *'Orkopiña'*, 'there on the hill', as the Virgin was seen ascending towards heaven. At the summit of the hill, the townspeople discovered a stone image of the Virgin, which was carried to the village church and thereafter known as the Virgen de Urkupiña.

Places to Stay & Eat At Estancia Marquina, four km north of Quillacollo on the Liriuni road, is the *Eco Hostal Los Nuevos Inkas* (☎ 41505, fax 61234), Casilla 318, Cochabamba. This unique place was conceived by the Movimiento Pachamama Universal as part of an experiment in ecologically and culturally sustainable tourism. It's

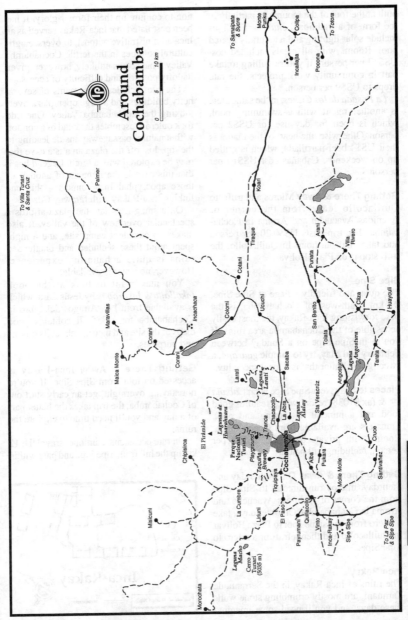

Around
Cochabamba

built at the foot of the mountain, partially in the form of a traditional *chullpa*. Facilities include solar lighting and a naturally heated pool. Rooms with all meals included cost US$12 per person; if you're willing to take part in community work projects, the rate drops to US$9 per person.

La Posada de los Cisnes, in the same area, is another resort with a swimming pool, which is open for day use for US$2 per person. Otherwise, the heart of the matter is their US$4 beef parrillada, which is grilled up on weekends. Cabañas cost US$10 per person.

Getting There & Away Micros and trufis to Quillacollo leave from the corner of Avenidas Ayacucho and Aroma in Cochabamba. The trip costs US$0.20 per person and takes half an hour. In Quillacollo, the trufi stop is on Plaza Bolívar.

Sipe Sipe

The quiet and friendly village of Sipe Sipe, 27 km south-west of Cochabamba, is the base for visiting Inca-Rakay, the most easily accessible of the Cochabamba area ruins. If you're in Sipe Sipe on a Sunday between February and May, try to sample *guarapo*, a sweet grape liquor that is a local speciality.

Places to Stay Near Sipe Sipe is *La Cabaña* (☎ & fax 81038) resort, which features good food and a mineral hot spring and pool. Transfers are available from Cochabamba. Rooms with private bath cost US$25 per person, including full board.

Getting There & Away On Wednesday and Saturday, micros run directly to Sipe Sipe from the corner of Avenidas Ayacucho and Aroma in Cochabamba. On other days, take a micro from the same spot to Plaza Bolívar in Quillacollo and then a trufi or a micro to Sipe Sipe.

Inca-Rakay

The ruins of Inca-Rakay, in the Serranía de Tarhuani, are mostly crumbling stone walls these days, and you'll need some imagina-

tion to conjure up their former glory. It has been postulated that Inca-Rakay served as an Inca administrative outpost, to oversee agricultural colonies in the fertile Cochabamba Valley. That seems unlikely, however, given its lofty position and difficulty of access.

The site includes the remains of several hefty buildings and a large open plaza overlooking the Cochabamba Valley. One odd rock outcrop resembles the head of a condor, with a natural passageway inside leading to the top. Just off the plaza area is a cave that may be explored with a torch. Legend has it that this cave is the remnant of another of those apocryphal Inca tunnels – this one linking Inca-Rakay with faraway Cuzco.

On a smog-free day, the plaza affords a spectacular overview of the valley. It also makes an excellent camp site, and a night spent amid these secluded and unattended ruins is quite a haunting experience. However, no water is available.

You may want to look at the book *Inkallajta & Inkaraqay* by Jesús Lara, which is available from Los Amigos del Libro in Cochabamba for US$5. It contains good maps of the site and theories about its origins and purposes.

Getting There & Away Inca-Rakay is accessed on foot from Sipe Sipe. If you're not staying overnight, get an early start out of Cochabamba; the trip takes the better part of a day and you'll need time to explore the ruins.

On rare occasions, camiones travel the 12 km up the hill from Sipe Sipe and pass within

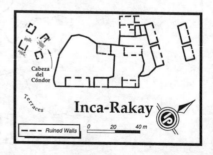

several hundred metres of Inca-Rakay, but otherwise, it's a four to five-km cross-country walk. If you've come to Cochabamba from the lowlands, allow a couple of days to acclimatise before tackling this uphill hike.

From the main plaza in Sipe Sipe, follow the road past the secondary school. From there the road narrows into a path and crosses a small ditch. Across the ditch, turn right onto the wider road. At this point you have a choice. If you stay on the road, it's a relatively easy 12-km uphill climb that will take about four hours if you're carrying a pack. You'll eventually come across a sign on the roadside pointing towards the ruins, which are hidden from view amid rocky outcrops and a clump of molle trees (which resemble willows); from the road, it's five minutes downhill to the ruins.

To follow the more direct route, straight up the mountain, it's a tiring two hour grunt. This route isn't straightforward and is at times very steep. From several hundred metres up the road from town, follow a water pipeline uphill to the first major ridge; there'll be a large ravine on your left. From there, bear to the right, following the ridge until you see a smaller ravine to the right. At this point, you'll be able to see Inca-Rakay atop a reddish hill in the distance, but from so far away it won't be obvious what you're looking at.

Cross the small ravine and follow it until you can see two adobe houses on the other side. In front you'll see a little hill with some minor ruins at the top. Climb the hill, cross the large flat area, and then climb up two more false ridges until you see Inca-Rakay.

Taquiña Brewery

In the hills along the road to Tiquipaya, 10 km north-west of Cochabamba, is the source of that refreshing brew, Taquiña. Brewery tours are conducted every day, but unless beer is your main interest, visit on a weekend and have a meal at the restaurant, which boasts a delicious view across the valley. Recommended menu specialities include trout, lamb, duck and *lechón* (suckling pig)–

washed down, of course, with the star tipple, and followed by a speciality ice-cream concoction. Taxis from Cochabamba cost about US$2.

Tiquipaya

The village of Tiquipaya, 40 minutes from Cochabamba, is known for its cultivation of flowers and strawberries, and its array of unusual festivals. At the end of April, there's an annual Chicha Festival; the second week in September sees the Trout Festival; around 24 September is the Flower Festival; and in the first week of November there's the Festival de la Wallunca, which features colourfully dressed traditional women from around Cochabamba department.

Places to Stay The mid-range *Hostal Tolavi* has cabañas constructed of perfumed wood, which occupy a garden-like setting among the trees. Meals are German-style and cost US$4 each. The hostal lies only three blocks from the trufi stop in Tiquipaya.

Getting There & Away Micros leave every half-hour from the corner of Avenidas Ladislao Cabrera and San Martín in Cochabamba.

Liriuni

At Liriuni, seven km north-west of Quillacollo on the Cerro Tunari route, you may want to stop at the Termas de Liriuni (Liriuni Hot Springs) for a good relaxing soak. Here you'll find the natural health resort, *Janajpacha* (☎ & fax 61234), Casilla 318, Cochabamba, which specialises in alternative medicine. Accommodation in double cabañas costs US$9 per person, including meals. Trufis run from Quillacollo on Sunday.

Payrumani

If you haven't already had your fill of Simon Patiño's legacy in Oruro and Cochabamba, you can visit Payrumani and tour the home actually occupied by the tin baron. This enormous white mansion, which could have been the inspiration for the television home of the Beverly Hillbillies, was named Villa Albina after his wife. Albina was presumably as fussy as her husband when it came to the finer things in life, and the elegant French decor of the main house and the Carrera-marble mausoleum seem typical of royalty – mineral or otherwise – anywhere in the world. In 1964, the estate was donated to the nonprofit Salesian Congregation by the Simon I Patiño University Memorial fund, which still represents the tin baron's heirs.

Villa Albina is open Monday to Friday from 12.30 to 3.30 pm and on Saturday from 9 to 11 am.

Getting There & Away To reach Payrumani, take trufi 211Z from Avenida Aroma in Cochabamba or from Plaza Bolívar in Quillacollo and get off at Villa Albina. It's only 22 km from Cochabamba, but getting there takes a couple of hours.

Vinto

Vinto, not to be confused with the tin smelter of the same name near Oruro, is best known for two annual fiestas. On 19 March, it celebrates the Fiesta de San José (or St Joseph, the patron saint of carpenters). The Fiesta de la Virgen del Carmen is celebrated on 16 July with folkloric groups, Masses, parades and military bands.

Getting There & Away The easiest access is by trufi 211Z from the corner of Avenidas Ayacucho and Aroma in Cochabamba. Micros run on Wednesday and Saturday from the same corner, but on other days, you have to change in Quillacollo.

La Angostura

The village of La Angostura, near the large reservoir of the same name, lies on the route to Tarata and is known mainly as a place to eat fish. Of the four informal restaurants, the best is away from the highway, over the bridge near the railway. Here you'll pay US$3.50 for excellent fish dishes with enough pejerrey, rice, salad and potato to fill

up two people. Take any micro (US$0.25) towards Tarata or Cliza and get off at the Angostura bridge.

En route, 18 km east of the city, is Lago del Edén Angostura, a small park and restaurant which is popular with families on weekends. Three km west of the park is an open-air restaurant called *Las Carmelitas*; at weekends, Señora Carmen Lopez serves up delicious cheese, egg, olive and onion *pukacapas*, baked on the spot in a large beehive oven. At US$0.30 each, they're one of Bolivia's best bargains.

Punata

The small market town of Punata, 48 km east of Cochabamba, is known for the finest chicha in all Bolivia. If you can't make it to the source, you can sample Punata chicha in Cochabamba from a small shop on the northern side of Avenida Aroma between Calles 25 de Mayo and Esteban Arce. Tuesday is market day. Punata is accessed by micros that depart every half-hour from the corner of Avenida República (the southern extension of Antezana) and Pulacayo, at Plaza Villa Bella, in Cochabamba.

Tarata & Huayculi

Tarata, 30 km south-east of Cochabamba, lives in infamy as the birthplace of the mad president General Mariano Melgarejo. The town has an enormous and interesting church, the Iglesia de San Pedro, and a worthwhile Thursday market specialising in ceramics. In Tarata, the Franciscan convent, which was founded in 1792 as a missionary training school, contains the ashes of San Severino, the patron saint of the village. In the nearby village of Huayculi, which is a village of potters and pottery painters, the air is thick with the scent of eucalyptus branches and leaves being burned in cylindrical firing kilns.

Micros leave Cochabamba hourly from Avenida Barrientos, between Manuripi and Guayaramerín, south of the railway station. There are no micros to Huayculi, but taxis from Cochabamba cost US$4.

Cliza

The Sunday market in Cliza is a good alternative to the utter Sunday shutdown in Cochabamba. It's a good place to sample squab, which is a local speciality. You can also avoid the bone-chilling early-morning camión departure to Torotoro by taking a micro to Cliza and picking up the Torotoro camión as it passes between 6.30 and 8 am. Micros to Cliza leave from the corner of Avenida Barrientos and Pulacayo in Cochabamba; the trip takes 25 minutes.

Arani

Arani, 53 km east of Cochabamba, stages a Thursday market where you'll find locally produced woollens. Up to 500 village women work as artesans creating colourful and practical articles for export. Six km south of Arani is the hamlet of Villa Rivero where both men and women weave magnificent carpets in zoomorphic patterns and high relief. Taxis from Arani cost US$3, from Punata there are micros for just US$0.20.

Bear in mind that purchasing weavings and carpets directly from the source rather than a shop will decrease the price and increase the artesan's percentage of the sale. A two-metre-square carpet, which requires 15 kg of wool and at least 15 days of spinning and weaving, sells for about US$40; in Cochabamba, the mark-up is at least 50%.

Arani is also known for *pan de Arani*, a bread concocted from a blend of grains to yield a distinct flavour. Look also at the intricately carved wooden altars in the church, which was formerly the seat of the Santa Cruz Bishopric.

On 24 August, Arani stages the Festividad de la Virgen de la Bella, which dates from colonial times.

Getting There & Away Micros to Arani leave from the corner of Avenida República and Plaza Villa Bella in Cochabamba.

INCALLAJTA

The nearest thing Bolivia has to Peru's Machu Picchu is the remote and little-visited site of Incallajta (meaning 'land of the Inca'), which lies 132 km east of Cochabamba on a flat mountain spur above the Río Machajmarka. This was the easternmost outpost of the Inca empire and after Tiahuanaco, it's the country's most significant archaeological site. The most prominent feature is the immense stone fortification that sprawls across alluvial terraces above the river, but at least 50 other structures are also scattered around the site.

Incallajta was probably founded by Inca Emperor Tupac Yupanqui, the commander who had previously marched into present-day Chile to demarcate the southern limits of the Inca empire. It's estimated that Incallajta was constructed sometime in the 1460s, as a measure of protection against attack by the Chiriguanos to the south-east. In 1525, the last year of the rule of Emperor Huayna Capac, the outpost was abandoned. This may have been due to a Chiriguano attack, but was more likely the result of increasing Spanish pressure and the unravelling of the empire, which fell seven years later.

The ruins were made known to the world in 1914 by Swedish zoologist and ethnologist Ernest Nordenskiold, who spent a week at the ruins, measuring and mapping them. However, they were largely ignored – except by ruthless treasure hunters – for the next 50 years, when the University of San Simón in Cochabamba started investigations. The road in was built in 1977 and the site became a national monument in 1988. The archaeological museum in Cochabamba is now working to restore the ruins and translate Nordenskiold's writing on Bolivia into Spanish.

For more information, pick up a copy of Jesús Lara's book *Inkallajta & Inkaraqay*, which is available from Los Amigos del Libro in Cochabamba. You need to read Spanish to get anything out of the text, but the site map is useful. Lara's original research was carried out in the 1920s, but wasn't published until 1967.

Organised Tours

Several Cochabamba agencies run tours to

COCHABAMBA

Incallajta, but only if they have a group large enough to make it worthwhile. The best is probably Viajes Fremen, which runs day tours for US$86/70 per person in groups of two/four people. For two day tours, the price jumps to US$171/128 per person with two/four people. Your best chances of joining a pre-organised tour will be on Friday.

Getting There & Away

Without your own transport, visiting Incallajta will prove inconvenient at best, and if you can't arrange lodging in private homes, you'll probably have to camp for two or three nights. From Cochabamba, take any camión or bus towards Sucre (along the old Santa Cruz highway) and get off at Monte Punku, 116 km east of Cochabamba. From here, unless a camión happens along, you'll probably have to walk. Turn south on the Pocona road at km 119, three km east of Monte Punku, then continue south for 13 km to Collpa. At the Koari turn-off, opposite a church on the left side of the road, turn west and follow the road uphill for 10 km. After crossing the Río Machajmarka, you'll enter the Incallajta archaeological park. Take plenty of water, food and warm clothing.

TOTORA

Totora, 140 km east of Cochabamba, huddles in a valley at the foot of Cerro Sutuchira, and may be the loveliest colonial village in the department. Accommodation is limited to the optimistically named *Gran Hotel Totora*, which is housed in an old colonial building near the bus stop. The charge is US$3 per person.

Totora lies on the main route to Sucre, but unfortunately, few travellers ever see it because the buses all run at night. Micros leave for Totora hourly from the corner of Avenida Montes and Esteban Arce in Cochabamba.

AIQUILE & MIZQUE

Aiquile and Mizque, two small towns 38 km apart in the Valles Altos of south-eastern Cochabamba department, are ideal for a peaceful and pastoral respite from the city noise.

Dusty little Aiquile, which is known for some of the best *charangos* produced in Bolivia, lies midway between Sucre and Cochabamba, in the Tipajara Mayu watershed. It sponsors a lively Sunday market, and services extend to post and ENTEL offices, and a dental and medical clinic. Entertainment is limited to a movie house showing old flicks. If you're feeling grimy, visit the El Cisne baths; for US$0.50 you'll get a 15-minute hot shower, sauna or steam bath.

Mizque, which is smaller and even dustier, enjoys a lovely pastoral setting on the Río Mizque north of Aiquile. The main attraction is simply the beauty of the Tucuna Valley; the perennial Río Tucuna joins the Río Mizque just east of town. Watch for the 100 or so endangered scarlet macaws – large red, blue and green parrots with 56-cm wingspans – which squawk and frolic in the early morning.

Special Events

A good fiesta to attend in Aiquile is that of the Virgen de Candelaria, which takes place on 2 February. In Mizque, there's the Fiesta del Señor de los Milagros on 14 September.

Places to Stay & Eat

For meals, Aiquile has a lovely family-run pensión called *La Tradición*. Accommodation is available at the basic *Aiquile Inn* on the main street, but watch out for vinchuca beetles. Other dirt-cheap options are *El Turista* and *Los Escudos*. There's also the decent *Hostal Campero*, which charges US$2 per person and serves meals. It's in an old colonial building surrounding a nice courtyard, and the owner Carlos is very personable and likes to chat with guests.

In Mizque, you'll find meals such as delicious sopita de arroz at *Doña Nati's*, or you can eat at the street stalls beside the church. The best accommodation is the clean, well-lit *dormitorio*, run by a Belgian Franciscan priest. It's just south of the football ground at the eastern end of town.

COCHABAMBA

Getting There & Away

Mizque and Aiquile lie on the main route between Cochabamba and Sucre, but buses between those two cities pass in the wee hours of the night when these already soporific little places are soundly asleep. Flota Aiquile has a service to both Mizque and Aiquile six times weekly from the corner of Avenida Montes and Esteban Arce in Cochabamba.

It's about a 60-minute drive between Mizque and Aiquile. You can readily thumb a ride on passing camiones, but be prepared for a real dust bath.

PARQUE NACIONAL TOROTORO

By road, Parque Nacional Tororoto lies eight hours and 198 km south-east of Cocha-bamba, in Potosí department. It's an absolute jewel, but like Incallajta, it's difficult or uncomfortable to reach without private transport. This promises to change, however, as the road is improved and more camiones do the run from Cochabamba.

Most of the treasures of Tororoto – caves, ruins, rock paintings, waterfalls and fossilised dinosaur tracks – are in the Parque Nacional Tororoto, which was created in 1988 and is now administered by the Asociación Conservacionista de Tororoto, which has an office in the village.

Dinosaur Tracks

Most visitors to Tororoto come for the palaeontology. The village, which sits in a wide section of a 20-km-long valley at 2600m elevation, is flanked by enormous inclined mudstone rock formations, bearing biped and quadruped dinosaur tracks from the Cretaceous period. As the road flattens out beside the stream north-west of Tororoto, it actually crosses the path of a group of three-toed tracks, each measuring about 25 cm long.

A short distance from the village, just beyond the Río Tororoto crossing, the area's largest tracks march up from just above the waterline. They were made by an enormous quadruped dinosaur, and measure 35 cm wide, 50 cm long and 20 cm deep – at a stride of nearly two metres!

Several hundred metres farther upstream from the crossing, a group of small three-toed tracks climb out of the water and under a layer of rocks. Five km upstream are more

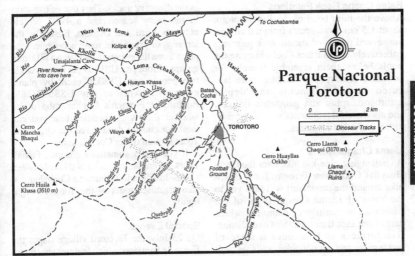

Parque Nacional Tororoto

tracks, and dinosaur bone fragments have been found in layers of red earth.

All the tracks in the Torotoro area were made in soft mud, which then solidified into mudstone. They were later uplifted and tilted by tectonic forces. For that reason, nearly all the tracks appear to lead uphill. The exception is the set known as the Carreras Pampa site, along the route to Umajalanta Cave. These tracks, which were made by three-toed biped dinosaurs, run in several different directions, suggesting a dance-like frolic.

Fossils

In a small side gully, an hour's walk west of Torotoro, on the Cerro de las Siete Vueltas (so-called because the trail twists seven times before reaching the peak), is a major deposit of sea fossils. At the base of the ravine, you may see petrified sharks teeth, while higher up, the limestone and sedimentary layers are set with fossils of ancient trilobites, echinoderms, gastropods, arthropods, cephalopods and brachiopods. The site is thought to date back about 350 million years. Another major sea-fossil site lies in the Quebrada Thajo Khasa, south-east of Torotoro.

Batea Cocha Rock Paintings

Above the third bend of the Río Torotoro, about 1.5 km downstream from the village, are several panels of ancient rock paintings collectively called Batea Cocha because the pools below them resemble troughs for pounding laundry. The paintings were executed in red pigments and depict anthropomorphic and geometric designs, and also fanciful representations of serpents, turtles and other creatures.

Llama Chaqui Ruins

A challenging nine-km hike over the Cerro Huayllas Orko from Torotoro (or a 19-km hike around the mountain) will take you to the ruins of Llama Chaqui (Foot of the Llama). The multilevel complex, which dates from Inca times, rambles over distinctive terraces and includes a maze of rectangular and semicircular walls, as well

as a fairly well-preserved watchtower. Given its strategic vantage point, it probably served as a military fortification, and may have been somehow related to Incallajta, farther north.

Gruta de Umajalanta

Seven km north-west of Torotoro, the Río Umajalanta disappears beneath a layer of limestone approximately 22m thick, forming the Gruta de Umajalanta, of which 4.5 km of passages have been explored. The walk takes two hours from the village. Inside are fanciful stalagmite and stalactite formations, underground lakes with blind catfish and several cascades and waterfalls. Other subterranean waterways flowing into the Río Umajalanta have been whimsically dubbed the Río Singani and the Río 7-Up. Together, they exit the cavern as the Río Chuflay.

Although the cave remains undeveloped, there are plans to install pathways, artificial lighting and stairs. To see it in a natural state, find a torch and a guide and go soon. Pick up the entrance key from the village shop.

Organised Tours

Viajes Fremen organises tours that visit the caves of Chilijusco and Umajalanta, as well as the dinosaur tracks. They use air transport in the rainy season and a 4WD vehicle between April and October. Basically, the larger your group, the more economical the price. For a three day all-inclusive 4WD tour, groups of four pay US$304 per person while two people pay US$356 each; by plane, groups of two/four pay US$573/288. Enquire at Fremen's Cochabamba office whether there's a scheduled tour you can join. For contact details, see the Organised Tours section under Cochabamba.

If you prefer something cheaper, Famali Tours, Avenida Ayacucho S-0471, between Calles Jordán and Calama in Cochabamba, also organises tours of the Torotoro highlights.

Special Events

On 25 July, the Torotoro village stages the Fiesta de Santiago, which features sheep sacrifices as well as Potosí's own *tinku* fights, in which participants literally beat the hell out of each other with their fists or worse. This may be a good time to look for transport to Torotoro, but certainly not the best for visiting the natural attractions.

Places to Stay & Eat

Thankfully, Torotoro isn't exactly prepared for mass tourism, but facilities are improving. There's now the *Alojamiento Trinidad* near the micro stop, which charges US$1.50 per person. Alternatively, visitors may lodge with private families or at the *Casa de la Prefectura*. There's no restaurant in the village and the *Tienda Santiago* sells only staples, so bring supplies from Cochabamba.

Getting There & Away

Air The Free Swedish Mission of Cochabamba flies into Torotoro from time to time and may have space for passengers. If you charter the plane, the flight costs US$150 for up to five passengers. Enquiries may be directed to Captain Arvindson (☎ 46289) in Cochabamba.

Bus Micros depart on Thursday and Sunday at about 6 am from the corner of Avenida República and Calle Punata, near the Mercado de Ferias, in Cochabamba. They return on Friday and Monday at 7 am from near the plaza in Torotoro. The trip takes at least nine hours and costs US$3 per person. During school holidays it's often booked out by student groups.

Camión During the dry season, there are a couple of weekly camiones between Cochabamba and Torotoro, departing at 5 am from the Mercado de Ferias in Cochabamba. The trip takes 10 to 12 hours each way and costs US$2.50 per person. You'll pass through several climatic zones, so bring a range of clothing.

Car & Motorcycle Don't try this trip in anything but a 4WD or a large camión – and not at all during the rainy season – because it involves fording the rather substantial Río

Caine. Follow the highway towards Sucre for 31 km, turn right and continue seven km to the village of Cliza. There's no petrol available beyond Cliza, so make sure you have enough for the return trip to Torotoro – about 400 km. Follow the Oruro road 10 km beyond Cliza and turn left onto the Torotoro road.

INCACHACA & THE CHAPARE ROAD

In the highlands, 93 km north-east along the Santa Cruz road from Cochabamba, you'll pass the large Corani reservoir, which was created to provide water for the city. On its shores is a popular weekend resort complex favoured by cochabambinos. Also look for the bizarre Casa de los Brujos (House of the Warlocks), an exceptional but now-dilapidated dwelling constructed by a local eccentric.

Farther down the valley is Incachaca (Inca House), which enjoys a Yungas-like microclimate that has covered the slopes with lush rainforest. A pleasant stop is at the waterfall that issues from the Ventana del Diablo (Devil's Window), where an underground aquifer reaches the surface.

Readers have also made the following suggestion:

A good place to see nice cloud forest is on the side road to Tablas Monte. Get off the Cochabamba-Villa Tunari bus at km 72 (painted on a blue wrecked car) and walk down the track. Early in the morning, one can see hooded mountain toucans, Andean guans and lots of other birds. It's good to camp near the track for a great early-morning view. It's possible to pick up a bus or camioneta to Cochabamba or Villa Tunari.
Quentin Given & Lorna Reith, UK

Organised Tours

From Cochabamba, Incachaca is accessible on any bus or micro going to Chapare. Viajes Fremen in Cochabamba organises day excursions to the Corani and the Ventana del Diablo for US$64/56 per person in a group of two/four people.

Getting There & Away

To visit Incachaca on your own, take a micro from Cochabamba and get off at the drugs

COCHABAMBA

check as you enter Chapare. From there, walk about 100m down the road, where you'll find an unpaved road leading up the mountain. Follow it up for about half an hour (or take a short cut along the power lines) until you reach the site. Try to allow yourself several hours to look around at the various items of interest: a small lake, a bridge over a deep gorge, an old hydroelectric plant and

of course, the Ventana del Diablo. To visit the last two, you'll have to report at the caretakers' office.

CHAPARE

For details on the Chapare region of northern Cochabamba department, see the Amazon Basin chapter.

Sucre

Any Bolivian who knows Sucre will tell you it's their nation's most beautiful city. As a result, its inhabitants have reverently bestowed upon it romantic-sounding nicknames: the Spanish equivalents of The Athens of America, The City of Four Names, The Cradle of Liberty and The White City of the Americas. At an altitude of 2790m, it enjoys a mild and comfortable climate nearly as appealing as that of Cochabamba.

Set in a valley surrounded by low mountains, Sucre is a small, pleasant city of 100,000 people, and it boasts numerous churches, museums and ancient mansions. Like the Netherlands, Libya and South Africa, Bolivia divides its bureaucracy between multiple capitals. Although La Paz has usurped most of the governmental power, the Supreme Court still convenes in Sucre and with some sort of twisted pride, *sureños* maintain that their city remains the real heart of Bolivian government.

Today, Sucre struggles to retain the flavour of its colonial heritage. All buildings within the central core of the city must be either whitewashed or painted white. The city remains a centre of learning and both Sucre and its university enjoy their reputations as focal points of liberal and progressive thought within the country.

Highlights
- Wander the streets of Sucre and soak up its colonial charms
- Follow in the path of the Incas from Chataquila's rocky ridgetop to its steep six-km descent into the tiny traditional village of Chaunaca
- Seek out the snake oil vendors and local *artesanía* at Tarabuco's colourful Sunday market
- Walk the brilliantly coloured green and violet hillsides of the Cráter de Maragua and thence south through the Cordillera de los Frailes to bathe in the 45°C waters of the Termas de Talula
- Seek out the beautiful and colourful Jalq'a and Candelaria weavings, which are among the world's finest

History

Throughout its history, Sucre has served as the administrative, legal, religious, cultural and educational centre of the easternmost Spanish territories, and in the 17th century it came to be known as the Athens of America.

Prior to Spanish domination, the town of Charcas, where Sucre now stands, was the indigenous capital of the valley of Choque-Chaca. It served as the residence of local religious, military and executive leaders and its jurisdiction extended to several thousand inhabitants. When the Spanish arrived, the entire area from Southern Peru to the Río de la Plata in present-day Argentina came to be known as Charcas.

In the early 1530s, Francisco Pizarro, the conquistador who felled the Inca empire, sent his brother Gonzalo to the Charcas region to oversee Indian mining activities and interests that might be valuable to the Spanish realm. Uninterested in the Altiplano, he concentrated on the highlands east of the main Andean Cordilleras. As a direct result, in 1538 the city of La Plata was founded by Pedro de Anzures, Marques de Campo

SUCRE

317

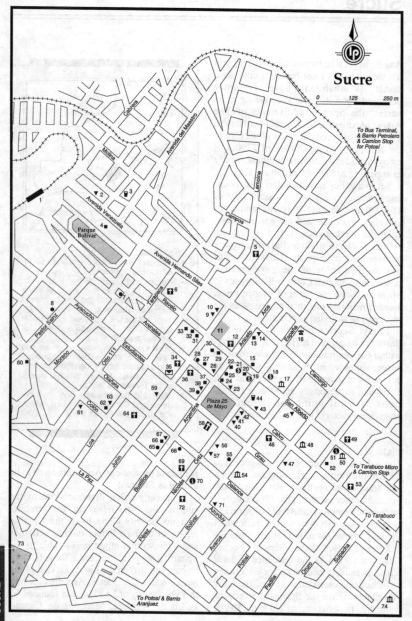

PLACES TO STAY		38	Palett Heladería-	28	Soliz Barber Shop
4	Hotel Municipal		Pastelería	29	Saico del Sur
	Simón Bolívar	40	Pizza Napolitana		Supermarket
13	Hostal San Francisco	41	Chifa Hong Kong	34	Iglesia de Santa
15	Residencial Bolivia	42	Las Vegas & Plaza		Mónica
20	Residencial Oriental	43	La Repizza	35	Post Office
22	Hostal Libertad	45	Piccolissimo	36	Iglesia de San Miguel
24	Grand Hotel	47	Kultur Café Berlin	39	Casa de la Libertad
29	Alojamiento La Plata	56	Bibliocafé	44	Andy Capp's
30	Residencial Charcas	57	Arco Iris		Wisquería
31	Alojamiento El Turista	59	El Tropezón	46	Iglesia de Santo
32	Alojamiento Anexo	61	Restaurant Delta		Domingo
	San José	63	El Batán	48	Museo & Convento
33	Residencial Bustillo	67	Churrasquería		de Santa Clara
37	Hostal Colonial		Argentina	49	Convento de Santa
52	Hotel Real Audiencia	71	El Solar		Teresa
60	Hostal Los Pinos			50	Museo Textil
62	Hotel Cruz de	**OTHER**			Etnográfico
	Popayán	1	Railway Station	51	Tourist Office &
66	Hostal Sucre	3	Discoteca Up-Down		Caserón de la
		5	Iglesia San Sebastián		Capellanía
PLACES TO EAT		6	Iglesia Santa Rita	53	Iglesia de San Lázaro
2	Piso Cero	7	Teatro Gran Mariscal	54	Museos Universitarios
9	Nova Pan		de Ayacucho	55	Laverap Laundry
10	Café Hacheh	8	Doña Máxima	58	Cathedral
13	El Germén		Artesanía	64	Iglesia de San Agustín
14	El Cedrón, Paso de	11	Market	65	LAB (Airline)
	los Toros, Burger	12	Iglesia de San	68	Instituto Geográfico
	Theos & Arabe		Francisco		Militar
	Ramadan	16	ENTEL	69	Convento de San
22	Arco's Coffee Shop	17	Museo de la Historia		Felipe Neri
23	Hamburguesas al		Natural	70	University Tourist
	Paso	18	Banco de Santa Cruz		Information Office
25	La Taverne & Jugos	19	Banco Nacional	72	Iglesia de la Merced
	Dumbo	21	Casa de Cambio	73	Cemetery
26	Bonbons Leblon		Ambar	74	Museo de la Recoleta
		27	AeroSur (Airline)		

Redondo, as the Spanish capital of the Charcas. As his Indian predecessors had done, he chose the warm, fertile and well-watered valley of Choque-Chaca for its site.

During the early 16th century, the Viceroyalty of Lima governed all Spanish territories in central and eastern South America. In 1559, King Phillip II created the Audiencia (Royal Court) of Charcas, with its headquarters in the city of La Plata, to administer the eastern territories. The Audiencia was unique in the New World in that it held both judicial authority and executive powers. The judge of the Audiencia also served as the chief executive officer. Governmental subdivisions within the district came under the jurisdiction of royal officers known as *corregidores*.

Until 1776, the Audiencia presided over Paraguay, south-eastern Peru, northern Chile and Argentina, and most of Bolivia. When Portuguese interests in Brazil threatened the easternmost Spanish-dominated regions, a new Viceroyalty, La Plata, was established in order to govern and ensure tight control. The city of La Plata thereby lost jurisdiction over all but the former Choque-Chaca, one of the four provinces of Alto Peru, which comprised leftover territories between the Viceroyalties of Lima and La Plata. The city's name was changed to Chuquisaca (the Spanish corruption of Choque-Chaca), presumably to avoid confusion between the city and the new Vice-royalty.

The city had received an archbishopric in 1609, according it theological autonomy. That, along with the establishment of the University of San Xavier in 1622 and the

1681 opening of a law school, Academía Carolina, fostered continued growth and development of liberal and revolutionary ideas and set the stage for 'the first cry of Independence in the Americas' on 25 May 1809. The mini-revolution set off the alarm throughout Spanish America and, like ninepins, the north-western South American republics were liberated by the armies of the military genius, Simón Bolívar.

After the definitive liberation of Peru at the battles of Junín and Ayacucho on 6 August and 9 December 1824, Alto Peru, historically tied to the Lima government, was technically free of Spanish rule. Historically, however, it had carried on closer relations with the La Plata government in Buenos Aires and disputes arose about what to do with the territory.

On 9 February 1825, Bolívar's second-in-command, General Antonio José de Sucre, drafted and delivered a declaration that stated in part:

The…Viceroyalty of Buenos Aires to which these provinces pertained at the time of the revolution of America lacks a general government which represents completely, legally, and legitimately the authority of all the provinces…Their political future must therefore result from the deliberation of the provinces themselves and from an agreement between the congress of Perú and that…in the Río de la Plata.

Bolívar, unhappy with this unauthorised act of sovereignty, rejected the idea but Sucre stood his ground, convinced that there was sufficient separatist sentiment in Alto Peru to back him up. As he expected, the people of the region refused to wait for a decision from the new congress to be installed in Lima the following year, and rejected subsequent invitations to join the Buenos Aires government.

On 6 August, the first anniversary of the Battle of Junín, independence was declared in the Casa de la Libertad at Chuquisaca and the new republic was christened 'Bolivia' after its liberator. On 11 August, the city's name was changed for the final time to Sucre in honour of the general who promoted the independence movement.

Difficult years followed in the Republic of Bolivia and at one stage, the Great Liberator became disenchanted with his namesake republic. After a particularly tumultuous period of political shuffling, he uttered: 'Hapless Bolivia has had four different leaders in less than two weeks! Only the kingdom of Hell could offer so appalling a picture discrediting humanity!'.

Information

Tourist Office The tourist office (☎ 35994), in the Caserón de la Capellanía, isn't terribly helpful, but the staff can answer specific questions. It's open from 8.30 am to noon and 2.30 to 6.30 pm. There's also a helpful university tourist office (☎ 23763) at Calle Nicolás Ortiz 182, which can provide expert student guides for city sightseeing. Clients pay only transport expenses and an optional tip. Pick up topo sheets of Chuquisaca department from the Instituto Geográfico Militar on Calle Dalence between Ortiz and Bustillos.

Immigration For visa extensions, go to the immigration office (☎ 32770) in the Palacio del Gobierno on the main plaza. This is one of the best places in Bolivia to extend visas, and the process is often completed in less than five minutes.

Money Casa de Cambio Ambar changes travellers cheques, but the Banco Nacional has better rates. Street moneychangers operate along Avenida Hernando Siles, behind the market. There are also quite a few businesses around town displaying 'Compro Dólares' signs, but they only change cash. Visa cash advances are available without ado at Casa de Cambio Ambar and at the Banco de Santa Cruz, on the corner of San Alberto and España.

Post & Communications The new post office is on the corner of Estudiantes and Junín. The ultramodern ENTEL office on the corner of Calle España and Urcillo opens at 8 am. The telephone code for Sucre is 064.

Cultural Centres The Instituto Cultural Boliviano Alemán (or Goethe Institut), at Kultur Café Berlin, has a selection of current German-language books and newspapers as well as a café and news from the German community. It's open Monday to Friday from 9.30 am to 12.30 pm and 3 to 9 pm and on Saturday from 9.30 am to 12.30 pm.

Similarly, Alliance Française (☎ 23599) at Avenida Aniceto Arce 35 keeps a supply of French-language reading material and newspapers and operates a restaurant, La Taverne. It also shows foreign films; for schedules, check the notice board at the north-west corner of the plaza.

The Centro Boliviano-Americano (☎ 30966), Calle Calvo 301 on the corner of Calle Potosí, brings Yankee culture to Sucre with its Rainbow Room Café and plenty of North American reading material.

The Centro Cultural Los Masis at Calle Bolívar 561 (☎ 23403) sponsors concerts and other cultural events, and has a small museum of local musical instruments. It also offers Quechua classes. It's open Monday to Friday from 10 am to noon and 3.30 to 9 pm.

Laundry For 90-minute laundry service, try Laverap at Calle Bolívar 617. It's open Monday to Saturday from 8 am to 8 pm and on Sunday and holidays from 9 am to 1 pm. The charge is US$2.50 per kg for washing, drying and ironing.

Dangers & Annoyances Harassment by bogus police is increasing in Sucre. If you do have a problem, report it to the tourist police (☎ 25983) or the Radio Patrulla (☎ 110).

Museums

Museo & Convento de Santa Clara The old Convento de Santa Clara, founded in 1639, has been converted into a museum of religious art. Its collection includes several works by Bolivian master, Melchor Pérez de Holguín and his Italian instructor, Bernardo de Bitti. In 1985 it was robbed, and several paintings and gold ornaments disappeared. One canvas that remains was apparently deemed too large to carry off, so the thieves

sliced a big chunk out of the middle and left the rest hanging – and it's still hanging just that way. If you're interested, the guides will demonstrate the still-functional 17th-century pipe organ.

The museum is open Monday to Friday from 9 to 11 am and 5 to 7 pm. On Saturday, you can visit from 10 am to noon. If it's closed, knock on the door on Calle Abaroa. Admission is US$1.

Museo de la Catedral The recently renovated Museo de la Catedral, beside the Capilla de la Virgen de Guadalupe, holds what is probably Bolivia's best collection of religious relics. Half of these were donated by one archbishop. Along with paintings and carvings, there are some priceless gold and silver religious articles set with rubies, emeralds and other precious stones. It's open Monday to Friday from 10 am to noon and 3 to 5 pm, and on Saturday from 10 am to noon. Admission is US$0.75.

Museos Universitarios The three university museums at Calle Bolívar 698 near Dalence make a worthwhile visit. When all is well in Sucre academia, they're open Monday to Friday from 9 am to noon and 2 to 6 pm, and on Saturday from 9 am to noon. Admission is US$1 and photography permits cost US$1.50 (but in the dim light, you'll need at least 200 ASA film). The affiliated Museo de Historia Natural on Calle San Alberto is open Monday to Friday from 8.30 am to noon and 2.30 to 5.30 pm.

Museo de Charcas The Museo de Charcas was founded in 1939 and occupies a home with 21 large rooms. It houses Bolivia's best known works of art, including some by Holguín, Padilla, Gamarra and Villavicencio. You'll also see ornate furniture that was handcrafted by Indians of the Jesuit missions.

Museo Antropológico The Anthropology Museum, founded in 1943, contains separate exhibits dealing with folklore, archaeology and ethnography. Highlights include mummies, skulls, and artefacts from the eastern jungles of Bolivia. There are also the usual collections of pottery, tools and textiles.

Museo de Arte Moderna The best of the three university museums is the Museum of Modern Art, which has good examples of modern Bolivian painting and sculpture, as well as pieces from around Latin America. Don't miss the handcrafted *charangos* by Bolivian artist and musician, Mauro Núñez, and the section devoted to native art.

Museo Textil Etnográfico Highly worthwhile is the Museo Textil Etnográfico, in the 17th-century Caserón de la Capellanía, which features itinerant art exhibitions, art workshops and a coffee shop serving local specialities.

The museum upstairs displays beautiful and practical weavings from both the Candelaria (Tarabuco) and Jalq'a (Potolo) traditions, among others, all beautifully and tastefully displayed in appropriate light and background colours. It's open Monday to Friday from 8.30 am to noon and 3 to 6 pm, and on Saturday from 9.30 am to noon. Admission is US$0.50. Scheduled cultural events are posted on the notice board at the north-western side of the main plaza.

On the inner patio is the Proyecto Textil ASUR (☎ 23841, fax 32194), a Swiss-funded project that markets locally produced weavings and ensures that a good share of the profits go to the artesans. If you have the time, however, it's more interesting (and cheaper) to visit the weaving villages and buy directly from the artesans.

La Recoleta The Recoleta, established by the Franciscan Order in 1601, overlooks the city of Sucre from the top of Calle Polanco. It has served not only as a convent and museum but also as a barracks and prison. In one of the stairwells is a plaque marking the spot where, in 1828, President D Pedro Blanco was assassinated. Outside are courtyard gardens brimming with colour and the renowned Cedro Milenario – the ancient

cedar – a huge tree that was once even larger than its current size. It is the only remnant of the cedars that were once abundant around Sucre.

The museum is worthwhile for its anonymous paintings and sculptures from the 16th to 20th centuries, including numerous interpretations of St Francis of Assisi.

The highlight is the church choir and its magnificent wooden carvings dating back to the 1870s, each one intricately unique. They represent the Franciscan, Jesuit and Japanese martyrs who were crucified in 1595 in Nagasaki, Japan.

La Recoleta is open from 9 to 11 am and 3 to 5 pm. Admission, including a guided tour, costs US$1. Check out the price list for religious services on the notice board at the entrance!

Churches
Cathedral The cathedral on the southern corner of the Plaza 25 de Mayo was begun in 1551 and although the original structure was completed 15 years later, major sections were added between 1580 and 1650. Of interest is the bell tower, a Sucre landmark, and the statues of the 12 Apostles and four patron saints of Sucre. The tower clock was ordered from London in 1650 and installed in 1772. The interior is rather overburdened with kitsch.

Around the corner is the Capilla de la Virgen de Guadalupe, which was completed in 1625. Encased in the altar is the Virgin de Guadalupe de la Extremadura, named after a similar image in Spain. She was originally painted by Fray Diego de Ocaña in 1601. The work was subsequently coated with highlights of gold and silver and adorned in robes encrusted with diamonds, amethysts, pearls, rubies and emeralds donated by wealthy colonial parishioners. The jewels alone are said to be worth millions of dollars and one wonders why the priceless Virgin's head is ringed with cheap incandescent Christmas bulbs!

The chapel and cathedral are open daily between 7 and 8 am. The Museo de la Catedral is described earlier in this section.

DEANNA SWANEY

The intricate carvings of La Recoleta

San Francisco The Iglesia de San Francisco at Calle Ravelo 1 was established in 1538 by Francisco de Aroca soon after the founding of La Plata. It began as a makeshift structure; the current church wasn't completed until 1581. In 1809, when the struggle for Bolivian independence got underway, a law passed by Mariscal Sucre transferred San Francisco's religious community to La Paz, and turned the building over to the army, to be used as a military garrison, market and customs hall. In 1838, the top floor collapsed, but it was rebuilt and later used as military accommodation. It wasn't re-consecrated until 1925.

Architecturally, the most interesting feature of San Francisco is its *mudéjar* ceiling. In the belfry is the Campana de la Libertad, Bolivia's Liberty Bell, which called patriots to revolution in 1825. The church is open daily from 7 to 9 am and 4 to 7 pm, and during Mass on weekends.

Convento de San Felipe Neri For evidence of why Sucre was nicknamed the White City of the Americas, visit the bell tower and tiled rooftop of the Convento de San Felipe Neri at Calle Nicolás Ortiz 165.

In the days when the building served as a monastery, asceticism didn't prevent the monks coming to meditate over the view; you can still see the stone seats on the roof terraces. The church was originally constructed of stone but was later covered with a layer of stucco. Gardens of poinsettias and roses are in the courtyard, and a nice painting of the Last Supper hangs in the stairwell.

In the catacombs are tunnels where priests and nuns once met clandestinely and where, during times of political unrest, guerrillas hid and circulated around the city. The building now functions as a parochial school.

The church and roof are open Monday to Friday from 4.30 to 6 pm. Visitors must first check in with the university tourist information office opposite San Felipe Neri and procure a guide (no charge). Admission is US$0.20, payable at the convent.

Santa Mónica The Iglesia de Santa Monica on the corner of Arenales and Calle Junín, begun in 1574, reveals Sucre's best example

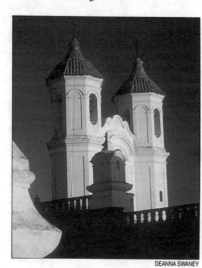

DEANNA SWANEY

Convento de San Felipe Neri

of mestizo architecture. It was originally intended to serve as the Monasterio de las Religiosas Mónicas for the Ermitañas de San Agustín, but the order ran into serious financial difficulties in the early 1590s, eventually resulting in its closure and conversion into a Jesuit school.

The building, which has recently been converted into a multipurpose civic auditorium, is open weekday afternoons after 3 pm and during special events. It is adorned with carvings of seashells, animals and human figures. The ceiling woodwork inside is impressive and the courtyard is one of the city's finest with lawns and a variety of semitropical plants.

San Miguel Built between 1612 and 1621, the Iglesia de San Miguel reflects mudéjar influences, mainly in the arched galleries around the courtyard and Doric columns supporting the choir. Originally a Jesuit church, it was re-dedicated when the order was expelled from Bolivia. Highlights include the painted ceiling, the silver altar and several period paintings and sculptures.

The interior is open Monday to Friday from 11.30 am to noon and during Mass on weekends.

La Merced Although it appears ordinary from the exterior, the Iglesia de la Merced on Calle Azurduy, diagonally opposite San Felipe Neri, contains the most beautiful interior of any church in Sucre and possibly in Bolivia. Because the order of La Merced left Sucre for Cuzco in 1826, taking its records with it, the founding date of the church is uncertain, but it's believed to have been sometime in the early 1550s. The building was completed no later than the early 1580s.

The Baroque-style altar and carved mestizo pulpit are decorated with filigree and gold inlay. Several paintings by the esteemed artist Melchor Pérez de Holguín – notably *El Nacimiento de Jesús*, *El Nacimiento de María* and a self-portrait of the artist rising from the depths of Purgatory – are on display, as are sculptures by other artists.

It seems La Merced has been decommissioned due to a shortage of priests, so a visit may prove tricky. It's meant to be open Monday to Friday from 10 to 11.30 am and 3 to 5.30 pm, but this is rarely the case. If it's not open, try knocking on the door during opening hours.

Santo Domingo The Baroque-style Iglesia de Santo Domingo at Calle Calvo 101 was constructed in the mid-16th century by the Dominican Order. During the war for Bolivian independence, the Spanish crown forced the church to liquidate its gold and silver in order to pay for the war effort. After the war, it was transformed into the official residence of the governor, and was also used as a post office. The building is now part of the University's Junín College, but one item of interest is a superb wooden carving of Christ.

San Lázaro The 1544 Iglesia de San Lázaro, on Calle Calvo between Padilla and Oruro, was the first church in the historical Audiencia de Charcas. The original building was constructed of simple adobe brick and covered with a roof of straw, but it has now been entirely reworked. Items of note include the original silverwork on the altar and several paintings attributed to the school of Polanco. It's open for Mass daily at 7 am.

Convento de Santa Teresa The brilliant white Convento de Santa Teresa, near the corner of Calle San Alberto and Potosí, belongs to an order of cloistered nuns. From 10 am to noon, they sell candied oranges, apples, figs and limes they've prepared.

Be sure to have a look at the Callejón de Santa Teresa, a lantern-lit alleyway that was once partially paved with human bones laid out in the shape of a cross. This gruesome motif was intended to remind passers-by of the inevitability of death. In the 1960s, it was re-paved with its current cobbles.

Casa de la Libertad

For a dose of Bolivian history, visit the Casa de la Libertad, the house on the main plaza where the Bolivian declaration of independence was signed on 6 August 1825. The building has been designated a national memorial in commemoration of this and other historical events. A replica of the actual document (the original is in the Sucre branch of the Banco Nacional!) and numerous other mementos of the era are on display.

The first score of Bolivian congresses were held in the Salon, originally a Jesuit chapel. Doctoral candidates were also examined here. Behind the pulpit hang portraits of Simón Bolívar, Hugo Ballivián and Antonio José de Sucre. General Bolívar said that this portrait by Peruvian artist José Gil de Castro was the most lifelike representation ever done of him.

The museum also includes portraits of presidents, military decorations, war and independence-related art and relics, and old governmental documents. The most memorable is a huge wooden bust of Bolívar carved by artist and musician Mauro Núñez. Note the magnificent gilded loft in the Aula de Independencia.

It's open Monday to Friday from 9 am to noon and 2.30 to 5.30 pm, and on Saturday from 9 am to noon. Admission costs US$1; photography permits cost an additional US$1.50.

Soliz Barber Shop

For a bit of nostalgia, have a look at the delightfully retro barber shop of Jaime Soliz, on the corner of Junín and Arenales. It's a vision from a 1930s silent film and men will receive a shave and haircut in the manner typical of that era. Note the early 20th-century furnishings and the wooden hobbyhorse where kiddies can amuse themselves before being shorn of their locks.

Cemetery

The enthusiasm surrounding Sucre's cemetery seems disproportionate to what's there. Locals make a point of reminding visitors not to miss it. 'See it,' they urge. 'It's wonderful.' Well, such assessments may be a tad excessive. Yes, there are some arches carved from poplar trees and there are unkempt gardens and mausoleums of wealthy colonial families, but it's a mystery why it should inspire such local fervour. Still, go and judge it for yourself, or some proud locals may be disappointed. To enliven the experience, you may want to hire one of the enthusiastic child guides who offer their services for US$0.50. To get there, take a taxi or *micro* 'A', or walk from the centre.

Cement Quarry Dinosaur Tracks

It seems that 60 million years ago, the site of Sucre's FANCESA cement quarry served as a sort of Grumman's Chinese Theatre for large and scaly types. When the grounds were being cleared, plant employees uncovered a layer of mudstone set with the tracks of tyrannosaurus rex and iguanodon, some of which measure up to 80 cm in diameter. There are also petrified remains of prehistoric algae and fish. The site, 10 km north of town, is open to the public on Saturday.

El Libertador

'There have been three great fools in history: Jesus, Don Quixote and I'. This is how Simón Bolívar summed up his life shortly before he died. The man who brought independence from Spanish rule to all of north-western South America – modern-day Venezuela, Colombia, Panama, Ecuador, Peru and Bolivia – died abandoned, rejected and poor.

Simón Bolívar was born on 24 July 1783. His father died five years later and his mother died when he was nine years old. The boy was brought up by his uncle and was given a tutor, Simón Rodríguez, an open-minded mentor who had a strong formative influence on his pupil.

In 1799, the young Bolívar was sent to Spain and France to continue his education. After having mastered French, he turned his attention to that country's literature. Voltaire and Rousseau became his favourite authors. Their works introduced him to the new, progressive ideas of liberalism and, as it turned out, would determine the course of his life.

In 1802, Bolívar married his Spanish bride, María Teresa Rodríguez del Toro, and a short time later the young couple sailed for Caracas, but eight months later, María Teresa died of yellow fever. Although Bolívar never remarried, he had many lovers. The most devoted of these was Manuela Sáenz, whom he met in Quito in 1822 and who stayed with him almost until his final days.

The death of María Teresa marked a drastic shift in Bolívar's destiny. He returned to France where he met with the leaders of the French Revolution, and then travelled to the USA to take a close look at the new order after the American Revolution. By the time he returned to Caracas in 1807, he was full of revolutionary theories and experiences taken from these two successful examples. It didn't take him long to join the clandestine, pro-independence circles.

At the time, disillusionment with Spanish rule was close to breaking into open revolt. On 19 April 1810, the Junta Suprema was installed in Caracas and, on 5 July 1811, the Congress declared independence. This turned out to be the beginning of a long and bitter war, most of which was to be orchestrated by Bolívar.

Simón Bolívar's military career began under Francisco de Miranda, the first Venezuelan leader of the independence movement. After Miranda was captured by the Spanish in 1812, Bolívar took over command. Battle followed battle with astonishing frequency until 1824. Of those battles personally directed by Bolívar, the independence forces won 35, including a few key ones: the Battle of Boyacá (7 August 1819), which secured the independence of Colombia; the Battle of Carabobo (24 June 1821), which brought freedom to Venezuela; and the Battle of Pichincha (24 May 1822), which led to the liberation of Ecuador.

In September 1822, the Argentine liberator General José de San Martín, who had occupied Lima, abandoned the city to the Spanish, and Bolívar took over the task of winning in Peru. On 6 August 1824, his army was victorious at the Battle of Junín and on 9 December 1824, General Antonio José de Sucre inflicted a final defeat at the Battle of Ayacucho. Peru, which included Alto Perú, had been liberated and the war was over. On 6 August 1825, the first anniversary of the Battle of Junín, Bolivia declared independence from Peru at Chuquisaca (Sucre) and the new republic was christened 'Bolivia', after the liberator.

Bolívar could now get down to his long-awaited dream: Gran Colombia, the unified state comprising Venezuela, Colombia (which then included Panama) and Ecuador, became reality. However, the task of setting the newborn state on its feet proved even more difficult than winning battles. 'I fear peace more than war', Bolívar wrote in a letter, aware of the difficulties ahead.

The main problem was the great racial and regional differences in Gran Colombia, which Bolívar, as president, was unable to hold together, even with strong central rule. Gran Colombia began to collapse from the moment of its birth. However, the president insisted upon holding the union together,

La Glorieta

After an extended tour of Europe, the wealthy entrepreneur Don Francisco Argandoña decided to build a home reflecting the various architectural traditions he'd encountered overseas. He commissioned the architect Antonio Camponovo to design a castle that incorporated a hotch-potch of European styles to be built on the outskirts of Sucre. The result was La Glorieta, an imposing mishmash that is difficult to discuss without passing judgement. Now a classic example of faded grandeur, it serves as the Lyceo Militar (military high school).

To get there, take a taxi or micro 'G' from the corner of Ravelo and Aniceto Arce and although it was rapidly slipping from his hands. The impassioned speeches for which he was widely known could no longer sway the growing opposition, and his glory and charisma faded.

In August 1828, he took drastic action: he ousted his vice-president Santander and assumed dictatorship, maintaining that 'Our America can only be ruled through a well managed, shrewd despotism'. His popularity waned further, as did his circle of friends and supporters, and a short time later, he miraculously escaped an assassination attempt in Bogotá. Disillusioned and in poor health, he resigned the presidency in early 1830 and planned to leave for Europe, just in time for the formal disintegration of Gran Colombia.

Venezuela broke away in 1830, approved a new Congress and banned Bolívar from his homeland. A month later, Antonio José de Sucre, Bolívar's closest friend, was assassinated in southern Colombia. These two news items reached Bolívar just as he was about to board a ship for France. Depressed and ill, he accepted the invitation of a Spaniard, Joaquín de Mier, to stay in his home in Santa Marta, Colombia.

Bolívar died on 17 December 1830 of pulmonary tuberculosis. A priest, a doctor and a few officers were by his bed, but none of these were his close friends. Joaquín de Mier donated one of his shirts to dress the body, as there had been none among Bolívar's humble belongings. So died perhaps the most important figure in the history of the South American continent.

It took the Venezuelan nation 12 years to acknowledge its debt to the man to whom it owed its freedom. In 1842, Bolívar's remains were brought from Santa Marta to Venezuela and deposited in the cathedral in Caracas. In 1876, they were solemnly transferred to the Pantheon in Caracas, where they now rest.

Today, Bolívar is once again a hero – his reputation polished and inflated to almost superhuman dimensions. His cult is particularly strong in Venezuela, but he's also widely venerated in the other nations he freed. His statue graces nearly every central city plaza and at least one street in every town bears his name.

El Libertador – as he was called at the beginning of his liberation campaigns and is also called today – was undoubtedly a man of extraordinary gifts. An idealist with a poetic mind and visionary ideas, his goal was not only to topple Spanish rule, but to create a unified America. This, of course, proved an impossible ideal, yet the military conquest of some five million sq km remains a phenomenal accomplishment. This inspired amateur with no formal training in war strategy won battles in a manner that still confounds the experts.

One of the final prophetic remarks in Bolívar's diary reads 'My name now belongs to history. It will do me justice'. And history has duly done so. ■

get off seven km south of town along the Potosí road. It's open Monday to Friday from 9 am to noon and 2 to 6 pm, and on Saturday from 9 am to noon. Admission is free but visitors must leave passports at the entrance.

Organised Tours

Most Sucre tour companies run Sunday excursions to Tarabuco, and a few also offer jaunts into the Cordillera de los Frailes.

To organise an adventure trek into the Cordillera de los Frailes or Cordillera de los Sombreros, or an incredible 10-day trek from Sucre to Torotoro, see local guide and trekking enthusiast Lucho Loredo, who lives in Barrio Petrolero. For contact details, see

Guides under the Cordillera de los Frailes section, later in this chapter.

Some other options include:

Altamira Tours
    Edificio Hostal Libertad, Aniceto Arce 99 (☎ & fax 23525)
Seatur
    Edificio Multicentro Céspedes, Plaza 25 de Mayo 25, Casilla 573 (☎ 21858, fax 32425)
SurAndes
    Nicolás Ortiz 6 (☎ 21983)
Turismo Sucre
    Calle Bustillo 117 (☎ 22936, fax 22677)

Special Events

Carnaval *Carnaval* in Sucre can be a pleasant experience, but beware of the pre-Lent water carnivals that take place on Sunday evenings in late January and early February, accompanied by processions and booming brass bands. They continue right up to Carnaval when they crescendo into madness. The object is to *mojar con agua* – that is, drench every passing thing – with water balloons. Foreign women are favourite targets.

Fiesta de la Virgen de Guadalupe On the evening of September 8, peasants sing and recite couplets to celebrate this festival. The following day, they dress in colourful costumes and parade around the main plaza carrying religious images and silver arches. It's a worthwhile event if you're in the area.

Fiesta de la Empanada The Fiesta de la Empanada, which takes place several times a year in the Casa de la Libertad, on the plaza, draws chefs and bakers from around the area, who compete for prizes with their original salteña and empanada recipes. The festival includes folkloric music, dancing, costumes and tables where artesans sell their handicrafts and weavings. The tourist office can provide specific dates.

Places to Stay – bottom end

Sucre is popular with visitors, so there's a choice of inexpensive accommodation and prices are negotiable. Most budget hotels are around the market and along Calles Ravelo and San Alberto.

A rock-bottom place is the cheap and basic *Alojamiento Anexo San José* (☎ 25572), on Calle Ravelo, but it's noisy and the walls don't go to the ceiling. Rooms cost US$2.30 per person. The friendly *Alojamiento El Turista* (☎ 23172), next door at Calle Ravelo 118, is musty and mediocre but at US$2.30 per person, it's good value for strict budgets. Try to get a room on the top floor; one even has a private bath. In the middle of nowhere, opposite the bus terminal, is the misnamed *Alojamiento Central* (☎ 23935), with rooms without bath for US$2.50 per person. It's only ten minutes from town on micro 'A'.

Residencial Oriental (☎ 21644) offers good value accommodation, charging US$3.80 per person without bath. For a double bed and bath, the charge is US$4 per person. The rooms are clean and there's TV in the reception area. Another cheap and convenient option is *Alojamiento La Plata*, with clean rooms, good hot showers and friendly staff. Rooms cost US$2.50 per person.

A popular backpackers' haunt is the friendly *Residencial Bustillo* (☎ 21560), on Calle Ravelo a block from the market. You'll pay US$3.80 per person without bath, which is good value if you don't mind the prison-like layout of the building.

The friendly *Hostal Charcas* (☎ 23972), Calle Ravelo 62, at the upper end of the bottom range, is a real winner and is among the best value for money in Sucre. Showers combine solar and electric heat, so hot water is available around the clock. Sparkling clean single/double rooms cost US$9/14.50 with bath and US$5.20/10 without bath.

Residencial Bolivia (☎ 24346) charges US$7.20/12.50 for a single/double with bath and US$5.20/8.25 without. The building once looked like someone had run amok with remaindered paint, but the resulting riot of colour has now been disappointingly obliterated by a wash of dull cream. It's centrally located but its facilities are fairly remote from the sleeping quarters, and the advertised breakfast isn't worth bothering with.

The rather oddly demeanoured *Hostal San Francisco* (☎ 22777) boasts clean rooms, private baths, a bright courtyard, sunny terraces and a German vegetarian restaurant. Single/double rooms cost US$8/12.50, including a marginally appetising breakfast of cold coffee and stale bread rolls with margarine.

Places to Stay – middle

The friendly and recently refurbished *Grand Hotel* (☎ 22104, fax 22461), at Aniceto Arce 61, represents excellent value. Single/double rooms, all with bath, TV, phone and breakfast, cost US$8.25/14.50. Rooms with double beds are US$11.50.

Hostal Sucre (☎ 21411, fax 31928) is one of Sucre's nicest – but not most expensive – places to stay. It has a lovely antique dining room and a sunny, flowery courtyard where you can kick back and read or catch up on letters. At US$16/20 for a single/double room, it's a rewarding splurge.

Hostal Libertad (☎ 23101, fax 30128) just a block from the plaza at Avenida Aniceto Arce 99, offers TV, telephone, piped music, private baths and a frigobar (bar fridge). Single/double rooms cost US$15.50/19.60. The spacious suite with huge wraparound windows and lots of light costs US$25 and would be ideal for two couples but unfortunately there's a bit of traffic noise. Breakfast is an additional US$1.50.

Hotel Municipal Simón Bolívar (☎ 21216, fax 24826) at Avenida Venezuela 1052 near Parque Bolívar is an average upmarket option with a lively beer garden called La Rotonda, which provides a bright counterpoint to the sombre dining room. Singles/doubles with bath, TV and telephone cost US$17/22.30, including breakfast.

The three-star *Hostal Cruz de Popayán* (☎ 25156), at Calle Loa 881, has a reputation for its charm and comfort, and is reminiscent of a Spanish parador or a Portuguese pousada. It's good value at US$17/22 for bright and spacious singles/doubles with bath. Breakfast in the courtyard is a real treat.

For a quiet retreat, there's *Hostal Los Pinos* (☎ 24403), at Calle Colón 502, which sits at the outer edge of town. This squeaky-clean place features cosy rooms and a beautiful courtyard and garden. Single/double rooms with bath and a good breakfast cost US$14.50/18.50.

Places to Stay – top end

The *Hostal Colonial* (☎ 24709, fax 21912) on Plaza 25 de Mayo receives four stars according to the Bolivian rating system. It lacks the character of the middle-range Hostal Sucre, but it's as central as a hotel can be. Singles/doubles cost US$21/26 and a luxury double suite is US$40.

Sucre's poshest hotel is the new *Hotel Real Audiencia* (☎ 30823, fax 32809), near the tourist office, which charges US$50/80 for single/double rooms with bath, TV, telephone and breakfast included.

Places to Eat

Sucre has a pleasant variety of quality restaurants and is a good place to spend time lolling around coffee shops and observing Bolivian university life.

For breakfast, try *Agencias Todo Fresco*, at Calle Ravelo 74 (the sign says 'Dillmann'), which is a bakery offering great bread, pastries, coffee, tea etc. The best places for salteñas are *El Patio*, at Calle San Alberto 18, and *Salteñas Miriam*, on Calle España. The latter does very good spicy beef or chicken salteñas.

Hamburguesas al Paso, on the plaza, and *Jugos Dumbo*, around the corner, open early to serve salteñas, coffee, tea, juice and licuados. The highly recommended *Arco's Coffee Shop* on Aniceto Arce near Ravelo also does breakfasts (US$1.50 to US$2.50) from 8 am, with juice, eggs and pancakes, and later, it moves into pizzas, burgers and healthy sandwiches (US$0.80 to US$1.20). The chicken and avocado sandwich is recommended.

The relatively posh *Palett Heladería-Pastelería* serves nice cakes, ice cream, coffee and other snacks, and *Nova Pan* does speciality breads, cakes and sticky doughnuts.

The market also provides some highlights.

Don't miss the fruit salads and juices, which are among the best in the country. You'll have to search for the correct stalls; they're tucked in an obscure corner of the ground floor. Try *jugo de tumbo* (juice of unripe yellow passion fruit) or any combination of melon, guava, pomelo, strawberry, papaya, banana, orange, lime etc. The vendors and their blenders always come up with something indescribably delicious. Upstairs in the market, you'll find good, filling meals in unusually sanitary conditions (for a market, anyway) for US$0.50 to US$0.75. For breakfast, you can enjoy a *pastel* (pastry) or *salteña* and a glass of *api* for as little as US$0.30.

For quick and cheap local *almuerzos* seven days a week, try *El Tropezón*, on Calle Junín near Estudiantes. Another lunch spot that's popular with locals is the *Restaurant Delta*. It has a bar and sunny courtyard, and features Bolivian standards and fresh juices.

Pizza Napolitana, on the plaza, plays good British and US music and does well as a hang-out for the under-21 university crowd, with ice cream and pizzas leading the menu selections. Drinks and coffee are on the expensive side, but a pizza large enough to fill two people costs only US$4.

Also excellent for pizza – as well as pasta, chicken, steak and even ribs – is *Kactus*, just off the plaza on Calle España. A host of chicken-and-chips shops are found along Avenida Hernando Siles between Tarapaca and Junín. The best are *Don Gerardo*, *Ce-Na II*, *Broaster la Pollita* and *Pollos Catalán*. Around the corner on Calle Loa you'll find four decent snack restaurants: *El Cedrón*, *El Paso de los Toros*, *Burger Theos* and *Arabe Ramadan* (is this meant to suggest you'd be better off fasting?).

La Repizza (☎ 32246) does meat or vegetarian pizzas, milanesas, pacumutus and pasta dishes, including vegetarian lasagne for US$1.60. The four-course *almuerzos* cost only US$1.20 and are very popular with university students.

Serious carnivores might want to head for the *Churrasquería Argentina*, which specialises in steak and other beef dishes. It's worth visiting for the menu alone, which manages such brilliant translations as 'Cow tit', 'English is juicy' and 'Do you want me to worm it?'.

At the long-running *Las Vegas*, on the plaza, the primarily meat-based meals are filling and adequate, but this place is a legend only in its own mind and the service has been described as a 'Latin Fawlty Towers'. For a snack, try the deservedly famous cheese *cuñapes*.

The *Restaurant Plaza*, next door, offers a similar menu and the outdoor balconies upstairs are also a great place to drink beer on a Sunday afternoon. Plusher restaurants with fine fare are *El Solar* (☎ 24341), on the corner of Calles Bolívar and Azurduy, and better still, *Piso Cero*, at Avenida Venezuela 1241. The latter serves huge portions of international and regional dishes costing no more than US$3.

An expensive but very good Chinese place is the *Chifa Hong Kong*, on the plaza. For upmarket Italian food, including lasagne, ravioli, cannelloni etc, there's *Piccolissimo* (☎ 23247), at Calle San Alberto 237. It's about as elegant as Sucre gets and although the extraordinary service tries to be pretentious, it joyfully fails. Plan on US$5 to US$7 per person, or more if you splurge on a bottle of Chilean wine. Afterwards, enjoy a cup of espresso or cappuccino – so good one could wax poetic about it!

The excellent Alliance Française restaurant, *La Taverne*, serves a mean ratatouille for US$1.50, as well as coq au vin, quiche Lorraine and other continental favourites. The menu reflects a laudable trilingual harmony: 'con eggs ou sin eggs'. And then there are the desserts. Films, usually French, are shown nightly. For more elegant international dining, try the *Restaurant El Batán*, beside the Hostal Cruz de Popayan.

There's also a quartet of Teutonic options. One of the nicest is *Bibliocafé*, with a dark but cosy atmosphere, good music and stacks of *Geo* and *Der Spiegel* magazines on the shelves. The pasta dishes are recommended, as is the banana, chocolate and cream crêpe.

It's only open in the evening and it gets crowded, so go early.

Another German alternative is the coffee shop and restaurant *Kultur Café Berlin* at Calle Avaroa 326. It's open for lunch from 12.30 to 3 pm. Don't miss the papas rellenas (potatoes with spicy fillings), which cost only US$0.30.

The third is Swiss-German *Arco Irís*, on Calle Nicolás Ortiz, near the plaza. The menu includes such delights as roeschti, fondue bourguignonne, Greek salad, mousse au chocolat and head-buzzing cappuccino, and vegetarian meals are available. Arco Irís stages weekend peñas featuring local musicians, and occasionally shows videos.

The fourth German option is the bright and airy *Restaurant Germén* at the Hostal San Francisco, which does excellent vegetarian dishes – tofu curry, vegie lasagne and pizza – and German-style gateaux and pastries. Vegetarian almuerzos are just US$1.50. There's also a book exchange but as you'd expect, most titles are in German. It's open daily from 3.30 to 8 pm.

A popular student hang-out with a Bolivian twist is the *Café Hacheh* at Pastor Sainz 241. Specialities include sandwiches and coffee and fruit juice.

For upmarket self-caterers, there's the marvel-ridden *Saico del Sur* supermarket on the corner of Avenida Aniceto Arce and Calle Ravelo. Here you'll find all the nasty prepackaged food items that you may have begun dreaming about (don't deny it!) – taco shells, Cadbury chocolate, Pringles potato chips, Reese's peanut butter cups – but at a premium.

Because Sucre is Bolivia's chocolate capital, there's plenty of scope for a sweet fix. For the best from Cadbury, Breick, Hershey's, Mars, Nestlé and other companies, a good choice is *Bonbons Leblon*, near the corner of Arenales and Aniceto Arce.

Entertainment

If you want to enjoy a bit of nightlife with the more affluent university crowds, try the *Discoteca Up-Down* on the corner of Gregorio Mendizábal and Franz Ruck, two blocks from Parque Bolívar. It's expensive and a bit snobbish, but there are few better choices. It's open from Thursday to Sunday and admission is US$2, including one drink.

Despite the name, don't roll up at *Andy Capp's Wisquería* in search of warm beer and Cockney hospitality. It's more of a basic local wheeler dealers' hang-out than a pleasant pub, and the red lighting inside does nothing to improve its reputation. The Chinese-Bolivian proprietors sell Brazilian cachaça for less than US$1 a glass.

On Plaza Pizarro, there's an opulent old opera house, the *Teatro Gran Mariscal de Ayacucho*. Cultural events are announced on the notice board on the north-west corner of the plaza. *Café Tertulias*, in the garden of the Casa de la Cultura, serves as a venue for cultural programmes and music and theatre productions. The tourist office and the Casa de la Cultura (☎ 21083) distribute a monthly calendar of events.

Things to Buy

A good place to look for quality weavings is the Proyecto Textil (☎ 23841, fax 32194) in the Caserón de la Capellanía. Prices are steep by Bolivian standards, but most of the profits are directed back to the artesans and the artistry and quality of the items justifies them. Plan on spending US$75 to US$125 for top-quality work. Alternatively, opt for the *oferta del mes*, the 'monthly sale item', which may be marked down to less than half the normal price; with some luck, you'll pick up a fabulous piece for as little as US$40.

If you prefer to buy genuine Candelaria and Jalq'a weavings that have not been produced expressly for tourists, visit the jam-packed cubbyhole of Doña Máxima in the Centro Comercial Guadalupe, Calle Junín 411. With hard bargaining, you'll find excellent deals on some incredible creations. In general, they're less decorative and more utilitarian than those sold to Proyecto Textil. If Doña Máxima isn't in the shop, ask around and someone will hunt her up.

Some of Bolivia's best charango makers are based around Sucre and several shops in town specialise in this instrument. Learning to play one is another matter but if you already play the guitar, you should be able to coax pleasant sounds from a charango. The artesan may even throw in a lesson or two. Try the shops at Calle Junín 1190 and Destacamento 59 but in the interest of endangered armadillos everywhere, please avoid armadillo-shell charangos.

Getting There & Away

Air LAB (☎ 22666) and AeroSur (☎ 24895) both have flights to and from La Paz (US$56), Cochabamba (US$35 – LAB only), Santa Cruz (US$41), Tarija (US$44 – LAB only), Camiri (US$89.50) and other towns. You can reach the airport on micro 'F' for US$0.10, or by taxi for US$1.50.

Bus The bus terminal is unfortunately not within walking distance of the centre, but is readily accessed by micro 'A'. However, the usually cramped micros can be full of luggage. Long-distance bus fares are usually lowered if you request a discount when buying the ticket.

There are numerous daily buses to Cochabamba (US$7, 12 hours), all of which leave around 6 or 7 pm; many of these continue on to Santa Cruz (US$10, 24 hours). Direct buses to Santa Cruz – those that pass through Samaipata rather than Cochabamba – leave only on Tuesday, Friday and Sunday (US$9, 18 hours) around noon.

Several companies leave daily for Potosí (US$3, 3½ hours) at 7 or 7.30 am and at 5 pm. When the road is passable, Flota Chaqueña does the rough but beautiful trip to Camiri on Tuesday and Friday at 7 am for US$12.50.

A number of *flotas* also connect Sucre with La Paz. Morning departures travel via Oruro (US$8, 20 hours) and arrive the following morning; most evening departures travel via Cochabamba and don't arrive until the following afternoon.

Camión *Camiones* for Punilla, Chataquila, Potolo, Ravelo and points north and west leave in the morning from the Río Quirpinchaca bridge, en route to the airport. There are usually two or three services daily to each destination, departing between 6 and 10 am. Camiones to Tarabuco, Candelaria, Padilla and points south and east leave from the stop on Avenida de las Américas. Micros and camiones to Potosí leave when full from the railway tracks at Avenida Ostria Gutiérrez.

Train The railway station is across the plaza/traffic circle north-west of Parque Bolívar on Calle Cabrera. The *ferrobus* to Potosí (US$4, 4½ hours), Oruro (US$8.50, nine hours) and La Paz (US$10.50, 12 hours) leaves on Wednesday and Sunday at 3 pm.

Getting Around

The Airport The airport, nine km north-west of town, is accessed by micro 'F' from Avenida Hernando Siles or by taxi for US$1 in a shared taxi or US$4 on your own. LAB no longer provides an airport shuttle.

Bus Lots of micros ply the city streets and all seem to congregate at or near the market between runs. They're usually quite crowded but Sucre is small, so you won't spend much time aboard. The most useful routes are those that climb the steep Avenida Grau hill to the Recoleta, and micro 'A', which goes to the main bus terminal. The standard fare for any route is US$0.15. Micros to the colonial village of Yotala leave from the cemetery and cost only US$0.15.

Taxi Taxis between any two points around the centre cost US$0.30 (B$1.50) per person. To outlying areas such as the bus terminal or Barrio Petrolero, you'll pay US$0.40 (B$2).

Around Sucre

TARABUCO

The village of Tarabuco lies at an elevation of 3200m, 65 dusty km (three hours by camión) south-east of Sucre. It enjoys a mild climate, just a bit cooler than Sucre's. Most *tarabuqueños* are involved in agriculture or textiles and the colourful handmade clothing

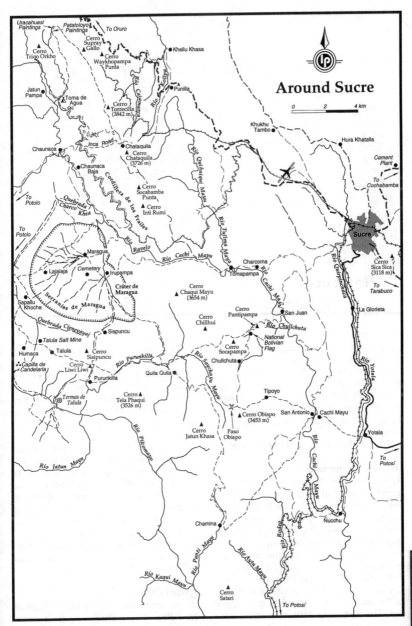

Around Sucre

Tarabuco map showing: To Sucre, Road to Sucre, Market, Tourist Office, Alojamiento Florida, ENTEL, Plaza, Police, Mass held here during Phujllay Festival, Traditional Food Market, Pukhara Ritual Ceremony Site, Tarabuco, scale 0 100 200 m

and weavings produced there are some of the most renowned in Bolivia.

On 12 March 1816, Tarabuco was the site of the Battle of Jumbati in which the village folk defended themselves under the leadership of a woman, Doña Juana Azurduy de Padilla, and liberated the town from Spanish forces.

The telephone code for Tarabuco is 0691.

Mercado Campesino

Apart from the Phujllay celebration, the main reason to visit Tarabuco is the colourful Sunday market where you can buy beautiful artesanía – *charangos*, pullovers, coca pouches, ponchos and weavings featuring geometric and zoomorphic designs. The colourful wares laid out in stalls around the plaza and on side streets lend a festive and lighthearted atmosphere to the entire place. It's worth going to see the unique costumes of the strolling charango-playing campesinos. The men wear distinct *monteras* (also known as *morriones*), which are leather hats patterned after those worn by the conquistadores. It's also interesting to seek out the snake oil vendors in the central market; they proclaim the universal curative powers of their wares surrounded by leftover bits of snakes and other (by this time) anonymous reptiles.

It's all quite touristy, however, drawing both organised groups and individual travellers, so even well-bargained prices tend to be high and sales tactics are somewhat less than passive. You'll have to learn to appreciate and admire skill and quality when it's being shoved up your nose. If it's all too overwhelming, you may want to visit other weaving villages in the area, such as Candelaria south-east of Tarabuco, or Ravelo and Potolo north-west of Sucre.

Special Events

In commemoration of the Battle of Jumbati, the village stages Phujllay (which means 'amusement' or 'play' in Quechua) on the second weekend of March. Over 60 communities show up in local costume. The celebration begins with a Quechua Mass and procession followed by the Pukhara ceremony, a Bolivian version of Thanksgiving. Folkloric dancers and musicians perform throughout the two-day weekend fiesta. It's one of Bolivia's largest festivals and is worth attending.

The smaller local celebration La Virgen de Rosario takes place in October, and features bullfights, Masses and parades.

Places to Stay & Eat

During Phujllay your chances of finding accommodation in Tarabuco are slim, so take camping equipment if you plan to stay the night. The ephemeral *Alojamiento Florida* (☎ 2233), half a block north of the plaza, charges US$3 per person for a grotty room and dirty communal facilities. The attached restaurant isn't too bad. A better option is the nameless *alojamiento* on the plaza, which is run by a friendly local woman who also charges US$3 per person.

Meals of chorizo, curry, charque kan and soup are available from street stalls during market hours. On the plaza you'll find a couple of basic restaurants.

Getting There & Away

Several Sucre agencies run Sunday tours to Tarabuco for less than US$15 per person. There's also a tourist bus, which costs US$2.20 and leaves Sucre on Sunday morning at 7 am from accommodation along Calles Ravelo and San Alberto. Unfortunately, it leaves Tarabuco at 12.30 pm, which is too early for most people.

If you'd prefer a bit more flexibility, camiones, micros and mini-buses leave when full from Avenida de las Américas in Sucre on Sunday between 6.30 and 9.30 am. To reach the stop, take micro 'B' or 'C'. The Tarabuco trip takes at least two hours along dusty roads. Micros/camiones charge US$1/0.80 per person.

Camiones returning to Sucre park at the top of the main plaza in Tarabuco. On

Sunday, they leave any time from 11 am to 3.30 pm but still wait until they're 'full' by local definition.

CORDILLERA DE LOS FRAILES

The Cordillera de los Frailes, the imposing serrated ridge in Sucre's backdrop, creates a formidable barrier between the departments of Chuquisaca and Potosí.

A great way to see the Cordillera is on foot. The map in this chapter can help with route planning, but trekking on your own isn't recommended and a local guide will be indispensable when it comes to route-finding or communicating with the Quechua-speaking campesinos. A guide will also help you avoid misunderstandings, minimise your impact and help you get a better feeling for local culture.

There are numerous walking routes through the Cordillera de los Frailes, some of which are marked on the 1:50,000 topo sheets *Sucre*, sheet 6536-IV, and *Estancia Chaunaca*, sheet 6537-III.

A recommended six-day circuit begins at Chataquila, on the ridge above Punilla, 25 km north-west of Sucre. It begins with a side-trip to Incamachay, then loops through Chaunaca, the Cráter de Maragua, the Termas de Talula and Quila Quila, taking in several Cordillera highlights before returning to Sucre from the south. Basic staples are available in Chaunaca. Soft drinks are sold at the Termas de Talula on weekends and are available sporadically in Quila Quila, but otherwise, there are no shops or meals nor is there accommodation anywhere on the circuit.

Guides

Several Sucre travel agencies offer quick jaunts into the Cordillera – for example, a two-day circuit from Chataquila to Incamachay and Chaunaca. For an extended trip, however, it's less expensive and probably more enjoyable to hire a private guide, who will allow you to customise your trip. Highly recommended are Sucre-based Lucho and Dely Loredo, who speak Quechua and

SUCRE

Spanish and are familiar with local customs, traditions and life in the campo. They can organise a range of custom itineraries, either camping or overnighting in homes or village schools.

One to seven-day organised treks including public transport from Sucre, and very simple meals, drinks and accommodation (or camping using your own equipment) cost US$15 to US$25 per person per day, depending on the group size. There's no phone; contact the Loredos by taking a US$0.40 taxi ride to their home at Barrio Petrolero, Calle Panamá final esquina Calle Comarapa 127.

Access

Camiones leave for Potolo via Punilla and Chataquila two or three times daily, before 10 am, from the Río Quirpinchaca bridge, between Sucre and the airport. To Chataquila takes two hours and costs US$0.75 per person.

To Quila Quila or the Termas de Talula or Quila Quila, buses and camiones depart from Barrio Aranjuez in Sucre on Saturday and Sunday mornings and return the same day in the afternoon. The standard fare is less than US$1.50 per person, but if you're boarding somewhere en route (especially on the return trip to Sucre), the charge may be as much as US$3.50.

The Route

Chataquila to Chaunaca On the rocky ridge top at Chataquila is a lovely stone chapel dedicated to the Virgen de Chataquila, a Virgin-shaped stone that has been dressed in a gown and placed on the altar.

From Chataquila, look around on the southern side of the road for an obvious notch in the rock, which issues onto a lovely pre-Hispanic route that descends steeply to the village of Chaunaca. The original route has been plagued by slides, but there are still lots of good paved sections and it's easy to follow. The six-km descent to Chaunaca takes about three hours.

At Chaunaca, you'll find a school, a tiny

church and several Mediterranean-style whitewashed houses, which were constructed in an international aid scheme that was less than successful Very basic supplies are available in an unlikely-looking hovel along the main road. Guides may organise accommodation in the school, but otherwise, try to camp away from the village to avoid disruption in this traditional area. The river beaches downstream are ideal for picnics or camping.

Incamachay Side Trip A worthwhile day trip from Chataquila leads to the two sets of ancient rock paintings collectively known as Incamachay. At the first major curve on the road west of Chataquila, a rugged track heads north along the ridge. For much of its length, the route is flanked by impossibly rugged rock formations, but it's relatively easy going until you've almost reached the paintings, where you face a bit of a scramble. The first set, Uracahuasi, lies well-ensconced inside a rock cleft between two stone slabs. The other more impressive panel, Patatoloyo, lies 15 minutes farther along beneath a rock overhang. Note that these sites would be virtually impossible to find without a guide.

From here, you can either return to Chataquila the way you came or continue downhill for about two hours until you strike the road at the Tomo de Agua aqueduct, where there's drinking water and a good camp site. From there, take the road six km to the Chataquila-Chaunaca road, where you can decide whether to ascend to Chataquila or descend to Chaunaca.

Chaunaca to the Cráter de Maragua Follow the road south from Chaunaca (not the one that continues towards Potolo) for about seven km, passing brilliantly coloured green and violet hillsides into the Cráter de Maragua. This unearthly natural formation, sometimes called the Umbligo de Chuquisaca or 'navel of Chuquisaca', features surreal settlements scattered across a red and violet crater floor, and bizarre slopes that culminate in gracefully symmetrical pale green arches called the Serranías de Maragua. It's one of the most bizarre places in all Bolivia.

Maragua to the Termas de Talula You can leave the Cráter de Maragua either to the south, through Irupampa and Sisipunku to Purinquilla, or west to Sapallu Khocha or Lajalaja.

The latter route will take you over some challenging up-and-down terrain studded with brilliant mica deposits to Hacienda Humaca, an isolated ghost oasis between high peaks, with mud ruins, palm trees and salty Río Khoya Mayu. From Humaca, access to the Termas de Talula, just five km away, requires two fords of the Río Pilcomayo. The crossing is safest in the morning when the water level is at its lowest.

If you opt for the route south from Maragua, you can reach the Talula by turning west at Purunkilla and sauntering four km down the road. No river fords are required.

The Talula hot springs issue into three pools with temperatures up to 45°C. There's no accommodation, but you can camp inside the crumbling bathhouse. On weekends, vendors sell soft drinks, but no meals are available. Admission to Talula is US$0.20 per day. The pools are drained and refilled on Friday evening, so a Saturday soak is more salubrious than one late in the week.

From the bathhouse, it's only 500m to where the Río Pilcomayo slides between the steep walls of Punkurani gorge. With more time, you can also cross the Río Pilcomayo and poke around the numerous rock painting sites above the opposite bank.

Termas de Talula to Sucre From Talula, the route back to Sucre begins by following the road (which was constructed to serve less than a dozen vehicles per week!) back up to Purunkilla. From there, it's five km of well-kept farmland to Quila Quila (spelt Quilla Quilla on the topo sheet). This crumbling and bizarrely beautiful ghost village is now being revived by Sucre people exchanging city life for an agricultural lifestyle. There's little of

interest here, but the enormous church does occupy an imposing position beneath the dramatic peak of 3526m Cerro Tela Phaqui. Soft drinks are sold at one home on the plaza, but no other supplies are available. Only on weekends, when day-trippers travel between Sucre and the Termas de Talula, does the village see any vehicular traffic.

Continuing back towards Sucre, the road climbs through a barren but colourful landscape of red hills and maguey to the pass at the foot of 3453m Cerro Obispo. Here, there's a choice. One is to turn off on the 12-km track through the Tipoyo and Hacienda Cachi Mayu to the colonial village of Yotala, which lies about 16 km south of Sucre on the main road.

Alternatively, continue another four km down the road past the rather idyllic and well-watered flower-growing village of Chullchuta, over the shoulder of Cerro Pantipampa. About 2.5 km farther along, look across the quebrada at the bands of red, yellow and green in the hillside, which form a natural Bolivian flag. From the crest, the road drops steeply down to Hacienda San Juan on the Río Cachi Mayu, where sand is extracted to make cement, then climbs up to the plateau for the final – and rather tedious – 11 km into Sucre.

Potolo

The village of Potolo is the origin of some of Bolivia's finest Jalq'a tradition weavings, particularly the renowned red and black (or magenta and black) animal-patterned pieces sold throughout the Andes and esteemed by experts worldwide.

Potolo lies about two days trekking from either Maragua or Chaunaca. Alternatively, several daily camiones leave for Potolo between 6 and 10 am from near the Río Quirpinchaca, the first bridge on the airport road near Sucre. The fare is US$1.20 per person and the trip takes at least three hours.

Supay Huasi

Among the most interesting rock paintings in the Cordillera de los Frailes are those at

Supay Huasi, the 'house of the devil'. These unusual zoomorphic and anthropomorphic images in ochre, white and yellow, include a white long-tailed animal, which could be a monkey; a hump-backed llama that bears a remarkable resemblance to a camel; a 12-cm two-headed creature, which may represent a pair of amorous canines; an ochre-coloured

40-cm man wearing a sun-like headdress; and several faded geometric figures and designs.

The paintings are about a 2½ hour walk upstream from the point where the Río Mama Huasi crosses the Ravelo road, north of Punilla. However, they're almost impossible to find without a local guide.

Potosí

I am rich Potosí,
The treasure of the world
And the envy of kings.

The renown of Potosí – its history and splendour as well as its tragedy and horror – is inextricably tied to silver. The above legend from the city's first coat of arms wasn't far off the mark, but then, any city with a mountain of silver in its backyard is certain to attract attention. The city was founded in 1545, following the discovery of ore in silver-rich Cerro Rico, and the veins proved so rich that the mines quickly became the world's most prolific.

Despite its setting at an altitude of 4090m (it's the world's highest city), Potosí blossomed, and towards the end of the 18th century, grew into the largest and wealthiest city in Latin America. Silver from Potosí underwrote the Spanish economy – and its monarch's extravagance – for over two centuries. Now, anything incredibly lucrative is said to 'vale un Potosí' (be worth a Potosí). A good example is the city of San Luís Potosí in central Mexico where silver was discovered in the 1600s. However, it never lived up to its Bolivian namesake.

Visitors to modern Potosí will find remnants of a grand colonial city – ornate churches, monuments, and colonial architecture – in a most unlikely setting.

Highlights

- Discover the grand colonial architectural heritage of Potosí from the days when this, the world's highest city, was larger than London or Shanghai
- Take in a grand vista of Potosí from the roof of Bolivia's oldest monastery, the Convento de San Francisco
- Witness the appalling conditions inside the Potosí Cooperative Mines
- Tour the historical treasures held behind metre-thick walls in the icy interior of the restored colonial mint, Casa Real de la Moneda – but whatever the weather, put on your thermal underwear first
- Bathe in the hot springs at Tarapaya

History

No one is certain how much silver has been extracted from Cerro Rico (the 'rich hill' in Potosí's backdrop) over its four centuries of productivity, but a popular boast was that the Spanish could have constructed a silver bridge to Spain and still had some left to carry across on it. The Spanish monarchs, who personally received 20% of the booty, were certainly worth more than a few pesetas.

Although the tale of how it all started probably takes liberties with the facts, it's as good a story as any; it begins in 1544 when a Peruvian Indian, Diego Huallpa, was tending his llamas. When he noticed that two of the beasts were missing, he set off to search for them. By nightfall, however, he still hadn't found them and the cold grew fierce, so Diego stopped to build a fire at the foot of the mountain known in Quechua as 'Potojsi' (meaning 'thunder' or 'explosion', although it might also have stemmed from potoj, 'the springs'). The fire grew so hot that the very earth beneath it started to melt, and shiny liquid oozed from the ground.

POTOSÍ

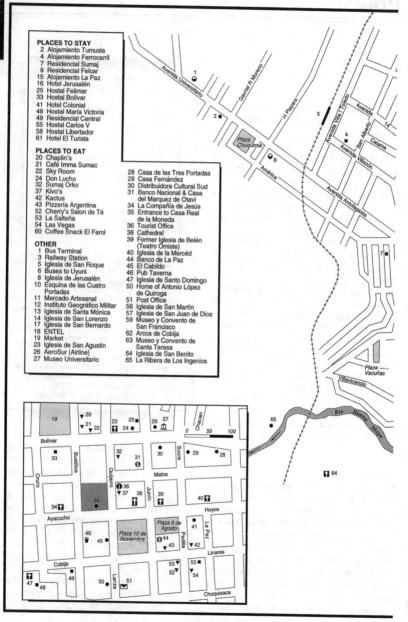

PLACES TO STAY
2 Alojamiento Tumusla
4 Alojamiento Ferrocarril
7 Residencial Sumaj
9 Residencial Felcar
15 Alojamiento La Paz
16 Hotel Jerusalén
25 Hostal Felimar
33 Hostal Bolívar
41 Hotel Colonial
48 Hostal María Victoria
49 Residencial Central
55 Hostal Carlos V
58 Hostal Libertador
61 Hotel El Turista

PLACES TO EAT
20 Chaplin's
21 Café Imma Sumac
22 Sky Room
24 Don Lucho
32 Sumaj Orko
37 Kivo's
42 Kactus
43 Pizzería Argentina
52 Cherry's Salon de Té
53 La Salteña
54 Las Vegas
60 Coffee Snack El Farol

OTHER
1 Bus Terminal
3 Railway Station
5 Iglesia de San Roque
6 Buses to Uyuni
8 Iglesia de Jerusalén
10 Esquina de las Cuatro
   Portadas
11 Mercado Artesanal
12 Instituto Geográfico Militar
13 Iglesia de Santa Mónica
14 Iglesia de San Lorenzo
17 Iglesia de San Bernardo
18 ENTEL
19 Market
23 Iglesia de San Agustín
26 AeroSur (Airline)
27 Museo Universitario

28 Casa de las Tres Portadas
29 Casa Fernández
30 Distribuidora Cultural Sud
31 Banco Nacional & Casa
   del Marquez de Otavi
34 La Compañía de Jesús
35 Entrance to Casa Real
   de la Moneda
36 Tourist Office
38 Cathedral
39 Former Iglesia de Belén
   (Teatro Omiste)
40 Iglesia de la Mercéd
44 Banco de La Paz
45 El Cabildo
46 Pub Taverna
47 Iglesia de Santo Domingo
50 Home of Antonio López
   de Quiroga
51 Post Office
56 Iglesia de San Martín
57 Iglesia de San Juan de Dios
59 Museo y Convento de
   San Francisco
62 Arcos de Cobija
63 Museo y Convento de
   Santa Teresa
64 Iglesia de San Benito
65 La Ribera de Los Ingenios

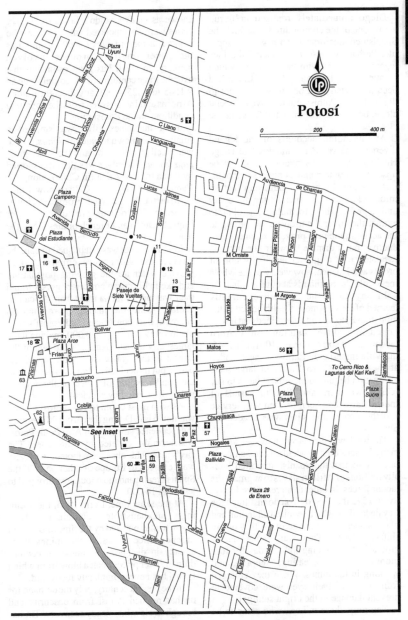

Potosí

Diego immediately realised he'd run across one of the commodities for which the Spanish conquerors had an insatiable appetite. Perhaps he also remembered the Inca legend associated with the mountain, which recounted that Inca ruler Huayna Capac had been instructed by a booming voice not to dig in the hill Potojsi, but to leave the metal alone, because it was intended for someone else.

At this point, accounts of the legend diverge. One version maintains that Diego Huallpa kept his discovery secret, lest he upset the mountain *apus*. Others say that his instincts got the best of him, and that he informed a friend, Huanca, of the discovery and together they formulated a plan to extract the silver themselves. According to the account, the vein proved extremely productive, but a dispute between the partners escalated into a quarrel about division of profits and Huanca, now weary of the whole mess, told the Spaniards about the mine.

In any case, the Spanish eventually learned of the enormous wealth buried in the mountain Potojsi, and determined that it warranted immediate attention. On 1 April (according to some sources, 10 April) 1545, the Villa Imperial de Carlos V was founded at the foot of Cerro Rico and large-scale excavation began. In the time it takes to say 'Get down there and dig', thousands of Indian slaves had been pressed into service and the first of the silver was headed for Spain.

The work was dangerous, however, and so many Indians died of accidents and silicosis pneumonia that the Spanish imported literally millions of African slaves to augment the labour forces. In order to increase productivity, in 1572 the Viceroy Toledo instituted the Ley de la Mita, which required all Indian and black slaves over the age of 18 to work in shifts of 12 hours. They would remain underground without seeing light of day for four months at a time, eating, sleeping, and working in the mines. When they emerged from a 'shift', their eyes were covered to prevent damage in the bright sunlight.

Naturally, these miners, who came to be known as *mitayos*, didn't last long. Heavy losses were also incurred among those who worked in the *ingenios* (smelting mills) as the silver smelting process involved mercury. In all, it has been estimated that over the three centuries of the colonial period – 1545 to 1825 – as many as eight million Africans and Indians died from the appalling conditions in the Potosí mines.

Inside the mines, silver was smelted in small ovens known as *huayrachinas*, which were fuelled with wood and the spiky grass *paja brava*. The silver was then transported by llama train to Arica (in Chile), along the Camino de Plata, or to Callao (now Lima, Peru) on the Pacific coast. From there, it was carried by ship to Spain, providing spoils for English, Dutch and French pirates along the way.

In 1672, a mint was established to coin the silver; reservoirs were constructed to provide water for the growing population; and exotic European consumer goods found their way up the llama trails from Arica and Callao. Amid the mania, more than 80 churches were constructed and Potosí's population grew to nearly 200,000, making it the largest city in Latin America and one of the largest in the world. One politician of the period put it succinctly: 'Potosí was raised in the pandemonium of greed at the foot of riches discovered by accident'.

As with most boom towns, Potosí's glory was not to last. During the early 19th-century Independence struggles in Alto Perú, Potosí was naturally coveted by both sides. The city's many churches were looted, its wealth was removed to Europe or other parts of the Spanish realm and the population dropped to less than 10,000.

At the same time, Cerro Rico, the seemingly inexhaustible mountain of silver, began to play out, and by the time of Bolivian independence in 1825, the mines were already in decline. The mid-19th century drop in silver prices dealt a blow from which Potosí has never completely recovered.

In the present century, only the demand for tin has rescued Potosí from obscurity and brought a slow but steady recovery. Tin has now taken over as Bolivia's major metallic export and *potosinos* are now mining previously discarded tailings for lead, zinc, copper and tin. Silver extraction continues on only a small scale, but reminders of the grand colonial city are still evident in the narrow streets, formal balconied mansions and ornate churches.

The mining reforms of 1952 brought the Pailaviri mine under government control and mining conditions improved immensely. Most of the Cerro Rico operations, however, are now in the control of miner-owned cooperatives. The government mine has closed, having been plagued by strikes, protests and general dissatisfaction, while the cooperatives continue operating under conditions that have changed shamefully little from the colonial period.

In 1987, UNESCO named Potosí a World Heritage Site in recognition of its rich and tragic history and its wealth of colonial architecture.

Orientation
Maps An office of the Instituto Geográfico Militar (☎ 26248), upstairs in the courtyard at Calle Sucre 78, sells topo sheets of all areas of Potosí department.

Information
Tourist Office The Senatur tourist office (☎ 25288), upstairs at the corner of Matos and Calle Quijarro, is theoretically open Monday to Friday from 9 am to noon and 3 to 6 pm, but it's a waste of time in a city where there are a number of better things to see and do. Some hotels, particularly Hotel El Turista and Hostal María Victoria, provide reliable tourist information for their guests.

Money Lots of businesses along Calle Bolívar and Calle Sucre change US dollars cash at a reasonable rate – look for the 'Compro Dólares' signs. Travellers cheques fetch a poor rate in Potosí – up to 10% below the official rate. On weekdays, you can change them at the Banco Nacional on Calle Junín for a very poor rate. At other times, try Casa Fernández, at Calle Sucre 10 or Casa

Shutt, Calle Matos 19. Visa cash advances are available at Banco de La Paz, on the plaza; you can receive the cash in bolivianos or US dollars.

Post & Communications The central post office is on Calle Lanza, a block south of the main plaza. The shop in the lobby sells postcards, but they're cheaper at Distribuidora Cultural Sud. The new ENTEL office occupies the corner of Frías and Camacho. The public fax number in Potosí is 24005. The telephone code is 062.

Film & Photography You'll find Fuji and Agfa slide film at Casa Fernández, Calle Sucre 10.

Laundry As usual, all hotels can organise laundry services for their guests. Failing that, try Lavandería La Veloz, on Calle Quijarro near the corner of Calle Matos.

Dangers & Annoyances If you're harassed by bogus police, contact the Radio Patrulla (☎ 110) or the tourist police (☎ 25288).

Casa Real de la Moneda
The Casa Real de la Moneda (Royal Mint) is the city's star attraction and one of South America's finest and most interesting museums. The first mint in Potosí was constructed on the present site of the Casa de Justicia in 1572 under orders of the Viceroy Toledo. The present building, which occupies an entire block near the cathedral, was built between 1753 and 1773 to control the minting of colonial coins right where the metal was mined. These coins, which bore the mint mark 'P', were known as *potosís*.

The exceptionally impressive building has been carefully restored. Its massive walls are more than a metre thick and it has not only functioned as a mint, but also done spells as a prison, a fortress and, during the Chaco War, as the headquarters of the Bolivian Army.

From the entrance, visitors are ushered into a courtyard where they're greeted by a stone fountain and a mask of Bacchus, the wine god, hung there in 1865 by Frenchman Eugenio Martin Moulon for reasons known only to him. In fact, this aberration looks more like an escapee from a children's fun fair, but it has somehow become a national icon.

The museum houses a host of historical treasures. Among them are the first locomotive used in Bolivia and a beautiful salon brimming with religious paintings (lots of blood). In the basement are a couple of still-functional hand-powered minting devices that were in use until 1869, when the minting machines were imported from Philadelphia. For the obligatory two-hour tours, which are conducted from Monday to Saturday at 9 am and 2 pm, foreigners pay US$1.75. Photography permits cost an extra US$2. Whatever the outside temperature, wear thermal underwear and several layers of clothing for the tour; the vast dungeon-like spaces in this building never feel the warmth of day!

Museo Universitario

The Museo Universitario Ricardo Bohorquez, on Calle Bolívar between Junín and Sucre, has a diverse but rather haphazard and mostly unlabelled collection of paintings, pottery, antiques, stuffed birds etc. It's open Monday to Friday, 10 am to noon and 3 to 5 pm; the US$1 admission helps support the university.

Calle Quijarro

North of the Iglesia de San Agustín, Calle Quijarro narrows as it winds between a wealth of colonial buildings, many with doorways graced by old family crests. It's thought that the bends in Calle Quijarro were an intentional attempt to inhibit the cold winds that would otherwise whistle through and chill everything in their path. (This concept is carried to extremes on the Pasaje de Siete Vueltas – 'the passage of seven turns' – which is an extension of Calle Ingavi, east of Junín.) During colonial times, Calle Quijarro was the street of potters, but it's now known for its hat makers. One shop worth visiting is that of Don Antonio Villa Chavarría, at Calle Quijarro 41. The intersec-

tion of Calles Quijarro and Modesto Omiste, farther north, has been dubbed the Esquina de las Cuatro Portadas because of its four decorative colonial doorways.

Museo & Convento de San Francisco

The Convento de San Francisco was founded in 1547 by Fray Gaspar de Valverde, making it the oldest monastery in Bolivia. Due to its inadequate size, it was demolished in 1707 and reconstructed over the following 19 years. A gold-covered altar from this building is now housed in the Casa Real de la Moneda. The statue of Christ that graces the present altar features hair that is said to grow miraculously and for some reason, the stone cupolas have been painted to resemble brick-work.

The museum has examples of typical religious art, including various paintings from the Escuela Potosina Indígena (Indigenous Potosí School), such as *The Erection of the Cross* by Melchor Pérez de Holguín, various mid-19th century works by Juan de la Cruz Tapia, and 25 scenes from the life of San Francisco de Asis. Another notable painting is a portrait of Antonio Lopez de Quiroga, a wealthy 17th-century philanthropist who donated generously to the Church.

It's open Monday to Friday from 10 am to noon and 2.30 to 5 pm, and on Saturday from 10 am to noon. Foreigners pay US$1.50. The highlight comes at the end, when you're ushered up the tower and onto the roof for a grand vista over Potosí. Photography permits cost an extra US$2 for cameras and US$3 for videos.

Museo & Convento de Santa Teresa

The oddly orange-coloured Carmelite Convento de Santa Teresa was founded in 1685 by Mother Josepha de Jesús y María and a band of nuns from the city of La Plata (now Sucre). The construction, which reflects heavy mestizo influence, was completed only seven years later, in 1692.

A visit to Santa Teresa may provide an unsettling vision into a hidden facet of the colonial Church. At the entrance you can still see the 17th-century wooden turnstile that sheltered the cloistered nuns from the outside world. Visitors to the convent may still hear them conducting prayers and songs from their self-imposed seclusion. The display of religious art is more interesting than most and includes works of Bolivia's most renowned artist, Melchor Pérez de Holguín, as well as a collection of morbid disciplinary and penitential paraphernalia (fortunately no longer in use), a skeleton in the old dining room ('ashes to ashes, dust to dust') and – as one correspondent put it – 'evidence of lots of flagellation'.

The museum is open Monday to Saturday from 8.30 am to noon and 2.30 to 6 pm. Admission and a one-hour guided tour costs US$2. Photography permits cost US$2/3 for cameras/videos. Visitors can also purchase *quesitos*, the marzipan sweets that have become a Potosí speciality.

Churches

Such was the wealth of colonial Potosí that over 80 churches were constructed in the city, and it's worth visiting the roof of the aforementioned Convento de San Francisco for a striking view over the urban forest of towers and spires.

Cathedral Construction of Potosí's cathedral, on Plaza 10 de Noviembre, was initiated in 1564 but the church wasn't officially founded until 1572 and wasn't finished until around 1600. The original building lasted until the early 19th century, when it mostly collapsed. During the reconstruction from 1808 to 1838, the original structure gained some neoclassical Greek and Spanish additions, courtesy of architect Fray Manuel Sanahuja.

The interior decor represents some of the finest in Potosí and merits a look around. Half-hour tours, which cost US$1 per person, are conducted Monday to Saturday from 9.30 to 10 am and Monday to Friday, between 1 and 3 pm.

San Bernardo This immense former church and convent on Plaza del Estudiante displays impressive Baroque architecture and an elaborate ornamented portal. The original structure dates back to 1590, but it was completely renovated in the late 1720s. The church immediately behind it is now occupied by a cinema.

Belén The former Iglesia de Belén, near the main plaza, with its three-tier Baroque façade, was constructed in 1735 as a church and later served as a hospital. It is now occupied by Teatro Omiste.

La Compañía de Jesús This Jesuit church, just over a block west of the main plaza on Ayacucho, is renowned for its ornate and beautiful bell tower. The present structure was completed in 1707 after the collapse of the original church, which had been built in 1590. Both the tower and the doorway are display examples of Baroque mestizo architecture.

San Benito The Iglesia de San Benito, which is laid out in the form of a Latin cross, features Byzantine domes and a distinctive mestizo doorway. From a distance, it resembles the traditional Christmas card rendition of the city of Bethlehem. The structure was begun in 1711 and completed in 16 years, which must have been a colonial construction record.

San Martín This rather ordinary-looking church on Calle Hoyos near Plaza Cervantes was built in the 1600s and is today run by the French Redemptionist Fathers. Inside is a veritable art museum, with at least 30 paintings beneath the choir area depicting the Virgin Mary and the 12 Apostles. The Virgin on the altarpiece wears clothing woven from silver threads. However, San Martín lies outside the centre and is often closed due to the risk of theft, so phone (☎ 23682) before traipsing out there. Your best chances of getting in will be on weekdays after 3.30 pm.

San Lorenzo The ornate Baroque mestizo portal of San Lorenzo is probably one of the most photographed subjects in Bolivia. It was carved in stone by master Indian

POTOSÍ

artesans in the 16th century, but the main structure wasn't completed until the bell towers were added in 1744. Inside are two Holguín paintings and handcrafted silver work on the altar. The church was renovated in 1987.

San Agustín San Agustín, with its elegant Renaissance doorway, is known for its eerie underground crypts and catacombs. To visit them, pick up a guide and the key at the tourist office; the charge is US$1 per person.

Other Churches Other churches of note include **Jerusalén** with its golden ornamentation and several paintings by Holguín, and **San Juan de Dios** which has stood since the 1600s despite its adobe construction. **La Merced** on Calle Hoyos is also lovely, with its carved pulpit and a beautiful 18th-century silver arch over the altarpiece. **Santo**

Erotic mestizo-design nymph, Iglesia de San Lorenzo

Domingo is currently under renovation, but it's worth a look to see the ornate portal and panelled ceiling. Pick up the key from Don Antonio at the corner shop across the Plazuela Santo Domingo from the church.

Other Buildings
The architecture of Potosí is unique in Bolivia and merits a stroll around the narrow streets to take in the ornate doorways and façades, as well as the covered wooden balconies that overhang the streets and provide an almost Alpine sense of cosiness to the city's bleak surroundings.

Architecturally worthy homes and monuments include El Cabildo (the old town hall) on Plaza 10 de Noviembre; the home of 17th-century miner, Antonio López de Quiroga, on Calle Lanza; the Casa de las Tres Portadas at Calle Bolívar 1052; the Palacio de Cristal at Calle Sucre 148-156; and the Arcos de Cobija (Arches of Cobija), on the street of the same name. These arches honour not the present-day capital of Pando, but the Pacific port of Cobija which now belongs to Chile. Just downhill from the first arch is the Ingenio Dolores, which bears a 1787 inscription.

On Calle Junín, between Matos and Bolívar, is an especially lovely and elaborate *portón mestizo*, or mestizo-style doorway, flanked by twisted columns. It once graced the home of the Marquez de Otavi, but now it ushers you into the Banco Nacional.

Los Ingenios
On the banks (*la ribera*) of the Río Huana Maya, in the upper Potosí barrios of Cantumarca and San Antonio, are some fine ruined examples of the ingenios. These were formerly used to extract silver from the ore hauled out of Cerro Rico. There were originally 33 mills along the stream and some of those that remain date back to the 1570s. Some of these were in use until the mid-1800s.

Each ingenio consists of a floor penetrated by shallow wells, called *buitrones*, where the ore was mixed with mercury and salt. The ore was then ground by millstones that were powered by water impounded in the 32 artificial Lagunas de Kari Kari, south-east of the city.

Organised Tours

Cooperative Mine Tours Visiting the cooperative mines may well be the most memorable experience you'll have in Bolivia, providing an opportunity to witness working conditions that should have gone out with the Middle Ages. You may be left in a state of shock (see the aside A Job from Hell.

Quite a few young Potosí men offer guided tours through the mines, and each tour agency has its own pool of guides. Some guides are well known and well tested, but you may also want to try out new and enthusiastic guides. Tours cost about US$5 to US$10 per person, increasing during periods of high demand. Mine visits aren't easy, and the low ceilings and steep, muddy passageways are best visited in your worst clothes. Temperatures can reach 45°C, and the altitude can be extremely taxing. You'll be exposed to noxious chemicals and gases including silica dust (the cause of silicosis), arsenic gas, acetylene vapours and other trapped mine gases, as well as asbestos deposits and the byproducts of acetylene combustion and the detonation of explosives. Anyone with doubts or medical problems should avoid these tours. The plus side is that you can speak with the friendly miners who will share their insights and opinions about their difficult lot. Surprisingly, most of them are miners by choice, carrying on family traditions by working there.

Mine tours begin with a visit to the miners' market, where they go to stock up on acetylene rocks, dynamite, cigarettes and other essentials. Although gifts are not expected, the miners will appreciate coca leaves and cigarettes, luxuries for which their meagre earnings are scarcely sufficient. Photography is permitted; you'll need a flash.

Mine tours run in the morning or afternoon and last from 2½ to five hours. The official rate is about US$10 per person, including guide, public transport from town and equipment: helmets, boots, lamps and jackets. For an abbreviated tour, or in the off season, you can negotiate rates as low as US$6. Wear sturdy clothing and carry water and a handkerchief/headscarf to filter some of the noxious substances you'll encounter underground. For information on specific tour agencies, see the Organised Tours section later in this chapter.

Other Tours There are lots of guided tours on offer in Potosí, and also lots of agencies offering them. In addition to the tours through the cooperative mines, popular options include several nearby hot springs, the ingenios, Hacienda Cayara and treks around the Lagunas de Kari Kari. Most agencies are professional, but there are a couple of fly-by-night operations, so seek recommendations from other travellers. Unless you're visiting off-season (October to May) or you're short of time, South-Western Circuit tours are probably better arranged in Uyuni (see the Uyuni section of the Southern Altiplano chapter).

Altiplano Tours
    Calle Ayacucho 19, Casilla 204 (☎ 27299, fax 25353). This recommended agency organises daily cooperative mine tours and day tours to the ingenios, Lagunas de Kari Kari, Tarapaya and local archaeological sites, as well as longer excursions to Torotoro, Sucre and the South-Western Circuit.
Koala Tours
    Calle Oruro 136, Casilla 33 (☎ 24708, fax 22092). With its blunt motto, 'Not for wimps or woosies', Koala Tours is probably the best known operator for cooperative mine tours. This is thanks mostly to Eduardo Garnica, who has become a sort of unofficial media spokesperson for the miners. A current project being promoted by this agency provides miners with a health care assistance post using medicines and other materials donated by tourists (a worthy benefactor for your unused stocks). For an additional US$1.60, you can enjoy a typical Bolivian lunch – quinoa soup, llama stew, rice, salad and potatoes – after your mine tour. This may be followed by a US$4 afternoon run to Tarapaya for a thermal bath to soak off the mine grime. The company also runs

tours to the Lagunas del Kari Kari, the ingenios and the South-Western Circuit.

Potosí Tours

Plaza Alonzo de Ibañez 16 (☎ 25786). This company offers all the standards: the cooperative mines, the ingenios, city tours, the Lagunas de Kari Kari, Tarapaya, Chaqui and the South-Western Circuit.

Trans-Amazonas

Calle Quijarro 12, Edificio Cámara de Mineria (☎ 25304, fax 27175). This company offers popular mine tours, which are led by the recommended guide, Raul Braulio Israel Mamani. The price of US$10 per person includes an excursion to the ingenios. Other options include city tours, Chapare, Tarapaya, Chaqui and South-Western Circuit tours. One/two-day treks around the Lagunas de Kari Kari cost US$10/20 per person, including food and overnights in the homes of local campesinos.

Victoria Tours

Calle Chuquisaca 148, Casilla 444 (☎ & fax 22132). This friendly new agency, which operates out of the Hostal María Victoria, runs inexpensive tours to the cooperative mine, the ingenios, and Tarapaya, as well as treks around the Lagunas de Kari Kari, and excursions to Torotoro and the South-Western Circuit.

Pailaviri The former government mine, Pailaviri, which is headquartered in Cerro Rico's most imposing structure, was the first mine in Potosí and has operated continuously since 1545. It descends through 17 levels to a depth of 480m, where temperatures soar to more than a stifling 50°C, and is laced with more than 5000 interconnected shafts. It was originally worked for silver,

---

A Job from Hell

In the cooperative mines on Cerro Rico, all work is done with primitive tools, and underground temperatures vary from below freezing – the altitude is over 4200m – to a stifling 45°C on the fourth and fifth levels. Miners, exposed to all sorts of noxious chemicals and gases, normally die of silicosis pneumonia within 10 years of entering the mines.

Contrary to popular rumour, women are admitted to many cooperative mines – only a few miners hang on to the tradition that women underground invite bad luck and, in many cases, the taboo applies only to miners' wives, whose presence in the mines would invite jealousy from Pachamama. In any case, lots of local women are consigned to picking through the tailings, gleaning small amounts of minerals that may have been missed. These women are known as *pailiris*, Quechua for 'those who select'.

Since cooperative mines are owned by the miners themselves, they must produce to make their meagre living. All work is done by hand with explosives and tools that must purchase themselves, including the acetylene lamps used to detect pockets of deadly carbon monoxide gas.

Miners prepare for their workday by socialising and chewing coca for several hours, beginning work at about 10 am. They work until lunch at 2 pm when they rest and chew more coca. For those who don't spend the night working, the day usually ends at 7 pm. On the weekend, each miner sells his week's production to the buyer for as high a price as he can negotiate.

Mine visitors will undoubtedly see a small, devilish figure occupying a small niche somewhere along the passageways. As most of the miners believe in a God in Heaven, they deduce that there must also be a devil beneath the earth in a place where it's hot and uncomfortable. Since Hell (according to the traditional description of the place) must not be far from the environment in which they work, they reason that the devil himself must own the minerals they're digging and dynamiting out of the earth. In order to appease this character whom they call Tío (Uncle) or Supay (never Diablo), they set up a little ceramic figurine in a place of honour.

On Friday nights a *cha'lla* is offered to invoke his goodwill and protection. A little alcohol is poured on the ground before the statue, lighted cigarettes are placed in his mouth and coca leaves are laid out within easy reach. Then, as in most Bolivian celebrations, the miners smoke, chew coca and proceed to drink themselves unconscious. While this is all taken very seriously, it also provides a bit of diversion from an extremely difficult existence. It's interesting that offerings to Jesus Christ are only made at the point where the miners can first see the outside daylight.

In most cooperative operations, there is a minimal medical plan in case of accident or silicosis (which is inevitable after seven to 10 years working underground) and a pension of about US$14.50 a month for those so incapacitated. Once a miner has lost 50% of his lung capacity to silicosis, he may retire, if he so wishes. In case of death, a miner's widow and children collect this pension. ■

but as with the cooperatives, it now produces mainly tin.

Pailaviri was run by the government until the early 1990s, and conditions until then contrasted sharply with those of the cooperatives. Salaried miners were provided with electric lamps, jackhammers and lifts, and enjoyed some measure of safety standards and favourable medical and pension plans. When it was taken over by the private Empresa Minera Sumaj Orcko in the early 1990s as part of the government capitalisation programme, miners were awarded severance pay of US$1000 for each year underground.

The selling off of Pailaviri and other mines illustrates the tragedy of mining in Bolivia. Given diminishing ore-metal ratios, limited investment capital, labour unrest and high-level corruption, the cost of implementing humane mining conditions may render operations noncompetitive and result in mass unemployment.

Special Events
Fiesta del Espíritu Fiesta del Espíritu, Potosí's most unusual event, takes place on the last three Saturdays of June and the first Saturday of August. It's dedicated to the honour of Pachamama, the earth mother, who the miners regard as the mother of all Bolivians.

Campesinos bring their finest llamas to the base of Cerro Rico to sell to the miners for sacrifice. The entire ritual is conducted according to a meticulous schedule. At 10 am, one miner from each mine purchases a llama and their families gather for the celebrations. At 11 am, everyone moves to the entrances of their respective mines. The miners chew coca and drink alcohol from 11 to 11.45 am then, at precisely 11.45 am, they prepare the llama for Pachamama by tying its feet and offering it coca and alcohol. At high noon, the llama meets its maker. As its throat is slit, the miners petition Pachamama for luck, protection and an abundance of minerals. The llama's blood is caught in glasses and splashed around the mouth of the mine in order to ensure Pachamama's attention, cooperation and blessing.

For the following three hours, the men chew coca and drink while the women prepare a llama parrillada. The meat is served traditionally with potatoes baked along with habas and oca in a small adobe oven. When the oven reaches the optimum temperature, it is smashed in on the food, which is baked beneath the hot shards. The stomach, feet and head of the llama are buried in a three-metre hole as a further offering to Pachamama, and then the music and dancing begin. In the evening, truckloads of semi-conscious celebrants are escorted home in transport provided by the honoured miner who secured the llama for his respective mine.

Fiesta de San Bartolomé (Chu'tillos) This rollicking celebration, best known as Chu'tillos, takes place on the final weekend of August or the first weekend of September and is marked by processions, student exhibitions, traditional costumes and folk dancing by people from all over the country. In recent years, it has even extended overseas, and featured musical groups and dance troupes from as far away as China and the USA. Given the amount of practicing going on during the week leading up to the festival, you'd be forgiven for assuming it actually started a week early.

Exaltación de la Santa Vera Cruz This festival, which falls on 14 September, honours Santo Cristo de la Vera Cruz. Activities focus on the church of San Lorenzo and the railway station. Silver cutlery features prominently, as do parades, duelling brass bands, dancing, costumed children and lots of alcohol.

Places to Stay
Only top-end hotels have heating and as there may be blanket shortages in cheaper accommodation, you might want to bring a sleeping bag. Unless your hotel has water tanks or goes through an arduous water-collection ritual every morning, water is available only between 7 and 11 am. Cheapie

places charge around US$0.50 extra for hot showers.

Places to Stay – bottom end

For the past decade, the favourite budget hotel has been the *Residencial Sumaj* (☎ 23336), near the Plaza del Estudiante. It's convenient to both the bus terminal and the railway station and although its appeal escapes many people, it keeps plugging along. Small, dark rooms without bath cost US$3 per person; a basic breakfast costs an additional US$1. Cooking is permitted in the two central meeting areas and there's even a TV to help you catch up on popular culture. Since the Sumaj has a reputation as 'the place where foreigners stay', guests may be pestered by would-be guides throwing their sales pitch at everyone who rolls up. Beware of thieves posing as guides.

Another budget favourite is the friendly *Hostal Carlos V* (☎ 25121) on Linares. This cosy old colonial building has a pleasant covered patio, but the 'hot' showers scarcely rate as tepid. Rooms cost US$3.50 per person.

Even nicer is the *Hostal María Victoria* (☎ 22132), a charming colonial home surrounding a classic courtyard at Calle Chuquisaca 148. Rooms cost a negotiable US$3 per person. Breakfast and snacks are available and the friendly and helpful staff really make travellers feel welcome. This place is destined to become a favourite so advance bookings are recommended.

Also recommended is *Hotel Jerusalén* (☎ 22600) at Calle Oruro 143, with a friendly, helpful staff, nice balconies and a mellow atmosphere. Single/double rooms without bath cost US$4.20/6.20; with bath, they're US$8.50/12.50.

The adequate *Residencial Central* (☎ 22207), on the corner of Bustillos and Cobija, in a quiet old part of town, has a traditional potosino overhanging balcony. Chilly rooms with piles of blankets cost US$3.50 per person. Although hot water is available with an hour's notice, it's of little benefit since the shower is effectively in the open air.

The good value *Hotel El Turista* (☎ 22492), at Calle Lanza 19, is a long-standing Potosí favourite. The friendly owner, Señor Luksic, provides reliable tourist information and some of Bolivia's best hot showers (between 6.30 and 11 am). Rooms cost US$7/11. For a superb view, request a room on the top floor.

Also recommended is *Residencial Felcar* (☎ 24966) at Serrudo 345, which offers clean rooms, free – and great – hot showers and a sunny patio. Rooms cost US$3 per person.

As its name would imply, *Alojamiento Ferrocarril* (☎ 24294) is adjacent to the railway station. It's among the friendliest of the bargain basement options, and has hot showers. Singles/doubles cost US$2.75/4. An old travellers' standard is *Alojamiento La Paz* (☎ 22632), at Calle Oruro 262, but guests often have shocking tales to tell about the showers! Rooms cost US$2.50 per person; the dodgy showers are extra.

Places to Stay – middle

The two-star *Hostal Felimar* (☎ 24357), a pleasant and centrally situated choice at Calle Junín 14, charges US$12.50/16.50 for single/double rooms with bath. It's solar powered and some upstairs rooms have balconies and a view over a fine colonial street.

The sparkling and recommended *Hostal Libertador* (☎ 27877) is at Calle Millares 58 Quiet, heated single/double rooms with bath cost US$21/27. Guests have access to the sunny patio and terrace, with a view over the town.

Another relatively upmarket choice is the four-star *Hotel Colonial* (☎ 24265, fax 27146), at Calle Hoyos 8, which occupies a lovely old colonial building near the main plaza. Singles/doubles with private bath and central heating cost US$21/27. Alternatively, there's *Hostal Bolívar* (☎ 25647) at Bolívar 772 opposite the market, which charges the same and also occupies a colonial home.

Places to Eat

Stalls in the *market comedor* serve inexpensive breakfasts of bread, pastries and coffee. The small heladería on the plaza (in the hideous grey building beside the cathedral) and a couple of small bakeries along Calle Padilla do American and continental breakfasts. *Pastelería Clofi*, at Calle Matos 30, serves breakfasts, sandwiches, pastries, cakes, tea and coffee. Most hotels and residenciales provide some sort of breakfast option, but almost everything else is locked up until mid-morning.

For great salteñas, check out *La Salteña*, at Linares and Padilla, or *Café Imma Sumac*, at Calle Bustillos 987. In the morning, street vendors sell meatless salteñas potosinas near Iglesia de San Lorenzo for US$0.20. Meat empanadas are sold around the market until early afternoon, and in the evening, street vendors sell cornmeal humintas.

Very nice pizzas and pasta are the emphasis at Italian-oriented *Kivo's*, beside the tourist office. Pizzas are also the speciality of the *Pizzería Argentina*, on Calle Linares just above the plaza.

Some of Potosí's best and most innovative meals are served at *Don Lucho*, which does pretty good almuerzos for US$3, including soup, salad, a main course and dessert. Dinners are even better, ranging from killer pasta to excellent filet mignon with béchamel sauce. For details of the Friday night peña, see the Entertainment section in this chapter.

Almost as good but more expensive is *Las Vegas*, near the corner of Calles Padilla and Linares. Its exhaustive four-course lunch specials run at about US$4; the house specialty is pique a lo macho. A good place for almuerzos is *Kactus*, at the corner of Calles Padilla and Linares.

The *Sumaj Orko*, at Calle Quijarro 46, does filling almuerzos of salad, soup, a meat dish and dessert for just US$1.50. In the evening, à la carte options include trucha al limón (lemon trout) and picante de perdíz (spicy partridge). The *Sky Room* restaurant near the market on Calle Bolívar has excellent mid-range beef and chicken specialities, including chicken in mushroom sauce, curried chicken and filet mignon.

An especially friendly choice is *Chaplin's*, on Calle Bustillos near the market. It serves delicious vegetarian lunches of vegetable noodle soup, pumpkin soup, spicy lentils, potatoes, rice, fruit juice and papaya for US$1.20 and is also popular for dinners. The Mexican señora prepares tasty nachos and, on Friday and Saturday evenings, serves excellent Mexican tacos.

For delicious, excellent value apfelstrudel, chocolate cake, lemon meringue pie *(pai de limón)* and other decadent cakes and pastries, or just a hot drink (sadly, they haven't yet discovered filter coffee), try the popular *Cherry's Salon de Té*, on Calle Padilla. It's open all afternoon and makes a good pit stop while you're out exploring the town. More low key is the *Coffee Snack El Farol*, opposite the Convento de San Francisco.

Entertainment

Don't miss the weekend peña at *Don Lucho* on Bolívar; it may well be Bolivia's most home-grown traditional music programme. If you're lucky, you may even hear the lively and driving music of the local group Arpegio Cinco, as well as examples of the unique nasal-sounding accompaniment to Potosí department's own *tinku* fights. The peña plays on Friday and Saturday nights, starting at 9 pm.

A popular drinking spot for foreigners and middle-class Bolivians is the *Pub Taverna* on Calle Bustillo. The sign reading 'Pub English' may be rather misleading, but it's warm inside and you'll sometimes hear good music.

For dancing, try the popular *Disco TK* at Calle Junín 7 or the *Charlie Fox Club*. A recommended upmarket pub is *Top Wisquería* on Plaza Alonzo de Ibañes, the wide spot in Calle Padilla just above the main plaza.

Things to Buy

Naturally, favoured Potosí souvenirs will include silver and tin articles available in stands near the market entrance on Calle Oruro; many of them were produced in the village of Caiza, south of Potosí. To give you some idea of prices, small dangly earrings cost about US$2 per set; larger ones go as high as US$5, hoop earrings are US$0.80 to US$1.50, and spoons and platters start between US$1.20 and US$1.50.

If your wallet is becoming a burden, try the Mercado Artesanal in Plaza Cornelio Saavedra, between Junín and Sucre, which sells musical instruments, exquisite weavings and a range of local crafts – but also a lot of tourist tat.

Artesanías Palomita at Avenida Serrudo 152 has been recommended for dolls, handmade traditional clothing and alpaca weavings. A bit cheaper are the smaller shops along Calle Sucre north of Calle Bolívar.

Getting There & Away

Air The LAB office (☎ 22361) is in the Hotel El Turista, Calle Lanza 19. Potosí boasts the world's highest commercial airport, Aeropuerto Capitán Rojas, but although the runway has recently been extended to 4000m to accommodate larger planes, the city isn't yet on the LAB or AeroSur timetables. That will probably change soon, but currently, your best option is to fly in or out of Sucre, which is three hours away by bus.

One way to fly to Potosí is on the plane that delivers newspapers from La Paz. It departs La Paz daily at around 9 am and may be booked through the Transamazonas agency (☎ 350411, fax 360923, La Paz) Office 3c, 3rd floor, Edificio V Centenario, Avenida 6 de Agosto, Casilla 14551, La Paz. The flight takes two hours and costs US$65 per person.

Bus All routes into Potosí are quite scenic, and arriving by day will always present a dramatic introduction to the city.

The bus terminal is a long way from the centre – at least half an hour on foot – but *micros* and minibuses run frequently from the centre and taxis cost only US$0.40. There are numerous buses to La Paz each evening (US$8, 10 to 12 hours). If you prefer to travel by day, Trans Bustillo has a 6.45 am bus to Oruro (US$4, seven hours), from

where you'll easily find a bus to La Paz. It also does frequent runs to Llallagua.

Buses leave for Tupiza (US$6.50, 12 hours) and Villazón (US$8, 14 hours) daily at 8.30 am and 6 pm. Buses to Tarija (and on to Yacuiba) run at 9.30 am, and at 2 and 4 pm (US$7, 12 hours).

Quite a few *flotas* leave for Sucre (US$3, 3½ hours) daily at 7 or 7.30 am and 5 pm. To buy an advance ticket without traipsing out to the bus terminal, visit the more central offices of Andesbus or Trans-Alave on Calle Bustillos, or Transtin or Real Audiencia on Plaza Arce. Between Sucre and Potosí, watch for the picturesque Puente Sucre with its castle-like buttresses just a km or so from the new bridge at the Río Pilcomayo crossing.

Buses to Uyuni (US$3.50, eight hours) depart between 9.30 am and noon from higher up on Avenida Antofagasta. (If you're travelling with Flota Transamericana, keep a vigilant watch on your luggage, as I've had several reports of problems.) The route to Uyuni is quite spectacular, passing through some mysterious-looking valleys and canyons with unusual vegetation and rock formations. At Ticatica, which is backed up by a stunning violet mountain amid classic badlands, you'll pass a prominent geothermal site with interesting travertine deposits.

Camión *Camiones* to Uyuni leave from roughly the same place as the bus. The cheapest way between Potosí and Sucre is by camión or micro. They leave from Plaza Uyuni when full; in the morning, that normally means every half-hour or so. However, the trip may not be particularly speedy, as one reader learned:

We waited at Plaza Uyuni for an hour for a camión to leave. It left at 3 pm, then took three hours to tour Potosí, passing by Plaza Uyuni five times, picked up around 30 more people and their stuff and finally arrived in Sucre at 5 am. That was 14 hours for a 3½-hour trip. Pure hell!

Train The *ferrobus* to Oruro (US$8.60/5.50, seven hours) and La Paz (US$11/8, 12 hours)

Cerro Rico and rooftops, Potosí (DS)

Left: Miner, Candelaria mine, Cerro Rico, Potosí (DS)
Right: Cerro Rico and rooftops, Potosí (RS)
Bottom: Trekking near Quila Quila, Chuquisaca (DS)

leaves on Wednesday and Sunday at 7.50 pm. The ferrobus to Sucre (US$4.10/3.30, four hours) departs on Wednesday and Sunday at 4.25 am. Prices given are for 1st/2nd (*pullman/especial*) class.

Getting Around

Bus Micros provide transport between the centre and the Cerro Rico mines, as well as the train and bus terminals. They're a bargain at less than US$0.15 per ride.

Taxi Taxis from the centre to the mines or the transport terminals charge around US$0.50. The main ranks are on the northern side of Plaza 10 de Noviembre. Coming from the bus terminal, hail a taxi from across the street, or you'll pay more.

Around Potosí

LAGUNAS & CORDILLERA DE KARI KARI

The artificial lakes of Kari Kari were constructed in the late 16th and early 17th centuries by 20,000 Indian slaves to provide water for the city and hydro power to run the city's 132 ingenios. In 1626, the retaining wall of Laguna San Idelfonso broke and caused an enormous flood that destroyed operations along La Ribera de los Ingenios and killed 2000 people. Of the 32 original lagunas, only 25 remain and all have been abandoned – except by waterfowl, which appreciate the incongruous surface water in this otherwise stark region.

Hiking

The easiest way to visit the lakes of Kari Kari is with a Potosí tour agency; see the Organised Tours section in the Potosí section. If you prefer to strike out on your own, carry food, water and warm clothing. There are several variations on the walking routes around the lagunas and into the Cordillera de Kari Kari. In a long day, you can have a good look around but it will be more

rewarding to camp overnight in the mountains.

Access is fairly easy. Either hitch out past Cerro Rico along the Tupiza road; you'll begin seeing the lakes on your left about eight km south-east of town, or alternatively, start walking east from Potosí's main plaza along Calle Hoyos. A few blocks beyond the Iglesia de San Martín, take a right fork and you'll eventually reach a track. Follow it south-east up the hill and eventually you'll reach Laguna San Idelfonso.

From here, either follow the track around the northern shore of the lake and continue up the valley or strike off eastward into the hills. The higher you go, the more spectacular the views become and the area is riddled with open mine entrances and remains of mining equipment.

On the valley route, you'll eventually pass a small ephemeral lake; here you should turn south and climb up a side valley to a pass with impressive views of distant high peaks, about six hours walking from Potosí. From here there are several routes back to town but the nicest is probably the way you came.

Alternatively, if you're prepared for an overnight stay, you can keep wandering. There are no difficult summits in the area and as long as you can catch sight of Cerro Rico, the route back to Potosí will be obvious. The only problem may be the altitude, which ranges from 4400 to 5000m. The Cordillera de Kari Kari is included on the IGM topo sheet *Potosí (East) – sheet 6435*, available from the IGM office in Potosí or La Paz.

HACIENDA CAYARA

For a peaceful retreat or some comfortable hill walking, visit Hacienda Cayara, 25 km down valley north-west of Potosí at an elevation of 3550m. This beautiful working farm, which is set amid lovely hills, produces vegetables and milk for the city. It dates back to colonial times, when it was owned by the Viceroy of Toledo. In the name of King Felipe II, its title was later handed to Don Juan de Tendones and was thence transferred to the Marquis de Otavi, whose coat of arms

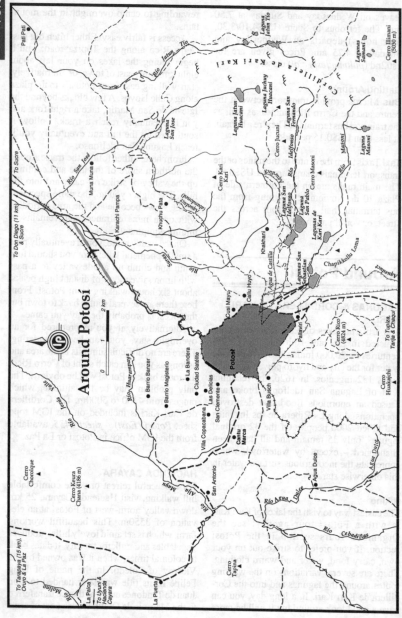

Around Potosí

the ranch still bears. In 1901, it was purchased by the English Aitken family, who still own it. They converted it into a hostal in 1992. 'Cayara' is the Aymara name for the *Puya raimondii* plant, which flowers after 100 years then decomposes.

The hostal is like a museum: an opulent colonial mansion furnished with original paintings and period furniture. Guests will have use of the fireplace and extensive library, which includes works dating to the 17th century. An English-speaking historian and agronomist will provide information about the site and answer questions about Bolivia and its history. For bookings, speak with either Señora Luchi or the owner, Señor Luis Aitken (☎ & fax 26389), in Potosí. Rooms with private bath cost US$15 per person. Meals are available for an extra charge.

Getting There & Away

You can organise your transport from Potosí when you make the reservation but it would actually be cheaper to go by taxi, especially if you're in a group; have the driver take the left fork to La Palca instead of heading right through the canyon toward Tarapaya.

BETANZOS

Set in a landscape of rugged, rocky mountains, the village of Betanzos lies about an hour from Potosí along the road to Sucre. It makes an excellent day trip, especially on Sundays when the market is in full swing. Many campesinos wearing local dress bring their harvests and handicrafts from the countryside.

Special Events

On 4 and 5 April, Betanzos celebrates the Fiesta de la Papa (Potato Festival). Although it isn't well known, reports indicate that it's a winner. Major musical groups travel to Betanzos from all over Bolivia to dance and play Andean folk music.

Places to Stay

The best option is the *Hotel Sucre*; the *Hotel Betanzos* is a real dump.

Getting There & Away

Camiones and micros leave for Betanzos from Plaza Uyuni in Potosí early in the morning, with extra departures on Sunday. All Sucre buses also pass Betanzos.

TARAPAYA

Belief in the curative powers of Tarapaya, the most frequently visited hot springs area around Potosí, dates back to Inca times. It even served as the holiday destination for Inca Huayna Capac, who would come all the way from Cuzco (now in Peru) to bathe.

Ojo del Inca

The most interesting site is the 30°C Ojo del Inca, a perfectly round green lake in a volcanic crater, 50m in diameter. Locals believe bathing is safe only in the morning due to the *remolinos* (whirlpools) that may develop early in the afternoon and cause drownings. Along the river below the crater are several *balnearios* (resorts) with medicinal thermal pools utilising water from the lake.

To reach Ojo del Inca, cross the bridge 400m before the Balneario de Tarapaya, turn left and walk about 200m. Just past the waterfall on the right, a trail that resembles a washed out road leads uphill. Follow it about 400m to the lake. The track may disappear at times into eroded gullies but if you keep walking uphill or along the streams that flow from the lake, you'll get there.

Places to Stay

Balneario Paraíso has a basic hostel for overnight guests and there's also a hotel at the Balneario de Tarapaya. Campers will find a number of level and secluded sites near the river; all water should be purified.

Getting There & Away

From Potosí, Tarapaya is a 15-km trip along asphalted highway. There are frequent camiones from Plaza Chuquimia near the bus terminal, charging US$0.50 per person. Taxis charge US$4 for up to four people.

Ask the driver to let you off at the bridge where the gravel road turns off. The

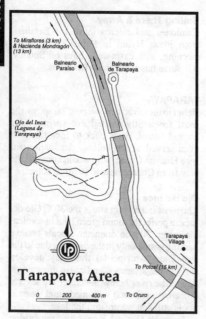

To Miraflores (3 km)
& Hacienda Mondragón
(13 km)

Balneario
Paraíso

Balneario
de Tarapaya

Ojo del Inca
(Laguna de
Tarapaya)

Tarapaya
Village

To Potosí (15 km)

Tarapaya Area

To Oruro

0   200   400 m

be a problem. On Sunday, potosinos come with loads of sugar, flour, rice and bread to exchange in the markets for potatoes, cheese, and local farm products. The climate is considerably more agreeable than in Potosí and superior quality handicrafts, such as weavings and blankets, are sold in small villages.

Places to Stay
The *Hotel Termas de Chaqui* has rooms for US$3 per person, including use of the hot pools. Non-guests may use the pools and sauna for US$1 per person. Chaqui village also has a couple of *alojamientos*, but they're three km downhill from the resort.

Getting There & Away
Chaqui is reached by micro or camión from Plaza Uyuni in Potosí for about US$0.50 per person. Alternatively, arrange transport through the Hotel Termas de Chaqui. Enquire at its Potosí office (☎ 22158) at Calle Chuquisaca 587. For other options, see the Organised Tours section under Potosí. From Sucre, you can visit Chaqui with the company Seatur (☎ 40909, Sucre), in the Edificio Multicentro Céspedes on the main plaza.

Getting there is one thing but returning to Potosí can be more difficult. Some drivers won't leave until there's sufficient interest.

DON DIEGO
The hot springs at Don Diego are along the Sucre road and can be reached by micro or camión from Plaza Uyuni, or on a Sucre bus. The resort has a hostel costing US$2 per person, including use of the baths.

Balneario de Tarapaya is 400m from the bridge along the paved road. Balneario Paraíso is over the bridge and 400m down the road to the right. Miraflores lies three km beyond Paraíso.

CHAQUI
Another major hot spring bubbles away three km uphill from the village of Chaqui, which lies two hours south-east of Potosí. The countryside around nearby Puna and Belen is particularly interesting but transport may

South Central Bolivia & the Chaco

Drier and more desolate than the country farther north, the people of the isolated highlands of Tarija department have historically identified and traded more with Argentina than with the rest of Bolivia. In fact, the department bills itself as the Andalucia de Bolivia, in reference to its dry, eroded badlands, neatly groomed vineyards and orchards, and white-stucco and red-tile architecture, all of which are reminiscent of the Iberian Peninsula. Here the people call themselves Chapacos and speak with the lilting dialect of European Spanish. In fact, the river flowing past the departmental capital is called the Guadalquivir!

In the far eastern regions of Tarija and Chuquisaca departments, the highlands roll down into the petroleum-rich scrublands and red earth of the Gran Chaco. Villamontes, a small place on the Santa Cruz-Yacuiba railway line, claims the distinction of being literally the country's hottest spot.

Highlights

- Spot the dogs with flowery collars before the Fiesta de San Roque in Tarija
- Find a prehistoric mammal on a fossil hunt in the Tarija badlands
- Cool down beside the 60m Coimata waterfall
- Make the rugged journey between Bolivia and Filadelfia (Paraguay), along the rough-and-ready Chaco Road
- Attend a fiesta to hear some of Tarija department's bizarre musical instruments

South Central Bolivia

In spite of Tarija's grand delusions about spiritual kinship with Andalucia, more urbanised Bolivians regard south central Bolivia as a half-civilised backwater, and tasteless jokes are told in La Paz with 'Chapaco' forming the standard butt of the humour. In rebuttal, the regionalistic southerners are quick to point out that in 1810, the year following Chuquisaca department's 'first cry of independence in the Americas', part of Tarija department declared independence from Spain and operated briefly under a sovereign government with its capital at Tarija.

In the southernmost 'toe' of Bolivia are oil-bearing veins and the lush sugar-cane producing valleys surrounding the town of Bermejo on the Argentine border.

TARIJA

Tarija, with a population of 90,000, lies at an elevation of 1924m. The valley climate resembles the 'eternal spring' of Cochabamba, although winter nights may be slightly cooler. As in most of Bolivia, the dry season lasts from April to November.

Tarija's distinctly Mediterranean flavour is evident in its climate, architecture and vegetation. Chapacos are proud to be accused of considering themselves more Spanish or Argentine than Bolivian; many *tarijeños* are descended from Argentine gauchos. Around the main plaza grow stately date palms, and the surrounding landscape has been wildly eroded by wind

357

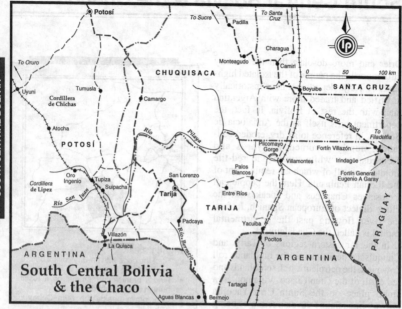

South Central Bolivia & the Chaco

and water into badlands that resemble parts of the Spanish meseta.

History

Tarija was founded on 4 July 1574 as La Villa de San Bernardo de Tarixa by Don Luis de Fuentes y Vargas under the orders of Viceroy Don Francisco de Toledo. In 1810, Tarija and the surrounding area declared independence from Spanish rule. Although the breakaways weren't taken very seriously by the Spanish, the situation did erupt into armed warfare on 15 April 1817. At the Batalla de la Tablada, the Chapacos won a major victory over the Spanish forces and Tarija's departmental holiday is now celebrated on 15 April.

In the early 1800s, Tarija actively supported Bolivia's struggle for independence, and although Argentina was keen to annex the agriculturally favourable area, Tarija opted to join the Bolivian Republic when it was established in 1825.

Information

Tourist Office The tourist office (☎ 25948), on the main plaza, Luis de Fuentes y Vargas, is very helpful with queries regarding sites both within the city and out of town. Maps of the town cost US$0.25.

Note that between 1 and 4 pm, Tarija becomes a virtual ghost town, so if you don't transact all your business in the morning, you'll have to wait until late afternoon.

Money The casas de cambio on Calle Bolívar, between Calle Sucre and Daniel Campos, change only US dollars and Argentine pesos. For travellers cheques, try Café Irubana in the central market or Ferretería El Lorito. The latter charges an extortionate 5 to 10% commission.

Post & Communications The modern central post office is on the corner of Calles Sucre and Virginio Lema, and ENTEL is on the corner of Virginio Lema and Daniel

Campos. It's open Monday to Saturday from 8 am to midnight and on Sunday from 8 am to 9 pm. Tarija's public fax number is 23402. Its telephone code is 066.

Churches

Cathedral The cathedral at the end of La Madrid, a block from the main plaza, contains the remains of prominent Chapacos, including Tarija's founder, Luis de Fuentes y Vargas. It was constructed in 1611 and expanded and embellished in 1925. By Bolivian standards, the interior is fairly ordinary.

San Francisco The Basílica de San Francisco, on the corner of Daniel Campos and La Madrid, was founded in 1606 and is now a national monument. The attached convent houses two libraries. The 16th-century convent library and archives, which may conjure up images from *The Name of the Rose*, may be used only by researchers with permission from the Franciscan order. The general reference library in the Ecclesiastical Documentation Centre contains all sorts of reference works, including lots of stuff on Bolivian archaeology. There's also a museum of religious painting, sculpture and artefacts, open weekdays from 8 am to 6 pm.

The office entrance is on Calle Ingavi between Daniel Campos and Suipacha. To arrange a visit, ask for Padre Maldini or Padre Lorenzo, or speak with the secretary. Admission is free.

San Roque Architecturally, Tarija's most unusual church is the 1887 Iglesia de San Roque, which crowns the hill at the end of General Bernardo Trigo. This imposing landmark is visible from all over town and its balcony once served as a lookout post.

San Juan The Iglesia de San Juan, at the top of Bolívar, was constructed in 1632. Here, the Spanish signed their surrender to the liberation army after the Batalla de la Tablada on 15 April 1817. The garden affords a sweeping view over Tarija and its dramatic backdrop of brown mountains.

Mirador Loma de San Juan

This park area above the tree-covered slopes of Loma de San Juan provides a sweeping view over the city and is a favourite with students, who spend their afternoons there studying and socialising. To get there climb Bolívar to its end, then turn right behind the hill and climb the footpath up the slope that faces away from the city.

Casa Dorada

The Casa Dorada (Gilded House), on the corner of Ingavi and General Bernardo Trigo, dates back to 1930 when it was one of the several homes of the wealthy Tarija landowner Moisés Navajas (who was a sort of Bolivian Teddy Roosevelt) and his wife, Esperanza Morales.

The building could be described as imposing, but amusingly, the exterior has been sloppily splashed with gold and silver paint and topped with a row of liberating angels, and the interior reflects equally questionable taste. The ground floor is painted a scintillating shade of purple and the frescoes could have been the work of precocious preschoolers. There's also a winning collection of lamps: rose lamps, peacock lamps, grape lamps, morning glory lamps and of course, crystal chandeliers that sprout light bulbs. Perhaps the most worthwhile relic is the *funola* (an early type of player piano), which produced music using a strip of perforated paper.

The building now belongs to the university and houses the Casa de la Cultura. It's open Monday to Friday from 8 am to noon and 2.30 to 6 pm. For brief guided tours, foreigners pay US$1.

Castillo de Moisés Navajas

The Castillo de Moisés Navajas, another of Moisés Navajas' homes, is an oddly prominent and deteriorating mansion on Bolívar between Junín and O'Connor. It is currently inhabited, but the owner does show visitors around. To visit, just ring the bell.

Zoo

The zoo lies on the western outskirts of town,

SOUTH CENTRAL BOLIVIA

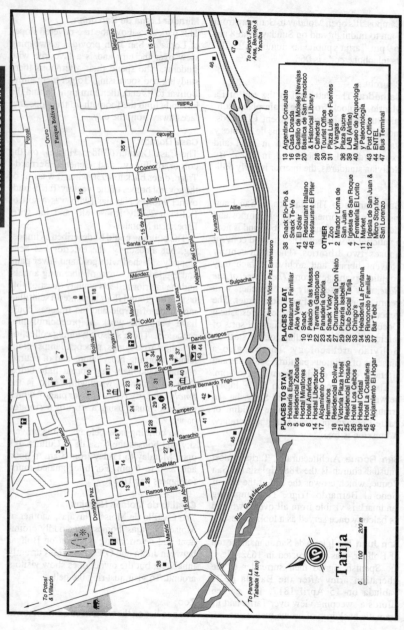

Tarija

0   100   200 m

To Airport, Fossil
Area, Bermejo &
Yacuiba

To Potosí
& Villazón

To Parque La
Tablada (4 km)

PLACES TO STAY
3   Hostería España
5   Residencial Zeballos
6   Hostal Miraflores
8   Hotel América
14 Hostal Libertador
17 Alojamiento Ocho
    Hermanos
18 Residencial Bolívar
21 Victoria Plaza Hotel
25 Residencial Rosario
26 Hotel Los Ceibos
39 Hostal Cristal
45 Hotel La Costañera
46 Alojamiento El Hogar

PLACES TO EAT
9   Restaurant Familiar
    Aloe Vera
10 Snack
15 Palacio de las Masas
22 Taverna Gattopardo
23 Panadería Gloria
24 Snack Vicky
27 Churrasquería Don Ñato
29 Pizzería Isabella
32 Club Social Tarija
33 Chingo's
35 Heladería La Fontana
37 Bar Tebit
38 Snack Pío-Pío &
    Snack Te-Ve
41 El Solar
42 Restaurant Italiano
46 Restaurant El Piter

OTHER
1   Zoo
2   Mirador Loma de
    San Juan
4   Iglesia de San Roque
7   Ferretería El Lorito
11 Market
12 Iglesia de San Juan &
    Micro Stop for
    San Lorenzo
13 Argentine Consulate
16 Casa Dorada
19 Castillo de Moisés Navajas
20 Basílica de San Francisco
28 Cathedral
30 Tourist Office
31 Plaza Luis de Fuentes
    y Vargas
36 Plaza Sucre
39 LAB (Airline)
40 Museo de Arqueología
    y Paleontología
43 Post Office
44 ENTEL
47 Bus Terminal

about 15 minutes walk from the centre, but the animals are mostly in poor condition and it's unkempt and depressing. The surrounding park is more pleasant and there's a nice children's playground. Admission is US$0.20.

Museo de Arqueología y Paleontología

The Archaeology & Palaeontology Museum, operated by the university, is on the corner of General Bernardo Trigo and Virginio Lema, one block from the main plaza. It provides a convenient overview of the prehistoric creatures and the early peoples that once inhabited the Tarija area.

Downstairs, you'll see the well-preserved remains of most of the animals: *Megatherium*, a giant ground sloth; *Mastodon*; *Glyptodon*, a giant prehistoric armadillo; *Macrauchenia*, a cross between a llama and a tapir; *Lestodon*, which resembled a giant-clawed aardvark; *Scelidotherium*, a small ground sloth; *Smilodon*, the sabre-toothed tiger; and *Toxodon*, a large and dozy-looking creature with buck teeth. Of note are the nearly complete *Glyptodon* carapace, and the tail and a superb hand of a *Megatherium*. Displays are accompanied by artistic representations of how the animals appeared in the flesh. The archaeological section displays ancient tools, weapons, copper items, textiles and pottery from all over southern Bolivia.

The rooms upstairs focus on history, geology and anthropology, containing displays of old household implements, weapons, an old piano and various prehistoric hunting tools, including a formidable-looking cudgel (which in Spanish is called a *rompecabezas*, 'break heads'). One interesting item is an old bit of presidential stationery, bearing the letterhead 'Mariano Melgarejo, President of the Republic of Bolivia, Major General of the Army, etc, etc, etc'. That is topped, however, by a hideously bizarre representation of the Antichrist made from nuts, seeds, grass, wool hair, shells, flowers, wood and lichen.

The museum is open from 8.30 am to noon and 2.30 to 6 pm. Admission is free but donations are gratefully accepted.

Parque La Tablada

Across the Río Guadalquivir, four km by road from Tarija, is the historic battlefield of La Tablada, where José Eustaquio 'Moto' Méndez and his forces defeated the Spanish royal armies in 1817. It's now a pleasant park and national monument. Take *micro* 'C' from the centre.

Wineries

The Tarija region is known for its wines, some of which are palatable and others of which will produce a spontaneous reaction of the facial muscles. To visit the wineries and cellars – and sample the product – enquire at their town offices: Kohlberg (Calle 15 de Abril O-275), Aranjuez (Calle 15 de Abril O-241), Casa Real (Calle 15 de Abril O-246) and Rujero (on the corner of La Madrid and Suipacha). The managers are friendly and you may be able to get a lift with the staff. Only the Aranjuez vineyard is close to town; Kohlberg and Casa Real are in Santana, 15 km from Tarija, and Rujero is near Concepción, about 20 km from town. The offices of Kohlberg, Aranjuez and Casa Real have small shops where they sell wine at factory prices. Rujero has separate shops at Ingavi E-311 and at O'Connor N-642. Besides the wine, all the wineries produce *singani*, a distilled grape spirit.

Special Events

The traditional dance La Rueda features at all annual fiestas in Tarija, as do the *chunchos*. These Bolivian versions of British Morris dancers are men who have vowed to the Virgin Mary to dance at festivities for anything from 10 to 50 years. Their colourful costumes, which are assembled from a variety of items, include half-length silk shirts, scarves, veils and stockings, clown shoes, gaudy silk hearts decorated with shells and polychrome feather top hats adorned with assorted bangles. As they dance and gyrate, they click small metal castanets in time with the music.

Charangos, guitars and flutes, popular elsewhere in the Andes, also feature promi-

Tarija Fossils

The Tarija area is a paradise for amateur palaeontologists who'd like to try their hand at fossil-hunting. The *quebradas* (ravines or washes) and badlands around the airport and across the highway along the pipeline are littered with the remains of prehistoric mammals, including early horses, *Mastodons*, *Megatheria* and three-metre long armadillo-like *Glyptodons*. However, because the area is severely eroded and every rainfall changes the face of the land, bones have been sloshed around for thousands of years and deposited haphazardly in the sedimentary layers. The more complete fossil bones lie loose or perched on pedestals of sediment, but it's rare to find a complete skeleton.

If you know what to look for, the profusion of specimens will probably seem overwhelming. The ubiquitous small blue 'stones' are well fossilised fragments of *Mastodon* bones, tusks and teeth; the crumbly rosettes which lie in heaps or are embedded in sediment are bits of *Glyptodon* carapace; and the small and rounded chalk-like 'pebbles' come from the hide of a *Megatherium*. Crania, pelvic bones and long bones of all these creatures are common, but the dry climate means that they normally haven't been well petrified and are quite fragile. Don't try to unearth them or they may crumble into dust as soon as the supporting soil is removed.

When you're wandering through the quebradas and badlands, carry water and wear good hiking footwear with lots of tread; the terrain is difficult and the unconsolidated silt is slippery, especially when it's wet. Please leave the specimens as you find them (it's illegal to remove them), and report any significant discoveries to the Museo de Arqueología y Paleontología in town. ■

Glyptodon

nently in the music-making. For a description of special Chapaco musical instruments, see the Arts section in the Facts about the Country chapter.

Carnaval Tarija's carnival is one of the most animated in Bolivia and is well worth attending. It's dedicated to good fun and the streets fill with joyful dancing, original Chapaco music and colourfully costumed country folk who come to town for the event. There's a Grand Ball in the main plaza after the celebration and the entire town turns out for dancing and performances by folkloric groups, bands and orchestras. Water balloons figure prominently in the festivities.

On the Sunday after Carnaval, the barrio near the cemetery enacts a bizarre 'funeral' in which the devil is burned and buried in preparation for Lent. Paid mourners lend the ritual a very morose air but they're actually lamenting that they must remain free of vice for the 40 days until Easter!

Rodeo Chapaco In keeping with its gaucho heritage, Tarija stages a rodeo in Parque La Tablada (across the river from Tarija) between 15 and 21 April. It includes all the standard cowboy events and prizes for the overall winner. To get there, take micro 'C' from the centre.

Fiesta de San Roque Tarija's best known festival is the Fiesta de San Roque, the patron saint of the city. Although San Roque's feast day falls on 16 August, when festively dressed canines (San Roque is also the patron saint of dogs) may be seen sporting flowery collars, the celebration begins on the first Sunday of September and continues for eight days. Celebrations begin with traditional musical performances and a chunchos procession; the costumes are highlighted with bright feathers, ribbons, glittering sequins and other small, bright objects. Participants masquerade as members of a Chaco tribe that has been recently converted to Christianity.

Fiesta de las Flores Another annual event

is the Fiesta de las Flores, a religious celebration dedicated to the Virgen de Rosario. It begins on the second Sunday in October, when a procession of the faithful led by an image of the Virgen de Rosario sets off from the Iglesia de San Juan. Along their route, they're showered with flower petals by the spectators. The highlight of the day is a colourful fair and bazaar in which the faithful spend lavishly for the benefit of the Church.

Places to Stay – bottom end
Camping When it isn't raining, the best camp sites are in the quebradas and fossil areas near the airport. If you don't mind being less secluded, perhaps walk down the far bank of the Río Guadalquivir, which is accessible via the bridge near the intersection of Calle 15 de Abril and Avenida Victor Paz Estenssoro.

Hotels The central and frequently recommended *Alojamiento Ocho Hermanos* (☎ 42111), at Calle Sucre N-782, offers tidy, pleasant singles/doubles for US$3.70/6.20 with shared bath. Laundry services are available, as they are at most Tarija hotels.

Residencial Zeballos (☎ 42068), at Calle Sucre N-920, has bright, comfortable rooms for US$4/7 per person without/with bath. It's friendly enough, but the obstreperous TV in the lounge may affect your assessment of this place.

Next door is *Hostal Miraflores* (☎ 43355), in a restored colonial-style building, which charges US$7/12 for singles/doubles with bath. Rooms without bath are US$3.70 per person. Unfortunately, rooms are in a dark warren at the back. VISA cards are accepted.

The *Residencial Rosario* (☎ 43942), on Calle Ingavi, a favourite haunt of volunteer workers, doesn't have the warmest atmosphere, but it's comfortable and good value at US$3.70/6 per person without/with bath. Advantages include the TV room and the reliable gas hot showers rather than the usual electrical attachment.

Residencial Bolívar (☎ 22741), Bolívar 256, features hot showers, a TV room and a sunny courtyard. Single/double rooms with

bath cost US$7.50/12.50; for a TV, add US$2. Note that the windows don't close properly, so take care of your valuables.

Just opposite is *Hotel América* (☎ 22627) – you won't miss the obtrusive sign hanging above the street. The atmosphere in this rather chaotic place is governed by the raucous bar downstairs. Rooms without/with bath cost US$3.20/6.40 per person.

Hostería España (☎ 43304), at Calle Alejandro Corrado 546, is a good all-round choice, with a nice flowery patio. Rooms without/with bath cost US$4/7 per person. Note, however, that even the private baths aren't attached to the rooms and require a jaunt across the patio.

Alojamiento El Hogar (☎ 43964), opposite the bus terminal, offers comfortable accommodation and a friendly, family-run atmosphere, but it's a good 20-minute walk from the centre. Rooms cost US$2.75 per person, with shared bath and hot water.

Places to Stay – middle
A passable central option is the welcoming *Hostal Libertador* (☎ 44231) at Bolívar O-649. Singles/doubles with bath, telephone and TV cost US$11.50/17.50. Breakfast is an additional US$1.

More central is the *Hostal Cristal* (☎ 25534), right on the main plaza. Singles/doubles cost US$25/35, with private bath and a continental breakfast. Rooms with double beds are US$38 and a 'honeymoon suite' with a pleasant view is US$40.

The *Victoria Plaza Hotel* (☎ 22600), on the corner of La Madrid and Sucre, is an upper mid-range option charging US$30/50 for singles/doubles with bath, TV, phone and frigobar. Rooms with a double bed cost US$45.

On the corner of Avenida Victor Paz Estenssoro and Calle JM Saracho is the pleasantly posh *Hostal La Costañera* (☎ 42851; fax 32640), which provides most amenities: heat, air-con, phone, cable TV and private parking. Rooms are excellent value at US$25/35 for a single/double, including a continental breakfast, and lower tariffs may be negotiated during the low season or for longer stays.

More expensive but not any nicer is the *Hotel Los Ceibos* (☎ 34430; fax 42461), on the corner of Avenida Victor Paz Estenssoro and Calle La Madrid. It offers the same amenities as Hostal La Costañera, but costs US$35/50 for singles/doubles, all of which have balconies overlooking the pool. Rooms with double beds are US$45 and suites (simply two normal rooms combined) cost US$90.

Places to Eat

North-east of the market, on the corner of Calle Sucre and Domingo Paz, street vendors sell local pastries and snacks unavailable in other parts of Bolivia, including delicious crêpe-like panqueques. In the back of the market, there's a section selling breakfast, and lots of stalls in the produce area sell fresh juices and licuados. Other meals are served upstairs.

At the *Palacio de las Masas*, on Campero near Bolívar, you'll find a variety of breads, cakes and pastries, including French-style baguettes, chocolate cake, cuñapes (cassava and cheese rolls) and both chocolate and meringue confections. *Panadería Gloria*, on Ingavi near Trigo, is also recommended for cakes, French bread, apple strudel and biscuits. Nearby, *Snack Vicky* serves snack meals and almuerzos for about US$1, and is OK for a quick bite. The generically named *Snack*, opposite the market, serves sandwiches, steak, milanesa, burgers, empanadas, salteñas and chicken. The diminutive *Snack Te Ve*, on Calle Sucre just off the plaza, is known for its excellent chile con carne.

The friendly Restaurant-Wiskería *Viejo Bar*, at Calle Madrid 356, on the main plaza, serves highly recommended home-made salteñas as well as great pizzas and burgers.

For lunch, the popular *El Solar* vegetarian restaurant, on the corner of Campero and Virginio Lema, is superb – if a bit freaky – and proudly caters to Tarija's New Age fringe. (In the affiliated office next door, you can indulge in the wonders of chro-

motherapy, aromatherapy, geotherapy, natural baths, psychic readings, group yoga sessions etc.) The restaurant experiments with such nontraditional practices as serving the dessert before the meal; you'd think you were in southern California! Four-course macrobiotic lunches are served from noon to 2 pm for US$1.20 and it's a real cow's delight; you can guzzle green alfalfa juice and graze on avocado salad, oat soup, bulgur wheat, cream of mango puree and straw tea. Go early to beat the herd.

A more terrestrial vegetarian choice is *Restaurant Familiar Aloe Vera*, on Daniel Campos between Bolívar and Domingo Paz. Almuerzos cost US$1.20 and it also sells health foods and natural products.

For more conservative lunches, try the *Club Social Tarija*, on the main plaza, which serves inexpensive almuerzos on weekdays. At *Chingo's*, also on the plaza, you'll find hefty Argentine beef parrillada with all the standard trimmings – rice, salad and potatoes – for about US$4.

The extremely popular Swiss and Czech-run *Taverna Gattopardo*, also on the plaza, is recommended for its pizza, pasta, burgers (among the best in Bolivia) and friendly, animated atmosphere. There's a stone-lined alcove at the back with straw on the floor and a nice social bar. When the weather's fine, you can sit outside and observe plaza life.

Another plaza pizzeria is *Isabella*, which is cheaper but more basic and lacks the ambience of the Gattopardo. Some claim that the Italian-run *Restaurant Italiano*, on Calle Alejandro del Carpio, serves some of the best Italian food in Bolivia. Most pasta dishes are a very reasonable US$2.50.

For Chinese meals, there's the high-brow *Bar Tebit* – probably intended to be 'Tibet' – which serves a decent lunch buffet for US$2. It's upstairs in the arcade on Virginio Lema near Sucre. Unfortunately, the management appears to be under a lot of stress, which can be off-putting. In the evening, you need a reservation for at least two people; if you turn up alone, you won't be served.

The *Restaurant El Piter*, near the bus terminal, emphasises such Tarija specialities as chancao (chicken with yellow pepper covered with tomato and onion sauce), saíce (hot meat and rice stew) and ranga (tripe with yellow pepper, potato, and tomato and onion sauce). The attached shop is a good place to pick up bottled water.

The *Rinconcito Familiar*, on the corner of 15 de Abril and Ejército, prides itself on being a family restaurant, and proclaims officially that drunks aren't welcome. It's open from 7 pm for good-value standards and pseudo-Italian pasta dishes.

Snack Pio-Pio, near the corner of Calles Sucre and 15 de Abril, is a local youth hang-out serving chicken and chips. *Heladería La Fontana*, on La Madrid, is good for ice-cream confections.

For meat dishes and an aquarium view (a few guppies and a stranded diver), try *Churrasquería Don Ñato*, at Calle 15 de Abril 842. It serves typical parrillada, zaraza (beef stomach), lomo, silpancho (milanesa pounded paper thin and deep fried) and milanesa de pollo, but the quality is hit or miss. Beware of grease in indigestible doses.

Entertainment

There's a peña on Friday at 9 pm at *Los Parrales* (☎ 24046), Calle Cochabamba 1154, in Barrio La Loma, not far from the Loma de San Juan. *Cabaña Don Pepe* (☎ 22426) at Daniel Campos and Avaroa occasionally stages a peña at the weekends; phone in advance for times.

Things to Buy

The best handcrafted souvenirs typical of Tarija would naturally be the unique musical instruments played in the area. It would be difficult to carry a *caña* or a *caja* around in your pack, but smaller instruments may be posted home.

For the best selection of Chapaco and Bolivian music, go to Disco Foto Rodríguez, on the corner of Calle Sucre and La Madrid. Some suggestions include the tape *Tarija y su Música* by various artists, and anything by the groups Los Trobadores Chapacos and Los Sapos Cantores de Tarija (the 'singing toads of Tarija').

Artesanías Vemar, touted by the tourist office, offers tacky primary school crafts and nothing of real interest. Try the Casa Folklórica on the corner of La Madrid and General Bernardo Trigo.

Getting There & Away

Air The Oriel Lea Plaza airport lies three km east of town along Avenida Victor Paz Estenssoro. LAB (☎ 45706), whose office is on the main plaza, connects Tarija with La Paz (US$87.50) and Cochabamba (US$64.50) daily except Sunday. It also flies to and from Santa Cruz (US$67) and Sucre (US$43).

Bus The bus terminal is a 20-minute walk from the city centre, east along Avenida Victor Paz Estenssoro. There's a problem with overcharging foreigners for bus tickets here, particularly with Flota Trans-Yacuiba. Before you pay for bus tickets, try to check the manifest and see what others are paying.

Several *flotas* run buses to Potosí, with connections to Oruro, Cochabamba and Sucre; they run daily in the afternoon (US$7, 12 hours). Buses to Villazón depart daily in the evening (US$3, 10 hours). It's a pity there are no daytime services, because the spectacular route passes through some incredible 'Wild West' mountain and canyon landscapes. About the best you can hope for is a full moon.

For Tupiza, there are daily evening departures (US$4, eight hours). To Yacuiba, Expreso Yacuiba and other buses leave daily between 6 and 7 pm (US$8, 12 hours). Unfortunately, this incredibly beautiful journey is also done at night and to see it by day, you'll have to find a *camión*. Flota Trans Gran Chaco leaves for Camiri (US$12, 13½ hours) on Monday, Thursday and Saturday at 6 pm. Heading towards Bermejo on the Argentine border, several flotas have daily departures between 7 and 10 am (US$3.50, seven hours).

Camión If you're heading for Villamontes, the best place to wait for a camión is at the *tranca* east of town. The road may be rough, but the scenery is fantastic, particularly between Entre Ríos and Palos Blancos, and near Villamontes, the road passes through the amazing Cañón del Pilcomayo (Pilcomayo Gorge). In the summer wet season, it may be easier to take the long way around through Argentina via Bermejo, Orán, Tartagal, Pocitos and Yacuiba.

For camiones to Potosí, Villazón, Yacuiba or Bermejo, take a taxi to the appropriate tranca and wait for a vehicle going your way. Use the north tranca for Villazón and Potosí and the south-east tranca for Yacuiba and Bermejo. You'll pay only slightly less than you would on the bus.

Getting Around

The Airport For taxis from the airport into town, step just outside the airport gate and you'll pay only US$0.40 (B$2) per person, less than half the price charged inside the airport. Otherwise, walk 100m across the main road and flag down a passing micro or *trufi*; either costs US$0.15 (B$0.60).

Bus City micros cost US$0.15 (B$0.60) per ride.

Taxi Tarija is small and you can walk just about anywhere. Taxis cost US$0.30 (B$1.50) within the centre, and US$0.40 (B$2) to the bus terminal. To the fossil areas or trancas, they charge about US$1 (B$5). A recommended radio taxi is Moto Méndez (☎ 24480).

AROUND TARIJA
San Jacinto

The 1700-hectare artificial lake of San Jacinto, seven km south-west of town, provides Tarija with water-related recreation close to home. There's a tourist complex with mid-range *cabañas*, canoe rental, a marginal restaurant, nice walks along the shore and surrounding ridges and some pleasant views. Micros leave every 20 minutes from the corner of Ingavi and Daniel Campos in Tarija, and on weekends hitching shouldn't be difficult. For more information,

contact the resort office (☎ 23179) in Comercial Villanueva at Campero 1025 in Tarija.

San Lorenzo

San Lorenzo, 15 km from Tarija, is a lovely colonial village with cobbled streets, carved balconies, a church built in 1709 and a flowery plaza with palm trees. It's best known, however, as the home of José Eustaquio 'Moto' Méndez, the hero of the Batalla de la Tablada, whose house has been turned into the Museo Moto Méndez. The museum displays his personal belongings, which he bequeathed to the people of Tarija and, as in so many such museums, his things have been left exactly as they were when he died. It's open Monday to Saturday from 9 am to 12.30 pm and 3 to 5 pm and on Sunday from 10 am to noon. Admission is US$0.30.

You can also head two km north to the Capilla de Lajas, a delicate chapel of exquisite proportions and fine colonial architecture. It was once the private chapel of the Méndez family and remains in private hands. Just to the north is the former home of Jaime Paz Zamora, with an adjacent billboard paying homage to the former president.

Special Events The popular Fiesta de San Lorenzo takes place on 10 August and features Chapaco musical instruments and dances.

Getting There & Away San Lorenzo lies on the Tupiza road. Micros and trufis leave from the Iglesia de San Juan in Tarija approximately every 10 minutes during the day. The fare is US$0.40. Along the route, you'll pass through the Parque Nacional las Barrancas, which was created in the 1960s to foster tree-planting and thereby control erosion in the crumbling fossil-rich badlands. (To reach only the park, take micro 'A' and get off at any of the park gates.)

Tomatitas, Coimata & Rincón de la Victoria

Another attraction is Tomatitas, with natural swimming holes and lots of little restaurants for Tarija day-trippers. The best swimming is immediately below the footbridge.

From Tomatitas, you can walk or hitch the five km to Coimata. Coming from Tarija, you should turn left off the main San Lorenzo road. After less than one km, you'll pass a cemetery on the left, which is full of flowers and brightly coloured crosses. Just beyond the cemetery, bear right and head for Coimata. Once there, turn left at the football ground and continue to the end of the road. Here you'll find a small cascade and swimming hole that makes a great Sunday escape from the city, as lots of *tarijeño* families can attest. From this point, you can follow a walking track 40 minutes upstream to the base of the two-tier Coimata Falls, which has a total drop of about 60m.

Another swimming hole and waterfall are found at Rincón de la Victoria, which lies about 6.5 km from Tomatitas in a green plantation-like setting. Instead of bearing right beyond the colourful cemetery, as you would for Coimata, follow the route to the left. From the fork, it's about five km to Rincón de la Victoria. If you wish to ascend the route leading up behind the falls, exercise extreme caution as it's steep and potentially slippery.

Micros to Tomatitas leave every few minutes from the western end of Avenida Domingo Paz in Tarija, and on weekends occasional trufis go all the way to Coimata. A taxi from Tomatitas to Coimata costs about US$5 with up to four people. Travelling from Tarija to Coimata costs around US$8.

Chorros de Jurina

The twin 40m waterfalls at Chorros de Jurina make an agreeable destination for a day trip from Tarija. The whole thing is set in a beautiful but unusual landscape, and, oddly, one waterfall cascades over white stone while the other pours over black stone. In late winter, however, they may be reduced to a mere trickle or even be dry.

The route from Tarija passes through some impressive rural landscapes. From near the flowery plaza in San Lorenzo, follow the Jurina road, which turns off beside the Casa

del Moto Méndez. Six km along, you'll pass a school on the left side. Turn left 200m beyond the school and follow that road another 2.5 km to the waterfalls.

From the end of the road, it's less than five minutes to the base of either waterfall. The one on the left is accessed by following the river upstream; for the other follow the track that leads from behind a small house.

Trufis leave for Jurina from near the Iglesia de San Juan in Tarija at around 8.30 am and 2.45 and 5 pm. Get off near the school and then walk the rest of the way. Hitching is feasible only on weekends.

El Valle de la Concepción

El Valle de la Concepción, or simply 'El Valle', as locals affectionately refer to it, is the heart of Bolivian wine and singani production and the town itself still bears lots of picturesque colonial elements. To visit the valley wineries, you need permission from Señor Navarro at the office of the Bodegas y Viñedos de la Concepción (☎ 25040), on the corner of La Madrid and Suipacha in Tarija. The Fiesta de la Uva takes place over three days in March, corresponding with the grape harvest.

El Valle lies off the route towards Bermejo, which means taking the right fork at the tranca east of Tarija. Trufis leave from Plaza Sucre in Tarija approximately every half-hour during the day and cost US$0.50.

Padcaya

Apart from an attractive church, a couple of buildings on the plaza and one other building (now a truck repair shop) with a plaster colonial façade peeling to its adobe innards, there's not much left of Padcaya's touted colonial heritage. It does have a nice setting, nestled in a hollow with lots of eucalyptus trees, but what makes Padcaya worthwhile is the trip itself – 50 km of lovely mountainous desert with green river valleys.

For an interesting walk from Padcaya, continue south along the road towards Chaguaya (not Bermejo – turn right at the tranca) for three km to a cluster of buildings called Cabildo. Tanning seems to be a major cottage industry, done the old-fashioned way with pits of vile-looking liquids and hides strung on lines.

At Cabildo, turn right on a llama road and continue until you pick up the river. Then walk five more km to where there's a cave with petroglyphs. This is a popular field trip for Tarija students. You'll probably need help to find the paintings, but don't ask a child to accompany you; locals believe that the devil inhabits this enchanting spot and don't allow their children to go near it.

Micros to Padcaya leave hourly from Plaza Sucre (Colón at 15 de Abril) and cost US$1. Most are marked 'P' to distinguish them from those going to Concepción, which are marked 'V'.

Chaguaya

In Chaguaya, 51 km south of Tarija near Padcaya, is the pilgrimage shrine, Santuario de la Virgen de Chaguaya. The Fiesta de la Virgen de Chaguaya begins on 15 August, with celebrations on the subsequent Sunday; alcohol is forbidden at this time. Pilgrims from all over Bolivia arrive during the following month, some on foot (including the annual 12-hour, 45-km procession from Tarija). Micros from Tarija to Padcaya and Chaguaya leave from the main bus terminal at 4 pm daily. The fare is US$1.

Tacshara

The area known as Tacshara lies high on the cold and windy Altiplano in western Tarija department. About 80 km south-west of Tarija, along the road to Villazón, several shallow flamingo-filled lagoons appear like jewels in the harsh, barren landscape, vegetated only by *thola* (a small desert bush) and spiky *paja brava*. Tarija's New Agers consider Tacshara to be a natural power site (indeed, it could easily be mistaken for a lost corner of Tibet). Highland people believe the lakes are haunted by spirit voices that call out at night, and that to be out after dark would invite disaster. Well, the night air *does* produce some eerie voice-like cries, but unimaginative people have ascribed the phenomenon to the distinctive sound of the wind rushing through thola bushes.

Along the eastern shores of the lagoons, the wind has heaped up large *arenales* (sand dunes). An interesting climb will take you to the symmetrical peak of Muyuloma, which rises about 1000m above the plain. The summit affords views across the lagoons and beyond to the endless expanses of the southern Altiplano. The return climb takes the better part of a day.

To get there, take a bus towards Villazón and get off at the sign announcing a Dutch aid project. Access is more daunting that it sounds, as buses all run at night when temperatures often drop well below freezing; all you'll be wanting is a warm tent and sleeping bag. It's about three km down that track to the lakes and a farther three km to the base of Muyuloma. The arenales lie between the lakes and the hills, approximately three km nearer Villazón. You'll need good warm clothing, food and camping gear.

BERMEJO

Bermejo, Bolivia's southernmost town, is a hot, muggy and dusty community 170 km south of Tarija on the banks of the Río Bermejo, at the south-west end of Bolivia's oil-bearing geologic formation. There's a YPFB (petroleum) compound that keeps many of the town's 15,000 or so residents busy. Bermejo also lies in the heart of a major sugar-cane producing region and there's a sugar refinery just outside town. Five km upriver from the YPFB, an international bridge over a canyon provides a highway link with the Argentine side.

There's little for the visitor but a Bolivian entry or exit stamp.

Information

Money The main street is lined with casas de cambio but none change travellers cheques so be sure to have Argentine pesos, US dollars cash or bolivianos on hand. It's wise to shop around for the best rate.

Dangers & Annoyances Bermejo's power

supply is turned off overnight, and the tap water is drawn straight from the murky river.

Comercio de Hormigas

About the only thing to do while waiting in the Argentine immigration queue is watch the comedy of errors associated with the *comercio de hormigas* (ant trade). The Argentine officer feigns ignorance of the intentions of the *contrabandistas* as they pass through the gate into the country.

Once the containers have been filled with wine, noodles, rice and what have you, they play the same game to return to Bolivia, passing through the gate while the officials are conversing or literally looking the other way. Occasionally something is confiscated or a sack of noodles is 'accidentally' broken on the ground, but nothing is taken too seriously. They'll be back the next day to try again.

Places to Stay & Eat

There isn't much choice of accommodation. The basic but clean *Residencial San Antonio* charges US$3.50 per person without bath. The owners are friendly and there's a decent restaurant attached. The clean white *Hotel El Turista* (☎ 61198) at Avenida Barranqueras 146, near immigration, has rooms with private bath and hot water for US$6 per person. There is no accommodation in Aguas Blancas.

Both the *Don Javiér* on the plaza and *Residencial San Antonio* serve standard Bolivian favourites for equally standard prices. Nothing is outstanding – just lomo, chicken, soup and rice – but there's a good *heladería* on the plaza.

Getting There & Away

Between Bermejo and Tarija, buses leave several times daily between 7 and 10 am. Under optimum conditions, the scenic trip takes seven hours.

From Aguas Blancas, Argentine buses to Orán depart hourly from the terminal opposite the immigration office. The trip costs US$2 and takes about an hour, depending on the time spent at the police inspection. From Orán, you can connect to Salta, Jujuy, Tucumán, Tartagal (the connection to Pocitos and Yacuiba) and Asunción (Paraguay).

Crossing the Border Bolivia is one hour behind Argentine time. Both the Bolivian and Argentine posts are open the same hours: 7 am to 4 pm *mas o menos* in Bolivia and a more reliable 8 am to 5 pm in Argentina.

The rowing-boat ferries across the river couldn't be more convenient; they charge US$0.20 per person and leave when full – which is about every 30 seconds. Don't forget to pick up an exit stamp before crossing the river.

Note that Bolivian immigration is closed at weekends; if you're leaving on Saturday or Sunday, get your exit stamp at immigration in Tarija.

The Chaco

The Chaco, an immense flat expanse of thorn scrub parcelled into vast *estancias*, takes in most of south-eastern Bolivia and western Paraguay, and spills into bits of neighbouring Argentina. The human population of this expansive region is limited to a handful of widely dispersed ranchers, isolated Indian groups, resourceful Mennonite colonists and troops at police and military posts.

What the Chaco lacks in up-and-down scenery, it makes up for with its colourful variety of flora and fauna. Butterflies and birds are abundant, and it's one of the dwindling South American strongholds of larger mammals such as the tapir, jaguar and peccary (locally called *javeli*).

The thorny scrub that characterises the Chaco's unusual flora is enlivened by brilliant flowering trees and bushes, including the yellow *carnival* bush, the yellow and white *huevo* and the pink or white thorny bottle tree, locally known as the *toboroche* or *palo borracho*, and the red-flowering *quebracho* or 'break-axe' tree. Beautiful quebracho wood, which is too heavy to float, is one of the Chaco's main exports. There are also numerous species of cactus.

History

Before the 1932-35 Chaco War, most of Paraguay north-east of the Paraguay and Pilcomayo rivers – encompassing about 240,680 sq km – and the 168,765-sq-km chunk of Argentina north of the Río Bermejo, lay within Bolivian territory.

The dispute between Bolivia and Paraguay, which led to the Chaco War, had its roots in Paraguay's formal 1842 declaration of independence, which omitted official demarcation of Paraguay's boundary with Bolivia. In 1878, the Hayes Arbitration designated the Río Pilcomayo as the boundary between Paraguay and Argentina, which was duly accepted. The empty land to the north, however, became a matter of dispute between Paraguay and Bolivia. Subsequent attempts at arbitration failed and Bolivia began pressing for a settlement.

After losing the War of the Pacific in 1884, Bolivia more than ever needed the Chaco as an outlet to the Atlantic via the Río Paraguay. Hoping that physical possession would be interpreted as official sovereignty, the Bolivian army set up a fort at Piquirenda on the Pilcomayo.

Arbitration attempts failed because Bolivia refused to relinquish rights to Fort Vanguardia, its only port on the Río Paraguay. Paraguay was unwilling to concede and, in 1928, the Paraguayan military seized the fort. Although the situation heated up, both sides maintained a conciliatory attitude, hoping that a military solution would not be necessary.

While negotiations were underway in Washington (the USA never could stay out of a good conflict), an unauthorised action on the part of the Bolivian military erupted into full-scale warfare. Casualties on both sides were heavy but the highland Bolivians, unaccustomed to the subtropical terrain, fared miserably. No decisive victory was reached, but the 1938 peace negotiations awarded most of the disputed territory to

Paraguay. Bolivia retained only the town of Villamontes, where, in 1934, it saw its most successful campaign of the war.

YACUIBA

Straddling the transition zone between the Chaco and the Argentine Pampa, Yacuiba is the easternmost border crossing on the Bolivian/Argentine frontier. It's the terminus for both the railway from Santa Cruz and the 10,000-barrels-a-day YPFB oil pipeline from Camiri. The railway line was constructed with Argentine capital according to the terms of a 10 February 1941 Bolivia-Argentina treaty, in which Bolivia agreed to export surplus petroleum to Argentina in exchange for a 580-km rail approach to the Buenos Aires-Pocitos line terminus. Although construction began immediately, it wasn't completed until the 1960s.

As a typical border town, Yacuiba has lots of shoddy commercial goods for sale and lots of shoppers scrambling to buy stuff nobody really wants or needs. The town and the surrounding area are really of little interest but you may be stranded here overnight, awaiting a train or a bus out.

Information

Money Yacuiba's main north-south street is flanked by several casas de cambio. None of them exchange travellers cheques, so heading north, you'll have to wait until Camiri or Santa Cruz and going south, until Embarcación (Argentina). When changing money, be on the lookout for counterfeit US dollar notes. Also, be sure to calculate the amount you should receive, and count it carefully before leaving the exchange window.

Telephone The telephone code for Yacuiba is 0682.

Dangers & Annoyances Thanks to heavy cross-border traffic, pickpocketing and petty theft is on the increase, especially in crowded shopping areas.

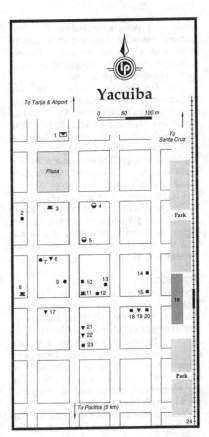

Yacuiba

To Tarija & Airport

0   50   100 m

To Santa Cruz

Plaza

Park

To Pocitos (5 km)

Park

PLACES TO STAY
10   Hotel Paris
12   Residencial Yacuiba
14   Hotel Valentín
15   Residencial San Martín
18   Residencial Aguaragüe
20   Alojamiento Ferrocarril
23   Hotel Monumental

PLACES TO EAT
3   Pepito's Café
6   La Pianola
8   Café El Negrito
11   TVO Expreso Café
17   Pizzería Chop
19   Parrilladas Ricardo
21   Swin
22   La Alhamba Confitería, El Mesón &
     Salón de Té San Silvestre

OTHER
1   Post Office & ENTEL
2   LAB (Airline)
4   Flota Gran Chaco Bus Terminal
5   Expreso Yacuiba Bus Terminal
7   TAM (Airline)
9   Casas de Cambio
13   Supermarket
16   Railway Station
24   Railway Terminus

(☎ 2317), opposite the railway station, with an attached bar/restaurant. Singles/doubles without bath are US$4/6 and rooms with double bed and private bath cost US$14.50. A double suite is a bargain at US$18.50.

The next best alternative is the older *Hotel Monumental* (☎ 2088), which isn't bad but occasionally has problems with the plumbing and electricity. In the newer section, singles/doubles cost US$9/14.50 and rooms with more than two beds are US$7 per person, all with bath. In the older annexe you'll pay US$3.50/5 for singles/doubles without bath and US$3 per person for rooms with more than two beds.

The new *Hotel Paris* (☎ 2182; fax 3059), beside the TVO Expreso Café, has singles/doubles with bath, air-con and frigobar for US$16.50/20.50.

Places to Eat

For a taste of Argentina north of the border – that means huge slabs of meat – try *Parrilladas Ricardo*. Typical Bolivian meals

Places to Stay

The number of hotels, bars and restaurants in Yacuiba is totally disproportionate to its size. Passable budget accommodation includes the *Residencial Aguaragüe*, which charges US$3/3.75 for a single/double without bath.

Other cheap dosshouses include *Alojamiento Ferrocarril* and *Residencial San Martín*. Both are very basic with shared bath and cold showers and charge US$2.30 per person. The *Residencial Yacuiba* charges US$3 per person for rooms with a hot water tap, and doubles with private bath are US$8.

A very good deal is *Hotel Valentín*

and decent breakfasts are available at the unfortunately named *Swin*, *La Pianola* and *Café El Negrito*. This last one is quite popular with locals. *TVO Expreso Café*, *Pepito's Café*, *Pizzería Chop*, *La Alhambra Confitería* and *Salón de Te San Silvestre* all serve snacks.

Getting There & Away

Air AeroSur operates a daily flight between Yacuiba and Santa Cruz (US$100.50). Unfortunately, LAB has suspended its service between Yacuiba and Tarija.

Bus & Camión Flota Trans Gran Chaco and Flota San Lorenzo each have daily services to Tarija for US$7, and several buses leave for Santa Cruz daily. This rather tiring journey can take up to 24 hours.

Most of the traffic to Villamontes follows the direct route along the foothills. Minibuses to Villamontes leave Yacuiba around mid-morning on weekdays and from Villamontes in the mid to late afternoon. For information and tickets, go to Galería Copacabana #15 in the Yacuiba shopping district. If you prefer a more scenic – as well as a longer and more uncertain – route to Villamontes, ride the Tarija bus as far as Palos Blancos and hitch or wait for a bus from there to Villamontes.

Shared taxis go to immigration at Pocitos (US$1 per person), five km away on the border. From the Argentine side, buses leave for Tartagal every two hours or so. In Yacuiba, you can pick up Argentine Veloz del Norte bus tickets to Salta, Jujuy, Tucumán, Buenos Aires or Santiago del Estero at the TVO Expreso Café. The Veloz del Norte bus terminal is in Pocitos (Argentina), just over the border.

Train The railway station ticket window opens at 8 am on the day of departure, but queue up at least one or two hours earlier. For up-to-date information on train departures, phone ☎ 2308. If you have a 2nd-class ticket to Santa Cruz, consider riding in the bodegas; it's a bit uncomfortable riding with all the freight, but you'll also meet some interesting people, including the contrabandistas who transport their mostly innocuous goods on the train. There's nothing risky about it – smuggling is considered an honourable profession here.

The *ferrobus* to Santa Cruz, via Villamontes, leaves Friday at 5 pm and arrives at 6 am the following day. The fares in 1st/2nd class are US$18.50/15.50. The *tren rápido* leaves on Tuesday and Saturday at 4.25 pm and costs US$12.75/10.75 for 1st/2nd-class seats. The *tren mixto* pulls only 2nd-class carriages and isn't particularly good value at US$10.75. It leaves Wednesday and Sunday at 5 pm and arrives the next day at 4 pm. Southbound, the ferrobus leaves Santa Cruz on Wednesday at 7 pm; the tren rápido on Monday and Friday at 3.40 pm; and the tren mixto on Wednesday and Sunday at 8.30 am.

POCITOS

The tiny village of Pocitos straddles the Bolivia-Argentina border, five km south of Yacuiba. From the Argentine side, buses depart approximately every two hours to Tartagal and Embarcación where you can make connections to Salta, Jujuy, Orán and Buenos Aires. Bear in mind that Bolivian time is one hour behind Argentine time. The Argentine bus terminals are just a couple of minutes walk from immigration.

You can take a shared taxi for the five-km trip between Yacuiba and the immigration post at Pocitos. The fare is US$1 per person regardless of the number of people. There's no consulate for either country.

PALOS BLANCOS

Comprising little more than a few bars and scattered houses overlooking a beautiful river, Palos Blancos oozes character. There's really little reason to visit, but it is a charming little place that could easily pass for a Hollywood Western movie set. Standing on the main street, you can almost see the outlaws galloping into town in a cloud of billowing dust.

Of some interest is the rustic church, a tumbledown, whitewashed mud building set in a colourful red and green landscape. An arch of cowbells outside is used to call the faithful to worship and the donation box is surrounded by wildflowers and prayer requests.

Places to Stay & Eat

There's no formal accommodation, but camp sites abound along the river. Minimal food services are available at the stores and bars opposite the church.

About 30 km east of Palos Blancos, towards Villamontes, is the recommended *Restaurant Guadalarajara*, which serves good fish. Behind it is a scenic 20m waterfall.

Getting There & Away

All buses and camiones between Villamontes, Yacuiba and Tarija pass through Palos Blancos, so finding transport is generally no problem in the dry season (March to October).

VILLAMONTES

Villamontes, Bolivia's main outpost in the true Chaco, prides itself on being the hottest place in the country – which doesn't seem amiss when the mercury rises above the 40°C mark and a hot, dry wind coats everything with a thick layer of red dust. As with the rest of the Chaco, it's famous for its wildlife, particularly small buzzing varieties like flies and mosquitoes.

The telephone code for Villamontes is 0684.

History

During Inca times, tribes of Guaraní Indians immigrated to western Chaco from present-day Paraguay, and their descendants now comprise most of the town's indigenous population.

Villamontes remained a small, lonely outpost until it emerged as a strategic Bolivian army stronghold during the Chaco War. The Paraguayans considered Villamontes their key to undisputed victory over the Bolivian resistance. In 1934, in the Battle of

Villamontes, the Bolivian army enjoyed its most significant victory of the war under the command of General Bernardino Bilbao Rioja and Major Germán Busch. The momentum gained in that battle allowed them to recapture portions of the eastern Chaco and some of the Santa Cruz department oil fields previously lost to Paraguay.

Cañón del Pilcomayo

At El Chorro Grande waterfall, in the beautiful Pilcomayo Gorge, fish are prevented from swimming farther upstream and *surubí*, *sábalo* and dorado are abundant and easily caught. This makes the area a favourite with anglers from all over the country. The prized dorado is particularly interesting because it has an odd hinge at the front of its jawbone, which allows the mouth to open wider horizontally.

There are great views from the restaurants along the Tarija road seven to 10 km west of town. There you can sample local fish dishes for about US$2.50.

To reach the gorge, take any Tarija-bound bus or petrol truck, or go by taxi to the tranca and hitch or walk from there (as usual, weekends are the best time to hitchhike). Where the road forks, bear right and continue another two km or so to the start of the gorge.

Special Events

Each year in August, Villamontes holds a fishing festival that focuses on the Río Pilcomayo.

Places to Stay

The basic *Hotel Pilcomayo* has no sign, so ask for the right doorway; rooms cost US$2 per person. Alternatively, there's the slightly more expensive *Residencial Raldes* (☎ 2545), near the railway line east of the main plaza. It's not that clean, but the grounds are nice and flowery. Rooms costs US$4 per person. The more appealing *Hotel El Rancho* is opposite the railway station two km north of town. Bungalows cost a reasonable US$5 per person.

Eight km out of town in the opposite direction, beside the Río Pilcomayo, is the

THE CHACO

friendly *Hotel Hoterma* (☎ 2373). It's good value at only US$3 per person and has access to superb fishing and some pleasant hot springs across the river. A boy with a rowing boat charges US$0.40 per person for the crossing.

Getting There & Away

Air The only air services to Villamontes are with TAM, which can be much less than reliable.

Bus & Camión Flota Trans Gran Chaco has one daily service to and from Tarija, and minibuses to Yacuiba leave Villamontes in the morning and return in the afternoon. Most bus services to Santa Cruz will be coming from Yacuiba and may be full.

Camiones going to Tarija, Yacuiba, Boyuibe, Palos Blancos, Camiri and Santa Cruz queue up along the strip marked 'Parada de Camiones', near the northern end of the market. If you're hitching towards Yacuiba it's worth taking a taxi to the southern tranca, five km south of town, and hitching from there.

Train Villamontes lies two hours by rail north of Yacuiba and 10 hours south of Santa Cruz. Taxis to the railway station, two km north of town, charge US$0.50 per person. The ferrobus passes on Friday at 7 pm northbound and on Thursday at 5 am southbound; the rápido stops on Tuesday and Saturday at 6.25 pm northbound and on Monday and Wednesday at 1.40 pm southbound; and the mixto drops in on Monday and Thursday at 7.30 pm northbound and on Wednesday and Sunday at 6.30 pm southbound.

BOYUIBE

Scarcely large enough to be called a town, Boyuibe sits on the fringes of the Chaco along the railway line three hours north of Villamontes and seven hours south of Santa Cruz. It serves mainly as a transit point. There are roads south to Villamontes, west to Camiri and east to Paraguay.

Places to Stay & Eat

Boyuibe has two hotels, the *Hotel Rosedal* and the *Hotel Guadalquivir*, both on the main street through town. Either can provide a basic bed to crash in, but they're not the best value for money at US$4 per person. For meals, your best option is *Pensión Boyuibe*, also on the main street.

Getting There & Away

Buses, colectivos and camiones from Boyuibe to Camiri, Villamontes and Yacuiba wait in front of the Tránsito office on the main street. The trip to Camiri takes only an hour on the newly asphalted road; the bus fare is US$1.50.

All trains between Santa Cruz and Yacuiba stop in Boyuibe. For more information, see Getting There & Away under Santa Cruz and Yacuiba.

THE CHACO ROAD

One of South America's great journeys stretches across the vast Gran Chaco between Filadelfia in Paraguay, and Boyuibe (or Santa Cruz) in Bolivia. Now that a couple of bus lines have taken up the Santa Cruz-Asunción run, the route has lost some of its romanticism, but most of the old uncertainties remain and you can be assured that it's still an exciting haul through raw, wild country. The road from Filadelfia to La Patria is good gravel, but between La Patria and the Bolivian border, it's little more than parallel deep sand ruts. However you go, expect a lot of jolts, bounces and repeated immigration, customs, police and military checkpoints before you can settle back and relax at journey's end.

However you look at it, this trip is still an adventure through one of the South America's wildest regions. In 1995, two friends and I travelled the Chaco Road in the bed of a camión carrying a load of uncured cowhide, which oozed rancid fat and saturated the 40°C heat with an aromatic bovine perfume. On one five-km stretch immediately south of Fortín General Eugenio A Garay, the crew and passengers had to spend 12 hours digging sand, cutting trees and laying branches to make the road passable. At the end of the day, the always jolly Bolivian crew rewarded the exhausted passengers – the three of us, a traveller from eastern Germany and a Colombian Hare Krishna devotee – with a delicious meal around a cowboy-style campfire.

The Chaco Road may be adventurous, but it's also fraught with bureaucracy and suspicion. Travellers heading from Bolivia to Paraguay by camión or private vehicle can pick up exit stamps from the military post at Boyuibe (along the railway south of the village) and from the immigration/police post on the highway about a km farther out.

At the Bolivian border post at Fortín Villazón, you'll have a passport check and you may receive another exit stamp. The Paraguayan border post is at Irindagüe, about five km farther along, but you pick up Paraguayan entry stamps at the military post, Fortín General Eugenio A Garay, about 15 km into Paraguay. Between there and Mariscal Estigarribia, there are a couple more checks, one at a remote police post and another at La Patria. At Mariscal Estigarribia, travellers coming from Bolivia may be subjected to a military inspection.

Travelling from Paraguay to Bolivia you'll have all the same checks, and you must also check in at both the immigration/police post and the military post in Boyuibe. If you're stopping overnight in Camiri, you must visit the immigration office in Camiri. However, you won't actually receive your length of stay stamps until you reach immigration in Santa Cruz, which you must do within 72 hours of entering the country.

Crossing the Chaco
Bus During winter, a couple of bus companies tackle the Chaco Road. In the wet season, the rough, sandy road becomes impassable quicksand and slimy mud. Flota Santa Ana runs from Asunción to Santa Cruz on Monday, Wednesday and Friday, conditions permitting. The office is upstairs at the main bus terminal in Asunción. There are no set departure times from Santa Cruz to Asunción; the best anyone can tell you is that buses leave from the main bus terminal in Santa Cruz sometime after they arrive there (which isn't necessarily a sure thing).

The more organised Servicio de Transporte y Excursiones (STEL) Turismo (☎ 26059) leaves the main bus terminal in Asunción on Tuesday at 4 pm. Its booking office is at Avenida República de Colombia 1050, Asunción. If you're coming from Filadelfia, you'll have to reserve a seat via Asunción and meet the bus at Cruce de los Pioneros on Tuesday at 8.30 pm by taking the connecting bus, which leaves Filadelfia at 6.45 pm. Book tickets at the STEL Turismo office on the main street in Filadelfia, one very long block east of the Esso station. If all goes well, the bus departs from Santa Cruz for Asunción sometime on Friday.

The trip takes a minimum of 40 hours and costs US$72 from Asunción and US$65 from Filadelfia. If you book a return ticket from Asunción to Santa Cruz (but few people who have done the trip one way would consider returning by the same route), the price includes a hotel discount in Santa Cruz.

Camión Overland travellers between Bolivia and Paraguay should allow a few days in Boyuibe or Filadelfia waiting for a truck. In the dry season, camiones leave for Mariscal Estigarribia and Filadelfia, the first major towns inside Paraguay, more or less weekly, but there's no set schedule. Ask around in Boyuibe for anyone who's going, or wait at the immigration/police post two km south of town.

Travelling from Paraguay to Bolivia, trucks run more or less every few days whenever the road is dry and passable. In Filadelfia, drivers park at the large vacant lot that lies 1½ enormous blocks east of the Esso station. Prospective travellers need only make arrangements with the drivers. Alternatively, you can wait at the military checkpoint at the southern entrance to Mariscal Estigarribia.

Passengers in either direction can expect to pay about US$10 to US$15 per person for the two to three-day trip.

ar & Motorcycle If you have access to a hardy 4WD vehicle, you can attempt this trip independently, but serious and thorough preparations are necessary. A supply of fuel, water, food, spare parts, tyres and so on is essential. There are no spares or fuel available until well into Paraguay, road conditions change with each rainfall and traffic is intermittent at best. If you break down, it may be days before someone passes by.

CAMIRI

Situated at the edge of the Chaco with a favourable climate, Camiri has grown phe-nomenally in recent years due to lucrative employment opportunities with the national oil company, YPFB (known affectionately as 'Yacimientos'). Camiri is a centre for the production of petroleum and natural gas and bills itself as the Capital Petrolífero de Bolivia.

History

In 1955, two pipelines were constructed to carry natural gas and petroleum to Yacuiba on the Argentine frontier. The following year, a 1.5 million dollar natural gas reinjec-tion plant was built by YPFB atop Cerro

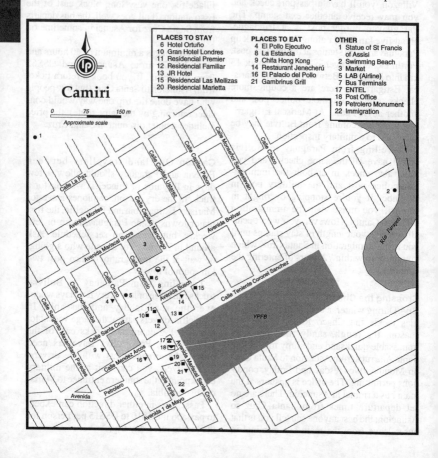

Camiri

0   75   150 m
Approximate scale

PLACES TO STAY
6 Hotel Ortuño
10 Gran Hotel Londres
11 Residencial Premier
12 Residencial Familiar
13 JR Hotel
15 Residencial Las Mellizas
20 Residencial Marietta

PLACES TO EAT
4 El Pollo Ejecutivo
8 La Estancia
9 Chifa Hong Kong
14 Restaurant Jenecherú
16 El Palacio del Pollo
21 Gambrinus Grill

OTHER
1 Statue of St Francis
   of Assisi
2 Swimming Beach
3 Market
5 LAB (Airline)
7 Bus Terminals
17 ENTEL
18 Post Office
19 Petrolero Monument
22 Immigration

Calle Monseñor Santiesteban
Calle Chaco
Calle Capitán Pabón
Calle La Paz
Calle Capitán Ugarte
Avenida Montes
Calle Capitán Manchego
Avenida Mariscal Sucre
Calle Comercio
Avenida Bolívar
Calle Teniente Coronel Sánchez
Río Parapetí
Calle Oruro
Avenida Busch
Calle Cochabamba
Calle Sargento Maximiliano Paredes
Calle Santa Cruz
Calle Méndez Arcos
Avenida Mariscal Santa Cruz
Calle Tarija
Avenida Petrolero
Avenida 1 de Mayo
YPFB

Sararenda to recover liquid petroleum gas by injecting natural gas into oil-bearing formations. Another plant to process this liquid petroleum gas was built and began functioning in 1968, and a refrigeration and dehydration plant to recover liquid petroleum was put into operation at nearby Taquiparenda in 1983. Decreased production closed it, however, after only three years of operation. Camiri has since experienced ups and downs in the industry but it remains the centre of Bolivia's fossil fuel production.

Information

Money Librería Ramirez will change cash and up to US$100 in travellers cheques. Hotel Ortuño changes US dollars cash at a relatively good rate and will sometimes also change travellers cheques.

Post & Communications The friendly post office, on Avenida Mariscal Santa Cruz, is a relic from the days when most people had a lot more time than they do now. The public fax number at ENTEL is 2202. The telephone code for Camiri is 0952.

Immigration Visitors who are coming from Paraguay must register with immigration on arrival. The office is on Avenida 1 de Mayo, downhill from Calle Tarija.

Things to See & Do

Camiri may not be well endowed with attractions, but the town is proud of its **YPFB plant**. Although there's no formal tour, visitors wanting to have a look at it should turn up at about 8 am and appear to be interested in oil. One item not to miss is the **Petrolero (oil workers') monument** in the middle of Avenida Petrolero, which is inscribed with the slightly excessive *Himno al Petrolero* (Hymn to the Oil Worker).

There are also a couple of nice **walks**. One will take you up to the statue of St Francis of Assisi on the top of the hill behind the market for a super view over the town and the surrounding hills. Another pleasant walk will take you down Avenida Mariscal Sucre to the Río Parapetí. On the bank, turn south and

walk several 100m downstream, where you'll find a clean sandy beach and a good, deepwater swimming hole.

Places to Stay

The friendly *Hotel Ortuño* (☎ 2288) on Calle Comercio charges US$3/4 per person for rooms without/with bath. Several of the Ortuño children have attended school in the USA and therefore speak English.

The immaculate *Residencial Premier* on Calle Santa Cruz (☎ 2204) charges US$4 per person for a room with a private bath and hot water whenever both water and electricity are available. Rooms without bath cost US$3. Try for one of the light and airy upstairs rooms, which open onto a leafy patio. Another decent choice is the *Residencial Las Mellizas* (☎ 2614) on the corner of Calle Capitán Manchego and Avenida Busch. Rooms cost US$4 per person with bath.

The *Residencial Marietta* (☎ 2254), at Avenida Petrolero 15, is slightly more expensive at US$4/5 per person without/with bath. It's owned by Ana and Federico Forfori. This place doubles as the Italian consulate and also houses the AeroSur office.

Camiri's most upmarket digs, the friendly *JR Hotel* (☎ 2200) may sometimes accommodate visiting oil barons, but prices are quite reasonable at US$13.50/23 for singles/doubles with bath, phone, heat, air-con and TV. Peripherals include an à la carte restaurant, a bright sitting area and good views of the surrounding hills.

Places to Eat

By Bolivian standards, Camiri has only a limited choice of restaurants. The one favoured by visiting business people is the *Gambrinus Grill* at Avenida Mariscal Santa Cruz 149, which specialises in international cuisine.

Some Camiri restaurants appear to keep inconsistent opening hours. On the rare occasions when it's open, *La Estancia*, on the corner of Calle Comercio and Avenida Busch, does almuerzos for US$1.50 and à la rte evening meals. The Chinese-oriented *Chifa Hong Kong*, on the plaza, also appears to be closed most evenings and the recommended *Restaurant Jenecherú* (the Arab Social Club), on Avenida Busch, never seems to be open. Maybe you'll have more luck.

If you need a grease fix, *El Palacio del Pollo*, near the plaza, and *El Pollo Ejecutivo* (yes, the executive chicken!), opposite the LAB office, serve chicken and chips in the evening only. For breakfast, street vendors on the corner of Avenida Bolívar and Calle Comercio, outside the market, sell coffee, tea, chocolate, bread and delicious licuados. Inside, you'll find good deals on basic meals.

Getting There & Away

Air The airport lies just outside town on the Sucre road. AeroSur has flights from Santa Cruz to Camiri (US$59) Monday to Friday at 6.30 am, returning at 7.55 am on the same days.

Bus & Camión Flota El Chaqueño, Trans Camiri (bizarrely psychedelic buses), Transportes Gran Chaco, Auto Transical, Flota Cordillera, Trans Guzmán and Transportes

San Silvestre all have services to Santa Cruz nightly between 5 and 6.30 pm.

Most buses to Yacuiba come through from Santa Cruz in the middle of the night and may already be full, but Flota El Chaqueño's Wednesday and Saturday service to Yacuiba, which leaves at 10 am, originates in Camiri.

Flota San Silvestre leaves for Villamontes on Tuesday and Saturday at 5 pm. Transportes Gran Chaco has a service to Tarija, with connections to Villamontes, Yacuiba, Tupiza and Bermejo. It leaves on Monday and Thursday at noon.

When the road is passable, Flota El Chaqueño leaves for Sucre on Tuesday and Friday at 6 am to arrive around midday the following day, depending on the normally very rough road conditions.

The Boyuibe road passes through some beautiful hilly Chaco scrub. Micros leave from Avenida Bolívar, four blocks uphill from the main market; the hour-long trip costs US$1.50. Camiones to Villamontes, Boyuibe, Yacuiba and Tarija leave from the tranca when full. It's quite a long uphill walk with luggage, but a taxi wil cost you only US$0.40.

Camiones to Santa Cruz and Sucre park along Calle Comercio beside the market and leave when full.

Santa Cruz

Since 1950, Santa Cruz has mushroomed from a backwater cattle-producing town to its present position as Bolivia's second city, with just under one million inhabitants – a big city on the fringe of a diminishing wilderness.

The area's economic and agricultural potential has attracted not only optimistic settlers from the highlands, but people from many other walks of life: it boasts a rice-growing Japanese colony, a settlement of Italians, Palestinians, Indian Sikhs and thousands of German-Canadian Mennonites fleeing governmental conflicts in Mexico and Belize. It has also been a haven for escaped Nazis (a rapidly diminishing group) and is now attracting throngs of Brazilian opportunists, foreign oil workers, agribusiness tycoons, drug traffickers, foreign researchers, missionaries and environmental activists.

Santa Cruz has also developed into a hub of transportation and trade, and the amount of money here is evident in the number of 12-bedroom homes, Toyota 4WDs, BMWs and other playthings not normally associated with Bolivia. The city is connected by rail with Argentina and Brazil and by road with Cochabamba, the Chaco and Trinidad. However, its longstanding reputation as a drug-trafficking mecca is now being eclipsed by a boom in tropical agriculture, and large corporate plantations of sugar, rice, cotton, soybeans and other warm-weather crops now dominate the vast lowlands east of the city, which only five years ago were covered with thick tropical forest.

Despite its phenomenal rate of growth, Santa Cruz retains traces of its dusty past, evident in its wide streets, frontier architecture and small-town atmosphere. It may have an international airport with direct flights to Miami, but forest-dwelling sloths still hang in the trees of the main plaza.

The overall climate is tropical, but because Santa Cruz sits in the transition zone

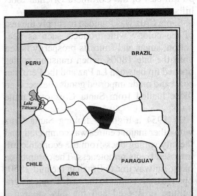

Highlights

- See tapirs, pumas and spectacled bears in the well-tended Santa Cruz zoo
- Watch the sloths hanging in Santa Cruz's Plaza 24 de Septiembre
- Acclimatise in the laid-back village of Samaipata and explore the pre-Inca ruins of El Fuerte
- Search for the blue-horned curassow in the Parque Nacional Amboró
- Enjoy a cosmopolitan choice of cuisines in the restaurants of Santa Cruz

between the Amazon rainforest, the highlands and the dry Chaco plains, it enjoys more sun and less stifling temperatures than the humid, rainy Amazon Basin farther north-west. During winter, rainfall occurs in 10-minute downpours, but a single summer deluge can last for days. Santa Cruz also experiences heavy winds that rarely subside and at times during winter, chilly winds called *surazos* blow in from Patagonia and the Argentine pampas.

History

Santa Cruz de la Sierra was founded in 1561 by Ñuflo de Cháves, a Spaniard who hailed from what is now Paraguay. The town originally lay 220 km east of its current location.

However, around the end of the 16th century, it proved too vulnerable to attack from local tribes and was moved to its present position, 50 km east of the Cordillera Oriental foothills.

Santa Cruz was founded to supply the rest of the colony with products such as rice, cotton, sugar and fruit. Its prosperity lasted until the late 1800s, when transport routes opened up between La Paz and the Peruvian coast and made imported goods cheaper than those hauled from Santa Cruz over mule trails.

In 1954 a highway linking Santa Cruz with other major centres was completed, and the city sprang back from the economic lull imposed by its remoteness. The completion of the railway line to Brazil in the mid-1950s opened trade routes to the east. Tropical agriculture prospered and the city entered a flurry of growth that has continued to the present day.

Orientation

The city is roughly oval in shape and is laid out in *anillos*, or rings, which form concentric circles around the city centre. Most commercial enterprises, hotels and restaurants lie within the 1st *(primer)* anillo, which focuses on the main plaza, 24 de Septiembre. The railway station lies within the 3rd anillo but is still only a half-hour walk from the centre. The 2nd to 7th anillos are mainly residential and industrial. Their tourist attractions include the zoo, the Río Piray and several markets, discos and fine restaurants.

Maps The two best city maps, *Multiplano Ilustrado*, which covers the 1st to 3rd anillos, and *Hotelería en Santa Cruz*, which features hotels and includes everything out to the 5th anillo, are available at the tourist offices for about US$2 each.

Information

Tourist Office There's a convenient tourist information office on the ground floor of the Palacio de la Prefectura, on the plaza. Alternatively, visit the office (☎ 368900, fax 368901) upstairs in the CORDECRUZ

building on Avenida Omar Chávez, several blocks south of the bus terminal. Both places are open weekdays from 8.30 am to noon and 2.30 to 6 pm.

For national park information, head out to the office of Fundación Amigos de la Naturaleza (FAN; ☎ 524921, fax 533389). It's behind a prominent white wall in La Nueve, about seven km west of Santa Cruz on the old Cochabamba road. To get there, take *micro* 44 from the corner of Avenidas Cañoto and Isabél la Católica.

Some street kiosks sell the *Guía de Santa Cruz*, which has good but patchy information about the city and its environs. It's in Spanish and costs about US$5.

Foreign Consulates Santa Cruz has several consulates, open weekdays only:

Argentina
    Banco de la Nación Argentina, Plaza 24 de Septiembre (☎ 324153); open 9 am to noon.
Brazil
    Avenida Busch 330 (☎ 344400); open 9.30 am to 12.30 pm and 3.30 to 6.30 pm
France
    Calle Avaroa 70 (☎ 334818); open 3 to 6.30 pm
Germany
    Avenida de las Américas 241 (☎ 324825); open 8.30 am to 1 pm
Netherlands
    Calle Buenos Aires 172 (☎ 340331); open 8.30 am to noon
USA
    Edificio Oriente, 3rd floor, Suite 313 (☎ 330725); open 9 to 11.30 am

Immigration The immigration office (☎ 332136) is at Calle España 383. It's open weekdays from 8.30 am to noon and 2.30 to 6 pm. If you're arriving overland from Paraguay, you must pick up a length of stay stamp. This stamp is free and there's an official anticorruption sign on the wall to this effect. If someone asks for money, just point to the sign.

Money You can change cash or travellers cheques at the casas de cambio on the main plaza, and at certain banks. Casas de cambio charge 3% commission to change travellers cheques. If you're changing at banks, which generally offer better rates, carry photocopies of your purchase slips. The Banco Económico on Calle Ayacucho will change travellers cheques to cash dollars for 1% commission. Count your cash before leaving the window, as short-changing is rife.

Visa cash advances are available at the Banco de Santa Cruz, Calle Junín 154. Street moneychangers congregate along Avenida Cañoto between Calles Ayacucho and Junín; at the intersection of Avenidas Cañoto and Irala, near the bus terminal; and occasionally around the main plaza.

Post & Communications The post office is half a block from the main plaza on Calle Junín.

The ENTEL office is on Warnes between Calles René Moreno and Chuquisaca. You can send a telegram abroad for B$1 per word. The public fax number is 112010. The telephone code for Santa Cruz is 03.

Travel Agencies Magri Turismo Limitada (☎ 345663, fax 366309), at Calle Ingavi 14, is the American Express representative. Before you can change American Express travellers cheques at the casas de cambio,

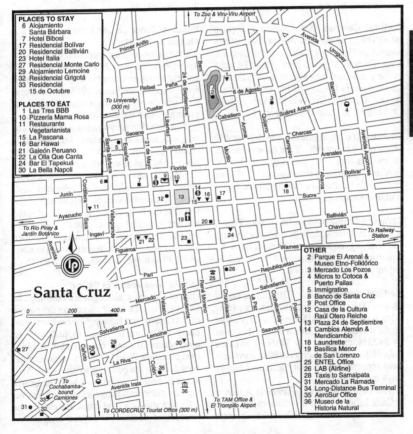

PLACES TO STAY
6 Alojamiento Santa Bárbara
7 Hotel Bibosi
17 Residencial Bolívar
20 Residencial Ballivián
23 Hotel Italia
27 Residencial Monte Carlo
29 Alojamiento Lemoine
32 Residencial Grigotá
33 Residencial 15 de Octubre

PLACES TO EAT
1 Las Tres BBB
10 Pizzería Mama Rosa
11 Restaurante Vegetarianista
15 La Pascana
16 Bar Hawai
21 Galeón Peruano
22 La Olla Que Canta
24 Bar El Tapekuá
30 La Bella Napoli

OTHER
2 Parque El Arenal & Museo Etno-Folklórico
3 Mercado Los Pozos
4 Micros to Cotoca & Puerto Pailas
5 Immigration
8 Banco de Santa Cruz
9 Post Office
12 Casa de la Cultura Raúl Otero Reiche
13 Plaza 24 de Septiembre
14 Cambios Alemán & Mendicambio
18 Laundrette
19 Basílica Menor de San Lorenzo
25 ENTEL Office
26 LAB (Airline)
28 Taxis to Samaipata
31 Mercado La Ramada
34 Long-Distance Bus Terminal
35 AeroSur Office
36 Museo de la Historia Natural

Santa Cruz

SANTA CRUZ

they must be certified at this office. American Express will receive post for their customers at Casilla 4438, Santa Cruz. See also Organised Tours later in this section.

Bookshops Los Amigos del Libro on Calle Velasco has Spanish, English, French and German-language books, as well as a good selection of local history and literature, and foreign news magazines. The Casa de la Cultura on the plaza sells work by Bolivian authors, from poetry and children's books to scientific research. The *Miami Herald*, *Time*, *Newsweek* and the brilliant Brazilian news magazine *Veja* are sold at street kiosks opposite the post office.

Cultural Centres The Alliance Française (☎ 333392), at Andrés Ibáñez 241, offers courses in French, Spanish and Portuguese. Their French-language library may be used by the public and they also sponsor talks and screen foreign films. The USA's equivalent is the Centro Boliviano-Americano (☎ 342299) at Calle Cochabamba 66.

Laundry The laundrette at Calle Bolívar 490 offers one-day service. If the door is closed, knock and they'll let you drop off clothes. Washing, drying and ironing costs US$1 per kg. There's another good laundrette on Santa Bárbara, south of Florida.

Camping Equipment La Jara Caza y Pesca, at Calle Bolívar 458, sells limited camping and fishing equipment. There's also El Aventurero on Calle Buenos Aires, which is run by an ex-pat American.

Medical Services The Clínica Japonesa (☎ 462031), on the 3rd anillo, *lado este* (east side), is recommended for good, inexpensive medical treatment. Clínica Angel Foianini (☎ 342211, emergency ☎ 345566), Avenida Irala 468, delivers quality care, but travellers have reported unnecessary tests and longer stays than necessary.

The best pharmacy is Farmacia América at Calle Libertad 333; it's efficient and inexpensive, and the English-speaking staff

know the products. Next door is the Policonsultorio Central, run by the recommended Dr Ana María Lopez, who trained in the USA and speaks English.

Dangers & Annoyances Although Santa Cruz has become considerably more relaxed in recent years, you must still carry your passport at all times. If you're caught without documents, you'll be fined US$50 and have to waste several hours at the police station while paperwork is shuffled.

Beware of bogus immigration officials, particularly at the railway station. If someone asks to see your passport, check their credentials.

Basílica Menor de San Lorenzo & Museo de la Catedral

Although the original cathedral on Plaza 24 de Septiembre was founded in 1605, the present structure dates back to 1845, and it wasn't consecrated until 1915. The decorative woodwork on the ceiling and silver plating around the altar are worth a look.

The cathedral museum has a collection of religious icons and artefacts but very little typical religious art. Most interesting are the many gold and silver relics from the Jesuit Guarayos missions north-east of Santa Cruz. There's also a collection of religious vestments and medallions, as well as one of the world's smallest books, a thumbnail-sized volume containing the Lord's Prayer in several languages. The museum is open Tuesday and Thursday from 8.30 am to noon and 2.30 to 6 pm. Admission is US$0.75.

Iglesia 'Viva Jesús El Señor'

One of the most incongruous buildings in Santa Cruz is the small church on the corner of Salvatierra and Izozog. Covered with coloured bathroom tiles and topped with an onion dome, it might not seem out of place along the Silk Road in Central Asia. Emblazoned across the building are the words *Viva Jesús El Señor* (Long Live Christ the Lord). On one outer wall hangs a large copper crucifix and above, a tiled cross. It's clearly the product of someone's devout imagination and merits at least a good look as you pass by.

Parque El Arenal & Museo Etno-Folklórico

Locals relax around the lagoon at Parque El Arenal. On an island in the lagoon, a bas-relief mural by renowned Bolivian artist Lorgio Vaca depicts historic and modern-day aspects of Santa Cruz. Inside the building is the newish Museo Etno-Folklórico, which displays a small collection of traditional art and artefacts from several *camba* (lowland) cultures.

Casa de la Cultura Raúl Otero Reiche

The chaotic corridors of the Casa de la Cultura, on the plaza, contain a rather informal and haphazardly arranged museum of Bolivian art. Although the paintings are poorly lit, originality runs high and it's a breath of fresh air if you've overdosed on the blood and flagellation typical of most Bolivian art. Especially look for the works of Vaca and other contemporary Bolivian artists such as Herminio Pedraza and Tito Kurasotto. It's open weekdays from 8.30 am to noon and 2.30 to 6 pm; admission is free.

Plaza 24 de Septiembre

The plaza is a great place to relax. One LP reader wrote:

Here you can kick back and watch folks, have your shoes shined, be asked to buy everything under the sun (and a few things you'd never think of, like Teenage Mutant Ninja Turtle marionettes). You can also engage in my favourite restful activity, sloth-watching. Keep your eyes peeled and you'll find a couple, grooming or eating or just hanging around. There are nearly always two of them in the trees opposite the cathedral.

Mary Ann Springer, USA

Museo de la Historia Natural

The Natural History Museum, in the old Immigration building on Avenida Irala, gives you the lowdown on the flora, fauna and geology of eastern Bolivia. Exhibits include pickled frogs and the usual stuffed animals, fish and birds, as well as informa-

Three-toed sloth

tion on seeds, wood, fruit, gardening and other lowland pursuits. The bug collections include specimens large enough to inspire psychosis or keep you out of rainforests forever. It's open daily from 9 am to noon and 3 to 6 pm. Admission is free but donations are gratefully accepted.

Zoo

The Santa Cruz zoo is one of the few on the continent that's worth the time and money.

Its collection is limited to South American birds, mammals and reptiles, and all appear to be humanely treated (although the llamas appear a little overdressed for the climate.) The zoo features endangered and exotic species such as tapirs, pumas, jaguars and spectacled bears. Sloths, which are too slow and lazy to escape successfully, are not confined to cages, and hang around in the trees, occasionally mustering enough energy for a slow crawl around the grounds.

It's open daily from 9 am to 7.30 pm; admission costs US$1. Take micros 76 or 77 from Calle Santa Bárbara or micros 8, 11 or 17 from El Arenal. Taxis for up to four people charge about US$1.50.

Río Piray

The Jardín Botánico (Botanical Garden) here was destroyed in a flood in the 1980s, and plans to renovate it developed into the creation of a park requiring less maintenance. The river banks are good for a picnic, especially on the weekend when local families make an outing of it, and there are stalls and a basic teahouse selling food.

To get there, take micro 6 or 9 from Avenida Cañoto, near the long-distance bus terminal, and get off at the western end of Avenida Roca y Coronado.

Organised Tours

Several companies offer organised tours. Amazonas Adventure Tours (☎ 422760, fax 422748), at 756 Avenida San Martín, 3rd anillo interno, Barrio Equipetrol, specialises in the remote Reserva de Vida Silvestre Ríos Blanco y Negro and the jungle resort at Perseverancia. Rosario Tours (☎ & fax 369656), at Calle Arenales 193, Casilla 683, has tours to sites all around Santa Cruz, including the Pantanal, the Jesuit missions, Parque Nacional Amboró, Los Espejillos, Samaipata and Dunas de Palmar.

Uimpex Travel (☎ 336001, fax 330785), at Calle René Moreno 226, is one of the oldest agencies in the area and also one of the most imaginative. It has recently expanded to include programmes around Bolivia's major cities, as well as the Panta-nal, the Jesuit missions, the Dunas de Palmar, Bermejo, Los Espejillos, Samaipata, Vallegrande/La Higuera and Parque Nacional Amboró. It also runs an amazing six-day excursion to the Los Fierros region of Parque Nacional Noel Kempff Mercado, and an eight-day jungle and river excursion around Magdalena and down the Río Itonama to Forte Principe da Beira (in Brazil). With a group of four participants, these last two excursions cost US$625 and US$950 per person, respectively.

Special Events

If you're in Santa Cruz for *Carnaval* (held the week before Lent), check out the Mau-Mau in the auditorium on the corner of Ibáñez and Calle 21 de Mayo. This annual event, which includes dancing, music shows and the coronation of the carnival queen, attracts more than 10,000 people.

Every couple of years in mid to late September, Santa Cruz hosts an enormous two-week *feria* where you can buy anything from a toothbrush or clothing to a new house, a combine harvester or a 20-tonne truck. To accommodate it, a temporary village is constructed, including banks, an ice cream parlour and an ENTEL office. It's worthwhile even if you're not shopping, especially at night when it takes on a carnival atmosphere as Bolivians stroll, browse, listen to music, eat, drink and have a good time. Admission is US$1.

Places to Stay – bottom end

If you don't feel like walking far when you arrive at the bus terminal, there is a good selection of cheap places nearby. Two blocks away on a crowded market street is the friendly *Residencial Grigotá* (☎ 337699), Calle Muchirí 15, where fairly clean rooms cost US$4 per person without bath. A double bed with private bath costs US$10.50. *Residencial Monte Carlo* (☎ 527776), at Ghiriguanos 190, sits in a quiet leafy street near Mercado La Ramada. (Their motto is 'the sensation of being at home'.) Rooms cost US$5 per person with a shared bath. Room 10, which is a very nice double, is

Top: Ski hut, Chacaltaya (RS)
Bottom: Beni home, near Río Tuichi (DS)

Top: Dusty street, Riberalta (RS)
Bottom: The upper Río Beni (RS)

US$10.50 with bath; add US$2 and you get a fan and TV.

Another nearby option is *Residencial 15 de Octubre* (☎ 342591), Calle Guaraní 33. It's more spartan than the Grigotá, but costs only US$3.50 per person without bath and US$8.25 with bath and a double bed. A more basic place in the bus terminal area is the *Alojamiento Lemoine* (☎ 346670), at Calle Lemoine 469. Rooms without bath cost US$3 per person, but it gets noisy.

If you prefer to be more central, the *Alojamiento Santa Bárbara* (☎ 321817), Calle Santa Bárbara 151, is fairly friendly and offers simple but comfortable accommodation and hot showers for US$4 per person. The *Alojamiento 24 de Septiembre* (☎ 321992) at Calle Santa Bárbara 79, isn't particularly clean or friendly but seems popular with young Bolivians. Singles/doubles cost US$6.20/8.25.

A longtime backpackers' favourite is the clean and bright *Residencial Bolívar* (☎ 342500), at Calle Sucre 131. With good breakfasts, inviting courtyard hammocks, wonderful hot showers and a couple of charming toucans (which have the run of the place), it's an excellent choice. Rooms without private bath cost US$5 per person and breakfast is an additional US$1. A good alternative is *Residencial Ballivián* (☎ 321960), which has a lovely courtyard and comfortable rooms. Rooms cost US$4 per person without bath. If you believe the rumours, Ché Guevara once stayed here. According to one reader, 'it's like staying at your grandmother's house: tile floors, sagging beds, pitcher and washbasin, chamber pot...and the advice is free but unobtrusive. She advised me to get married and have at least one kid to pass on my name'.

The *Residencial Charcas* (☎ 349400), at Calle Camiri 171 near Mercado Siete Calles, is a good friendly choice. Singles/doubles without bath are US$6.20 and doubles with bath cost US$8.24.

Places to Stay – middle

Santa Cruz has a growing number of mid-range hotels, which are very reasonably priced and cater mainly to business travellers.

The very central *Hotel Bibosi* (☎ 348548, fax 348887), Calle Junín 218, has a cheery proprietor, clean, spacious rooms and a great rooftop view. Singles/doubles with fan, telephone, bath and breakfast cost US$15.50/25. Beside the Bibosi, at Calle Junín 214, is *Hotel Amazonas* (☎ 334583). Rooms with TV and private bath cost US$11.50/15.50.

The ultra-clean *Hotel Copacabana* (☎ 321845, fax 330757), at Junín 217 is showing signs of wear, but it's still good value at US$6.20/10 for rooms without bath and US$15.50/23 with bath (US$21/30 with air-con). The pleasant and centrally located *Hotel Italia* (☎ 323119), at Calle René Moreno 167, charges US$20/30 for rooms with air-con, TV, phones and hot showers.

The main plus at the *Hotel Viru Viru* (☎ 335298), at Junín 338, is its swimming pool. Singles/doubles with bath, TV and breakfast cost US$14.50/23 (US$18.50/29 with air-con). Another good-value place with a pool is the bright and friendly *Hotel La Siesta* (☎ 349775, fax 330146), at Calle Vallegrande 17, where rooms with breakfast cost US$12.50/19.

The *Hotel Felimar* (☎ 34667,; fax 323232), Calle Ayacucho 445, offers clean and carpeted singles/doubles with air-con and a buffet breakfast for US$20/27. At Calle Camiri 71, Gran Hotel Mediterráneo (☎ 338804, fax 361344), charges US$17.50/29 for rooms, with breakfast. Large family rooms accommodating four people are US$48.50.

Near the bus terminal, within a few metres of each other, are the fairly nice twin hotels, *Virgen de Cotoca* (☎ 333239) and *España* (☎ 330558), which are under the same management. Both charge US$13.50 for doubles with fan and bath.

Places to Stay – top end

The five-star *Hotel Los Tajibos* (☎ 421000, fax 426994) has a nightclub, swimming pools, a health club, racquetball courts, a casino, a massage parlour, fountains and tropical gardens. The major drawback is its distance from the centre, out on Avenida San Martín in Barrio Equipetrol (3rd anillo). Singles/doubles cost US$130/150 and non-smoking rooms are available.

Places to Eat

When it comes to culinary matters, cosmopolitan Santa Cruz won't disappoint. There are quite a few options and the food is generally of high quality, but at the better places prices are high.

For a simple and inexpensive breakfast, try the markets *La Ramada* and *Los Pozos*. The licuado de papaya or guineo con leche – puréed papaya or banana with milk, whipped in a blender and served cold – costs only US$0.40. It's hard to tear yourself away after only one glass! You'll also find meals during the day, but you may be put off by the heat around the cooking areas. Mercado Los Pozos is especially good for unusual tropical fruits; try some of the more exotic ones such as guaypurú and ambaiba. For inexpensive roast chicken, churrasco, chips and fried plantains, stroll down Avenida Cañoto (also known as Pollo Alley), where there are dozens of nearly identical grill restaurants. The *30 de Marzo* and *Pollos a la Leña* are recommended.

A popular spot for ice cream, sundaes, cakes, burgers and other light meals or just speciality coffee is the bright *Bar Hawai*, one block east of the plaza. Other choices include *Kivón*, at Ayacucho 267 and *Dumbo*, near Independencia and Ayacucho. *California Donuts*, at Calle Independencia 481, serves coffee, burgers and sticky doughnuts. The best chocolatier – and a testament to the city's cosmopolitan atmosphere – is *Confetti* at Calle René Moreno 184.

Inexpensive vegetarian almuerzos and dinners are served at *Restaurant Familiar Vegetariano*, Calle Velasco 225, and *Restaurant Vegetarianista* near the corner of Ayacucho and Cordillera Sara. The latter serves healthy almuerzos for US$1.75. The popular *La Pascana*, on the plaza, dishes up huge four-course meals (platos fuertes) for

US$4. Try the surubí à la thermidor for US$4.50.

The health food shop, *La Alternativa* (☎ 421238), at Antonio Vaca Diez 75, specialises in organically grown produce, juices, wholemeal bread, cakes, biscuits, yoghurt, natural medicines, textiles and candles, as well as advice on Bolivia's ecology movement and natural alternative lifestyles. For more mainstream – but not cheap – self-catering, try *Supermercado Santa Cruz* on the corner of Cuellar and 24 de Septiembre.

The popular *Pizzería Mama Rosa*, across from the plaza, offers good pizzas, chicken dishes, Mexican burgers, hot dogs and other meat dishes and fast foods. It's open daily from noon to midnight. Another plaza option, the quiet *Restaurant Plaza*, at Calle Libertad 116, is recommended for its soup and US$1.50 almuerzos. Other favourite lunch spots with locals include the *Galeón Peruano* and *La Olla Que Canta*, which are side by side on Calle Ingavi, near Calle España. They're always full and serve good food for very good prices. A four-course almuerzo at either costs US$1.60.

In the morning, *Café España*, near the corner of Calles Junín and 21 de Mayo, serves breakfasts, salteñas, empanadas and coffee. For lunch, you'll get four courses plus a soft drink for US$1.80. The *Burger House*, on Avenida Cristóbal de Mendoza 45 (2nd anillo), serves a range of burgers and sandwiches, including Swiss, English, Mexican and Italian.

The cosy Swiss/Bolivian-owned *Bar El Tapekuá* (☎ 343390), on the corner of Calles Ballivián and La Paz, serves pub meals from Wednesday to Saturday evenings. The musician owner appreciates good music, and from Thursday to Saturday there are live performances for a US$1 cover charge. Phone in advance to find out what's on.

La Bella Napoli, on Independencía in a rustic barn six blocks south of the plaza, serves fine pasta dishes – including ravioli, canelloni and lasagne – on chunky hardwood tables, but it's not cheap and it's a dark walk back to the centre at night.

An alternative for excellent Italian cuisine is *Michelangelo's* (☎ 348403), housed in a romantically dark, wooden home, complete with fireplaces and marble floors, at Calle Chuquisaca 102. There must be something about Italian Renaissance artists (or perhaps Ninja Turtles), because there's also *Leonardo's*, on Calle Warnes, where you can enjoy a cosy candlelit dinner in a beautiful old converted mansion.

The *Bicho Gustoso* (☎ 336181), on the 2nd anillo at Avenida Cristóbal de Mendoza 38, specialises in seafood and Brazilian cuisine, as well as Spanish and Italian dishes. Another fine place to splurge is *Crêperie El Boliche*, on Calle Arenales between Murillo and Beni. You can choose from crêpe dishes, salads, ice cream confections, cakes and cocktails for about US$11 per person. Tropical specialities from the Beni lowlands are the forte of the *Restaurant Bar Borjano* (☎ 424187), opposite the main entrance to the zoo.

A recommended fish restaurant is *El Pez Gordo* (☎ 361921) at Avenida Uruguay 783, near Suárez Arana (by the German cemetery, at the northern end of the 1st anillo). Opposite Parque El Arenal is the oddly named *Las Tres BBB*, which serves ceviche and other fish dishes. A third option for local fish dishes, including an excellent fish soup, is *El Surubí* (☎ 427884), on the 2nd anillo at Avenida Cristóbal de Mendoza 640.

If you're craving Mexican food, try *Tequila's Bar Restaurant* (☎ 432186), a midrange place at Cristóbal de Mendoza 605 (northern end of the 2nd anillo) or *Tacos Mexicanos*, at Avenida Argentina 377 in the 2nd anillo. Within walking distance of the centre, there's *Cactus* (☎ 336429) at Avenida Uruguay 642. The food is excellent and it's open daily for lunch and dinner. A fair attempt at Mexican food is *The Jungle*, at Calle Cordillera 346. It's open Tuesday to Sunday from 11 am to 2 pm and from 6.30 to 11.30 pm.

An unforgettable Japanese option – serving sushi, sashimi, tempura and a vast range of exceptional Japanese specialities – is *Yorimichi* (☎ 347717), at Avenida Busch 548. Although pricey, this place gets lots of votes (including mine) for the best restaurant in Santa Cruz. Bookings are recommended.

Steak is the speciality at *El Fogón* (☎ 329675), Avenida Viedma 436, and it is repeatedly recommended as being among the best for parrillada and other Argentine specialities. Meaty American cuisine, barbecue, apple pie and alcohol feature at *Bob's Place BBQ* (☎ 335451), Avenida Irala 333. Another recommended place for steak and salad is *El Cuadril* (☎ 340295) at Avenida Uruguay 454, about 20 minutes on foot from the plaza. *El Camba Futre* (☎ 424205), at Cristóbal de Mendoza 543, specialises in eastern Bolivian dishes, including majado de charque, ají de lengua, queperí and rapi al jugo. It isn't cheap, but you'll get a taste for local cuisine.

For Chinese, good choices include *El Mandarin* (☎ 348288), Calle Sucre 209; *Mandarin II* (☎ 335340), Avenida Irala 679; and *New Hong Kong* (☎ 328956) at Ballivián 131. Not far from the bus terminal, at Avenida Grigotá 37, *Churrasquería Asia* (☎ 533969) serves Chinese meals, and beef dishes with an Asian twist.

Entertainment

Pubs, Nightclubs & Discos A good source for the latest information on Santa Cruz night spots is the free booklet *Noche Cruceña*, which is published at Calle Vallegrande 15. You can pick it up there or at the tourist office.

Santa Cruz has a disproportionate number of discos and karaoke bars, which reflects the city's liberal, cosmopolitan character. Most night spots are outside the central area, so you'll need a taxi (US$1 to US$2). Cover charges start at about US$2; if you need to conserve funds, avoid the bar. Most places open at 9 pm but don't warm up until 11 pm, then continue until 3 am. For the younger set, the 'in' club at the moment seems to be *Palladium*, on the main drag in Barrio Equipetrol. *Club Chaplin*, on Calle Las Azucenas in Barrio Urbari is highly regarded by locals as both a comedy club and dinner venue.

SANTA CRUZ

One of the most pleasant drinking establishments is *Bar El Tapekuá* (☎ 343390) on the corner of Calles Ballivián and La Paz (see Places to Eat). *Picasso's* (☎ 349149) on Avenida Irala features a variety of live musical programmes, such as piano recitals, guitar music and jazz concerts. *La Cueva del Ratón* (☎ 326163), at Calle La Riva 173, is also relatively central and offers live music on most weekends.

There's also a clutch of trendy bars, nightclubs and karaoke venues with exotic names that attract the more affluent youth. Among them are *Tarousch*, on the corner of Avenida Irala and Calle Colón; *Bahamas*, at Avenida El Trompillo 645; and *Mauna Loa* – 'open the hole week', says the ad – which is known for high prices, weak drinks and kinky strip shows. The only *casino* is at Hotel Los Tajibos.

Cinema The city also has a number of cinemas, and the films are generally better than elsewhere in Bolivia. For schedules and venues, see the daily newspapers *El Deber* and *El Mundo*.

Things to Buy

There are artesanía shops scattered around town, where you can buy beautiful Western-style clothing made of llama and alpaca wool. Mercado Los Pozos is good for inexpensive basketry, but if you're after genuine indigenous articles, the Altiplano is a better area to look.

Woodcarvings made from the tropical hardwoods *morado* and *guayacán* are unique to the Santa Cruz area. Although morado is less expensive than guayacán, you'll still pay at least US$20 for a nice piece. Relief carvings on *tari* nuts are also interesting and make easily transportable souvenirs.

For those who love Jesuit mission artwork, you can commission a wonderful wooden angel carving, of the type seen in the mission churches. See Señora Ángela Muñoz at La Misión (☎ 328143), Calle René Moreno 60. They're not cheap – US$80 to US$100 each – but they're awesomely beautiful, hand-carved and painted by Chiquitanos Indians in the missions. Commissions take about a month.

Local Indians also make beautiful macramé *llicas*, bags of root fibres. Santa Cruz leatherwork is expert, but unfortunately most items are adorned with kitsch designs and slogans. There are also some lovely ceramic pieces for sale, but they're difficult to transport.

Getting There & Away

Air Viru-Viru international airport, 15 km north of the centre, handles domestic and international flights. Both LAB (☎ 344411), on the corner of Warnes and Chuquisaca, and AeroSur (☎ 364446), on the corner of Calle Colón and Avenida Irala, have daily services to Cochabamba (US$53), La Paz (US$90.50), Sucre (US$41), Trinidad (US$56.50) and most other Bolivian cities.

LAB also has international services to Manaus, São Paulo, Belo Horizonte, Rio de Janeiro, Caracas, Panama City and Miami; VARIG (☎ 346994), Calle Junín 284, has flights to Rio de Janeiro and São Paulo; American Airlines (☎ 341314), Calle Beni 202, flies to Miami; and Aerolíneas Argentinas (☎ 339776), Plaza 24 de Septiembre, flies to Buenos Aires. LAB also connects Santa Cruz to Lima (Peru), and Arica and Santiago (Chile), all via La Paz.

AeroSur flies daily and LAB flies on Monday, Wednesday and Friday to Puerto Suárez (US$86), opposite Corumbá (Brazil). These flights let you avoid the uncertainties of rail travel to Brazil, but they fill up quickly, so book as far ahead as possible.

Bus The long-distance bus terminal is on the corner of Avenidas Cañoto and Irala. There are plenty of daily services to Cochabamba (US$7, 12 hours), from where you'll find easy connections to La Paz, Oruro, Sucre, Potosí and even Tarija. Most flotas offer both morning and evening services to Cochabamba.

Several companies offer a direct service to Sucre (that is, they don't pass through Cochabamba) in the afternoon on Monday,

Wednesday and Saturday (US$8). From Sucre, lots of buses continue to Potosí. Most services to Camiri and Yacuiba depart about mid-afternoon. Buses to Comarapa and Vallegrande leave in the morning and afternoon; for example, Transportes Señor de los Milagros has departures at 9.30 am and 2 and 6 pm.

Flota Chiquitano leaves nightly at 7 pm for San Ramón, San Javier, Concepción, Santa Rosa de la Roca and San Ignacio. The trip takes 10 hours and costs US$10.50. On Saturday, it continues to San Miguel, which costs an additional US$1. To San Matías, Flota Transical Velasco leaves daily in the evening from its Calle Velasco terminal, two blocks north of Avenida Irala.

To Trinidad and beyond, a number of nightly buses leave between 5.30 and 7 pm (US$8, 12 hours). Although the road is theoretically open year-round, at least to Trinidad, the trip gets rough in the rainy season. Flota Trans-Tropico can get you all the way to San Borja (US$19), Rurrenabaque (US$23), Reyes (US$25), Santa Rosa (US$27), Riberalta (US$31) and Guayaramerín (US$33).

BALUT has international services to Chile and Argentina, and in the dry season both Flota Santa Ana and STEL Turismo have services to Asunción via the infamous Chaco road.

Smaller micros and *trufis* to Viru-Viru (the international airport), Montero (with connections to Buena Vista, Yapacaní and Okinawa), Cotoca, San Juan, Limoncito, La Angostura, Samaipata, Mairana, Comarapa, Siberia and other communities in Santa Cruz department also depart regularly from, or near, the main terminal.

Camión Camiones to Cochabamba depart from Avenida Grigotá, near the 3rd anillo, and some cargo traffic still uses the old road via Samaipata and Siberia. Alternatively, take micro 17 to the *tranca* 12 km west of town where all traffic must stop. You'll pay from US$2 to US$4 for the 16-hour trip. Be prepared with warm clothing!

Train The new railway station, on Avenida Brasil just inside the 3rd anillo, is only 10 minutes from the centre on micro 12 or 13; you can catch them on Avenida Cañoto near the bus terminal, or along Calle Sucre. The Red Oriental (eastern network) is comprised of two railway lines: one to Quijarro on the Brazilian border, and another to Yacuiba on the Argentine border.

In spite of the sparkling new station, Bolivian rail travel still has its quirks. At the time of writing, rail tickets could only be purchased on the day of departure. Whatever anyone tells you about the ticket window at the station, it keeps no specific hours and it's unlikely to open before 8 am. There are still tense queues for seats, and securing tickets may involve some unpleasant elbowing. For Bracha tickets (US$21 to Quijarro, including meals), go to the office at Calle Florida 11, on the corner of 24 de Septiembre.

When demand is high, tickets can be hard to come by and carriages may be so crowded with people and luggage that there's no room to sit anyway. It's wise to chain and padlock your luggage to the racks, especially at night. The alternative to fighting for a ticket is to stake out a place in the *bodegas* (boxcars) and purchase a 2nd-class ticket from the acrobatic conductor for 20% more than the ticket window price.

To Argentina The *ferrobus* to Yacuiba (US$18.50/15.50 in 1st/2nd class) leaves Santa Cruz on Wednesday at 7 pm and Yacuiba on Friday at 5 pm. The *tren rápido* (US$12.80/10.70) runs on Monday and Friday at 3.40 pm from Santa Cruz, and the *tren mixto* (US$14.60/12.40) on Wednesday and Sunday at 8.30 am. From Santa Cruz to Yacuiba, the bodegas are empty, but on the return they're brimming with Argentine goods and aren't as comfortable.

To Brazil The rough and ready railway line between Santa Cruz and Quijarro accommodates the affectionately named Death Train, which at times leaps around on the tracks like a bucking bronco. The line passes through soya plantations, lowland forest, scrubland

SANTA CRUZ

and oddly shaped mountains on its way to the steamy, sticky Pantanal on the frontier.

Highlights of the trip include the long bridge over the Río Grande. As the train from the frontier chugs into the outskirts of Santa Cruz, it's interesting to watch passengers jettison hundreds of baskets, parcels and boxes of contraband from the train, to be retrieved by friends waiting with vehicles alongside the tracks just prior to arrival – and customs inspections – at the station.

Carry enough mosquito repellent for coping with long and unexplained stops in low-lying, swampy areas. A pleasant place to break the 16 to 20-hour journey is at San José de Chiquitos (see the Eastern Lowlands chapter), but getting an onward ticket may be problematic.

The optimistically named *Expreso del Oriente* leaves on Monday, Wednesday and Friday at 1.50 pm eastbound and on Tuesday, Thursday and Saturday at 1.45 pm westbound (US$20.50/17 in 1st/2nd class). It also carries the Bracha carriage (US$25), which may be booked through Santa Cruz travel agencies or through Bracha offices in Santa Cruz and La Paz (see Train in the Getting Around chapter). The tren rápido (US$16.70/14.50 in 1st/2nd class) runs on Tuesday and Sunday at 1.50 pm eastbound and Monday and Thursday at 1.45 pm westbound. The tren mixto (US$12.50 in 2nd class) runs Monday and Friday at 9.15 am eastbound and on Tuesday and Saturday at 6.30 pm westbound. Freight trains pulling at least one open boxcar at the end may run at any time on any day, and cost US$12.50.

Taxis from Quijarro to the Brazilian border (US$1 per person), two km away, meet arriving trains. You can change dollars or bolivianos into *reais* (pronounced 'hey-ICE') on the Bolivian side, but the boliviano rate is poor. Note that there's no Brazilian consulate in Quijarro, so if you need a visa, pick it up in Santa Cruz. Officially, yellow fever certificates are required to enter Brazil from Bolivia.

Getting Around
The Airport The frequent minibus service

from the Viru-Viru terminal costs US$0.75 and takes half an hour. Taxis for up to four people cost US$4. This airport has been notorious for drug-related activities, but the city is now trying to improve its image.

Bus There is a good system of city micros connecting the transportation terminals and all the anillos with the centre. The fare is US$0.17 (B$0.80) per ride. Micros and colectivos to small towns around Santa Cruz leave from the north end of the bus terminal.

Taxi Generally, Santa Cruz taxis are slightly more expensive than in highland Bolivia. The official rate is US$0.50 (B$2.50) to anywhere in the 1st anillo and US$1 (B$5) to the 2nd anillo, including the railway station. If you have several people or lots of luggage, however, drivers may expect up to 50% more.

You can hire private long-distance taxis to sites of interest around Santa Cruz from City Tours Santa Cruz (☎ 537332), 3rd anillo interno s/n, opposite Comercio Chiriguano. Some sample fares for up to four people are: Cotoca (US$15), Samaipata (US$70), Vallegrande (US$160), Yapacaní (US$80), Los Espejillos (US$60) and the Dunas de Palmar (US$30).

Around Santa Cruz

DUNAS DE PALMAR
These large sand dunes, 16 km (about 45 minutes) south of Santa Cruz on the road to Palmasola, are popular on weekends. The largest is Loma Chivato. There's an artificial lake and freshwater lagoons where locals swim, picnic and ride motorcycles. There are plans to improve the road and build facilities at the site but, as yet, nothing has happened.

Getting There & Away
Take the micro marked 'Palmar' from the corner of Avenidas Grigotá and Cañoto in

Santa Cruz and get off at the turn-off for 'las lomas de arena'. From there, it's an eight-km walk along a 4WD track to the dunes, but if you go on Sunday, there's a good chance of catching a lift. Alternatively, you can go with City Tours Santa Cruz (☎ 537332) for US$30 for up to four people. If you're driving, you'll need 4WD.

COTOCA

In the mid-1700s, two woodsmen discovered a miraculous image in a tree trunk 20 km east of Santa Cruz by. In 1799, in honour of this image, an opulent church was constructed. Each year on 8 December, the Virgin's discovery is celebrated in the Fiesta de la Virgen de Cotoca, which draws thousands of pilgrims from Bolivia and beyond. At this time, Santa Cruz residents who are grateful for answers to special petitions customarily walk to the shrine overnight from Santa Cruz.

The telephone code for Cotoca is 0388.

Getting There & Away

Micros leave for Cotoca approximately every 10 minutes from the El Deber building, on the corner of Oruro and Suárez Arana in Santa Cruz. The trip takes 35 minutes.

PUERTO PAILAS

Puerto Pailas, 40 minutes along the railway line east of Santa Cruz, is the base of operations for a growing Sikh colony, which is building a temple amid agricultural and reforestation projects. The areas near the railway line could win international competitions for the volume of trash on the ground – the streets are literally paved with plastic bags. It's truly a sight to behold.

Puerto Pailas lacks any sort of tourist infrastructure, but private accommodation is available for about US$1 per person. On Sunday they stage horse races at 5 pm.

Getting There & Away

From Santa Cruz, you can ride the train to

SANTA CRUZ

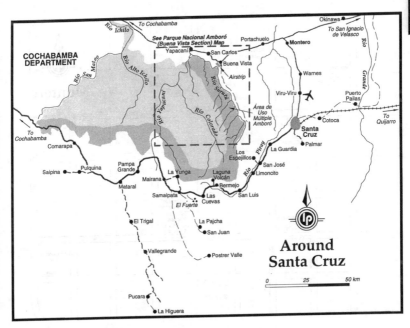

Around Santa Cruz

Puerto Pailas or take a camión from Cotoca or the micro (US$0.30) from in front of the El Deber building on the corner of Oruro and Suárez Arana.

MONTERO

The rapidly growing community of Montero, named after the Independence war hero General Marceliano Montero, sprawls across the flat agricultural lands north of Santa Cruz. Its immediate surroundings are planted with bananas, sugar cane and rice. Soybeans, sesame and peanuts, which are used to produce vegetable oils, are also cultivated. With a population of 60,000, it's one of the largest cities in the Bolivian lowlands.

The telephone code for Montero is 092.

Market

The market in Montero defies description, but I'll try. It is surely the filthiest in Bolivia and if the trash, insects and discarded animal parts don't make you retch, the sewage, dogs and festering stagnant water will. Keep clear unless you just want the experience of seeing something so revolting.

Places to Stay & Eat

Accommodation is in basic alojamientos which cost about 60% of what you would pay for equivalent places in Santa Cruz. Alojamientos *Central*, *Tarija*, *Bolívar* and *Tropical* are all marked on the map. The Central appears to be clean and pleasant. Near here is a self-service laundrette, which is useful considering that clothing hung out in this humid climate normally sours before it's dry. There's also the new and recommended *Alojamiento Pinocho* (☎ 20305), which has singles/doubles with air-con, TV and private bath for US$9/12.

There are several cubbyhole restaurants serving Bolivian standards. *Pollo Paté*, on Calle Florida, does chicken and chips, and you can get ice cream and snacks at *Heladería Dany* and *Kivón* on the main

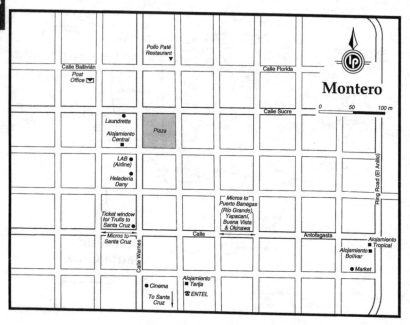

Montero

plaza. If nothing seems appealing, go to the market where you'll lose your appetite altogether!

Getting There & Away

Micros and trufis (US$1) leave for Montero from the Santa Cruz bus terminal every 10 minutes, and transport back to Santa Cruz queues up two blocks south of the plaza, on Calle Antofagasta. Along the route from Santa Cruz, note the sculpture of the man with an ox-drawn banana cart in the roundabout in Warnes. It's known fittingly as *El Carretero*.

Micros to Puerto Banegas, Yapacaní, Buena Vista, Okinawa and other villages also leave from Calle Antofagasta, four blocks west of the market.

OKINAWA

Okinawa, the Japanese rice-growing colony north-east of Montero makes an interesting excursion. This colony is comprised mainly of Japanese immigrants who arrived after WWII and received 50 hectares each from the government for opening up the then inhospitable eastern lowlands. Farming equipment was provided by the US government. Unfortunately, recent competition from big agrobusinesses has meant a decline in smaller farms and the colony is on the wane as settlers migrate in search of greener pastures.

The Okinawa turn-off, north of Montero, is marked by an enormous Japanese-style parasol. Near Okinawa is Puerto Banegas, on the Río Grande. When the water level is high, it may be possible to catch a boat from here to Trinidad, but it's not a well-established cargo route. Micros between Montero and either Okinawa or Puerto Banegas cost US$1.

YAPACANÍ

Another possible destination is the bridge over the Río Yapacaní, 85 km from Montero on the new Cochabamba road. Along the river is a row of haphazardly built eating establishments serving surubí and other fresh fish from the river. Sadly, they also cook up more exotic species like *jochi* (agouti) and *tatu* (armadillo). These places are normally washed away by flooding in the rainy season and must be rebuilt each year, so you probably won't have much luck between November and March.

BUENA VISTA

Buena Vista, two hours north-west of Santa Cruz, makes an ideal staging point for trips into the forested lowland section of Parque Nacional Amboró.

Information

For information on Parque Nacional Amboró, visit the BID office (☎ 2032), in the large compound 1½ blocks south of the plaza. Here you can book park *cabañas* for US$2 per person per day and hire guides into the park for about US$5 per day.

For their guests, Hotel Amboró and Residencial Nadia also provide reliable park information.

The telephone code for Buena Vista is 0932.

Iglesia de los Santos Desposorios

The Jesuit mission of Buena Vista was founded in 1694 as La Misión de los Desposorios de San José, the fifth mission in the Viceroyalty of Perú. The need for a church was recognised and 29 years later, after a search for a high-standing location with sufficient water and potential crop land, the first building was finally constructed.

By late 1750, 700 Chiraguano Indians had been converted to Christianity and the Swiss Jesuit missionary and architect Padre Martin Schmid saw the need for a new church. In 1767, the current structure was completed. When the Jesuits were expelled from Bolivia later that year, the administration passed to the Bishop of Santa Cruz.

Although the building is now deteriorating, it has a lovely classic form and merits a quick visit. During Buena Vista's tricentennial celebrations in 1994, plans were announced to establish a church museum.

Río Surutú & Santa Bárbara

Río Surutú is a popular excursion for locals. There's a pleasant sandy beach ideal for picnics, swimming and camping during the dry season. From Buena Vista, it's an easy three-km walk to the river bend nearest town. The opposite bank is the boundary of Parque Nacional Amboró.

A good longer option is the six-hour circuit walk through the community of Santa Bárbara, which takes you through pleasant and partially forested tropical plantation country. From Buena Vista, follow the unpaved road to Santa Bárbara and ask there for the Ucurutú track, which leads to a lovely river beach on the Río Ucurutú. After a picnic and a dip, you can return to Buena Vista via the Huaytú road.

Special Events

The local fiesta, the Día de los Santos Desposorios, which features bullfights, food stalls and general merrymaking, starts on 26 October. There's also a Rice Festival that takes place in early May, following the rice harvest.

Places to Stay & Eat

If you want a couple of days relaxation, you can't beat the friendly *Hotel Amboró* (☎ & fax 2054), Casilla 2097, Santa Cruz, about two km south-west of Buena Vista. It enjoys a lush setting on a ridge overlooking Parque Nacional Amboró and is home to a variety of tropical vegetation and birdlife. Rooms with private bath and hot water cost US$20 per person for bed and breakfast, and US$30 per

person with a hearty full board (reduced rates are available for groups and long stays). Meals feature sushi and Indian, Thai and Brazilian specialities; for nonguests, they cost US$2 each. Camping is also possible. There's no sign for Hotel Amboró, so either phone for directions from the ENTEL office in Buena Vista or find a motorcycle taxi from the main plaza. Beware of people who offer informal accommodation and claim to be from Hotel Amboró!

More basic accommodation is available in Buena Vista itself for US$2.70 per person at *Residencial Nadia* (☎ 2049), Calle Mariano Sancedo Sevilla 180. The owner is a former park ranger and a good source of information on Amboró.

Things to Buy

For a typical souvenir, go to the Jipijapa shop, a block west of the plaza, which sells creations – lampshades, handbags, boxes, panama hats etc – made from *jipijapa*, the fronds of the cyclanthaceae fan palm *(Carludovica palmata)*.

Getting There & Away

Shared taxis from Santa Cruz cost US$3 per person to either Buena Vista or Yapacaní. They leave from behind the long-distance bus terminal. You can also take a micro from Santa Cruz to Montero and there change to a Buena Vista micro.

PARQUE NACIONAL Y ÁREA DE USO MÚLTIPLE AMBORÓ

The 430,000-hectare Amboró National Park lies in a unique geographic position at the confluence of three distinct ecosystems: the Amazon Basin, the northern Chaco and the Andes. The park was originally created in 1973 as the Reserva de Vida Silvestre Germán Busch, with an area of just 180,000 hectares. In 1984, thanks to the efforts of British ornithologist Robin Clarke and Bolivian biologist Noel Kempff Mercado, it was given national park status and in 1990 was expanded to 630,000 hectares. In late 1995, however, amid controversy surrounding *campesino* colonisation inside park boundaries, it was pared down to its current size (see the Struggle for Amboró aside).

Its range of habitats means that both highland and lowland species are found here. All species native to Amazonia, except those of the Beni savannas, are represented, including the spectacled bear, which is now close to extinction. Jaguars, capybaras, river otters, agoutis, tapirs, deer, peccaries and various monkeys still exist in relatively large numbers, and over 700 species of birds have been identified. The unfortunately tasty mutún *(Mitu tuberosa)*, or razor-billed curassow, is still native to the area, and even rare quetzals have been spotted. The park is also one of the only remaining habitats of the rare and endangered blue-horned curassow *(Crax unicornis)*, also known as the unicorn bird.

Buena Vista Area

The BID office is at Buena Vista. Here, you can collect information, book cabañas, hire guides and organise transport to the park perimeter.

Access to the eastern part of the Área de Uso Múltiple Amboró requires a crossing

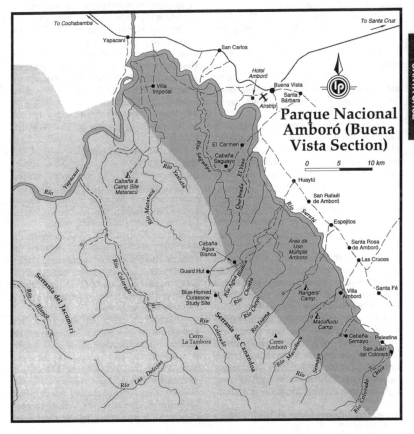

Parque Nacional Amboró (Buena Vista Section)

over the Río Surutú, either in a vehicle or on foot. Depending on the rainfall and weather, the river may be anywhere from knee to waist-deep.

Río Macuñucu The Río Macuñucu route is the most popular into the Área de Uso Múltiple, and begins at Las Cruces, 35 km south-east of Buena Vista. From there, it's six or seven km to the Río Surutú, where you must drive or wade across. Just beyond the opposite bank you'll reach the village of Villa Amboró. Here you'll pick up a track that continues several km through the trees and homesteads and past a few cattle gates to the banks of the Río Macuñucu.

Four km farther upstream is the *Macuñucu rangers' camp*, which has a sleeping loft costing US$2 per day, including the use of rudimentary cooking facilities. The main camp activity is sitting beside the river and waiting for wildlife to wander past. Jaguar and puma tracks are frequently seen along the riverbank, but large cats are rarely observed.

The track continues upriver through thick forest for about two hours, then disappears into the river course. Continue upstream another hour or so, hopping over river stones past beautiful red rocks, cliffs and overhangs. Beyond a particularly narrow canyon, which confines hikers to the river, you'll reach a large rock overhang accommodating up to 10 campers. If you have a tent, the sandy river beaches also make pleasant camp sites.

At this point, the upriver walk becomes increasingly difficult and entails negotiating some large and slippery river boulders and scrambling past obstructing landslides. Several hours of heavy slogging upstream from the cave is a nice waterfall and another potential camp site. The very daring can continue the increasingly treacherous boulder hopping to more overhangs farther upstream. The terrain becomes increasingly rugged, so a guide is recommended for overnight or extended trips above the waterfall.

Río Isama & Cerro Amboró The Río Isama route turns off at the village of Espejitos, 28 km from Buena Vista, and provides access to the base of 1300m Cerro Amboró, the bulbous peak for which the park is named. It's possible to climb to the summit, but it's a difficult trek and a guide is essential.

Upper Saguayo The objective of this route is the study site on the upper Río Saguayo, where researchers rediscovered the rare blue-horned curassow, once thought to be extinct. It's very rough going in places – in fact, it may well be overgrown by the time you read this – so prospective hikers need a guide and a good machete. Without a 4WD to take you to the end of the motorable track, the return trip requires about five days.

The hike begins at the mouth of the Río Chonta. To get there, drive or take the micro 23 km to Huaytú, south-east of Buena Vista. Here, turn right (south-west) and continue five km to the Río Surutú. In the dry season, you can ford the river by vehicle or on foot. From the opposite bank, it's 12 km along the 4WD track to the end of the motorable track at the ranch belonging to Don Arnaldo Hurtado.

From the ranch, keep going a short distance along the track to the Agua Blanca cabaña, watching along the way for herons, toucans, parrots, kingfishers and other colourful birds. If the route to the study site proves impassable, this makes a pleasant base for a couple of days exploring.

Beyond the cabaña, the track crosses the 'red line', the new boundary between the Área de Uso Múltiple and the Parque Nacional Amboró, and descends through thick forest to the Río Saguayo. On the bluff above the opposite bank is an abandoned guard hut and a viable camp site.

Alternatively, after an hour from Don Hurtado's ranch, watch for a dim path leading off to the right. If it isn't totally overgrown, it will also take you to the guard hut, passing first through mixed forest and overgrown fields. Just beyond a derelict house is a large area of *curichi* marsh, which is home to the *tojo*, or yellow-rumped cacique *(Cacicus cela)*, whose bizarre cry sounds remarkably like a manual cash register ringing up a purchase.

If you do get as far as the guard hut, look for a trail heading upstream. Under optimum conditions, it entails boulder hopping and wading, but at last report, one critical section which detoured around a particularly deep river pool was overgrown and impassable, so this is probably as far as you'll go.

If the way has been cleared again, you can also explore distracting side trips up clear streams and observe an amazing variety of birdlife: tanagers, orpendolas (blackbirds), honeycreepers, hummingbirds, warblers, herons and a host of others. After about five hours, you'll reach the abandoned hut which served as the research base for the blue-horned curassow, but you'll need a great deal of luck to see one. This is also ideal habitat for the colourful military macaw.

The downhill return to the road is the same way you came; on foot, this takes about two days from the research camp and one long day from the Cabaña Agua Blanca.

Mataracú From near Yapacaní, on the main Cochabamba road, a 4WD track heads south across the Río Yapacaní into the northern reaches of the Área de Uso Múltiple Amboró and after about 18 rough km, rolls up to the Mataracú cabaña and camp site. This is the only Amboró cabaña accessible by motor vehicle. Naturally, it can also be reached on foot. Except in the driest part of the year, however, crossing the Río Yapacaní may be a problem.

Samaipata Area

Samaipata (see the Around Santa Cruz map) sits outside the southern boundary of the Área de Uso Múltiple Amboró, and is the best access point for the Andean section of

SANTA CRUZ

The Struggle for Amboró

The location of Parque Nacional Amboró is a mixed blessing; although it's conveniently accessible to visitors, it also lies practically within spitting distance of Santa Cruz, Bolivia's second-largest city, and squarely between the old and new Cochabamba-Santa Cruz highways. At a time when even the remote parks of the Amazon Basin are coming under threat, this puts Amboró in an especially vulnerable position.

The first human settlers in the area were Chiriguano and Yuracare Indians, who occupied the lowlands, while Altiplano peoples, such as the Aymara, probably settled parts of the highland areas. Although agriculture was introduced after the arrival of the Spanish in the late 16th century, the remote Amboró region remained untouched until the late 20th century, when unemployed opportunity seekers began migrating from the highlands in search of land.

When Parque Nacional Amboró was created in 1973, its charter included a clause forbidding settlement and resource exploitation. Unfortunately for naturalists and conservationists, hunters, loggers and campesino settlers continue to pour in – many of them displaced from the Chapare region by the US Drug Enforcement Agency – and the north-eastern area is already settled, cultivated and hunted out. For poor farmers, cultivation practices have changed little since the 1500s and slash and burn agriculture is still the prevailing method.

Although FAN has attempted to train committed *guardaparques* (rangers) and educate people about the values of wilderness, more land is lost every year and the future of Parque Nacional Amboró is far from certain. In 1995, conflicts between colonists and authorities heated up and, as a result, the park was informally redefined to include only land which lay 400m beyond the most remote cultivated field, effectively shrinking the protected area by about 200,000 hectares.

In July of the same year, campesinos pressing for official recognition of their rights to occupy the land prevented tourists and researchers from entering the park. The following October, with regional elections coming up, the government abandoned the struggle and issued an official decree reducing the park by over 200,000 hectares. The decommissioned area was then redesignated as the Área de Uso Múltiple Amboró, which effectively opens it up for agriculture, settlement, mineral exploration and timber extraction. The affected portion includes a band across the southern area from Comarapa to Samaipata, all of the eastern bit up to the headwaters of the Surutú tributaries, and parts of the far north. ■

the former park. There's really no infrastructure, and public facilities and walking tracks are still in the planning stages.

To visit the area, pass by the FAN office in Samaipata to radio the park guards and let them know you're coming. They're normally happy to act as guides for a day or so, but your visit will be limited by their schedules.

The road uphill from Samaipata ends at a small cabin, and from there, it's a four-hour walk to a camping spot near the boundary between the primary forest and the Andean cloud forest. From this point, you can continue an hour farther into the park, but you'll need a guide and a good machete.

If you can't find a guide, a recommended two-day walk is the 23-km traverse between Samaipata and Mairana via the hamlet of La Yunga. Most of the route is depicted on the IGM 1:50,000 topo sheet *Mairana – 6839-IV*. Samaipata appears at the northern edge of *Samaipata – 6839-III*.

For more information, see Organised Tours in the Samaipata section later in this chapter.

Mairana Area

From Mairana, it's seven km uphill along a walking track to the hamlet of La Yunga, where there's a guest hut owned by FAN. It sits in a particularly lush region of the Área de Uso Múltiple Amboró, surrounded by tree ferns and other cloud forest vegetation. From La Yunga, a 16-km forest traverse connects with the main road near Samaipata.

To enter the park here, visit the guard post at the south end of the football ground in La Yunga. Access to Mairana is by micro or camión from Santa Cruz or Samaipata.

Comarapa Area

Four km north-west of the town of Comarapa (ie towards Cochabamba) is a little-used entrance to the Área de Uso Múltiple Amboró. After the road crosses a pass between a hill and a ridge with a telephone tower, look for the minor road turning off to the north-east (right) at the hamlet of Khara Huasi. This road leads uphill to verdant

stands of cloud forest, which blanket the peaks.

Other worthwhile visits in this area include the 36-sided Pukhara de Tuquipaya, a set of pre-Inca ruins on the summit of Cerro Comanwara, 1.5 km from Comarapa; and the colonial village of Pulquina Arriba, several km east of Comarapa.

Organised Tours

For a list of companies running guided excursions into the park, see Organised Tours in the Santa Cruz section. Alternatively, speak with the people at Hotel Amboró in Buena Vista, who occasionally run their own trips.

Places to Stay

Inside the park, you'll find five wilderness *cabañas* you can rent for US$2 per person

Blue-horned currassow

per day. They're very basic, so you'll need your own sleeping bag. The most popular and accessible cabaña is the one on the Río Macuñucu. Others are found on the lower Río Semayo, above the Río Mataracú, on the Río Agua Blanca, and on the lower Río Saguayo. For bookings and information, see the BID office in Buena Vista.

Getting There & Away
Every morning a bus heads south from Buena Vista, running beside the Río Surutú, which forms Amboró's eastern boundary. This boundary provides access to several rough routes and tracks which lead southwest into the interior, following tributaries of the Río Surutú: the Quebrada El Yeso, and the Ríos Agua Blanca/Chonta/Cheyo, Isama, Macuñucu, Semayo and Colorado Chico. Note that all access to the park along this road will require a crossing of the Río Surutú.

SANTA CRUZ TO SAMAIPATA
Los Espejillos
Los Espejillos is a popular retreat 26 km west of Santa Cruz. Its name, which means 'the little mirrors', is derived from the surrounding smooth black rock, polished by a small mountain river. The site, which features cascades and refreshing swimming holes, lies across the Río Piray about six km north of the highway.

Catch any micro or trufi going towards Santiago del Torno, Limoncito, La Angostura or Samaipata, and get off just beyond the village of San José. From here, Los Espejillos is a six-km walk or hitch, north along the 4WD track. Saturday and Sunday are the best days for catching lifts from the turn-off.

Bermejo
Bermejo, about 85 km south-west of Santa Cruz on the Samaipata road, is marked by a hulking slab of red rock known as Cueva de los Monos, which is flaking and chipping into nascent natural arches.

Laguna Volcán
The intriguing crater lake, Laguna Volcán, lies six km uphill to the north of Bermejo. It was once a popular stopover for migrating ducks, but in the late 1980s it was purchased by a *cruceño* who cleared all the vegetation around it and consequently banished the wildlife as well. It makes a pleasant walk from the highway. Coming from Santa Cruz, take a micro or trufi towards Samaipata and get off one km beyond Bermejo; the route is signposted.

Las Cuevas
Las Cuevas is 100 km south-west of Santa Cruz. If you walk upstream on a clear path for about 15 minutes, you'll reach two lovely waterfalls which spill into eminently swimmable lagoons bordered by sandy beaches. It's a touch of paradise.

SAMAIPATA
The village of Samaipata, at 1660m in the foothills of the Cordillera Oriental, is a popular weekend destination for cruceños and a great place to hole up for a couple of days. This quiet village has also attracted a few foreign settlers and lowland Bolivians, and a cosmopolitan society is developing. If you're coming from the lowlands, it's also a good place to begin acclimatisation by degrees. The main attraction is the pre-Inca ceremonial site of El Fuerte, 10 km east of the village (see Around Samaipata).

Samaipata is one of the few places where the guerrilla band of Ché Guevara actually had a taste of revolutionary success. On 6 July 1967, three months before their leader's death, the band rolled into town in a lorry they'd stopped on the highway. In his journals, Ché recounts:

The men went in...to Samaipata, where they captured two soldiers and the chief of the post, Lieutenant Vacaflor. The sergeant was forced to give the password and a lightning action captured the post with its ten soldiers after a brief exchange of fire with a soldier who resisted. They succeeded in taking five Mausers and one ZB30 and drove away with the ten prisoners, leaving them naked one km from Samaipata...The

SANTA CRUZ

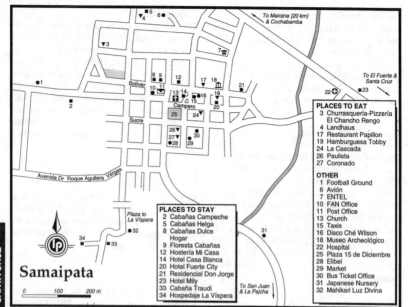

Samaipata

PLACES TO EAT
3 Churrasquería-Pizzería
   El Chancho Rengo
4 Landhaus
17 Restaurant Papillon
19 Hamburguesa Tobby
24 La Cascada
26 Paulista
27 Coronado

OTHER
1 Football Ground
6 Avión
7 ENTEL
10 FAN Office
11 Post Office
13 Church
15 Taxis
16 Disco Ché Wilson
18 Museo Archeológico
22 Hospital
25 Plaza 15 de Diciembre
28 Elibel
29 Market
30 Bus Ticket Office
31 Japanese Nursery
32 Mahikari Luz Divina

PLACES TO STAY
2 Cabañas Campeche
5 Cabañas Helga
8 Cabañas Dulce
   Hogar
9 Floresta Cabañas
12 Hostería Mi Casa
14 Hotel Casa Blanca
20 Hotel Fuerte City
21 Residencial Don Jorge
23 Hotel Mily
33 Cabaña Traudi
34 Hospedaje La Víspera

0   100   200 m

action took place in front of the whole town and a group of travellers, so the news will spread like wildfire.

Information

For information and route advice on Parque Nacional Amboró, try the FAN office one block from the church.

The post office in Samaipata only delivers mail; they can't accept outgoing post (and if they did, it would probably never be heard from again). The telephone code for Samaipata is 0944.

Museo Arqueológico

Samaipata's small archaeological museum makes an interesting visit, but it offers little explanation of the El Fuerte site. It does have a few Tiahuanaco artefacts and some local pottery. It's open daily from 9 am to noon and 2.30 to 6.30 pm. Admission is US$1.

Japanese Nursery

The Japanese nursery on the hillside above Samaipata has beautiful Japanese gardens, and many varieties of vegetables and flowers are grown here. The two friendly Japanese families living at the nursery are pleased to show visitors around their projects.

On the hill, along the road towards Hospedaje La Víspera, the Japanese religious sect Mahikari grows and sells fresh vegetables. For US$1, you can be blessed with the 'energy' of the Mahikari Luz Divina (divine light).

Organised Tours

The Hospedaje La Víspera (☎ & fax 6082) runs several exciting adventure tours into wonderfully remote places south of Samaipata. One is the alternative 'back route' trek to the El Fuerte ruins, which includes a six-hour walk and a refreshing dip in a mountain stream, as well as a guided tour of the ruins and vehicle transport back to Samaipata. The cost per group of up to four or five people is US$75.

Another option is a return-trip horseback tour from Samaipata through San Juan del Rosario, La Pajcha, Postrer Valle, Tierras Nuevas, La Ladera, Quirusillas (where there's a nice mountain lake), Hierbas Buenas, Valle Abajo and back to Samaipata. The route passes through some lovely mountain country, and part of it runs along pre-Hispanic paving. The per person price depends on the size of the group, but the average charge for this week-long trip, including horses, camping equipment, food and guides, is US$500 per person with three or more people. If you wish to do this circuit route as a walking trek (about 10 days), La Víspera offers advice and maps for US$10, and also hires out camping and cooking equipment. Tents cost US$5 per day.

A four-day variation follows part of this route to Vallegrande (in the footsteps of Ché Guevara), with a rest day in Vallegrande and vehicle transport back to Samaipata. This option costs US$250 per person with three or more people.

Places to Stay

Camping Bolivia's leap into European style camping begins at *Achira Kamping* at Km 112, eight km east of Samaipata. It has cabañas, camp sites, baths, showers and washing sinks, as well as a social hall with a restaurant and games room. Contact the Achira Sierra Resort (☎ 522288), Urbari Racquet Club, Barrio Urbari, 506 Calle Igmiri 590, Santa Cruz. More basic camping is available at the secluded *Mama Pasquala's*, set in a beautiful valley around some great swimming holes. It lies 500m upstream from the river crossing en route to El Fuerte. Camp sites/cabañas cost US$1/2 per person.

Self-Contained Cabañas & Guesthouses

A quiet and relaxing choice is the *Hospedaje La Víspera*, on an experimental biological farm 800m from the plaza. The Dutch owners rent horses (US$5 an hour or US$25

a day) and organise trips (see Organised Tours earlier in this section), and guests can arrange to be picked up from the centre in the Eco-Movil, a horse-drawn cart made by Mennonites. The self-contained guesthouse, which accommodates up to 15 people, is clean and warm, and enjoys a commanding view across the valley. On weekdays/weekends, it costs US$26/37 for up to six people, plus US$4 for each additional person. Book through Tropical Tours (☎ 361428) in Santa Cruz. When there's space, they'll accept backpackers for US$6 per person. Bring a torch (flashlight), as there's no street lighting between the village and the guesthouse.

More upmarket is the tasteful *Cabañas Helga* (☎ 6033), behind the Restaurant Landhaus near the landmark *avión* (aeroplane), on the hill. Each cabaña has cooking and bathroom facilities, and accommodates up to five people in two bedrooms, making it ideal for families. Used as doubles, the cabañas cost US$30; with five people, they're US$45.

Hotels The basic but very friendly *Hotel Fuerte City* (☎ 6118) is a good choice for budget travellers. Rooms without bath cost US$4.50 per person, including a continental breakfast.

The equally friendly *Residencial Don Jorge* (☎ 6086) charges US$4/5 per person for rooms without/with bath, including a continental breakfast. Guests may also book almuerzos (US$1.50) and dinners (US$3).

The *Hotel Casa Blanca* (☎ 6076), also on the main street, has basic rooms with private bath for US$5 per person, with breakfast.

The clean and recommended *Hotel Mily* (☎ 6151), on the main highway, charges US$5 per person. An especially playful dog enlivens the scene, but there's constant traffic noise.

On the main street, Calle Bolívar, is the *Hostería Mi Casa* (☎ 6061) with a nice garden and passable accommodation. Rooms without bath, including lunch and a choice of breakfast or dinner, cost US$10 per person.

Places to Eat

For snacks, try the hamburgers, chicken and delicious jugo de mandarina at the friendly *Hamburguesa Tobby*. The inexpensive and down-to-earth *Restaurant Papillon* serves three meals daily, as well as snacks and beer anytime.

You'll find great pizza and home-baked goodies at the cosy and interestingly decorated *Churrasquería-Pizzería El Chancho Rengo*. *Paulista*, on the plaza, serves Brazilian food. *Restaurant Coronado* does basic Bolivian meals all day, as does *La Cascada*, which appears to be open only on weekends.

If you're up for a European gourmet-style meal, try the *Landhaus*, near the avión at the northern end of town. This place is superb value by anyone's standard and the food is unforgettable. It's open Thursday to Sunday evening. The door is sometimes locked – just knock and they'll open up. The attached *Postrería Helga*, run by the chef's wife, sells good German baked goods and real coffee.

Tasty international and criollo dishes are available at *Mi Casa* (☎ 6061), at Calle Bolívar 98. Daily almuerzos cost only US$2.50; for a major meal, it's wise to book in advance. If the door is locked, just ring the bell.

Entertainment

A slice of Santa Cruz teenage nightlife is transported to Samaipata each weekend and revived at the popular *Disco Ché Wilson*. Anyone over 21 or so will probably prefer the weekend disco at the *Landhaus* (see Places to Eat), which cranks up as the restaurant winds down. Children may enjoy the playground area beside the avión.

Things to Buy

The Elibel shop sells postcards, magazines, books and home-made marmalade.

Getting There & Away

Expreso Santa Cruz trufis leave for Samaipata when full, from the corner of Avenida Cañoto and Calle Parapeti, near the bus terminal in Santa Cruz. They carry up to four passengers and cost US$3 per person.

Weekends are best for getting away quickly. Alternatively, micros leave the bus terminal in Santa Cruz at 8 am and 4 pm, and cost US$2.30. The trip takes 2½ hours each way.

Transport to Santa Cruz can be booked from the ticket office on Campero; there are departures at 6 am and 6 pm. A minibus leaves at 2 pm. If you don't mind possibly having to stand, it's easier to wait on the road for a passing micro coming from Comarapa, Mairana or Vallegrande. There are also plenty of camiones.

If you're heading to Mairana, Comarapa, Siberia, Vallegrande or Cochabamba, finding transport is a bit trickier, but if you wait on the main highway, a micro or camión will eventually come along.

AROUND SAMAIPATA
El Fuerte

Samaipata's main attraction is El Fuerte, which is most likely the remains of a pre-Inca ceremonial site. It occupies a hilltop about 10 km from Samaipata and affords a commanding view across the rugged transition zone between the Andes and low-lying areas farther east.

Early conquerors assumed the site had been used for defence, hence its Spanish name, 'the fort'. In 1832, French naturalist Alcides d'Orbigny visited the site and decided that the pools and parallel canals had been used for washing gold. In 1936, German anthropologist Leo Pucher described it as an ancient temple to the serpent and the jaguar.

Recently, the place has gained a New Age following, and in one of his fits of extraterrestrial fancy, Erich von Daniken visited El Fuerte and proclaimed that it was a take-off and landing ramp for ancient spacecraft. One can hardly blame him; take a look into the valley below and you'll see a large flying saucer which has landed – and remains – on the grounds of Achira Kamping, a European-style camping complex.

In fact, no one knows the exact purpose of El Fuerte. The site has been radiocarbon dated at approximately 1500 BC. There are no standing buildings but the remains of 500 dwellings have been discovered in the immediate vicinity and ongoing excavation reveals more every day. The main site, which is almost certainly of religious significance, is a 100m-long stone slab with a variety of sculpted features: seats, tables, a conference circle, troughs, tanks, conduits and *hornecinos* (niches), which are believed to have held idols. Zoomorphic designs on the slab include a raised relief of a puma and numerous serpents, which probably represented fertility. Most intriguing are the odd parallel grooves which appear to shoot off into the sky and inspired von Daniken's UFO launch ramp hypothesis.

About 300m down an obscure track behind the main ruin is El Hueco, a sinister hole in the ground which appears all the more menacing by the concealing vegetation and sloping ground around it. It's almost certainly natural, but three theories have emerged about how it might have been used:

that it served as a water storage cistern; that it functioned as an escape-proof prison; or that it was part of a subterranean communication system between the main ruin and its immediate surroundings. El Hueco has been partially explored, but the project was abandoned when excavators heard mysterious sounds emanating from the walls. Openings of suspected side passages are now blocked with earth.

El Fuerte is open daily from 9 am to 5 pm. Admission is US$2 (students US$1). On weekends, snacks and refreshments are served from trailers outside the entrance.

Getting There & Away Hitching from Samaipata is easiest on weekends – especially Sunday – but the 20-km return walk also makes a rewarding day trip. Follow the main highway back towards Santa Cruz for 3.5 km and turn right at the sign pointing uphill to 'Ruinas de El Fuerte'. From there, it's five scenic km to the summit. Watch for

SANTA CRUZ

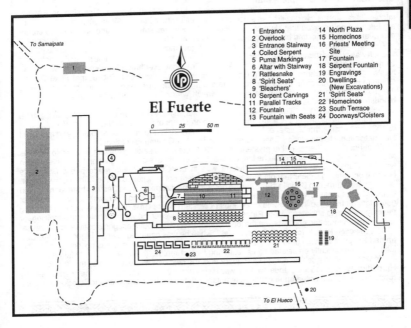

1 Entrance	14 North Plaza
2 Overlook	15 Homecinos
3 Entrance Stairway	16 Priests' Meeting
4 Coiled Serpent	Site
5 Puma Markings	17 Fountain
6 Altar with Stairway	18 Serpent Fountain
7 Rattlesnake	19 Engravings
8 'Spirit Seats'	20 Dwellings
9 'Bleachers'	(New Excavations)
10 Serpent Carvings	21 'Spirit Seats'
11 Parallel Tracks	22 Homecinos
12 Fountain	23 South Terrace
13 Fountain with Seats	24 Doorways/Cloisters

El Fuerte

To Samaipata

To El Hueco

small condors, and in the morning and afternoon for the flocks of commuting parakeets that chatter overhead.

Taxis for the return trip, including a 1½-hour stop at the ruins, cost US$8 for up to four people.

La Pajcha

La Pajcha, a series of three beautiful waterfalls on a turbid mountain river, has a sandy beach for swimming and some inviting camp sites. It lies 42 km (one to two hours by jeep) south of Samaipata, towards San Juan, then seven km on foot off the main road. The site is now privately owned, so there may soon be a charge to visit. You'll occasionally find transport from Samaipata, but unless you have guaranteed transport back, take camping gear and plenty of food.

Archaeological Sites

The Samaipata region abounds in painted caves and semi-explored archaeological sites, including examples at Mairana, Pampagrande, Mataral, Saipina and others. Access is extremely difficult, but if you're adequately motivated, it's simply a matter of speaking with locals or just exploring.

VALLEGRANDE

Set in the Andean foothills at 2100 metres, Vallegrande enjoys a lovely temperate climate. Like most rural towns in Bolivia, life starts up at about 4.30 am, when the micros start arriving from the *campo*, delivering people to the markets. The daily market at the plaza begins about 5 am, but the weekly feria is on Sunday. Nearly every week, there's some sort of small fiesta at the

---

Ché Guevara – a 'Complete Man'

Ernesto 'Ché' Guevara de la Serna was born on 14 June 1928 in Rosario, Argentina, to wealthy middle-class parents. He qualified as a doctor at the University of Buenos Aires, but turned revolutionary because he believed that idealism, sacrifice and violent revolution were the only ways to create an equal society. Rejecting his comfortable life, he set off to travel penniless around Latin America.

Guevara held a minor position in the Communist government of Jacobo Arbenz in Guatemala in 1954. It was around this time that he earned his nickname, Ché, after the Argentine habit of punctuating sentences with that word, meaning 'buddy'. After the CIA-aided overthrow of Arbenz the following year, he fled to Mexico, where he and his first wife, Peruvian socialist Hilda Gadea, met Fidel Castro. Guevara decided his calling was to bring about a worldwide socialist revolution, first by overthrowing the dictatorship of Fulgencio Batista in Cuba, which was accomplished, after much struggle and bloodshed on both sides, on 2 January 1959.

Through the late 1950s, Guevara worked as a doctor, military commander and adviser in Castro's revolutionary forces. In 1959, Castro appointed him president of the Banco Nacional de la Cuba, and in 1961 he became the Minister of Industry and was responsible for land redistribution and industrial nationalisation. He persuaded Castro to ally Cuba to other Communist nations.

What happened then is rather mysterious. In 1965, the ever-zealous Guevara decided to take his Marxist message to Africa. Before he left, Castro required him to sign a resignation from his affiliation with the Cuban government. While Guevara was in the Congo, Castro made public Guevara's resignation, making it clear that his African activities were not sanctioned by the Cuban government.

When he returned to Cuba in 1965, feeling betrayed and disappointed at Castro's bureaucratisation of the Marxist ideal, Ché turned back to Latin America. The following year, with a motley band of guerrillas, he marched into the wild rural lands of western Santa Cruz department, bent on inspiring the campesinos to social rebellion. Rather than support, however, he was met only with suspicion, or was ignored altogether, and not even the local Communist party would recognise or take up his cause.

The rejection took its toll. On 8 October 1967, when he was captured near La Higuera by the CIA-trained troops of Bolivian military dictator René Barrientos Ortuño, Guevara was no longer the T-shirt icon, but a pathetically emaciated figure, suffering from chronic asthma, arthritis and malnutrition.

He was taken to a schoolroom in La Higuera and, the next day, was executed by the Bolivian army. His body was flown to Vallegrande, where it was displayed until the following day in the hospital laundry room. Local women noted an uncanny resemblance to the Catholic Christ and took locks of his hair

sportsground, featuring traditional music and dancing.

After Ché Guevara was executed in La Higuera, his body was brought to Vallegrande and buried beneath the airstrip, and most visitors to the town are passing through on a pilgrimage to La Higuera. Otherwise, Vallegrande is little more than a great spot to relax and walk in the hills.

Information
The *alcaldía* (☎ 2149; fax 2091) is keen to promote tourism in Vallegrande and is happy to answer queries. For any sort of cultural or historical information, see Señor Licenciado Adhemar Sandoval at the Casa de la Cultura. The telephone code for Vallegrande is 0942.

Places to Stay & Eat
There are three places to stay in Vallegrande:

Alojamiento Teresita (☎ 2151) and *Residencial Vallegrande*, both of which charge US$5 per person, and *Hotel Ganadero*, which costs US$6 per person.

Among the best places for a meal are *El Acuario* on the plaza, which features the local speciality, pique a lo macho, and the chicken joint, *La Casita*, on Calle Bolívar. The cheap pensión, *Los Chinos*, near the police station, serves almuerzos and cenas for about US$1.

Getting There & Away
From the terminal in Santa Cruz, Transportes Señor de los Milagros has departures daily at 9.30 am and 2 and 6 pm; smaller flotas leave from near the corner of Avenidas Irala and Cañoto. Expreso Vallegrande goes from Isabél la Católica. From Samaipata, an unreliable Vallegrande bus leaves at about 2 pm,

as mementos. His hands, which were cut off to prevent fingerprint identification, were smuggled to Cuba by a Bolivian journalist and remain there in an undisclosed location. That night, he was buried with his comrades in an unmarked grave to deny him a place of public homage. In 1995, General Vargas, one of the soldiers who carried out the burial, revealed that the grave was beneath the airstrip in Vallegrande. The Bolivian government is now calling for exhumation of the body, and both the Cubans and Argentines want it brought home to their respective countries.

Ché's final speech, relayed from the Bolivian forest via the Tri-Continental Conference in Havana, in April 1967, became a rallying cry around the world: 'Wherever death may surprise us, let it be welcome, provided that this, our battle cry, may have reached some receptive ear and another hand be extended to wield our weapons and other men be ready to intone the funeral dirge with the staccato singing of machine guns and new battle cries of war and victory. *Venceremos* (We shall overcome).'

For more on Ché's life – straight from the horse's mouth – look for *Bolivian Diary*, which was written during the final months of his life, or his myth-shattering book *The Motorcycle Diaries* (translated by Ann Wright, Verso, 1995), which presents a less politically correct side of this enduring legend. ■

SANTA CRUZ

but otherwise you'll have to just stand out on the road and wait for something headed west. If the vehicle that stops isn't going to Vallegrande, go as far as Mataral and hitch south from there. From Cochabamba, there are daily buses at 8.30 pm with Jumbo Bus Ballivián.

PUCARA & LA HIGUERA

To reach La Higuera, the site of Ché Guevara's final struggle and execution, you must first go to Vallegrande and catch a micro to Pucara, which follows a very rough road and takes four to six hours. From Pucara, a new road winds through the mountains to La Higuera and is passable to vehicles. There aren't any vehicles, however, and on foot the trip takes seven or eight hours. On horseback, it's five hours.

On the plaza in Pucara, a grizzled campesino runs the local bar/tienda, and his daughter serves meals in a basic *comedor*. They're both very kind, and if you buy the man a couple of beers, he'll probably start talking about Ché or suggest people who hire horses to go to La Higuera. They also have a room to let on the roof at the back of the house, with marvellous views over the mountains and the upper Río Grande.

Approaching La Higuera, you see the long *barranca* where Ché was captured. Apart from that, there's little to see in the village but the schoolroom – now the local clinic – where Ché was kept before being executed. In the village, there's a small bar/shop where you can buy a beer and speak with locals about the event – and also about the outsiders who turn up every October for the anniversary of the shoot out.

La Higuera has no formal accommodation, so you may wind up camping, but unless you're invited to do otherwise, select a spot well outside the village.

The Eastern Lowlands

The vast, sparsely populated lowlands of the Bolivian Oriente take in all of crescent-shaped south-eastern Bolivia. They're bounded on the west by the foothills of the Cordillera; on the north by Llanos de Guarayos; and on the south and east by the international boundaries of Paraguay and Brazil.

The land is generally flat, broken only by long, low ridges and odd monolithic mountains. Much of the territory lies soaking under vast marshes like the Bañados del Izozog (which has been proposed as a national park by native Guaraní people), deep in the wilderness, or the magnificent Pantanal on the Brazilian frontier. Mostly, however, it serves as a transition zone between the hostile, thorny Chaco scrubland in the south and the low jungle-like forests and savannas of the Amazon Basin to the north.

The film *The Mission*, which was set in the South American Jesuit missions, spawned an awakening of interest in Jesuit work in the interior regions of the continent. Perhaps the height of mission architecture is represented in the unique and well-preserved churches of south-eastern Bolivia. The most interesting and accessible are those at Concepción, San Javier, San Miguel de Velasco, Santa Ana de Velasco, San Rafael de Velasco and San José de Chiquitos, all of which lie in the lowlands north and east of Santa Cruz.

Culturally and economically, the Oriente looks toward Brazil rather than La Paz, and the 'Death Train' between Santa Cruz and Quijarro on the Brazilian border is the lifeline; over this dilapidating link flows a stream of commerce and undocumented imports.

History

In the days when eastern Bolivia was still unsurveyed and largely unorganised territory, the Jesuits established an autonomous religious state in Paraguay. From there, they

Highlights

- Travel little-known backroads in search of colourful birds, butterflies and tropical vegetation
- Visit San Miguel de Velasco, which has the best restored church on the Jesuit mission circuit
- Admire the beautiful interior of the mission church at San Rafael de Velasco
- Wander through San José de Chiquitos and its unique mission church complex
- Cross into Brazil to visit the tranquil 'Cidade Branca' (White City) of Corumbá and the nearby Brazilian Pantanal

spread outwards, founding missions and venturing into wilderness that had been previously unexplored by other Europeans. The northern reaches of this territory were inhabited by tribes of Indians –including the Chiquitanos, Chiriguanos, Moxos, and Guaraníes.

Each mission became an experiment in community life for groups of people who had lived by their wits from time immemorial. The Jesuits established what they considered the optimum community hierarchy. Each population unit, known as a *reducción*, was headed by two or three Jesuit priests. To each of these reducciones a military unit was

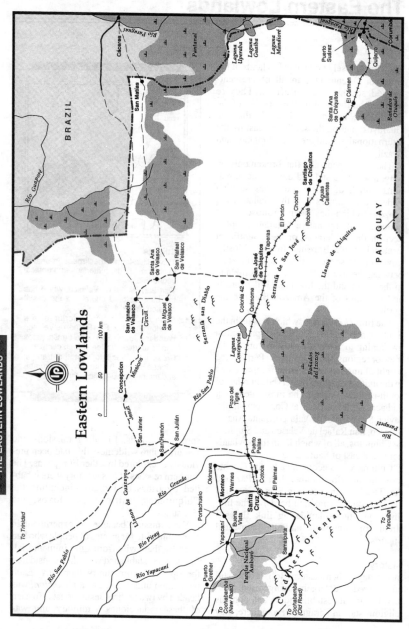

attached, and for a time, the Jesuit armies were the strongest and best trained on the continent. In fact, these units created a formidable barrier/buffer zone between the Spanish in the west and the Portuguese in Brazil.

The Indians, who were traditionally hunters and gatherers, were instructed in the principles of agriculture and forcibly settled into an agricultural economy. Over the years, a trade network was established between these lowland communities and the Quechua and Aymara in the highlands. Cotton, honey, beeswax and artwork were exchanged for raw silver mined in the highlands.

In addition to economic ventures, the Jesuits promoted education and culture among the tribes. With Jesuit training, the Indians became accomplished artesans and produced outstanding work in both silver and wood, handcrafting the renowned violins and harps that now feature in traditional Paraguayan music. At the height of this revolutionary cultural transition, the Indians were giving concerts and dances and even performing Italian Baroque opera in the heart of the wilderness!

Naturally, the Indians were also thrust heart and soul into Christianity. Local rituals and belief systems were suppressed by the priests and the people were coerced into European culture, philosophy and lifestyle. The coup was so complete that today very little is known about the pre-Jesuit cultures of the South American interior.

By the mid-1700s political strife in Europe had escalated into a power struggle between the Church and the governments of France, Spain and Portugal. When the Spanish in South America fully realised the extent of Jesuit influence and got wind of all the wealth being produced in the wilderness, they decided the Jesuits had usurped too much power from the State. In 1767, caught in a crossfire of political babble and religious dogma, the missions were disbanded and King Carlos III signed the Order of Expulsion, which expelled the Jesuits from the continent.

During the period leading up to Bolivian independence in 1825, the eastern regions of the Spanish colonies were largely ignored. Possession of the hostile lowlands and the hazy boundaries between Alto Peru, the Viceroyalty of La Plata and Portuguese territory was of little concern. Although agriculture was thriving in the Santa Cruz area, the Spanish remained intent upon extracting every scrap of mineral wealth that could be squeezed from the rich and more hospitable highlands.

Jesuit Missions Circuit

North of San José de Chiquitos in the Llanos de Chiquitos and Llanos de Guarayos, an unpaved road between Santa Cruz and San José de Chiquitos circuits through several of the most prominent Jesuit missions.

From Santa Cruz, the route heads east across the Río Grande (on the railway bridge!) to Puerto Pailas, then north to San Julián, where it crosses the Río San Pablo. There it turns east into the agricultural and ranching lands around San Javier and Concepción. Eventually, the farmland gently gives way to the wild, scrubby forest country around San Ignacio.

At San Ignacio, the route enters the Velasco province mission complex, which includes the missions of San Ignacio, San Miguel, Santa Ana and San Rafael. About 150 km south of San Rafael, through scrub forest and low-lying wetlands, lies San José de Chiquitos.

The main attractions in most of these villages are, of course, the mission churches, whose incongruous architecture was intended to represent a Christian voice in the wilderness. The missions at San Javier, San Rafael and Concepción were originally designed by Martin Schmidt, a Swiss missionary, musician and architect who was born in Baar in 1694 and worked with the local Indians from 1730 to the mid-1700s. An enormous renovation project is currently underway, directed by Swiss architect Hans

Roth, whose headquarters are in Concepción.

SAN RAMÓN

Although dusty San Ramón lacks a mission church, it's a significant crossroads between Santa Cruz, Trinidad, the missions and Brazil. It may be the site of a new gold mine, but anything taken out of the ground is quickly transported somewhere else.

Places to Stay & Eat

Hotel Manguari, two blocks from the plaza on the Trinidad road, charges US$5 per person for basic facilities. For meals, wander the few metres to the recommended *Boliche de Arturo*.

Getting There & Away

Buses to Trinidad pass between 10 pm and midnight, as do those headed east to San Ignacio. The first bus leaves for Santa Cruz at 7 am, but camiones also run relatively frequently.

SAN JAVIER

San Javier, the oldest mission on the circuit, was founded in 1692. Martin Schmidt arrived in 1730 and founded the region's first music school and workshop to produce violins, harps and harpsichords. He also designed the present church, which was constructed between 1749 and 1752. It sits on a forested ridge with a commanding view over the surrounding low hills. Restoration work moved along slowly on a meagre budget, but the church was finally completed in 1992. The newly restored building appears pleasantly old.

San Javier is also proud of its cheese factory, which can be visited. North-west of town, 14 km away, are some inviting hot springs for bathing; you can reach them on a motorcycle taxi for US$6.50. A farther six km along is a pool and waterfall, Los Tumbos de Suruquizo, also suitable for swimming.

The telephone code for San Javier is 0963.

Places to Stay & Eat

Totaitu (☎ & fax 344700, Santa Cruz), probably the poshest accommodation in the missions, is on a dairy farm four km northwest of town. Cabañas for four/six/eight people cost US$60/80/100 on weekends, with a US$20 discount on weekdays. Camping is also available. Amenities include a pool, golf and tennis; hikers can do some lovely day walks and there are horses and mountain bikes for hire to explore the area. The booking office is in the Casco Viejo arcade in Santa Cruz.

In town, you can choose between *Alojamiento Ame-Tauna*, on the plaza, which charges US$4.50 per person with comfortably cool rooms and shared facilities, and *Alojamiento San Javier* (☎ 5038), which has simple rooms for US$4 per person.

Restaurants include *El Turista*, which is frequented by mission-bound tour groups, as well as the more down-to-earth *La Pascana*, *El Snack* and *El Ganadero*.

Getting There & Away

All buses between Santa Cruz and San Ignacio pass through San Javier, 77 km (one hour) west of Concepción and 231 km (five hours) from Santa Cruz.

CONCEPCIÓN

Concepción lies 175 km (four hours by bus) west of San Ignacio in an agricultural and cattle-ranching area. The main appeal is the friendliness and tranquillity of the village. Possibly because it's the nerve centre for all the mission restoration projects, the church, which was founded in 1709, has been excessively restored and appears to have fallen prey to kitsch tendencies, with gaudy plastic decor and a Disney-like atmosphere. Despite the intimidating signs on the gate, it's interesting to visit the restoration workshops behind the mission.

Places to Stay & Eat

Concepción's choice of budget accommodation includes *Alojamiento Westfalia* and *Residencial 6 de Agosto*, both of which cost

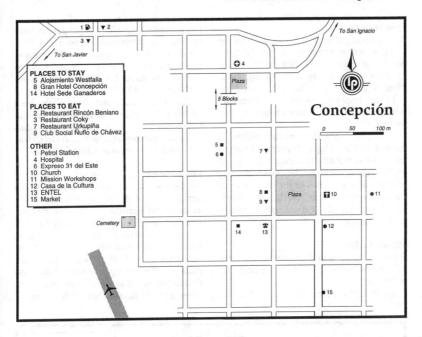

PLACES TO STAY
5 Alojamiento Westfalia
8 Gran Hotel Concepción
14 Hotel Sede Ganaderos

PLACES TO EAT
2 Restaurant Rincón Beniano
3 Restaurant Coky
7 Restaurant Urkupiña
9 Club Social Nuflo de Chávez

OTHER
1 Petrol Station
4 Hospital
6 Expreso 31 del Este
10 Church
11 Mission Workshops
12 Casa de la Cultura
13 ENTEL
15 Market

Concepción

under US$5 per person. The most upmarket place is the three-star *Gran Hotel Concepción* (☎ 324193; fax 364723, Santa Cruz), which charges US$20/30 for singles/doubles. The hotel features a nice patio with an exotic garden and carved wooden pillars reminiscent of the Jesuit style. *Hotel Sede Ganaderos* is also recommended.

Some recommended restaurants include the *Coky*, the inexpensive *Urkupiña*, the *Rincón Beniano* and *Club Social Ñuflo de Cháves*, which has bargain set meals, music on Friday nights and bats in the rafters.

Getting There & Away
All buses between Santa Cruz and San Ignacio pass through Concepción. Coming from Trinidad, take a Santa Cruz bus and get off at San Ramón, where you can pick up a bus to Concepción and points east.

Micros leave for San Javier (US$1) and Santa Cruz (US$5) daily at 7 am. Otherwise, wait near the petrol station and flag down whatever may be passing.

SAN IGNACIO
The first mission church at San Ignacio de Velasco, which was founded in 1748, was once the largest and perhaps the most elaborate of all the missions. Unfortunately, the original structure was demolished in the 1950s and replaced by a modern abomination. Realising they'd made a hash of it the first time, they've now decided to have another go at it. It was still under re-restoration at the time of research, so who knows what you'll find? All that remains of the original building are the altar and the wooden pillars.

The town still has a large indigenous population and remains the 'capital' and commercial centre of the Jesuit missions.

The telephone code for San Ignacio is 0962.

THE EASTERN LOWLANDS

Things to See

An interesting feature of San Ignacio are the large **wooden crosses** that have been erected at intersections just off the plaza, creating an appealing effect. Only 700m from the church – and visible from the plaza – is the imposing **Guapomó reservoir**, where you can swim or hire a boat and putter around.

Also check out the **wooden pillars** in front of the Casa Miguel Areijer on the plaza; one pillar is beautifully carved with a group of Bolivian musicians. The owner intended to carve all the posts, but the city preferred the plain colonial style and there are doubts about whether the carved pillar will be allowed to stay.

Places to Stay

Because San Ignacio is the commercial heart of the missions district, there's a choice of accommodation.

Casa Suiza, seven blocks west of the plaza, has rooms for US$10 per person, with meals. The proprietor, Señora Cristina, speaks German and Spanish and can organise horse riding, fishing trips and visits to surrounding haciendas. She also has a wonderful library of books.

The *Hotel Palace* and *Hotel Plaza*, both on the plaza, charge US$6.20 per person. Other basic and inexpensive possibilities include *Alojamiento Guapomó*, *Hotel Oriental*, *Hotel 31 de Julio* and *Hotel Misión*.

Places to Eat

On the plaza are *Restaurant Acuario*, which specialises in asados griegos (Greek grill – a variation on parrillada); *Pizzería Pauline*, serving acceptable pizza; *Parrillada Las Palmares*, with beef dishes; and *Snack Marcelito*, with more down-to-earth offerings. *Hamburguesas Chachi*, 2½ blocks south of the plaza, also does a range of snacks. You'll also find decent meals at the market, one block west and three blocks south of the plaza.

PLACES TO STAY
1 Casa Suiza
3 Hotel 31 de Julio
4 Hotel Palace
7 Hotel Plaza
8 Hotel Misión
13 Alojamiento Guapomó
14 Hotel Oriental

PLACES TO EAT
6 Restaurant Acuario
10 Pizzería Pauline
11 Snack Marcelito
15 Parrillada Las Palmares
20 Hamburguesas Chachi

OTHER
2 Church
5 AeroSur (Airline)
9 Flota Trans Jao/Trans Brasil
12 Flota Chiquitano
16 Expreso 31 del Este
17 Police
18 Market
19 Flota Transical Velasco
21 ENTEL
22 Flota Trans Bolivia-Micros to San Miguel & San Rafael
23 Veloz del Este Micro Stop
24 'Town Gate' Shrine
25 Camión Stop
26 Kiosk

Lago Guapomó

To Concepción

Plaza

San Ignacio

0   100   200 m

To San Miguel

To Santa Ana

THE EASTERN LOWLANDS

Getting There & Away

Air LAB flies from Santa Cruz to San Ignacio International (!) Airport on Monday, Wednesday and Friday at 7.30 am, and returns to Santa Cruz on the same days at 8.35 am. The one-way fare is US$23. Transbrasil airline connects San Ignacio with Cáceres, Brazil.

Bus, Micro & Camión If you're bussing it to San Ignacio, cover your luggage or it will arrive in a thick coating of red dust. Most buses and micros leave from near the market.

Flota Chiquitano leaves Santa Cruz for San Ignacio via San Javier, Concepción and Santa Rosa de la Roca, daily at 7 pm (11 hours, US$8.40). There's only one rest stop and it's just outside Santa Cruz, at Cotoca, so deal with all your bodily necessities there. On Fridays, the bus continues to San Miguel, 40 km and one hour away. The fare is US$1.

Coming from Trinidad, take a Santa Cruz bus and get off at San Ramón (usually in the middle of the night). There, you can hitch or wait for an eastbound bus to San Ignacio.

Flota Universal connects San Ignacios with San José de Chiquitos, via San Miguel and San Rafael, at around 10 am on Monday, Wednesday and Friday. In the dry season, Flota Transical Velasco, Expreso 31 del Este and Trans Jao/Trans Brasil leave daily for San Matías, on the Brazilian border. There you'll find connections to Cáceres and Cuiabá. They normally leave early to mid-morning.

The Flota Trans-Bolivia micro departs daily to San Miguel (half an hour, US$1) and San Rafael at about 8 am, passing through dusty campo and marshland.

SAN MIGUEL

The village of San Miguel de Velasco, lost in the scrub 39 km from San Ignacio, seems to be permanently on siesta. Its church, which was founded in 1721, is the most accurately restored of all the Bolivian Jesuit missions. Its spiral pillars, carved wooden altar with a flying San Miguel, extravagant golden pulpit, religious artwork, toy-like bell tower

and elaborately painted façade are simply superb.

It wasn't designed by Martin Schmidt but it does reflect his influence and is generally considered the most beautiful of the Jesuit missions in Bolivia. During the restoration, which took place from 1978 to 1984, they set up workshops and trained local artesans, probably much as the Jesuits did two centuries before. The artesans remained and they now work in cooperatives making furniture and carvings, such as small carved cedar chests painted in pastels.

The best time to photograph the church is in the morning light. The nightly Mass at 7 pm will also give you an interesting local perspective.

Places to Stay & Eat

The basic but acceptable *Alojamiento Pascana*, on the plaza, charges US$3 per person and the attached restaurant serves simple meals and cold drinks. The *Alojamiento Pardo*, just off the plaza, charges the same, but you may have to chase up the owner to get a room. If you'd prefer to camp, speak with the religious community at the church, who can direct you to a suitable site.

Getting There & Away

The Flota Trans-Bolivia micro leaves daily at 8.30 am for San Ignacio, then returns, and leaves at 9.30 am for San Rafael. It then passes back through San Miguel at around noon, before returning to San Ignacio. It's also easy to travel to San Ignacio with the camionetas that buzz around town honking for passengers in the early morning and after lunch.

SANTA ANA

The mission at the tiny Chiquitano village of Santa Ana de Velasco, 25 km north of San Rafael, was established in 1755. The church, with its earthen floor and palm-frond roof, is more rustic than the others, and recalls the preliminary churches constructed by the Jesuit missionaries upon their arrival. In fact,

DEANNA SWANEY

Interior of the Jesuit mission church, San Miguel

the building itself is post-Jesuit, but the interior contains exquisite religious carvings and paintings.

Given its age, the original structure is in remarkable condition. Sadly, its ongoing 'renovation' is more utilitarian than preservationist and is limited to 'band-aid' repairs made as bits of the building collapse. So far, the work has been done by unskilled labour using cheap modern materials and techniques, but there are now well-conceived plans to professionally restore it to its original state.

Getting There & Away
You shouldn't have problems finding transport from either San Ignacio or San Rafael. Most days, micros run between San Ignacio and San Rafael, via Santa Ana. Because most traffic now uses this route, hitching is also a possibility.

SAN RAFAEL
San Rafael de Velasco lies 150 km (five to six hours by micro or camión) north of San José de Chiquitos. Founded in 1696 and constructed between 1740 and 1748, it was the first of the mission churches to be completed. In the 1970s and 1980s, the building was restored by the same Swiss architects responsible for the restoration of the San José de Chiquitos church.

The interior is particularly beautiful, and the original paintings and woodwork remain intact. The pulpit is covered with a layer of lustrous mica, the ceiling is of reeds and the spiral pillars were carved from *cuchi* (ironwood or *Argania sideroxylon*) logs. San Rafael is the only mission church to retain the original room style, with cane sheathing. Of perhaps the most interest are the lovely music-theme paintings in praise of God along the entrance wall, which include depictions of a harp, flute, bassoon, horn and maracas.

Places to Stay & Eat
At the corner of the main road and the street running south from the church is *Alojamiento San Rafael* (no sign), and there's another *alojamiento* on the plaza itself. Both are very basic and charge US$2.50 per person.

Getting There & Away
The best place to wait for lifts south to San José de Chiquitos or north to Santa Ana, San Miguel or San Ignacio is on the main road in front of Alojamiento San Rafael. In the morning, buses run in both directions. To reach Santa Ana, use the right fork north of town.

SAN JOSÉ DE CHIQUITOS
One of the most accessible of the Jesuit missions, San José de Chiquitos was named for the Chiquitanos Indians who were the original inhabitants of the area. The Jesuits arrived sometime in the mid-1740s, and construction of the magnificent mission church

that today dominates the town was begun around 1750.

San José de Chiquitos surprises its few visitors with the atmosphere and beauty of an Old West frontier town, complete with dusty streets and footpaths shaded by pillar-supported roofs. Flanked on the south by a low escarpment and on the north by flat soggy forest, San José is developing into the cattle ranching centre of the deep Oriente, and oil exploration is an ongoing concern. There's also a lively trade in undocumented goods from Brazil.

Information

Money The small corner store two blocks from the main plaza changes US dollars cash if they have sufficient bolivianos on hand. You'll probably be limited by cash availability to about US$50 at a time.

Dangers & Annoyances The electricity goes off from 2 to 6.30 am, and all the ventilation fans grind to a halt. If you've never experienced a night in a sauna, now you can.

Jesuit Mission Church

Even if you've had your fill of ho-hum monuments to New World colonialism, the beautiful stone Jesuit mission church in San José de Chiquitos is unique in South America and won't fail to impress. Although the main altar is nearly identical to those in other nearby missions and vague similarities to churches in Poland and Belgium have been noted, there is no conclusive evidence about the source of its unusual exterior design.

The Jesuits could not find a ready source of limestone for making cement mortar, so they built with wood and mud plaster. The church compound consists of four principal buildings arranged around the courtyard and occupying an entire city block. The bell tower was finished in 1748, the *funerario*, or Death Chapel, is dated 1752 and the *parroquio*, or living area, was completed in 1754. It is believed, however, that only the façades were completed before the Jesuits

were expelled in 1767. All construction work was done by the Chiquitano Indians under Jesuit direction. The doors, some of the altar work and one magnificent bench seat were hand-carved in wood by expert Chiquitano artesans.

Massive renovations and restorations have been underway for the past decade (this is rather reminiscent of colonial days, when church construction often required an entire lifetime!) and the altar is currently a series of bare, empty niches.

Plaza

The *toboroche* trees on the town's huge plaza were once occupied by a family of sloths, but a flowering of the trees several years ago sent them off to search for leafier pickings. They now shelter noisy green parrots and during the rainy season, the ground beneath hops with thousands of frogs and large toads. Note also the bust of Ñuflo de Chavez, founder of Santa Cruz, and the rather odd and erotic fountain off to one side of the plaza; it's a safe bet you won't see anything like it in highland Bolivia!

In 1993, some politicians donated paving blocks to improve the dirt streets around the plaza and keep down the dust, but neglected to provide funds for placing them, so stacks of hexagonal concrete paving blocks lie stacked around the plaza. The same thing happened in San Miguel and San Rafael.

Chiquitano Monument

The people of the area seem to be proud of the indigenous heritage of San José and to prove it they've erected a monument of an archetypal Chiquitano maiden, with her obligatory water jar, at the entrance to town.

Santa Cruz la Vieja Walk

Just south of town, the road passes beneath an archway supported by bikini-clad ferro-concrete nymphs welcoming you to the old Santa Cruz highway (the route to the original Santa Cruz de la Sierra). These beauties were obviously designed by the same person responsible for the Chiquitano maiden and the plaza fountain. About a km farther along, through dusty ranchland, you'll pass an abandoned schoolhouse from bygone days. After three km or so, the road enters more jungle-like vegetation, which supports throngs of squawking green parrots.

Along this road, four km south of town, is the Parque Histórico Santa Cruz la Vieja, but there's little to see other than an abandoned guard house. Over the road is a small park where locals go to cool off in a murky green swimming pool. Admission is US$1 per person but the walk itself is more appealing than the pool. In the forest nearby is a waterfall, the source of San José's drinking water; it's a cool spot sheltered from the tropical heat, but swarms of biting insects may limit you to a fleeting visit. Carry insect repellent and wear good shoes and trousers to protect your feet and legs from ferocious ants.

If you continue another two to three km up the switchbacks onto the escarpment, you'll have a far-ranging view of San José and the surrounding plains. Farther along are some nice eroded landscapes.

Cerro Turubo
Another possible day takes you to the forested summit of Cerro Turubo, the prominent peak that rises to the east of town.

Places to Stay
The *Alojamiento San Silvestre* (☎ 2041), opposite the railway station, charges US$3 per person with breakfast. Double rooms have private baths. Guests may use the billiard table, but beware of the stereo system that swallowed South America.

Despite its lackadaisical staff, the best place to stay is *Hotel Raquelita* (☎ 2037) on the plaza, which has a laundry service, fans and sparkling clean facilities. The rates schedule is rather complicated, but essentially, it works out to about US$4/5 per person without/with bath.

The cheapest place is the very basic *Posada Vallegrandina*, which isn't recommended. If you prefer to camp, ask the priest at the mission church whether you can pitch a tent in the courtyard.

Places to Eat
There's a good clean *snack bar* in the Hotel Raquelita where you'll get a mean guineo con leche and excellent home-made ice cream. It's worth a look to see the unusual wall decor, especially the bizarre simian representation of General Idi Amin with brightly painted toenails.

The *Sombrero é Sao*, next door, serves chicken and beef dishes with rice, chips and salad. It's a great spot to sit outside and down a couple of cold brews. Another decent spot for an evening meal is the cheaper *Casa é Paila*, around the corner, but it's rarely open.

Pollo Pio-Pio, on the plaza, serves up chicken and chips but is notorious for overcharging foreigners. A better choice is *Pollo Barbaroja*, a few metres farther along.

Watch for the army of lads who emerge from plaza doorways selling salteñas in the morning and cheese bread in the afternoon from heaped trays, tellingly recycled from blue Santa Fe lard tins. There are also some informal restaurant stalls near the railway station, which serve snacks and inexpensive lunch and dinner specials. On Mondays, the Mennonites come into town from the colonies and sell home-made cheese, butter, bread and produce. Mineral water is sold at one of the kiosks near the railway station.

Getting There & Away
Bus & Camión There are currently no bus or micro services between San José de Chiquitos and Santa Cruz. You must first reach San Ignacio and pick up transport from there. On Monday, Wednesday and Friday at 10 am, micros leave for San José de Chiquitos from the market in San Ignacio; they return on Tuesday, Thursday and Saturday.

If you prefer to take your chances with a camión to San Rafael, Santa Ana, or San Ignacio, wait at the tranca beyond the railway line 300m north of town. In the dry season, camiones go to San Ignacio with some regularity – there are usually at least a couple every day. Plan on about US$5 per person as far as San Ignacio.

To San Rafael &
San Ignacio

To Cemetery
& Military Post

**San José
de Chiquitos**

0   100   200 m

0.8 km
approx

To Parque Histórico Santa
Cruz la Vieja & Waterfall

PLACES TO STAY
6 Alojamiento San Silvestre
10 Posada Vallegrandina
18 Hotel Raquelita

PLACES TO EAT
4 Food Stalls & Bars
16 Case é Paila
17 Sombrero é Sao
19 Pollo Pio-Pio
20 Pollo Barbaroja

OTHER
1 Tranca
2 Flota Universal
3 Petrol Station
5 Railway Station
7 Hospital
8 Satellite Dish
9 Chiquitano Monument
11 Pharmacy
12 Shop to Exchange Cash
13 Police
14 AeroSur (Airline)
15 Market
21 Jesuit Mission Complex
22 ENTEL
23 School & Football Ground
24 Ferro-Concrete Nymphs
25 Old Schoolhouse

THE EASTERN LOWLANDS

Train The easiest way to travel between San José de Chiquitos and Santa Cruz or Quijarro is on the 'Death Train'. Most trains arrive and depart at night, which is a shame because this area is the most scenic on the eastern railway line.

The *Expreso del Oriente* passes on Monday, Wednesday and Friday at 9 pm eastbound and on Tuesday, Thursday and Saturday at 9.45 pm westbound. The fare is US$11/9 for 1st/2nd class to either Santa Cruz or Quijarro. The *tren rápido* passes on Tuesday and Sunday at 9.50 pm eastbound and Monday and Thursday at 9.45 pm west-

bound, and costs US$8/7 in 1st/2nd class to either end of the line. The *tren mixto* passes on Monday and Friday at 8.15 pm eastbound and on Tuesday and Saturday at 5.30 pm westbound; the fare is US$8 to Santa Cruz or Quijarro. Freight trains run at any time and you can simply hop into the passenger *bodega* and pay the 2nd class fare of US$8 to either Santa Cruz or Quijarro.

Buying train tickets is a slow process and you'll need your passport. Intermediate stations such as San José de Chiquitos receive only a few ticket allotments, and tickets are sold only on the day of departure (or, in the case of departures in the wee hours, on the previous day). The *boletería* opens whenever the ticket seller rolls up, which may be any time from 6 am to noon.

COLONIA 42

Although it's best not viewed as a tourist attraction, the Mennonite colony, Colonia 42, which is 42 km north of San José de Chiquitos, makes for an interesting cultural side trip. This is only one of numerous Mennonite colonies in Bolivia, but it's by far the most conservative. Others are scattered around the entire Oriente, including Santa Cruz and farther north towards the Beni, as well as throughout Paraguay, northern Argentina and south-western Brazil.

The highly traditional Mennonites belong to a religious sect founded by Menno Simons, a 16th-century Dutch reformer. They speak a German dialect known as Platt-Deutsch, which is actually more of a German-Dutch hybrid.

Despite this very conservative colony's Canadian roots, few of the Mennonites speak English and many don't even speak Spanish. The *menonos*, as they're known by locals, are easily recognised by their dress. The men all wear hats and identical blue or green overalls, and the women, who are required to appear inconspicuous and unadorned, wear head coverings and plain monocoloured knee-length dresses. The Mennonites live in simple farmhouses typical of the North American Midwest and travel about in horse-drawn carts. Most of the farm work is done by hand or by draught animals.

Visitors to the colony should respect the privacy of the colonists. Many prefer not to have their photos taken and a few, especially the women, wish to avoid contact with the outside world.

History

The Mennonites in Colonia 42 originally came from Saskatchewan, Canada. They set out from there in search of a place where they could practise their religion, farm their land and live out peaceful and self-sufficient lives

without the influences of modern society. They originally found such a place in Belize, Central America, but hassles with the Belizean government in the mid-70s sent them off again in search of a home.

Recognising the agricultural potential of the Bolivian Oriente, thousands came to the wilderness north and east of Santa Cruz. They cleared vast tracts of forest and recreated a rustic cross between the north German plain and the North American Midwest in the heart of Bolivia. So far the Bolivian government has appreciated the role that the Mennonites have played in opening up previously uninhabited territory, but as more and more highland Bolivians look toward the Oriente for economic opportunities, their unique situation may become threatened.

Getting There & Away

San José de Chiquitos merchants trade with the colony, buying milk, cheese, butter and poultry from the Mennonites on a regular basis. Usually, at least one camión does the run each day. If you'd like to ride along, wait at the tranca north of town before 9 am. Expect to pay between US$2 and US$3.50 per person for the return trip.

Far Eastern Bolivia

ROBORÉ

The town of Roboré, about four hours along the railway east of San José de Chiquitos, began in 1916 as a military outpost, and the military presence is still a bit overwhelming. You can probably imagine what happens when a lot of bored soldiers posted in the middle of nowhere encounter tourists in a town that rarely sees outsiders. The situation seems to have improved over the past few years, but it's still best not to appear conspicuous.

Río Roboré

The cool and clean Río Roboré, which flows through town, offers some pleasant and refreshing swimming. You may want to move several hundred metres upstream from the bridge to avoid the curious eyes of local crowds.

Los Balnearios

A highly recommended visit is to 'El Balneario', a mountain stream with a waterfall and natural swimming hole. It's a two-hour walk each way from town and you'll need a local guide to find it. Alternatively, there's another closer swimming hole that is accessible by taxi for US$1.50 return.

Santiago de Chiquitos

In the cultural sense, the Jesuit mission at Santiago de Chiquitos, 20 km from Roboré, is more interesting than San José de Chiquitos. It's set in the hills and the cooler climate provides a welcome break from the tropical heat of the lowlands. By taxi, the return trip from Roboré costs US$10 for up to four people. Camiones and military vehi-

cles occasionally do the run from the east end of town for US$1 per person each way.

Aguas Calientes

The 40 to 41°C thermal baths at Aguas Calientes, 31 km east of Roboré, are popular with Bolivian visitors who believe in their curative powers. The Santa Cruz-Quijarro train stops in Aguas Calientes and camiones leave from the eastern end of town, charging US$1.10 per person. Taxis charge US$12 for up to four passengers. There's no accommodation, so the baths are best visited on a day trip.

Chochís

Chochís, two stops towards San José de Chiquitos along the railway line, has a lovely church.

El Portón

Between Roboré and San José de Chiquitos, the railway line passes through a bizarre and

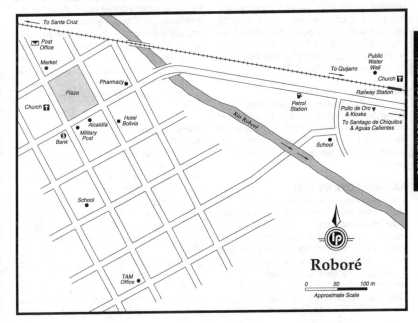

THE EASTERN LOWLANDS

beautiful region of wilderness hills and monoliths. Unfortunately, most trains pass at night. If you're keen to see the best of it, the most convenient station is El Portón, which lies immediately west of the spectacular and oft-photographed rock pillar of the same name. There are no tourist facilities so carry food and camping gear.

Places to Stay

Roboré's only accommodation option is the *Hotel Bolivia*, which is half a block from the plaza. Doubles cost US$3/5 without/with bath. If you're waiting for an evening train, they'll let you keep the room for the normal rate less a US$1 discount.

Places to Eat

For breakfast, you can't beat the terrace of the *Hotel Bolivia*, where you'll get coffee, eggs, bread rolls and jam for about US$0.75. For other meals, check out the *Pollo de Oro*, near the railway station, where local dogs have left a maze of paw prints in the blue concrete patio floor. In the evening, this place livens up appreciably; the scratchy stereo system and alcohol-assisted celebrating will provide a bit of diversion to accompany the inevitable wait for the typical *tren atrasado* (late train)!

Getting There & Away

By train, Roboré lies about four hours west of Quijarro and the same distance (time wise) east of San José de Chiquitos. For departure times, see the Getting There & Away information in the Santa Cruz and Quijarro sections.

BAÑADOS DEL IZOZOG

The vast Bañados del Izozog wetland, in the heart of the wilderness, is perhaps Bolivia's most enigmatic site. On the map, it lies buried in the heart of the seemingly inaccessible expanse of territory between San José de Chiquitos and the Paraguayan border. Currently, the local Guaraní Indians, in conjunction with the Bolivian Ministerio de Desarollo, the World Bank, the Swiss government, the Wildlife Conservation Society and the Armonía Foundation, are asking the Bolivian government to protect this ecological treasure in the form of a two million-hectare national park and wildlife reserve.

Of the total area, the proposal stipulates that 800,000 hectares would go to the *guaraníes* and 300,000 hectares to the neighbouring Ayoreos tribe. The proposal hasn't yet met with much enthusiasm in the federal government, but environmentalists agree that Izozog is the one area of Bolivia that desperately needs some sort of protection before it's discovered by developers.

Currently, the only access into this fabulous region is by 4WD or on foot from El Tinto, on the railway line west of San José de Chiquitos. This is a true wilderness and there are no facilities or services anywhere in the area.

PUERTO SUÁREZ

If it could only get its act together, Puerto Suárez, set in a watery wilderness with some of the densest wildlife populations on the continent, could be a legitimately profitable and attractive centre. Instead, it's infamous as the place where São Paulo car thieves dump their spoils and 80% of the community is in some way involved in illicit dealings. In short, it's a hell-hole and not a place to linger.

The telephone code for Puerto Suárez is 0976.

Places to Stay

At US$6.20 for a double, the *Hotel Beby* (☎ 2290) probably offers the best value. Alternatively, you could try *Hotel Sucre* (☎ 2069), *Hotel Palace* (☎ 2098) or *Hotel Ejecutivo* (☎ 2270).

The brand new five-star *El Pantanal Hotel Resort Casino* (☎ & fax 2020), is at Arroyo Concepción outside Puerto Suárez. Six-day packages, including flights from Santa Cruz, all meals, accommodation, a one-day cruise on the Río Paraguay, duty-free shopping and a pop over the border to Corumbá, costs US$690/1256 for one/two people. The current programme may attract Bolivian interest, but foreigners would probably expect more emphasis on the Pantanal and wildlife-viewing. For information, contact Tajibos Tours (☎ 439046, fax 426994), Santa Cruz.

Getting There & Away
Air AeroSur has daily flights between Santa Cruz and Puerto Suárez, and LAB flights depart Monday, Wednesday and Friday. TAM has a Friday morning flight from Santa Cruz to Puerto Suárez and returns on Saturday morning. All these flights are popular, so it's wise to reserve at the earliest opportunity. In Corumbá (Brazil), you can reserve tickets from Puerto Suárez to Santa Cruz for about 20% more than you'd pay in Bolivia. The price includes transport between Corumbá and the airport.

Train Puerto Suárez is on the railway 15 km west of Quijarro. See the Quijarro Getting There & Away section for more information.

QUIJARRO
Quijarro, a muddy collection of shacks at the eastern terminus of the Death Train, sits on slightly higher and drier ground than Puerto Suárez and serves as the border crossing between Bolivia and Corumbá (Brazil). Visitors heading east will be treated to a wonderful preview of Corumbá; from muddy Quijarro, it appears on a hill in the distance, a dream city of sparkling white towers rising above the vast green expanses of the Pantanal. In Mutún, just south of Quijarro, what may be the richest deposits of iron manganese on the continent are currently being developed.

The telephone code for Quijarro is 0978.

The Bolivian Pantanal
The Hotel Santa Cruz in Quijarro organises boat tours through the unspoilt, wildlife-rich wetlands of the Bolivian Pantanal and provides an alternative to the well-visited and controversially managed Brazilian side. A comfortable three-day excursion, including transport, food and accommodation (on the boat) costs about US$100 per person.

Places to Stay & Eat
The nicest accommodation is at the friendly *Hotel Santa Cruz* (☎ 2113), two blocks from the railway station, which charges US$12/18 for clean, air-conditioned single/double rooms. Book through Hotel Amazonas in Santa Cruz. The three-star *Hotel Oasis* (☎ 2159) offers pleasant rooms for the same rates.

More basic accommodation is available for US$3 per person at the small alojamientos to the left as you exit the railway station. Lots of good inexpensive restaurants are lined up along the street perpendicular to the railway station entrance.

Getting There & Away
Train By rail, the trip between Quijarro and Santa Cruz takes anywhere from 16 to 23 hours, depending on which train you take. The *Expreso del Oriente* leaves Quijarro on Tuesday and Saturday at 2.15 pm and costs US$20.50/17 in 1st/2nd class. The tren rápido leaves on Monday and Thursday at 1.45 pm and costs US$16.70/14.50 in 1st/2nd class. The slow and cumbersome tren mixto chugs out on Tuesday and Saturday at 6.30 pm. You can only buy 2nd class tickets, which cost US$12.50. You'll pay the same to ride in a bodega on a freight train.

You may have the same problems buying tickets in Quijarro as in Santa Cruz. If you're in a hurry, Quijarro taxi drivers sometimes have scalped tickets for sale at inflated prices. Before buying anything, make sure the tickets are valid for the correct day and have not been punched already.

For some Bolivian-style luxury book a seat on the *Expreso Especial Bracha*, which is attached to the *Expreso del Oriente* and costs US$25. This deteriorating railway car offers air-conditioning, videos and food service.

To Brazil When the train pulls into Quijarro, a lineup of taxis waits to take new arrivals to the border. The border post is only two km from the station, so if you can't bargain the drivers down to something reasonable – say

US$0.75 per person – you can always start walking.

Some travellers report being charged up to US$10 for Bolivian exit stamps, but this is entirely unofficial; politely explain that you understand there is no official charge for the stamp, and appear prepared to wait.

Just over the bridge, you pass through Brazilian customs. From there, city buses will take you into Corumbá. Brazilian entry stamps are now given at the disorganised immigration office on the Praça da Rèpública, Rua 13 de Junho between Rua Antônio João and Rua Antônio Maria Coelho. It's open until 5 pm. You may also have to check in with the Polícia Federal at the *rodoviária* (long-distance bus terminal, pronounced 'haw-daw-VYAHR-ya'), a few blocks from the centre.

Technically, travellers arriving in Brazil from Bolivia need a yellow fever vaccination certificate. Officials don't always ask for one, but when they do, the rule is inflexibly enforced. In a pinch, there's a clinic in Corumbá that provides the vaccine. You can change US dollars cash or travellers cheques at the Banco do Brasil, two blocks from Praça Independência.

To reach the Bolivian border from Corumbá, catch a bus from Praça Independência, opposite the cathedral. If you're entering Bolivia, you can change Brazilian reais and US dollars at the frontier (you may have problems with US$100 notes, which are frequently counterfeited). Have your requisite amount readily and discreetly available.

SAN MATÍAS

The border town of San Matías is the main Bolivian access point into the northern Brazilian Pantanal. Travellers between Cáceres and Bolivia must pick up Brazilian entry or exit stamps from the Polícia Federal office at Rua Antônio João 160 in Cáceres. On the Bolivian side, you'll have to hunt up the immigration officer; otherwise, pick up your entry or exit stamp in Santa Cruz.

Places to Stay

You're limited to the *Hotel San José*, which charges US$4 per person for very basic, stifling accommodation. The best restaurant, which serves a very limited menu, is *BB's* (it stands for Bolivia/Brazil – cute).

Getting There & Away

The Bolivian military airline TAM has a return flight between Santa Cruz and San Matías on Thursday mornings.

There's a bus from Cáceres to San Matías (US$10, two hours) at 5 am Monday to Saturday and on Sunday at 7 am; it returns immediately after arriving. From Santa Cruz, Flota Transical Velasco and Expreso 31 del Este buses go to San Matías via San Ignacio every evening. The trip takes 22 to 24 hours.

Amazon Basin

Although it lies over 1000 km upstream from the great river, Bolivia's portion of the Amazon Basin better preserves the classic image many travellers associate with that river than the real thing itself. While Brazilian rainforests continue to suffer heavy depredation, the archetypal Amazon forests of northern Bolivia remain relatively intact. Although facing similar threats, they still offer a glimpse of the deep and mysterious Eden (they've also been called the Green Hell!) that calls from the glossy pages of travel brochures.

History

The Beni, Pando and surrounding areas have weathered continuous human immigration and boom-bust cycles. Only a few original forest-dwelling tribes remain, and even fewer continue their traditional subsistence hunting-and-gathering lifestyles. Indigenous peoples occupying the western regions of the Bolivian Amazon were conquered early on by the Incas.

Then came the Spanish, who wandered all over the Americas following rumours of a mystical city of unimaginable wealth, which they called El Dorado (The Gilded One). One such tale was of Paititi, an incredibly opulent land east of the Andean Cordillera near the source of the Río Paraguai. It was said to be governed by a particularly affluent king named El Gran Moxo. Though the would-be looters scoured the region for traces of the coveted booty, they found nothing but a few primitive and hostile tribes and muddy jungle villages. There was not a single street paved with gold nor a single royal treasury brimming with precious gems and metals. In the mid-17th century, the Spanish turned elsewhere in their quest for El Dorado.

The Jesuits The Spanish may have found nothing in the Moxos region that interested them, but the Jesuits did. The area was rich

Highlights

- Take a jungle or pampas trip from Rurrenabaque
- Spend a few days exploring the Reserva Biosférica del Beni
- Enjoy a slow river trip down the Río Mamoré between Trinidad and Guayaramerín
- Hike in the biologically diverse Noel Kempff Mercado National Park
- Join in the Fiesta del Santo Patrono de Moxos, held at San Iganacio de Moxos each 31 July
- Relax, go for a hike or swim in the idyllic natural swimming holes in the rainforest near Villa Tunari
- Canoe on the Río Beni between Guanay and Rurrenabaque

in souls ripe for the plucking by the messengers of the Christian god. Their first mission in the Moxos was founded at Loreto in 1675. The first significant European penetration of these lowlands was staged by these hardy missionaries.

The Jesuits set up a society similar to the one they would establish in the Llanos de Chiquitos and Llanos de Guarayos during the following century. They imposed Christianity and taught the indigenous people European ways – metal and leatherwork,

423

The Amazon Basin

weaving, basketry, writing, reading, printing and so on. They recognised a natural expertise in woodcarving, which developed into the brilliant carvings now characteristic of the missions. They imported herds of cattle and horses to remote outposts, and thanks to the prolific natural vegetation, the animals fared well. The descendants of these herds still thrive throughout most of the Beni department.

From the Indians, the Jesuits learned about agricultural methods in the tropical and often flooded lowlands. They, in turn, introduced unfamiliar crops, and the Beni today produces bananas, coffee, tobacco, cotton, cacao, peanuts and a host of other warm-weather crops.

After the expulsion of the Jesuits in 1767, the Franciscan and Dominican missionaries and the opportunistic settlers who followed brought only slavery and disease to the indigenous peoples. The vast, steamy forests and plains of northern Bolivia saw little other activity for 50 years.

The Rubber Boom The migration of the Suárez family from Santa Cruz to Trinidad in the late 19th century marked the beginning of serious economic exploitation of the region. While Suárez senior was occupied with cattle ranching, young Nicolás Suárez set off to explore the inhospitable wilderness of Bolivia's northern hinterlands (at the time, this included a sizeable portion of what is now western Brazil). He developed a substantial business dealing in quinine, derived from the bark of the cinchona tree.

When the rubber boom descended upon Amazonian Brazil, it was a simple matter for Suárez to arrange a system for transporting rubber around the Mamoré rapids into Brazil, and thence down the Río Madeira to the Amazon and the Atlantic. Before the turn of the century, the Suárez family owned about six million hectares of lowland real estate. However, a good proportion of these holdings lay in the remote Acre territory, which Bolivia lost to Brazil in 1903. Although a large percentage of the Suárez fortune was lost with the Acre, and Bolivia's rubber boom ground to a halt, the family was by no means devastated.

The Cocaine Trade Less than a century later, a member of the Suárez family came to control another booming industry. Coca, the leaf revered by the highland Indians for its ability to stave off the discomforts of altitude, thirst, hunger, discontent and stress, grows primarily in the Yungas mountains north of La Paz and in the Chapare region of the northern Cochabamba department. The Yungas produce the more palatable leaves while the Chapare crop is more bitter-tasting. Local Indians prefer the former for everyday consumption, while the Chapare coca has a worldwide market. Dried, soaked in kerosene and mashed into a pasty pulp, the leaves are treated with hydrochloric and sulphuric acid until they form a foul-smelling brown base. Further treatment with ether creates cocaine.

So profitable is the cocaine industry that 60% (and probably more) of Bolivia's informal gross national product is derived from it, and the country has become synonymous with large-scale production of illicit substances.

By the mid-1980s, the USA was consuming so much Bolivian cocaine that the US government decided something had to be done about it. Realising that it would be unpopular to bomb its own people, the USA threatened drastic DEA (Drug Enforcement Agency) action should the Bolivian government not cooperate with US military action aimed at curtailing cocaine production. When then US President Ronald Reagan

Coca leaf

proposed some joint cleaning up of the remote reaches of the Beni and Chapare regions, Bolivian President Victor Paz Estenssoro agreed to go along with their plans.

The operation was prematurely leaked to the press, however, giving remote processing labs sufficient warning to clear out before the bombs arrived. Only minor damage was done and the US government found itself in a rather embarrassing situation.

In 1987 the Bolivian army failed to arrest the elusive Roberto Suárez Gomez, when it noisily raided his ranch by helicopter, ruining the element of surprise. In Suárez's absence, the Bolivian government sentenced him to 12 years in prison, and in 1988 Bolivian soldiers, sent in quietly and under cover of night, managed to arrest the cocaine king while he slept.

Modern Bolivian Amazonia Despite all the attention focused on the environment and the drugs issue, northern Bolivia is not all cocaine and rainforest. Cattle ranching con-

tinues on a large scale, especially in the savannas north and west of Trinidad.

The region's main highways are Amazon tributaries – the Mamoré, Ichilo, Beni, Madre de Dios and Guaporé, to name but a few – which elsewhere would be considered great rivers in their own right. Along these jungle waterways, riverboats, barges, buckets and bathtubs are the predominant means of transport for passengers, freight, vehicles and livestock. Villages are still thin on the ground and some remote tribes have had only minimal contact with modern civilisation. All that is changing, however, with the recent spate of road construction leading to an influx of highland settlers and a subsequent upsurge in logging and land clearance.

Chapare Region

The word Chapare is synonymous with coca and DEA attempts to eradicate it, which have resulted in a few messy confrontations between *campesinos*, the DEA and the Bolivian government. The Bolivian media frequently exposes cases of human rights abuse and disregard for property. Although it isn't inherently unsafe to travel in the Chapare, violence may flare up at any time, especially in more remote areas. Currently, it's probably best not to stray too far off the Cochabamba-Santa Cruz highway.

VILLA TUNARI

The spectacular route from Cochabamba to Villa Tunari passes between peaks and mountain lakes before dropping steeply into deep, steaming valleys and levelling out into remnants of tropical forest. Villa Tunari is mainly a tropical resort for cold-weary highlanders, and a quiet spot to relax, hike, and swim in cool rivers. In the wet season, there's a small waterfall on the Río Chapare behind the public toilets.

A good independent walk is to the friendly village of Majo Pampa. Follow the route towards Hotel El Puente and turn right about

---

Hero or Bad Guy?

Roberto Suárez Gomez, the great-nephew of Nicolás Suárez, amassed a fortune from the cocaine trade. Throughout Bolivia, people perpetuate legends of the philanthropic deeds performed by this enigmatic man, who became a folk hero among his compatriots. One story has him landing unannounced in a Piper aircraft at Reyes airport, walking into a particularly poor neighbourhood and flinging large quantities of cash into the air for the local people. From there, he reportedly proceeded to the local drinking establishment and declared open bar for the evening.

Other tales speak of his donations to rural schools, development projects and health clinics. And, of course, now and again he's been known to make significant contributions to the federal government.

The life of Suárez Gomez reads like a spy novel in which the hero (or bad guy, depending on your point of view) always stays one step ahead of the CIA – or, in this case, the US Drug Enforcement Agency (DEA). ■

THE AMAZON BASIN

150m before the hotel. After you cross the river, it's about eight km farther along.

The telephone code is 0411.

Organised Tours

Villa Tunari is a main focus for the Dutch tour operator, Viajes Fremen (☎ 59392, Cochabamba), which arranges tours, accommodation, river trips and other activities at out-of-the-way sites. The tours aren't cheap, but do offer good value. Programmes include the Cuevas de los Pájaros Nocturnos (Caves of the Night Birds), in the Carrasco portion of Parque Nacional Amboró, where you'll see the rare nocturnal *guáchero (Steatornis caripensis)*, also known as the oilbird. This four-hour excursion includes a short slog through the rainforest and a thrilling crossing of the Río San Mateo on a single cable. With four people, it costs US$12 per person; with two people, it's US$19.

All-day rainforest walks, including guide and refreshments, cost US$15 per person with two people. You can also take an excursion to Todos Santos, an abandoned Italian colony near Puerto Aurora, which has been swallowed by lush forest greenery. All that remains is a church tower and the ruins of the old hospital. It lies 55 km from Villa Tunari on the Río Chapare. This trip costs US$34 per person, with four people.

Alternatively, you can hire a private guide for walks around the rainforest. A recommended guide is Marcelo Ondarza (☎ 4102). A suggested trip is to the newly established Parque Machia, which takes in great views, waterfalls and the small village of Copacabana. You return to Villa Tunari by canoe. Ondarza also organises longer and more adventurous trips to Parque Nacional Isiboro-Sécure using local transport. He asks US$25 per day for small groups and US$15 if you're alone. He's very knowledgeable about the area and can also provide insight into the Chapare coca problem.

Special Events

In the first week of August, Villa Tunari stages the Feria Regional del Pescado, in which a wide variety of lowland fish dishes are served up. Recipes feature *pacu*, dorado, *surubí* (catfish) and others.

Places to Stay & Eat

Viajes Fremen (☎ 59392, Cochabamba) operates *Hotel El Puente*, a forest retreat four km from Villa Tunari, near the point where the Ríos San Mateo and Espíritu Santo join to form the Río Chapare. It is delightfully hidden in a remnant island of rainforest. The highlight is a walk around Los Pozos, 14 idyllic natural swimming holes, deep in the forest along the river, where you're guaranteed to see fluttering blue morpho butterflies.

El Puente is a great place to spend a few days mellowing out and savouring the slow tropical pace. Prices are considerably lower if you book in Bolivia rather than overseas. Booked from Cochabamba, single/double cabañas cost US$22/28 and family rooms with one double bed and two twin beds are US$45. On weekdays, you'll get special deals, which include accommodation and full board for US$21 per person, with a minimum of three people. Otherwise, excellent meals cost US$3 for a full American breakfast, and US$4 each for lunch and dinner. To reach the hotel, catch a passing micro east of Villa Tunari; get off at the first turn-off after the second bridge, turn right and continue for two km through the forest to the hotel. Taxis from the centre charge about US$4 for up to four people.

The *Hotel Las Palmas*, east of town, charges US$24 for a double cabaña and US$10 per person for the dormitory, including access to the swimming pool. The attached restaurant serves well-prepared locally caught fish. Another option is the friendly *Hotel Las Vegas*, which also serves good meals. Rooms cost US$5 per person. Around the cobbled plaza in the Villa Tunari are *La Querencia*, which charges US$3 per person, and a nameless pink-and-blue *alojamiento* with rooms for US$2.50 per person.

Along the main road in Villa Tunari is a string of small food stalls selling good, inexpensive tropical fare.

THE AMAZON BASIN

Getting There & Away

Bus and micro offices are sandwiched amid the line of food stalls along the main highway. From Cochabamba, any micro to Puerto Villarroel or *flota* to Santa Cruz will pass through Villa Tunari. The fare is US$2 for the five to six-hour trip. Flota 7 de Junio leaves for Villa Tunari (US$2.60, five hours) from the terminal on Avenida República near 16 de Julio at least once every morning and at 1 and 4 pm.

From Villa Tunari to Santa Cruz, several services operate in the early afternoon, but most Santa Cruz traffic departs in the evening. To Cochabamba, micros leave at 8.30 am.

PUERTO VILLARROEL

The muddy tropical settlement of Puerto Villarroel, one of northern Bolivia's major river ports, lies several hours north-east of Villa Tunari. Although it's little more than a collection of tumbledown wooden hovels, a military installation, a YPFB (petroleum) plant and a loosely defined port area, it's both a vital transportation terminal and a gateway to the Amazon lowlands. If you just want a quick look at the rainforests, the trip to Puerto Villarroel is an easy two-day return trip from Cochabamba.

Bring lots of insect repellent and wear strong old shoes with lots of tread. Even in the dry season, the muddy streets of Puerto Villarroel will crawl up past your ankles.

Organised Tours

Viajes Fremen (☎ 59392) in Cochabamba organises three-day all-inclusive speedboat trips on the Ichilo between Puerto Villarroel and Trinidad, for US$330 per person with two people and US$237 with at least six people.

Places to Stay

There are only two hotels in Puerto Villarroel, both on the main street, and neither will win any awards. Fortunately, if you've arranged river transport to Trinidad

you're normally permitted to sleep on the boat.

Rooms at the very basic *Alojamiento Petrolero* are constructed of raw boards and scraps of wood pieced haphazardly together – the roof leaks and the beds get wet. If that's not enough, there's a rodent problem, the doors don't lock and strangers may wander in at all hours. There are no showers but there is a toilet in the banana grove out the back. For these conditions you'll pay US$1.50 per person.

The *Hotel Hannover* has a pleasant shady courtyard, lawn furniture, a restaurant and a disco/bar. This place is ideal for people who want to dance all night, because the noise level makes it impossible to sleep. You may ultimately decide it's a case of 'if you can't beat 'em, join 'em!'

A third choice is upstairs in the *ENTEL building*, which offers informal accommodation for US$2 per person.

Places to Eat

There are half a dozen acceptable restaurant shacks along the main street, offering mainly fish and chicken. For good empanadas, snacks, hot drinks and juice, try the market on the main street.

Getting There & Away

Bus & Camión Micros to Puerto Villarroel are marked 'Chapare' and leave from the corner of Avenidas 9 de Abril and Oquendo, near Laguna Alalay, in Cochabamba. The first one sets off at about 6.30 am and subsequent buses depart when full. The fare is US$2.20. The first *micro* back from Puerto Villarroel to Cochabamba leaves at 7 am from the bus stop on the main street. *Camiones* leave from the same place at any hour of the day, especially when there are boats in port.

Buses running between Cochabamba and Santa Cruz do not stop at Puerto Villarroel.

Boat Two types of local boats run between Puerto Villarroel and Trinidad. The small family-run cargo boats that putter up and down the Ríos Ichilo and Mamoré normally

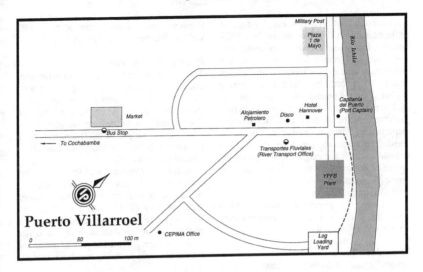

only travel by day and reach Trinidad in six to eight days. Larger commercial craft travel day and night and do the run in as little as four days.

The average fare to Trinidad on either type of boat is about US$25, including food. The quality of food varies from boat to boat, but overall the shipboard diet consists of fish, dried meat, masaco and fruit. Some boats may also offer turtle eggs, but as turtles are an endangered species in parts of the Bolivian Amazon, you might consider declining them. Even if your passage includes meals, it's wise to carry emergency rations in case the food proves too unexciting for your tastes. You can buy a passage without food for a few dollars less.

Hammocks are sold in Cochabamba markets, but it may be cheaper to buy one from a river traveller going in the opposite direction or to pick one up in Santa Cruz. Few boats along the Ichilo make cabins available to passengers. For further information, see the Getting Around chapter, or Getting There & Away in the Trinidad section later in this chapter.

The port captain's office, the CEPIMA office and the Transportes Fluviales (River Transport) office in Puerto Villarroel will all provide sketchy departure information on cargo transporters. You shouldn't have more than a three or four-day wait unless military exercises or labour strikes shut down cargo transport.

PARQUE NACIONAL ISIBORO-SÉCURE

Created in 1965, this 1.2 million-hectare national park occupies a large triangle between the Ríos Isiboro and Sécure and the Serranías Sejerruma, Mosetenes and Yanakaka. It takes in mountains, rainforest and savanna and was once (and in remoter sections, still is) home to profuse wildlife. An obscure 1905 Department of Cochabamba resolution opening the region to settlement means much of it has been overrun by humans and the wildlife has been almost wiped out.

Settlers have either displaced or exterminated the formerly large Indian population, which consisted primarily of Yuracarés, Chimanes, Sirionos and Trinitarios. Although stringent protection measures have been proposed, nothing has come of them.

Unfortunately, the park also lies along cocaine-producing and drug-running routes, so independent visitors must exercise extreme caution. Thanks to ruthless DEA activity, foreigners may be considered *anti-cocaleros* and hence fair game. It's very dangerous unless you have all the proper letters of recommendation from people higher-up in the coca-growers' association.

There's also a dispute over whether Isiboro-Sécure is part of Cochabamba department (Chapare) or whether it lies in the Beni. The suspected presence of oil in the region – which is being explored by all the major oil companies – makes the issue all the more relevant. In this book, the park is included under Chapare.

Although few people will be inclined to visit the park, increased awareness may improve conditions there.

Organised Tours

Viajes Fremen (☎ 59392, Cochabamba) runs eight-day boat trips from Trinidad to Laguna Bolivia, which is the most interesting destination in the park. The itinerary includes stops at riverside settlements, various forest walks, horseback rides, wildlife viewing and a canoe trip on the Río Ichoa. At present, this is the only truly safe way to visit the park, and is probably the easiest and most pleasant way to promote its preservation. Tours cost US$998 per person, with three to five people. If you have a group of nine or more, you'll pay just US$730 per person. These rates include accommodation in Trinidad before and after the trip as well as transfers, meals, transport and a guide. You can also hire a private guide (see Organised Tours under Villa Tunari, earlier in this chapter).

A rewarding alternative is offered by the indigenous peoples' organisation Confederación Indígena del Chaco, Amazonia y Oriente-Boliviano (CIDOB) and one of its branches, the Central de Pueblos Indígenas del Beni (CPIB). One branch of the latter, in turn, deals with the needs of the Yuracaré people. The leader of this group is the very amicable Marcial Fabricano, who sees sensitive tourism in the region as an economic benefit for the native people. If you're interested in organising a trip into the park with a native guide, contact him at the CPIB Cabildo Indígena (☎ 21575) in Trinidad.

Getting There & Away

This area is inaccessible between November and March because of flooding. If you wish to attempt an independent trip, take a bus from the end of Avenida Oquendo in Cochabamba to the village of Eterezama, which has an alojamiento. There, look for a camión to Isinuta, which also has alojamiento accommodation.

In Isinuta, you must wait for yet another camión to the Trinitarios Moxos community of Santísima Trinidad (not to be confused with the city of Trinidad farther north). Unless you're very lucky, to continue north of there – through Aroma, Ycoya and Río Moleto and deeper into the park's forests and savannas – will probably involve travelling on foot.

Western Bolivian Amazon

RURRENABAQUE

Rurrenabaque, a bustling little frontier settlement on the Río Beni, is the loveliest village in the Bolivian lowlands, and its changing moods can be magical. The sunsets are normally superb, and at night, dense clouds of fog roll down the river and create beautiful effects, especially at full moon.

The original people of the area, the Tacana, were one of the few lowland tribes that resisted Christianity and Western-style civilisation. It was the Tacana who were responsible for the name Beni, which means 'wind'. The name Rurrenabaque (locally shortened to just 'Rurre') is derived from Arroyo Inambaque, the Hispanicised version of the Tacana word 'SuseInambaque', which means the 'Ravine of Ducks'. The main draw for tourists to Rurrenabaque is the surrounding rainforest and pampa, which still supports Amazonian wildlife in relatively large numbers.

Rurrenabaque features prominently in the journals of the British explorer Colonel Percy Harrison Fawcett, and is also the setting of the book *Back from Tuichi*, the story of the 1981 rescue of Israeli Yossi Ginsberg, who was lost in the rainforest on an ill-fated expedition.

Information

There's no bank, but you can change travellers cheques and US dollars cash with Tico Tudela at Hotel Tuichi.

Any hotel or other business in Rurrenabaque may be contacted by leaving a message at the ENTEL office (☎ 2205). The telephone code is 0832.

Electricity services are sporadic.

Things to See & Do

Most of Rurrenabaque's appeal is natural beauty, and it's worth spending a day or two here. Behind the town is a low but steep hill affording a **view** across the seemingly endless Beni lowlands. It may be climbed via a track that begins near the *colegio* (secondary school).

Another nice excursion is to **El Chorro**, an idyllic pool and waterfall about one km up the Beni from town. A track leads from the wet sand beach to this favourite swimming and picnicking spot. The beach and track are accessible only by boat; enquire at Agencia Fluvial. On a rock rising out of the river opposite El Chorro is an ancient serpent engraving that was intended as a warning to travellers. When the water reached serpent level, the Beni was considered unnavigable.

You can cool off in the green-but-clean

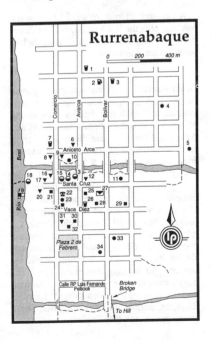

PLACES TO STAY
21	Hotel Berlin
24	Hotel El Porteño
25	Hotel Tuichi
28	Hotel Rurre
29	Alojamiento Aurora
30	Hotel Santa Ana
32	Hotel Taquara

PLACES TO EAT
6	Brostería Chorito
8	Pensión Ramos & Rincón Cochabambino
9	Buen Gusto
12	Heladería Bambi
16	Sede Social
17	Las Playas
20	La Chocita
31	Restaurant Illimani

OTHER
1	Bar El Resbalón
2	Petrol Station
3	Bar La Pascañita
4	Mercado Campsino
5	Military Base
7	Bar El Tropezón
10	Market
11	Balneario El Ambaiba
13	Flota Yungueña
14	Trufis to Reyes
15	Trans-Totaí Buses
18	Ferry to San Buenaventura
19	Agencia Fluvial Floating Dock
22	ENTEL
23	Eco-Tours
25	Agencia Fluvial
26	Discoteca Aqui Me Quedo
27	Post Office
33	LAB (Airline)
34	Secondary School

THE AMAZON BASIN

pool at the friendly Balneario El Ambaiba. It costs US$2 per person, but there's a garden bar with music, and a resident blue-and-yellow macaw, who's always good for a chat.

Organised Tours

Jungle Trips For an introduction to the wilder side of Bolivia, you can't beat a jungle trip from Rurrenabaque. The Bolivian rainforest is full of more interesting and unusual things than you'd ever imagine. The guides, most of whom have been reared in the area, are knowledgeable about the fauna, flora and forest lore and can explain animals' habits and habitats and demonstrate the uses of some of the thousands of plant species, including the forest's natural remedies for colds, fever, cuts, insect bites, diarrhoea and so on.

Trips are tailored to travellers' specific interests and no two are alike. You can explore the forest floor, fish, track tapirs and jaguars at night, or make a show of catching (and releasing) an alligator with your bare hands. To get the most out of a trip, a minimal knowledge of Spanish is requisite.

A standard trip begins by canoe upstream along the Río Beni as it winds between high, steep hills. Then you ascend the Río Tuichi, visiting various camps and taking shore walks along the way. There's plenty of time for swimming and relaxing as well as hiking and exploring. On the return trip, group construction of a large log raft provides for a hair-raising descent.

The trips, which aren't as touristy as they may sound, normally last from three to six days and include canoe transport, guides and food. Accommodation is on the river sand beneath a tarpaulin tent and a mosquito net.

Groups must form themselves so you may want to organise four or five people before leaving La Paz or Coroico (see Organised Tours below for agencies, costs etc). Most essential is a strong mosquito repellent. For other guidelines on what to take, see the What to Bring section in the Facts for the Visitor chapter.

Pampas Trips If you're more interested in

birds and animals than visiting the rainforest, you may want to opt for the pampas trip, which takes in the wetland savannas north of Rurrenabaque. It includes guided walks and both daytime and evening wildlife-viewing trips by boat. You can also try your hand at piranha fishing.

The normal three-day option begins with a three to four-hour bus ride to Santa Rosa and nearby Laguna Colorada. In the evening, you travel by boat across the lake to the Dormitorio de los Aves, a large tree which sustains an enormous bird colony.

On the second day, you travel by bus to the upper Río Yacuma, then by boat for three to four hours, watching along the way for a variety of birds and riverine wildlife, such as dolphins, caymans, monkeys and anaconda. After setting up camp on the riverbank, you go out in a boat by lantern light to search for eyes in the darkness. The last day includes a wildlife-viewing walk through the marshes and the return to Rurrenabaque by boat and bus.

A two-day alternative would take in the bus trip, plus the last two days of the three-day excursion (see Organised Tours below for agencies, costs etc).

Other Tours Several tour agencies organise jungle and pampas tours from Rurrenabaque, and each one has its own strong points. The two main ones – Eco-Tours and Agencia Fluvial – are both very good choices, but each offers a different experience. Contact either on ☎ 2205.

Agencia Fluvial, owned by Tico Tudela, runs jungle tours up the Río Tuichi and pampas tours to the area around Santa Rosa. The agency is based at the popular backpackers' digs, Hotel Tuichi, which makes it relatively easy to assemble a group. Tours are popular and well organised, with an emphasis on keeping several jumps ahead of hunters and logging concerns. The company's current project is to open up the wild and ecologically significant Laguna Rogagua, north-west of Santa Rosa. Some guides speak minimal English.

Eco-Tours, on Calle Comercio opposite Hotel Berlin, was formed by the Mamani brothers – Leoncio, Israel (Negro), Irguen, Nicolás and Uinmar. Some of the brothers are former guides of Agencia Fluvial and are familiar with the sort of experiences independent visitors want. They've all grown up in the forest and are well versed in local rainforest lore; Negro is an especially recommended guide. Note that mainly because of the public nature of the office, it's best not to deposit your belongings there while you're away.

Both Eco-Tours and Agencia Fluvial organise two to four-day jungle trips along the Río Tuichi for US$25 per day, or pampas trips along the Río Yacumo for US$30 per day. With Eco-Tours, there's a 5% discount if you pay with US-dollar travellers cheques, and with a large group you can add a bit of swimming and volleyball at Laguna Colorada, near Santa Rosa, for no extra charge.

From January to May, Eco-Tours also runs canoe trips up the remote Río Erasama, also known as the Río Hondo, which has so far escaped the scale of hunting and logging suffered by the more accessible Río Tuichi.

Transamazonas (☎ 350411, fax 360923), Office 3C, Edificio V Centenario, 3rd floor, Avenida 6 de Agosto (opposite the university), Casilla 14551, La Paz, is a third player. The Rurrenabaque office is on Calle Comercio. This agency also runs jungle and pampas trips, but it emphasises customised group tours which may last from three days to a month and focus on just about anything you'd like: bird-watching, botany, trekking, canoeing, jungle survival, native cultures and natural medicines. For groups of five to eight people, the charge is US$25 per person per day; English-speaking guides should be requested in advance.

Places to Stay

The favourite travellers' haunt is the friendly *Hotel Tuichi* on Calle Avaroa, run by Tico and Eli Tudela, which features laundry service, cooking facilities, and hammocks and tables in a pleasant garden. It's a good place to form tour groups if you're using

Agencia Fluvial. Rooms cost US$2.50/3 per person without/with bath, but they can't be prebooked. There's electricity from 11.30 am to 11.45 pm, which means that the fans work through the heat of the day. On 20 June each year, the hotel celebrates the Día de los Turistas, which began as a joke and has escalated into an annual event; it's worth checking out.

The equally welcoming *Hotel Rurre* (☎ 795917, La Paz) is also recommended. Rooms cost US$3/5 per person without/with bath, and simple dormitory rooms are just US$2 per person.

The basic *Hotel Santa Ana* has a nice courtyard with tables for enjoying the sun and drinking Yungas coffee, and cooking is permitted. Rooms without bath cost US$3 per person. However, cost-cutting measures mean that fans work for only a couple of hours each evening. Guests must also supply their own toilet paper.

The *Hotel Berlin*, near the river, offers friendly but rather unkempt accommodation for US$2/3 per person without/with bath and cold showers. The wall facing the thatched restaurant is graced with a mural of a German warship being tossed about the waves before a Río Beni shoreline!

The *Hotel El Porteño*, which is frequented by Bolivian travellers, charges US$6 per person for a room with private bath and hot water, and US$4 per person with a toilet and cold shower only. Dormitory rooms accommodating up to five people are US$2 per person. Rates are negotiable during slow periods, but beware of overcharging at other times.

The most upmarket place is the *Hotel Taquara*, on the main plaza, where relatively luxurious rooms with fans, private baths and inevitably mouldy carpet go for US$15 per person. It's geared toward petroleum executives and fly-in foreign tour groups.

Places to Eat

Everywhere in Rurre, you'll find excellent freshly brewed Yungas coffee, and fresh bread is available in the green-painted shop on the corner of Calles Avaroa and Santa

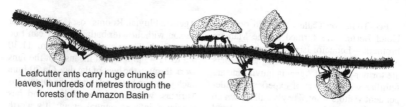

Leafcutter ants carry huge chunks of leaves, hundreds of metres through the forests of the Amazon Basin

Cruz. The *Hotel Berlin* serves nice inexpensive breakfasts, tropical specialities and Bolivian standards in a garden-like setting. If you want to try masaco, order it the day before. The *Sede Social*, on Calle Comercio, serves drinks and set meals for just US$1 per person.

Several fish restaurants occupy wooden shelters along the riverfront: *La Chocita* and *Las Playas* are sporadically good, depending on the prevailing temperament and the catch of the day. They're also good places to sample masaco. The friendly *Heladería Bambi* is highly recommended for toasted sandwiches, burgers, snacks, ice cream, soda and beer, all of which go down well on a typically hot and sticky Rurre afternoon.

Pensión Ramos, *Rincón Cochabambino* and *Buen Gusto*, all in the same stretch of Calle Comercio, serve almuerzos and cenas. The last is the pick of the bunch, with a typical cena of soup, main course, rice and salad for US$0.80. *Brostería Chorito* concentrates on chicken and standard meat dishes and *Restaurant Illimani* has all the old Bolivian favourites.

Entertainment

If you're looking for nightlife in Rurre, you're scraping the barrel. You'll find several bars – among them *El Resbalón*, *La Pascañita* and *El Tropezón*. The most popular disco is *Aquí me Quedo* and there are two video cinemas, one on Calle Comercio and one on Avaroa, but that's about it.

Things to Buy

Rurrenabaque is a good place to pick up hammocks, which sell for US$7 for a single and US$13 for a double. Finely woven quality mosquito nets start at about US$11.

Getting There & Away

Air Although it makes little sense, there's a new airport at Rurrenabaque, which hopes to attract international flights.

The flight from La Paz to Rurrenabaque is glorious on a clear day. The plane passes between 6000m peaks as it climbs over the spine of the Cordillera Real, then flies over the Yungas, where the land dramatically drops away and opens onto the forested expanses of the Amazon Basin. In theory, TAM has US$45 Monday flights between La Paz and Rurre, via Apolo. They leave La Paz at 10 am and from Rurre at 12.15 pm. In reality, they're often cancelled.

Bus When the roads are dry, several flotas run daily between Rurrenabaque and La Paz (US$12.50, 18 hours). If you want to get off at Yolosa (for Coroico), you'll pay US$9.30. There are also daily runs to Trinidad (US$9, eight hours) via Yucumo, San Borja and San Ignacio de Moxos. Trans-Totaí buses leave for Riberalta (US$14.50, 13 hours) and Guayaramerín (US$16.50, 15 hours) on Wednesday and Sunday, and Trans-Guaya Tours goes on Friday. *Trufis* to Reyes leave when full from the corner of Comercio and Santa Cruz.

Boat Thanks to the Guayaramerín road, river-cargo transport down the Beni to Riberalta is now very limited (see Riberalta later in this chapter), and there's no traffic at all during periods of low water. If you do find something, plan on four or five days at about US$5 per day for the 1000-km trip, including meals. Going the opposite direction, the journey takes as many as 10 days. Enquire at the disco Aquí me Quedo.

Unless the river is very low, motorised canoe transport upriver to Guanay is much easier to come by; you'll pay about US$20 per person for the 10-hour trip. Enquire at the Hotel Tuichi. See also Getting There & Away under Guanay in the Cordilleras & Yungas chapter.

Cargo transport is rare between Guanay and Rurrenabaque, and a new bridge has left Puerto Linares cut off from all but small canoe traffic.

Taxi ferries to San Buenaventura, on the opposite shore of the Río Beni, depart from the riverbank when full and cost US$0.20.

SAN BUENAVENTURA

On the La Paz department bank of the Río Beni, opposite Rurrenabaque, is the laid-back tropical town of San Buenaventura. Since residents mostly conduct their business across the river in Rurre, nothing much is going on in San Buenaventura, and that's the way they seem to like it. There is the disco Musica Buena near the ferry landing, which hums at weekends, and if you're looking for fine Beni leather wallets and bags, visit the well-known shop of leather artesan Manuel Pinto.

Places to Stay

The only accommodation is the very basic *Alojamiento Florida*, which charges US$2 per person.

Getting There & Away

There's no road link to San Buenaventura; you have to take the ferry across the Río Beni (see the Rurrenabaque section).

PARQUE NACIONAL ALTO MADIDI

The Río Madidi watershed, which has been slated for oil exploration, contains one of the most intact ecosystems in South America, and part of it is protected by the new Parque Nacional Alto Madidi. The park takes in a range of wildlife habitats, from steaming lowland rainforests to Andean peaks reaching up to 5500m. It's thought that the park is home to more than 1000 species of birds – over 10% of all known species in the world.

The populated portions of the park along the Río Tuichi have been given a special UNESCO distinction allowing indigenous people to continue their traditional lifestyles using forest resources.

The greatest threat to the park is from logging activity, both around the Tuichi and in the colonisation areas at the northern end of the park, near Ixiamas.

There are currently plans to establish a simple tourist complex at Laguna Chalalan, a lovely oxbow lake by the Tuichi near San José de Uchupiamonas. If it happens, it will rival Peru's Parque Nacional Manu as one of the world's best places to observe rainforest species.

Getting There & Away

Most of the national park is inaccessible, which is why it remains a treasure. Agencia Fluvial in Rurrenabaque can arrange guides to take you up the Tuichi and over the hills into the Madidi headwaters. Plan on at least seven days for this spectacular trip. The more adventurous can hire a guide in Apolo and hike down into the park, but this is an arduous trip (getting to Apolo is an adventure in itself) which is only for the fit and well-prepared.

REYES & SANTA ROSA

Both Reyes and Santa Rosa, as yet relatively undiscovered by tourists, have lovely lagoons with myriad birds, alligators and other local wildlife. Reyes is only half an hour from Rurrenabaque, and Santa Rosa, with its attractive Laguna Rogagua, is 1½ hours farther on. Currently, Agencia Fluvial in Rurrenabaque is attempting to set up organised excursions to Laguna Rogagua.

Places to Stay & Eat

In Reyes, you can stay at the *Residencial 6 de Enero* and arrange horse rentals for trips around the lagoons with Señor Saúl Simons. At Santa Rosa there's the *Hotel Oriental*, and the same Simons family also organises horse rentals. For decent meals in Santa Rosa, go to the very amenable *Restaurant El Triángulo*.

TAWA Tours in La Paz operates its own jungle camp, *Santa Rosa Camp*, five minutes walk from lovely Laguna Santa Rosa. Accommodation in comfortable but rustic cabañas is US$24 per person per day, including full board, and they organise a range of activities and tours (it will help if you speak French). For prebooked guests, river transfers from Rurrenabaque cost US$150 for up to 10 people. For details, see Organised Tours under La Paz.

Getting There & Away
All buses between La Paz and Riberalta pass through both Reyes and Santa Rosa.

YUCUMO
The main thing to know about Yucumo, a frontier eldorado for development-crazed settlers, is how to get there and away as quickly as possible. It lies at the intersection of the La Paz-Guayaramerín road and the Trinidad turn-off.

The road between Rurrenabaque and Yucumo passes through once thick rainforest. Now every second building is a sawmill or chainsaw dealer; cattle graze among the tree stumps on increasingly barren land; and logging trucks penetrate the deepest recesses of the forest on an expanding network of rough-hewn tributary tracks bulldozed by donated machinery.

It's a nice walk along the road south of town; then follow the walking track which turns left at the bridge. You may see scarlet macaws.

Places to Stay
If you're trapped for the night, you can stay at *Alojamiento Las Palmeras* or *Alojamiento Yucumo*, both of which charge US$2 per person.

Getting There & Away
All buses travelling between Rurrenabaque and La Paz or Trinidad pass through Yucumo. Alternatively, it's not too difficult to find a camión going in the right direction.

Once in Yucumo, connect with the white camionetas, which will take you through the savanna to San Borja in less than an hour

(US$1.50). In San Borja, you'll find camiones and buses to the Reserva Biosférica del Beni, San Ignacio de Moxos and Trinidad.

SAN BORJA
With a penchant for illicit dealings, San Borja takes on a dark cast, and travellers may sense unsettling vibes. However, it's dangerous only to those involved in the cocaine trade.

The telephone code for San Borja is 0848.

Things to See & Do
There's not a lot to keep you occupied around San Borja, but the town's prosperity is revealed in the rather palatial homes which rise on the block behind the church.

A long day walk along the relatively little-travelled road west of town will take you through an area of **wetlands** and small ponds frequented by numerous species of tropical birds. You may see rheas, jabirus and other storks, limpkins, spoonbills, hawks, caracaras and a host of other birds.

Places to Stay
Top of the hotel heap is the friendly and clean *Hotel San Borja*, at the corner of the plaza, which charges US$4.10/6.20 per person without/with bath.

The *Hotel Trópico* is acceptable but less elegant, with constant noise and only screen windows to keep the mosquitoes at bay. It charges US$2 per person with shared hot showers.

The *Hotel Victoria* opposite the Hotel Trópico also charges US$2 per person with bath, but it's a bit of a dump. The more pleasant and lively *Residencial San Luis*, two blocks from the plaza, also charges US$2 per person without bath.

Places to Eat
One of the best options is the courtyard restaurant at the *Hotel San Borja*. Meals are fairly standard but there's ceaseless entertainment provided by caged parrots and

other birds, whose constant babble resembles the sound of a schoolyard at break time.

One block off the plaza is the popular *La Pascana de Camba* where it's lomo, lomo, lomo – as well as an assortment of lesser incarnations – all orchestrated by pounding rock music and slobbering drunks. It's not memorable but it's about the best you'll find.

Getting There & Away

Air AeroSur (☎ & fax 3185) flies between Trinidad and San Borja daily except Wednesday and Sunday.

Bus & Camión Along the road between San Borja and San Ignacio de Moxos, look for wildlife and birds: herons, jabiru storks, cormorants, birds of prey, egrets and countless others. You may also spot capybaras and pink river dolphins at small river crossings.

The transport terminals line up on the street south of the plaza. They belong to a syndicate so when one decides not to travel, they're all obligated to suspend service. Private vehicle owners also queue up to await passengers along the same street and only charge a bit more than the syndicate.

Camionetas Trans-Moxos leaves daily for Trinidad and Santa Cruz; the fare is US$2.50 to the Reserva Biosférica del Beni, US$4 to San Ignacio de Moxos, US$8 to Trinidad and US$16.50 to Santa Cruz for a seat in the back of a pick-up. For a bit extra, you can ride in the cab.

Transportadora 10 de Febrero runs 'Mini-Jumbo' tourist buses to La Paz on Tuesday and Thursday, and pick-ups to San Ignacio and Trinidad daily. Several other companies also go to San Ignacio and Trinidad, and pick-ups frequently depart for the one-hour run to Yucumo, which costs US$1.50 per person.

Car & Motorcycle If you're Trinidad-bound, remember the Mamoré balsa crossing closes at 6 pm and you need five to six hours to reach it from San Borja. There's no accommodation on either side of the crossing.

RESERVA BIOSFÉRICA DEL BENI

Created by Conservation International in 1982 as a loosely protected natural area, the 334,200-hectare Beni Biosphere Reserve was recognised by UNESCO in 1986 as a 'Man & the Biosphere Reserve'. The follow-

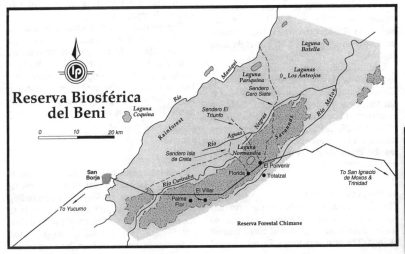

ing year, it received official Bolivian Congressional recognition through a debt trade agreement with the Bolivian government (see Ecology & Environment in Facts about the Country).

The abutting Reserva Forestal Chimane (Chimane Forest Reserve), a 1.15 million-hectare buffer zone and Indian reserve, has also been set aside for sustained subsistence use by the 1200 Chimane people living inside it. The combined areas are home to at least 500 species of tropical bird as well as more than 100 species of mammal, including monkeys, jaguars, deer, two species of peccary, river otters, foxes, anteaters and bats.

In September 1990, the Chimane reserve was threatened when the government opened it up to logging interests. In response, 700 Chimanes and representatives of other tribes staged a 'March for Dignity and Territory' from Trinidad to La Paz to protest what would amount to the wholesale destruction of their land and its flora and fauna. Logging concessions were rezoned but not altogether revoked.

Information

Admission to the reserve is US$5 for foreigners and US$3.50 for Bolivian citizens. Guides cost US$3 per day if you provide their food (US$5 otherwise). Horse rentals are also available for US$6 per eight-hour day.

Scientific personnel wishing to carry out research here should address enquiries to Ms Carolina Zumarán, Outreach Program Coordinator, Beni Biological Station, Bolivian Academy of Natural Sciences (fax 352071), PO Box 5829, La Paz, Bolivia. Other visitors should contact Conservación Internacional; see the Environment & Ecology section in the Facts about the Country chapter.

Visiting the Reserve

The El Porvenir station lies in the savannas quite a distance from the true rainforest, so walks around the station will be of limited interest. The best way to see the reserve and

observe its wildlife is to hire a guide and explore the primary and secondary-growth rainforests north of the savanna areas. To reach the northern areas of the reserve, allow at least four days travel from El Porvenir.

The best time to visit is in June and July when there's little rain and days are clear; bring warm clothing to protect yourself from the occasional *surazo*, a cold south wind. During the rainy season, days are hot, rainy, muggy and miserable with mosquitoes. In August and September, the atmosphere becomes sombre with the smoke from *chaqueo* (see the aside on the next page).

Laguna Normandia

The most popular destination, the savanna lake, Laguna Normandia, lies only two hours walk from El Porvenir. It's chock-a-block with rare black caymans *(caimanes negros)* – 400 at last count – which are descendants of specimens originally destined to become shoes and handbags. When the breeder's leather business failed, the caymans were left to fend for themselves and the vast majority perished from neglect, crowding and hunger. The survivors were confiscated by Bolivian authorities and, with the aid of a US$20,000 grant from the French, were airlifted into Laguna Normandia.

The caymans have no interest in humans so it's safe to observe them at close range; if you're dubious, hire a guide to accompany you. There's a rowing boat at the lake for public use – and close-up cayman viewing – but the shore is quite muddy and launching it will involve slogging through slime. A family living along the route sells refreshing *pomelo* drinks to hikers.

The Rainforest

Beyond Laguna Normandia, a guide is required. Certified guides from El Porvenir are good value at US$7 per day, including food. From the lake, it's a four-hour walk to the margin of the secondary-growth rainforest. There you'll find a bug-infested *campamento* beside a clean, inviting stream

The Big Smoke, Fire & Rain

Every year in September, the skies over Bolivia fill with a thick pall of smoke, obscuring the air, cancelling flights, aggravating allergies and causing respiratory problems and conjunctivitis all around the country. Illimani disappears from the La Paz skyline and the view of the Cordillera Real from Lake Titicaca is lost. Fly into Trinidad or Guayaramerín and you won't see the ground until you're on it.

This is a result of *chaqueo*, the slashing and burning of the rainforest for agricultural and grazing land. In some places, forest is burned in the mistaken belief that the smoke will rise and become clouds, thus ensuring good rains for the coming season. The World Bank estimates that each year, Bolivia loses 115,000 to 200,000 hectares of forest in this way.

Although the burnt vegetable matter initially provides rich nutrients for crops, those nutrients aren't replenished, and the land becomes barren after two or three years. Such a plot requires 15 years to become productive again and that's too long for farmers to wait, so they pull up stakes and search for more forest to burn.

Beni ranchers have long set fire to the savannas annually to encourage the sprouting of new grass. Now, however, some of the most dramatic deforestation is occurring along the highways of the northern frontier, around Cobija, Riberalta and Guayaramerín. In the mid-1980s, this was largely virgin wilderness accessible only by air and river; the new roads connecting the region to La Paz have turned it into a free-for-all. Forest is being consumed by expanding cattle ranches, and only charred tree stumps remain.

Forestry statutes prohibit burning of the forest, but it is impossible to enforce effectively in an area as vast as the Bolivian lowlands. What's more, the practice has been going on for hundreds of years. When relatively few people were farming the lowlands, the effects of chaqueo were minimal. However, Bolivia's current annual population growth rate of 2.4% means that an additional 170,000 people must be fed each year, and as most of this growth is in the rural sector, more farmers' children are looking for land of their own.

Although the long-term implications aren't yet known (but you'll get a good idea by looking at the devastated Brazilian states of Acre and Rondônia), the Bolivian government has implemented a programme aimed at teaching forest fire control and encouraging lowland farmers to minimise chaqueo in favour of alternatives – presumably mulching and composting – which don't drain the soil of nutrients. ∎

---

where you can pitch a tent. It's an ideal swimming spot.

A further four hours walk through secondary forest takes you to the primary forest. The first camp site is beside a river with an established fire pit and lots of birds and alligators. You'll need a tent. The river water is good to drink and there's a chance of observing peccaries and several species of monkey.

Totaizal & Reserva Forestal Chimane

Only a stone's throw from the road, 40 minutes walk from El Porvenir, is Totaizal. This friendly and well-organised village of 140 people lies hidden in the forest of the Chimane reserve. The Chimane are one of Bolivia's best known nomadic forest tribes, and are currently being driven from their ancestral lands by lumber companies and highland settlers. Skilful hunters, they also

catch fish with natural poisons and are particularly adept at avoiding the stickier drawbacks of wild honey collection. People living in the settlement of Ocho Cero, four hours walk from Totaizal, trudge into the village to sell bananas.

Local guides can take you into the deeper recesses of the reserve. Before venturing into this traditional area, please read the Gift Giving aside in the Facts for the Visitor chapter.

Places to Stay & Eat

Although El Porvenir isn't equipped for large numbers of visitors, it does offer accommodation and meals. It's a good idea to make advance arrangements through the Bolivian Academy of Natural Sciences (see Information in this section). Foreigners pay a US$6 entrance fee, US$6 per person for a

THE AMAZON BASIN

bed and an additional US$6 for three meals. Meals are good, but not opulent, and it's OK to bring food from elsewhere. With your own food and tent, you may be able to negotiate the daily rate down to about US$3 per person.

Getting There & Away
The Beni Biosphere Reserve station El Porvenir, lies 200m off the highway just an hour east of San Borja, so access is straightforward. Several companies operate camiones and camionetas between San Borja, San Ignacio de Moxos and Trinidad. Reserve personnel charge US$3 per person for transport from San Borja.

SAN IGNACIO DE MOXOS
This Moxos Indian village 89 km west of Trinidad was founded as San Ignacio de Loyola by the Jesuits in 1689. In 1760 the village suffered pestilence and had to be shifted to its present location on higher and healthier ground.

Although the Jesuits were expelled from South America in 1767, Jesuit priests are now returning not only to work among the Moxos but also to strike an understanding between the Moxos, the dispossessed Chimane people and the newly arriving settlers and loggers.

Despite all the outside factions in the Beni, San Ignacio de Moxos remains a friendly and tranquil agricultural village with an ambience quite distinct from any other in Bolivia. The people speak an indigenous dialect known locally as Ignaciano, and their lifestyles, traditions and foods are unique in the country.

Things to See & Do
In the main plaza there is a **monument** to Chirípieru, El Machetero Ignaciano, with his crown of feathers and formidable-looking hatchet. The relatively recent church on the plaza is filled with local art and Ignaciano religious murals.

At the **museum** in the Casa Belén near the north-west corner of the plaza, you can see elements of both the Ignaciano and Moxos cultures, including the bajones, or immense zampoñas (flutes), introduced by the Jesuits.

North of town is the large **Laguna Isirere**, a great lake for swimming and fishing, but it's accessible only by hitching from town. There is profuse bird life and the possibility of seeing larger species as well.

Special Events
Annually, 31 July is the first day of the huge Fiesta del Santo Patrono de Moxos, in honour of the sacred protector of the Moxos. As in most Bolivian fiestas, the celebration includes games, music, dancing and drinking. The festivities culminate at 2 pm on the final day of the fiesta, when wildly clad dancers led by El Machetero himself proceed from the church, accompanied by fiddles and woodwind instruments.

Places to Stay & Eat
The friendly Residencial 31 de Julio, one block off the plaza, charges US$2 per person for clean and basic accommodation (prices double during the Fiesta del Santo Patrono). Residencial 22 de Abril, on the plaza to the right of the church, is known for its good breakfasts. It charges US$2 per person and hot water is occasionally available. The recommended Residencial Don Joaquín, at the corner of the plaza near the church, has a nice patio and charges US$3/5 per person without/with bath.

Other similarly priced places include Residencial Tamarindo and Residencial 14 de Septiembre, which are both on the main street.

During the fiesta, visitors are permitted to set up tents at established sites in the environs of town.

The recommended eating establishment is the wonderfully friendly Restaurant Don Chanta on the corner of the plaza. Don't miss the Ignaciano specialities: chicha de camote (sweet potato chicha) and the interesting sopa de joco (beet and pumpkin soup). Another good dining choice is Restaurant Cherlis, also on the plaza.

THE AMAZON BASIN

Getting There & Away

From Trinidad, micros and camionetas (US$2.50, three hours) leave for San Ignacio when full from the terminals on Avenida Mariscal Santa Cruz, and camiones leave in the morning from the east end of Calle La Paz near the river. There's good forest scenery all along the way, but be prepared for delays of about half an hour at the Río Mamoré balsa crossing between Puerto Barador and Puerto Ganadero. The crossing costs US$6 per vehicle and closes at 6 pm. There's no accommodation on either side so check the timing before setting out between San Ignacio and Trinidad.

From March to October, it takes two or three hours from Trinidad, including the balsa crossing, but in the summer rainy season the road may become impassable.

Eastern Bolivian Amazon

TRINIDAD

The tropical city of Trinidad, at an altitude of 237m, looks somewhat like Santa Cruz did 20 years ago and is now the Beni capital and the nerve centre of the Bolivian Amazon. Although not Bolivia's most prepossessing city – the open sewers are a nauseating health hazard – Trinidad's population has now passed 60,000 and is growing.

Only 14° latitude south of the equator, Trinidad has a humid tropical climate. The seasons are less pronounced than in other parts of Bolivia and temperatures are uniformly hot year-round. Most of the rain falls during the summer in unrelenting downpours. Although winter is drier than summer, it also sees a good measure of precipitation.

History

The city of La Santísima Trinidad (the Most Holy Trinity) was founded in 1686 by Padre Cipriano Barace as the second Jesuit mission in the flatlands of the southern Beni. It was originally constructed on the banks of the Río Mamoré 14 km from its present location, but floods and pestilence along the riverbanks necessitated relocation. In 1769 it was moved to the Arroyo de San Juan, which now divides the city in two.

Orientation

Don't rely too heavily on street names in Trinidad. They've been changed several times over the past decade, and it seems that no two maps agree on the current names. Fortunately, the city isn't too big and the confusion caused by this will be minimal. Of note, Avenida Mariscal Santa Cruz is sometimes known as Avenida Pedro Ignacio Muiva, and Calle Junín is sometimes called Calle Pedro de la Rocha.

Information

Money You'll find street moneychangers on Avenida 6 de Agosto between Calle Nicolás Suárez and Avenida 18 de Noviembre, but they only deal in US dollars cash. You can change travellers cheques for a 2% commission at the friendly and efficient Banco Sur, half a block from the plaza beneath the old Hotel Ganadero.

Post & Communications Service at the main post office, just off the plaza, moves at a suitably tropical pace. The public fax number is 24100. The telephone code for Trinidad is 046.

Laundry When your clothes can no longer cope with the sticky heat, drop in at the Lavandería Pro-Vida on Calle Felix Sattori.

Dangers & Annoyances Trinidad's open sewers are enough to make anyone retch – except perhaps the three-metre boa constrictor we found swimming in one. Be especially careful at night.

In recent years, Trinidad has been a centre of the DEA's anti-drug activities in Bolivia. Although the focus has now shifted south to Chapare, the Beni still sees sporadic action. And people haven't forgotten 1991, when the DEA occupied the city and behaved objectionably. Don't be surprised if locals

Trinidad

react bemusedly – or are even a bit resentful – toward foreigners.

Plaza Moto Rally

If you want to participate in the Trinidad social scene or you're after a touch of US-style nostalgia, spend an evening (particularly on a Sunday) on the balcony of the Heladería Kivón ice-cream parlour and watch the motorcycles cruising around the plaza. It's all a bit like *American Graffiti* with a tropical twist. The whole affair is refereed by a police officer who sits in a huge wooden chair and conjures up red, yellow and green traffic lights by touching an electric wire against one of three nails.

Also on the plaza, watch for the several lethargic sloths that inhabit the trees, and note the statue of Ballivián, which bears the Beni coat of arms. The unusual plaza fountain – a mishmash of carved Indians, pink dolphins, puma heads and buzzards – is also worth a photo.

Zoo

Trinidad's small zoo is at the university and has specimens of indigenous tropical animals.

PLACES TO STAY		PLACES TO EAT		12	ENTEL
2	Hotel Bajío	6	El Moro	13	Post Office
4	Alojamiento Ortiz	7	El Pacumutu	21	Motorcycle Rental
9	Residencial Forestero	11	Heladería Iglu		(Two Locations)
14	Hotel Copacabana	19	Snack Brasilia	22	Plaza General José
15	Residencial Colonial	20	Carlitos		Ballivián
16	Gran Hotel Moxos	23	Heladería Kivón	26	Immigration
17	Hotel Monte Verde	24	La Casona	27	Cathedral
18	Hotel Beni	37	El Dragón Chino	28	Banco Sur
19	Hotel Paulista			29	Micros to San Ignacio
25	Mi Residencia	**OTHER**			de Moxos
31	Residencial 18 de	1	Airport	30	Motos de Alquiler
	Noviembre	3	Laundrette	32	LAB (Airline)
33	Residencial Palermo	5	Police	36	Mercado Municipal
34	Hotel Avenida	8	Mercado Fátima	38	Transportes Fluviales
35	Hotel Yacuma	10	Bus Terminal	39	Mercado Pompeya

Organised Tours

Although it's difficult to arrange a jungle trip on your own, a couple of Trinidad tour agencies run excursions into the city's hinterlands. One of these is Turismo Moxos (☎ 21141), 114 Avenida 6 de Agosto, which organises tours to San Ignacio de Moxos and Loreto as well as canoe and horseback safaris into more remote areas. Prices are about US$20 per person per day.

Viajes Fremen (☎ 22276), Calle Loreto, on the corner of Calle Riberalta, is a Cochabamba-based agency specialising in river cruises on the relatively posh 'Flotel' *Reina de Enin*. This Dutch hotel boat based at Puerto Barador does excursions of three to six nights on the Mamoré, with stops at places of interest. For groups of fewer than 10 people, a three-night excursion costs about US$268 per person while six-night tours are US$440 per person. Rates include transport, sleeping quarters, tours and guide. Per-person prices are lower for larger groups.

Places to Stay – bottom end

The budget travellers' favourite is probably *Hotel Yacuma* (☎ 22249), a sort of faded Graham Greene tropical outpost. Basic rooms without/with bath cost US$3/5 per person. Snacks are served on the quiet patio, which is a great place to pass a sultry afternoon.

Another good choice is the clean and central *Hotel Paulista* (☎ 20018), which charges US$5/9.50 for single/double rooms without bath (US$8.25/13.50 with bath). The simple *Residencial Forestero* (☎ 20802), opposite the bus terminal on Calle Viados Pinto, charges US$2.50/5 per person without/with bath.

The cheapest decent place is *Alojamiento Ortiz*, which charges US$3 per person. Trinidad also has a crop of medium-to-worse budget hotels strung along Avenida 6 de Agosto. The best appears to be the spartan but clean *Residencial Palermo* (☎ 20472), two blocks from the plaza, which charges US$2.40/4.10 per person without/with bath. The nicer *Hotel Beni* (☎ 20522) charges US$10.30/13.50 for singles/doubles with bath, fan, phone and TV. A bit farther down is *Hotel Avenida* (☎ 22356), which charges US$6.20 per person with private bath. The friendly but not entirely clean *Residencial 18 de Noviembre* (☎ 21272) charges US$3/4 per person without/with bath. Hammocks are available for lounging around the patio.

Places to Stay – middle

A recommended mid-range place is *Hotel Monte Verde* (☎ 22750, fax 22044). With a bit of friendly bargaining, you can get singles/doubles with bath and fan for US$15.50/21, including a continental breakfast. For US$25/35, you'll get a fridge, TV, air-con and gas hot showers.

Although expensive, one of the cleanest

THE AMAZON BASIN

mid-range options is *Mi Residencia* (☎ 21529, fax 22464) at Calle Manuel Limpias 76, half a block from the post office. They charge US$25/35 for a single/double, including breakfast, and US$52 for a double suite.

The three-star *Hotel Bajío* (☎ 22400, fax 20030) at Calle Nicolás Suárez 520 is good value at US$19/30 for singles/doubles with fan and private bath. With air-con you'll pay US$26/36. All rates include a continental breakfast, and guests have access to the swimming pool and sauna.

Places to Stay – top end
For many years, Trinidad's 'business' digs was the four-star Hotel Ganadero, which, ironically, was occupied by the DEA in 1991. The hotel closed down in 1995, however, and if or when it will reopen is anyone's guess.

By default, the current business travellers' choice is the four-star *Gran Hotel Moxos* (☎ 22240, 20002), where singles/doubles with TV and air-con cost US$45/60. A suite costs US$100. Credit cards are accepted.

Places to Eat
If budget is a major concern, go to the *Mercado Municipal*. For a pittance, you can pick up tropical fruits and try the local speciality, arroz con queso (rice with cheese), plus kebab, yuca, plantain and salad.

Light meals, full breakfasts, ice cream, cakes, sweets, pastries, sandwiches, coffee and juice are served at *Heladería Kivón*, the local youth hang-out on the plaza. It's open when everything else is closed, including mornings and Saturday afternoon.

Also on the plaza are *La Casona* pizzería and *Carlitos*, which specialises in that Beni forte, parrillada. Nearby *Snack Brasilia* does a standard menu of good, inexpensive lunch options. Another snack option, *Heladería Iglu*, is worth visiting for its amazing jungle courtyard setting alone.

Since Trinidad is the heart of cattle country, it's a practical place to indulge in beef. *El Pacumutu*, on Avenida Velasco between Bolívar and Cespedes, specialises in meat dishes and is very popular with

locals. Pacumutus are chopped chunks of beef marinated in salt and lime juice and barbecued on a skewer; even if you get a medio (half) for two people, it'll still be too much, especially with the trimmings. There's also a nice dining room at the Hotel Bajío which does beef dishes.

For something different, try *El Dragón Chino* on Calle Cipriano Barace opposite the Mercado Municipal. Although it's run by a woman from Beijing, the food is 'Bolivianised'. For excellent local fish specialities, try *El Moro*, on the corner of Avenidas Bolívar and Velasco. It's just a short hike from the centre, but after dark, you may want to catch a taxi. Better still, head out to Puerto Barador, where makeshift restaurants serve up the catch of the day.

Getting There & Away
Air The LAB office (☎ 20595) is on Avenida Santa Cruz, and TAM (☎ 20855) is on Avenida Bolívar between 18 de Noviembre and Avenida Santa Cruz and has a notice board that keeps travellers up-to-date on flight changes and cancellations – useful in the rainy season. In addition to the US$1.75 AASANA tax, there's an airport tax of US$0.60, which ostensibly goes to support senior citizens and finance public works.

LAB (☎ 20595) and AeroSur (☎ 20765) both fly to La Paz (US$57), Cochabamba (US$48), Santa Cruz (US$56.50), Riberalta (US$71), Guayaramerín (US$71) and Cobija (US$100). LAB also has several weekly flights to San Joaquín (US$35.50), Magdalena (US$32.50) and San Ramón (US$32). AeroSur flies to San Borja (US$57).

Bus & Camioneta In the dry season, numerous flotas depart nightly for Santa Cruz from the main bus terminal, at the corner of Calles Pinto and Rómulo Mendoza. The most luxurious is Flota Copacabana (☎ 22193), which has heating, air-con, videos, refreshments and a steward. The trip costs US$15 and under optimum conditions takes 11 to 12 hours.

Several companies leave for San Borja,

Down the Lazy River

River trips from Trinidad will carry you to the heart of Bolivia's greatest wilderness area, where you'll experience the mystique and solitude for which the Amazon is renowned. For optimum enjoyment, go during the dry season, which lasts roughly from May to September.

Although the scenery along the northern rivers changes little, the diversity of plant and animal species along the shore picks up any slack in the pace of the journey. The longer your trip, the deeper you'll gaze into the forest darkness and the more closely you'll scan the riverbanks for signs of movement. Free of the pressures and demands of active travel, you'll have time to relax and savour the passing scene.

Meals on the river consist mainly of *masaco, charque*, rice, noodles, thin soup and bananas in every conceivable form. In general, the food is pretty good, but after a couple of days you'd probably appreciate having brought some alternative nourishment. It's a good idea to bring your own water or some form of water purification.

Make sure you discuss sleeping arrangements with the captain before setting out. Passengers usually have to bring their own hammocks (available in Trinidad) but you may be allowed to sleep on deck or on the roof of the boat. Don't forget to bring a sleeping bag or a blanket as well, especially in the winter when jungle nights can be surprisingly chilly. If you're fortunate enough to be going on a boat that travels through the night, a mosquito net isn't necessary, but if your boat ties up at night and you don't have one, your night will range from being miserable to unbearable. ■

Rurrenabaque and La Paz daily between 9 and 10 am. On Tuesday, Thursday and Sunday at 10 am, Flota 8 de Diciembre goes to Guayaramerín, via Riberalta, for US\$25. Guaya Tours goes to Cobija, via Riberalta, on Monday and Thursday for US\$38; Trans Trópico (☎ 22216) does the same haul on Monday, Wednesday and Friday.

Micros and camionetas run to San Ignacio de Moxos (US\$2.50, three hours) when full from the small terminals on Avenida Mariscal Santa Cruz, several blocks south of the Pompeya bridge, and from the agency on Calle La Paz, near Avenida 18 de

Noviembre. Camionetas to San Borja cost US\$8 in the cab or US\$7 in the back.

Boat Trinidad isn't actually on the bank of a navigable river; Puerto Barador lies on the Río Mamoré, 13 km away, and Puerto Almacén is on the Ibare, eight km from town. Camionetas charge US\$1 to Puerto Almacén and US\$2 to Puerto Barador.

If you're looking for river transport north along the Mamoré to Guayaramerín, or south along the Mamoré and Ichilo to Puerto Villarroel, enquire at the Transportes Fluviales office on Calle Mamoré, or at the Distrito Naval – the navy sails comfortably to Puerto Villarroel three times monthly – on Avenida 6 de Agosto near Matías Carrasco. If nothing turns up, check departure schedules with the Capitanía del Puerto at Puerto Barador. Alternatively, head for Puerto Barador and enquire around the riverboats themselves. See Puertos Almacén & Barador in the Around Trinidad section.

The Guayaramerín run takes a week or less (larger boats do it in three to four days) and costs about US\$25, including food. To Puerto Villarroel, smaller boats take eight to 10 days. The Mamoré route to Guayaramerín or Puerto Villarroel will cost about US\$25 to US\$30 per person, including food.

Getting Around

The Airport The airport is on the north-west edge of town, a half-hour walk from the centre. Motorcycle taxis charge about US\$0.85, but it's not easy balancing a large pack while perched behind the driver. The standard rate for car taxis carrying up to four people is US\$1, but you will have to insist on this price.

Motorcycle You may consider hiring a motorcycle to visit the river ports or surrounding area. All you'll need is a regular driving licence from home.

Motorcycle taxi drivers are happy to take the day off and hire out their bikes. They'll want US\$2 per hour or US\$18 for a 24-hour day. They hang out around the south-west corner of the plaza. Alternatively, you can

Around Trinidad

hire motorcycles at Motos de Alquiler for about US$2 per hour, US$10 for six hours or US$20 per 24-hour day. It's open daily from 7 am to 11 pm.

Taxi Motorcycle taxis around town cost US$0.30 (B$1.50) while car taxis charge US$0.40 (B$2). A taxi to the airport or bus terminal costs US$1.

For taxis to outlying areas, phone Radio Taxi Progreso Beniano (☎ 22759). It's important to know the distances involved and bargain well for a good rate, which should be about US$5 per hour for up to four

people. Be sure to include any waiting time you'll need to visit the sites.

AROUND TRINIDAD
Loma Suárez
Although it's of little real interest, Loma Suárez is a local landmark and a good motor-cycle destination. This artificial mound, nine km from Trinidad on the banks of the Ibare, was first known as Loma Mocovi. When it was purchased by the Suárez brothers, it was renamed Loma Ayacucho. Later, it came to be known as Loma Suárez through common usage. There's a military post at the loma and you'll have to pass a checkpoint if you want to continue past it to Chuchini.

Transport in this direction from Trinidad leaves from the petrol station 15 minutes walk from town beyond the Pompeya bridge. If you're trying to reach Chuchini, you'll probably have to walk the five km from Loma Suárez.

Santuario Chuchini
In the Llanos de Moxos, between San Ignacio de Moxos and Loreto, over 100 km of canals and causeways, and hundreds of *lomas* (artificial mounds), embankments – and more fanciful prehistoric earthworks depicting people and animals – cross the forested landscape. One anthropomorphic figure is over two km from head to toe: a rainforest variation on Peru's famed Nazca Lines. These structures were originally built to permit cultivation in a seasonally flooded area.

According to archaeologists, the prehis-toric structures of the Beni were constructed by the Paititi tribe 5500 years ago, and provide evidence of much larger pre-Colum-bian populations than were previously suspected. Figurines, pottery, ceramic stamps, human remains and even tools made from stone imported to the region were buried inside the mounds. It's likely that the ancient civilisations of the Beni were the source of the legends of Gran Paititi.

The Santuario Chuchini, 14 km from Trin-idad, is one of the few easily accessible

Paititi sites. The name means 'the jaguar's lair' (*madriguera del tigre* in Spanish). This camp sits on an eight-hectare artificial loma, which is only one of numerous lomas dotted throughout the surrounding forest. From the camp, you can take short walks in the rainforest to lagoons with profuse bird life, caymans, and other larger animals.

In 24 hours, we saw capybaras, alligators, puma, several species of monkey, macaws, squirrels and lots of extraordinary birds. The noise of hundreds of macaws coming to roost at dusk was amazing and was only eclipsed by the dawn chorus of macaws, howler monkeys, jaguars, etc. BUT the mosquitoes were the most ferocious we have ever met.
Quentin Given & Lorna Reith, UK

The camp has shady, covered picnic sites, trees, children's swings and a variety of native plants, birds and animals, but the main attraction is the onsite archaeological museum which displays articles excavated from the loma. Family members guide visitors around the exhibits and explain the general thinking on the subject of Paititi. Items uncovered here include bizarre statues with distinctly Mongol queues and slanted eyes. One piece appears to be a female figure wearing a bikini, but it's actually presumed to be identification of specific body areas rather than an article of clothing.

Chuchini may be a lovely place, but unfortunately, foreign visitors are now charged an unreasonable US$10 per person just to get in.

Places to Stay & Eat Bungalows are overpriced at US$60 per person, even though the price includes meals. If you're not staying, exotic dishes are available in the restaurant; the food is great, but again, it's pricey. If you prefer just a snack, ask for the tasty chipilo (fried green plantain chips). Further information is available from Lorena Hinojoso (☎ 21968), Calle 25 de Noviembre 199, Trinidad, Beni, Bolivia.

Getting There & Away Hitching is best on Sunday, though you may have to walk the final five km from Loma Suárez. It's also a good motorcycle destination.

Laguna Suárez

This large, artificial lake five km from Trinidad reaches only 1.5 metres in depth. Constructed by the Paititis, Laguna Suárez was originally known as Socoreno or 'lagoon of animals'. It's a relaxing spot and is popular on Sunday when local families turn out to picnic, drink in the bar and eat lunch at the lakeside Restaurant Tapacaré. Children swim in the pool, canoe and play football and volleyball. Watch for the resort's pet *tapacaré*, a large bird similar to a secretary bird. This one hangs around the restaurant suffering abuse from children.

Getting There & Away There's no public transport; you'll have to walk, take a taxi, hire a motorcycle or hitch. Follow the ring road toward Santa Cruz and turn right at a small, white police post. From there, it's four km to the lake. Admission to the resort is US$0.30 per person and pool use costs US$1. Kayak rental is US$1.20/2 per hour for a single/double. Motorboats rent for US$7 per hour.

Puertos Almacén & Barador

You may enjoy visiting one of the rickety fish restaurants in Puerto Almacén, eight km from Trinidad. This pointless little place is now the proud owner of a massive concrete bridge, and vehicles no longer have to be shunted across on balsas.

You may prefer to continue four km farther to Puerto Barador. There you can observe pink river dolphins in small Mamoré tributaries or sample fresh fish at one of several pleasant portside restaurants. One of the best is *El Pantanal*, which serves excellent surubí for US$2.50. It's very popular with Bolivians, especially on Sunday.

Getting There & Away Taxis from Trinidad to either port cost about US$10 each way, but camiones and camionetas leave frequently from Avenida Mariscal Santa Cruz, 1½ blocks south of Pompeya bridge in Trinidad.

THE AMAZON BASIN

Any bus going to San Ignacio de Moxos will pass both Puerto Almacén and Puerto Barador en route. The fare to Puerto Almacén should be about US$0.80; to Puerto Barador it's US$1.20.

See Getting There & Away in the Trinidad section earlier in this chapter for information about boat travel.

LORETO

Loreto, the first Jesuit mission in the Beni lowlands, was founded in 1675. From 4 to 7 October 1959, the statue image of Nuestra Señora de Loreto wept, as witnessed by the entire town, and Loreto, 54 km south of Trinidad, has become a pilgrimage site.

ASUNCIÓN DE GUARAYOS

This small Jesuit Indian settlement, with a very nice old church, lies on the Santa Cruz-Trinidad road, five to eight hours from Trinidad. The town is known for its *maricas*, little palm-leaf backpacks woven by the locals.

MAGDALENA

One of the loveliest towns in Bolivian Amazonia is Magdalena, which lies 220 km north-east of Trinidad in the heart of vast, low-lying forest and pampa beside the Río Itonamas. It was founded by the Jesuits in 1720, and was the northernmost of the Bolivian missions. Today, the atmosphere is more than *tranquilo* – the only local vehicles are horse or ox-drawn carts.

The area is rich in birds and other wildlife and has yet to be discovered by tourism. About 30 minutes upstream is the inviting Laguna Baíqui, which is a good spot for a picnic and is accessible by boat from town; expect to pay about US$1 per person.

Magdalena's biggest festival, Santa María de Magdalena, takes place on 22 July. The telephone code for Magdalena is 0855.

Places to Stay & Eat

The best accommodation is *Hotel San Carlos*, which charges US$8 per person for rooms with private bath. The more basic

Residencial Sylvana charges US$5 per person. For good standard meals, go to *El Edén*, near the airport.

Getting There & Away

LAB has flights daily except Wednesday and Friday between Magdalena and some combination of the following: Trinidad, Guayaramerín, San Joaquín and San Ramón.

There's a very poor road to Trinidad, but it's impassable in the wet season and the only public transport is the odd camión.

SANTA ANA DEL YACUMA

Originally known as San Lorenzo, Santa Ana del Yacuma, north-west of Trinidad, was founded by the Jesuits in 1693. This low-lying town is surrounded by a dyke to prevent flooding during the diluvian rainy seasons.

Traditionally a cattle town, it is now a booming cocaine-processing and trafficking capital and one of the few towns to organise resistance to American DEA forces. In June 1991, an intensive DEA cleanup of Santa Ana netted 10 homes, 15 labs, 28 aeroplanes, assorted supplies and spare parts, and 110 kg of cocaine base, but no-one was arrested; processors, traffickers and their Colombian accessories had all melted into the forest.

The Club Social on the plaza is now the country home of drug baron Roberto Suárez. The movers and shakers are here!

The telephone code is 0484.

Getting There & Away

Although it's accessible by boat or air from Trinidad, Santa Ana del Yacuma is scarcely worth a special trip and, as one might imagine, foreigners aren't particularly welcome anyway. If you find yourself landed here, check out the crop of blossoming palaces in the centre and the extravagant new air terminal that graces the airstrip of this remote settlement.

PERSEVERANCIA & RESERVA DE VIDA SILVESTRE RÍOS BLANCO Y NEGRO

The 1.4 million-hectare Ríos Blanco y Negro

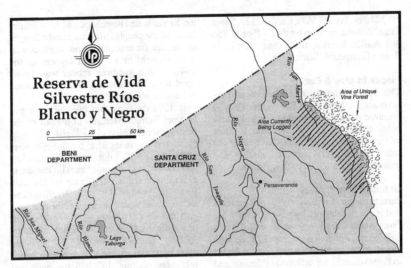

Reserva de Vida Silvestre Ríos Blanco y Negro

0   25   50 km

BENI DEPARTMENT

SANTA CRUZ DEPARTMENT

Río San Martín

Río Negro

Río San Joaquín

Área Currently Being Logged

Area of Unique Vine Forest

Perseverancia

Río San Miguel

Río Blanco

Lago Taborga

Wildlife Reserve was created in 1990. It lies in the heart of Bolivia's largest wilderness area and contains vast tracts of undisturbed rainforest with myriad species of plants and animals, including giant anteaters, peccaries, tapirs, jaguars, bush dogs, marmosets, river otters, capuchin monkeys, caymans, squirrel monkeys, deer and capybara. There are also curassows, six varieties of macaw and over 300 other bird species.

The area's only settlement, the privately owned *estancia* of Perseverancia, lies 350 km north of Santa Cruz. It started as a centre of rubber production in the 1920s and continued until the last *seringueros* (rubber tappers) left in 1972. When the airstrip was completed, professional hunters went after river otters and large cats. By 1986, the estancia had again been abandoned, and it remained so until the tourist resort was set up in 1989.

In the mid-1990s, Moira logging concerns began encroaching on the eastern portion of the reserve. USAid is currently recommending that loggers clear the forest rather than cut selective trees. The idea is that it's preferable to have a total loss over a small area than partial loss of a large area.

Organised Tours

Amazonas Adventure Tours has established a wilderness lodge and a research and conservation centre at Perseverancia. It's open and accessible to visitors only during the dry season, between March and October. They offer wilderness walks, horse trekking and dugout canoe trips, as well as plant identification, bird-watching and wildlife spotting activities, including a night at a *salitral* (salt lick) waiting for large animals.

Visits to Perseverancia are not cheap, but anyone who can manage the splurge will not regret it. Since a large portion of the total cost goes toward the plane ride from Santa Cruz, travellers in larger groups will pay less per person and similarly, those who factor their flight costs over a longer stay will pay less per day. For packages booked overseas, individuals in groups of four, for example, will pay US$963 from Santa Cruz for a seven-day stay including accommodation, all meals, transport and guided activities at the reserve. For two people, the same trip will cost US$1275 per person.

For further information on tours, prices, access, accommodation or research possibilities, contact Amazonas Adventure Tours

(☎ 324099, fax 337587), Casilla 2527, Santa Cruz, Bolivia, or drop by their office at 756 3rd Anillo Interno, Calle San Martín, in Barrio Equipetrol, Santa Cruz.

Places to Stay & Eat
The lodge, chalets and kitchen at Perseverancia overlook the Río Negro. They're constructed of wood, mud bricks and *jatata* palm thatching. Only the chalets have private baths, but all rooms have access to solar hot showers. Accommodation and meals are included in package prices.

Getting There & Away
Perseverancia is a privately owned estancia that is accessible only by prior arrangement. From Santa Cruz it's a 1½-hour flight in a light plane, which departs from El Trompillo airport to the south of the city. Return flights to Perseverancia are included in the tour and lodging packages.

There's now a 100-km track between Asención de Guarayos and Perseverancia but it's not passable by vehicle, even in the dry season. On foot, it will probably take you about five days to get from Asención de Guarayos to Perseverancia.

PARQUE NACIONAL NOEL KEMPFF MERCADO
Remote Noel Kempff Mercado National Park lies in the northernmost reaches of Santa Cruz department, between the Serranía de Huanchaca (also called Caparuch) and the banks of the Río Guaporé (marked Río Iténez on some maps). Not only is it one of South America's most spectacular parks, it also takes in a range of dwindling habitats, lending it world-class ecological significance. The park encompasses the most dramatic scenery in northern Bolivia – rivers, rainforests, waterfalls, plateaux and rugged 500m escarpments – as well as a broad spectrum of Amazonian flora and fauna (see the accompanying aside).

History
This 700,000-hectare park, originally known as Huanchaca, was created in 1979 to protect the Serranía de Huanchaca and its wildlife. Many of the people living around the fringes of the park are descended from workers who were brought in as rubber tappers in the 1940s. When synthetic rubber was developed, their jobs disappeared and they turned to hunting and agriculture.

In 1988 the name was officially changed to Noel Kempff Mercado in honour of the distinguished Bolivian biologist who was murdered by renegades on 5 September 1986, along with pilot Juan Cochamanidis and environmental guide Franklin Parada, at a remote park airstrip east of the Río Paucerna. In May 1995, two Brazilians and a Colombian were convicted of the murders.

Although the riverine section of the park has suffered from the activities of drug-runners, hunters, mahogany loggers and other opportunists, the vast interior remains relatively pristine. In 1995 the park was expanded westward to the Río Tarvo in its southern reaches.

Information
Responsibility for park conservation and infrastructure is currently in the hands of Fundación Amigos de la Naturaleza (FAN), which operates with the aid of Nature Conservancy and USAid. For information, contact the office (☎ 524921, fax 533389) in La Nueve, seven km west of Santa Cruz.

A good source of information on independent travel in the park is the mayor of San Ignacio de Velasco (see the Eastern Lowlands chapter), who is on the park board of directors and believes increased tourism will mean improved conservation practices and be a boost to the local economy. You'll find her at city hall in San Ignacio, or just ask around town.

Admission to the park is US$30 per person.

When to Go There's no right season to visit the park. The wet season is great for river travel, especially if you want to boat up to the two big waterfalls. The wettest months are from December to February. The dry season is obviously better for vehicles, but in the late winter months, smoke from forest burning can obliterate the scenery, especially from mid-August to October. March to June is pleasant and not overly hot or rainy, and from October to December, the spring blooms add another fabulous dimension.

Dangers & Annoyances Your biggest concern will be insects. During rainy periods, the mosquitoes are fierce and voracious and tiny *garapatilla* ticks can be especially annoying. Beware especially of the blood-sucking sandfly, which carries leishmaniasis (see the Health section in the Facts for the Visitor chapter). These flies are a real pest at some camp sites, particularly in the high forest around Huanchaca I. Fortunately, they're only wet-season pests.

Between September and December there's a phenomenal bee hatch-out, when the bees seek out human camp sites for salt. At such times, it's not unusual to have as many as 10,000 bees hanging around a single site, so if you're allergic, avoid the park during these months. The best way to avoid attracting such numbers is to change camp sites daily.

Leafcutter ants may also become a problem, and although their six-inch-wide forest highways, choked with trains of leaf-bearing workers, can be fascinating to watch, they also seem to thrive on the rip-stop nylon used in tents. In fact, they can destroy a tent in less than an hour – even while you're sleeping. Don't set up camp anywhere near an ant trail. If that isn't enough, termites have a taste for backpacks that have been left lying on the ground.

Fire is also a concern. The main natural fire season in the park is from July to November, and since the savanna doesn't burn every year, the amount of dead vegetation is substantial. Never cook or even camp in grassland habitat, no matter how flat and inviting, and never leave a cooking fire unattended, even in the forest.

Surface water in the park is delicious and safe to drink, but if you're worried about contamination, it's still a good idea to purify

The Lost World

Although it's commonly assumed Sir Arthur Conan Doyle's classic *The Lost World* was set among the *tepuis* (flat-topped mountains) of Amazonian Venezuela, it was actually inspired by the Bolivian plateaux and escarpments in the region of Parque Nacional Noel Kempff Mercado.

In his journals, British explorer Colonel Percy Harrison Fawcett, who was commissioned by the Bolivian government early this century to survey the boundary between Bolivia and Brazil, wrote the following:

Above us towered the Ricardo Franco Hills, flat-topped and mysterious, their flanks scarred by deep *quebradas*. Time and the foot of man had not touched these summits. They stood like a lost world, forested to their tops, and the imagination could picture the last vestiges there of an age long vanished. Isolated from the battle with changing conditions, monsters from the dawn of man's existence might still roam those heights unchallenged, imprisoned and protected by unscaleable cliffs. So thought Conan Doyle when later in London I spoke of these hills and showed him photographs of them. He mentioned an idea for a novel on Central South America and asked for information. The fruit of it was his *Lost World* in 1912, appearing as a serial in the *Strand Magazine*, and subsequently in the form of a book that achieved widespread popularity. ■

your water. Surface water can be scarce between August and November.

Guides If Noel Kempff Mercado National Park is to survive the ravages of logging, hunting and other destructive exploitation, it's essential to demonstrate that conservation is worthwhile, and there's no better way to do so than to hire a local guide. In addition to showing you the way, helping with camp chores and keeping you out of trouble, they'll also channel tourist money directly into their local communities.

Indigenous guides are available at La Florida, Porvenir and Piso Firme. The going rate is US$5 to US$10 per group per day.

La Florida

One of the best access points for the park is

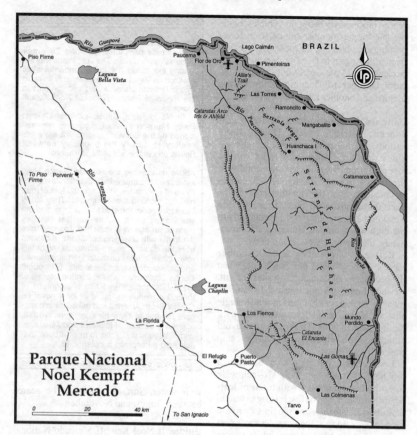

Parque Nacional
Noel Kempff
Mercado

0   20   40 km

the village of La Florida, home to Aserradero Moira, one of the region's largest and most prominent sawmills. It's an easy walk to the park entrance at Los Fierros. The 40-km hike will take you through pleasant forest along a good logging road that's open to vehicular traffic from April to December. Allow two days for the walk and be sure to carry plenty of water.

Los Fierros

Campamento Los Fierros lies near the park entrance, within hiking distance of the Huanchaca Plateau, and gives access to all the most interesting sites in this part of the park.

It has an airstrip and basic accommodation (see Places to Stay & Eat). However, the camp is being upgraded by FAN and it's likely that prices will climb. For those on a budget, the best option is to take a tent.

Catarata El Encanto

The objective of most visitors to Los Fierros is Catarata El Encanto, a spectacular 150m waterfall that spills off the Serranía de Huanchaca. It makes an enchanting three-day return hike from Los Fierros; with a vehicle or a mountain bike, it's a long and tiring day trip. The trip can also be extended with a hike up onto the plateau.

If you're on foot, go with someone who knows the route or hire a guide at Los Fierros, since it's very easy to get lost. The hike begins along the 4WD track that heads east from Los Fierros. On the way, you'll pass through high Amazonian forest, seasonally flooded 'termite savanna' (plains dotted with termite mounds) and the threatened *cerrado* savanna.

Once you've crossed the savanna area, continue until you reach a fork in the road; take the one on the left (there should be a sign, but don't count on it). This abandoned logging road passes through some attractive forest and with luck, you should see spider monkeys.

Eventually, you'll reach a brook (go ahead, take a drink; the water is good). Here the logging road ends and you follow a trail which runs alongside the stream to the foot of the waterfall. It's a beautiful spot, so please don't disturb anything.

On the way to the waterfall, while you're still in the termite savanna, you'll see a small track that turns left (north-east) off the road and leads through the cerrado and forest to the foot of the escarpment. From here, it's a 500m climb up a steep and poorly designed footpath onto the plateau. On the way, you'll pass through dry forest on the lower slopes and cerrado and bamboo groves on the upper slopes. Once at the top, you're ushered onto a spectacular grassy plain dotted with unusual rock outcrops which lend it the name *campo rupestre*. There are also plenty of islands of gallery forest which would serve as excellent camp sites.

Don't attempt to do both hikes in a single day – it's impossible. In fact, it's best to allow two days for each – three if you expect to see anything. Unfortunately, there is no integrated system of trails on top of the plateau. You can explore a bit, but you must return to Los Fierros the way you came.

Serranía de Huanchaca

Those with financial resources can fly into one of two remote airstrips at the abandoned drug-processing laboratories Huanchaca I and Las Gamas. The former lies on the northern end of the plateau amid cerrado savanna dotted with islands of Amazonian forest. From there, it's a short day hike to the upper reaches of the Río Paucerna, which is a fast-running blackwater river. Strong swimmers will be OK, but drag yourself out before you reach the Arco Irís waterfall! Las Gamas is a beautiful place at the southern end of the escarpment, which may soon have trail access from Los Fierros.

Río Paucerna

The two spectacular 80m waterfalls, Arco Irís and Federico Ahlfeld, are on the Río Paucerna above Campamento Paucerna. The river is great for swimming, and if you go out by boat at night with a powerful torch, you're bound to see large numbers of caymans and alligators. For the best results, hold the torch at eye-level, so the shine off the animals' retinas is directed straight back at you.

The waterfalls are currently accessed by motor launch from Flor de Oro. The trip takes about five hours each way, depending upon water levels. Low water normally closes off the Río Paucerna to boat traffic between July and early December, when the waterfalls are of limited interest anyway. You can also hike to the falls from Lago Caimán (see later in this section). Road access from Flor de Oro is planned for the future.

Monster fans will be interested in one local legend, which describes a four-metre shark-like fish called the Paraíba that supposedly inhabits the Río Paucerna. Its existence has apparently been confirmed by diving Brazilian *garimpeiros* (gold prospectors).

Piso Firme & Porvenir

Piso Firme is a pleasant little place with several alojamientos, restaurants and a small shop selling staples – rice, salt, sardines etc. There's an occasional barge service between Piso Firme and Pimenteiras, which takes 12 hours. Pimenteiras is only a short boat ride from Flor de Oro, making this an alternative to the expensive flight. Porvenir is just a tiny village with no lodging, but you'll usually find something to eat.

Flor de Oro

From Piso Firme, it's four hours up the Río Guaporé to Campamento Paucerna, near the confluence of the Ríos Paucerna and Guaporé. From there, it's 30 km upriver to Flor de Oro, where FAN runs a tourist lodge (see Places to Stay & Eat later in this section). Around the camp, you'll find examples of termite savanna, degraded cerrado and riverine flooded forest which affords superb bird-watching opportunities. Sightings of pink river dolphins are almost guaranteed.

It's a 30-minute hike along the trail from Flor de Oro to Lago Caimán, which is the trailhead for Allie's Trail to the plateau and waterfalls. FAN intends to construct a light road from Flor de Oro to the Río Paucerna waterfalls, but until that happens, visitors wanting to see the falls must either take Allie's Trail to the falls from Lago Caimán or go by boat up the Río Paucerna.

Lago Caimán & Allie's Trail

Lago Caimán, 30 minutes on foot upstream from Flor de Oro, is a superb spot for bird-watching and seeing caymans. A small hut

The maned wolf has long, stilt-like legs that enable it to bound through tall grass in pursuit of armadillos and similar-sized mammals

was built here several years ago by the Wildlife Conservation Society and is occupied on and off by research teams.

A little-known highlight of the park is the spectacular Allie's Trail, which is named after the Peace Corps volunteer who constructed it in the early 1990s. It begins at Lago Caimán and climbs up through dry forest, with great scenery along the edges of the escarpment. It then wanders through dwarf evergreen forest and high forest until it eventually passes the Arco Irís and Federico Ahlfeld waterfalls. If you've made previous arrangements with FAN, they'll pick you up here by boat; alternatively, walk back the way you came. For the entire return hike, allow about four days: 1½ days each way, plus one day to spend relaxing and pottering around the waterfalls.

Organised Tours

Uimpex Travel (☎ 336001, fax 330785), Calle René Moreno 226, Santa Cruz, offers all-inclusive six-day trips from Santa Cruz to Los Fierros and Catarata El Encanto for US$625 per person, with at least four people. Groups of more than eight pay only US$473.

Places to Stay & Eat

Campamento Los Fierros, in the south-western part of the park and 10 km directly west of the escarpment, sleeps up to 100 people. It has dormitories, running water, showers, cooking facilities and two or three permanent park rangers (who love to have company). Up to now, use of the facilities has been free to researchers, but current renovations by FAN are scheduled to result in a room and board charge of US$25 per night for researchers and probably considerably more for other visitors. Your best alternative is to bring your own tent, sleeping bag, food and cooking stove.

The luxury class *Eco-Lodge* at Flor de Oro is considerably more plush than Los Fierros, and charges from US$85 to US$125 per person per day, including meals. Book directly through FAN or make arrangements with one of the Santa Cruz travel agencies organising park tours. To explore the river,

Wildlife of Noel Kempff Mercado National Park

Noel Kempff Mercado National Park is both spectacularly scenic and ecologically extraordinary because of the diversity of its habitat. It contains elements of five distinct ecosystems – broadleaf evergreen forest, dry forest, inundated forest, dry savanna and inundated savanna – each of which is composed of numerous distinct biological communities.

Recent studies put the number of mammal species at 140, birds at 600, reptiles at 75 and frogs at 63. In addition, researchers have collected more than 260 different species of fish from park rivers, and it's estimated that the park supports over 4000 plant species, including dozens of orchid varieties and some of the last remnants of cerrado vegetation in South America. This makes Noel Kempff Mercado one of the biologically richest parks in the world, surpassed only by parks in the Andean foothills (such as Manu in Peru or Alto Madidi in Bolivia), which have the advantage by their 3000m altitudinal ranges.

Patient and observant visitors are likely to see a rich variety of wildlife. If you're very lucky, you may even see a jaguar. Note, however, that full-time researchers only see them perhaps twice in a year. More predictably observed is the maned wolf, which is found mainly around Los Fierros. It's the most endangered species in the park – not to mention the most glamorous. Go out onto the termite savanna in the early morning and the odds are that you'll see one when they come to the road culverts to drink. You can sometimes hear them barking at night. The best time is June and July. Also relatively easy to see are the pampas deer. These are most readily observed on the track up onto the plateau from Los Fierros, or around Las Gamas.

In the rivers, you'll see alligators, caimans, pink river dolphins and perhaps even a rare river otter. Also around are peccaries, tapirs and spider monkeys, which are frequently observed around Lago Caimán, Catarata El Encanto and along the plateau track from Los Fierros. Less common are howler monkeys, giant anteaters, bush dogs, short-eared dogs and giant armadillos, all of which are considered endangered or threatened species.

And don't forget your binoculars – Noel Kempff Mercado has more bird species than all of North America! Especially interesting are the very rare grassland species that are largely restricted to Brazil but are becoming threatened there by conversion of their cerrado habitat to cattle ranches and soybean farms. Species that will get birders' juices flowing include the rusty-necked piculet, Zimmer's tody tyrant, the ocellated crake, the rufous-winged antshrike, the long-tailed tyrant, the campo miner, the blue finch, the black and tawny seedeater and a host of others. For the nonenthusiast, there is easy bird-watching at Flor de Oro along the river. The guans and curassows are especially tame as there hasn't been much hunting pressure in recent years.

Timothy J Killeen, Bolivia

you can hire four-person boats from here for a rather steep US$30 per hour.

Two other minor encampments, *Las Torres* and *Mangabalito*, up the Río Guaporé from Campamento Paucerna and Flor de Oro, are accessible by boat. They protect the park from illicit Brazilian resource exploitation.

Getting There & Away

Land access to the park is possible only in the dry season, roughly between May and October. The best place to look for transport is San Ignacio de Velasco, which is a US$8 bus ride or a US$50 commercial flight from Santa Cruz.

Air Although remote airstrips exist all around the park, the main access fields are at La Florida, Los Fierros, Piso Firme and Flor de Oro. The easiest – and most expensive – way into the park is by chartered five-seater aero taxi from Santa Cruz. FAN charges US$220 per hour and Los Fierros is five hours return flying time (you must pay the pilot's trip back to Santa Cruz). With four or five people, the cost doesn't look too bad. Another possibility is with SAMAIR, a group of American missionary pilots who charge US$165 per hour. The environmental organisation Armonía (☎ 522919, fax 324971), Casilla 3081, Santa Cruz, also runs air services and charges even lower rates.

The cheapest air option, however, is to go by bus to San Ignacio and hire pilot Fernando Aguirre. He lives on the plaza and anyone can tell you where to find him. The return flight from San Ignacio takes only 2½ to three hours, so the savings are substantial.

Bus The only bus that approaches within striking distance of the park is the one from San Ignacio to Piso Firme, near the north-western corner of the park. It occasionally passes through La Florida, but not always, so if you're heading for Los Fierros, try to convince the driver to drop you there.

A more radical but relatively convenient alternative is the Brazilian connection to Lago Caimán and Flor de Oro. (Note,

however, that the nearest place to pick up a Brazilian visa is in Santa Cruz.) From Santa Cruz or San Ignacio, you can catch a bus to San Matías on the Brazilian border, and then on to Cáceres, four hours into Brazil. From there, catch another bus to Vilhena in the southern part of Rondônia state, where you'll find daily buses to Pimenteiras, which lies opposite Lago Caimán and about 20 minutes by boat upstream from Flor de Oro.

Car & Motorcycle The best way to reach the park is with your own vehicle, which can be hired in Santa Cruz for about US$50 per day. Alternatively, catch a bus to Concepción or San Ignacio de Velasco and ask around about renting an old pick-up with driver, for which you'll pay about half the commercial rate. They'll drop you at the park but you must find your own way back (which will probably amount to hitching).

Hitching The main overland access is from Santa Cruz via Santa Rosa de la Roca, but without a private 4WD vehicle, it's a complicated route. From San Ignacio, which is accessible on daily buses from Santa Cruz, it's 220 km north to La Florida, where the park road turns off toward Los Fierros, 40 km to the east.

Your best hope of a lift to La Florida will be with logging trucks, but you may also get lucky and connect with park employees. There's also quite a lot of research traffic, but don't count on a lift, as their vehicles are nearly always full.

Logging trucks will also get you to Piso Firme, which lies on the Río Paraguá 178 km north of La Florida and about 22 hours nonstop by road from Santa Cruz.

When you want to head back south, it will simply be a matter of standing by the road or hanging around a lumber mill. Alternatively, try hooking into the local radio network – all villages have a radio and established hours of contact – and asking the operator to check for trucks travelling south. Be prepared to pay for a ride.

Boat From Piso Firme, which may be

reached by bus from San Ignacio, there's an occasional barge service to Pimenteiras, Brazil (12 hours). From there, it's just a 30-minute boat ride to Flor de Oro.

There's also a fair amount of Brazilian cargo transport along the Ríos Mamoré and Guaporé between Guajará-Mirim and Costa Marques, in the Brazilian state of Rondônia, and Vila Bela in the state of Mato Grosso. Although river transport passes Paucerna, Las Torres and Mangabalito, access to the Bolivian shore is limited to small independent boat owners. As yet, there's no immigration officer in the park, so after your visit, you'll probably have to return to Brazil or head straight for immigration in Santa Cruz.

Northern Frontier

GUAYARAMERÍN

Guayaramerín, on the Río Mamoré opposite the Brazilian town of Guajará-Mirim, is a rail town where the railway never arrived. The line that would have connected the Río Beni town of Riberalta and the Brazilian city of Porto Velho was completed only as far as Guajará-Mirim and never reached Bolivian territory.

Historically, the area was a centre of rubber production, and Nicolás Suárez had his rubber exporting headquarters at Cachuela Esperanza, 40 km north-west of Guayaramerín. From there, he transported cargo overland past the Mamoré rapids to the Río Madeira and shipped it downstream to the Amazon, the Atlantic and on to markets in Europe and North America. (Also see Guajará-Mirim later in this chapter.)

This typically friendly Amazon town of 14,000 people serves as a river port and a back door between Bolivia and Brazil. It's actually the northern terminus for river transport along the Río Mamoré, thanks to the same rapids that plagued the rubber boomers and rendered the river unnavigable just a few km to the north.

Of late, Guayaramerín has sprung to life with a thriving commercial trade. Although it retains its frontier atmosphere, the town is growing quickly – a constant stream of motorcycles buzz around the streets, and the shops are overflowing with electronic and bootlegged goods from China and Taiwan.

Information

Tourist Office There's a tourist office (of sorts) at the port – there's no tourist literature, but the staff will gladly help with general information. The telephone code for Guayaramerín is 0855.

Foreign Consulates There's an efficient Brazilian consulate one block east of the main plaza. It's open weekdays from 9 am to 1 pm and will issue visas on the same day. Visas are free for US and Australian citizens, but Canadians must pay US$40 and French citizens US$50.

Money US dollars cash and travellers cheques may be exchanged at the Hotel San Carlos for a decent rate or at the Agencia de Viajes Amazonas for a lower rate. Alternatively, moneychangers hang around the port area and change US dollars cash, *reais* and *bolivianos*.

Organised Tours

The Agencia de Viajes Amazonas (☎ & fax 2544), on Plaza Hernán Roca, runs five-hour city tours (US$35) of Guayaramerín and Guajará-Mirim, as well as day tours to Cachuela Esperanza (US$40).

Places to Stay

The most mellow budget place is the *Hotel Litoral* (☎ 2016), near the airport, which charges US$3 per person for clean rooms with private baths and refreshingly tepid showers. Rooms with double beds are US$8.25 with bath. In the courtyard there's a snack bar and a very popular TV set that plays Brazilian *novelas* (soap operas) to a full house.

Opposite is the quiet and shady *Hotel Santa Ana* (☎ 2206), with similar amenities

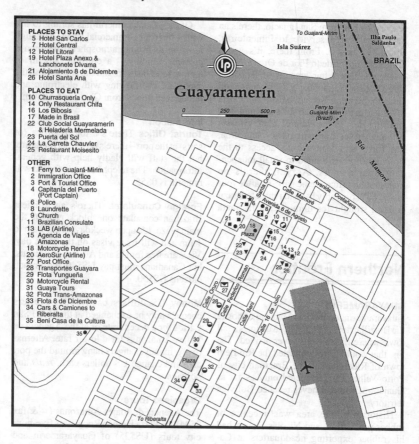

PLACES TO STAY
5 Hotel San Carlos
7 Hotel Central
12 Hotel Litoral
19 Hotel Plaza Anexo &
    Lanchonete Divama
21 Alojamiento 8 de Diciembre
26 Hotel Santa Ana

PLACES TO EAT
10 Churrasquería Only
14 Only Restaurant Chifa
16 Los Bibosis
17 Made in Brasil
22 Club Social Guayaramerín
    & Heladería Mermelada
23 Puerta del Sol
24 La Carreta Chauvier
25 Restaurant Moisesito

OTHER
1 Ferry to Guajará-Mirim
2 Immigration Office
3 Port & Tourist Office
4 Capitanía del Puerto
   (Port Captain)
6 Police
8 Laundrette
9 Church
11 Brazilian Consulate
13 LAB (Airline)
15 Agencia de Viajes
    Amazonas
18 Motorcycle Rental
20 AeroSur (Airline)
27 Post Office
28 Transportes Guayara
29 Flota Yungueña
30 Motorcycle Rental
31 Guaya Tours
32 Flota Trans-Amazonas
33 Flota 8 de Diciembre
34 Cars & Camiones to
    Riberalta
35 Beni Casa de la Cultura

Guayaramerín

0   250   500 m

for US$5 per person without bath and US$8.25 for a room with a bath and double bed.

The seedy *Hotel Central* (☎ 2042), on Calle Santa Cruz, charges US$4 per person. It's a low-budget option with shared baths and no double beds. Even cheaper is *Alojamiento 8 de Diciembre*, which charges US$3 per person. The *Hotel Plaza Anexo* (☎ 2086), on the plaza, has clean rooms with bath and a pleasant ambience for US$5 per person.

If you can't cope with the heat, the *Hotel*

San Carlos (☎ 2419, fax 2150) has a swimming pool, as well as a restaurant, sauna (redundant in Guayaramerín), hydromassage, billiards room and 24-hour hot water. Singles/doubles with bath, TV and air-con cost US$21/31 with breakfast.

Places to Eat
Guayaramerín has two restaurants called 'Only', and they both got it wrong! *Churrasquería Only*, a barn-sized place with an extensive international menu and a cool outdoor garden, is probably the Beni's best

restaurant, and is very popular with Brazilians. The smaller, more languid and overpriced *Only Restaurant Chifa*, a block off the plaza, serves fish, meat and pseudo-Chinese dishes – but very slowly. The quality is just acceptable.

A recommended lunch and dinner place near the plaza is *Made in Brasil*, which provides home cooking for the town's many Brazilian expats. At lunch, you can get an enormous prato feito (almuerzo, Brazilian style); on Wednesday, they cook up baião de dois com carne de sol; and on weekends, you can sample Brazil's national dish, feijoada carioca. Regular offerings include pizza, fish, chicken and beef, as well as surubí and peixe dorada (golden fish) from the Mamoré. They also serve the best rice in all Bolivia. Prices, however, which are quoted in reais, are generally higher than in Bolivian establishments. It's open daily from 7 am to 10 pm.

Out of town is the very good restaurant *Sujal*; motorcycle taxis will get you there for US$0.30. *Heladería Mermelada*, on the plaza, has mountainous fruit and ice-cream creations, while *Los Bibosis*, on the plaza, is popular for drinks and snacks and most of the town's lager louts spend their days here. A good informal place for lunch or dinner is *La Carreta Chauvier*.

For Bolivian specialities and alcohol in a nice leafy setting, there's *Restaurant Moisesito*, beside the Hotel Santa Ana. A good value choice for set meals is the *Club Social Guayaramerín*, which is in the same building as Heladería Mermelada. The *Puerta del Sol* is frequently recommended by locals, but it's rather overrated; the food is only average and foreigners are often overcharged.

Things to Buy

Currently, Guayaramerín is enjoying a commercial blitz, thanks to its designation as a duty-free zone (authorities couldn't fight the illicit trade, so they decided to sanction it). The town is extremely popular with crowds of Brazilians, who pop over to shop for bargains at a fraction of what they'd pay at home, and all market prices are quoted in reais. As a result, commerce in once-thriving Guajará-Mirim, across the river, has all but dried up. There's nothing of exceptional interest, but Guayaramerín is a good place to pick up fake Adidas bags, Indian drawstring skirts and imitation brand-name electronic goods. If you prefer *artesanía*, visit Caritas, across the airfield, which sells locally produced wooden carvings for reasonable prices.

Getting There & Away

Air Guayaramerín's airport is right at the edge of town. AeroSur (☎ 2201) has a daily flight at 9 am to Trinidad (US$84.50), with same-day connections to Santa Cruz (US$127), La Paz ($131.50) and Cobija (US$169). LAB (☎ 2140) flies four times a week to Cochabamba (US$96.50); on Thursday and Sunday to Santa Cruz (US$124.50); and on Tuesday and Saturday to La Paz (US$136.50). You can also fly to or from Cobija (US$57) on Monday and Friday. The LAB office isn't yet on the computer line, so it's wise to book flights elsewhere or you risk not getting a seat.

Bus Bus services to and from Guayaramerín (with the exception of Riberalta) operate only during the dry season – roughly from May to October. Most terminals are at the southern end of town, beyond the market.

Several companies have services to Riberalta (US$2, three hours); each has two to four departures daily. In the dry season, Flota Yungueña has services to Rurrenabaque (US$16.50, 15 hours) and La Paz (US$27, 35 hours), via Santa Rosa and Reyes, daily except Monday and Saturday at 8 am.

Transportes Guayara has departures to Cobija (US$15.50, 14 hours) on Monday, Wednesday and Friday at 7 am. Trans-Amazonas goes to Trinidad on Thursday at 8.30 am and Flota Yungueña does the same run on Monday, Thursday and Sunday at 7.30 am.

Beware of bus services cancelling trips. If tickets aren't sold out, the run may be cancelled.

Camión & Car Cars and camiones to Riberalta leave from opposite the 8 de Diciembre bus terminal. Camiones charge the same as buses but make the trip in less time. If you'd like to travel a bit more comfortably, cars charge US$5 and spare you exposure to the choking red dust that gets into everything. To Cobija, YPFB petrol trucks and a white Volvo freight carrier depart occasionally from the same place as the camiones to Riberalta.

Boat From the port, cargo boats leave more or less daily for Trinidad, a five to seven-day trip up the Río Mamoré. Expect to pay about US$35 with food. A notice board outside the port captain's office lists departures. For more information, see under Trinidad earlier in this chapter.

Brazil Even if you aren't travelling to Brazil, you can pop across the Río Mamoré and visit Guajará-Mirim. Between early morning and 6.30 pm, frequent motorboat ferries cross the river between the two ports; they cost US$0.80 (B$4) from Bolivia and US$1.50 (BR$1.50) from Brazil. After hours, there are only express motorboats charging US$4 to US$5.50 per boat. There are no restrictions on crossing between Guayaramerín and Guajará-Mirim, but to travel farther into Brazil or to enter Bolivia here, you'll have to complete border formalities.

The Bolivian immigration office is at the port. On the Brazilian side, you pass through customs at the port in Guajará-Mirim and have your passport stamped at the port. They may also ask you to visit the Polícia Federal, on Avenida Presidente Dutra, five blocks from the port. Leaving Brazil, you may also need to pick up a stamp at the Bolivian Consulate in Guajará-Mirim.

Although officials don't always check, technically everyone needs a yellow-fever vaccination certificate to enter Brazil here. If you don't have one, there's a convenient and relatively sanitary clinic at the port on the Brazilian side. The medical staff use an air gun rather than a hypodermic needle.

For information about onward travel into Brazil, see Getting There & Away in the Guajará-Mirim section below.

Getting Around

Guayaramerín is small enough to walk just about anywhere. There are no automobile taxis, but motorcycle taxis and *tuk-tuks* charge US$0.30 (B$1.50) to anywhere around town.

Motorcycles for exploring the surrounding area may be hired from the main plaza for about US$2 per hour, but you can negotiate lower rates on all-day rentals. Plan on about US$20 for 24 hours. Don't be tempted to take a swig of the stuff sold in Coke bottles on the street; it's motorcycle petrol!

GUAJARÁ-MIRIM (BRAZIL)

Guajará-Mirim and Guayaramerín, on the Brazil-Bolivia border, have gone through a reversal of roles in recent years. Although the Brazilian town is now quiet and subdued by Brazilian standards, the upgrading of the roads to Porto Velho and Riberalta has brought an economic boom to Guayaramerín.

On the Brazilian side of the river, the Portuguese words *onde fica* (pronounced AWN-gee FEE-ca), meaning 'where is', will go a long way, and the ubiquitous *gracias* becomes *obrigado* (bree-GAH-doo) if you're a man, or *obrigada* (bree-GAH-dah) if you're a woman.

History

In 1907, the US company May, Jeckyll & Randolph began work on a 364-km railway to link the village of Santo Antônio on the Rio Madeira to the Bolivian town of Riberalta. The original idea was to compensate Bolivia for the loss of the Acre territory, which was annexed by Brazil in 1903, by providing a transport outlet to the Atlantic which was otherwise blocked by the Mamoré rapids 25 km north of Guayaramerín. German, Jamaican and Cuban workers, and even Panama Canal hands, were brought in to work on the project. When the track was finished in 1912, more than 6000 workers had perished from

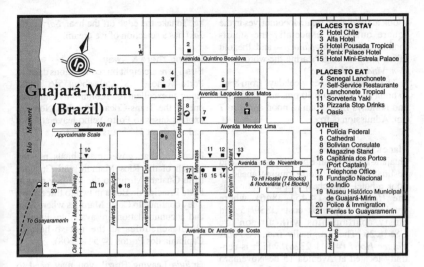

Guajará-Mirim
(Brazil)

Rio Mamoré

0   50   100 m
Approximate Scale

Avenida Quintino Bocaiúva

Avenida Leopoldo dos Matos

Avenida Costa Marques

Avenida Mendez Lima

Avenida 15 de Novembro

Avenida Constituição

Avenida Presidente Dutra

Avenida P. Menezes

Avenida Benjamin Constant

Avenida Dr Antônio de Costa

Avenida Dom Pedro

Old Madeira - Mamoré Railway

To Guayaramerín

To HI Hostel (7 Blocks)
& Rodoviária (14 Blocks)

PLACES TO STAY
2   Hotel Chile
3   Alfa Hotel
5   Hotel Pousada Tropical
12 Fenix Palace Hotel
15 Hotel Mini-Estrela Palace

PLACES TO EAT
4   Senegal Lanchonete
7   Self-Service Restaurante
10 Lanchonete Tropical
11 Sorveteria Yaki
13 Pizzaria Stop Drinks
14 Oasis

OTHER
1   Polícia Federal
6   Cathedral
8   Bolivian Consulate
9   Magazine Stand
16 Capitânia dos Portos
    (Port Captain)
17 Telephone Office
18 Fundação Nacional
    do Indio
19 Museu Histórico Municipal
    de Guajará-Mirim
20 Police & Immigration
21 Ferries to Guayaramerín

malaria, yellow fever, gunfights and accidents, and the railway came to be known as *A Via do Diablo* (the Devil's line).

Since the railroad never arrived at Riberalta, and the world market price of rubber plummeted while it was still under construction, the line became a white elephant before it was even put into operation. Still, both Guajará-Mirim and Porto Velho are the products of the project. Today the road between Porto Velho and Guajará-Mirim uses the railway bridges, but the line itself is used only occasionally as a tourist novelty from the Porto Velho end.

Marcio Souza chronicles the brutal story in his book, *Mad Maria*, mandatory reading for anyone interested in how a small parcel of the Green Hell was briefly conquered.

Information
Bolivian Consulate If you're entering Bolivia and require a visa, there's a Bolivian Consulate (☎ 541 2862) on Avenida Costa Marques 495. It's open weekdays from 7.30 am to 12.30 pm. Every nationality that requires a visa has its own rate, but these rates apply only at this consulate: Canadians (US$40); New Zealanders (US$38); Bel-

gians (US$35); Japanese and Portuguese (US$30); Dutch (US$25); and Australians, Mexicans and Greeks (free). Have two photographs ready.

Telephone The telephone code for Guajará-Mirim is 069.

Museu Histórico Municipal de Guajará-Mirim
The marginally interesting museum in the old railway station on Avenida 15 de Novembro focuses on regional history and contains the remains of some of Rondônia's fiercely threatened wildlife. Particularly interesting are a tree full of moth-eaten dead animals; a brilliant butterfly collection; a hair-raising assortment of enormous bugs; a huge anaconda that stretches the length of the main salon; a *sucurí*, the snake of your nightmares; an eye-opening history of Brazilian currency inflation; a stamp display in which Hungary is identified as Belgium; and a hideous but lovable turtle that inhabits one aquarium.

The museum's collection of photographs has an especially intriguing portrayal of an Indian attack taken in the 1960s. Also have

THE AMAZON BASIN

a look at the classic steam locomotives in the square outside – especially the smart-looking *Hidelgardo Nunes* – and the old railway water tower bearing the words *Seja Bem Vindo* ('Welcome').

The museum is open weekdays from 8 am to noon and 2.30 to 6.30 pm, and weekends and holidays from 9 am to noon and 3 to 7 pm. Admission is free.

Places to Stay

Guajará-Mirim is quite popular as a weekend destination, so it's worth ringing ahead to book a hotel. The cheapest place in town is the *Hotel Chile* (☎ 451 3846), where single/double quartos cost US$9/15 and musty apartamentos with air-con are US$18/26. The marginally friendly *Fenix Palace Hotel* (☎ 541 2326), which is centrally located at Avenida 15 de Novembro 459, has quartos at US$10/18 and apartamentos for US$18/30, including an electric fan. Across the road, the popular *Hotel Mini-Estrela Palace* (☎ 541 2399) charges US$20/35 for single/double apartamentos with air-con and breakfast.

The *Hotel Pousada Tropical* (☎ 541 3308) is quite comfortable, and it has single/double apartamentos with fan for US$15/30 and air-con doubles for US$35; during slack periods, you can easily negotiate a 10% discount.

More upmarket, the *Alfa Hotel* (☎ 541 3121) charges US$27/40 for single/double apartamentos, including breakfast.

Places to Eat

Universally recommended as Guajará-Mirim's best restaurant is the *Oasis*, next door to the Hotel Mini-Estrela Palace. Across the road, *Pizzaría Stop Drinks* has a wide range of pizzas and is popular at night. In fact, some of the clientele stop and drink all night long.

For other Brazilian-style treats – mostly fast food – a couple of decent lanchonetes (lunch counters) are *Senegal* and *Tropical*. The novel *Self-Service Restaurante* offers pizzas, lunches and snacks for a set price per kg. To take the edge off the heat, *Sorvetería Yaki* has a selection of ice cream.

Getting There & Away

Bus There are eight bus connections daily to Porto Velho (US$10.50, about 5½ hours) along an excellent road commonly known as one of the Trans-Coca highways. Nonstop express buses to Porto Velho leave at 2 pm and cut about 1½ hours off the trip.

Boat Brazilian government boats ply the stretch of the Ríos Mamoré and Guaporé from Guajará-Mirim to the military post at Forte Príncipe da Beira in two to three days. They continue to Costa Marques where food and accommodation are available. Enquire about schedules at the not-so-helpful Capitânia dos Portos (☎ 541 2208).

Bolivia Leaving Brazil, you may need to have your passport stamped at the Bolivian consulate in Guajará-Mirim before getting a Brazilian exit stamp at the port. Once across the Río Mamoré, pick up an entrance stamp from Bolivian immigration at the ferry terminal. Motor ferries leave from the port every few minutes and cost US$1.25. For further information, see the section on Guayaramerín earlier in this chapter.

CACHUELA ESPERANZA

Now all but abandoned, this tiny Río Beni settlement 40 km north-west of Guayaramerín was the capital of the economic empire built by Nicolás Suárez. Its location was dictated by the Beni and Mamoré rapids, which halted all Atlantic-bound traffic.

In its heyday, Cachuela Esperanza (meaning Rapids of Hope) was a self-contained marvel: homes and offices were clean and modern and the private hospital and doctors were the finest and best equipped in Bolivia. Suárez imported North American limousines for his personal use on roads he built himself, and a theatre was constructed so that an invitation could be extended to the opera star Theda Bara. Everything had to be imported up the Madeira and Mamoré, then disassembled and carried past the rapids;

Suárez even brought in a steam locomotive, which today graces the centre.

The town has now been partially restored. You can see the small, white church, which was built high on an outcrop of solid rock overlooking the rapids, and the remains of Nicolás Suárez's home (he died in 1940). Ironically, the town's main – and mutually incompatible – pursuits are now logging and brazil nut gathering.

Organised Tours

An Italian-Australian, John Zenari, who has been active in the restoration work, offers tours to Cachuela Esperanza. He can be contacted at the Hotel Litoral (☎ 2246) in Guayaramerín.

Places to Stay

Accommodation is available in the *Canadian Hotel*, a tropical-bungalow sort of place built around the turn of the century from imported Canadian pine. A new option is the *Hotel Esperanza* (☎ 2201), Casilla 171, Guayaramerín, run by Alois Schwartmüller. This well-appointed jungle-lodge-style hotel has singles/doubles for US$20/30, with breakfast. For bookings, contact American Tours (☎ 374204, fax 328584, La Paz), Edificio Avenida, Casilla 2568, La Paz.

Getting There & Away

Transportes Beni connects Guayaramerín with Cachuela Esperanza, but runs according to no fixed schedule.

RIBERALTA

Riberalta sits at an elevation of 175m on the banks of the Río Beni near its confluence with the Madre de Dios and on the highway linking La Paz to Guayaramerín, making it a hub of sorts. It's the major town in Bolivia's northern frontier region, with a rapidly increasing population that is currently about 50,000.

It was once a thriving centre of rubber production, but with increased competition from Asian countries and the development of synthetics, that industry declined, and since the opening of the road link to La Paz,

Riberalta's importance as a river port has also declined. The town has fallen back on its current mainstay industry: the cultivation, production and export of brazil nuts and brazil nut oil.

Information

Money As a service to travellers, Brother Casimiri at the vicarage changes US dollars cash, travellers cheques and verifiable personal cheques. Although there are lots of 'compro dólares' signs in shops around town, they change only cash, and at a lower rate.

Post & Communications The post office and ENTEL office are near the main plaza. Riberalta's public fax number is 472242. The telephone code is 0852.

Dangers & Annoyances Riberalta's municipal water supply is contaminated and the heat and open sewers make its atmosphere rather pungent. Drink only bottled or well-purified water.

Things to See & Do

Riberalta is a pleasant enough town, but it doesn't have a lot for visitors and in the paralysing heat of the day, strenuous activity is suspended and locals search out the nearest hammock.

If you're feeling motivated, don't miss the novel **motorcycle monument** on Avenida Nicolás Suárez, with riders fashioned from machine parts; one passenger is a shoeshine kid.

For some minor amusement, stroll past the bizarre **Mogul palace** that has appeared beside the Residencial El Pauro. Although the prevailing theme is Rajasthani, the architecture schizophrenically integrates Roman columns and arches, a couple of lounging lions and some raised-relief palm trees, as well as an odd grassy knoll, which sprouts from the roof.

Alternatively, you can hire a motorcycle and explore surrounding jungle tracks or take a swim in the river; locals will know where it's safe. At **Puerto Beni-Mamoré**, within walking distance of the centre, you can watch the hand-carving and construction of small boats and dugouts by skilled artesans. Two km east of the plaza, along Ejército Nacional, you can visit an old **rubber plantation**, see coffee being roasted and visit a carpentry workshop. Riberalta carpenters specialise in high-quality rocking chairs and other furniture made from tropical hardwoods.

The **Parque Mirador la Costañera**, on Riberalta's river bluff, overlooks a broad, sweeping curve of the Río Beni and affords the standard Amazonian view across water and rainforest. The African-style river steamer *Tahuamanu*, inaugurated in 1899 and used in the Acre War (1900-04) and the Chaco War (1932-35), stands planted in cement here 20m above the river. It was the first and last steamer used in the Bolivian Amazon.

The **Mario Vargas brazil nut factory**, one of many in Riberalta, is happy to conduct tours of its operations. Here over 6000 Riberalta women enjoy a cracking career smashing brazil nuts. Once extracted, the nuts are dried for 24 hours prior to shipment to prevent their going rancid, and the shells are hauled off to massive dumps to be turned into road-building and patching material. In 1994 the region exported eight million kg of the nuts. Perhaps the most significant thing about this industry is that it's a renewable harvest in rainforests that might otherwise fall to loggers. So go out and buy more brazil nuts!

Tumichúcua once served as the Summer Institute of Linguistics of the Wycliffe Bible Society and as the headquarters for translation of the Bible into local indigenous languages. When the work was finished, most of the Indians left and the site and school were turned over to the Bolivian government. With a pleasant lake and picnic site, it's now Riberalta's get-away-from-it-all spot. The lake lies 25 km from town on the road towards Santa Rosa. To get there, it's easiest to catch a lift on weekends, particularly with the camionetas that leave from the Plaza del Periodista, south-east of the centre.

It should also be straightforward catching a lift back to town.

Places to Stay

The cheapest place to stay is *Alojamiento Navarro*, which is popular with itinerant workers. Male or female dormitory accommodation costs US$1.50 per person (don't leave your things in your room). Doubles are US$3. It's a US$0.30 motorcycle taxi ride from the centre. This neighbourhood, which isn't on the municipal water system, has the only good tap water in Riberalta. Another cheapie, which is more central, is the friendly but grotty *Residencial El Pauro* (☎ 452). Rooms with bath cost US$3 per person and there are a couple of rooms with double beds for US$5.

The best value option is probably the spotless *Residencial Los Reyes* (☎ 8018), near the airport. It costs US$3 per person for a room without bath and US$5/8.40 for a single/double with bath. You also get a cool and shady area to while away the heat of the afternoon. Iced water and hot coffee are always available. Its only drawback is the disco on the corner, which rollicks until late on weekends.

The friendly *Alojamiento Comercial Lazo* (☎ 8326), which has a talkative parrot who's especially chatty in the early morning, has basic singles/doubles for US$4.10/6.20 with bath, and US$3/4 without. Rooms with ratty air-con are US$12.50/21.

Residencial Katita (☎ 386), a friendly and welcoming new place with a public restaurant, charges just US$3 per person. A good lower mid-range choice is *Hotel Amazonas* (☎ 339), the local business travellers hotel, where the tropical atmosphere is nicely enhanced by the two resident jochis (agoutis). Single/double rooms with private bath and hot showers are US$6.20/11. The charge for a carpeted three-bed suite with TV is US$25.

The quirky *Hotel Colonial* (☎ 212) isn't the best, but it's quite friendly and always well-meaning. Rooms cost US$5/7.50 per person with cold/hot showers and breakfast. A real plus is the breakfast of toast, eggs and

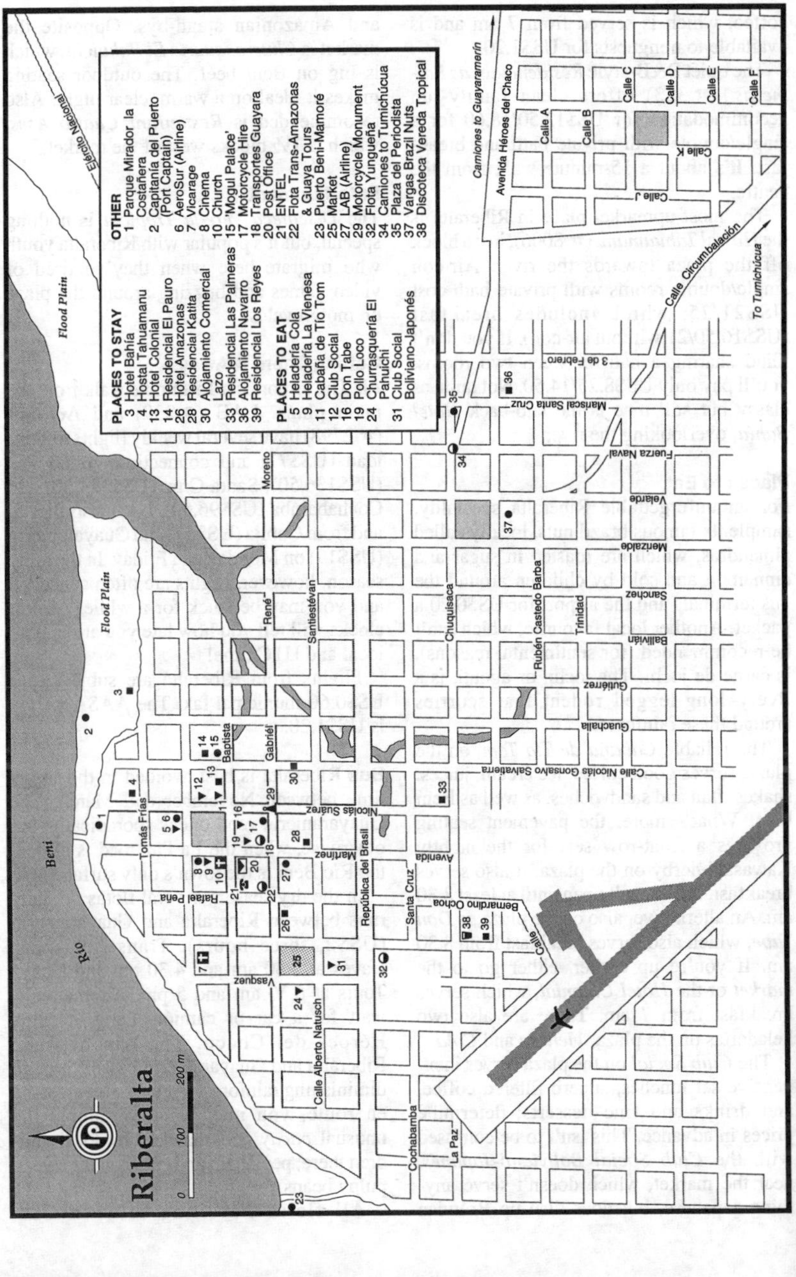

Riberalta
0 100 200 m
PLACES TO STAY
3 Hotel Bahía
4 Hostal Tahuamanu
13 Hotel Colonial
14 Residencial El Pauro
26 Hotel Amazonas
28 Residencial Katita
30 Alojamiento Comercial Lazo
33 Residencial Las Palmeras
36 Alojamiento Navarro
39 Residencial Los Reyes
PLACES TO EAT
5 Heladería Cola
9 Heladería La Vienesa
11 Cabaña de Tío Tom
12 Club Social
16 Don Tabe
19 Pollo Loco
24 Churrasquería El Pahuichi
31 Club Social Boliviano-Japonés
OTHER
1 Parque Mirador la Costañera
2 Capitanía del Puerto (Port Captain)
6 AeroSur (Airline)
7 Vicarage
8 Cinema
10 Church
15 'Mogul Palace'
17 Motorcycle Hire
18 Transportes Guayara
20 Post Office
21 ENTEL
22 Flota Trans-Amazonas & Guaya Tours
23 Puerto Beni-Mamoré
25 Market
27 LAB (Airline)
29 Motorcycle Monument
32 Flota Yungueña
34 Camiones to Tumichúcua
35 Plaza del Periodista
37 Vargas Brazil Nuts
38 Discoteca Vereda Tropical
Río Beni
Flood Plain
Flood Plain
Flood Plain
Eletrico Nacional
Camiones to Guayaramerín
Avenida Héroes del Chaco
Calle Circumbalación
To Tumichúcua
Calle Alberto Natusch
Vasquez
Rafael Peña
Martínez
Tomás Frías
Nicolás Suárez
República del Brasil
Santa Cruz
Avenida Bernardino Ochoa
Calle
Cochabamba
La Paz
Chuquisaca
Rubén Castedo Barba
Trinidad
Ballivián
Gutiérrez
Guachalla
Calle Nicolás Gonsalvo Salvatierra
Sanchez
Menzalde
Velarde
Fuerza Naval
Mariscal Santa Cruz
3 de Febrero
Moreno
René
Santiestévan
Gabriel
Baptista
Calle A
Calle B
Calle C
Calle D
Calle E
Calle F
Calle J
Calle K

THE AMAZON BASIN

coffee, which is served from 7 am and is available to nonguests for US$1.20.

The quiet B&B-style *Residencial Las Palmeras* (☎ 353) offers clean family-run accommodation for US$12.50/18.60 for a single/double with private bath and breakfast. It's about a 15-minute walk from the centre.

The most upmarket place in Riberalta is the *Hostal Tahuamanu* (☎ 8006), just a block off the plaza towards the river. Air-con single/double rooms with private bath cost US$21/25, which includes breakfast (US$16.50/21 without air-con). If you don't mind sharing a bath between two rooms, you'll pay only US$8.25/14.50. Not quite as classy but still nice is the laid-back *Hotel Bahía*, overlooking the river.

Places to Eat

For an unforgettable Riberalta speciality, sample its famous brazil nuts, locally called almendras, which are roasted in sugar and cinnamon and sold by children around the bus terminals and the airport for US$0.20 a packet. Another local favourite, which can't be recommended (for sentimental reasons), is carne de jochi. The jochi, or agouti, is a lively long-legged rodent that scurries around these rainforests.

The reliable *Cabaña de Tío Tom*, on the plaza, serves good coffee, ice cream, juices, shakes, flan and sandwiches, as well as Beni beef. What's more, the pavement seating provides a front-row seat for the nightly Kawasaki derby on the plaza. It also serves breakfast, but doesn't open until at least 8.30 am. An alternative, also on the plaza, is *Don Tabe*, which also serves breakfast from 8.30 am. If you're up earlier, either go to the *market* or the *Hotel Colonial*, which serves breakfast from 7 am. There are also two heladerías on the plaza, *Vienesa* and *Cola*.

The *Club Social* on the plaza serves inexpensive set lunches, superb filtered coffee, and drinks and fine desserts; determine prices in advance. This isn't to be confused with the *Club Social Boliviano-Japonés*, near the market, which doesn't serve anything Japanese, but does dish up Bolivian

and Amazonian stand-bys. Opposite the market is *Churrasquería El Pahuichi*, which is big on Beni beef. The outdoor seating makes it ideal on a warm, clear night. Also recommended is *Restaurant Cuatro Ases*, which is 1½ blocks west of the market.

Entertainment

The *Discoteca Vereda Tropical* is nothing special, but it's popular with Riberalta youth who migrate here when they've tired of video games and buzzing around the plaza on motorcycles.

Getting There & Away

Air The airport is a 15-minute walk from the main plaza. LAB (☎ 239) and AeroSur (☎ 2798) have several weekly flights to Trinidad (US$71) and connections to La Paz (US$136.50), Santa Cruz (US$124.50) and Cochabamba (US$96.50). LAB also flies to and from Cobija (US$57) and Guayaramerín (US$19) on Monday and Friday. In the rainy season, however, flights are often cancelled and you may be stuck for a while. Airport clocks will tell you how late you are in both local and UTC time!

Flights from Riberalta are subject to a US$0.60 municipal tax. The AASANA tax is US$1.20.

Bus Riberalta is best avoided in the soggy time between November and March. The Guayaramerín road opens sporadically, but otherwise, when the La Paz road is closed, the Río Beni is the town's only surface link.

In the dry season, several flotas do daily runs between Riberalta and Guayaramerín (US$2, three hours). Trans-Amazonas leaves at 7.30 am and 4.30 pm and Guaya Tours at 6.30 am and 5 pm. Alternatively, wait for a car or camión along Avenida Héroes del Chaco. The trip between Riberalta and Guayaramerín passes through diminishing rainforest. At the balsa crossing en route, you may want to sample the unusual pacay pods hawked by local children there; peel them and chew on the sweet, pulpy beans.

All flotas travelling between Guayaramerín (US$2, three hours) and Cobija (US$12.50, 12 hours), Rurrenabaque (US$14.50, 12 hours) and La Paz (US$25, 33 hours) also stop en route at their Riberalta terminals. Guaya Tours has services to Santa Rosa, Reyes, Yucumo and Rurrenabaque, with connections to San Borja, Trinidad and Santa Cruz, on Tuesday, Thursday, Saturday and Sunday. It also goes to Trinidad (US$21, 17 hours) daily at 9.30 am. In addition, Trans-Pando Turismo leaves for Cobija from the Hotel Amazonas on Wednesday, Friday and Sunday at 7 am.

Boat The Beni passes through countless twisting km of virgin rainforest and provides the country's longest single river trip. Unfortunately, boats upriver to Rurrenabaque are now rare and, in any case, they normally only run when the road becomes impassable (October to May). For departure information, check the notice board at the Capitanía del Puerto at the northern end of Calle Guachalla. Plan on US$20 to US$35 for the five to eight-day trip.

Getting Around
Motorcycle taxis will take you anywhere for US$0.30. *Colectivos*, which are rare, cost US$0.20 per person.

You can also hire a motorcycle from the *taxistas* on the corner of Nicolás Suárez and Gabriel René Moreno. The going rate is about US$20 per 24-hour day. You'll need your home driving licence.

RIBERALTA TO COBIJA
Just a few years ago, the route between Riberalta and Cobija was a penetration-standard track negotiated only by hardy 4WD vehicles and large, high-clearance camiones. Nowadays, it's a good, high-speed gravel track, which connects the once-isolated Pando department with the rest of the country, and in the several years that it has been open, the road has attracted unprecedented development. Virgin rainforest is being cleared at a rate of knots and scarcely a scrap remains untouched.

At Peña Amarilla, just a couple of hours

out of Riberalta, the route crosses the Río Beni by balsa raft. On the western bank, to the south of the road, is a friendly woman who sells *empanadas* and other snacks at fair prices.

The most interesting river crossing on the trip is over the great Madre de Dios, which is a river of truly Amazonian proportions. The eastern port is a small backwater tributary, which after a few hundred metres issues into the great river itself; along the way, listen for the intriguing jungle chorus. The upstream crossing takes about 45 minutes.

The last major balsa crossing is over the Río Orthon, at Puerto Rico. Here the balsas cross slightly downstream, dodging swimmers as they go. From Puerto Rico to Cobija, development is rampant, and almost nothing has escaped being cleared, burned, logged, settled and turned into cattle pasture. The scene is of charred giants, a forest of stumps and smoking bush; and at some times of the year the sun looks like an egg yolk through all the thick smoke.

COBIJA
Tropical Cobija, with about 15,000 people, sits on a sharp bend of the Río Acre and serves as the capital of the Pando, Bolivia's youngest department. The name of the town means 'blanket', and not surprisingly, the climate creates the sensation of being smothered beneath a whopping great duvet. With 1770 mm of precipitation annually, it's the rainiest spot in Bolivia.

Cobija was founded in 1906 under the name of Bahia, and in the 1940s experienced a boom as a rubber-producing centre. When that industry declined, so did Cobija's fortunes and the town was reduced to little more than a forgotten village, tucked away in the farthermost corner of the republic. The Pando should have included Vaca Diéz province, with Riberalta as the capital of the new department and Cobija left out in the cold. When Riberalta opted to stay with the Beni department, Cobija didn't protest.

The only town plan of Cobija is over a decade old and lots of the streets depicted on it are now overgrown by jungle. In fact, it

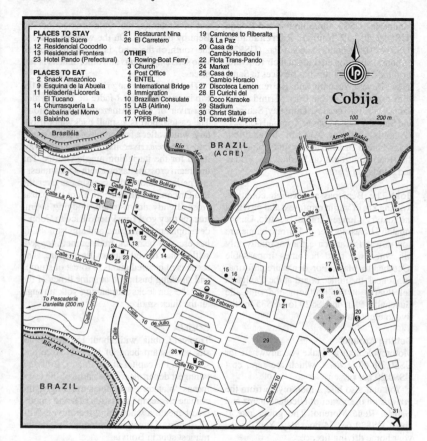

PLACES TO STAY
7 Hostería Sucre
12 Residencial Cocodrilo
13 Residencial Frontera
23 Hotel Pando (Prefectural)

PLACES TO EAT
2 Snack Amazónico
9 Esquina de la Abuela
11 Heladería-Licorería
   El Tucano
14 Churrasquería La
   Cabaíña del Momo
18 Baixinho
21 Restaurant Nina
26 El Carretero

OTHER
1 Rowing-Boat Ferry
3 Church
4 Post Office
5 ENTEL
6 International Bridge
8 Immigration
10 Brazilian Consulate
15 LAB (Airline)
16 Police
17 YPFB Plant
19 Camiones to Riberalta
   & La Paz
20 Casa de
   Cambio Horacio II
22 Flota Trans-Pando
24 Market
25 Casa de
   Cambio Horacio
27 Discoteca Lemon
28 El Curichi del
   Coco Karaoke
29 Stadium
30 Christ Statue
31 Domestic Airport

Cobija

0   100   200 m

once appeared that the town might some day be entirely swallowed up, but with the new road and a spate of ambitious projects, the town's fortunes may be turning around. First off, there's a brand new Japanese-funded hospital; unfortunately, it's believed that 80% of the funding for this project somehow went missing. Then there's the new high-tech brazil nut processing plant just outside town: in contrast, funding for this project mysteriously materialised from nowhere. Cobija is also the site of a new international airport, which accommodates 727s and hopes to attract flights along the popular route between Miami and Santa Cruz. The big question is, why?

Information

Tourist Office On the plaza there's a Pando tourist office that operates sporadically, but it wasn't staffed at the time of writing.

Brazilian Consulate For those who need a visa to enter Brazil, there is a consulate (☎ 2188) on the corner of Calle Beni and Avenida Fernández Molina. It's open weekdays from 8.30 am to 12.30 pm.

Immigration Bolivian immigration is in the Prefectural building on the main plaza. The office opens at 9 am on weekdays but the immigration officer is often taken with wanderlust, so you may have to hunt him down to get your entry or exit stamp.

Money Casa de Cambio Horacio changes reais, bolivianos and US dollars at official rates, and will occasionally change travellers cheques for an inordinate 10% commission.

Post & Communications The post office is on the plaza and the ENTEL office is a block from here, towards the river. Cobija's public fax number is 2292. The telephone code is 0842.

Things to See

Cobija isn't laid out in a grid pattern but rambles over a series of hills, giving it a certain desultory charm. Of interest in the centre are the remaining tropical **wooden buildings**, which are now giving way to modern brick, concrete and plaster. There are still a few nice old structures around the plaza and on the outskirts, and lovely avenues of royal palms around the plaza. It's also worth dropping by the **church**, which is open most of the day, for a look at the series of naive paintings from the life of Christ.

In Cobija's hinterlands, you can visit rubber and brazil nut plantations, and there are also several lakes and places to observe rainforest wildlife, but transport is difficult. The very adventurous can hire a motorised dugout and head upriver from nearby Porvenir to visit remote villages around the Peruvian border, but it's recommended you take a guide with experience in navigating the overgrown and convoluted waterways.

If you're really bored, check out the monument in front of the old hospital. It commemorates an apocryphal local youth who, during the Brazilian takeover of the Acre, shot a flaming arrow and set the fire that sent invading Brazilians packing back across the river.

Special Events

Cobija holds a Feria de Muestras, featuring local artesans, from 18 to 27 August. It takes place at the extreme western end of town, near the Río Acre.

Places to Stay

The friendly, Spanish-run *Hotel Pando* (☎ 2230), also known as the Hotel Prefectural, has nice breezy singles/doubles with fans, comfy beds and private bath for US$12.50/14.50, including breakfast. Try to meet the chatty parrots and take a look at the jaguar skins and the 8.5m anaconda stretched across the reception area.

The *Residencial Frontera* (☎ 2740) is clean but a bit overpriced, with rooms at US$5 per person without bath and US$10 for a double bed with bath. Rates include breakfast. It's pleasant if you can get a room with a window onto the patio.

The *Residencial Cocodrilo* (☎ 2215) charges US$3/8.50 per person for clean but far from opulent rooms without/with bath. Rates include breakfast. The pleasant *Hostería Sucre* (☎ 2797), just off the plaza, charges US$10.50/14.50 for singles/doubles with bath and breakfast.

Places to Eat

In the early morning, the market sells chicken empanadas, but that's about all in the way of prepared food. Nothing stays fresh very long in this sticky climate, and most people wouldn't touch the meat sold in the market. There are, however, lots of fresh fruits and vegetables and tinned Brazilian products. On the plaza, there's a juice bar serving refrescos de frutas.

The restaurant *Esquina de la Abuela*, on Avenida Fernández Molina, is Cobija's nicest restaurant, and has outdoor tables. Fresh, well-cooked chicken and meat dishes cost US$3 to US$4. If you really want to pig out, finish off with an ice-cream sundae at *Heladería y Licorería El Tucano*, over the road.

On the same street, about five minutes walk from the city centre, is *Churrasquería La Cabaína del Momo*, also known as Tío

A Wild Sloth Chase

In his book *In Patagonia*, Bruce Chatwin describes visiting a cave in which he finds the remains of a human-sized ground sloth that was clearly not a fossil. For as long as anyone can remember, forest Indians of Brazil, Bolivia and Peru have reported seeing such a creature, which they call *mapinguari*, and maintain that it has a special chemical spray defence that is capable of paralysing its enemies.

Scientists call the creature *Mylodontid*, and in 1994 American ornithologist Dr David Oren conducted scores of interviews with forest-dwellers regarding the creature. All the interviewees came up with basically the same story: that mapinguari lived only in the deepest forest, had shaggy red hair, club feet, long claws, powerful jaws, a booming cry, an ape-like face and a particular fondness for palm hearts (yes, fortunately, it's a vegetarian). It also has bony armour plating embedded in the skin, much as its presumed predecessor, the *Megatherium*. Dr Oren concluded there were enough signs of its existence to warrant a scientific investigation, but we're still waiting for further evidence. ■

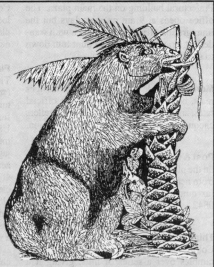

Leos. Here you can eat churrasco (US$2) at tables on a raised balcony. A recommended restaurant specialising in beef is the long-standing *El Carretero*.

For lunch and dinner, you may enjoy the *Pescadería Danielita* (☎ 2658), which specialises in freshwater fish dishes. Sadly, at lunch it's a hang-out for obnoxious drunks and women may feel uncomfortable. Another good choice is the *Restaurant Baixinho* (the name is Portuguese for 'shorty'), which is run by an affable chap who's at least two metres tall.

Entertainment

Cobija isn't exactly a hopping place. Most local youth hang out at the *Discoteca Lemon* or across the street at the *El Curichi del Coco* karaoke bar.

Getting There & Away

Air Amazingly, Cobija has two airports. Most traffic uses the domestic airport, which lies just outside town. The new international airport, with its 2000m asphalted runway, is used mainly in the wet season.

AeroSur (☎ 2562), which has an office at the Hotel Pando, flies daily to Trinidad (US$98.50), with same-day connections to La Paz (US$144) and Santa Cruz (US$140). Next-day connections are available from Trinidad to Guayaramerín, Riberalta and San Borja.

The LAB office (☎ 2170) is on Avenida Fernández Molina, near the Policía Nacional. LAB has two flights weekly to and from La Paz (US$134), and another two flights weekly with stops in Riberalta (US$57), Guayaramerín (US$57), Trinidad (US$100) and Cochabamba (US$146). If you're on the LAB Fokker that flies this run, look for the golden plaque that hangs over the seat occupied by the pope on his most recent visit to Bolivia.

Bus With the opening of the road to Riberalta, there's now a surface connection to La Paz. There are buses to Riberalta

(US$12.50, 12 hours) leaving at 6 am daily. From there, you can connect with services to Guayaramerín, Rurrenabaque, Trinidad and La Paz. Purchase tickets at Trans Guaya Tours, near the Hotel Pando. Flota Cobija micros connect Cobija with the village of Porvenir, 30 km (about one hour) to the south. They depart three times daily and cost US$0.60.

Camión In the dry season, you can travel directly between La Paz and Cobija by camión for a well-bargained US$30 to US$40. In the wet season, camiones may still get through, but plan on at least three hot, wet days to reach the highlands.

Brazil Travellers to or from Brazil need entry/exit stamps from immigration in Cobija and from the Polícia Federal, just outside Brasiléia. A yellow-fever vaccination certificate is required to enter Brazil from Cobija, but there's no vaccination clinic in Brasiléia, so if your health records aren't in order, you'll have to track down a private physician.

It's a rather long up-and-down slog from Cobija across the bridge to Brasiléia. You can take a taxi, but negotiate the fare in advance. For about US$3.50, the driver will take you to the Polícia Federal in Brasiléia, wait while you complete immigration formalities, then take you to the centre or to the rodoviária (bus terminal). From the centre of Brasiléia to Cobija, taxis try to charge double the Bolivian price.

Alternatively, take the rowing-boat ferry across the Río Acre for US$0.40 (B$2) per person from Bolivia and US$0.50 (BR$0.50) from Brazil. At the Brazilian landing, you're greeted by a topiary turkey; from there, it's one km to the rodoviária and another 1.5 km to the Polícia Federal.

Peru For the adventurous traveller, access to Peru from Cobija is possible via two routes. Note, however, that Peru's Madre de Dios department has recently been the stage for operations of Sendero Luminoso (Shining Path) guerrillas, as well as the site of drug-running, lawless gold-digging and other renegade activities.

The first option is to cross into Brazil at Brasiléia and take a bus from there to Assis Brasil, which lies 90 km west. There's one hotel in Assis Brasil – the *Assis Brasil Palace Hotel* (☎ 548 1045) on Rua Eneide Batista. For meals, try *Restaurante Seridó* at Rua Valério Magalhães 62, or the *Bar & Restaurante Petisco* on Rua Raimundo Chaar.

Across the Río Acre from Assis Brasil is the muddy Peruvian settlement of Iñapari, where you must check into Peru with the police. From Iñapari, there's a road (of sorts) to Puerto Maldonado, which is accessible from Cuzco by the Peruvian road system. For practical purposes, however, the Iñapari-Puerto Maldonado road is impassable to all but pedestrian or motorcycle traffic. From the Iñapari airport, seven km from the village, you can fly to Puerto Maldonado on a Grupo Ocho military cargo flight for about US$30. From Puerto Maldonado, it's US$60 to Cuzco with Faucett or AeroPerú.

In the wet season, from December to February, you can reach Puerto Maldonado by cargo boat from Porvenir, south of Cobija. At other times, you may be able to hitch south from Porvenir to the road's end at Chivé, on the Río Madre de Dios near Puerto Heath. There you can hire a small boat to Puerto Pardo on the Peru border. After securing a Bolivian exit stamp, link up with a cargo boat or arrange informal river transport farther up the Madre de Dios to Puerto Maldonado – and Peruvian immigration – at the port. In a cargo boat, you'll pay US$5 to US$10 for the one-day trip from the border to Puerto Maldonado, but prepare for long waits, especially during periods of low water. Chartering a boat will cost about US$100.

Getting Around
Motorcycle or automobile taxis around Cobija charge a set US$0.40 to anywhere in town, including the domestic airport. Taxis to the international airport cost US$3. The taxi fare over the bridge to Brasiléia is US$1.

Around Brasiléia (Brazil)

0   250   500 m
Approximate Scale

To Rio Branco

Immigration &
Policía Federal ★

Kador Hotel

BRAZIL

Río
Acre

Rodoviária

To Assis Brasil

Arroyo   Bahía

Brasiléia

Ferry

Praça

BOLIVIA

Cobija

AROUND COBIJA

About 150 km south of Cobija, on the Chivé road, is **Lago Bay**, a freshwater lake for picnicking and fishing near the Río Manuripi. The *Complejo Turístico* rents basic cabañas. Access is easiest on weekends. To get there, hitch in a private vehicle or camión (US$3), or take a taxi (US$15), as far as San Silvestre, 60 km from Cobija. From there, you'll find small boats to take you the 1½-hour trip down the Río Manuripi to Lago Bay.

BRASILÉIA (BRAZIL)

Brasiléia, in the state of Acre, is the small Brazilian border town across the Río Acre from Cobija. The western end of town has a sort of rustic tropical charm and there's an attempt at civic pride in the topiary along the main street (which features round, cuboid and animal-shaped trees), but otherwise, Brasiléia has nothing of interest to travellers save an immigration stamp into or out of Brazil and a bus to somewhere else.

The Polícia Federal is two km from the centre. Dress neatly – no shorts allowed – or they may refuse to stamp your passport. The

office is open daily from 8 am to noon and 2 to 5 pm. For information on crossing the border, see Brazil in Getting There & Away under Cobija.

Information

There's a Bolivian Consulate in Brasiléia at Rua Major Salinas 205. It's open weekdays from 8 to 11 am. The post office is near the Río Acre ferry landing. Brasiléia is one hour behind Cobija. The telephone code for Brasiléia is 068.

If you're changing money in Brasiléia, be sure to check official tourist rates before handing money over to a shopkeeper. None of the banks in Brasiléia accepts travellers cheques.

Places to Stay & Eat

If you're stuck in Brasiléia, try the *Hotel Fronteira* (☎ 546 3134), opposite the church in the centre. For a single or double quarto/apartamento, the cost is US$10/15, including access to satellite TV. The *Restaurante Carioca* beside the hotel serves drinks, chicken and beef dishes and prato feito, a veritable feast of Brazilian carbohydrates!

Pousada las Palmeras (☎ 546 3284), also in the centre, has single/double apartamentos with air-con, TV and bar fridge for US$18/25. Less opulent rooms with just a fan are US$11/20. Guests are provided with free transfers to the airport or rodoviária. The *Junior Hotel*, farther down the main street, charges US$8/13 for single/double quartos and US$20/23 for apartamentos.

Alternatively, there's the *Hotel Kador* (☎ 546 3283), at Avenida Santos Dumont 25, on the road between the international bridge and the Polícia Federal. Single/double apartamentos cost US$10/15. Just over the road is the *Pizzaria Ribeira*. Another pleasant place for meals is the *Restaurante Brasiléia*, a nice, clean little place on the main street.

Getting There & Away

From the rodoviária, four buses run daily to Rio Branco (US$11, six hours), and from

THE AMAZON BASIN

there you'll find flights and bus connections to points all over Brazil. In the dry season (June to October), buses go to Assis Brasil. During the rainy season, you may be able to organise a ride with a truck; contact Transport Acreana in Brasiléia. For information about crossing the border, see Getting There & Away under Cobija in this chapter.

Glossary

abra – opening; refers to a mountain pass, usually flanked by steep high walls

achachilas – *Aymara* mountain spirits, believed to be ancestors of the people, who look after their *ayllus* and provide bounty from the earth

alcaldía – municipal hall

almuerzo – economical set lunch, which usually consists of three or more courses

Altiplano – (High Plain); the largest expanse of level (and in places arable) land in the Andes; extends from Bolivia into southern Peru, north-western Argentina and northern Chile

anillos – literally 'rings'; the name used for main orbital roads in some Bolivian cities

anticuchos – beef-heart shishkebabs

apacheta – mound of stones on a mountain peak or pass; travellers carry a stone from the valley to place on top of the heap as an offering to the *apus*

api – syrupy form of *chicha morada* made from maize, lemon, cinnamon and sugar

apu – mountain spirit who provides protection for travellers and water for crops, often associated with a particular *nevado*

arenales – sand dunes

artesanía – locally handcrafted items

ayllus – loosely translates as 'tribe'; native groups inhabiting a particular area

Aymara or **Kolla** – indigenous Indian people of Bolivia; Aymara also refers to the language of these people

azulejos – decorative tiles, so-named because most early Iberian azulejos were blue and white

barrio – district or neighbourhood

bodega – boxcar, carried on some trains, in which 2nd class passengers can travel

bofedales – swampy alluvial grasslands in the *puna* and *Altiplano* regions, where *Aymara* people pasture their llamas and alpacas

boletería – ticket window

bolivianos – Bolivian people; also, Bolivian unit of currency

brazuelo – shoulder (of meat)

buna – giant rainforest ant, over one cm long

buñuelo – type of doughnut dipped in sugar syrup

cabaña – cabin

cama matrimonial – double bed

camarín – niche in which a religious image is displayed

camba – Bolivian person from the eastern lowlands; some highlanders use this term for anyone from the Beni, Pando or Santa Cruz departments

cambista – street moneychanger

camino – road, path, way

camión – flat-bed truck; a popular form of local transport

camioneta – pick-up or other small truck; a form of local transport

cancha – open space in an urban area, often used for market activities; football ground

casilla – post office box

cédula de identidad – identity card

cena – set dinner menu, which is usually a very economical option

cerrado – sparsely forested scrub savanna; an endangered habitat that may be seen in Parque Nacional Noel Kempff Mercado

cerro – hill; this term is often used to refer to mountains, which is a laughably classic case of understatement given their altitudes!

chairo – mutton or beef soup with *chuños*, potatoes and *mote*

chacra – cornfield

cha'lla – offering or toast to an indigenous deity

chancao – chicken with yellow pepper and tomato and onion sauce; a Tarija specialty

Chapacos – residents of Tarija; used proudly by *tarijeños* and in misguided jest by other Bolivians

chaqueo – annual burning of Amazonian rainforest to clear agricultural and grazing land; there's a mistaken belief that the smoke from chaqueo forms clouds and ensures good rains.

charango – traditional Bolivian ukelele-type instrument

charque kan – meat jerky served with mashed *choclo*

chicha – popular beverage that is often alcoholic; made from such ingredients as *yuca*, sweet potato and maize

chicharrón de cerdo – fried pork

choclo – large-grain Andean maize

Cholo(a) – *Quechua* or *Aymara* person who has migrated to the city but continues to wear traditional dress

chompa – jumper, sweater

chullo – traditional pointed woollen hat, usually with earflaps

chullpa – *Kolla* funerary tower

chuños – freeze-dried potatoes

churrasco – steak

colectivo – minibus or collective taxi

Colla – alternative spelling for *Kolla*

comedor – dining hall

comercio de hormigas – literally 'ant trade'; smuggling of goods from Argentina into Bolivia on the backs of peasants

COMIBOL – Corporación Minera Boliviana (Bolivian Mining Corporation)

confitería – snack bar

contrabandista – smuggler

cordillera – mountain range

cuñapes – cassava and cheese rolls

DEA – Drug Enforcement Agency; US drug offensive body sent to Bolivia to enforce coca-crop substitution programmes and to apprehend drug magnates

denuncia – affidavit

edificio – building

Ekeko – household god of abundance; the name means 'dwarf' in *Aymara*

empanada – meat or cheese pasty

ENFE – Empresa Nacional de Ferroviarios (Bolivian national railroad authority)

ENTEL – Empresa Nacional de Telecomuni-caciones (Bolivian national communications commission)

especial – 2nd class

esquina or abbreviated as **esq** – corner

estancia – extensive grazing establishment

falso conejo – literally 'false rabbit'; greasy, animal-based dish

FAN – Fundación Amigos de la Naturaleza

feria – fair, market

ferretería – hardware shop

ferrobus – bus on bogies

flota – long-distance bus

fricasé – pork soup, a La Paz specialty

garapatillas – tiny ticks that are the bane of the northern plateaux and savanna grass-lands

gaseosa – soft drink

guardaparque – national park ranger

hechicería – traditional *Aymara* witchcraft

hornecinos – niches commonly found in Andean ruins, presumably used for the placement of idols and/or offerings

iglesia – church

Inca – dominant indigenous civilisation of the Central Andes at the time of the Spanish conquest; refers both to the people and to their leader

ingenio – mill; in Potosí, it refers to one of the 33 silver smelting plants along the Río de la Ribera, where metal was extracted from low-grade ore by crushing it in a solution of salt and mercury

jardín – garden

jochi – agouti: an agile, long-legged rodent of the Amazon basin

Kallahuayas – itinerant traditional healers and fortune-tellers of the remote Cordillera Apolobamba

koa – sweet-smelling incense bush *(Senecio mathewsii)*, which grows on Isla del Sol and other parts of the *Altiplano* and is used as an incense in *Aymara* ritual; also refers to a similar-smelling domestic plant *Mentha pulegium*, which was introduced by the Spanish

Kolla – another name for *Aymara*

Kollasuyo – *Inca* name for Bolivia, the 'land

of the *Kolla*', or *Aymara* people; the Spanish knew the area as Alto Peru, 'upper Peru'

LAB – Lloyd Aéreo Boliviano (national airline)
La Diablada – the 'Dance of the Devils': a renowned Bolivian carnival held in Oruro
lago – lake
laguna – lagoon; shallow lake
legía – alkaloid usually made of potato and *quinoa* ash which is used to draw the drug from coca leaves when chewed
licuado – fruit shake
liquichiris – harmful spirits who suck out a person's vitality, causing death for no visible reason
llajhua – hot tomato sauce
llanos – plains
llapa – bargaining practice in which a customer agrees to a final price provided the vendor augments the item being sold
llareta – combustible salt-tolerant moss growing on the *salares* of the Southern Altiplano that oozes a turpentine-like jelly used by locals as stove fuel
locoto – small, hot pepper pods
loma – mound or hillock, sometimes artificial
lomo – loin (of meat)

Manco Capac – the first *Inca* emperor
mariguí – small biting fly of the Amazon lowlands
masaco – *charque* served with mashed plantain, yuca and/or maize; a Bolivian Amazon staple
mate – tea
mercado – market
mestizo – person of Spanish-American and American-Indian parentage or descent
micro – small bus or minibus
milanesa – fairly greasy type of beef or chicken schnitzel
mobilidad – any sort of motor vehicle
mote – freeze-dried maize
mudéjar – Spanish name for architecture displaying Moorish influences

nevado – snow-capped mountain peak

oca – tough edible tuber similar to a potato

Pachamama – the *Aymara* and *Quechua* earth mother
pacumutu – enormous chunks of beef grilled on a skewer, marinated in salt and lime juice, with cassava, onions and other trimmings; this dish originated in Beni department
pahuichi – straw-thatched home with reed walls; a common dwelling in Beni department
paja brava – spiky grass
panqueques – pancakes
parrillada – meat grill or barbecue
peña – folk music programme
piso – floor
pomelo – grapefruit
pongaje – nonfeudal system of peonage inflicted on the Bolivian peasantry; it was abolished after the April Revolution of 1952
prato feito – Portuguese for 'full plate': a veritable feast of Brazilian carbohydrates, including *maccarão* (pasta), *arroz e feijão* (beans and rice) and *farofa* (manioc flour); available in places along the Brazilian border.
pukacapa – circular *empanada* filled with cheese, olives etc
pullman – 1st class
puna – high open grasslands of the *Altiplano*

quebrada – ravine or wash, usually dry
Quechua – highland *(Altiplano)* indigenous language of Ecuador, Peru and Bolivia; language of the *Incas*
quena – simple reed flute
queñua – dwarf tree that can survive at elevations over 5000m; it can grow higher than any other tree in the world
quinoa – highly nutritious grain similar to sorghum, used to make flour and thicken stews; grown at high elevations
quirquincho – armadillo carapace used in the making of *charangos*; nickname for residents of Oruro.

ranga – tripe with yellow pepper, potato and tomato and onion sauce; a Tarija specialty
real – Brazilian unit of currency, pronounced

'hey-OW'; the plural is *reais*, pronounced 'hey-ICE'

refugio – mountain hut

río – river

saíce – hot meat and rice stew

salar – salt pan or salt desert

salteña – meat and vegetable pasty, originally created in Salta, Argentina, but now a staple in the Bolivian diet

SENATUR – Secretaria Nacional de Turismo (Bolivian national tourism authority)

seringueros – rubber tappers in the Amazon region

silpancho – similar to *milanesa*, only pounded even thinner and allowed to absorb even more grease

singani – distilled grape spirit

soroche – altitude sickness; invariably suffered by newly arrived visitors to highland Bolivia

surazo – cold wind blowing into lowland Bolivia from Patagonia and the Argentine pampa

Tahuatinsuyo – the *Inca* name for their empire

tambo – wayside inn, market and meeting place selling staple domestic items; the New World counterpart of the caravanserai

taxista – taxi driver

termas – hot springs

terminal terrestre – long-distance bus terminal

thimpu – spicy lamb and vegetable stew

thola – small desert bush

tienda – small shop, usually family-run

tinku – ritual fight that is a form of martial art and takes place primarily in northern Potosí department during festivals; the blood that is shed during these fights is considered an offering to *Pachamama*

totora – type of reed; used as a building material in the Titicaca region

tranca – highway police post, usually found at city limits

tren expreso – reasonably fast train that has 1st and 2nd class carriages, a dining room and a passenger *bodega*

tren mixto – very slow goods train; only 2nd class is available and most passengers travel in *bodegas*

tren rápido – slow train that stops at every station

trufi – collective taxi or minibus that travels along a set route

tucumana – cube-shaped pastry stuffed with meat, olives, eggs, raisins and other goodies, which originated in Tucuman, Argentina; served as a morning snack in parts of Bolivia

viscacha – small long-tailed rabbit-like rodent, *Lagidium viscacia*, which is related to the chinchilla; inhabits rocky outcrops on the high *Altiplano*

wiskería – classy bar

yareta – see *llareta*

yatiri – traditional *Aymara* healer/priest or witch doctor

yuca – cassava (manioc) tuber

zampoña – pan flute made of hollow reeds of varying lengths, lashed together side by side; features in most traditional music performances

Index

TEXT

Map references are in **bold** type

accommodation 104-6
Achacachi 210, 211, 248
Achura 187
acute mountain sickness 77-8
African-Bolivian people 190, 200
Agua Blanca Cabaña 396

Aguas Blancas (Arg) 369
Aguas Calientes 419
Aiquile 312-13
air travel
Asia 121
Australia & New Zealand 119
elsewhere in South America 121
Europe 119-21
the USA 118-19

departure tax 124
glossary 117
to/from Bolivia 115
within Bolivia 127
Allie's Trail 454
Altiplano 20-1, 26-7
altitude sickness 76-7
Alto Madidi National Park 28, 435

BOXED ASIDES

Thanks

Thanks to all the following travellers and others (apologies if we have misspelled your name) who took the time to write to us about their experiences in Bolivia.

Duanna Aguirre, Garry Alderson, Madeleine Basler-Tschopp, Gordon Biggar, Steve Boucher, M Bozolo, Daniel Buck, Pablo Caballero, Damaris Carlisle, Mariano Chmiel, Lizzet Delgado Cina, Chiaras Clauti, Louise Cyr, Anne Bois d'Enghien, Ann De Schryver, Nicolas de Vulpillieres, Lizzet Delgado, Janet Donald, Lisa Durham, Leanne Dyck, Tim Eyre, W Falcone, R Farnell, Barbara Fisher, Gregory Frux, Mary Ellen Galante, Richard Gamble, F Gates, Massimo Giannini, Parc Gilles, Jonathon Goldstein, Andor Gomml, Wenceslao Gorchs, David Grayce, Geoffrey Groesbeck, Otto Grolig, Thomas Gummermann, Andrew Hanson, Catherine Hesse-Swain, Lucy Holbrook, Lawrence Hribar, Ann Jenkins, Shirley Johnson, Ian G Jones, Kryss Katsiavriades, Heidi Konecny, Evangelos Kotsopoulos, Susanne Langer, Ida Larsen, Howard A. LeVaux, James A Lind, Katherine Long, Therese Lung, Dr Renata Lysy, Sandy Main, Helen Marieskind, Jeremy Martin, Franco Mazzarella, Ann Michiclsen, Andreas Muheim, Ann & Bruce Palmer, Matthew Parris, A. Phillips, Paul Pichler, Sandra Poston, Robert Poynton, Juan Carlos Querejazu, J D Rabbit, Lorna Reith, L Robertson, Remi Salles, Riaguel Garcia Salmones, Raul Sanjines, Mr J. Scherer, Florian Schindelmann, Geert Job Sevink, Vincent Smith, Greg Stace, Julian Stanley, Petra Stettler, Chris Sullivan, Brian Sunesen, Marlene Taussig, Ryan Taylor, Jane Taylor, Mike Truman, Arjan van Bentem, Benjamin van Every, Christine Vauden Wuickef, Frederique Verbiest, Hugo Vernhout, Ruth Von Armeln, Andrew Wain, Candice Weaver, Paula Weinstein, Marcel Wenneker, James Westerman, Tom Williams, Ron Wilmoth, Ed Wright, Mark Zimmerman.

LONELY PLANET JOURNEYS

JOURNEYS is a unique collection of travellers' tales – published by the company that understands travel better than anyone else. It is a series for anyone who has ever experienced – or dreamed of – the magical moment when they encountered a strange culture or saw a place for the first time. They are tales to read while you're planning a trip, while you're on the road or while you're in an armchair, in front of a fire.

JOURNEYS books will catch the spirit of a place, illuminate a culture, recount a crazy adventure, or introduce a fascinating way of life. They will always entertain, and always enrich the experience of travel.

ISLANDS IN THE CLOUDS
Travels in the Highlands of New Guinea
Isabella Tree

This is the fascinating account of a journey to the remote and beautiful Highlands of Papua New Guinea and Irian Jaya. The author travels with a PNG Highlander who introduces her to his intriguing and complex world. *Islands in the Clouds* is a thoughtful, moving book, full of insights into a region that is rarely noticed by the rest of the world.

'One of the most accomplished travel writers to appear on the horizon for many years ... the dialogue is brilliant' – Eric Newby

LOST JAPAN
Alex Kerr

Lost Japan draws on the author's personal experiences of Japan over a period of 30 years. Alex Kerr takes his readers on a backstage tour: friendships with Kabuki actors, buying and selling art, studying calligraphy, exploring rarely visited temples and shrines ... The Japanese edition of this book was awarded the 1994 Shincho Gakugei Literature Prize for the best work of non-fiction.

'This deeply personal witness to Japan's wilful loss of its traditional culture is at the same time an immensely valuable evaluation of just what that culture was'
– Donald Richie of the Japan Times

THE GATES OF DAMASCUS
Lieve Joris
Translated by Sam Garrett

This best-selling book is a beautifully drawn portrait of day-to-day life in modern Syria. Through her intimate contact with local people, Lieve Joris draws us into the fascinating world that lies behind the gates of Damascus.

'A brilliant book ... Not since Naguib Mahfouz has the everyday life of the modern Arab world been so intimately described' – William Dalrymple

SEAN & DAVID'S LONG DRIVE
Sean Condon

Sean and David are young townies who have rarely strayed beyond city limits. One day, for no good reason, they set out to discover their homeland, and what follows is a wildly entertaining adventure that covers half of Australia. Sean Condon has written a hilarious, offbeat road book that mixes sharp insights with deadpan humour and outright lies.

'Funny, pithy, kitsch and surreal ... This book will do for Australia what Chernobyl did for Kiev, but hey you'll laugh as the stereotypes go boom' – Andrew Tuck, Time Out

LONELY PLANET TRAVEL ATLASES

Lonely Planet has long been famous for the number and quality of its guidebook maps. Now we've gone one step further and in conjunction with Steinhart Katzir Publishers produced a handy companion series: Lonely Planet travel atlases – maps of a country produced in book form.

Unlike other maps, which look good but lead travellers astray, our travel atlases have been researched on the road by Lonely Planet's experienced team of writers. All details are carefully checked to ensure the atlas corresponds with the equivalent Lonely Planet guidebook.

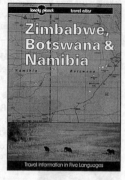

The handy atlas format means no holes, wrinkles, torn sections or constant folding and unfolding. These atlases can survive long periods on the road, unlike cumbersome fold-out maps. The comprehensive index ensures easy reference.

- full-colour throughout
- maps researched and checked by Lonely Planet authors
- place names correspond with Lonely Planet guidebooks
  – no confusing spelling differences
- legend and travelling information in English, French, German, Japanese and Spanish
- size: 230 x 160 mm

Available now:
Thailand; India & Bangladesh; Vietnam; Zimbabwe, Botswana & Namibia

Coming soon:
Chile; Egypt; Israel; Laos; Turkey

LONELY PLANET TV SERIES & VIDEOS

Lonely Planet travel guides have been brought to life on television screens around the world. Like our guides, the programmes are based on the joy of independent travel, and look honestly at some of the most exciting, picturesque and frustrating places in the world. Each show is presented by one of three travellers from Australia, England or the USA and combines an innovative mixture of video, Super-8 film, atmospheric soundscapes and original music.

Videos of each episode – containing additional footage not shown on television – are available from good book and video shops, but the availability of individual videos varies with regional screening schedules.

Video destinations include: Alaska; Australia (Southeast); Brazil; Ecuador & the Galápagos Islands; Indonesia; Israel & the Sinai Desert; Japan; La Ruta Maya (Yucatán, Guatemala & Belize); Morocco; North India (Varanasi to the Himalaya); Pacific Islands; Vietnam; Zimbabwe, Botswana & Namibia.

Coming soon: The Arctic (Norway & Finland); Baja California; Chile & Easter Island; China (Southeast); Costa Rica; East Africa (Tanzania & Zanzibar); Great Barrier Reef (Australia); Jamaica; Papua New Guinea; the Rockies (USA); Syria & Jordan; Turkey.

The Lonely Planet TV series is produced by:
Pilot Productions
Duke of Sussex Studios
44 Uxbridge St
London W8 7TG UK

Lonely Planet videos are distributed by:
IVN Communications Inc
2246 Camino Ramon
California 94583, USA

107 Power Road, Chiswick
London W4 5PL UK

Music from the TV series is available on CD & cassette.
For ordering information contact your nearest Lonely Planet office.

PLANET TALK

Lonely Planet's FREE quarterly newsletter

We love hearing from you and think you'd like to hear from us.

When...is the right time to see reindeer in Finland?
Where...can you hear the best palm-wine music in Ghana?
How...do you get from Asunción to Areguá by steam train?
What...is the best way to see India?

For the answer to these and many other questions read PLANET TALK.

Every issue is packed with up-to-date travel news and advice including:

* a letter from Lonely Planet co-founders Tony and Maureen Wheeler
* go behind the scenes on the road with a Lonely Planet author
* feature article on an important and topical travel issue
* a selection of recent letters from travellers
* details on forthcoming Lonely Planet promotions
* complete list of Lonely Planet products

To join our mailing list contact any Lonely Planet office.

Also available: Lonely Planet T-shirts. 100% heavyweight cotton.

LONELY PLANET ONLINE

Get the latest travel information before you leave or while you're on the road

Whether you've just begun planning your next trip, or you're chasing down specific info on currency regulations or visa requirements, check out the Lonely Planet World Wide Web site for up-to-the-minute travel information.

As well as travel profiles of your favourite destinations (including interactive maps and full-colour photos), you'll find current reports from our army of researchers and other travellers, updates on health and visas, travel advisories, and the ecological and political issues you need to be aware of as you travel.

There's an online travellers' forum (the Thorn Tree) where you can share your experiences of life on the road, meet travel companions and ask other travellers for their recommendations and advice. We also have plenty of links to other Web sites useful to independent travellers.

With tens of thousands of visitors a month, the Lonely Planet Web site is one of the most popular on the Internet and has won a number of awards including GNN's Best of the Net travel award.

http://www.lonelyplanet.com

LONELY PLANET PRODUCTS

Lonely Planet is known worldwide for publishing practical, reliable and no-nonsense travel information in our guides and on our web site. The Lonely Planet list covers just about every accessible part of the world. Currently there are eight series: *travel guides*, *shoestring guides*, *walking guides*, *city guides*, *phrasebooks*, *audio packs*, *travel atlases* and *Journeys* – a unique collection of travellers' tales.

EUROPE

Austria • Baltic States & Kaliningrad • Baltic States phrasebook • Britain • Central Europe on a shoestring • Central Europe phrasebook • Czech & Slovak Republics • Denmark • Dublin city guide • Eastern Europe on a shoestring • Eastern Europe phrasebook • Finland • France • Greece • Greek phrasebook • Hungary • Iceland, Greenland & the Faroe Islands • Ireland • Italy • Mediterranean Europe on a shoestring • Mediterranean Europe phrasebook • Paris city guide • Poland • Prague city guide • Russia, Ukraine & Belarus • Russian phrasebook • Scandinavian & Baltic Europe on a shoestring • Scandinavian Europe phrasebook • Slovenia • St Petersburg city guide • Switzerland • Trekking in Greece • Trekking in Spain • Ukrainian phrasebook • Vienna city guide • Walking in Switzerland • Western Europe on a shoestring • Western Europe phrasebook

NORTH AMERICA

Alaska • Backpacking in Alaska • Baja California• California & Nevada • Canada • Hawaii • Honolulu city guide • Los Angeles city guide • Mexico • Miami • New England • Pacific Northwest USA • Rocky Mountain States • San Francisco city guide • Southwest USA • USA phrasebook

CENTRAL AMERICA & THE CARIBBEAN

Central America on a shoestring • Costa Rica • Eastern Caribbean • Guatemala, Belize & Yucatán: La Ruta Maya • Jamaica

SOUTH AMERICA

Argentina, Uruguay & Paraguay • Bolivia • Brazil • Brazilian phrasebook • Buenos Aires city guide • Chile & Easter Island • Colombia • Ecuador & the Galápagos Islands • Latin American Spanish phrasebook • Peru • Quechua phrasebook • Rio de Janeiro city guide • South America on a shoestring • Trekking in the Patagonian Andes • Venezuela

Travel Literature: Full Circle: A South American Journey

ALSO AVAILABLE:

Travel with Children • Traveller's Tales

AFRICA

Arabic (Moroccan) phrasebook • Africa on a shoestring • Cape Town city guide • Central Africa • East Africa • Egypt & the Sudan • Ethiopian (Amharic) phrasebook • Kenya • Morocco • North Africa • South Africa, Lesotho & Swaziland • Swahili phrasebook • Trekking in East Africa • West Africa • Zimbabwe, Botswana & Namibia • Zimbabwe, Botswana & Namibia travel atlas